Student Solutions Manual
for Stewart/Redlin/Watson's

Precalculus
Mathematics for Calculus

Fourth Edition

John A. Banks
Evergreen Valley College,
San Jose City College

BROOKS/COLE
— ✦ —
™
THOMSON LEARNING

Australia • Canada • Mexico • Singapore • Spain • United Kingdom • United States

BROOKS/COLE

THOMSON LEARNING

Assistant Editor: *Carol Ann Benedict*
Marketing Manager: *Karin Sandberg*
Marketing Communications: *Samantha Cabaluna*
Marketing Assistant: *Darcie Pool*
Editorial Assistant: *Molly Nance*

Production Coordinator: *Dorothy Bell*
Cover Design: *Roy R. Neuhaus*
Cover Illustration: *Bill Ralph*
Print Buyer: *Christopher Burnham*
Printing and Binding: *Webcom Limited*

For more information about this or any other Brooks/Cole product, contact:
BROOKS/COLE
511 Forest Lodge Road
Pacific Grove, CA 93950 USA
www.brookscole.com
1-800-423-0563 (Thomson Learning Academic Resource Center)

Printed in Canada

10   9   8   7   6   5   4   3

ISBN 0-534-38544-3

Table of Contents

Chapter One
Exercises 1.1

1. Commutative Property for addition.

3. Associative Property for addition.

5. Distributive Property.

7. $3(x+y) = 3x + 3y$

9. $4(2m) = (4 \cdot 2)m = 8m$

11. $-\dfrac{5}{2}(2x - 4y) = -\dfrac{5}{2}(2x) + \dfrac{5}{2}(4y) = -5x + 10y$

13. (a) $\dfrac{4}{13} + \dfrac{3}{13} = \dfrac{7}{13}$

(b) $\dfrac{3}{10} + \dfrac{7}{15} = \dfrac{9}{30} + \dfrac{14}{30} = \dfrac{23}{30}$

15. (a) $\dfrac{2}{5} \div \dfrac{9}{10} = \dfrac{2}{5} \cdot \dfrac{10}{9} = \dfrac{4}{9}$

(b) $\left(4 \div \dfrac{1}{2}\right) - \dfrac{1}{2} = \left(4 \cdot \dfrac{2}{1}\right) - \dfrac{1}{2} = 8 - \dfrac{1}{2} = 7\dfrac{1}{2}$ or $\dfrac{15}{2}$

17. (a) False

(b) True

19. (a) False

(b) True

21. (a) $x > 0$

(b) $t < 4$

(c) $a \geq \pi$

(d) $-5 < x < \frac{1}{3}$

(e) $|p - 3| \leq 5$

23. (a) $A \cup B = \{1, 2, 3, 4, 5, 6, 7, 8\}$

(b) $A \cap B = \{2, 4, 6\}$

25. (a) $A \cup C = \{1, 2, 3, 4, 5, 6, 7, 8, 9, 10\}$

(b) $A \cap C = \emptyset$

27. (a) $B \cup C = \{x \mid x \leq 5\}$

(b) $B \cap C = \{x \mid -1 < x < 4\}$

29. $(-3, 0) = \{x \mid -3 < x < 0\}$

31. $[2, 8) = \{x \mid 2 \leq x < 8\}$

33. $[2, \infty) = \{x \mid x \geq 2\}$

35. $x \leq 1 \quad \Leftrightarrow \quad x \in (-\infty, 1]$

37. $-2 < x \leq 1 \quad \Leftrightarrow \quad x \in (-2, 1]$

39. $x > -1 \quad \Leftrightarrow \quad x \in (-1, \infty)$

41. $(-2, 0) \cup (-1, 1) = (-2, 1)$

43. $[-4, 6] \cap [0, 8) = [0, 6]$

45. $(-\infty, -4) \cup (4, \infty)$

47. (a) $|100| = 100$

(b) $|-73| = 73$

49. (a) $\left||-6| - |-4|\right| = |6 - 4| = |2| = 2$

(b) $\dfrac{-1}{|-1|} = \dfrac{-1}{1} = -1$

51.   (a) $|(-2) \cdot 6| = |-12| = 12$ (b) $\left|\left(-\frac{1}{3}\right)(-15)\right| = |5| = 5$

53.   (a) $|17 - 2| = 15$ (b) $|21 - (-3)| = |21 + 3| = |24| = 24$

      (c) $\left|-\frac{3}{10} - \frac{11}{8}\right| = \left|-\frac{12}{40} - \frac{55}{40}\right| = \left|-\frac{67}{40}\right| = \frac{67}{40}$

55.   (a) Let $x = 0.777\dots$. So,   (b) Let $x = 0.2888\dots$. So,

$$10x = 7.7777\dots$$
$$\underline{x = 0.7777\dots}$$
$$9x = 7 \qquad \text{Thus } x = \tfrac{7}{9}.$$

$$100x = 28.8888\dots$$
$$\underline{10x = \;\; 2.8888\dots}$$
$$90x = 26 \qquad \text{Thus } x = \tfrac{26}{90} = \tfrac{13}{45}.$$

      (c) Let $x = 0.575757\dots$. So,

$$100x = 57.5757\dots$$
$$\underline{x = \;\; 0.5757\dots}$$
$$99x = 57 \qquad \text{Thus } x = \tfrac{57}{99} = \tfrac{19}{33}.$$

57.   (a) Is $\frac{1}{28}x + \frac{1}{34}y \le 15$ when $x = 165$ and $y = 230$? We have
$\frac{1}{28}(165) + \frac{1}{34}(230) = 5.89 + 6.76 = 12.65 \le 15$, so yes the car can travel 165 city miles and 230 highway miles without running out of gas.

      (b) Here we must solve for y when $x = 280$. So $\frac{1}{28}(280) + \frac{1}{34}y = 15 \quad \Leftrightarrow \quad 10 + \frac{1}{34}y = 15$
$\Leftrightarrow \quad \frac{1}{34}y = 5 \quad \Leftrightarrow \quad y = 170$. Thus the car can travel up to 170 highway miles without running out of gas.

59. $\frac{1}{2} + \sqrt{2}$ is irrational. Since the sum of two rational numbers is rational (see Exercise 58), if $\frac{1}{2} + \sqrt{2}$ was rational, then the $\left(\frac{1}{2} + \sqrt{2}\right) + \left(-\frac{1}{2}\right) = \sqrt{2}$ is rational. But this is a contradiction. In general the sum of a rational number and an irrational number is irrational.

Zero is rational and the product of zero and any real number is zero.

If the rational number is not zero, $\frac{a}{b} \ne 0$, then the product of it and any irrational number, w, is irrational. Again, if we assume the product is rational, say $\frac{a}{b} \cdot w = \frac{c}{d}$, then since $\frac{a}{b} \ne 0$, we have $\frac{b}{a} \ne 0$ so $\frac{b}{a}\left(\frac{a}{b} \cdot w\right) = \frac{b}{a} \cdot \frac{c}{d} \quad \Leftrightarrow \quad w = \frac{bc}{ad}$ which is rational. But w is irrational.

61.   (a) Construct the number $\sqrt{2}$ on the number line by transferring the length of the hypotenuse of a right triangle with legs of length 1 and 1.

      (b) Construct a right triangle with legs of length 1 and 2. By the Pythagorean Theorem, the length of the hypotenuse is $\sqrt{1^2 + 2^2} = \sqrt{5}$. Then transfer the length of the hypotenuse to the number line.

      (c) Construct a right triangle with legs of length $\sqrt{2}$ and 2, (construct $\sqrt{2}$ as in part (a)). By the Pythagorean Theorem, the length of the hypotenuse is $\sqrt{(\sqrt{2})^2 + 2^2} = \sqrt{6}$. Then transfer the length of the hypotenuse to the number line.

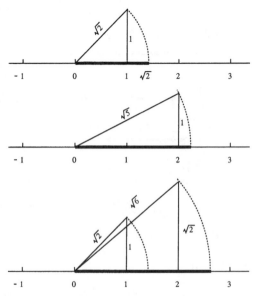

Exercises 1.2

1. $\dfrac{1}{\sqrt{17}} = 17^{-1/2}$ 　　　　　　　3. $4^{2/3} = \sqrt[3]{4^2} = \sqrt[3]{16}$ 　　　　5. $a^{3/5} = \sqrt[5]{a^3}$

7. (a) $(-2)^4 = 16$ 　　　　　　　　　　　　(b) 　$-2^4 = -16$
   (c) $(-2)^0 = 1$

9. (a) $2^4 5^{-2} = \dfrac{2^4}{5^2} = \dfrac{16}{25}$ 　　　　　　(b) 　$\dfrac{10^7}{10^4} = 10^{7-4} = 10^3 = 1000$
   (c) $\left(2^3 \cdot 2^2\right)^2 = \left(2^5\right)^2 = 2^{10} = 1024$

11. (a) $\sqrt{\dfrac{4}{9}} = \dfrac{\sqrt{4}}{\sqrt{9}} = \dfrac{2}{3}$ 　　　　　　(b) 　$\sqrt[4]{256} = \sqrt[4]{4^4} = 4$

   (c) $\sqrt[6]{\dfrac{1}{64}} = \sqrt[6]{\dfrac{1}{2^6}} = \dfrac{\sqrt[6]{1}}{\sqrt[6]{2^6}} = \dfrac{1}{2}$

13. (a) $\left(\dfrac{4}{9}\right)^{-1/2} = \left(\dfrac{2^2}{3^2}\right)^{-1/2} = \dfrac{2^{-1}}{3^{-1}} = \dfrac{3}{2}$

   (b) $(-32)^{2/5} = \left[(-2)^5\right]^{2/5} = (-2)^2 = 4$

   (c) $(-125)^{-1/3} = \left[(-5)^3\right]^{-1/3} = (-5)^{-1} = \frac{1}{-5} = -\frac{1}{5}$

15. When $x = 3$, $y = 4$, $z = -1$ we have $\sqrt{x^2 + y^2} = \sqrt{3^2 + 4^2} = \sqrt{9 + 16} = \sqrt{25} = 5$.

17. When $x = 3$, $y = 4$, $z = -1$ we have
$$(9x)^{2/3} + (2y)^{2/3} + z^{2/3} = (9 \cdot 3)^{2/3} + (2 \cdot 4)^{2/3} + (-1)^{2/3} = \left(3^3\right)^{2/3} + \left(2^3\right)^{2/3} + (1)^{1/3}$$
$$= 3^2 + 2^2 + 1 = 9 + 4 + 1 = 14.$$

19. $\sqrt[3]{108} - \sqrt[3]{32} = 3\sqrt[3]{4} - 2\sqrt[3]{4} = \sqrt[3]{4}$ 　　　21. $\sqrt{245} - \sqrt{125} = 7\sqrt{5} - 5\sqrt{5} = 2\sqrt{5}$

23. $a^9 a^{-5} = a^{9-5} = a^4$ 　　　　　　　　　25. $\left(12x^2 y^4\right)\left(\frac{1}{2}x^5 y\right) = \left(12 \cdot \frac{1}{2}\right)x^{2+5}y^{4+1} = 6x^7 y^5$

27. $\dfrac{x^9 (2x)^4}{x^3} = 2^4 \cdot x^{9+4-3} = 16x^{10}$

29. $b^4\left(\dfrac{1}{3}b^2\right)\left(12b^{-8}\right) = \dfrac{12}{3}b^{4+2-8} = 4b^{-2} = \dfrac{4}{b^2}$

31. $(rs)^3 (2s)^{-2} (4r)^4 = r^3 s^3 2^{-2} s^{-2} 4^4 r^4 = r^3 s^3 2^{-2} s^{-2} 2^{2 \cdot 4} r^4 = 2^{-2+8} r^{3+4} s^{3-2} = 2^6 r^7 s = 64r^7 s$

33. $\dfrac{\left(6y^3\right)^4}{2y^5} = \dfrac{6^4 y^{3 \cdot 4}}{2y^5} = \dfrac{6^4}{2} y^{12-5} = 648y^7$

35. $\dfrac{\left(x^2 y^3\right)^4 \left(xy^4\right)^{-3}}{x^2 y} = \dfrac{x^8 y^{12} x^{-3} y^{-12}}{x^2 y} = x^{8-3-2} y^{12-12-1} = x^3 y^{-1} = \dfrac{x^3}{y}$

37. $\dfrac{\left(xy^2z^3\right)^4}{\left(x^3y^2z\right)^3} = \dfrac{x^4y^8z^{12}}{x^9y^6z^3} = x^{4-9}y^{8-6}z^{12-3} = x^{-5}y^2z^9 = \dfrac{y^2z^9}{x^5}$

39. $\left(\dfrac{q^{-1}rs^{-2}}{r^{-5}sq^{-8}}\right)^{-1} = \dfrac{qr^{-1}s^2}{r^5s^{-1}q^8} = q^{1-8}r^{-1-5}s^{2-(-1)} = q^{-7}r^{-6}s^3 = \dfrac{s^3}{q^7r^6}$

41. $x^{2/3}x^{1/5} = x^{(10/15+3/15)} = x^{13/15}$

43. $(4b)^{1/2}\left(8b^{2/5}\right) = \sqrt{4} \cdot 8b^{1/2}b^{2/5} = 16b^{(5/10+4/10)} = 16b^{9/10}$

45. $\left(c^2d^3\right)^{-1/3} = c^{-2/3}d^{-1} = \dfrac{1}{c^{2/3}d}$ 47. $\left(y^{3/4}\right)^{2/3} = y^{(3/4)\cdot(2/3)} = y^{1/2}$

49. $\left(2x^4y^{-4/5}\right)^3\left(8y^2\right)^{2/3} = 2^3x^{12}y^{-12/5}8^{2/3}y^{4/3} = 2^{3+2}x^{12}y^{(-12/5+4/3)} = \dfrac{32x^{12}}{y^{16/15}}$ (Note that

$8^{2/3} = \left(8^{1/3}\right)^2 = 2^2$.)

51. $\left(\dfrac{x^6y}{y^4}\right)^{5/2} = \dfrac{x^{15}y^{5/2}}{y^{10}} = x^{15}y^{5/2-10} = x^{15}y^{-15/2} = \dfrac{x^{15}}{y^{15/2}}$

53. $\left(\dfrac{3a^{-2}}{4b^{-1/3}}\right)^{-1} = \dfrac{3^{-1}a^2}{4^{-1}b^{1/3}} = \dfrac{4a^2}{3b^{1/3}}$

55. $\dfrac{(9st)^{3/2}}{(27s^3t^{-4})^{2/3}} = \dfrac{27s^{3/2}t^{3/2}}{9s^2t^{-8/3}} = 3s^{3/2-2}t^{3/2+8/3} = 3s^{-1/2}t^{25/6} = \dfrac{3t^{25/6}}{s^{1/2}}$

57. $\sqrt[4]{x^4} = |x|$ 59. $\sqrt[3]{x^3y} = \left(x^3\right)^{1/3}y^{1/3} = x\sqrt[3]{y}$

61. $\sqrt[5]{a^6b^7} = a^{6/5}b^{7/5} = a \cdot a^{1/5}b \cdot b^{2/5} = ab\sqrt[5]{ab^2}$

63. $\sqrt[3]{\sqrt{64x^6}} = (8|x^3|)^{1/3} = 2|x|$

65. (a) $\dfrac{1}{\sqrt{6}} = \dfrac{1}{\sqrt{6}} \cdot \dfrac{\sqrt{6}}{\sqrt{6}} = \dfrac{\sqrt{6}}{6}$ (b) $\sqrt{\dfrac{x}{3y}} = \dfrac{\sqrt{x}}{\sqrt{3y}} = \dfrac{\sqrt{x}}{\sqrt{3y}} \cdot \dfrac{\sqrt{3y}}{\sqrt{3y}} = \dfrac{\sqrt{3xy}}{3y}$

   (c) $\sqrt{\dfrac{3}{20}} = \dfrac{\sqrt{3}}{2\sqrt{5}} \cdot \dfrac{\sqrt{5}}{\sqrt{5}} = \dfrac{\sqrt{3}\sqrt{5}}{10} = \dfrac{\sqrt{15}}{10}$

67. (a) $\dfrac{1}{\sqrt[3]{x}} = \dfrac{1}{\sqrt[3]{x}} \cdot \dfrac{\sqrt[3]{x^2}}{\sqrt[3]{x^2}} = \dfrac{\sqrt[3]{x^2}}{x}$ (b) $\dfrac{1}{\sqrt[5]{x^2}} = \dfrac{1}{\sqrt[5]{x^2}} \cdot \dfrac{\sqrt[5]{x^3}}{\sqrt[5]{x^3}} = \dfrac{\sqrt[5]{x^3}}{x}$

   (c) $\dfrac{1}{\sqrt[7]{x^3}} = \dfrac{1}{\sqrt[7]{x^3}} \cdot \dfrac{\sqrt[7]{x^4}}{\sqrt[7]{x^4}} = \dfrac{\sqrt[7]{x^4}}{x}$

69. (a) $69,300,000 = 6.93 \times 10^7$ (b) $0.000028536 = 2.8536 \times 10^{-5}$
   (c) $129,540,000 = 1.2954 \times 10^8$

71. (a) $3.19 \times 10^5 = 319{,}000$ (b) $2.670 \times 10^{-8} = 0.0000000267$
   (c) $7.1 \times 10^{14} = 710{,}000{,}000{,}000{,}000$

73. (a) $5{,}900{,}000{,}000{,}000$ mi $= 5.9 \times 10^{12}$ mi (b) 0.0000000000004 cm $= 4 \times 10^{-13}$ cm

(c)   33 billion billion molecules $= 33 \times 10^9 \times 10^9 = 3.3 \times 10^{19}$ molecules

75. $(7.2 \times 10^{-9})(1.806 \times 10^{-12}) = 7.2 \times 1.806 \times 10^{-9} \times 10^{-12} \approx 13.0 \times 10^{-21} = 1.3 \times 10^{-20}$

77. $\dfrac{1.295643 \times 10^9}{(3.610 \times 10^{-17})(2.511 \times 10^6)} = \dfrac{1.295643}{3.610 \times 2.511} \times 10^{9+17-6} \approx 0.1429 \times 10^{19} = 1.429 \times 10^{19}$

79. $\dfrac{(0.0000162)(0.01582)}{(594621000)(0.0058)} = \dfrac{(1.62 \times 10^{-5})(1.582 \times 10^{-2})}{(5.94621 \times 10^8)(5.8 \times 10^{-3})} = \dfrac{1.62 \times 1.582}{5.94621 \times 5.8} \times 10^{-5-2-8+3}$

     $0.074 \times 10^{-12} = 7.4 \times 10^{-14}$

81.   Since one light year is 5.9×10^{12} mile, Centauri is about $4.3 \times 5.9 \times 10^{12} \approx 2.54 \times 10^{13}$ miles or 25,400,000,000,000 miles

83.   Volume $= (average\ depth)(area) = (3.7 \times 10^3 \text{ m})(3.6 \times 10^{14} \text{ m}^2)\left(\frac{10^3 \text{ liters}}{\text{m}^3}\right) \approx 1.33 \times 10^{21}$ liters

85. $\begin{array}{l} number\ of \\ molecules \end{array} = (5 \cdot 10 \cdot 3)(10^3)(22.4)(6.02 \times 10^{23}) \approx 2.03 \times 10^{30}$

87.   First convert 1135 feet to miles. This gives $1135 \text{ ft} = 1135 \cdot \frac{1 \text{ mile}}{5280 \text{ feet}} = 0.215$ mi. Thus the distance you can see is given by $D = \sqrt{2rh + h^2} = \sqrt{2(3960)(.215) + (.215)^2} = \sqrt{1702.8} = 41.3$ miles.

89.   (a)

n	1	2	5	10	100
$2^{1/n}$	$2^{1/1} = 2$	$2^{1/2} = 1.414$	$2^{1/5} = 1.149$	$2^{1/10} = 1.072$	$2^{1/100} = 1.007$

     So when n gets large, $2^{1/n}$ decreases to 1.

     (b)

n	1	2	5	10
$\left(\frac{1}{2}\right)^{1/n}$	$\left(\frac{1}{2}\right)^{1/1} = 0.5$	$\left(\frac{1}{2}\right)^{1/2} = 0.707$	$\left(\frac{1}{2}\right)^{1/5} = 0.871$	$\left(\frac{1}{2}\right)^{1/10} = 0.933$

100
$\left(\frac{1}{2}\right)^{1/100} = 0.993$

     So when n gets large, $\left(\frac{1}{2}\right)^{1/n}$ increases to 1.

91.   (a) $\dfrac{18^5}{9^5} = \left(\dfrac{18}{9}\right)^5 = 2^5 = 32$

     (b) $20^6 \cdot (0.5)^6 = (20 \cdot 0.5)^6 = 10^6 = 1,000,000$

93.   Using $v = \dfrac{1}{10}c$ in the formula $m = \dfrac{m_0}{\sqrt{1 - \frac{v^2}{c^2}}}$, we get: $m = \dfrac{m_0}{\sqrt{1 - \frac{\left(\frac{1}{10}c\right)^2}{c^2}}} = \dfrac{m_0}{\sqrt{1 - \frac{1}{100}}}$. Thus

     $m = \dfrac{1}{\sqrt{\frac{99}{100}}}m_0 = \dfrac{10\sqrt{11}}{33}m_0$. So the rest mass of the spaceship is multiplied by $\dfrac{10\sqrt{11}}{33} \approx 1.005$.

     Using $v = \frac{1}{2}c$ in the formula, we get: $m = \dfrac{m_0}{\sqrt{1 - \frac{\left(\frac{1}{2}c\right)^2}{c^2}}} = \dfrac{m_0}{\sqrt{1 - \frac{1}{4}}}$. Thus

     $m = \dfrac{1}{\sqrt{\frac{3}{4}}}m_0 = \dfrac{2\sqrt{3}}{3}m_0$. So the rest mass of the spaceship is multiplied by $\dfrac{2\sqrt{3}}{3} \approx 1.15$.

Using $v = 0.9c$ in the formula, we get: $m = \dfrac{m_0}{\sqrt{1 - \frac{(.9c)^2}{c^2}}} = \dfrac{m_0}{\sqrt{1 - .81}}$. Thus

$m = \frac{1}{\sqrt{0.19}}m_0 \approx 2.29m_0$. So the rest mass of the spaceship is multiplied by $\frac{1}{\sqrt{0.19}} \approx 2.29$. As the

spaceship travels very close to the speed of light, $v \to c$, so the term $\dfrac{v^2}{c^2}$ approaches 1. So $\sqrt{1 - \dfrac{v^2}{c^2}}$

approaches 0, and we obtain $m = \dfrac{m_0}{\text{very small number}}$, which means $m = (\text{very large number})m_0$.

Hence the mass of the space ship becomes arbitrarily large as its speed approaches the speed of light.

The actual value of the speed of light does not affect the calculations.

Exercises 1.3

1. $(3x^2 + x + 1) + (2x^2 - 3x - 5) = 5x^2 - 2x - 4$

3. $(x^3 + 6x^2 - 4x + 7) - (3x^2 + 2x - 4) = x^3 + 6x^2 - 4x + 7 - 3x^2 - 2x + 4 = x^3 + 3x^2 - 6x + 11$

5. $8(2x + 5) - 7(x - 9) = 16x + 40 - 7x + 63 = 9x + 103$

7. $2(2 - 5t) + t^2(t - 1) - (t^4 - 1) = 4 - 10t + t^3 - t^2 - t^4 + 1 = -t^4 + t^3 - t^2 - 10t + 5$

9. $\sqrt{x}(x - \sqrt{x}) = x^{1/2}(x - x^{1/2}) = x^{1/2}x - x^{1/2}x^{1/2} = x^{3/2} - x$

11. $y^{1/3}(y^2 - 1) = y^{1/3}y^2 - y^{1/3} = y^{7/3} - y^{1/3}$

13. $(3t - 2)(7t - 5) = 21t^2 - 15t - 14t + 10 = 21t^2 - 29t + 10$

15. $(x + 2y)(3x - y) = 3x^2 - xy + 6xy - 2y^2 = 3x^2 + 5xy - 2y^2$

17. $(1 - 2y)^2 = 1 - 4y + 4y^2$

19. $(2x^2 + 3y^2)^2 = (2x^2)^2 + 2(2x^2)(3y^2) + (3y^2)^2 = 4x^4 + 12x^2y^2 + 9y^4$

21. $(2x - 5)(x^2 - x + 1) = 2x^3 - 2x^2 + 2x - 5x^2 + 5x - 5 = 2x^3 - 7x^2 + 7x - 5$

23. $(x^2 - a^2)(x^2 + a^2) = (x^2)^2 - (a^2)^2 = x^4 - a^4$ (the difference of squares)

25. $\left(\sqrt{a} - \dfrac{1}{b}\right)\left(\sqrt{a} + \dfrac{1}{b}\right) = (\sqrt{a})^2 - \left(\dfrac{1}{b}\right)^2 = a - \dfrac{1}{b^2}$ (the difference of squares)

27. $(1 + a^3)^3 = 1 + 3(a^3) + 3(a^3)^2 + (a^3)^3 = 1 + 3a^3 + 3a^6 + a^9$ (perfect cube)

29. $(x^2 + x - 2)(x^3 - x + 1) = x^5 - x^3 + x^2 + x^4 - x^2 + x - 2x^3 + 2x - 2$
$= x^5 + x^4 - 3x^3 + 3x - 2$

31. $(1 + x^{4/3})(1 - x^{2/3}) = 1 - x^{2/3} + x^{4/3} - x^{6/3} = 1 - x^{2/3} + x^{4/3} - x^2$

33. $(3x^2y + 7xy^2)(x^2y^3 - 2y^2) = 3x^4y^4 - 6x^2y^3 + 7x^3y^5 - 14xy^4$
$= 3x^4y^4 + 7x^3y^5 - 6x^2y^3 - 14xy^4$ (arranging in decreasing powers of x)

35. $12x^3 + 18x = 6x(2x^2 + 3)$

37. $6y^4 - 15y^3 = 3y^3(2y - 5)$

39. $x^2 - 2x - 8 = (x - 4)(x + 2)$

41. $y^2 - 8y + 15 = (y - 5)(y - 3)$

43. $2x^2 + 5x + 3 = (2x + 3)(x + 1)$

45. $9x^2 - 36x - 45 = 9(x^2 - 4x - 5) = 9(x - 5)(x + 1)$

47. $6x^2 - 5x - 6 = (3x + 2)(2x - 3)$

49. $4t^2 - 12t + 9 = (2t - 3)^2$

51. $r^2 - 6rs + 9s^2 = (r - 3s)^2$

53. $x^2 - 36 = (x - 6)(x + 6)$

55. $49 - 4y^2 = (7 - 2y)(7 + 2y)$

57. $(a + b)^2 - (a - b)^2 = [(a + b) - (a - b)][(a + b) + (a - b)] = (2b)(2a) = 4ab$

59. $x^2(x^2 - 1) - 9(x^2 - 1) = (x^2 - 1)(x^2 - 9) = (x - 1)(x + 1)(x - 3)(x + 3)$

61. $t^3 + 1 = (t + 1)(t^2 - t + 1)$

63. $8x^3 - 125 = (2x)^3 - 5^3 = (2x - 5)[(2x)^2 + (2x)(5) + 5^2] = (2x - 5)(4x^2 + 10x + 25)$

65. $x^6 - 8y^3 = (x^2)^3 - (2y)^3 = (x^2 - 2y)[(x^2)^2 + (x^2)(2y) + (2y)^2] = (x^2 - 2y)(x^4 + 2x^2y + 4y^2)$

67. $x^3 + 2x^2 + x = x(x^2 + 2x + 1) = x(x + 1)^2$

69. $x^4 + 2x^3 - 3x^2 = x^2(x^2 + 2x - 3) = x^2(x - 1)(x + 3)$

71. $y^3 - 3y^2 - 4y + 12 = (y^3 - 3y^2) + (-4y + 12) = y^2(y - 3) + (-4)(y - 3) = (y - 3)(y^2 - 4)$
    $= (y - 3)(y - 2)(y + 2)$ (factor by grouping)

73. $2x^3 + 4x^2 + x + 2 = (2x^3 + 4x^2) + (x + 2) = 2x^2(x + 2) + (1)(x + 2) = (x + 2)(2x^2 + 1)$
    (factor by grouping)

75. $(x - 1)(x + 2)^2 - (x - 1)^2(x + 2) = (x - 1)(x + 2)\Big[(x + 2) - (x - 1)\Big] = 3(x - 1)(x + 2)$

77. $y^4(y + 2)^3 + y^5(y + 2)^4 = y^4(y + 2)^3\Big[(1) + y(y + 2)\Big] = y^4(y + 2)^3(y^2 + 2y + 1)$
    $= y^4(y + 2)^3(y + 1)^2$

79. $x^{5/2} - x^{1/2} = x^{1/2}(x^2 - 1) = \sqrt{x}(x - 1)(x + 1)$

81. Start by factoring out the power of x with the smallest exponent, that is, $x^{-3/2}$. So
    $$x^{-3/2} + 2x^{-1/2} + x^{1/2} = x^{-3/2}(1 + 2x + x^2) = \frac{(1 + x)^2}{x^{3/2}}.$$

83. Start by factoring out the power of $(x^2 + 1)$ with the smallest exponent, that is, $(x^2 + 1)^{-1/2}$. So
    $$(x^2 + 1)^{1/2} + 2(x^2 + 1)^{-1/2} = (x^2 + 1)^{-1/2}\Big[(x^2 + 1) + 2\Big] = \frac{x^2 + 3}{\sqrt{x^2 + 1}}.$$

85. Start by factoring $y^2 - 7y + 10$, and then substitute $a^2 + 1$ for y. This gives
    $(a^2 + 1)^2 - 7(a^2 + 1) + 10 = \Big[(a^2 + 1) - 2\Big]\Big[(a^2 + 1) - 5\Big] = (a^2 - 1)(a^2 - 4)$
    $= (a - 1)(a + 1)(a - 2)(a + 2).$

87. $3x^2(4x - 12)^2 + x^3(2)(4x - 12)(4) = x^2(4x - 12)[3(4x - 12) + x(2)(4)]$
    $= 4x^2(x - 3)(12x - 36 + 8x) = 4x^2(x - 3)(20x - 36) = 16x^2(x - 3)(5x - 9)$

89. $3(2x - 1)^2(2)(x + 3)^{1/2} + (2x - 1)^3\left(\frac{1}{2}\right)(x + 3)^{-1/2}$
    $= (2x - 1)^2(x + 3)^{-1/2}\Big[6(x + 3) + (2x - 1)\left(\frac{1}{2}\right)\Big] = (2x - 1)^2(x + 3)^{-1/2}\left(6x + 18 + x - \frac{1}{2}\right)$
    $= (2x - 1)^2(x + 3)^{-1/2}\left(7x + \frac{35}{2}\right)$

91. (a) $\frac{1}{2}[(a + b)^2 - (a^2 + b^2)] = \frac{1}{2}[a^2 + 2ab + b^2 - a^2 - b^2] = \frac{1}{2}(2ab) = ab.$

    (b) $(a^2 + b^2)^2 - (a^2 - b^2)^2 = [(a^2 + b^2) - (a^2 - b^2)][(a^2 + b^2) + (a^2 - b^2)]$
    $= (a^2 + b^2 - a^2 + b^2)(a^2 + b^2 + a^2 - b^2) = (2b^2)(2a^2) = 4a^2b^2$

(c)   LHS $= (a^2 + b^2)(c^2 + d^2) = a^2c^2 + a^2d^2 + b^2c^2 + b^2d^2$

     RHS $= (ac + bd)^2 + (ad - bc)^2 = a^2c^2 + 2abcd + b^2d^2 + a^2d^2 - 2abcd + b^2c^2$
     $= a^2c^2 + a^2d^2 + b^2c^2 + b^2d^2$

     So LHS $=$ RHS, that is, $(a^2 + b^2)(c^2 + d^2) = (ac + bd)^2 + (ad - bc)^2$.

(d) $4a^2c^2 - (c^2 - b^2 + a^2)^2 = (2ac)^2 - (c^2 - b^2 + a^2)$

$$= \left[(2ac) - (c^2 - b^2 + a^2) \right]\left[(2ac) + (c^2 - b^2 + a^2) \right] \text{ (the difference of squares)}$$

$$= (2ac - c^2 + b^2 - a^2)(2ac + c^2 - b^2 + a^2)$$

$$= \left[b^2 - (c^2 - 2ac + a^2) \right]\left[(c^2 + 2ac + a^2) - b^2 \right] \text{ (regrouping)}$$

$$= \left[b^2 - (c - a)^2 \right]\left[(c + a)^2 - b^2 \right] \text{ (perfect squares)}$$

$$= [b - (c - a)][b + (c - a)][(c + a) - b][(c + a) + b] \text{ (each factor is a difference of}$$
$$\text{squares)}$$

$$= (b - c + a)(b + c - a)(c + a - b)(c + a + b)$$

$$= (a + b - c)(-a + b + c)(a - b + c)(a + b + c)$$

(e) $x^4 + 3x^2 + 4 = (x^4 + 4x^2 + 4) - x^2 = (x^2 + 2)^2 - x^2 = \left[(x^2 + 2) - x \right]\left[(x^2 + 2) + x \right] = (x^2 - x + 2)(x^2 + x + 2)$

93. (a) $528^2 - 527^2 = (528 - 527)(528 + 527) = 1(1055) = 1055$

   (b) $122^2 - 120^2 = (122 - 120)(122 + 120) = 2(242) = 484$

   (c) $1020^2 - 1010^2 = (1020 - 1010)(1020 + 1010) = 10(2030) = 20{,}300$

   (d) $49 \cdot 51 = (50 - 1)(50 + 1) = 50^2 - 1 = 2500 - 1 = 2499$

   (e) $998 \cdot 1002 = (1000 - 2)(1000 + 2) = 1000^2 - 2^2 = 1{,}000{,}000 - 4 = 999{,}996$

95. (a) $A^4 - B^4 = (A^2 - B^2)(A^2 + B^2) = (A - B)(A + B)(A^2 + B^2)$

       $A^6 - B^6 = (A^3 - B^3)(A^3 + B^3)$ (the difference of squares)
           $= (A - B)(A^2 + AB + B^2)(A + B)(A^2 - AB + B^2)$ (difference and sum of cubes)

   (b) $12^4 - 7^4 = 20{,}736 - 2{,}401 = 18{,}335$

       $12^6 - 7^6 = 2{,}985{,}984 - 117{,}649 = 2{,}868{,}335$

   (c) $18{,}335 = 12^4 - 7^4 = (12 - 7)(12 + 7)(12^2 + 7^2) = 5(19)(144 + 49) = 5(19)(193)$

       $2{,}868{,}335 = 12^6 - 7^6 = (12 - 7)(12 + 7)[12^2 + 12(7) + 7^2][12^2 - 12(7) + 7^2]$
           $= 5(19)(144 + 84 + 49)(144 - 84 + 49) = 5(19)(277)(109)$

97. (a) $x^4 + x^2 - 2 = (x^2 - 1)(x^2 + 2) = (x - 1)(x + 1)(x^2 + 2)$

   (b) $x^4 + 2x^2 + 9 = (x^4 + 6x^2 + 9) - 4x^2 = (x^2 + 3)^2 - (2x)^2 = [(x^2 + 3) - 2x][(x^2 + 3) + 2x]$
         $= (x^2 - 2x + 3)(x^2 + 2x + 3)$

   (c) $x^4 + 4x^2 + 16 = (x^4 + 8x^2 + 16) - 4x^2 = (x^2 + 4)^2 - (2x)^2$
         $= [(x^2 + 4) - 2x][(x^2 + 4) + 2x] = (x^2 - 2x + 4)(x^2 + 2x + 4)$

   (d) $x^4 + 2x^2 + 1 = (x^2 + 1)^2$

Exercises 1.4

1. $\dfrac{x-2}{x^2-4} = \dfrac{x-2}{(x-2)(x+2)} = \dfrac{1}{x+2}$

3. $\dfrac{x^2+6x+8}{x^2+5x+4} = \dfrac{(x+2)(x+4)}{(x+1)(x+4)} = \dfrac{x+2}{x+1}$

5. $\dfrac{y^2+y}{y^2-1} = \dfrac{y(y+1)}{(y-1)(y+1)} = \dfrac{y}{y-1}$

7. $\dfrac{2x^3-x^2-6x}{2x^2-7x+6} = \dfrac{x(2x^2-x-6)}{(2x-3)(x-2)} = \dfrac{x(2x+3)(x-2)}{(2x-3)(x-2)} = \dfrac{x(2x+3)}{2x-3}$

9. $\dfrac{t-3}{t^2+9} \cdot \dfrac{t+3}{t^2-9} = \dfrac{(t-3)(t+3)}{(t^2+9)(t-3)(t+3)} = \dfrac{1}{t^2+9}$

11. $\dfrac{x^2+7x+12}{x^2+3x+2} \cdot \dfrac{x^2+5x+6}{x^2+6x+9} = \dfrac{(x+3)(x+4)}{(x+1)(x+2)} \cdot \dfrac{(x+2)(x+3)}{(x+3)(x+3)} = \dfrac{x+4}{x+1}$

13. $\dfrac{2x^2+3x+1}{x^2+2x-15} \div \dfrac{x^2+6x+5}{2x^2-7x+3} = \dfrac{2x^2+3x+1}{x^2+2x-15} \cdot \dfrac{2x^2-7x+3}{x^2+6x+5} =$
$\dfrac{(2x+1)(x+1)}{(x-3)(x+5)} \cdot \dfrac{(2x-1)(x-3)}{(x+1)(x+5)} = \dfrac{(2x+1)(2x-1)}{(x+5)(x+5)} = \dfrac{(2x+1)(2x-1)}{(x+5)^2}$

15. $\dfrac{\dfrac{\dfrac{x^3}{x+1}}{x}}{x^2+2x+1} = \dfrac{x^3}{x+1} \cdot \dfrac{x^2+2x+1}{x} = \dfrac{x^3(x+1)(x+1)}{(x+1)x} = x^2(x+1)$

17. $\dfrac{x/y}{z} = \dfrac{x}{y} \cdot \dfrac{1}{z} = \dfrac{x}{yz}$

19. $\dfrac{1}{x+5} + \dfrac{2}{x-3} = \dfrac{x-3}{(x+5)(x-3)} + \dfrac{2(x+5)}{(x+5)(x-3)} = \dfrac{x-3+2x+10}{(x+5)(x-3)} = \dfrac{3x+7}{(x+5)(x-3)}$

21. $\dfrac{1}{x+1} - \dfrac{1}{x+2} = \dfrac{x+2}{(x+1)(x+2)} + \dfrac{-(x+1)}{(x+1)(x+2)} = \dfrac{x+2-x-1}{(x+1)(x+2)} = \dfrac{1}{(x+1)(x+2)}$

23. $\dfrac{x}{(x+1)^2} + \dfrac{2}{x+1} = \dfrac{x}{(x+1)^2} + \dfrac{2(x+1)}{(x+1)(x+1)} = \dfrac{x+2x+2}{(x+1)^2} = \dfrac{3x+2}{(x+1)^2}$

25. $u+1+\dfrac{u}{u+1} = \dfrac{(u+1)(u+1)}{u+1} + \dfrac{u}{u+1} = \dfrac{u^2+2u+1+u}{u+1} = \dfrac{u^2+3u+1}{u+1}$

27. $\dfrac{1}{x^2} + \dfrac{1}{x^2+x} = \dfrac{1}{x^2} + \dfrac{1}{x(x+1)} = \dfrac{x+1}{x^2(x+1)} + \dfrac{x}{x^2(x+1)} = \dfrac{2x+1}{x^2(x+1)}$

29. $\dfrac{2}{x+3} - \dfrac{1}{x^2+7x+12} = \dfrac{2}{x+3} - \dfrac{1}{(x+3)(x+4)} = \dfrac{2(x+4)}{(x+3)(x+4)} + \dfrac{-1}{(x+3)(x+4)}$
$= \dfrac{2x+8-1}{(x+3)(x+4)} = \dfrac{2x+7}{(x+3)(x+4)}$

31. $\dfrac{1}{x+3} + \dfrac{1}{x^2-9} = \dfrac{1}{x+3} + \dfrac{1}{(x-3)(x+3)} = \dfrac{x-3}{(x-3)(x+3)} + \dfrac{1}{(x-3)(x+3)}$

$= \dfrac{x-2}{(x-3)(x+3)}$

33. $\dfrac{2}{x} + \dfrac{3}{x-1} - \dfrac{4}{x^2-x} = \dfrac{2}{x} + \dfrac{3}{x-1} - \dfrac{4}{x(x-1)} = \dfrac{2(x-1)}{x(x-1)} + \dfrac{3x}{x(x-1)} + \dfrac{-4}{x(x-1)}$

$= \dfrac{2x-2+3x-4}{x(x-1)} = \dfrac{5x-6}{x(x-1)}$

35. $\dfrac{1}{x^2+3x+2} - \dfrac{1}{x^2-2x-3} = \dfrac{1}{(x+2)(x+1)} - \dfrac{1}{(x-3)(x+1)}$

$= \dfrac{x-3}{(x-3)(x+2)(x+1)} + \dfrac{-(x+2)}{(x-3)(x+2)(x+1)}$

$= \dfrac{x-3-x-2}{(x-3)(x+2)(x+1)} = \dfrac{-5}{(x-3)(x+2)(x+1)}$

37. $\dfrac{\dfrac{x}{y} - \dfrac{y}{x}}{\dfrac{1}{x^2} - \dfrac{1}{y^2}} = \dfrac{\dfrac{x^2-y^2}{xy}}{\dfrac{y^2-x^2}{x^2y^2}} = \dfrac{x^2-y^2}{xy} \cdot \dfrac{x^2y^2}{y^2-x^2} = \dfrac{xy}{-1} = -xy$. An alternative method is to multiply

the numerator and denominator by the common denominator of both the numerator and denominator, in this case x^2y^2.

$\dfrac{\dfrac{x}{y} - \dfrac{y}{x}}{\dfrac{1}{x^2} - \dfrac{1}{y^2}} = \dfrac{\left(\dfrac{x}{y} - \dfrac{y}{x}\right)}{\left(\dfrac{1}{x^2} - \dfrac{1}{y^2}\right)} \cdot \dfrac{x^2y^2}{x^2y^2} = \dfrac{x^3y - xy^3}{y^2-x^2} = \dfrac{xy(x^2-y^2)}{y^2-x^2} = -xy$

39. $\dfrac{1+\dfrac{1}{c-1}}{1-\dfrac{1}{c-1}} = \dfrac{\dfrac{c-1}{c-1}+\dfrac{1}{c-1}}{\dfrac{c-1}{c-1}+\dfrac{-1}{c-1}} = \dfrac{\dfrac{c}{c-1}}{\dfrac{c-2}{c-1}} = \dfrac{c}{c-1} \cdot \dfrac{c-1}{c-2} = \dfrac{c}{c-2}$. Using the alternative method we

obtain:

$\dfrac{1+\dfrac{1}{c-1}}{1-\dfrac{1}{c-1}} = \dfrac{\left(1+\dfrac{1}{c-1}\right)}{\left(1-\dfrac{1}{c-1}\right)} \cdot \dfrac{c-1}{c-1} = \dfrac{c-1+1}{c-1-1} = \dfrac{c}{c-2}$.

41. $\dfrac{\dfrac{5}{x-1} - \dfrac{2}{x+1}}{\dfrac{x}{x-1} + \dfrac{1}{x+1}} = \dfrac{\dfrac{5(x+1)}{(x-1)(x+1)} + \dfrac{-2(x-1)}{(x-1)(x+1)}}{\dfrac{x(x+1)}{(x-1)(x+1)} + \dfrac{x-1}{(x-1)(x+1)}} = \dfrac{\dfrac{5x+5-2x+2}{(x-1)(x+1)}}{\dfrac{x^2+x+x-1}{(x-1)(x+1)}}$

$= \dfrac{3x+7}{(x-1)(x+1)} \cdot \dfrac{(x-1)(x+1)}{x^2+2x-1} = \dfrac{3x+7}{x^2+2x-1}$

Alternatively,

$$\frac{\dfrac{5}{x-1}-\dfrac{2}{x+1}}{\dfrac{x}{x-1}+\dfrac{1}{x+1}}=\frac{\left(\dfrac{5}{x-1}-\dfrac{2}{x+1}\right)}{\left(\dfrac{x}{x-1}+\dfrac{1}{x+1}\right)}\cdot\frac{(x-1)(x+1)}{(x-1)(x+1)}=\frac{5(x+1)-2(x-1)}{x(x+1)+(x-1)}$$

$$=\frac{5x+5-2x+2}{x^2+x+x-1}=\frac{3x+7}{x^2+2x-1}.$$

43. $\dfrac{x^{-2}-y^{-2}}{x^{-1}+y^{-1}}=\dfrac{\dfrac{1}{x^2}-\dfrac{1}{y^2}}{\dfrac{1}{x}+\dfrac{1}{y}}=\dfrac{\dfrac{y^2}{x^2y^2}-\dfrac{x^2}{x^2y^2}}{\dfrac{y}{xy}+\dfrac{x}{xy}}=\dfrac{y^2-x^2}{x^2y^2}\cdot\dfrac{xy}{y+x}=\dfrac{(y-x)(y+x)xy}{x^2y^2(y+x)}=\dfrac{y-x}{xy}$

Alternatively,

$$\frac{x^{-2}-y^{-2}}{x^{-1}+y^{-1}}=\frac{\left(\dfrac{1}{x^2}-\dfrac{1}{y^2}\right)}{\left(\dfrac{1}{x}+\dfrac{1}{y}\right)}\cdot\frac{x^2y^2}{x^2y^2}=\frac{y^2-x^2}{xy^2+x^2y}=\frac{(y-x)(y+x)}{xy(y+x)}=\frac{y-x}{xy}.$$

45. $\dfrac{1}{1+a^n}+\dfrac{1}{1+a^{-n}}=\dfrac{1}{1+a^n}+\dfrac{1}{1+a^{-n}}\cdot\dfrac{a^n}{a^n}=\dfrac{1}{1+a^n}+\dfrac{a^n}{a^n+1}=\dfrac{1+a^n}{1+a^n}=1$

47. $\dfrac{\dfrac{1}{a+h}-\dfrac{1}{a}}{h}=\dfrac{\dfrac{a}{a(a+h)}-\dfrac{a+h}{a(a+h)}}{h}=\dfrac{\dfrac{a-a-h}{a(a+h)}}{h}=\dfrac{-h}{a(a+h)}\cdot\dfrac{1}{h}=\dfrac{-1}{a(a+h)}$

49. $\dfrac{\dfrac{1-(x+h)}{2+(x+h)}-\dfrac{1-x}{2+x}}{h}=\dfrac{\dfrac{(2+x)(1-x-h)}{(2+x)(2+x+h)}-\dfrac{(1-x)(2+x+h)}{(2+x)(2+x+h)}}{h}$

$$=\dfrac{\dfrac{2-x-x^2-2h-xh}{(2+x)(2+x+h)}-\dfrac{2-x-x^2+h-xh}{(2+x)(2+x+h)}}{h}=\dfrac{-3h}{(2+x)(2+x+h)}\cdot\dfrac{1}{h}$$

$$=\dfrac{-3}{(2+x)(2+x+h)}$$

51. $\sqrt{1+\left(\dfrac{x}{\sqrt{1-x^2}}\right)^2}=\sqrt{1+\dfrac{x^2}{1-x^2}}=\sqrt{\dfrac{1-x^2}{1-x^2}+\dfrac{x^2}{1-x^2}}=\sqrt{\dfrac{1}{1-x^2}}=\dfrac{1}{\sqrt{1-x^2}}$

53. $\dfrac{3(x+2)^2(x-3)^2-(x+2)^3(2)(x-3)}{(x-3)^4}=\dfrac{(x+2)^2(x-3)[3(x-3)-(x+2)(2)]}{(x-3)^4}$

$$=\dfrac{(x+2)^2(3x-9-2x-4)}{(x-3)^3}=\dfrac{(x+2)^2(x-13)}{(x-3)^3}$$

55. $\dfrac{2(1+x)^{1/2}-x(1+x)^{-1/2}}{1+x}=\dfrac{(1+x)^{-1/2}[2(1+x)-x]}{1+x}=\dfrac{x+2}{(1+x)^{3/2}}$

57. $\dfrac{3(1+x)^{1/3}-x(1+x)^{-2/3}}{(1+x)^{2/3}}=\dfrac{(1+x)^{-2/3}[3(1+x)-x]}{(1+x)^{2/3}}=\dfrac{2x+3}{(1+x)^{4/3}}$

59. $\dfrac{2}{3+\sqrt{5}} = \dfrac{2}{3+\sqrt{5}} \cdot \dfrac{3-\sqrt{5}}{3-\sqrt{5}} = \dfrac{2\left(3-\sqrt{5}\right)}{9-5} = \dfrac{2\left(3-\sqrt{5}\right)}{4} = \dfrac{3-\sqrt{5}}{2}$

61. $\dfrac{2}{\sqrt{2}+\sqrt{7}} = \dfrac{2}{\sqrt{2}+\sqrt{7}} \cdot \dfrac{\sqrt{2}-\sqrt{7}}{\sqrt{2}-\sqrt{7}} = \dfrac{2\left(\sqrt{2}-\sqrt{7}\right)}{2-7} = \dfrac{2\left(\sqrt{2}-\sqrt{7}\right)}{-5} = \dfrac{2\left(\sqrt{7}-\sqrt{2}\right)}{5}$

63. $\dfrac{1-\sqrt{5}}{3} = \dfrac{1-\sqrt{5}}{3} \cdot \dfrac{1+\sqrt{5}}{1+\sqrt{5}} = \dfrac{1-5}{3\left(1+\sqrt{5}\right)} = \dfrac{-4}{3\left(1+\sqrt{5}\right)}$

65. $\dfrac{\sqrt{r}+\sqrt{2}}{5} = \dfrac{\sqrt{r}+\sqrt{2}}{5} \cdot \dfrac{\sqrt{r}-\sqrt{2}}{\sqrt{r}-\sqrt{2}} = \dfrac{r-2}{5\left(\sqrt{r}-\sqrt{2}\right)}$

67. $\sqrt{x^2+1} - x = \dfrac{\sqrt{x^2+1}-x}{1} \cdot \dfrac{\sqrt{x^2+1}+x}{\sqrt{x^2+1}+x} = \dfrac{x^2+1-x^2}{\sqrt{x^2+1}+x} = \dfrac{1}{\sqrt{x^2+1}+x}$

69. $\dfrac{16+a}{16} = \dfrac{16}{16} + \dfrac{a}{16} = 1 + \dfrac{a}{16}$, so the statement is true.

71. This statement is false. For example, take $x = 2$, then LHS $= \dfrac{2}{4+x} = \dfrac{2}{4+2} = \dfrac{2}{6} = \dfrac{1}{3}$, while RHS $= \dfrac{1}{2} + \dfrac{2}{x} = \dfrac{1}{2} + \dfrac{2}{2} = \dfrac{3}{2}$, and $\dfrac{1}{3} \neq \dfrac{3}{2}$.

73. This statement is false. For example, take $x = 0$ and $y = 1$. Then substituting into the left side we obtain LHS $= \dfrac{x}{x+y} = \dfrac{0}{0+1} = 0$, while the right side yields RHS $= \dfrac{1}{1+y} = \dfrac{1}{1+1} = \dfrac{1}{2}$, and $0 \neq \frac{1}{2}$.

75. This statement is true: $\dfrac{-a}{b} = (-a)\left(\dfrac{1}{b}\right) = (-1)(a)\left(\dfrac{1}{b}\right) = (-1)\left(\dfrac{a}{b}\right) = -\dfrac{a}{b}$.

77. This statement is false. For example, take $x = -2$. Then LHS $= \dfrac{x^2+1}{x^2+x-1} = \dfrac{(-2)^2+1}{(-2)^2+(-2)-1}$ $= \dfrac{4+1}{4-2-1} = \dfrac{5}{1} = 5$, while RHS $= \dfrac{1}{x-1} = \dfrac{1}{(-2)-1} = \dfrac{1}{-3} = -\dfrac{1}{3}$, and $5 \neq -\dfrac{1}{3}$.

79. (a) $R = \dfrac{1}{\dfrac{1}{R_1} + \dfrac{1}{R_2}} = \dfrac{1}{\dfrac{1}{R_1} + \dfrac{1}{R_2}} \cdot \dfrac{R_1 R_2}{R_1 R_2} = \dfrac{R_1 R_2}{R_2 + R_1}$

   (b) Substituting $R_1 = 10$ ohms and $R_2 = 20$ ohms yields $R = \dfrac{(10)(20)}{(20)+(10)} = \dfrac{200}{30} \approx 6.7$ ohms.

81. No, squaring $\dfrac{2}{\sqrt{x}}$ changes its value by a factor of $\dfrac{2}{\sqrt{x}}$.

83. (a) $A + B$　　　　(b) AB　　　　(c) $A^{1/3}$　　　　(d) A/B

Exercises 1.5

1. (a) $3(4) + 7 \overset{?}{=} 5(4) - 1$

    $12 + 7 \overset{?}{=} 20 - 1$ Yes, a solution.

    (b) $3\left(\frac{3}{2}\right) + 7 \overset{?}{=} 5\left(\frac{3}{2}\right) - 1$

    $\frac{9}{2} + 7 \overset{?}{=} \frac{15}{2} - 1$ No, not a solution.

3. (a) $1 - [2 - (3 - \{2\})] \overset{?}{=} 4\{2\} - (6 + \{2\})$

    $1 - [2 - (1)] \overset{?}{=} 8 - 8$

    $1 - (1) \overset{?}{=} 0$ Yes, a solution.

    (b) $1 - [2 - (3 - \{22\})] \overset{?}{=} 4\{22\} - (6 + \{22\})$

    $1 - [2 - (-19)] \overset{?}{=} 88 - 28$

    $1 - (21) \overset{?}{=} 60$ No, not a solution.

5. $3x - 5 = 7 \quad \Leftrightarrow \quad 3x = 12 \quad \Leftrightarrow \quad x = 4$

7. $x - 3 = 2x + 6 \quad \Leftrightarrow \quad -9 = x$

9. $-7w = 15 - 2w \quad \Leftrightarrow \quad -5w = 15 \quad \Leftrightarrow \quad w = -3$

11. $\frac{1}{2}y - 2 = \frac{1}{3}y \quad \Leftrightarrow \quad 3y - 12 = 2y$ (multiply both sides by the LCD, 6) $\Leftrightarrow \quad y = 12$

13. $2(1 - x) = 3(1 + 2x) + 5 \quad \Leftrightarrow \quad 2 - 2x = 3 + 6x + 5 \quad \Leftrightarrow \quad 2 - 2x = 8 + 6x \quad \Leftrightarrow$
    $-6 = 8x \quad \Leftrightarrow \quad x = -\frac{3}{4}$

15. $4\left(y - \frac{1}{2}\right) - y = 6(5 - y) \quad \Leftrightarrow \quad 4y - 2 - y = 30 - 6y \quad \Leftrightarrow \quad 3y - 2 = 30 - 6y \quad \Leftrightarrow$
    $9y = 32 \quad \Leftrightarrow \quad y = \frac{32}{9}$

17. $x^2 + 2x - 8 = 0 \quad \Leftrightarrow \quad (x - 2)(x + 4) = 0 \quad \Leftrightarrow \quad x - 2 = 0$ or $x + 4$. Thus $x = 2$ or $x = -4$.

19. $2y^2 + 7y + 3 = 0 \quad \Leftrightarrow \quad (2y + 1)(y + 3) = 0 \quad \Leftrightarrow \quad 2y + 1 = 0$ or $y + 3 = 0$. Thus $y = -\frac{1}{2}$ or
    $y = -3$.

21. $6x^2 + 5x = 4 \quad \Leftrightarrow \quad 6x^2 + 5x - 4 = 0 \quad \Leftrightarrow \quad (2x - 1)(3x + 4) = 0 \quad \Leftrightarrow \quad 2x - 1 = 0$ or
    $3x + 4 = 0$. If $2x - 1 = 0$, then $x = \frac{1}{2}$; if $3x + 4 = 0$, then $x = -\frac{4}{3}$.

23. $x^2 + 2x - 2 = 0 \quad \Leftrightarrow \quad x^2 + 2x = 2 \quad \Leftrightarrow \quad x^2 + 2x + 1 = 2 + 1 \quad \Leftrightarrow \quad (x + 1)^2 = 3 \quad \Rightarrow$
    $x + 1 = \pm\sqrt{3} \quad \Leftrightarrow \quad x = -1 \pm \sqrt{3}$.

25. $x^2 + x - \dfrac{3}{4} = 0 \quad \Leftrightarrow \quad x^2 + x = \dfrac{3}{4} \quad \Leftrightarrow \quad x^2 + x + \dfrac{1}{4} = \dfrac{3}{4} + \dfrac{1}{4} \quad \Leftrightarrow \quad \left(x + \dfrac{1}{2}\right)^2 = 1 \quad \Rightarrow$
    $x + \frac{1}{2} = \pm 1 \quad \Leftrightarrow \quad x = -\frac{1}{2} \pm 1$, so $x = -\frac{3}{2}$ or $x = \frac{1}{2}$.

27. $2x^2 + 8x + 1 = 0 \quad \Leftrightarrow \quad x^2 + 4x + \frac{1}{2} = 0 \quad \Leftrightarrow \quad x^2 + 4x = -\frac{1}{2} \quad \Leftrightarrow \quad x^2 + 4x + 4 = -\frac{1}{2} + 4$
    $\Leftrightarrow \quad (x + 2)^2 = \frac{7}{2} \quad \Rightarrow \quad x + 2 = \pm\sqrt{\frac{7}{2}} \quad \Leftrightarrow \quad x = -2 \pm \frac{\sqrt{14}}{2}$.

29. $x^2 + 12x - 27 = 0 \quad \Leftrightarrow \quad x^2 + 12x = 27 \quad \Leftrightarrow \quad x^2 + 12x + 36 = 27 + 36 \quad \Leftrightarrow$
    $(x + 6)^2 = 63 \quad \Rightarrow \quad x + 6 = \pm 3\sqrt{7} \quad \Leftrightarrow \quad x = -6 \pm 3\sqrt{7}$.

31. $3x^2 + 6x - 5 = 0$ $\Leftrightarrow$ $x^2 + 2x - \frac{5}{3} = 0$ $\Leftrightarrow$ $x^2 + 2x = \frac{5}{3}$ $\Leftrightarrow$ $x^2 + 2x + 1 = \frac{5}{3} + 1$
$\Leftrightarrow$ $(x+1)^2 = \frac{8}{3}$ $\Rightarrow$ $x + 1 = \pm\sqrt{\frac{8}{3}}$ $\Leftrightarrow$ $x = -1 \pm \frac{2\sqrt{6}}{3}$.

33. $2y^2 - y - \frac{1}{2} = 0$ $\Rightarrow$ $y = \dfrac{-b \pm \sqrt{b^2 - 4ac}}{2a} = \dfrac{-(-1) \pm \sqrt{(-1)^2 - 4(2)\left(-\frac{1}{2}\right)}}{2(2)} = \dfrac{1 \pm \sqrt{1 + 4}}{4}$
$= \dfrac{1 \pm \sqrt{5}}{4}$.

35. $10y^2 - 16y + 5 = 0$ $\Rightarrow$ $x = \dfrac{-b \pm \sqrt{b^2 - 4ac}}{2a} = \dfrac{-(-16) \pm \sqrt{(-16)^2 - 4(10)(5)}}{2(10)}$
$= \dfrac{16 \pm \sqrt{256 - 200}}{20} = \dfrac{16 \pm \sqrt{56}}{20} = \dfrac{16 \pm 2\sqrt{14}}{20} = \dfrac{8 \pm \sqrt{14}}{10}$.

37. $3x^2 + 2x + 2 = 0$ $\Rightarrow$ $x = \dfrac{-b \pm \sqrt{b^2 - 4ac}}{2a} = \dfrac{-(2) \pm \sqrt{(2)^2 - 4(3)(2)}}{2(3)}$
$= \dfrac{-2 \pm \sqrt{4 - 24}}{6} = = \dfrac{-2 \pm \sqrt{-20}}{6}$. Since the discriminant is less than 0, the equation has no real solutions.

39. $\dfrac{1}{x - 1} + \dfrac{1}{x + 2} = \dfrac{5}{4}$ $\Leftrightarrow$ $4(x - 1)(x + 2)\left(\dfrac{1}{x - 1} + \dfrac{1}{x + 2}\right) = 4(x - 1)(x + 2)\left(\dfrac{5}{4}\right)$ $\Leftrightarrow$
$4(x + 2) + 4(x - 1) = 5(x - 1)(x + 2)$ $\Leftrightarrow$ $4x + 8 + 4x - 4 = 5x^2 + 5x - 10$ $\Leftrightarrow$
$5x^2 - 3x - 14 = 0$ $\Leftrightarrow$ $(5x + 7)(x - 2) = 0$. If $5x + 7 = 0$, then $x = -\frac{7}{5}$; if $x - 2 = 0$, then
$x = 2$. The solutions are $-\frac{7}{5}$ and 2.

41. $\dfrac{x^2}{x + 100} = 50$ $\Rightarrow$ $x^2 = 50(x + 100) = 50x + 5000$ $\Leftrightarrow$ $x^2 - 50x - 5000 = 0$ $\Leftrightarrow$
$(x - 100)(x + 50) = 0$ $\Leftrightarrow$ $x - 100 = 0$ or $x + 50 = 0$. Thus $x = 100$ or $x = -50$. The
solutions are 100 and -50.

43. $\dfrac{x + 5}{x - 2} = \dfrac{5}{x + 2} + \dfrac{28}{x^2 - 4}$ $\Rightarrow$ $(x + 2)(x + 5) = 5(x - 2) + 28$ $\Leftrightarrow$
$x^2 + 7x + 10 = 5x - 10 + 28$ $\Leftrightarrow$ $x^2 + 2x - 8 = 0$ $\Leftrightarrow$ $(x - 2)(x + 4) = 0$ $\Leftrightarrow$
$x - 2 = 0$ or $x + 4 = 0$ $\Leftrightarrow$ $x = 2$ or $x = -4$. However, $x = 2$ is inadmissible since we can't
divide by 0 in the original equation, so the only solution is -4.

45. $\sqrt{2x + 1} + 1 = x$ $\Leftrightarrow$ $\sqrt{2x + 1} = x - 1$ $\Rightarrow$ $2x + 1 = (x - 1)^2$ $\Leftrightarrow$
$2x + 1 = x^2 - 2x + 1$ $\Leftrightarrow$ $0 = x^2 - 4x = x(x - 4)$. Potential solutions are $x = 0$ and $x - 4$
$\Leftrightarrow$ $x = 4$. These are only potential solutions since *squaring* is not a reversible operation. We
must check each potential solution in the original equation.
Checking $x = 0$: $\sqrt{2(0) + 1} + 1 \overset{?}{=} (0)$, $\sqrt{1} + 1 \overset{?}{=} 0$, NO!
Checking $x = 4$: $\sqrt{2(4) + 1} + 1 \overset{?}{=} (4)$, $\sqrt{9} + 1 \overset{?}{=} 4$, $3 + 1 \overset{?}{=} 4$, Yes. The only solution is $x = 4$.

47. $2x + \sqrt{x + 1} = 8$ $\Leftrightarrow$ $\sqrt{x + 1} = 8 - 2x$ $\Rightarrow$ $x + 1 = (8 - 2x)^2$ $\Leftrightarrow$
$x + 1 = 64 - 32x + 4x^2$ $\Leftrightarrow$ $0 = 4x^2 - 33x + 63 = (4x - 21)(x - 3)$. Potential solutions are
$x = \frac{21}{4}$ and $x = 3$. Substituting each of these solutions into the original equation, we see that $x = 3$
is a solution, but $x = \frac{21}{4}$ is not. Thus 3 is the only solution.

49. Let $w = x^2$. Then $x^4 - 13x^2 + 40 = (x^2)^2 - 13x^2 + 40 = 0$ becomes $w^2 - 13w + 40 = 0$ $\Leftrightarrow$ $(w - 5)(w - 8) = 0$. So $w - 5 = 0$ $\Leftrightarrow$ $w = 5$, and $w - 8 = 0$ $\Leftrightarrow$ $w = 8$. When $w = 5$, we have $x^2 = 5$ $\Rightarrow$ $x = \pm\sqrt{5}$. When $w = 8$, we have $x^2 = 8$ $\Rightarrow$ $x = \pm\sqrt{8} = \pm 2\sqrt{2}$. The solutions are $\pm\sqrt{5}$ and $\pm 2\sqrt{2}$.

51. $2x^4 + 4x^2 + 1 = 0$. The LHS is the sum of two nonnegative numbers and a positive number, so $2x^4 + 4x^2 + 1 \geq 1 \neq 0$. This equation has no real solutions.

53. Let $u = x^{2/3}$. Then $0 = x^{4/3} - 5x^{2/3} + 6$ becomes $u^2 - 5u + 6 = 0$ $\Leftrightarrow$ $(u - 3)(u - 2) = 0$ $\Leftrightarrow$ $u - 3 = 0$ or $u - 2 = 0$. If $u - 3 = 0$, then $x^{2/3} - 3 = 0$ $\Leftrightarrow$ $x^{2/3} = 3$ $\Rightarrow$ $x = \pm 3^{3/2}$. If $u - 2 = 0$, then $x^{2/3} - 2 = 0$ $\Leftrightarrow$ $x^{2/3} = 2$ $\Rightarrow$ $x = \pm 2^{3/2}$. The solutions are $\pm 3^{3/2}$ and $\pm 2^{3/2}$.

55. $4(x + 1)^{1/2} - 5(x + 1)^{3/2} + (x + 1)^{5/2} = 0$ $\Leftrightarrow$ $\sqrt{x + 1}[4 - 5(x + 1) + (x + 1)^2] = 0$ $\Leftrightarrow$ $\sqrt{x + 1}(4 - 5x - 5 + x^2 + 2x + 1) = 0$ $\Leftrightarrow$ $\sqrt{x + 1}(x^2 - 3x) = 0$ $\Leftrightarrow$ $\sqrt{x + 1} \cdot x(x - 3) = 0$ $\Leftrightarrow$ $x = -1$ or $x = 0$ or $x = 3$. The solutions are $-1, 0$, and 3.

57. Let $u = x^{1/6}$. (We choose the exponent $\frac{1}{6}$ because the LCD of 2, 3, and 6 is 6.) Then $x^{1/2} - 3x^{1/3} = 3x^{1/6} - 9$ $\Leftrightarrow$ $x^{3/6} - 3x^{2/6} = 3x^{1/6} - 9$ $\Leftrightarrow$ $u^3 - 3u^2 = 3u - 9$ $\Leftrightarrow$ $0 = u^3 - 3u^2 - 3u + 9 = u^2(u - 3) - 3(u - 3) = (u - 3)(u^2 - 3)$. So $u - 3 = 0$ or $u^2 - 3 = 0$. If $u - 3 = 0$, then $x^{1/6} - 3 = 0$ $\Leftrightarrow$ $x^{1/6} = 3$ $\Leftrightarrow$ $x = 3^6 = 729$. If $u^2 - 3 = 0$, then $x^{1/3} - 3 = 0$ $\Leftrightarrow$ $x^{1/3} = 3$ $\Leftrightarrow$ $x = 3^3 = 27$. The solutions are 729 and 27.

59. $|2x| = 3$. So $2x = 3$ $\Leftrightarrow$ $x = \frac{3}{2}$ or $2x = -3$ $\Leftrightarrow$ $x = -\frac{3}{2}$.

61. $|x - 4| = 0.01$. So $x - 4 = 0.01$ $\Leftrightarrow$ $x = 4.01$ or $x - 4 = -0.01$ $\Leftrightarrow$ $x = 3.99$.

63. $PV = nRT$ $\Leftrightarrow$ $R = \dfrac{PV}{nT}$

65. $\dfrac{1}{R} = \dfrac{1}{R_1} + \dfrac{1}{R_2}$ $\Leftrightarrow$ $R_1 R_2 = R R_2 + R R_1$ (multiply both sides by the LCD, $R R_1 R_2$). Thus $R_1 R_2 - R R_1 = R R_2$ $\Leftrightarrow$ $R_1(R_2 - R) = R R_2$ $\Leftrightarrow$ $R_1 = \dfrac{R R_2}{R_2 - R}$

67. $\dfrac{ax + b}{cx + d} = 2$ $\Leftrightarrow$ $ax + b = 2(cx + d)$ $\Leftrightarrow$ $ax + b = 2cx + 2d$ $\Leftrightarrow$ $ax - 2cx = 2d - b$ $\Leftrightarrow$ $(a - 2c)x = 2d - b$ $\Leftrightarrow$ $x = \dfrac{2d - b}{a - 2c}$

69. $a^2 x + (a - 1) = (a + 1)x$ $\Leftrightarrow$ $a^2 x - (a + 1)x = -(a - 1)$ $\Leftrightarrow$ $(a^2 - (a + 1))x = -a + 1$ $\Leftrightarrow$ $(a^2 - a - 1)x = -a + 1$ $\Leftrightarrow$ $x = \dfrac{-a + 1}{a^2 - a - 1}$

71. $V = \dfrac{1}{3}\pi r^2 h$ $\Leftrightarrow$ $r^2 = \dfrac{3V}{\pi h}$ $\Rightarrow$ $r = \pm\sqrt{\dfrac{3V}{\pi h}}$

73. $a^2 + b^2 = c^2$ $\Leftrightarrow$ $b^2 = c^2 - a^2$ $\Rightarrow$ $b = \pm\sqrt{c^2 - a^2}$

75. $D = b^2 - 4ac = (-6)^2 - 4(1)(1) = 32$. Since D is positive, this equation has two real solutions.

77. $D = b^2 - 4ac = (2.20)^2 - 4(1)(1.21) = 4.84 - 4.84 = 0$. Since $D = 0$, this equation has one real solution.

79. Using $h_0 = 288$, we solve $0 = -16t^2 + 288$, for $t \geq 0$. So $0 = -16t^2 + 288 \Leftrightarrow 16t^2 = 288$ $\Leftrightarrow t^2 = 18 \Rightarrow t = \pm\sqrt{18} = \pm 3\sqrt{2}$. Thus it takes $3\sqrt{2} \approx 4.24$ seconds for the ball the hit the ground.

81. We are given $v_o = 40$ ft/s

    (a) Setting $h = 24$, we have $24 = -16t^2 + 40t \Leftrightarrow 16t^2 - 40t + 24 = 0 \Leftrightarrow$
        $8(2t - 3)(t - 1) = 0 \Leftrightarrow t = 1$ or $t = 1\frac{1}{2}$. Therefore, the ball reaches 24 feet in 1 second
        (on the ascent) and again after $1\frac{1}{2}$ seconds (on its descent).

    (b) Setting $h = 48$, we have $48 = -16t^2 + 40t \Leftrightarrow 16t^2 - 40t + 48 = 0 \Leftrightarrow$
        $2t^2 - 5t + 6 = 0 \Leftrightarrow t = \frac{5 \pm \sqrt{25-48}}{4} = \frac{5 \pm \sqrt{-23}}{4}$. However, since the discriminant $D < 0$,
        there are no real solutions, and hence the ball never reaches a height of 48 feet.

    (c) The greatest height h is reached only once. So $h = -16t^2 + 40t \Leftrightarrow 16t^2 - 40t + h = 0$
        has only one solution. Thus $D = (-40)^2 - 4(16)(h) = 0 \Leftrightarrow 1600 - 64h = 0 \Leftrightarrow$
        $h = 25$. So the greatest height reached by the ball is 25 feet.

    (d) Setting $h = 25$, we have $25 = -16t^2 + 40t \Leftrightarrow 16t^2 - 40t + 25 = 0 \Leftrightarrow$
        $(4t - 5)^2 = 0 \Leftrightarrow t = 1\frac{1}{4}$. Thus the ball reaches the highest point of its path after $1\frac{1}{4}$
        seconds.

    (e) Setting $h = 0$ (ground level), we have $0 = -16t^2 + 40t \Leftrightarrow 2t^2 - 5t = 0 \Leftrightarrow$
        $t(2t - 5) = 0 \Leftrightarrow t = 0$ (start) or $t = 2\frac{1}{2}$. So the ball hits the ground in $2\frac{1}{2}$ seconds.

83. (a) The fish population on January 1, 1992 corresponds to $t = 0$, so
        $F = 1000(30 + 17(0) - (0)^2) = 30,000$. To find when the population will again reach this
        value, we set $F = 30,000$, giving $30000 = 1000(30 + 17t - t^2) = 30000 + 17000t - 1000t^2$
        $\Leftrightarrow 0 = 17000t - 1000t^2 = 1000t(17 - t) \Leftrightarrow t = 0$ or $t = 17$. Thus the fish
        population will again be the same 17 years later, that is, on January 1, 2009.

    (b) Setting $F = 0$, we have $0 = 1000(30 + 17t - t^2) \Leftrightarrow t^2 - 17t - 30 = 0 \Leftrightarrow$
        $t = \frac{17 \pm \sqrt{289+120}}{-2} = \frac{17 \pm \sqrt{409}}{-2} = \frac{17 \pm 20.22}{2}$. Thus $t \approx -1.612$ or $t \approx 18.612$. Since $t < 0$ is
        inadmissible, it follows that the fish in the lake will have died out 18.612 years after January 1,
        1992, that is on Aug. 12, 2010.

85. Let d be the distance from the lens to the object. Then the distance from the lens to the image is
    $d - 4$. So substituting $F = 4.8$, $x = d$, and $y = d - 4$, and then solving for x, we have
    $\frac{1}{4.8} = \frac{1}{d} + \frac{1}{d - 4}$. Now we multiply by the LCD, $4.8d(d - 4)$, to get
    $d(d - 4) = 4.8(d - 4) + 4.8d \Leftrightarrow d^2 - 4d = 9.6d - 19.2 \Leftrightarrow 0 = d^2 - 13.6d + 19.2$
    $\Rightarrow d = \frac{13.6 \pm 10.4}{2}$. So $d = 1.6$ or $d = 12$. Since $d - 4$ must also be positive, the object is 12
    cm from the lens.

87. Since the total time is 3 s, we have $3 = \frac{\sqrt{d}}{4} + \frac{d}{1090}$. Letting $w = \sqrt{d}$, we have $3 = \frac{1}{4}w + \frac{1}{1090}w^2$
    $\Leftrightarrow \frac{1}{1090}w^2 + \frac{1}{4}w - 3 = 0 \Leftrightarrow 2w^2 + 545w - 6540 = 0 \Rightarrow w = \frac{-545 \pm 591.054}{4}$.
    Since $w \geq 0$, we have $\sqrt{d} = w \approx 11.51$, so $d = 132.56$. The well is 132.6 ft deep.

89. When we multiplied by x, we introduced $x = 0$ as a solution. When we divided by $x - 1$, we are
    really dividing by 0, since $x = 1 \Leftrightarrow x - 1 = 0$.

91. $x^2 - 9x + 20 = (x - 4)(x - 5) = 0$, so $x = 4$ or $x = 5$. The roots are 4 and 5. The product is
$4 \cdot 5 = 20$, and the sum is $4 + 5 = 9$.

$x^2 - 2x - 8 = (x - 4)(x + 2) = 0$, so $x = 4$ or $x = -2$. The roots are 4 and -2. The product is
$4 \cdot (-2) = -8$, and the sum is $4 + (-2) = 2$.

$x^2 + 4x + 2 = 0$, so using the quadratic formula, $x = \dfrac{-4 \pm \sqrt{4^2 - 4(1)(2)}}{2(1)} = \dfrac{-4 \pm \sqrt{8}}{2}$

$= \dfrac{-4 \pm 2\sqrt{2}}{2} = -2 \pm \sqrt{2}$. The roots are $-2 - \sqrt{2}$ and $-2 + \sqrt{2}$. The product is
$(-2 - \sqrt{2}) \cdot (-2 + \sqrt{2}) = 4 - 2 = 2$, and the sum is $(-2 - \sqrt{2}) + (-2 + \sqrt{2}) = -4$.

In general, if $x = r_1$ and $x = r_2$ are roots, then
$x^2 + bx + c = (x - r_1)(x - r_2) = x^2 - r_1 x - r_2 x + r_1 r_2 = x^2 - (r_1 + r_2)x + r_1 r_2$. Equating the
coefficients, we get $c = r_1 r_2$ and $b = -(r_1 + r_2)$.

Exercises 1.6

1. If n is the first integer, then $n + 1$ is the middle integer, and $n + 2$ is the third integer. So the sum of the three consecutive integers is $n + (n + 1) + (n + 2) = 3n + 3$.

3. If x dollars are invested at 7% simple interest, then each year you will receive $0.07x$ dollars in interest. After two years, this amounts to $2(0.07x) = 0.14x$ dollars.

5. Since w is the width of the rectangle, the length is $w + 5$. The perimeter is
    $2 \times length + 2 \times width = 2(w + 5) + 2(w) = 4w + 10$.

7. If x is the gallons of pure water added, the mixture will contain 25 oz of salt and $3 + x$ gallons of water. Thus the concentration is $\dfrac{25}{3 + x}$.

9. Let x be the first integer. Then $x + 1$ and $x + 2$ are the next consecutive integers. So
    $x + (x + 1) + (x + 2) = 336 \quad \Leftrightarrow \quad 3x + 3 = 336 \quad \Leftrightarrow \quad 3x = 333 \quad \Leftrightarrow \quad x = 111$. Thus the consecutive integers are 111, 112, and 113.

11. Let n be one number. Then the other number must be $55 - n$, since $n + (55 - n) = 55$. Because the product is 684, we have $(n)(55 - n) = 684 \quad \Leftrightarrow \quad 55n - n^2 = 684 \quad \Leftrightarrow \quad n^2 - 55n + 684 = 0 \quad \Rightarrow$
    $$n = \frac{-(-55) \pm \sqrt{(-55)^2 - 4(1)(684)}}{2(1)} = \frac{55 \pm \sqrt{3025 - 2736}}{2} = \frac{55 \pm \sqrt{289}}{2} = \frac{55 \pm 17}{2}. \text{ So}$$
    $n = \frac{55+17}{2} = \frac{72}{2} = 36$ or $n = \frac{55-17}{2} = \frac{38}{2} = 19$. In either case, the two numbers are 19 and 36.

13. Let m be the amount invested at $4\frac{1}{2}$%. Then $12{,}000 - m$ is the amount invested at 4%.
    Since *total interest* = (*interest earned at* $4\frac{1}{2}$%) + (*interest earned* at 4%), we have
    $525 = 0.045m + 0.04(12{,}000 - m) \quad \Leftrightarrow \quad 525 = 0.045m + 480 - 0.04m \quad \Leftrightarrow \quad 45 = 0.005m$
    $\Leftrightarrow \quad m = \frac{45}{0.005} = 9{,}000$. Thus \$9,000 is invested at $4\frac{1}{2}$%, and $\$12{,}000 - 9{,}000 = \$3{,}000$ is invested at 4%.

15. Let r be the annual interest rate. Then $3500r = 262.50 \quad \Leftrightarrow \quad r = \frac{262.50}{3500} = 0.075$. Thus the \$3500 must be invested at 7.5%.

17. Let x be her monthly salary. Since her *annual salary* = $12 \times$ (*monthly salary*) + (*Christmas bonus*) we have $97{,}300 = 12x + 8{,}500 \quad \Leftrightarrow \quad 88{,}800 = 12x \quad \Leftrightarrow \quad x \approx 7{,}400$. Her monthly salary is \$7,400.

19. Let h be the amount that Craig inherits. So $(x + 22{,}000)$ is the amount that he invests and doubles. Thus $2(x + 22{,}000) = 134{,}000 \quad \Leftrightarrow \quad 2x + 44{,}000 = 134{,}000 \quad \Leftrightarrow \quad 2x = 90{,}000 \quad \Leftrightarrow$
    $x = 45{,}000$. So Craig inherits \$45,000.

21. Let x be the hours the assistant work. Then $2x$ is the hours the plumber worked. Since the
    labor charge = *plumber's labor* + *assistant's labor*, we have
    $4025 = 45(2x) + 25x \quad \Leftrightarrow \quad 4025 = 90x + 25x \quad \Leftrightarrow \quad 4025 = 115x \quad \Leftrightarrow \quad x = \frac{4025}{115} = 35$
    Thus the assistant works for 35 hours, and the plumber works for $2 \times 35 = 70$ hours.

23. All ages are in terms of the daughter's age 7 years ago. Let y be age of the daughter 7 years ago. Then $11y$ is the age of the movie star 7 years ago. Today, the daughter is $y + 7$, and the movie star

is $11y + 7$. But the movie star is also 4 times his daughter's age today. So $4(y + 7) = 11y + 7$ $\Leftrightarrow$ $4y + 28 = 11y + 7$ $\Leftrightarrow$ $21 = 7y$ $\Leftrightarrow$ $y = 3$. Thus the movie star's age today is $11(3) + 7 = 40$ years.

25. Let p be the number of pennies. Then p is the number of nickels and p is the number of dimes. So the *value of the coins in the purse = value of the pennies + value of the nickels + value of the dimes*. Thus $1.44 = 0.01p + 0.05p + 0.10p$ $\Leftrightarrow$ $1.44 = 0.16p$ $\Leftrightarrow$ $p = \frac{1.44}{0.16} = 9$. So the purse contains 9 pennies, 9 nickels, and 9 dimes.

27. Let l be the length of the garden. Since *area = width · length*, we obtain the equation $1125 = 25l$ $\Leftrightarrow$ $l = \frac{1125}{25} = 45$ ft. So the garden is 45 feet long.

29. Let x be the length of a side of the square plot. As shown in the figure to the right,
area of the plot = area of the building +
                                area of the parking lot
So $x^2 = 60(40) + 12,000 = 2,400 + 12,000 = 14,400$ $\Rightarrow$ $x = \pm 120$. So the plot of land is 120 feet by 120 feet.

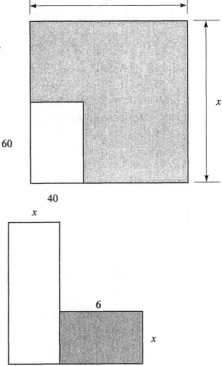

31. The figure can be broken up into two rectangles. Since the total area equals the sum of the areas of the rectangles, we have $144 = 10x + 6x$ $\Leftrightarrow$ $144 = 16x$ $\Leftrightarrow$ $9 = x$. Thus the length of x is 9 cm.

33. This shape is a trapezoid whose area is given by the formula $area = \dfrac{base_1 + base_2}{2} \times height$.
Substituting 1 for the top base, $x + 1$ for the bottom base, and x for height, we have
$1200 = \dfrac{1 + (1 + x)}{2} x = \dfrac{1}{2}(x + 2)x$ $\Leftrightarrow$ $2400 = x^2 + 2x$ $\Leftrightarrow$ $x^2 + 2x - 2400 = 0$ $\Leftrightarrow$ $(x + 50)(x - 48) = 0$. So $x = -50$ or $x = 48$. Since x represents a length, x is positive, so $x = 48$ cm.

35. Let w be the width of the garden in feet. We use the perimeter to express the length of the garden in terms of width. Since the *perimeter = 2 × width + 2 × length*, we have $200 = 2w + 2length$ $\Leftrightarrow$ $2length = 200 - 2w$ $\Leftrightarrow$ $length = 100 - w$. Using the formula for area, we have $2400 = w(100 - w) = 100w - w^2$ $\Leftrightarrow$ $w^2 - 100w + 2400 = 0$ $\Leftrightarrow$ $(w - 40)(w - 60) = 0$. So $w - 40 = 0$ $\Leftrightarrow$ $w = 40$. or $w - 60 = 0$ $\Leftrightarrow$ $w = 60$. If $w = 40$, then

$length = 100 - 40 = 60$. And if $w = 60$, then $length = 100 - 60 = 40$. So the length is 60 feet and the width is 40 feet.

37. We have that the volume is 180 ft^3, so $x(x-4)(x+9) = 180$ $\Leftrightarrow$ $x^3 + 5x^2 - 36x = 180$ $\Leftrightarrow$ $x^3 + 5x^2 - 36x - 180 = 0$ $\Leftrightarrow$ $x^2(x+5) - 36(x+5) = 0$ $\Leftrightarrow$ $(x+5)(x^2 - 36) = 0$ $\Leftrightarrow$ $(x+5)(x+6)(x-6) = 0$ $\Rightarrow$ $x = 6$ is the only positive solution. So the box is 2 feet by 6 feet by 15 feet.

39. Let x be the width of the strip. Then the length of the mat is $20 + 2x$, and the width of the mat is $15 + 2x$. Thus $perimeter = 2 \times length + 2 \times width$ $\Leftrightarrow$ $102 = 2(20 + 2x) + 2(15 + 2x)$ $\Leftrightarrow$ $102 = 40 + 4x + 30 + 4x$ $\Leftrightarrow$ $102 = 70 + 8x$ $\Leftrightarrow$ $32 = 8x$ $\Leftrightarrow$ $x = 4$. Thus the strip of mat is 4 inches wide.

41. Let x be the grams of silver added. The weight of the rings is $5 \times 18 \, \text{g} = 90 \, \text{g}$.

	5 rings	Pure silver	mixture
grams	90	x	$90 + x$
rate (% gold)	0.90	0	0.75
value	0.90(90)	$0x$	$0.75(90 + x)$

So $0.90(90) + 0x = 0.75(90 + x)$ $\Leftrightarrow$ $81 = 67.5 + 0.75x$ $\Leftrightarrow$ $0.75x = 13.5$ $\Leftrightarrow$ $x = \frac{13.5}{0.75} = 18$. Thus 18 grams of silver must be added to get the required mixture.

43. Let x be the liters of coolant removed and replaced by water.

	60% antifreeze	60% antifreeze (removed)	water	mixture
liters	3.6	x	x	3.6
rate (% antifreeze)	0.60	0.60	0	0.50
value	0.60(3.6)	$-0.60x$	$0x$	0.50(3.6)

so $0.60(3.6) - 0.60x + 0x = 0.50(3.6)$ $\Leftrightarrow$ $2.16 - 0.6x = 1.8$ $\Leftrightarrow$ $-0.6x = -0.36$ $\Leftrightarrow$ $x = \frac{-0.36}{-0.6} = 0.6$. Thus 0.6 liters must be removed and replaced by water.

45. Let c be the concentration of fruit juice in the cheaper brand. The new mixture that Jill makes will consist of 650 ml of the original fruit punch and 100 ml of the cheaper fruit punch.

	Fruit Punch	Cheaper FP	mixture
ml	650	100	750
concentration	0.50	c	0.48
juice	$0.50 \cdot 650$	$100c$	$0.48 \cdot 750$

So $0.50 \cdot 650 + 100c = 0.48 \cdot 750$ $\Leftrightarrow$ $325 + 100c = 360$ $\Leftrightarrow$ $100c = 35$ $\Leftrightarrow$ $c = 0.35$. Thus the cheaper brand is only 35% fruit juice.

47. Let d be the distance from the lamppost, in meters. Using similar triangles, $\dfrac{d+5}{6} = \dfrac{5}{2}$ $\Leftrightarrow$ $d + 5 = 15$ $\Leftrightarrow$ $d = 10$. Thus the man is 10 meters from the lamppost.

49. Let w be the width of the lot in feet. Then the length is $w + 6$. Using the Pythagorean Theorem, we have $w^2 + (w+6)^2 = (174)^2$ $\Leftrightarrow$ $w^2 + w^2 + 12w + 36 = 30276$ $\Leftrightarrow$ $2w^2 + 12w - 30240 = 0$ $\Leftrightarrow$ $w^2 + 6w - 15120 = 0$ $\Leftrightarrow$ $(w + 126)(w - 120) = 0$. So either $w + 126 = 0$ in which case $w = -126$, which is not possible, or $w - 120 = 0$ in which case $w = 120$. Thus the width is 120 feet and the length is 126 feet.

51. Let x be the distance from the fulcrum to where the mother sits. Then substituting the known values into the formula given, we have $100(8) = 125x$ $\Leftrightarrow$ $800 = 125x$ $\Leftrightarrow$ $x = 6.4$. So the mother should sit 6.4 feet from the fulcrum.

53. Let t be the time in minutes it would take Candy and Tim if they work together. Candy delivers the papers at a rate of $\frac{1}{70}$ of the job per minute, while Tim delivers the paper at a rate of $\frac{1}{80}$ of the job per minute. The sum of the fractions of the job that each can do individually in one minute equals the fraction of the job they can do working together. So we have $\dfrac{1}{t} = \dfrac{1}{70} + \dfrac{1}{80}$ $\Leftrightarrow$ $560 = 8t + 7t$ $\Leftrightarrow$ $560 = 15t$ $\Leftrightarrow$ $t = 37\frac{1}{3}$ minutes. Thus it would take them $37\frac{1}{3}$ minutes if they worked together.

55. Let t be the time, in hours, it takes Karen to paint a house alone. Then working together, Karen and Betty can paint a house in $\frac{2}{3}t$ hours. The sum of their individual rates equals their rate working together, so $\dfrac{1}{t} + \dfrac{1}{6} = \dfrac{1}{\frac{2}{3}t}$ $\Leftrightarrow$ $\dfrac{1}{t} + \dfrac{1}{6} = \dfrac{3}{2t}$ $\Leftrightarrow$ $6 + t = 9$ $\Leftrightarrow$ $t = 3$. Thus it would take Karen 3 hours to paint a house alone.

57. Let t be the time, in hours it takes Irene to wash all the windows. Then it takes Henry $t + \frac{3}{2}$ hours to wash all the windows, and the sum of the fraction of the job per hour they can do individually equals the fraction of the job they can do together. Since 1 hour 48 minutes $= 1 + \frac{48}{60} = 1 + \frac{4}{5} = \frac{9}{5}$, we have $\dfrac{1}{t} + \dfrac{1}{t + \frac{3}{2}} = \dfrac{1}{\frac{9}{5}}$ $\Leftrightarrow$ $\dfrac{1}{t} + \dfrac{2}{2t + 3} = \dfrac{5}{9}$ $\Rightarrow$ $9(2t + 3) + 2(9t) = 5t(2t + 3)$ $\Leftrightarrow$ $18t + 27 + 18t = 10t^2 + 15t$ $\Leftrightarrow$ $10t^2 - 21t - 27 = 0$ $\Leftrightarrow$ $t = \dfrac{-(-21) \pm \sqrt{(-21)^2 - 4(10)(-27)}}{2(10)} = \dfrac{21 \pm \sqrt{441 + 1080}}{20} = \dfrac{21 \pm 39}{20}$. So $t = \dfrac{21 - 39}{20} = -\frac{9}{10}$ or $t = \frac{21+39}{20} = 3$. Since $t < 0$ is impossible, all the windows are washed by Irene alone in 3 hours and by Henry alone in $3 + \frac{3}{2} = 4\frac{1}{2}$ hours.

59. Let t be the time in hours after takeoff until the planes pass each other. When the planes pass each other, the total distance they have traveled will equal 2550 km.

	Rate	Time	Distance
K.C. $\rightarrow$ S.F.	800	t	$800t$
S.F. $\rightarrow$ K.C.	900	t	$900t$

So $800t + 900t = 2550$ $\Leftrightarrow$ $1700t = 2550$ $\Leftrightarrow$ $t = 1.5$. Therefore, they will pass each other 1.5 hours after takeoff.

61. Let t be the time in hours that Wendy spent on the train. Then $\frac{11}{2} - t$ is the time in hours that Wendy spent on the bus. Using the equation $total\ distance = \left(\substack{distance\ traveled \\ by\ bus}\right) + \left(\substack{distance\ traveled \\ by\ train}\right)$, and the table

	Rate	Time	Distance
By train	40	t	$40t$
By bus	60	$\frac{11}{2} - t$	$60\left(\frac{11}{2} - t\right)$

we get the equation $300 = 40t + 60\left(\frac{11}{2} - t\right)$ $\Leftrightarrow$ $300 = 40t + 330 - 60t$ $\Leftrightarrow$ $-30 = -20t$ $\Leftrightarrow$ $t = \frac{-30}{-20} = 1.5$ hours. So the time spent on the train is $5.5 - 1.5 = 4$ hours.

63. Let r be the speed of the plane from Montreal to Los Angeles. Then $r + 0.20r = 1.20r$ is the speed of the plane from Los Angeles to Montreal.

	Rate	Time	Distance
Montreal to L.A.	r	$\dfrac{2500}{r}$	2500
L.A. to Montreal	$1.2r$	$\dfrac{2500}{1.2r}$	2500

Using the equation *total time* $= \left(\begin{smallmatrix} time\ traveling \\ Montreal\ to\ LA \end{smallmatrix} \right) + \left(\begin{smallmatrix} time\ traveling \\ LA\ to\ Montreal \end{smallmatrix} \right)$, we have

$9\frac{1}{6} = \dfrac{2500}{r} + \dfrac{2500}{1.2r} \quad \Leftrightarrow \quad \dfrac{55}{6} = \dfrac{2500}{r} + \dfrac{2500}{1.2r} \quad \Leftrightarrow \quad 55 \cdot 1.2r = 2500 \cdot 6 \cdot 1.2 + 2500 \cdot 6$

$\Leftrightarrow \quad 66r = 18000 + 15000 \quad \Leftrightarrow \quad 66r = 33000 \quad \Leftrightarrow \quad r = \dfrac{33000}{66} = 500.$ Thus the plane flew

at a speed of 500 mph on the trip from Montreal to Los Angeles.

65. Let x be the rate, in mi/h, at which the salesman drove between Ajax and Barrington.

Cities	Distance	Rate	Time
Ajax $\rightarrow$ Barrington	120	x	$\dfrac{120}{x}$
Barrington $\rightarrow$ Collins	150	$x + 10$	$\dfrac{150}{x+10}$

We have used the equation *Time* $= \frac{Distance}{Rate}$ to fill in the "Time" column of the table. Since the second part of the trip took 6 min. (or $1/10$ hours) more than the first, we can use the *Time* column to get the equation $\dfrac{120}{x} + \dfrac{1}{10} = \dfrac{150}{x+10} \quad \Rightarrow \quad 120(10)(x+10) + x(x+10) = 150(10x)$

$\Leftrightarrow \quad 1200x + 12000 + x^2 + 10x = 1500x \quad \Leftrightarrow \quad x^2 - 290x + 12000 = 0 \quad \Leftrightarrow$

$x = \dfrac{-(-290) \pm \sqrt{(-290)^2 - 4(1)(12000)}}{2} = \dfrac{290 \pm \sqrt{84100 - 48000}}{2} = \dfrac{290 \pm \sqrt{36100}}{2} =$

$\frac{290 \pm 190}{2} = 145 \pm 95.$ Hence, the salesman drove either 50 mi/h or 240 mi/h between Ajax and Barrington. (The first choice seems more likely!)

67. Let x be the number of people originally intended to take the trip. Then originally, the cost of the trip is $\dfrac{900}{x}$. After 5 people cancel, there are now $x - 5$ people, each paying $\dfrac{900}{x} + 2$. Thus

$900 = (x - 5)\left(\dfrac{900}{x} + 2 \right) \quad \Leftrightarrow \quad 900 = 900 + 2x - \dfrac{4500}{x} - 10 \quad \Leftrightarrow \quad 0 = 2x - 10 - \dfrac{4500}{x}$

$\Leftrightarrow \quad 0 = 2x^2 - 10x - 4500 = (2x - 100)(x + 45).$ Thus either $2x - 100 = 0$, so $x = 50$, or $x + 45 = 0$, $x = -45$. Since the number of people on the trip must be positive, originally 50 people intended to take the trip.

69. Let x be the length, in miles, of the abandoned road to be used. Then the length of the abandoned road not used is $40 - x$, and the length of the new road is $\sqrt{10^2 + (40 - x)^2}$ miles, by the Pythagorean Theorem. Since the cost of the road is *cost per mile* $\times$ *number of miles*, we have

$100,000x + 200,000\sqrt{x^2 - 80x + 1700} = 6,800,000 \quad \Leftrightarrow \quad 2\sqrt{x^2 - 80x + 1700} = 68 - x.$

Squaring both sides, we get $4x^2 - 320x + 6800 = 4624 - 136x + x^2 \quad \Leftrightarrow$

$3x^2 - 184x + 2176 = 0 \quad \Leftrightarrow \quad x = \frac{184 \pm \sqrt{33856 - 26112}}{6} = \frac{184 \pm 88}{6} \quad \Leftrightarrow \quad x = \frac{136}{3}$ or $x = 16.$ Since

$45\frac{1}{3}$ is longer than the existing road, 16 miles of the abandoned road should be used. A completely new road would have length $\sqrt{10^2 + 40^2}$, (let $x = 0$), and would cost $\sqrt{1700} \times 200{,}000 \approx 8.3$ million dollars. So no, it would not be cheaper.

71. Let x be the height of the pile in feet. Then the diameter is $3x$ and the radius is $\dfrac{3x}{2}$ feet. Since the

volume of the cone is 1000 ft^3, we have $\dfrac{\pi}{3}\left(\dfrac{3x}{2}\right)^2 x = 1000 \quad \Leftrightarrow \quad \dfrac{3\pi x^3}{4} = 1000 \quad \Leftrightarrow$

$x^3 = \dfrac{4000}{3\pi} \quad \Leftrightarrow \quad x = \sqrt[3]{\dfrac{4000}{3\pi}} \approx 7.52$ feet.

73. Let l be the length of the lot in feet. Then the length of the diagonal is $l + 10$. We apply the Pythagorean Theorem with the hypotenuse as the diagonal. So $l^2 + 50^2 = (l + 10)^2 \quad \Leftrightarrow$ $l^2 + 2500 = l^2 + 20l + 100 \quad \Leftrightarrow \quad 20l = 2400 \quad \Leftrightarrow$ $l = 120$. Thus the length of the lot is 120 feet.

75. Let r be the radius of the running track. The running track consists of 2 semicircles and 2 straight sections 110 yards long, so we get the equation $2\pi r + 220 = 440 \quad \Leftrightarrow \quad 2\pi r = 220 \quad \Leftrightarrow$ $r = \dfrac{110}{\pi} = 35.03$. Thus the radius of the semicircle is about 35 yards.

77. Let y be the circumference of the circle, so $360 - y$ is the perimeter of the square. Use the circumference to find the radius, r, in terms of y: $y = 2\pi r \quad \Rightarrow \quad r = \dfrac{y}{2\pi}$. Thus the area of the

circle is $\pi\left(\dfrac{y}{2\pi}\right)^2 = \dfrac{y^2}{4\pi}$. Now if the perimeter of the square is $360 - y$, the length of each side is

$\frac{1}{4}(360 - y)$, and the area of the square is $\left(\frac{360-y}{4}\right)^2$. Setting these areas equal, we obtain

$\dfrac{y^2}{4\pi} = \left(\dfrac{360 - y}{4}\right)^2 \quad \Leftrightarrow \quad \dfrac{y}{2\sqrt{\pi}} = \dfrac{360 - y}{4} \quad \Leftrightarrow \quad 2y = 360\sqrt{\pi} - \sqrt{\pi}\,y \quad \Leftrightarrow$

$(2 + \sqrt{\pi})y = 360\sqrt{\pi}$. Therefore, $y = \dfrac{360\sqrt{\pi}}{2 + \sqrt{\pi}} \approx 169.1$. Thus one wire is 169.1 in long and the

other is 190.9 in long.

79. Let x equal the original length of the reed in cubits. Then $x - 1$ is the piece that fits 60 times along the length of the field, that is, the length is $60(x - 1)$. The width is $30x$. Then converting cubits to ninda, we have $375 = 60(x - 1) \cdot 30x \cdot \frac{1}{12^2} = \frac{25}{2}x(x - 1) \quad \Leftrightarrow \quad 30 = x^2 - x \quad \Leftrightarrow$ $x^2 - x - 30 = 0 \quad \Leftrightarrow \quad (x - 6)(x + 5) = 0$. So $x = 6$ or $x = -5$. Since x must be positive, the original length of the reed is 6 cubits.

Exercises 1.7

1. $x = -1$: $2(-1) + 10 \overset{?}{>} 8$. No, $8 \not> 8$. $x = 0$: $2(0) + 10 \overset{?}{>} 8$. Yes.

    $x = \frac{1}{2}$: $2(\frac{1}{2}) + 10 \overset{?}{>} 8$. Yes. $x = \sqrt{2}$: $2(\sqrt{2}) + 10 \overset{?}{>} 8$. Yes.

    $x = 2$: $2(2) + 10 \overset{?}{>} 8$. Yes.   The solutions are 0, $\frac{1}{2}$, $\sqrt{2}$, and 2.

3. $x = -1$: $\dfrac{1}{(-1)} \overset{?}{\le} \dfrac{1}{2}$. Yes, $-1 \le \frac{1}{2}$. $x = 0$: $\dfrac{1}{(0)} \overset{?}{\le} \dfrac{1}{2}$. No, the LHS is undefined.

    $x = \frac{1}{2}$: $\dfrac{1}{(\frac{1}{2})} \overset{?}{\le} \dfrac{1}{2}$. No. $x = \sqrt{2}$: $\dfrac{1}{(\sqrt{2})} \overset{?}{\le} \dfrac{1}{2}$. No.

    $x = 2$: $\dfrac{1}{(2)} \overset{?}{\le} \dfrac{1}{2}$. Yes.   The solutions are -1 and 2.

5. $2x \le 7$ $\Leftrightarrow$ $x \le \frac{7}{2}$.   Interval: $(-\infty, \frac{7}{2}]$.   Graph:

7. $2x - 5 > 3$ $\Leftrightarrow$ $2x > 8$ $\Leftrightarrow$ $x > 4$.   Interval: $(4, \infty)$.

    Graph:

9. $7 - x \ge 5$ $\Leftrightarrow$ $-x \ge -2$ $\Leftrightarrow$ $x \le 2$.   Interval: $(-\infty, 2]$.

    Graph:

11. $2x + 1 < 0$ $\Leftrightarrow$ $2x < -1$ $\Leftrightarrow$ $x < -\frac{1}{2}$.   Interval: $\left(-\infty, -\frac{1}{2}\right)$.

    Graph:

13. $3x + 11 \le 6x + 8$ $\Leftrightarrow$ $3 \le 3x$ $\Leftrightarrow$ $1 \le x$.   Interval: $[1, \infty)$.

    Graph:

15. $\frac{1}{2}x - \frac{2}{3} > 2$ $\Leftrightarrow$ $\frac{1}{2}x > \frac{8}{3}$ $\Leftrightarrow$ $x > \frac{16}{3}$.   Interval: $\left(\frac{16}{3}, \infty\right)$.

    Graph:

17. $4 - 3x \le -(1 + 8x)$ $\Leftrightarrow$ $4 - 3x \le -1 - 8x$ $\Leftrightarrow$ $5x \le -5$ $\Leftrightarrow$ $x \le -1$.

    Interval: $(-\infty, -1]$.   Graph:

19. $2 \le x + 5 < 4$ $\Leftrightarrow$ $-3 \le x < -1$.   Interval: $[-3, -1)$.

    Graph:

21. $-1 < 2x - 5 < 7$ $\Leftrightarrow$ (add 5 to each expression) $4 < 2x < 12$ $\Leftrightarrow$ (divide each expression

    by 2) $2 < x < 6$. Interval: $(2, 6)$.   Graph:

23. $-2 < 8 - 2x \le -1$ $\Leftrightarrow$ $-10 < -2x \le -9$ $\Leftrightarrow$ $5 > x \ge \frac{9}{2}$ $\Leftrightarrow$ $\frac{9}{2} \le x < 5$.

    Interval: $\left[\frac{9}{2}, 5\right)$.   Graph:

25. $(x - 2)(x - 5) > 0$. The expression on the left of the inequality changes sign where $x = 2$ and where $x = 5$. Thus we must check the intervals in the following table.

Interval	$(-\infty, 2)$	$(2, 5)$	$(5, \infty)$
Sign of $x - 2$	$-$	$+$	$+$
Sign of $x - 5$	$-$	$-$	$+$
Sign of $(x - 2)(x - 5)$	$+$	$-$	$+$

From the table, the solution set is $\{x \mid x < 2 \text{ or } 5 < x\}$.

Interval: $(-\infty, 2) \cup (5, \infty)$.   Graph:

27. $x^2 - 3x - 18 \leq 0 \iff (x + 3)(x - 6) \leq 0$. The expression on the left of the inequality changes sign where $x = 6$ and where $x = -3$. Thus we must check the intervals in the following table.

Interval	$(-\infty, -3)$	$(-3, 6)$	$(6, \infty)$
Sign of $x + 3$	$-$	$+$	$+$
Sign of $x - 6$	$-$	$-$	$+$
Sign of $(x + 3)(x - 6)$	$+$	$-$	$+$

From the table, the solution set is $\{x \mid -3 \leq x \leq 6\}$.

Interval: $[-3, 6]$.   Graph:

29. $2x^2 + x \geq 1 \iff 2x^2 + x - 1 \geq 0 \iff (x + 1)(2x - 1) \geq 0$. The expression on the left of the inequality changes sign where $x = -1$ and where $x = \frac{1}{2}$. Thus we must check the intervals in the following table.

Interval	$(-\infty, -1)$	$(-1, \frac{1}{2})$	$(\frac{1}{2}, \infty)$
Sign of $x + 1$	$-$	$+$	$+$
Sign of $2x - 1$	$-$	$-$	$+$
Sign of $(x + 1)(2x - 1)$	$+$	$-$	$+$

From the table, the solution set is $\{x \mid x \leq -1 \text{ or } \frac{1}{2} \leq x\}$.

Interval: $(-\infty, -1] \cup \left[\frac{1}{2}, \infty\right)$.   Graph:

31. $3x^2 - 3x < 2x^2 + 4 \iff x^2 - 3x - 4 < 0 \iff (x + 1)(x - 4) < 0$. The expression on the left of the inequality changes sign where $x = -1$ and where $x = 4$. Thus we must check the intervals in the following table.

Interval	$(-\infty, -1)$	$(-1, 4)$	$(4, \infty)$
Sign of $x + 1$	$-$	$+$	$+$
Sign of $x - 4$	$-$	$-$	$+$
Sign of $(x + 1)(x - 4)$	$+$	$-$	$+$

From the table, the solution set is $\{x \mid -1 < x < 4\}$.

Interval: $(-1, 4)$.   Graph:

33. $x^2 > 3(x + 6) \iff x^2 - 3x - 18 > 0 \iff (x + 3)(x - 6) > 0$. The expression on the left of the inequality changes sign where $x = 6$ and where $x = -3$. Thus we must check the intervals in the following table.

Interval	$(-\infty, -3)$	$(-3, 6)$	$(6, \infty)$
Sign of $x + 3$	$-$	$+$	$+$
Sign of $x - 6$	$-$	$-$	$+$
Sign of $(x + 3)(x - 6)$	$+$	$-$	$+$

From the table, the solution set is $\{x \mid x < -3 \text{ or } 6 < x\}$.

Interval: $(-\infty, -3) \cup (6, \infty)$.   Graph:

35. $x^2 < 4 \quad \Leftrightarrow \quad x^2 - 4 < 0 \quad \Leftrightarrow \quad (x+2)(x-2) < 0.$ The expression on the left of the inequality changes sign where $x = -2$ and where $x = 2$. Thus we must check the intervals in the following table.

Interval	$(-\infty, -2)$	$(-2, 2)$	$(2, \infty)$
Sign of $x + 2$	$-$	$+$	$+$
Sign of $x - 2$	$-$	$-$	$+$
Sign of $(x + 2)(x - 2)$	$+$	$-$	$+$

From the table, the solution set is $\{x|\ -2 < x < 2\}$.

Interval: $(-2, 2)$.   Graph:

37. $-2x^2 \le 4 \quad \Leftrightarrow \quad -2x^2 - 4 \le 0 \quad \Leftrightarrow \quad -2(x^2 + 1) \le 0.$ Since $x^2 + 1 > 0$, $-2(x^2 + 1) \le 0$ for all x.   Interval: $(-\infty, \infty)$ Graph:

39. $\dfrac{x - 3}{x + 1} \ge 0.$ The expression on the left of the inequality changes sign where $x = -1$ and where $x = 3$. Thus we must check the intervals in the following table.

Interval	$(-\infty, -1)$	$(-1, 3)$	$(3, \infty)$
Sign of $x + 1$	$-$	$+$	$+$
Sign of $x - 3$	$-$	$-$	$+$
Sign of $\dfrac{x - 3}{x + 1}$	$+$	$-$	$+$

From the table, the solution set is $\{x|\ x < -1 \text{ or } x \le 3\}$. Since the denominator cannot equal 0 we must have $x \ne -1$.

Interval: $(-\infty, -1) \cup [3, \infty)$.   Graph:

41. $\dfrac{4x}{2x + 3} > 2 \quad \Leftrightarrow \quad \dfrac{4x}{2x + 3} - 2 > 0 \quad \Leftrightarrow \quad \dfrac{4x}{2x + 3} - \dfrac{2(2x + 3)}{2x + 3} > 0 \quad \Leftrightarrow \quad \dfrac{-6}{2x + 3} > 0.$ The expression on the left of the inequality changes sign where $x = -\dfrac{3}{2}$. Thus we must check the intervals in the following table.

Interval	$\left(-\infty, -\frac{3}{2}\right)$	$\left(-\frac{3}{2}, \infty\right)$
Sign of -6	$-$	$-$
Sign of $2x + 3$	$-$	$+$
Sign of $\dfrac{-6}{2x + 3}$	$+$	$-$

From the table, the solution set is $\left\{x|\ x < -\dfrac{3}{2}\right\}$.

Interval: $\left(-\infty, -\dfrac{3}{2}\right)$.   Graph:

43. $\dfrac{2x + 1}{x - 5} \le 3 \quad \Leftrightarrow \quad \dfrac{2x + 1}{x - 5} - 3 \le 0 \quad \Leftrightarrow \quad \dfrac{2x + 1}{x - 5} - \dfrac{3(x - 5)}{x - 5} \le 0 \quad \Leftrightarrow \quad \dfrac{-x + 16}{x - 5} \le 0.$ The expression on the left of the inequality changes sign where $x = 16$ and where $x = 5$. Thus we must check the intervals in the following table.

Interval	$(-\infty, 5)$	$(5, 16)$	$(16, \infty)$
Sign of $-x + 16$	$+$	$+$	$-$
Sign of $x - 5$	$-$	$+$	$+$
Sign of $\dfrac{-x + 16}{x - 5}$	$-$	$+$	$-$

From the table, the solution set is $\{x \mid x < 5 \text{ or } x \geq 16\}$. Since the denominator cannot equal 0, we must have $x \neq 5$.

Interval: $(-\infty, 5) \cup [16, \infty)$.   Graph:

45. $\dfrac{4}{x} < x \Leftrightarrow \dfrac{4}{x} - x < 0 \Leftrightarrow \dfrac{4}{x} - \dfrac{x \cdot x}{x} < 0 \Leftrightarrow \dfrac{4 - x^2}{x} < 0 \Leftrightarrow$

$\dfrac{(2 - x)(2 + x)}{x} < 0.$ The expression on the left of the inequality changes sign where $x = 0$, where $x = -2$, and where $x = 2$. Thus we must check the intervals in the following table.

Interval	$(-\infty, -2)$	$(-2, 0)$	$(0, 2)$	$(2, \infty)$
Sign of $2 + x$	$-$	$+$	$+$	$+$
Sign of x	$-$	$-$	$+$	$+$
Sign of $2 - x$	$+$	$+$	$+$	$-$
Sign of $\dfrac{(2 - x)(2 + x)}{x}$	$+$	$-$	$+$	$-$

From the table, the solution set is $\{x \mid -2 < x < 0 \text{ or } 2 < x\}$.

Interval: $(-2, 0) \cup (2, \infty)$.   Graph:

47. $1 + \dfrac{2}{x + 1} \leq \dfrac{2}{x} \Leftrightarrow 1 + \dfrac{2}{x + 1} - \dfrac{2}{x} \leq 0 \Leftrightarrow \dfrac{x(x + 1)}{x(x + 1)} + \dfrac{2x}{x(x + 1)} - \dfrac{2(x + 1)}{x(x + 1)} \leq 0 \Leftrightarrow$

$\dfrac{x^2 + x + 2x - 2x - 2}{x(x + 1)} \leq 0 \Leftrightarrow \dfrac{x^2 + x - 2}{x(x + 1)} \leq 0 \Leftrightarrow \dfrac{(x + 2)(x - 1)}{x(x + 1)} \leq 0.$ The expression

on the left of the inequality changes sign where $x = -2$, where $x = -1$, where $x = 0$, and where $x = 1$. Thus we must check the intervals in the following table.

Interval	$(-\infty, -2)$	$(-2, -1)$	$(-1, 0)$	$(0, 1)$	$(1, \infty)$
Sign of $x + 2$	$-$	$+$	$+$	$+$	$+$
Sign of $x - 1$	$-$	$-$	$-$	$-$	$+$
Sign of x	$-$	$-$	$-$	$+$	$+$
Sign of $x + 1$	$-$	$-$	$+$	$+$	$+$
Sign of $\dfrac{(x + 2)(x - 1)}{x(x + 1)}$	$+$	$-$	$+$	$-$	$+$

Since $x = -1$ and $x = 0$ yield undefined expressions, we cannot include them in the solution. From the table, the solution set is $\{x \mid -2 \leq x < -1 \text{ or } 0 < x \leq 1\}$.

Interval: $[-2, -1) \cup (0, 1]$.   Graph:

49. $\dfrac{6}{x - 1} - \dfrac{6}{x} \geq 1 \Leftrightarrow \dfrac{6}{x - 1} - \dfrac{6}{x} - 1 \geq 0 \Leftrightarrow \dfrac{6x}{x(x - 1)} - \dfrac{6(x - 1)}{x(x - 1)} - \dfrac{x(x - 1)}{x(x - 1)} \geq 0 \Leftrightarrow$

$\dfrac{6x - 6x + 6 - x^2 + x}{x(x - 1)} \geq 0 \Leftrightarrow \dfrac{-x^2 + x + 6}{x(x - 1)} \geq 0 \Leftrightarrow \dfrac{(-x + 3)(x + 2)}{x(x - 1)} \geq 0.$ The

expression on the left of the inequality changes sign where $x = 3$, where $x = -2$, where $x = 0$, and where $x = 1$. Thus we must check the intervals in the following table.

Interval	$(-\infty, -2)$	$(-2, 0)$	$(0, 1)$	$(1, 3)$	$(3, \infty)$
Sign of $-x + 3$	$+$	$+$	$+$	$+$	$-$
Sign of $x + 2$	$-$	$+$	$+$	$+$	$+$
Sign of x	$-$	$-$	$+$	$+$	$+$
Sign of $x - 1$	$-$	$-$	$-$	$+$	$+$
Sign of $\dfrac{(-x+3)(x+2)}{x(x-1)}$	$-$	$+$	$-$	$+$	$-$

From the table, the solution set is $\{x \mid -2 \le x < 0 \text{ or } 1 < x \le 3\}$. The points $x = 0$ and $x = 1$ are excluded from the solution set because they make the denominator zero.

Interval: $[-2, 0) \cup (1, 3]$ Graph: $\quad$ -2 $\quad$ 0 $\quad$ 1 $\quad$ 3

51. $\dfrac{x+2}{x+3} < \dfrac{x-1}{x-2} \quad \Leftrightarrow \quad \dfrac{x+2}{x+3} - \dfrac{x-1}{x-2} < 0 \quad \Leftrightarrow \quad \dfrac{(x+2)(x-2)}{(x+3)(x-2)} - \dfrac{(x-1)(x+3)}{(x-2)(x+3)} < 0 \quad \Leftrightarrow$

$\dfrac{x^2 - 4 - x^2 - 2x + 3}{(x+3)(x-2)} < 0 \quad \Leftrightarrow \quad \dfrac{-2x - 1}{(x+3)(x-2)} < 0$. The expression on the left of the inequality

changes sign where $x = -\frac{1}{2}$, where $x = -3$, and where $x = 2$. Thus we must check the intervals in the following table.

Interval	$(-\infty, -3)$	$\left(-3, -\frac{1}{2}\right)$	$\left(-\frac{1}{2}, 2\right)$	$(2, \infty)$
Sign of $-2x - 1$	$+$	$+$	$-$	$-$
Sign of $x + 3$	$-$	$+$	$+$	$+$
Sign of $x - 2$	$-$	$-$	$-$	$+$
Sign of $\dfrac{-2x-1}{(x+3)(x-2)}$	$+$	$-$	$+$	$-$

From the table, the solution set is $\left\{x \mid -3 < x < -\frac{1}{2} \text{ or } 2 < x\right\}$.

Interval: $\left(-3, -\frac{1}{2}\right) \cup (2, \infty)$.   Graph: $\quad$ -3 $\quad$ $-\frac{1}{2}$ $\quad$ 2

53. $x^4 > x^2 \quad \Leftrightarrow \quad x^4 - x^2 > 0 \quad \Leftrightarrow \quad x^2(x^2 - 1) > 0 \quad \Leftrightarrow \quad x^2(x-1)(x+1) > 0$. The expression on the left of the inequality changes sign where $x = 0$, where $x = 1$, and where $x = -1$. Thus we must check the intervals in the following table.

Interval	$(-\infty, -1)$	$(-1, 0)$	$(0, 1)$	$(1, \infty)$
Sign of x^2	$+$	$+$	$+$	$+$
Sign of $x - 1$	$-$	$-$	$-$	$+$
Sign of $x + 1$	$-$	$+$	$+$	$+$
Sign of $x^2(x-1)(x+1)$	$+$	$-$	$-$	$+$

From the table, the solution set is $\{x \mid x < -1 \text{ or } 1 < x\}$
Interval: $(-\infty, -1) \cup (1, \infty)$.   Graph: $\quad$ -1 $\quad$ 1

55. $|x| < 7 \quad \Leftrightarrow \quad -7 < x < 7$. Interval: $(-7, 7)$.   Graph: $\quad$ -7 $\quad$ 7

57. $|x - 5| \le 3 \quad \Leftrightarrow \quad -3 \le x - 5 \le 3 \quad \Leftrightarrow \quad 2 \le x \le 8$. Interval: $[2, 8]$.
Graph: $\quad$ 2 $\quad$ 8

59. $|x + 5| < 2 \quad \Leftrightarrow \quad -2 < x + 5 < 2 \quad \Leftrightarrow \quad -7 < x < -3$. Interval: $(-7, -3)$.
Graph: $\quad$ -7 $\quad$ -3

61. $|2x - 3| \leq 0.4$ $\Leftrightarrow$ $-0.4 \leq 2x - 3 \leq 0.4$ $\Leftrightarrow$ $2.6 \leq 2x \leq 3.4$ $\Leftrightarrow$ $1.3 \leq x \leq 1.7$.

Interval: $[1.3, 1.7]$.   Graph:
1.3   1.7

63. $\left|\dfrac{x - 2}{3}\right| < 2$ $\Leftrightarrow$ $-2 < \dfrac{x - 2}{3} < 2$ $\Leftrightarrow$ $-6 < x - 2 < 6$ $\Leftrightarrow$ $-4 < x < 8$.

Interval: $(-4, 8)$.   Graph:
-4   8

65. $4|x + 2| - 3 < 13$ $\Leftrightarrow$ $4|x + 2| < 16$ $\Leftrightarrow$ $|x + 2| < 4$ $\Leftrightarrow$ $-4 < x + 2 < 4$ $\Leftrightarrow$

$-6 < x < 2$. Interval: $(-6, 2)$.   Graph:
-6   2

67. Inserting the relationship $C = \frac{5}{9}(F - 32)$, we have $20 \leq C \leq 30$ $\Leftrightarrow$ $20 \leq \frac{5}{9}(F - 32) \leq 30$
$\Leftrightarrow$ $36 \leq F - 32 \leq 54$ $\Leftrightarrow$ $68 \leq F \leq 86$.

69. $128 + 16t - 16t^2 \geq 32$ $\Leftrightarrow$ $-16t^2 + 16t + 96 \geq 0$ $\Leftrightarrow$ $-16(t^2 - t - 6) \geq 0$ $\Leftrightarrow$
$-16(t - 3)(t + 2) \geq 0$. The expression on the left of the inequality changes sign at $x = -2$, at
$t = 3$, and at $t = -2$. However, $t \geq 0$, so the only endpoint is $t = 3$. Thus we check the intervals in
the following table.

Interval	$(0, 3)$	$(3, \infty)$
Sign of -16	$-$	$-$
Sign of $t - 3$	$-$	$+$
Sign of $t + 2$	$+$	$+$
Sign of $-16(t - 3)(t + 2)$	$+$	$-$

So $0 \leq t \leq 3$.

71. $240 > v + \dfrac{v^2}{20}$ $\Leftrightarrow$ $\frac{1}{20}v^2 + v - 240 < 0$ $\Leftrightarrow$ $(\frac{1}{20}v - 3)(v + 80) < 0$. The expression in the
inequality changes sign at $v = 60$ and $v = -80$. However, since v represents the speed, we must
have $v \geq 0$.

Interval	$(0, 60)$	$(60, \infty)$
Sign of $\frac{1}{20}v - 3$	$-$	$+$
Sign of $v + 80$	$+$	$+$
Sign of $(\frac{1}{20}v - 3)(v + 80)$	$-$	$+$

So Kerry must drive less than 60 mph.

73. Let x be the *average miles driven a day*. Each day the cost of Plan A is $30 + 0.10x$, and the cost of
Plan B is 50. Plan B saves money when $50 < 30 + 0.10x$ $\Leftrightarrow$ $20 < 0.1x$ $\Leftrightarrow$ $200 < x$. So
Plan B saves money when you average more than 200 miles a day.

75. (a) Let x be the number of $3 increases. Then the number of seats sold is $120 - x$. So
$P = 200 + 3x$ $\Leftrightarrow$ $3x = P - 200$ $\Leftrightarrow$ $x = \frac{1}{3}(P - 200)$. Substituting for x we have
that the number of seats sold is $120 - x = 120 - \frac{1}{3}(P - 200) = -\frac{1}{3}P + \frac{560}{3}$.

(b) $90 \leq -\frac{1}{3}P + \frac{560}{3} \leq 115$ $\Leftrightarrow$ $270 \leq 360 - P + 200 \leq 345$ $\Leftrightarrow$
$270 \leq -P + 560 \leq 345$ $\Leftrightarrow$ $-290 \leq -P \leq -215$ $\Leftrightarrow$ $290 \geq P \geq 215$. Putting this
into standard order, we have $215 \leq P \leq 290$. So the ticket prices are between $215 and $290.

77. If the customer buys x pounds of coffee at $6.50 per pound, then his cost c will be $6.50x$. Thus
$x = \frac{c}{6.5}$. Since the scale's accuracy is ± 0.03 lb, and the scale shows 3 lb, we have
$3 - 0.03 \leq x \leq 3 + 0.03$ $\Leftrightarrow$ $2.97 \leq \frac{c}{6.5} \leq 3.03$ $\Leftrightarrow$ $(6.50)2.97 \leq c \leq (6.50)3.03$ $\Leftrightarrow$

$19.305 \le c \le 19.695$. Since the customer paid $19.50, he could have been over- or undercharged by as much as $19\frac{1}{2}¢$.

79.   Let x be the length of the garden. Using the fact that the perimeter is 120 ft, we must have $2x + 2width = 120 \quad \Leftrightarrow \quad width = 60 - x$. Now since the area must be at least 800 ft^2, we have $800 < x(60 - x) \quad \Leftrightarrow \quad 800 < 60x - x^2 \quad \Leftrightarrow \quad x^2 - 60x + 800 < 0 \quad \Leftrightarrow$ $(x - 20)(x - 40) < 0$. The expression in the inequality changes sign at $x = 20$ and $x = 40$. However, since x represents length, we must have $x > 0$.

Interval	$(0, 20)$	$(20, 40)$	$(40, \infty)$
Sign of $x - 20$	$-$	$+$	$+$
Sign of $x - 40$	$-$	$-$	$+$
Sign of $(x - 20)(x - 40)$	$+$	$-$	$+$

The length of the garden should be between 20 and 40 feet.

81.   For $\sqrt{16 - 9x^2}$ to be defined as a real number we must have $16 - 9x^2 \ge 0 \quad \Leftrightarrow$ $(4 - 3x)(4 + 3x) \ge 0$. The expression in the inequality changes sign at $x = \frac{4}{3}$ and $x = -\frac{4}{3}$.

Interval	$\left(-\infty, -\frac{4}{3}\right)$	$\left(-\frac{4}{3}, \frac{4}{3}\right)$	$\left(\frac{4}{3}, \infty\right)$
Sign of $4 - 3x$	$+$	$+$	$-$
Sign of $4 + 3x$	$-$	$+$	$+$
Sign of $(4 - 3x)(4 + 3x)$	$-$	$+$	$-$

Thus $-\frac{4}{3} \le x \le \frac{4}{3}$.

83.   For $\left(\dfrac{1}{x^2 - 5x - 14}\right)^{1/2}$ to be defined as a real number we must have $x^2 - 5x - 14 > 0 \quad \Leftrightarrow$ $(x - 7)(x + 2) > 0$. The expression in the inequality changes sign at $x = 7$ and $x = -2$.

Interval	$(-\infty, -2)$	$(-2, 7)$	$(7, \infty)$
Sign of $x - 7$	$-$	$-$	$+$
Sign of $x + 2$	$-$	$+$	$+$
Sign of $(x - 7)(x + 2)$	$+$	$-$	$+$

Thus $x < -2$ or $7 < x$, and the solution set is $(-\infty, -2) \cup (7, \infty)$.

85.   We are given $\dfrac{a}{b} < \dfrac{c}{d}$, where a, b, c, and d are all positive. So multiplying by d, we get $\dfrac{ad}{b} < c$ and so by Rule 1 for Inequalities, $a + \dfrac{ad}{b} < a + c \quad \Leftrightarrow \quad \dfrac{ab + ad}{b} < a + c \quad \Leftrightarrow \quad \dfrac{a}{b}(b + d) < a + c$ $\Leftrightarrow \quad \dfrac{a}{b} < \dfrac{a + c}{b + d}$, since $b + d$ is positive. Similarly, $\dfrac{a}{b} < \dfrac{c}{d} \quad \Leftrightarrow \quad a < \dfrac{bc}{d} \quad \Leftrightarrow$ $a + c < \dfrac{bc}{d} + c \quad \Leftrightarrow \quad a + c < \dfrac{bc}{d} + \dfrac{dc}{d} \quad \Leftrightarrow \quad a + c < \dfrac{c}{d}(b + d) \quad \Leftrightarrow \quad \dfrac{a + c}{b + d} < \dfrac{c}{d}$, since $b + d > 0$. Combining the two inequalities, $\dfrac{a}{b} < \dfrac{a + c}{b + d} < \dfrac{c}{d}$.

87.   The rule we want to apply here is "$a < b \Rightarrow ac < bc$ if $c > 0$ and $a < b \Rightarrow ac > bc$ if $c < 0$". Thus we cannot simply multiply by x, since we don't yet know if x is positive or negative, so in solving $1 < \dfrac{3}{x}$, we must consider two cases

Case 1: $x > 0$ Then multiplying all sides by x, we have $x < 3$. Together with our initial condition, we have $0 < x < 3$.

Case 2: $x < 0$ Then multiplying all sides by x, we have $x > 3$. But $x < 0$ and $x > 3$ have no elements in common, so this gives no additional solutions.

Hence, the only solutions are $0 < x < 3$.

89. (a) $(-2, 5) < (-1, 4) < (0, 2) < (2, -3) < (2, 0) < (2, 5) < (4, -2)$.

     (b) $S = \{(x, y) \mid (0, 3) < (x, y)\}$.
          By the definition, $(0, 3) < (x, y)$
          if $0 < x$ or if $0 = x$ and $3 < y$.

          $T = \{(x, y) \mid (-2, 2) < (x, y) \leq (4, 0)\}$.
          Now $(-2, 2) < (x, y) \leq (4, 0)$
          if $-2 < x \leq 4$, or
          if $-2 = x$ and $2 < y$, or
          if $x = 4$ and $y \leq 0$.

Exercises 1.8

1.

3. (a)

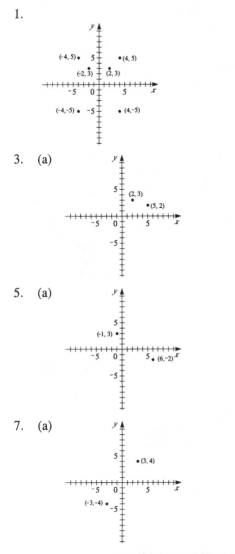

(b) $d = \sqrt{(2-5)^2 + (3-2)^2}$

$\qquad = \sqrt{(-3)^2 + (1)^2} = \sqrt{10}$

(c) midpoint: $\left(\frac{2+5}{2}, \frac{3+2}{2}\right) = \left(\frac{7}{2}, \frac{5}{2}\right)$

5. (a)

(b) $d = \sqrt{(6-(-1))^2 + (-2-3)^2}$

$\qquad = \sqrt{7^2 + (-5)^2} = \sqrt{49 + 25} = \sqrt{74}$

(c) midpoint: $\left(\frac{6-1}{2}, \frac{-2+3}{2}\right) = \left(\frac{5}{2}, \frac{1}{2}\right)$

7. (a)

(b) $d = \sqrt{(3-(-3))^2 + (4-(-4))^2}$

$\qquad = \sqrt{6^2 + 8^2} = \sqrt{36 + 64} = \sqrt{100}$

$\qquad = 10$

(c) midpoint: $\left(\frac{3+(-3)}{2}, \frac{4+(-4)}{2}\right) = (0, 0)$

9. $d(A, B) = \sqrt{(1-5)^2 + (3-3)^2} = \sqrt{(-4)^2} = 4.$

$d(A, C) = \sqrt{(1-1)^2 + (3-(-3))^2} = \sqrt{(6)^2} = 6.$

$d(C, D) = \sqrt{(1-5)^2 + (-3-(-3))^2} = \sqrt{(-4)^2} = 4.$

Thus the area of the rectangle is $4 \cdot 6 = 24.$

11. From the graph, the quadrilateral $ABCD$ has a pair of parallel sides,

so $ABCD$ is a trapezoid. The area is $\left(\dfrac{b_1 + b_2}{2}\right) h$. From the graph

we see that $b_1 = d(A,\,B) = \sqrt{(1-5)^2 + (0-0)^2} = \sqrt{4^2} = 4$;

$b_2 = d(C,\,D) = \sqrt{(4-2)^2 + (3-3)^2} = \sqrt{2^2} = 2$; and h is

the difference in y-coordinates $= |3 - 0| = 3$. Thus the area of the

trapezoid is $\left(\dfrac{4+2}{2}\right) 3 = 9$.

13.   15.   17.

19.   21.

23. $d(0, A) = \sqrt{(6-0)^2 + (7-0)^2} = \sqrt{6^2 + 7^2} = \sqrt{36 + 49} = \sqrt{85}$.

$d(0, B) = \sqrt{(-5-0)^2 + (8-0)^2} = \sqrt{(-5)^2 + 8^2} = \sqrt{25 + 64} = \sqrt{89}$.

Thus point A is closer to the origin.

25. $d(P, R) = \sqrt{(-1-3)^2 + (-1-1)^2} = \sqrt{(-4)^2 + (-2)^2} = \sqrt{16 + 4} = \sqrt{20} = 2\sqrt{5}$.

$d(Q, R) = \sqrt{(-1-(-1))^2 + (-1-3)^2} = \sqrt{0 + (-4)^2} = \sqrt{16} = 4$. Thus point Q is closer to
point R.

27. Since we do not know which pair are isosceles, we find the length of all three sides.

$d(A, B) = \sqrt{(-3-0)^2 + (-1-2)^2} = \sqrt{(-3)^2 + (-3)^2} = \sqrt{9+9} = \sqrt{18} = 3\sqrt{2}$.

$d(C, B) = \sqrt{(-3-(-4))^2 + (-1-3)^2} = \sqrt{1^2 + (-4)^2} = \sqrt{1 + 16} = \sqrt{17}$.

$d(A, C) = \sqrt{(0-(-4))^2 + (2-3)^2} = \sqrt{4^2 + (-1)^2} = \sqrt{16 + 1} = \sqrt{17}$. So sides AC and CB
have the same length.

29. (a) Here we have $A = (2, 2)$, $B = (3, -1)$ and $C = (-3, -3)$. So

$d(A, B) = \sqrt{(3-2)^2 + (-1-2)^2} = \sqrt{1^2 + (-3)^2} = \sqrt{1+9} = \sqrt{10}$;

$d(C, B) = \sqrt{(3-(-3))^2 + (-1-(-3))^2} = \sqrt{6^2 + 2^2} = \sqrt{36 + 4} = \sqrt{40} = 2\sqrt{10}$;

$$d(A, C) = \sqrt{(-3-2)^2 + (-3-2)^2} = \sqrt{(-5)^2 + (-5)^2} = \sqrt{25+25} = \sqrt{50} = 5\sqrt{2}.$$

Since $[d(A, B)]^2 + [d(C, B)]^2 = [d(A, C)]^2$, we conclude that the triangle is a right triangle.

(b)   The area of the triangle is $\frac{1}{2} \cdot d(C, B) \cdot d(A, B) = \frac{1}{2} \cdot \sqrt{10} \cdot 2\sqrt{10} = 10$.

31. $d(A, B) = \sqrt{(3-(-1))^2 + (11-3)^2} = \sqrt{4^2 + 8^2} = \sqrt{16+64} = \sqrt{80} = 4\sqrt{5}$.

$d(B, C) = \sqrt{(5-3)^2 + (15-11)^2} = \sqrt{2^2 + 4^2} = \sqrt{4+16} = \sqrt{20} = 2\sqrt{5}$.

$d(A, C) = \sqrt{(5-(-1))^2 + (15-3)^2} = \sqrt{6^2 + 12^2} = \sqrt{36+144} = \sqrt{180} = 6\sqrt{5}$.   So

$d(A, B) + d(B, C) = d(A, C)$, and the points are collinear.

33.   The midpoint of AB is $C' = \left(\dfrac{1+3}{2}, \dfrac{0+6}{2} \right) = (2, 3)$. So the length of the median CC' is

$d(C, C') = \sqrt{(2-8)^2 + (3-2)^2} = \sqrt{37}$.   The midpoint of AC is $B' = \left(\dfrac{1+8}{2}, \dfrac{0+2}{2} \right)$

$= \left(\frac{9}{2}, 1 \right)$. So the length of the median BB' is $d(B, B') = \sqrt{\left(\frac{9}{2} - 3 \right)^2 + (1-6)^2} = \dfrac{\sqrt{109}}{2}$. The

midpoint of BC is $A' = \left(\dfrac{3+8}{2}, \dfrac{6+2}{2} \right) = \left(\dfrac{11}{2}, 4 \right)$. So the length of the median AA' is

$d(A, A') = \sqrt{\left(\frac{11}{2} - 1 \right)^2 + (4-0)^2} = \dfrac{\sqrt{145}}{2}$.

35.   (a)

(b)   The midpoint of AC is $\left(\frac{-2+7}{2}, \frac{-1+7}{2} \right) = \left(\frac{5}{2}, 3 \right)$, and the midpoint of BD is $\left(\frac{4+1}{2}, \frac{2+4}{2} \right) = \left(\frac{5}{2}, 3 \right)$.

(c)   Since the they have the same midpoint, we conclude the diagonals bisect each other.

37.   (a)   The point $(5, 3)$ is shifted to $(5+3, 3+2) = (8, 5)$.

(b)   The point (a, b) is shifted to $(a+3, b+2)$.

(c)   Let (x, y) be the point that is shifted to $(3, 4)$. Then $(x+3, y+2) = (3, 4)$. Setting the x-coordinates equal, we get $x + 3 = 3 \iff x = 0$. Setting the y-coordinates equal, we get $y + 2 = 4 \iff y = 2$. So the point is $(0, 2)$.

(d) $A = (-5, -1)$ so $A' = (-5+3, -1+2) = (-2, 1)$;

$B = (-3, 2)$ so $B' = (-3+3, 2+2) = (0, 4)$;

$C = (2, 1)$ so $C' = (2+3, 1+2) = (5, 3)$.

39. $(0, 0)$: $0 \overset{?}{=} 2(0) + 3 \iff 0 \overset{?}{=} 3$ No. $\left(\frac{1}{2}, 4 \right)$: $4 \overset{?}{=} 2\left(\frac{1}{2} \right) + 3 \iff 4 \overset{?}{=} 1 + 3$ Yes.

$(1, 4)$: $4 \overset{?}{=} 2(1) + 3 \iff 4 \overset{?}{=} 2 + 3$ No.

So $\left(\frac{1}{2}, 4 \right)$ is on the graph of this equation.

41. $(0, 0)$: $2(0) - 0 + 1 \overset{?}{=} 0 \iff 1 \overset{?}{=} 0$ No. $(1, 0)$: $2(0) - 1 + 1 \overset{?}{=} 0 \iff -1 + 1 \overset{?}{=} 0$ Yes.

$(-1, -1)$: $2(-1) - (-1) + 1 \overset{?}{=} 0 \iff -2 + 1 + 1 \overset{?}{=} 0$ Yes.

So $(1, 0)$ and $(-1, -1)$ are points on the graph of this equation.

43.

x	y
-4	-4
-2	-2
0	0
1	1
2	2
3	3
4	4

$y = 0 \quad \Rightarrow \quad x = 0$. So the x-intercept is 0, and the y-intercept is also 0.

x-axis symmetry: $(-y) = x \quad \Leftrightarrow \quad -y = x$, which is not the same as $y = x$, so not symmetric with respect to the x-axis.

y-axis symmetry: $y = (-x) \quad \Leftrightarrow \quad y = -x$, which is not the same as $y = x$, so not symmetric with respect to the y-axis.

Origin symmetry: $(-y) = (-x)$ is the same as $y = x$, so it is symmetric with respect to the origin.

45.

x	y
-3	-4
-2	-3
-1	-2
0	-1
1	0
2	1
3	2

$y = 0 \quad \Rightarrow \quad 0 = x - 1 \quad \Leftrightarrow \quad x = 1$, so the x-intercept is 1, and $x = 0 \quad \Rightarrow \quad y = 0 - 1 = -1$, so the y-intercept is -1.

x-axis symmetry: $(-y) = x - 1 \quad \Leftrightarrow \quad -y = x - 1$, which is not the same as $y = x - 1$, so not symmetric with respect to the x-axis.

y-axis symmetry: $y = (-x) - 1 \quad \Leftrightarrow \quad y = -x - 1$, which is not the same as $y = x - 1$, so not symmetric with respect to the y-axis.

Origin symmetry: $(-y) = (-x) - 1 \quad \Leftrightarrow \quad -y = -x - 1 \quad \Leftrightarrow \quad y = x + 1$, which is not the same as $y = x - 1$, so not symmetric with respect to the origin.

47. Solve for y: $-y = -3x + 5 \quad \Leftrightarrow \quad y = 3x - 5$.

	y
-2	-11
-1	-8
0	-5
1	-2
2	1
3	4
4	7

$y = 0 \quad \Rightarrow \quad 0 = 3x - 5 \quad \Leftrightarrow \quad 3x = 5 \quad \Leftrightarrow \quad x = \frac{5}{3}$, so x-intercept is $\frac{5}{3}$, and $x = 0 \quad \Rightarrow \quad y = 3(0) - 5 = -5$, so y-intercept is -5.

x-axis symmetry: $3x - (-y) = 5 \quad \Leftrightarrow \quad 3x + y = 5$, which is not the same as $3x - y = 5$, so not symmetric with respect to the x-axis.

y-axis symmetry: $3(-x) - y = 5 \quad \Leftrightarrow \quad -3x - y = 5$, which is not the same as $3x - y = 5$, so not symmetric with respect to the y-axis.

Origin symmetry: $3(-x) - (-y) = 5 \quad \Leftrightarrow \quad -3x + y = 5$ which is not the same as $3x - y = 5$, so not symmetric with respect to the origin.

49.

x	y
-3	-8
-2	-3
-1	0
0	1
1	0
2	-3
3	-8

$y = 0 \Rightarrow 0 = 1 - x^2 \quad \Leftrightarrow \quad x^2 = 1 \quad \Rightarrow \quad x = \pm 1$, so the x-intercepts are 1 and -1, and $x = 0 \Rightarrow y = 1 - (0)^2 = 1$, so the y-intercept is 1.

x-axis symmetry: $(-y) = 1 - x^2 \quad \Leftrightarrow \quad -y = 1 - x^2$, which is not the same as $y = 1 - x^2$, so not symmetric with respect to the x-axis.

y-axis symmetry: $y = 1 - (-x)^2 \quad \Leftrightarrow \quad y = 1 - x^2$, so it is symmetric with respect to the y-axis.

Origin symmetry: $(-y) = 1 - (-x)^2 \quad \Leftrightarrow \quad -y = 1 - x^2$ which is not the same as $y = 1 - x^2$. Not symmetric with respect to the origin.

51. $4y = x^2 \iff y = \frac{1}{4}x^2$

x	y
-6	9
-4	4
-2	1
0	0
2	1
4	4
3	2

$y = 0 \implies 0 = \frac{1}{4}x^2 \iff x^2 = 0 \implies x = 0$, so the x-intercept is 0, and $x = 0 \implies y = \frac{1}{4}(0)^2 = 0$, so the y-intercept is 0.

x-axis symmetry: $(-y) = \frac{1}{4}x^2$, which is not the same as $y = \frac{1}{4}x^2$, so not symmetric with respect to the x-axis.

y-axis symmetry: $y = \frac{1}{4}(-x)^2 \iff y = \frac{1}{4}x^2$, so it is symmetric with respect to the y-axis.

Origin symmetry: $(-y) = \frac{1}{4}(-x)^2 \iff -y = \frac{1}{4}x^2$, which is not the same as $y = \frac{1}{4}x^2$, so not symmetric with respect to the origin.

53.

x	y
-4	7
-3	0
-2	-5
-1	-8
0	-9
1	-8
2	-5
3	0
4	7

$y = 0 \implies 0 = x^2 - 9 \iff x^2 = 9 \implies x = \pm 3$, so the x-intercepts are 3 and -3, and $x = 0 \implies y = (0)^2 - 9 = -9$, so the y-intercept is -9.

x-axis symmetry: $(-y) = x^2 - 9$, which is not the same as $y = x^2 - 9$, so not symmetric with respect to the x-axis.

y-axis symmetry: $y = (-x)^2 - 9 \iff y = x^2 - 9$, so it is symmetric with respect to the y-axis.

Origin symmetry: $(-y) = (-x)^2 - 9 \iff -y = x^2 - 9$, which is not the same as $y = x^2 - 9$, so not symmetric with respect to the origin.

55.

x	y
0	0
$\frac{1}{4}$	$\frac{1}{2}$
1	1
2	$\sqrt{2}$
4	2
9	3
16	4

$y = 0 \implies 0 = \sqrt{x} \iff x = 0$. so the x-intercept is 0, and $x = 0 \implies y = \sqrt{0} = 0$, so the y-intercept is 0. Since we are graphing real numbers and $\sqrt{x}$ is defined to be a non-negative number, the equation is not symmetric with respect to the x-axis nor with respect to the y-axis. Also, the equation is not symmetric with respect to the origin.

57.

x	y
-3	3
-2	2
-1	1
0	0
1	1
2	2
3	3

$y = 0 \implies 0 = |x| \iff x = 0$, so the x-intercept is 0, and $x = 0 \implies y = |0| = 0$, so the y-intercept is 0. Since $y \geq 0$, the graph is not symmetric with respect to the x-axis.

y-axis symmetry: $y = |-x| = |x|$, so the graph is symmetric with respect to the y-axis.

Since $y \geq 0$, the graph is not symmetric with respect to the origin.

59.

x	y
-6	-2
-4	0
-2	2
0	4
2	2
4	0
6	-2

$y = 0 \Rightarrow 0 = 4 - |x| \Leftrightarrow |x| = 4 \Rightarrow x = \pm 4$, so the x-intercepts are -4 and 4, and $x = 0 \Rightarrow$ $y = 4 - |0| = 4$, so the y-intercept is 4.

x-axis symmetry: $(-y) = 4 - |x| \Leftrightarrow y = -4 + |x|$, which is not the same as $y = 4 - |x|$, so not symmetric with respect to the x-axis.

y-axis symmetry: $y = 4 - |-x| = 4 - |x|$, so it is symmetric with respect to the y-axis.

Origin symmetry: $(-y) = 4 - |-x| \Leftrightarrow y = -4 + |x|$, which is not the same as $y = 4 - |x|$, so not symmetric with respect to the origin.

61.

x	y
-3	81
-2	16
-1	1
0	0
1	1
2	16
3	81

$y = 0 \Rightarrow 0 = x^4 \Rightarrow x = 0$, so the x-intercept is 0, and $x = 0 \Rightarrow y = 0^4 = 0$, so the y-intercept is 0.

x-axis symmetry: $(-y) = x^4 \Leftrightarrow y = -x^4$, which is not the same as $y = x^4$, so not symmetric with respect to the x-axis.

y-axis symmetry: $y = (-x)^4 = x^4$, so it is symmetric with respect to the y-axis.

Origin symmetry: $(-y) = (-x)^4 \Leftrightarrow -y = x^4$, which is not the same as $y = x^4$, so not symmetric with respect to the origin.

63. x-axis symmetry: $(-y) = x^4 + x^2 \Leftrightarrow y = -x^4 - x^2$, which is not the same as $y = x^4 + x^2$, so not symmetric with respect to the x-axis.

y-axis symmetry: $y = (-x)^4 + (-x)^2 = x^4 + x^2$, so it is symmetric with respect to the y-axis.

Origin symmetry: $(-y) = (-x)^4 + (-x)^2 \Leftrightarrow -y = x^4 + x^2$, which is not the same as $y = x^4 + x^2$, so not symmetric with respect to the origin.

65. x-axis symmetry: $x^2(-y)^2 + x(-y) = 1 \Leftrightarrow x^2y^2 - xy = 1$, which is not the same as $x^2y^2 + xy = 1$, so not symmetric with respect to the x-axis.

y-axis symmetry: $(-x)^2y^2 + (-x)y = 1 \Leftrightarrow x^2y^2 - xy = 1$, which is not the same as $x^2y^2 + xy = 1$, so not symmetric with respect to the y-axis.

Origin symmetry: $(-x)^2(-y)^2 + (-x)(-y) = 1 \Leftrightarrow x^2y^2 + xy = 1$, so it is symmetric with respect to the origin.

67. x-axis symmetry: $(-y) = x^3 + 10x \Leftrightarrow y = -x^3 - 10x$, which is not the same as $y = x^3 + 10x$, so not symmetric with respect to the x-axis.

y-axis symmetry: $y = (-x)^3 + 10(-x) \Leftrightarrow y = -x^3 - 10x$, which is not the same as $y = x^3 + 10x$, so not symmetric with respect to the y-axis.

Origin symmetry: $(-y) = (-x)^3 + 10(-x) \Leftrightarrow -y = -x^3 - 10x \Leftrightarrow y = x^3 + 10x$, so it is symmetric with respect to the origin.

69. Symmetric with respect to the y-axis.   71. Symmetric with respect to the origin.

73. Using $h = 2$, $k = -1$, and $r = 3$, we get $(x - 2)^2 + (y - (-1))^2 = 3^2$ $\Leftrightarrow$ $(x - 2)^2 + (y + 1)^2 = 9$.

75. Using $h = -1$ and $k = 5$ we get $(x - (-1))^2 + (y - 5)^2 = r^2$ $\Leftrightarrow$ $(x + 1)^2 + (y - 5)^2 = r^2$. Next, using the point $(-4, -6)$, we solve for r^2. This gives $(-4 + 1)^2 + (-6 - 5)^2 = r^2$ $\Leftrightarrow$ $130 = r^2$. Thus, the equation of the circle is $(x + 1)^2 + (y - 5)^2 = 130$.

77. Since the circle is tangent to the x-axis, it must contain the point $(7, 0)$, so the radius is the change in the y-coordinates. That is, $r = |-3 - 0| = 3$. So the equation of the circle is $(x - 7)^2 + (y - (-3))^2 = 3^2$, which is $(x - 7)^2 + (y + 3)^2 = 9$.

79. From the figure, the center of the circle is at $(-2, 2)$. The radius is the change in the y-coordinates, so $r = |2 - 0| = 2$. Thus the equation of the circle is $(x - (-2))^2 + (y - 2)^2 = 2^2$, which is $(x + 2)^2 + (y - 2)^2 = 4$.

81. Completing the square gives $x^2 + y^2 - 2x + 4y + 1 = 0$ $\Leftrightarrow$
$x^2 - 2x + \underline{\ \ } + y^2 + 4y + \underline{\ \ } = -1$ $\Leftrightarrow$
$x^2 - 2x + \left(\frac{-2}{2}\right)^2 + y^2 + 4y + \left(\frac{4}{2}\right)^2 = -1 + \left(\frac{-2}{2}\right)^2 + \left(\frac{4}{2}\right)^2$ $\Leftrightarrow$
$x^2 - 2x + 1 + y^2 + 4y + 4 = -1 + 1 + 4$ $\Leftrightarrow$ $(x - 1)^2 + (y + 2)^2 = 4$.
Thus, the center is $(1, -2)$, and the radius is 2.

83. Completing the square gives $x^2 + y^2 + 6y + 2 = 0$ $\Leftrightarrow$ $x^2 + y^2 + 6y + \underline{\ \ } = -2$ $\Leftrightarrow$
$x^2 + y^2 + 6y + \left(\frac{6}{2}\right)^2 = -2 + \left(\frac{6}{2}\right)^2$ $\Leftrightarrow$ $x^2 + y^2 + 6y + 9 = -2 + 9$ $\Leftrightarrow$ $x^2 + (y + 3)^2 = 7$.
Thus, the center is at $(0, -3)$, and the radius is $\sqrt{7}$.

85. Completing the square gives $x^2 + y^2 + 2x + y + 1 = 0$ $\Leftrightarrow$ $x^2 + 2x + \underline{\ \ } + y^2 + y = -1$ $\Leftrightarrow$
$x^2 + 2x + \left(\frac{2}{2}\right)^2 + y^2 + y + \left(\frac{1}{2}\right)^2 = -1 + 1 + \left(\frac{1}{2}\right)^2$ $\Leftrightarrow$ $x^2 + 2x + 1 + y^2 + y + \frac{1}{4} = \frac{1}{4}$ $\Leftrightarrow$
$(x + 1)^2 + \left(y + \frac{1}{2}\right)^2 = \frac{1}{4}$. Thus, the center is at $\left(-1, -\frac{1}{2}\right)$, and the radius is $\frac{1}{2}$.

87. $\{(x, y) \mid x^2 + y^2 \le 1\}$. This is the set of points inside (and on) the circle $x^2 + y^2 = 1$.

89. Completing the square gives $x^2 + y^2 - 4y - 12 = 0$ $\Leftrightarrow$ $x^2 + y^2 - 4y + \underline{\ \ } = 12$ $\Leftrightarrow$
$x^2 + y^2 - 4y + \left(\frac{-4}{2}\right)^2 = 12 + \left(\frac{-4}{2}\right)^2$ $\Leftrightarrow$ $x^2 + (y - 2)^2 = 16$. Thus, the center is $(0, 2)$, and the

radius is 4. So the circle $x^2 + y^2 = 4$, with center $(0,0)$ and radius 2, sits completely inside the larger circle. Thus, the area is $\pi 4^2 - \pi 2^2 = 16\pi - 4\pi = 12\pi$.

90. We solve the equation $6 = \dfrac{2+x}{2}$ to find the x coordinate of B: $6 = \dfrac{2+x}{2}$ $\Leftrightarrow$ $12 = 2 + x$

$\Leftrightarrow$ $x = 10$. Likewise, for the y coordinate of B, we have $8 = \dfrac{3+y}{2}$ $\Leftrightarrow$ $16 = 3 + y$ $\Leftrightarrow$

$y = 13$. Thus $B = (10,\ 13)$.

93. Completing the square gives $x^2 + y^2 + ax + by + c = 0$ $\Leftrightarrow$

$x^2 + ax + \underline{} + y^2 + by + \underline{} = -c$ $\Leftrightarrow$

$x^2 + ax + \left(\dfrac{a}{2}\right)^2 + y^2 + by + \left(\dfrac{b}{2}\right)^2 = -c + \left(\dfrac{a}{2}\right)^2 + \left(\dfrac{b}{2}\right)^2$ $\Leftrightarrow$

$\left(x + \dfrac{a}{2}\right)^2 + \left(y + \dfrac{b}{2}\right)^2 = -c + \dfrac{a^2 + b^2}{4}$.

This equation represents a circle only when $-c + \dfrac{a^2 + b^2}{4} > 0$. This equation represents a point

when $-c + \dfrac{a^2 + b^2}{4} = 0$, and this equation represents the empty set when $-c + \dfrac{a^2 + b^2}{4} < 0$.

When the equation represents a circle, the center is $\left(-\dfrac{a}{2}, -\dfrac{b}{2}\right)$, and the radius is

$$\sqrt{-c + \dfrac{a^2 + b^2}{4}} = \dfrac{1}{2}\sqrt{a^2 + b^2 - 4ac}.$$

95. (a) Symmetric about the x-axis.   (b) Symmetric about the y-axis.

              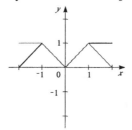

(c) Symmetric about the origin.

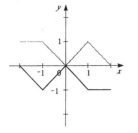

Exercises 1.9

1. $y = x^4 + 2$

   (a) $[-2, 2]$ by $[-2, 2]$ (b) $[0, 4]$ by $[0, 4]$

   (c) $[-8, 8]$ by $[-4, 40]$ (d) $[-40, 40]$ by $[-80, 800]$

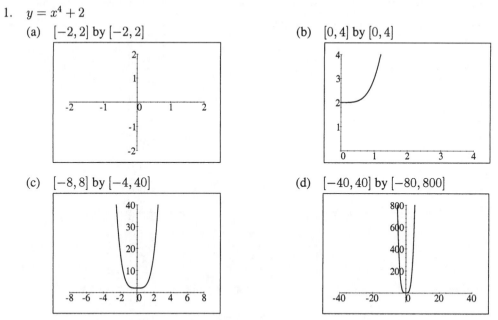

The viewing rectangle in part (c) produces the most appropriate graph of the equation.

3. $y = 100 - x^2$

   (a) $[-4, 4]$ by $[-4, 4]$ (b) $[-10, 10]$ by $[-10, 10]$

   (c) $[-15, 15]$ by $[-30, 110]$ (d) $[-4, 4]$ by $[-30, 110]$

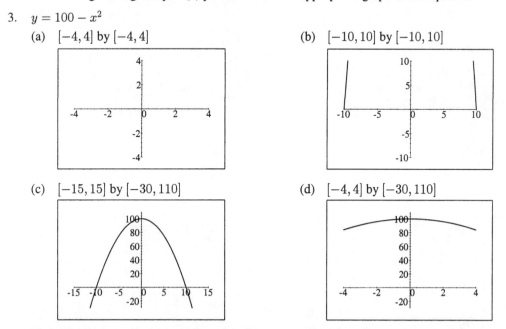

The viewing rectangle in part (c) produces the most appropriate graph of the equation.

5. $y = 10 + 25x - x^3$

(a) $[-4, 4]$ by $[-4, 4]$ (b) $[-10, 10]$ by $[-10, 10]$

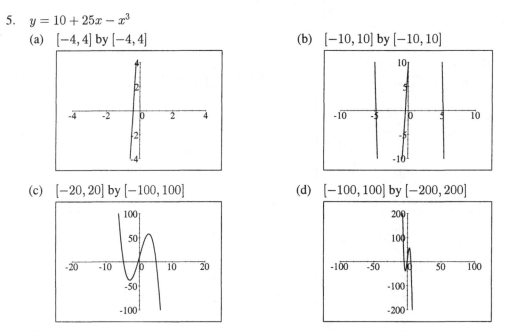

(c) $[-20, 20]$ by $[-100, 100]$ (d) $[-100, 100]$ by $[-200, 200]$

The viewing rectangle in part (c) produces the most appropriate graph of the equation.

7. $y = 100x^2$
    $[-2, 2]$ by $[-10, 400]$

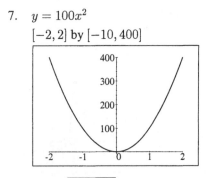

9. $y = 4 + 6x - x^2$
    $[-4, 10]$ by $[-10, 20]$

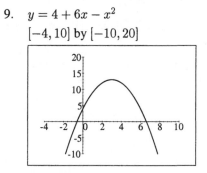

11. $y = \sqrt[4]{256 - x^2}$. We require that
     $256 - x^2 \geq 0 \quad \Rightarrow \quad -16 \leq x \leq 16$,
     so we graph $y = \sqrt[4]{256 - x^2}$ in the
     viewing rectangle $[-20, 20]$ by $[-1, 5]$.

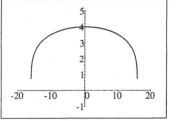

13. $y = 0.01x^3 - x^2 + 5$
     $[-50, 150]$ by $[-2000, 2000]$

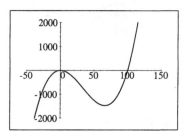

15. $y = x^4 - 4x^3$
$[-4, 6]$ by $[-50, 100]$

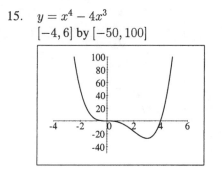

17. $y = 1 + |x - 1|$; $[-3, 5]$ by $[-1, 5]$

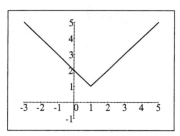

19. $x^2 + y^2 = 9 \iff y^2 = 9 - x^2 \implies$
$y = \pm\sqrt{9 - x^2}$. So we graph the functions
$y_1 = \sqrt{9 - x^2}$ and $y_2 = -\sqrt{9 - x^2}$ in the
viewing rectangle $[-6, 6]$ by $[-4, 4]$.

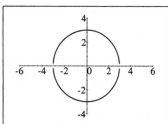

21. $4x^2 + 2y^2 = 1 \iff 2y^2 = 1 - 4x^2 \iff$
$y^2 = \dfrac{1 - 4x^2}{2} \implies y = \pm\sqrt{\dfrac{1 - 4x^2}{2}}$. So we graph
the functions $y_1 = \sqrt{\dfrac{1 - 4x^2}{2}}$ and $y_2 = -\sqrt{\dfrac{1 - 4x^2}{2}}$ in
the viewing rectangle $[-1.2, 1.2]$ by $[-0.8, 0.8]$.

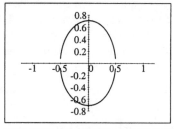

23. Although the graphs of $y = -3x^2 + 6x - \frac{1}{2}$ and
$y = \sqrt{7 - 7x^2/12}$ appear to intersect in the viewing
rectangle $[-4, 4]$ by $[-1, 3]$, there are no points of
intersection. You can verify that this is not an intersection
by zooming in.

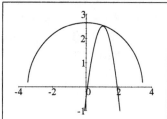

25. The graphs of $y = 6 - 4x - x^2$ and $y = 3x + 18$
appear to have two points of intersection in the
viewing rectangle $[-6, 2]$ by $[-5, 20]$. You can verify
that $x = -4$ and $x = -3$ are exact solutions.

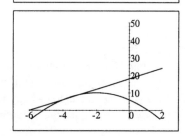

27. Algebraically: $x - 4 = 5x + 12$ $\Leftrightarrow$ $-16 = 4x$ $\Leftrightarrow$
     $x = -4$.
     Graphically: We graph the two equations $y_1 = x - 4$ and
     $y_2 = 5x + 12$ in the viewing rectangle $[-6, 4]$ by $[-10, 2]$.
     Zooming in we see that solution is $x = -4$.

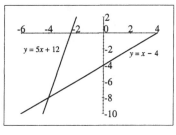

29. Algebraically: $\dfrac{2}{x} + \dfrac{1}{2x} = 7$ $\Leftrightarrow$ $2x\left(\dfrac{2}{x} + \dfrac{1}{2x}\right) = 2x(7)$
     $\Leftrightarrow$ $4 + 1 = 14x$ $\Leftrightarrow$ $x = \frac{5}{14}$.
     Graphically: We graph the two equations $y_1 = \dfrac{2}{x} + \dfrac{1}{2x}$ and
     $y_2 = 7$ in the viewing rectangle $[-2, 2]$ by $[-2, 28]$.
     Zooming in we see that solution is $x \approx 0.36$.

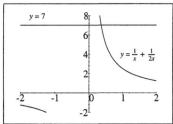

31. Algebraically: $x^2 - 32 = 0$ $\Leftrightarrow$ $x^2 = 32$ $\Rightarrow$ $x = \pm\sqrt{32} = \pm 4\sqrt{2}$.
     Graphically: We graph the equation $y_1 = x^2 - 32$ and
     determine where this curve intersects the x-axis. We use
     the viewing rectangle $[-10, 10]$ by $[-5, 5]$.
     Zooming in, we see that solutions are $x \approx 5.66$
     and $x \approx -5.66$.

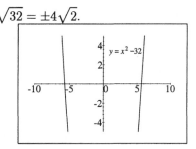

33. Algebraically: $16x^4 = 625$ $\Leftrightarrow$ $x^4 = \frac{625}{16}$ $\Rightarrow$ $x = \pm\frac{5}{2} = \pm 2.5$.
     Graphically: We graph the two equations $y_1 = 16x^4$ and
     $y_2 = 625$ in the viewing rectangle $[-5, 5]$ by $[610, 640]$.
     Zooming in we see that solutions are $x = \pm 2.5$.

35. Algebraically: $(x - 5)^4 - 80 = 0$ $\Leftrightarrow$ $(x - 5)^4 = 80$ $\Rightarrow$ $x - 5 = \pm\sqrt[4]{80} = \pm 2\sqrt[4]{5}$ $\Leftrightarrow$
     $x = 5 \pm 2\sqrt[4]{5}$.
     Graphically: We graph the equation $y_1 = (x - 5)^4 - 80$ and
     determine where this curve intersects the x-axis. We use
     the viewing rectangle $[-1, 9]$ by $[-5, 5]$.
     Zooming in, we see that solutions are $x \approx 2.01$ and $x \approx 7.99$.

37. We graph $y = x^2 - 7x + 12$ in the viewing rectangle $[0, 6]$ by $[-0.1, 0.1]$. The solutions are $x = 3.00$ and 4.00.

39. We graph $y = x^3 - 6x^2 + 11x - 6$ in the viewing rectangle $[-1, 4]$ by $[-0.1, 0.1]$. The solutions are $x = 1.00$, $x = 2.00$, and $x = 3.00$.

41. We first graph

$y = x - \sqrt{x+1}$ in the viewing rectangle $[-1, 5]$ by $[-0.1, 0.1]$ and find that the solution is near 1.6. Zooming in, we see that solutions is $x \approx 1.62$.

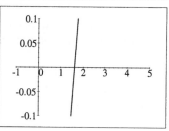

43. We graph $y = x^{1/3} - x$ in the viewing rectangle $[-3, 3]$ by $[-1, 1]$. The solutions are $x = -1.00$, $x = 0.00$, and $x = 1.00$.

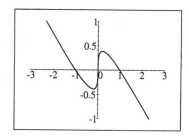

45. $x^3 - 2x^2 - x - 1 = 0$, so we start by graphing the function $y = x^3 - 2x^2 - x - 1$ in the viewing rectangle $[-10, 10]$ by $[-100, 100]$. There appear to be two solutions, one near $x = 0$ and another one between $x = 2$ and $x = 3$.

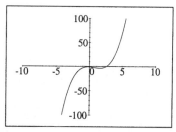

We then use the viewing rectangle $[-1, 5]$ by $[-1, 1]$ and zoom into the only solution at $x \approx 2.55$.

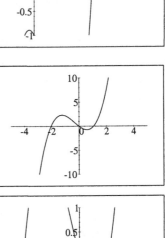

47. $x(x-1)(x+2) = \frac{1}{6}x \quad \Leftrightarrow \quad x(x-1)(x+2) - \frac{1}{6}x = 0.$
We start by graphing the function $y = x(x-1)(x+2) - \frac{1}{6}x$ in the viewing rectangle $[-5, 5]$ by $[-10, 10]$. There appear to be three solutions.

We then use the viewing rectangle $[-2.5, 2.5]$ by $[-1, 1]$ and zoom into the solutions at $x \approx -2.05$, $x = 0.00$, and $x \approx 1.05$.

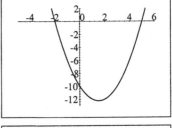

49. We graph $y = x^2 - 3x - 10$ in the viewing rectangle $[-5, 6]$ by $[-12, 2]$. Thus the solution to the inequality is: $[-2.0, 5.0]$.

51. Since $x^3 + 11x \leq 6x^2 + 6 \quad \Leftrightarrow \quad x^3 - 6x^2 + 11x - 6 \leq 0$, we graph $y = x^3 - 6x^2 + 11x - 6$ in the viewing rectangle $[0, 5]$ by $[-5, 5]$. The solution set is $(-\infty, 1.0] \cup [2.0, 3.0]$.

53. Since $x^{1/3} \le x \iff x^{1/3} - x < 0$, we graph
$y = x^{1/3} - x$ in the viewing rectangle $[-3, 3]$ by $[-1, 1]$.
From this, we find that the solution set is $(-1.0, 0) \cup (1.0, \infty)$.

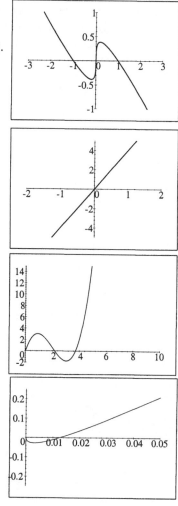

55. Since $(x+1)^2 < (x-1)^2 \iff (x+1)^2 - (x-1)^2 < 0$,
we graph $y = (x+1)^2 - (x-1)^2$ in the viewing rectangle
$[-2, 2]$ by $[-5, 5]$. The solution set is $(-\infty, 0)$.

57. As in Example 4, we graph the equation
$y = x^3 - 6x^2 + 9x - \sqrt{x}$ in the viewing rectangle $[0, 10]$ by
$[-2, 15]$. We see the two solutions found in Example 4
and what appears to be an additional solution near $x = 0$.

In the viewing rectangle $[0, 0.05]$ by $[-0.25, 0.25]$, we
find two more solutions at $x \approx 0.01$ and $x = 0$. We can
verify that $x = 0$ is an exact solution by substitution.

59. Calculators follow the following order of operations: exponents are applied before division and
division is applied before addition. Therefore, $Y_1 = x{\char94}1/3$ is interpreted as
$y = (x{\char94}1)/3 = \dfrac{x{\char94}1}{3} = \frac{1}{3}x$, which is the equation of a line. Likewise, $Y_2 = x/x + 4$ is interpreted as
$y = (x/x) + 4 = 1 + 4 = 5$, again, the equation of a line. The student should have entered the
following information into his calculator:

$\quad Y_1 = x{\char94}(1/3)$

$\quad Y_2 = x/(x+4)$.

61. (a) We graph $y_1 = x^3 - 3x$ and $y_2 = k$ for $k = -4, -2, 0,$ 2, and 4 in the viewing rectangle $[-5, 5]$ by $[-10, 10]$. The number of solutions and the solutions are shown in the table below.

k	number of solutions	Solutions
-4	1	$x \approx -2.20$
-2	2	$x = -2, x = 1$
0	3	$x \approx \pm 1.73, x = 0$
2	2	$x = -1, x = 2$
4	1	$x \approx 2.20$

(b) The equation $x^3 - 3x = k$ will have one solution for all $k < -2$ or $k > 2$, it will have exactly two solutions when $k = \pm 2$, and it will have three solutions for $-2 < k < 2$.

Exercises 1.10

1. $m = \dfrac{y_2 - y_1}{x_2 - x_1} = \dfrac{4 - 0}{2 - 0} = \dfrac{4}{2} = 2.$

3. $m = \dfrac{y_2 - y_1}{x_2 - x_1} = \dfrac{0 - 2}{10 - 2} = \dfrac{-2}{8} = -\dfrac{1}{4}.$

5. $m = \dfrac{y_2 - y_1}{x_2 - x_1} = \dfrac{4 - 12}{2 - 4} = \dfrac{-8}{-2} = 4.$

7. $m = \dfrac{y_2 - y_1}{x_2 - x_1} = \dfrac{6 - (-3)}{-1 - 1} = \dfrac{9}{-2} = -\dfrac{9}{2}.$

9. For ℓ_1, we find two points, $(-1, 2)$ and $(0, 0)$ that lie on the line. Thus the slope of ℓ_1 is
$m = \dfrac{y_2 - y_1}{x_2 - x_1} = \dfrac{2 - 0}{-1 - 0} = -2.$ For ℓ_2, we find two points $(0, 2)$ and $(2, 3)$. Thus, the slope of ℓ_2
is $m = \dfrac{y_2 - y_1}{x_2 - x_1} = \dfrac{3 - 2}{2 - 0} = \dfrac{1}{2}.$ For ℓ_3 we find the points $(2, -2)$ and $(3, 1)$. Thus, the slope of ℓ_3
is $m = \dfrac{y_2 - y_1}{x_2 - x_1} = \dfrac{1 - (-2)}{3 - 2} = 3.$ For ℓ_4, we find the points $(-2, -1)$ and $(2, -2)$. Thus, the
slope of ℓ_4 is $m = \dfrac{y_2 - y_1}{x_2 - x_1} = \dfrac{-2 - (-1)}{2 - (-2)} = \dfrac{-1}{4} = -\dfrac{1}{4}.$

11. First we find two points, $(0, 4)$ and $(4, 0)$ that lie on the line. So the slope is $m = \frac{0-4}{4-0} = -1.$ Since
the y-intercept is 4, the equation of the line is $y = mx + b = -1x + 4.$ So $y = -x + 4$, or
$x + y - 4 = 0.$

13. We choose the two intercepts as points, $(0, -3)$ and $(2, 0)$. So the slope is $m = \frac{0-(-3)}{2-0} = \frac{3}{2}.$ Since
the y-intercept is -3, the equation of the line is $y = mx + b = \frac{3}{2}x - 3$, or $3x - 2y - 6 = 0.$

15. Using the equation $y - y_1 = m(x - x_1)$, we get $y - 3 = 1(x - 2)$ $\Leftrightarrow$ $-x + y = 1$ $\Leftrightarrow$
$x - y + 1 = 0.$

17. Using the equation $y - y_1 = m(x - x_1)$, we get $y - 7 = \frac{2}{3}(x - 1)$ $\Leftrightarrow$ $3y - 21 = 2x - 2$ $\Leftrightarrow$
$-2x + 3y = 19$ $\Leftrightarrow$ $2x - 3y + 19 = 0.$

19. First we find the slope, which is $m = \dfrac{y_2 - y_1}{x_2 - x_1} = \dfrac{6 - 1}{1 - 2} = \dfrac{5}{-1} = -5.$ Substituting into
$y - y_1 = m(x - x_1)$, we get $y - 6 = -5(x - 1)$ $\Leftrightarrow$ $y - 6 = -5x + 5$ $\Leftrightarrow$
$5x + y - 11 = 0.$

21. Using $y = mx + b$, we have $y = 3x + (-2)$ or $3x - y - 2 = 0.$

23. We are given two points, $(1, 0)$ and $(0, -3)$. Thus, the slope is
$m = \dfrac{y_2 - y_1}{x_2 - x_1} = \dfrac{-3 - 0}{0 - 1} = \dfrac{-3}{-1} = 3.$ Using the y-intercept, we have $y = 3x + (-3)$ or $y = 3x - 3$
or $3x - y - 3 = 0.$

25. Since the equation of a horizontal line passing through (a, b) is $y = b$, the equation of the horizontal
line passing through $(4, 5)$ is $y = 5.$

27. Since $x + 2y = 6 \iff 2y = -x + 6 \iff y = -\frac{1}{2}x + 3$, the slope of this line is $-\frac{1}{2}$. Thus, the line we seek is given by $y - (-6) = -\frac{1}{2}(x - 1) \iff 2y + 12 = -x + 1 \iff x + 2y + 11 = 0$.

29. Any line parallel to $x = 5$ will have undefined slope and be of the form $x = a$. Thus the equation of the line is $x = -1$.

31. First find the slope of $2x + 5y + 8 = 0$. This gives $2x + 5y + 8 = 0 \iff 5y = -2x - 8 \iff y = -\frac{2}{5}x - \frac{8}{5}$. So the slope of the line that is perpendicular to $2x + 5y + 8 = 0$ is $m = -\frac{1}{-2/5} = \frac{5}{2}$. The equation of the line we seek is $y - (-2) = \frac{5}{2}(x - (-1)) \iff 2y + 4 = 5x + 5 \iff 5x - 2y + 1 = 0$.

33. First find the slope of the line passing through $(2, 5)$ and $(-2, 1)$. This gives $m = \frac{1-5}{-2-2} = \frac{-4}{-4} = 1$, and so the equation of the line we seek is $y - 7 = 1(x - 1) \iff x - y + 6 = 0$.

35. (a)

(b) $y - 1 = \frac{3}{2}(x - (-2)) \iff 2y - 2 = 3(x + 2) \iff 2y - 2 = 3x + 6 \iff 3x - 2y + 8 = 0$.

37.

Each of the lines contains the point $(3, 2)$ because the point $(3, 2)$ satisfies each equation $y = 2 + m(x - 3)$.

39. $x + y = 3 \iff y = -x + 3$. So the slope is -1, and the y-intercept is 3.

41. $x + 3y = 0 \iff 3y = -x \iff y = -\frac{1}{3}x$. So the slope is $-\frac{1}{3}$, and the y-intercept is 0.

43. $\frac{1}{2}x - \frac{1}{3}y + 1 = 0 \quad \Leftrightarrow \quad -\frac{1}{3}y = -\frac{1}{2}x - 1$
    $\Leftrightarrow \quad y = \frac{3}{2}x + 3$. So the slope is $\frac{3}{2}$, and the
    y-intercept is 3.

45. $y = 4$ can also be expressed as $y = 0x + 4$.
    So the slope is 0, and the y-intercept is 4.

47. $3x - 4y = 12 \quad \Leftrightarrow \quad -4y = -3x + 12$
    $\Leftrightarrow \quad y = \frac{3}{4}x - 3$. So the slope is $\frac{3}{4}$, and the
    y-intercept is -3.

49. $3x + 4y - 1 = 0 \quad \Leftrightarrow \quad 4y = -3x + 1$
    $\Leftrightarrow \quad y = -\frac{3}{4}x + \frac{1}{4}$. So the slope is $-\frac{3}{4}$, and
    the y-intercept is $\frac{1}{4}$.

51. We first plot the points to find the pairs of points that determine each
    side. Next we find the slopes of opposite sides.

    The slope of AB is $\frac{4-1}{7-1} = \frac{3}{6} = \frac{1}{2}$, and the slope of DC is
    $\frac{10-7}{5-(-1)} = \frac{3}{6} = \frac{1}{2}$. Since these slope are equal, these two sides are parallel.

    The slope of AD is $\frac{7-1}{-1-1} = \frac{6}{-2} = -3$, and the slope of BC is
    $\frac{10-4}{5-7} = \frac{6}{-2} = -3$. Since these slope are equal, these two sides are
    parallel.

    Hence $ABCD$ is a parallelogram.

53. We first plot the points to find the pairs of points that determine each
     side. Next we find the slopes of opposite sides.

     The slope of AB is $\frac{3-1}{11-1} = \frac{2}{10} = \frac{1}{5}$, and the slope of DC is
     $\frac{6-8}{0-10} = \frac{-2}{-10} = \frac{1}{5}$. Since these slope are equal, these two sides are
     parallel.

     Slope of AD is $\frac{6-1}{0-1} = \frac{5}{-1} = -5$, and the slope of BC is
     $\frac{3-8}{11-10} = \frac{-5}{1} = -5$. Since these slope are equal, these two sides are
     parallel.

     Since (slope of AB) × (slope of AD) = $\frac{1}{5} \times (-5) = -1$, the first two sides are each perpendicular
     to the second two sides. So the sides form a rectangle.

55. We need the slope and the midpoint of the line AB. The midpoint of AB is $\left(\frac{1+7}{2}, \frac{4-2}{2}\right) = (4, 1)$,
     and the slope of AB is $m = \frac{-2-4}{7-1} = \frac{-6}{6} = -1$. The slope of the perpendicular bisector will have
     slope $\frac{-1}{m} = \frac{-1}{-1} = 1$. Using the point-slope form, the equation of the perpendicular bisector is
     $y - 1 = 1(x - 4)$ or $x - y - 3 = 0$.

57. (a) We start with the two points $(a, 0)$ and $(0, b)$. The slope of the line that contains them is
          $\frac{b-0}{0-a} = -\frac{b}{a}$. So the equation of the line containing them is $y = -\frac{b}{a}x + b$ (using the slope-
          intercept form). Dividing by b (since $b \neq 0$) gives $\frac{y}{b} = -\frac{x}{a} + 1$ $\Leftrightarrow$ $\frac{x}{a} + \frac{y}{b} = 1$.

     (b) Setting $a = 6$ and $b = -8$, we get $\frac{x}{6} + \frac{y}{-8} = 1$ $\Leftrightarrow$ $4x - 3y = 24$ $\Leftrightarrow$
          $4x - 3y - 24 = 0$.

59. Let h be the change in your horizontal distance, in feet. Then $-\frac{6}{100} = \frac{-1000}{h}$ $\Leftrightarrow$
     $h = \frac{100,000}{6} \approx 16,667$. So the change in your horizontal distance is about $16,667$ feet.

61. (a) The slope is $0.0417D = 0.0417(200) = 8.34$. It represents the increase in dosage for each
          one-year increase in the child's age.

     (b) When $a = 0$, $c = 8.34(0 + 1) = 8.34$ mg.

63. (a) 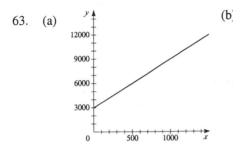   (b) The slope is the cost per toaster oven, $6. The y-intercept,
                                             $3000, is the monthly fixed cost, the cost that is incurred no
                                             matter how many toaster ovens are produced.

65. (a) Using n in place of x and t in place of y, we find that the slope is $\frac{t_2 - t_1}{n_2 - n_1} = \frac{80 - 70}{168 - 120} = \frac{10}{48}$
          $= \frac{5}{24}$. So the linear equation is $t - 80 = \frac{5}{24}(n - 168)$ $\Leftrightarrow$ $t - 80 = \frac{5}{24}n - 35$ $\Leftrightarrow$
          $t = \frac{5}{24}n + 45$.

     (b) When $n = 150$, the temperature is approximately given by $t = \frac{5}{24}(150) + 45 = 76.25°F$
          $\approx 76°F$.

67. (a) We are given $\dfrac{\text{change in pressure}}{10 \text{ feet change in depth}} = \dfrac{4.34}{10} = 0.434$. Using P for pressure and d for depth, and using the point $P = 15$ when $d = 0$, we have $P - 15 = 0.434(d - 0)$ ⇔ $P = 0.434d + 15$.

   (b) When $P = 100$, then $100 = 0.434d + 15$ ⇔ $0.434d = 85$ ⇔ $d = 195.9$ feet. Thus the pressure is 100 lb/in^3 at a depth of approximately 196 feet.

69. (a) Using d in place of x and C in place of y, we find the slope $= \dfrac{C_2 - C_1}{d_2 - d_1} = \dfrac{460 - 380}{800 - 480} = \dfrac{80}{320}$ $= \frac{1}{4}$. So the linear equations is $C - 460 = \frac{1}{4}(d - 800)$ ⇔ $C - 460 = \frac{1}{4}d - 200$ ⇔ $C = \frac{1}{4}d + 260$.

   (b) Substituting $d = 1500$ we get $C = \frac{1}{4}(1500) + 260 = 635$. Thus, the cost of driving 1500 miles is $635.

   (c)

   The slope of the line represents the cost per mile, $0.25.

   (d) The y-intercept represents the fixed cost, $260.

   (e) It is a suitable model because you have fixed monthly costs such as insurance and car payments, as well as costs that occur as you drive, such as gasoline, oil, tires, etc., and the cost of these for each additional mile driven is a constant.

71. (a) Viewing rectangle is $[0, 50]$ by $[0, 30]$.

   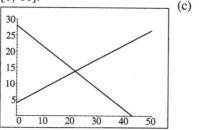

   (b) $(p, y) = (21.82, 13.82)$

   (c) Setting the two equations equal to each other we have $-0.65p + 28 = 0.45p + 4$ ⇔ $24 = 1.1p$ ⇔ $p = 21.8181...$ So the price is $21.82. Substituting we find $y = 0.45(21.82) + 4 = 13.82$.

73. Slope is the rate of change of one variable per unit change in another variable. So if the slope is positive, then the temperature is rising. Likewise, if the slope is negative then the temperature is decreasing. If the slope is 0, then the temperature is not changing.

Review Exercises for Chapter 1

1. Commutative Property for addition.

3. Distributive Property.

5. $[-2, 6) = \{x \mid -2 \leq x < 6\}$

7. $x \geq 5 \iff x \in [5, \infty)$

9. $|3 - |-9|| = |3 - 9| = |-6| = 6$

11. $2^{-3} - 3^{-2} = \dfrac{1}{8} - \dfrac{1}{9} = \dfrac{9}{72} - \dfrac{8}{72} = \dfrac{1}{72}$

13. $216^{-1/3} = \dfrac{1}{216^{1/3}} = \dfrac{1}{\sqrt[3]{216}} = \dfrac{1}{6}$

15. $\dfrac{\sqrt{242}}{\sqrt{2}} = \sqrt{\dfrac{242}{2}} = \sqrt{121} = 11$

17. $2^{1/2} 8^{1/2} = \sqrt{2} \cdot \sqrt{8} = \sqrt{16} = 4$

19. $\dfrac{x^2(2x)^4}{x^3} = \dfrac{x^2 \cdot 16x^4}{x^3} = 16x^{2+4-3} = 16x^3$

21. $(3xy^2)^3 \left(\tfrac{2}{3} x^{-1} y\right)^2 = 27x^3 y^6 \cdot \tfrac{4}{9} x^{-2} y^2 = 27 \cdot \tfrac{4}{9} x^{3-2} y^{6+2} = 12xy^8$

23. $\sqrt[3]{(x^3 y)^2 y^4} = \sqrt[3]{x^6 y^4 y^2} = \sqrt[3]{x^6 y^6} = x^2 y^2$

25. $\dfrac{x}{2 + \sqrt{x}} = \dfrac{x}{2 + \sqrt{x}} \cdot \dfrac{2 - \sqrt{x}}{2 - \sqrt{x}} = \dfrac{x\left(2 - \sqrt{x}\right)}{4 - x}$. Here simplify means to rationalize the denominator.

27. $\dfrac{8r^{1/2} s^{-3}}{2r^{-2} s^4} = 4r^{(1/2)-(-2)} s^{-3-4} = 4r^{5/2} s^{-7} = \dfrac{4r^{5/2}}{s^7}$

29. $78{,}250{,}000{,}000 = 7.825 \times 10^{10}$

31. $\dfrac{ab}{c} \approx \dfrac{(0.00000293)(1.582 \times 10^{-14})}{2.8064 \times 10^{12}} = \dfrac{(2.93 \times 10^{-6})(1.582 \times 10^{-14})}{2.8064 \times 10^{12}}$
$= \dfrac{2.93 \cdot 1.582}{2.8064} \times 10^{-6-14-12} \approx 1.65 \times 10^{-32}$

33. $12x^2 y^4 - 3xy^5 + 9x^3 y^2 = 3xy^2(4xy^2 - y^3 + 3x^2)$

35. $x^2 + 3x - 10 = (x + 5)(x - 2)$

37. $4t^2 - 13t - 12 = (4t + 3)(t - 4)$

39. $25 - 16t^2 = (5 - 4t)(5 + 4t)$

41. $x^6 - 1 = (x^3 - 1)(x^3 + 1) = (x - 1)(x^2 + x + 1)(x + 1)(x^2 - x + 1)$

43. $x^{-1/2} - 2x^{1/2} + x^{3/2} = x^{-1/2}(1 - 2x + x^2) = x^{-1/2}(1 - x)^2 = x^{-1/2}(x - 1)^2$

45. $4x^3 - 8x^2 + 3x - 6 = 4x^2(x - 2) + 3(x - 2) = (4x^2 + 3)(x - 2)$

47. $(x^2 + 2)^{5/2} + 2x(x^2 + 2)^{3/2} + x^2 \sqrt{x^2 + 2} = (x^2 + 2)^{1/2}((x^2 + 2)^2 + 2x(x^2 + 2) + x^2)$
$= \sqrt{x^2 + 2}(x^4 + 4x^2 + 4 + 2x^3 + 4x + x^2) = \sqrt{x^2 + 2}(x^4 + 2x^3 + 5x^2 + 4x + 4)$
$= \sqrt{x^2 + 2}(x^2 + x + 2)^2$

49. $(2x+1)(3x-2) - 5(4x-1) = 6x^2 - 4x + 3x - 2 - 20x + 5 = 6x^2 - 21x + 3$

51. $(1+x)(2-x) - (3-x)(3+x) = 2 + x - x^2 - (9-x^2) = 2 + x - x^2 - 9 + x^2 = -7 + x$

53. $x^2(x-2) + x(x-2)^2 = x^3 - 2x^2 + x(x^2 - 4x + 4) = x^3 - 2x^2 + x^3 - 4x^2 + 4x$
$= 2x^3 - 6x^2 + 4x$

55. $\dfrac{x^2 + 2x - 3}{x^2 + 8x + 16} \cdot \dfrac{3x + 12}{x - 1} = \dfrac{(x+3)(x-1)}{(x+4)(x+4)} \cdot \dfrac{3(x+4)}{(x-1)} = \dfrac{3(x+3)}{x+4}$

57. $\dfrac{x^2 - 2x - 15}{x^2 - 6x + 5} \div \dfrac{x^2 - x - 12}{x^2 - 1} = \dfrac{(x-5)(x+3)}{(x-5)(x-1)} \cdot \dfrac{(x-1)(x+1)}{(x-4)(x+3)} = \dfrac{x+1}{x-4}$

59. $\dfrac{1}{x-1} - \dfrac{2}{x^2 - 1} = \dfrac{1}{x-1} - \dfrac{2}{(x-1)(x+1)} = \dfrac{x+1}{(x-1)(x+1)} - \dfrac{2}{(x-1)(x+1)}$
$= \dfrac{x+1-2}{(x-1)(x+1)} = \dfrac{x-1}{(x-1)(x+1)} = \dfrac{1}{x+1}$

61. $\dfrac{\dfrac{1}{x} - \dfrac{1}{2}}{x-2} = \dfrac{\dfrac{2}{2x} - \dfrac{x}{2x}}{x-2} = \dfrac{2-x}{2x} \cdot \dfrac{1}{x-2} = \dfrac{-1(x-2)}{2x} \cdot \dfrac{1}{x-2} = \dfrac{-1}{2x}$

63. $\dfrac{\sqrt{6}}{\sqrt{3}+\sqrt{2}} = \dfrac{\sqrt{6}}{\sqrt{3}+\sqrt{2}} \cdot \dfrac{\sqrt{3}-\sqrt{2}}{\sqrt{3}-\sqrt{2}} = \dfrac{3\sqrt{2} - 2\sqrt{3}}{3-2} = 3\sqrt{2} - 2\sqrt{3}$

65. $7x - 6 = 4x + 9 \quad \Leftrightarrow \quad 3x = 15 \quad \Leftrightarrow \quad x = 5$

67. $\dfrac{x+1}{x-1} = \dfrac{3x}{3x-6} = \dfrac{3x}{3(x-2)} = \dfrac{x}{x-2} \quad \Leftrightarrow \quad (x+1)(x-2) = x(x-1) \quad \Leftrightarrow$
$x^2 - x - 2 = x^2 - x \quad \Leftrightarrow \quad -2 = 0$. Since this last equation is never true, there are no real solutions to the original equation.

69. $x^2 - 9x + 14 = 0 \quad \Leftrightarrow \quad (x-7)(x-2) = 0 \quad \Leftrightarrow \quad x = 7 \text{ or } x = 2$.

71. $2x^2 + x = 1 \quad \Leftrightarrow \quad 2x^2 + x - 1 = 0 \quad \Leftrightarrow \quad (2x-1)(x+1) = 0$. So either $2x - 1 = 0 \quad \Leftrightarrow$
$2x = 1 \quad \Leftrightarrow \quad x = \frac{1}{2}$; or $x + 1 = 0 \quad \Leftrightarrow \quad x = -1$.

73. $0 = 4x^3 - 25x = x(4x^2 - 25) = x(2x-5)(2x+5) = 0$. So either $x = 0$; or $2x - 5 = 0 \quad \Leftrightarrow$
$2x = 5 \quad \Leftrightarrow \quad x = \frac{5}{2}$; or $2x + 5 = 0 \quad \Leftrightarrow \quad 2x = -5 \quad \Leftrightarrow \quad x = -\frac{5}{2}$.

75. $3x^2 + 4x - 1 = 0 \quad \Rightarrow \quad x = \dfrac{-b \pm \sqrt{b^2 - 4ac}}{2a} = \dfrac{-(4) \pm \sqrt{(4)^2 - 4(3)(-1)}}{2(-3)}$
$= \dfrac{-4 \pm \sqrt{16 + 12}}{-6} = \dfrac{-4 \pm \sqrt{28}}{-6} = \dfrac{-4 \pm 2\sqrt{7}}{6} = \dfrac{2(-2 \pm \sqrt{7})}{-6} = \dfrac{-2 \pm \sqrt{7}}{3}$.

77. $\dfrac{x}{x-2} + \dfrac{1}{x+2} = \dfrac{8}{x^2 - 4} \quad \Leftrightarrow \quad x(x+2) + (x-2) = 8 \quad \Leftrightarrow \quad x^2 + 2x + x - 2 = 8 \quad \Leftrightarrow$
$x^2 + 3x - 10 = 0 \quad \Leftrightarrow \quad (x-2)(x+5) = 0 \quad \Leftrightarrow \quad x = 2 \text{ or } x = -5$. However, since $x = 2$
makes the expression undefined, we reject this solution. Hence the only solution is $x = -5$.

79. $|x - 7| = 4 \quad \Leftrightarrow \quad x - 7 = \pm 4 \quad \Leftrightarrow \quad x = 7 \pm 4$, so $x = 11$ or $x = 3$.

81. Let x be the number of pounds of raisins. Then the number of pounds of nuts is $50 - x$.

	raisins	nuts	mixture
pounds	x	$50 - x$	50
rate (cost per pound)	3.20	2.40	2.72
value	$3.20x$	$2.40(50 - x)$	$2.72(50)$

So $3.20x + 2.40(50 - x) = 2.72(50)$ $\Leftrightarrow$ $3.20x + 120 - 2.40x = 136$ $\Leftrightarrow$ $0.8x = 16$ $\Leftrightarrow$ $x = 20$. Thus the mixture uses 20 pounds raisins and $50 - 20 = 30$ pounds of nuts.

83. Let r be the rate the woman runs in mi/h. Then she cycles at $r + 8$ mi/h.

	Rate	Time	Distance
Cycle	$r + 8$	$\dfrac{4}{r+8}$	4
Run	r	$\dfrac{2.5}{r}$	2.5

Since the total time of the workout is 1 hour, we have $\dfrac{4}{r+8} + \dfrac{2.5}{r} = 1$. Multiplying by $2r(r+8)$, we get $4(2r) + 2.5(2)(r+8) = 2r(r+8)$ $\Leftrightarrow$ $8r + 5r + 40 = 2r^2 + 16r$ $\Leftrightarrow$ $0 = 2r^2 + 3r - 40$ $\Rightarrow$ $r = \dfrac{-3 \pm \sqrt{(3)^2 - 4(2)(-40)}}{2(2)} = \dfrac{-3 \pm \sqrt{9 + 320}}{4} = \dfrac{-3 \pm \sqrt{329}}{4}$.

Since $r \geq 0$, we reject the negative value. She runs at $r = \dfrac{-3 + \sqrt{329}}{4} \approx 3.78$ mi/h.

85. Let t be the time it would take Abbie to paint a living room if she works alone. It would take Beth $2t$ hours to paint the living room alone, and it would take $3t$ for Cathie to paint the living room. Thus Abbie does $\dfrac{1}{t}$ of the job per hour, Beth does $\dfrac{1}{2t}$ of the job per hour, and Cathie does $\dfrac{1}{3t}$ of the job per hour. So $\dfrac{1}{t} + \dfrac{1}{2t} + \dfrac{1}{3t} = 1$ $\Leftrightarrow$ $6 + 3 + 2 = 6t$ $\Leftrightarrow$ $6t = 11$ $\Leftrightarrow$ $t = \dfrac{11}{6}$. So it would Abbie 1 hour and 50 minutes to paint the living room alone.

87. $3x - 2 > -11$ $\Leftrightarrow$ $3x > -9$ $\Leftrightarrow$ $x > -3$.   Interval: $(-3, \infty)$.

Graph:

89. $x^2 + 4x - 12 > 0$ $\Leftrightarrow$ $(x - 2)(x + 6) > 0$. The expression on the left of the inequality changes sign where $x = 2$ and where $x = -6$. Thus we must check the intervals in the following table.

Interval	$(-\infty, -6)$	$(-6, 2)$	$(2, \infty)$
Sign of $x - 2$	$-$	$-$	$+$
Sign of $x + 6$	$-$	$+$	$+$
Sign of $(x - 2)(x + 6)$	$+$	$-$	$+$

Interval: $(-\infty, -6) \cup (2, \infty)$.   Graph:

91. $\dfrac{x - 4}{x^2 - 4} \leq 0$ $\Leftrightarrow$ $\dfrac{x - 4}{(x - 2)(x + 2)} \leq 0$. The expression on the left of the inequality changes sign where $x = -2$, where $x = 2$, and where $x = 4$. Thus we must check the intervals in the following table.

Interval	$(-\infty, -2)$	$(-2, 2)$	$(2, 4)$	$(4, \infty)$
Sign of $x - 4$	$-$	$-$	$-$	$+$
Sign of $x - 2$	$-$	$-$	$+$	$+$
Sign of $x + 2$	$-$	$+$	$+$	$+$
Sign of $\dfrac{x-4}{(x-2)(x+2)}$	$-$	$+$	$-$	$+$

Since the expression is not defined when $x = \pm 2$, we exclude these values and the solution is $(-\infty, -2) \cup (2, 4]$.   Graph: ![number line graph from -2 to 4]

93. $|x - 5| \le 3 \quad \Leftrightarrow \quad -3 \le x - 5 \le 3 \quad \Leftrightarrow \quad 2 \le x \le 8$. Interval: $[2, 8]$.
Graph: ![number line from 2 to 8]

95. $x^2 - 4x = 2x + 7$. We graph the equations $y_1 = x^2 - 4x$ and $y_2 = 2x + 7$ in the viewing rectangle rectangle $[-10, 10]$ by $[-5, 25]$. Using Zoom and/or Trace, we get the solutions $x = -1$ and $x = 7$.

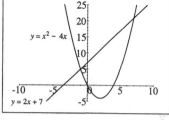

97. $4x - 3 \ge x^2$. We graph the equations $y_1 = 4x - 3$ and $y_2 = x^2$ in the viewing rectangle $[-5, 5]$ by $[0, 15]$. Using Zoom and/or Trace, we find the points of intersection are at $x = 1$ and $x = 3$. Since we want $4x - 3 \ge x^2$, the solution is the interval $[1, 3]$.

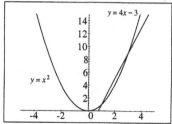

99. (a)

![graph with points (-5, 12) and (2, 0)]

(b) The distance from P to Q is
$$d(P, Q) = \sqrt{(-5 - 2)^2 + (12 - 0)^2}$$
$$= \sqrt{49 + 144} = \sqrt{193}.$$

(c) The midpoint is $\left(\frac{-5+2}{2}, \frac{12+0}{2}\right) = \left(-\frac{3}{2}, 6\right)$.

(d) The line has slope $m = \frac{12-0}{-5-2} = -\frac{12}{7}$, and has equation $y - 0 = -\frac{12}{7}(x - 2) \quad \Leftrightarrow$
$y = -\frac{12}{7}x + \frac{24}{7} \quad \Leftrightarrow \quad 12x + 7y - 24 = 0.$

(e)   The radius of this circle was found in part (b).
It is $r = d(P, Q) = \sqrt{193}$. So the equation is

$$(x - 2)^2 + (y - 0)^2 = \left(\sqrt{193}\right)^2 \quad \Leftrightarrow$$

$$(x - 2)^2 + y^2 = 193.$$

101.

103. $d(A, C) = \sqrt{(4 - (-1))^2 + (4 - (-3))^2} = \sqrt{(4 + 1)^2 + (4 + 3)^2} = \sqrt{74}$ and

$d(B, C) = \sqrt{(5 - (-1))^2 + (3 - (-3))^2} = \sqrt{(5 + 1)^2 + (3 + 3)^2} = \sqrt{72}$. Therefore, B is closer
to C.

105.   The center is $C = (-5, -1)$, and the point $P = (0, 0)$ is on the circle. The radius of the circle is
$r = d(P, C) = \sqrt{(0 - (-5))^2 + (0 - (-1))^2} = \sqrt{(0 + 5)^2 + (0 + 1)^2} = \sqrt{26}$. Thus, the equation
of the circle is $(x + 5)^2 + (y + 1)^2 = 26$.

107. $x^2 + y^2 + 2x - 6y + 9 = 0 \quad \Leftrightarrow \quad (x^2 + 2x) + (y^2 - 6y) = -9 \quad \Leftrightarrow$
$(x^2 + 2x + 1) + (y^2 - 6y + 9) = -9 + 1 + 9 \quad \Leftrightarrow \quad (x + 1)^2 + (y - 3)^2 = 1$. This equation
represents a circle with center at $(-1, 3)$ and radius 1.

109. $x^2 + y^2 + 72 = 12x \quad \Leftrightarrow \quad (x^2 - 12x) + y^2 = -72 \quad \Leftrightarrow \quad (x^2 - 12x + 36) + y^2 = -72 + 36$
$\Leftrightarrow \quad (x - 6)^2 + y^2 = -36$. Since the left side of this equation must be greater than or equal to
zero, this equation has no graph.

111. $y = 2x - 3$
x-axis symmetry: $(-y) = 2 - 3x \quad \Leftrightarrow \quad y = -2 + 3x$, which is not the same as the original
equation, so not symmetric with respect to the x-axis.
y-axis symmetry: $y = 2 - 3(-x) \quad \Leftrightarrow \quad y = 2 + 3x$, which is not the same as the original
equation, so not symmetric with respect to the y-axis.
Origin symmetry: $(-y) = 2 - 3(-x) \quad \Leftrightarrow \quad -y = 2 + 3x \quad \Leftrightarrow \quad y = -2 - 3x$, which is not the
same as the original equation, so not symmetric with respect
to the origin.
Hence the graph has no symmetry.

x	y
-2	8
0	2
$\frac{2}{3}$	0

113. $x + 3y = 21 \quad \Leftrightarrow \quad y = -\frac{1}{3}x + 7$

x-axis symmetry: $x + 3(-y) = 21 \quad \Leftrightarrow \quad x - 3y = 21$, which is not the same as the original equation, so not symmetric with respect to the x-axis.

y-axis symmetry: $(-x) + 3y = 21 \quad \Leftrightarrow \quad x - 3y = -21$, which is not the same as the original equation, so not symmetric with respect to the y-axis.

Origin symmetry: $(-x) + 3(-y) = 21 \quad \Leftrightarrow \quad x + 3y = -21$, which is not the same as the original equation, so not symmetric with respect to the origin.

Hence the graph has no symmetry.

x	y
-3	8
0	7
21	0

115. $y = 16 - x^2$

x-axis symmetry: $(-y) = 16 - x^2 \quad \Leftrightarrow \quad y = -16 + x^2$, which is not the same as the original equation, so not symmetric with respect to the x-axis.

y-axis symmetry: $y = 16 - (-x)^2 \quad \Leftrightarrow \quad y = 16 - x^2$, which is the same as the original equation, so its is symmetric with respect to the y-axis.

Origin symmetry: $(-y) = 16 - (-x)^2 \quad \Leftrightarrow \quad y = -16 + x^2$, which is not the same as the original equation, so not symmetric with respect to the origin.

Hence, the graph is symmetric with respect to the y-axis.

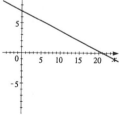

x	y
-3	7
-1	15
0	16
1	15
3	7

117. $x = \sqrt{y}$

x-axis symmetry: $x = \sqrt{-y}$, which is not the same as the original equation, so not symmetric with respect to the x-axis.

y-axis symmetry: $(-x) = \sqrt{y} \quad \Leftrightarrow \quad x = -\sqrt{y}$, which is not the same as the original equation, so not symmetric with respect to the y-axis.

Origin symmetry: $(-x) = \sqrt{-y}$, which is not the same as the original equation, so not symmetric with respect to the origin.

Hence, the graph has no symmetry.

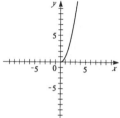

x	y
0	0
1	1
2	4
3	9

119. $y = x^2 - 6x$
Viewing rectangle $[-10, 10]$ by $[-10, 10]$.

121. $y = x^3 - 4x^2 - 5$
Viewing rectangle $[-4, 10]$ by $[-30, 20]$.

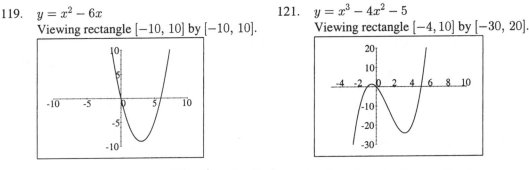

123.   The line has slope $m = \frac{-4+6}{2+1} = \frac{2}{3}$, and so, by the point-slope formula, the equation is
$y + 4 = \frac{2}{3}(x - 2) \quad \Leftrightarrow \quad y = \frac{2}{3}x - \frac{16}{3} \quad \Leftrightarrow \quad 2x - 3y - 16 = 0$.

125.   The x-intercept is 4, and the y-intercept is 12, so the slope is $m = \frac{12-0}{0-4} = -3$. Therefore, by the slope-intercept formula, the equation of the line is $y = -3x + 12 \quad \Leftrightarrow \quad 3x + y - 12 = 0$.

127.   We first find the slope of the line $3x + 15y = 22$. This gives $3x + 15y = 22 \quad \Leftrightarrow$
$15y = -3x + 22 \quad \Leftrightarrow \quad y = -\frac{1}{5}x + \frac{22}{15}$. So this line has slope $m = -\frac{1}{5}$, as does any line parallel to it. Then the parallel line passing through the origin has equation $y - 0 = -\frac{1}{5}(x - 0) \quad \Leftrightarrow$
$x + 5y = 0$.

129.   Here the center is at $(0,0)$, and the circle passes through the point $(-5, 12)$, so the radius is
$r = \sqrt{(-5 - 0)^2 + (12 - 0)^2} = \sqrt{25 + 144} = \sqrt{169} = 13$. The equation of the circle is
$x^2 + y^2 = 13^2 \quad \Leftrightarrow \quad x^2 + y^2 = 169$. The line shown is the tangent that passes through the point
$(-5, 12)$, so it is perpendicular to the line through the points $(0, 0)$ and $(-5, 12)$. This line has slope
$m_1 = \frac{12-0}{-5-0} = -\frac{12}{5}$. The slope of the line we seek is $m_2 = -\frac{1}{m_1} = -\frac{1}{-12/5} = \frac{5}{12}$. Thus, the
equation of the tangent line is $y - 12 = \frac{5}{12}(x + 5) \quad \Leftrightarrow \quad y - 12 = \frac{5}{12}x + \frac{25}{12} \quad \Leftrightarrow$
$y = \frac{5}{12}x + \frac{169}{12} \quad \Leftrightarrow \quad 5x - 12y + 169 = 0$.

Chapter 1 Test

1. (a) $[-2, 5)$

   (7, ∞)

   (b) $x \leq 3 \Leftrightarrow x \in (-\infty, 3]$ $\qquad$ $0 < x \leq 8 \Leftrightarrow x \in (0, 8]$

   (c) Distance $= |-12 - 39| = |-51| = 51$

2. (a) $(-3)^4 = 81$ $\qquad\qquad$ (b) $-3^4 = -81$

   (c) $3^{-4} = \dfrac{1}{3^4} = \dfrac{1}{81}$ $\qquad\qquad$ (d) $\dfrac{5^{23}}{5^{21}} = 5^{23-21} = 5^2 = 25$

   (e) $\left(\dfrac{2}{3}\right)^{-2} = \dfrac{3^2}{2^2} = \dfrac{9}{4}$ $\qquad\qquad$ (f) $16^{-3/4} = \left(2^4\right)^{-3/4} = 2^{-3} = \dfrac{1}{8}$

3. (a) $186{,}000{,}000{,}000 = 1.86 \times 10^{11}$ $\qquad$ (b) $0.0000003965 = 3.965 \times 10^{-7}$

4. (a) $\sqrt{200} - \sqrt{32} = 10\sqrt{2} - 4\sqrt{2} = 6\sqrt{2}$

   (b) $(3a^2b^3)(4ab^2)^2 = 3a^2b^3 \cdot 4^2 a^2 b^4 = 48a^4b^7$

   (c) $\left(\dfrac{3x^{3/2}y^3}{x^2y^{-1/2}}\right)^{-2} = \dfrac{3^{-2}x^{-3}y^{-6}}{x^{-4}y^1} = \tfrac{1}{9}x^{-3-(-4)}y^{-6-1} = \tfrac{1}{9}xy^{-7} = \dfrac{x}{9y^7}$

   (d) $\dfrac{x^2 + 3x + 2}{x^2 - x - 2} = \dfrac{(x+1)(x+2)}{(x+1)(x-2)} = \dfrac{x+2}{x-2}$

   (e) $\dfrac{x^2}{x^2 - 4} - \dfrac{x+1}{x+2} = \dfrac{x^2}{(x-2)(x+2)} - \dfrac{x+1}{x+2} = \dfrac{x^2}{(x-2)(x+2)} + \dfrac{-(x+1)(x-2)}{(x-2)(x+2)}$

   $= \dfrac{x^2 - (x^2 - x - 2)}{(x-2)(x+2)} = \dfrac{x+2}{(x-2)(x+2)} = \dfrac{1}{x-2}$

   (f) $\dfrac{\frac{y}{x} - \frac{x}{y}}{\frac{1}{y} - \frac{1}{x}} = \dfrac{\frac{y}{x} - \frac{x}{y}}{\frac{1}{y} - \frac{1}{x}} \cdot \dfrac{xy}{xy} = \dfrac{y^2 - x^2}{x - y} = \dfrac{(y-x)(y+x)}{x-y} = \dfrac{-(x-y)(y+x)}{x-y} = -(y+x)$

5. $\dfrac{\sqrt{10}}{\sqrt{5} - 2} = \dfrac{\sqrt{10}}{\sqrt{5} - 2} \cdot \dfrac{\sqrt{5} + 2}{\sqrt{5} + 2} = \dfrac{\sqrt{50} + 2\sqrt{10}}{5 - 4} = \dfrac{5\sqrt{2} + 2\sqrt{10}}{1} = 5\sqrt{2} + 2\sqrt{10}$

6. (a) $3(x+6) + 4(2x-5) = 3x + 18 + 8x - 20 = 11x - 2$

   (b) $(x+3)(4x-5) = 4x^2 - 5x + 12x - 15 = 4x^2 + 7x - 15$

   (c) $\left(\sqrt{a} + \sqrt{b}\right)\left(\sqrt{a} - \sqrt{b}\right) = \left(\sqrt{a}\right)^2 - \left(\sqrt{b}\right)^2 = a - b$

   (d) $(2x+3)^2 = (2x)^2 + 2(2x)(3) + (3)^2 = 4x^2 + 12x + 9$

   (e) $(x+2)^3 = (x)^3 + 3(x)^2(2) + 3(x)(2)^2 + (2)^3 = x^3 + 6x^2 + 12x + 8$

7. (a) $4x^2 - 25 = (2x - 5)(2x + 5)$

(b) $2x^2 + 5x - 12 = (2x - 3)(x + 4)$

(c) $x^3 - 3x^2 - 4x + 12 = x^2(x - 3) - 4(x - 3) = (x - 3)(x^2 - 4) = (x - 3)(x - 2)(x + 2)$

(d) $x^4 + 27x = x(x^3 + 27) = x(x + 3)(x^2 - 3x + 9)$

(e) $3x^{3/2} - 9x^{1/2} + 6x^{-1/2} = 3x^{-1/2}(x^2 - 3x + 2) = 3x^{-1/2}(x - 2)(x - 1)$

(f) $x^3 y - 4xy = xy(x^2 - 4) = xy(x - 2)(x + 2)$

8. (a) $x + 5 = 14 - \frac{1}{2}x \iff 2x + 10 = 28 - x \iff 3x = 18 \iff x = 6$

(b) $\dfrac{2x}{x + 1} = \dfrac{2x - 1}{x} \iff (2x)(x) = (2x - 1)(x + 1) \ (x \neq -1, x \neq 0) \iff$

$2x^2 = 2x^2 + x - 1 \iff 0 = x - 1 \iff x = 1$

(c) $x^2 - x - 12 = 0 \iff (x - 4)(x + 3) = 0$. So $x = 4$ or $x = -3$.

(d) $2x^2 + 4x + 1 = 0 \implies x = \dfrac{-4 \pm \sqrt{4^2 - 4(2)(1)}}{2(2)} = \dfrac{-4 \pm \sqrt{16 - 8}}{4} = \dfrac{-4 \pm \sqrt{8}}{4}$

$= \dfrac{-4 \pm 2\sqrt{2}}{4} = \dfrac{-2 \pm \sqrt{2}}{2}$.

(e) $\sqrt{3 - \sqrt{x + 5}} = 2 \implies 3 - \sqrt{x + 5} = 4 \iff -1 = \sqrt{x + 5}$. Squaring both sides
again, we get $1 = x + 5 \iff x = -4$. But this does not satisfy the original equation, so
there is no solution. (You must always check your final answers if you have squared both sides
when solving an equation, since extraneous answers may be introduced.)
*Some students might stop at the statement $-1 = \sqrt{x + 5}$ and recognize that this is
impossible, so there can be no solution.

(f) $x^4 - 3x^2 + 2 = 0 \iff (x^2 - 1)(x^2 - 2) = 0$. So $x^2 - 1 = 0 \iff x = \pm 1$ or
$x^2 - 2 = 0 \iff x = \pm \sqrt{2}$. Thus the solutions are $x = -1, x = 1, x = -\sqrt{2}$, and
$x = \sqrt{2}$.

(g) $3|x - 4| - 10 = 0 \iff 3|x - 4| = 10 \iff |x - 4| = \frac{10}{3} \iff x - 4 = \pm\frac{10}{3} \iff$
$x = 4 \pm \frac{10}{3}$. So $x = 4 - \frac{10}{3} = \frac{2}{3}$ or $x = 4 + \frac{10}{3} = \frac{22}{3}$. Thus the solutions are $x = \frac{2}{3}$ and
$x = \frac{22}{3}$.

9. Let t be the time (in hours) it took Mary to drive from Amity to Belleville. Then $4.4 - t$ is the time
it took Mary to drive from Belleville to Amity. Since then distance from Amity to Belleville equals
the distance from Belleville to Amity we have $50t = 60(4.4 - t) \iff 50t = 264 - 60t \iff$
$110t = 264 \iff t = 2.4$ hours. Thus the distance is $50(2.4) = 120$ miles.

10. Let w be the width of the parcel of land. Then $w + 70$ is the lenght of the parcel of land. Then
$w^2 + (w + 70)^2 = 130^2 \iff w^2 + w^2 + 140w + 4900 = 16900 \iff$
$2w^2 + 140w - 12000 = 0 \iff w^2 + 70w - 6000 = 0 \iff (w - 50)(w + 120) = 0$. So
$w = 50$ or $w = -120$. Since $w \geq 0$, the width is $w = 50$ ft and the length is $w + 70 = 120$ ft.

11. (a) $-4 < 5 - 3x \leq 17 \iff -9 < -3x \leq 12 \iff 3 > x \geq -4$. Expressing in standard
form we have: $-4 \leq x < 3$. Interval: $[-4, 3)$ Graph:

(b) $x(x - 1)(x + 2) > 0$. The expression on the left of the inequality changes sign when $x = 0$,
$x = 1$, and $x = -2$. Thus we must check the intervals in the following table.

Interval	$(-\infty, -2)$	$(-2, 0)$	$(0, 1)$	$(1, \infty)$
Sign of x	$-$	$-$	$+$	$+$
Sign of $x - 1$	$-$	$-$	$-$	$+$
Sign of $x + 2$	$-$	$+$	$+$	$+$
Sign of $x(x-1)(x-2)$	$-$	$+$	$-$	$+$

From the table, the solution set is $\{x \mid -2 < x < 0 \text{ or } 1 < x\}$

Interval: $(-2, 0) \cup (1, \infty)$.   Graph:

(c) $|x - 4| < 3$ is equivalent to $-3 < x - 4 < 3$ $\Leftrightarrow$ $1 < x < 7$.

Interval: $(1, 7)$.   Graph:

(d) $\dfrac{2x - 3}{x + 1} \le 1$ $\Leftrightarrow$ $\dfrac{2x - 3}{x + 1} - 1 \le 0$ $\Leftrightarrow$ $\dfrac{2x - 3}{x + 1} - \dfrac{x + 1}{x + 1} \le 0$ $\Leftrightarrow$ $\dfrac{x - 4}{x + 1} \le 0$. The
expression on the left of the inequality changes sign where $x = -4$ and where $x = -1$. Thus
we must check the intervals in the following table.

Interval	$(-\infty, -1)$	$(-1, 4)$	$(4, \infty)$
Sign of $x - 4$	$-$	$-$	$+$
Sign of $x + 1$	$-$	$+$	$+$
Sign of $\dfrac{x - 4}{x + 1}$	$+$	$-$	$+$

Since $x = -1$ makes the expression in the inequality undefined, we exclude this value.

Interval: $(-1, \ 4]$ Graph:

12. $5 \le \frac{5}{9}(F - 32) \le 10$ $\Leftrightarrow$ $9 \le F - 32 \le 18$ $\Leftrightarrow$ $41 \le F \le 50$. Thus the medicine is to be
stored at a temperature between 41°F to 50°F.

13.   For $\sqrt{6x - x^2}$ to be defined as a real number $6x - x^2 \ge 0$ $\Leftrightarrow$ $x(6 - x) \ge 0$. The expression on
the left of the inequality changes sign when $x = 0$ and $x = 6$. Thus we must check the intervals in
the following table.

Interval	$(-\infty, 0)$	$(0, 6)$	$(6, \infty)$
Sign of x	$-$	$+$	$+$
Sign of $6 - x$	$+$	$+$	$-$
Sign of $x(6 - x)$	$-$	$+$	$-$

From the table, we see that $\sqrt{6x - x^2}$ is defined when $0 \le x \le 6$.

14.   (a) $x^3 - 9x - 1 = 0$. We graph the equation
$y = x^3 - 9x - 1$ in the viewing rectangle
$[-5, 5]$ by $[-5, 10]$. We find that the points of
intersection occur at $x \approx -2.94, -0.11, 3.05$.

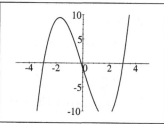

(b) $x^2 - 2 \le |x + 1|$. We graph the equations $y_1 = x^2 - 2$ and $y_2 = |x + 1|$ in the viewing rectangle $[-5, 5]$ by $[-5, 10]$. We find that the points of intersection occur at $x \approx -1.62$ and $x \approx 2.30$. Since we want $x^2 - 2 \le |x + 1|$, the solution is the interval $[-1.62, 2.30]$.

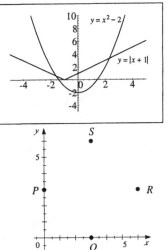

15. (a) There are several ways to determine the coordinates of S. The diagonals of a square have equal length and are are perpendicular. The diagonal PR is horizontal and has length is 6 units. So the diagonal QS is vertical and also has length 6. Thus the coordinates of S are $(3, 6)$.

(b) The length of PQ is $\sqrt{(0-3)^2 + (3-0)^2} = \sqrt{18} = 3\sqrt{2}$. So the area of $PQRS$ is $(3\sqrt{2})^2 = 18$.

16. (a)

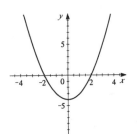

(b) The x-intercept occurs when $y = 0$, so $0 = x^2 - 4 \iff x^2 = 4 \implies x = \pm 2$. The y-intercept occurs when $x = 0$, so $y = -4$.

(c) x-axis symmetry: $(-y) = x^2 - 4 \iff y = -x^2 + 4$, which is not the same as the original equation, so not symmetric with respect to the x-axis.

y-axis symmetry: $y = (-x)^2 - 4 \iff y = x^2 - 4$, which is the same as the original equation, so it is symmetric with respect to the y-axis.

Origin symmetry: $(-y) = (-x)^2 - 4 \iff -y = x^2 - 4$, which is not the same as the original equation, so not symmetric with respect to the origin.

17. (a) The distance from A to B is
$$d(AB) = \sqrt{(-7-5)^2 + (4+12)^2} = \sqrt{144 + 256} = \sqrt{400} = 20.$$

(b) The midpoint is $\left(\frac{-7+5}{2}, \frac{4-12}{2}\right) = (-1, -4)$.

(c) The line has slope $m = \frac{4+12}{-7-5} = \frac{16}{-12} = -\frac{4}{3}$, and its equation is $y - 4 = -\frac{4}{3}(x + 7) \iff y = -\frac{4}{3}x - \frac{28}{3} + 4 = -\frac{4}{3}x - \frac{16}{3}$. Thus the equation is $y = -\frac{4}{3}x - \frac{16}{3} \iff 4x + 3y + 16 = 0$.

(d) The perpendicular bisector has slope $m = -\dfrac{1}{-(4/3)} = \dfrac{3}{4}$ and contains the midpoint $(-1, -4)$.

Thus, from the point-slope formula, the equation is $y + 4 = \frac{3}{4}(x + 1) \iff y + 4 = \frac{3}{4}x + \frac{3}{4}$ $\iff y = \frac{3}{4}x + \frac{3}{4} - 4 = \frac{3}{4}x - \frac{13}{4}$. Therefore, the equation is $y = \frac{3}{4}x - \frac{13}{4} \iff 3x - 4y - 13 = 0$.

(e) $(x-5)^2 + (y+12)^2 = 13^2$ $\Leftrightarrow$ $(x-5)^2 + (y+12)^2 = 169$

(f) The length of a diameter of this circle was found in part (a), so the radius is $r = \frac{20}{2} = 10$. The center is the midpoint found in part (b), so the equation is $(x+1)^2 + (y+4)^2 = 10^2$ $\Leftrightarrow$ $(x+1)^2 + (y+4)^2 = 100$.

18. (a) $x^2 + (y-4)^2 = 9$ $\Leftrightarrow$ $x^2 + (y-4)^2 = 3^2$
The center is $(0, 4)$, and the radius is 3.

(b) $x^2 + y^2 - 6x + 10y + 9 = 0$ $\Leftrightarrow$
$(x^2 - 6x) + (y^2 + 10y) = -9$ $\Leftrightarrow$
$(x^2 - 6x + 9) + (y^2 + 10y + 25) = -9 + 9 + 25$
$\Leftrightarrow$ $(x-3)^2 + (y+5)^2 = 5^2$
The center is $(3, -5)$, and the radius is 5.

19. $3x - 4y + 24 = 0$ $\Leftrightarrow$ $-4y = -3x - 24$
$\Leftrightarrow$ $y = \frac{3}{4}x + 6$.
The slope is $\frac{3}{4}$, and the y-intercept is 6.

20. (a) We first find the slope of the line $2x + 6y = 17$. This gives $2x + 6y = 17$ $\Leftrightarrow$ $6y = -2x + 17$ $\Leftrightarrow$ $y = -\frac{1}{3}x + \frac{17}{6}$. Thus, this line has slope $m = -\frac{1}{3}$, as does any line parallel to it. Then the parallel line passing through the point $(-2, 3)$ has the equation $y - 3 = -\frac{1}{3}(x+2)$ $\Leftrightarrow$ $3y - 9 = -x - 2$ $\Leftrightarrow$ $x + 3y - 7 = 0$. (You can also find this equation by substituting the point $(-2, 3)$ into the equation $2x + 6y = c$ and solving for c.)

(b) This line contains the points $(-3, 0)$ and $(0, 12)$. Thus, the slope of the line containing these points is $m = \frac{12-0}{0+3} = 4$, and so the equation is $y = 4x + 12$ $\Leftrightarrow$ $4x - y + 12 = 0$. (You can also use the two-intercept form of a line: $\frac{x}{a} + \frac{y}{b} = 1$ $\Rightarrow$ $\frac{x}{-3} + \frac{y}{12} = 1$.)

21. (a) When $x = 2{,}500$, $C = 7(2{,}500) + 17{,}500 = 17{,}500 + 17{,}500 = \$35{,}000$.

(b) The slope represents the cost of producing one more blender, \$7. The C-intercept, \$17,500, represents the fixed cost.

Principles of Problem Solving

1. Let d be the distance traveled to and from work. Let t_1 and t_2 be the times for the trip from home to work and the trip from work to home, respectively. Using $time = \dfrac{distance}{rate}$, we get $t_1 = \dfrac{d}{50}$ and $t_2 = \dfrac{d}{30}$. Since $average\ speed = \dfrac{distance\ traveled}{total\ time}$, we have $average\ speed = \dfrac{2d}{t_1 + t_2} = \dfrac{2d}{\frac{d}{50} + \frac{d}{30}}$

    $\Leftrightarrow \quad average\ speed = \dfrac{150(2d)}{150\left(\frac{d}{50} + \frac{d}{30}\right)} = \dfrac{300d}{3d + 5d} = \dfrac{300}{8} = 37.5$ mi/h.

3. We use the formula $d = rt$ (distance = rate $\times$ time). Since the car and the van each travel at a speed of 40 mi/h, they approach each other at a combined speed of 80 mi/h. (The distance between them decreases at a rate of 80 mi/h.) So the time spent driving till they meet is $t = \dfrac{d}{r} = \dfrac{120}{80} = 1.5$ hours. Thus, the fly flies at a speed of 100 mi/h for 1.5 hours, and therefore travels a distance of $d = rt = (100)(1.5) = 150$ miles.

5. $\left(\sqrt{3 + 2\sqrt{2}} - \sqrt{3 - 2\sqrt{2}}\right)^2 = 3 + 2\sqrt{2} - 2 \cdot \sqrt{\left(3 + 2\sqrt{2}\right)\left(3 - 2\sqrt{2}\right)} + 3 - 2\sqrt{2}$

    $= 6 - 2 \cdot \sqrt{9 - 8} = 6 - 2 = 4$. Therefore, $\sqrt{3 + 2\sqrt{2}} - \sqrt{3 - 2\sqrt{2}} = \sqrt{4} = 2$.

7. By placing two amoebas into the vessel, we skip the first simple division which took 3 minutes. Thus when we place two amoebas into the vessel, it will take $60 - 3 = 57$ minutes for the vessel to be full of amoebas.

9. The statement is false. Here is one particular counterexample:

	Player A	Player B
First half	1 hit in 99 at-bats: average $= \frac{1}{99}$	0 hit in 1 at-bat: average $= \frac{0}{1}$
Second half	1 hit in 1 at-bat: average $= \frac{1}{1}$	98 hits in 99 at-bats: average $= \frac{98}{99}$
Entire season	2 hits in 100 at-bats: average $= \frac{2}{100}$	99 hits in 100 at-bats: average $= \frac{99}{100}$

11. **Method 1:**
    After the exchanges, the volume of liquid in the pitcher and in the cup is the same as it was to begin with. Thus, any coffee in the pitcher of cream must be replacing an equal amount of cream that has ended up in the coffee cup.

    Method 2:
    Alternatively, look at the drawing of the spoonful of coffee and cream mixture being returned to the pitcher of cream. Suppose it is possible to separate the cream and the coffee, as shown. Then you can see that the coffee going into the cream occupies the same volume as the cream that was left in the coffee.

    cream
    coffee

    Method 3 (an algebraic approach):
    Suppose the cup of coffee has y spoonfuls of coffee. When one spoonful of cream is added to the coffee cup, the resulting mixture has the following ratios:

    $$\frac{cream}{mixture} = \frac{1}{y+1} \qquad \frac{coffee}{mixture} = \frac{y}{y+1}$$

So, when we remove a spoonful of the mixture and put it into the pitcher of cream, we are really removing $\dfrac{1}{y+1}$ of a spoonful of cream and $\dfrac{y}{y+1}$ spoonful of coffee. Thus the <u>amount</u> of <u>cream</u> left in the mixture (cream in the coffee) is $1 - \dfrac{1}{y+1} = \dfrac{y}{y+1}$ of a spoonful. This is the same as the <u>amount</u> of <u>coffee</u> we added to the cream.

13. (a) $(\text{Baby} + \text{Uncle}) + \text{Mother} = \text{Uncle} + \text{Mother} = \text{Uncle}$

(b) $\text{Father} \cdot (\text{Grandpa} + \text{Aunt}) = \text{Father} \cdot \text{Grandpa} = \text{Father}$

(c)   <u>Commutative:</u> $x + y = (\text{older of } x \text{ and } y) = (\text{older of } y \text{ and } x) = y + x$
$x \cdot y = (\text{younger of } x \text{ and } y) = (\text{younger of } y \text{ and } x) = y \cdot x$
<u>Associative:</u> $(x + y) + z = (\text{older of } x \text{ and } y) + z = \text{older of } (\text{older of } x \text{ and } y) \text{ and } z = \text{older}$
of x and y and z; $x + (y + z) = x + (\text{older of } y \text{ and } z) = \text{older of } x \text{ and } (\text{older of } y \text{ and } z)$
$= \text{older of } x \text{ and } y \text{ and } z$. So $(x + y) + z = x + (y + z)$
$(x \cdot y) \cdot z = (\text{younger of } x \text{ and } y) \cdot z = \text{younger of } (\text{younger of } x \text{ and } y) \text{ and } z = \text{younger of } x$
and y and z; $x \cdot (y \cdot z) = x \cdot (\text{younger of } y \text{ and } z) = \text{younger of } x \text{ and } (\text{younger of } y \text{ and } z)$
$= \text{younger of } x \text{ and } y \text{ and } z$. So $(x \cdot y) \cdot z = x \cdot (y \cdot z)$.
<u>Distributive:</u>   We consider three cases:
Case (i), x is oldest of x, y, and z. Then $x \cdot (y + z) = y + z$ and $x \cdot y + x \cdot z = y + z$, so
$x \cdot (y + z) = x \cdot y + x \cdot z$.
Case (ii), y is oldest. Then $x \cdot (y + z) = x \cdot y = x$ and $x \cdot y + x \cdot z = x + x \cdot z = x$ (since
$x \cdot z$ is no older than x by definition). Thus, $x \cdot (y + z) = x \cdot y + x \cdot z$.
Case (iii), z is oldest: then $x \cdot (y + z) = x \cdot z = x$ and $x \cdot y + x \cdot z = x \cdot y + x = x$ (since
$x \cdot y$ is no older than x by definition). Thus, $x \cdot (y + z) = x \cdot y + x \cdot z$.

(d)   Again we consider three cases.
Case (i), x is oldest of x, y, and z. Then $x + (y \cdot z) = x$. Also, $x + y = x$ and $x + z = x$, so
$(x + y) \cdot (x + z) = x \cdot x = x$. Thus, $x + (y \cdot z) = (x + y) \cdot (x + z)$.
Case (ii), y is oldest of x, y, and z. Then $y \cdot z = z$, and so $x + (y \cdot z) = x + z$. Also,
$x + y = y$, so $(x + y) \cdot (x + z) = y \cdot (x + z) = x + z$. Thus, $x + (y \cdot z) = (x + y) \cdot (x + z)$.
The proof in the third case, when z is the oldest, is similar to the case when y is the oldest.
No, the property does not hold for real numbers. For example, if $x = y = z = 1$, then
$1 + (1 \cdot 1) \neq (1 + 1) \cdot (1 + 1)$.

15. Let $r_1 = 8$.
$r_2 = \frac{1}{2}\left(8 + \frac{72}{8}\right) = \frac{1}{2}(8 + 9) = 8.5$
$r_3 = \frac{1}{2}\left(8.5 + \frac{72}{8.5}\right) = \frac{1}{2}(8.5 + 8.471) = 8.485$
$r_4 = \frac{1}{2}\left(8.485 + \frac{72}{8.485}\right) = \frac{1}{2}(8.485 + 8.486) = 8.485$
Thus $\sqrt{72} \approx 8.49$.

17. We continue the pattern. Three parallel cuts produce 10 pieces. Thus, each new cut produces an additional 3 pieces. Since the first cut produces 4 pieces, we get the formula $f(n) = 4 + 3(n - 1)$, $n \geq 1$. Since $f(142) = 4 + 3(141) = 427$, we see that 142 parallel cuts produce 427 pieces.

19. $8^{15} \cdot 5^{37} = (2^3)^{15} \cdot 5^{37} = 2^{45} \cdot 5^{37} = 2^8 \cdot 2^{37} \cdot 5^{37} = 2^8 \cdot 10^{37} = 256 \times 10^{37}$. Therefore, the number has $3 + 37 = 40$ digits.

21.   Since $x^3 + y^3 = (x+y)(x^2 - xy + y^2)$, we need to determine the value of xy.

$$x + y = 1 \quad \Leftrightarrow \quad x^2 + xy \qquad\;\; = x$$
$$x + y = 1 \quad \Leftrightarrow \quad \underline{\qquad\;\; xy + y^2 = y}$$
$$x^2 + 2xy + y^2 = x + y$$

So $4 + 2xy = 1 \quad \Leftrightarrow \quad xy = -\frac{3}{2}$. Thus $x^3 + y^3 = (x+y)(x^2 - xy + y^2) = (1)(4 + \frac{3}{2}) = \frac{11}{2}$.

23.   We know that $\sqrt{2}$ is irrational. Now $\sqrt{2}^{\sqrt{2}}$ is either rational or irrational. If $\sqrt{2}^{\sqrt{2}}$ is rational, we would be done because we would have found an irrational number raised to an irrational number which is rational. If $\sqrt{2}^{\sqrt{2}}$ is not rational, then consider $\left(\sqrt{2}^{\sqrt{2}}\right)^{\sqrt{2}} = \sqrt{2}^{\sqrt{2}\cdot\sqrt{2}} = \sqrt{2}^2 = 2$. So, again we would have found an irrational number (namely $\sqrt{2}^{\sqrt{2}}$) raised to an irrational number (namely $\sqrt{2}$) which is rational (namely 2).

25.   You can see infinitely far in this forest, because if your vision is blocked by a tree (at the rational point (a, b), say), then the slope of the line of sight from you to this tree is $\frac{b-0}{a-0} = \frac{b}{a}$, which is a rational number. Thus if you look along a line of irrational slope, you will see infinitely far.

27.   We consider four cases corresponding to each quadrant.

Case (i), $x \geq 0$ and $y \geq 0$: $|x| + |y| \leq 1$ becomes $x + y \leq 1$.
Case (ii), $x \leq 0$ and $y \geq 0$: $|x| + |y| \leq 1$ becomes $-x + y \leq 1$.
Case (iii), $x \geq 0$ and $y \leq 0$: $|x| + |y| \leq 1$ becomes $x - y \leq 1$.
Case (iv), $x \leq 0$ and $y \leq 0$: $|x| + |y| \leq 1$ becomes $-x - y \leq 1$
$$\Leftrightarrow \quad x + y \geq -1.$$

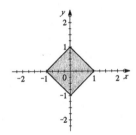

Chapter Two
Exercises 2.1

1. $f(x) = 7x + 2$

3. $f(x) = (x - 4)^2$

5. Divide by 2, then add 7.

7. Square, multiply by 3, then subtract 2.

9. Machine diagram for $f(x) = \sqrt{x}$.

11. $f(x) = 2x^2 + 1$

x	$f(x)$
-1	$2(-1)^2 + 1 = 3$
0	$2(0)^2 + 1 = 1$
1	$2(1)^2 + 1 = 3$
2	$2(2)^2 + 1 = 9$
3	$2(3)^2 + 1 = 19$

13. $f(1) = 2(1) + 1 = 3$; $f(-2) = 2(-2) + 1 = -3$; $f(\frac{1}{2}) = 2(\frac{1}{2}) + 1 = 2$;
    $f(a) = 2(a) + 1 = 2a + 1$; $f(-a) = 2(-a) + 1 = -2a + 1$;
    $f(a + b) = 2(a + b) + 1 = 2a + 2b + 1$.

15. $g(2) = \dfrac{1 - (2)}{1 + (2)} = \dfrac{-1}{3} = -\dfrac{1}{3}$; $g(-2) = \dfrac{1 - (-2)}{1 + (-2)} = \dfrac{3}{-1} = -3$; $g(\dfrac{1}{2}) = \dfrac{1 - (\frac{1}{2})}{1 + (\frac{1}{2})} = \dfrac{\frac{1}{2}}{\frac{3}{2}} = \dfrac{1}{3}$;
    $g(a) = \dfrac{1 - (a)}{1 + (a)} = \dfrac{1 - a}{1 + a}$; $g(a - 1) = \dfrac{1 - (a - 1)}{1 + (a - 1)} = \dfrac{1 - a + 1}{1 + a - 1} = \dfrac{2 - a}{a}$;
    $g(-1) = \dfrac{1 - (-1)}{1 + (-1)} = \dfrac{2}{0}$, so $g(-1)$ is not defined.

17. $f(0) = 2(0)^2 + 3(0) - 4 = -4$; $f(2) = 2(2)^2 + 3(2) - 4 = 8 + 6 - 4 = 10$;
    $f(-2) = 2(-2)^2 + 3(-2) - 4 = 8 - 6 - 4 = -2$;
    $f(\sqrt{2}) = 2(\sqrt{2})^2 + 3(\sqrt{2}) - 4 = 4 + 3\sqrt{2} - 4 = 3\sqrt{2}$;
    $f(x + 1) = 2(x + 1)^2 + 3(x + 1) - 4 = 2x^2 + 4x + 2 + 3x + 3 - 4 = 2x^2 + 7x + 1$;
    $f(-x) = 2(-x)^2 + 3(-x) - 4 = 2x^2 - 3x - 4$.

19. $f(-2) = 2|-2-1| = 2(3) = 6;$ $f(0) = 2|0-1| = 2(1) = 2;$ $f(\frac{1}{2}) = 2|\frac{1}{2}-1| = 2(\frac{1}{2}) = 1;$
     $f(2) = 2|2-1| = 2(1) = 2;$ $f(x+1) = 2|(x+1)-1| = 2|x|;$
     $f(x^2+2) = 2|(x^2+2)-1| = 2|x^2+1| = 2x^2+2$ (since $x^2+1 > 0$).

21. Since $-2 < 0$, we have $f(-2) = (-2)^2 = 4$. Since $-1 < 0$, we have $f(-1) = (-1)^2 = 1$. Since
     $0 \geq 0$, we have $f(0) = 0+1 = 1$. Since $1 \geq 0$, we have $f(1) = 1+1 = 2$. Since $2 \geq 0$, we have
     $f(2) = 2+1 = 3$.

23. Since $-4 \leq -1$, we have $f(-4) = (-4)^2 + 2(-4) = 16 - 8 = 8$. Since $-\frac{3}{2} \leq -1$, we have
     $f\left(-\frac{3}{2}\right) = \left(-\frac{3}{2}\right)^2 + 2\left(-\frac{3}{2}\right) = \frac{9}{4} - 3 = -\frac{3}{4}$. Since $-1 \leq -1$, we have
     $f(-1) = (-1)^2 + 2(-1) = 1 - 2 = -1$. Since $0 > -1$, we have $f(0) = 0$. Since $1 > -1$, we
     have $f(1) = 1$.

25. $f(x+2) = (x+2)^2 + 1 = x^2 + 4x + 4 + 1 = x^2 + 4x + 5;$
     $f(x) + f(2) = x^2 + 1 + (2)^2 + 1 = x^2 + 1 + 4 + 1 = x^2 + 6$.

27. $f(x^2) = x^2 + 4;$ $[f(x)]^2 = [x+4]^2 = x^2 + 8x + 16$.

29. $f(a) = 3(a) + 2 = 3a + 2;$ $f(a+h) = 3(a+h) + 2 = 3a + 3h + 2;$
     $\dfrac{f(a+h) - f(a)}{h} = \dfrac{(3a+3h+2) - (3a+2)}{h} = \dfrac{3a+3h+2-3a-2}{h} = \dfrac{3h}{h} = 3$.

31. $f(a) = 5;$ $f(a+h) = 5;$ $\dfrac{f(a+h) - f(a)}{h} = \dfrac{5-5}{h} = 0$.

33. $f(a) = 3 - 5a + 4a^2;$ $f(a+h) = 3 - 5(a+h) + 4(a+h)^2$
     $= 3 - 5a - 5h + 4(a^2 + 2ah + h^2) = 3 - 5a - 5h + 4a^2 + 8ah + 4h^2;$
     $\dfrac{f(a+h) - f(a)}{h} = \dfrac{(3 - 5a - 5h + 4a^2 + 8ah + 4h^2) - (3 - 5a + 4a^2)}{h}$
     $= \dfrac{3 - 5a - 5h + 4a^2 + 8ah + 4h^2 - 3 + 5a - 4a^2}{h} = \dfrac{-5h + 8ah + 4h^2}{h} = \dfrac{h(-5 + 8a + 4h)}{h}$
     $= -5 + 8a + 4h$.

35. (a) $C(10) = 1500 + 3(10) + 0.02(10)^2 + 0.0001(10)^3 = 1500 + 30 + 2 + 0.1 = 1532.1$
          $C(100) = 1500 + 3(100) + 0.02(100)^2 + 0.0001(100)^3 = 1500 + 300 + 200 + 100 = 2000$

     (b) $C(10)$ represents the cost of producing 10 yards of fabric and $C(100)$ represents the cost of
          producing 100 yards of fabric.

     (c) $C(0) = 1500 + 3(0) + 0.02(0)^2 + 0.0001(0)^3 = 1500$

37. (a) $D(0.1) = \sqrt{2(3960)(0.1) + (0.1)^2} = \sqrt{792.01} \approx 28.14$ miles
          $D(0.2) = \sqrt{2(3960)(0.2) + (0.2)^2} = \sqrt{1584.04} \approx 39.8$ miles

     (b) 1135 feet $= \frac{1135}{5280}$ miles ≈ 0.215 miles.
          $D(0.215) = \sqrt{2(3960)(0.215) + (0.215)^2} = \sqrt{1702.846} \approx 41.27$ miles

     (c) $D(7) = \sqrt{2(3960)(7) + (7)^2} = \sqrt{55489} \approx 235.56$ miles

39. (a) $v(0.1) = 18500(0.25 - 0.1^2) = 4440$, $v(0.4) = 18500(0.25 - 0.4^2) = 1665$.

    (b) That it flows much fast (about 2.75 times faster) 0.1 cm from the center than 0.1 cm from the edge.

    (c)

r	$v(r)$
0.1	4440
0.2	3885
0.3	2960
0.4	1665
0.5	0

41. (a) Since $0 \leq 5{,}000 \leq 10{,}000$ we have $T(5{,}000) = 0$. Since $10{,}000 < 12{,}000 \leq 20{,}000$ we have $T(12{,}000) = 0.08(12{,}000) = 960$. Since $20{,}000 < 25{,}000$ we have $T(25{,}000) = 1600 + 0.15(25{,}000) = 1{,}975$.

    (b) There is no tax on \$5,000, a tax of \$960 on \$12,000 income, and a tax of \$5,350 on \$25,000.

45. $f(x) = 2x$. Since there is no restrictions, the domain is the set of real numbers.

45. $f(x) = 2x$. The domain is restricted by the exercise to $[-1, 5]$.

47. $f(x) = \dfrac{1}{x - 3}$. Since the denominator cannot equal 0 we have $x - 3 \neq 0 \quad \Leftrightarrow \quad x \neq 3$. Thus the domain is $\{x \mid x \neq 3\}$. In interval notation, the domain is $(-\infty, 3) \cup (3, \infty)$.

49. $f(x) = \dfrac{x + 2}{x^2 - 1}$. Since the denominator cannot equal 0 we have $x^2 - 1 \neq 0 \quad \Leftrightarrow \quad x^2 \neq 1 \quad \Rightarrow \quad x \neq \pm 1$. Thus the domain is $\{x \mid x \neq \pm 1\}$. In interval notation, the domain is $(-\infty, -1) \cup (-1, 1) \cup (1, \infty)$.

51. $f(x) = \sqrt{x - 5}$. We require $x - 5 \geq 0 \quad \Leftrightarrow \quad x \geq 5$. Thus the domain is $\{x \mid x \geq 5\}$. The domain can also be expressed in interval notation as $[5, \infty)$.

53. $f(t) = \sqrt[3]{t - 1}$. Since the odd root is defined for all real numbers, the domain is the set of real numbers.

55. $h(x) = \sqrt{2x - 5}$. Since the square root is defined as a real number only for non-negative numbers, we require that $2x - 5 \geq 0 \quad \Leftrightarrow \quad 2x \geq 5 \quad \Leftrightarrow \quad x \geq \frac{5}{2}$. So the domain is $\{x \mid x \geq \frac{5}{2}\}$. In interval notation, the domain is $[\frac{5}{2}, \infty)$.

57. $g(x) = \dfrac{\sqrt{2 + x}}{3 - x}$. We require $2 + x \geq 0$, and the denominator cannot equal 0. Now $2 + x \geq 0$ $\Leftrightarrow \quad x \geq -2$, and $3 - x \neq 0 \quad \Leftrightarrow \quad x \neq 3$. Thus the domain is $\{x \mid x \geq -2 \text{ and } x \neq 3\}$, which can be expressed in interval notation as $[-2, 3) \cup (3, \infty)$.

59. $g(x) = \sqrt[4]{x^2 - 6x}$. Since the input to an even root must be non-negative, we have $x^2 - 6x \geq 0$ $\Leftrightarrow \quad x(x - 6) \geq 0$. Using the method of Section 3.7, we have

	$(-\infty, 0)$	$(0, 6)$	$(6, \infty)$
Sign of x	$-$	$+$	$+$
Sign of $x - 6$	$-$	$-$	$+$
Sign of $x(x - 6)$	$+$	$-$	$+$

Thus the domain is $(-\infty, 0] \cup [6, \infty)$.

61. This person appears to gain weight steadily until the age of 21 when this person's weight gain slows down. At age 30, this person experiences a sudden weight loss, but recovers, and by about age 40, this person's weight seems to level off at around 200 pounds. It then appears that the person dies at about age 68. The sudden weight loss could be due to a number of reasons, among them major illness, weight loss program, etc.

63.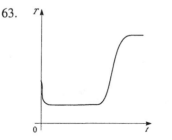

65. A won the race. All runners finished the race. Runner B fell, but got up and finished the race.

67. The sales of Christmas cards will increase sharply approximately from October to December and decrease sharply from January to September.

69. (a) At 6 A.M. the graph shows that the power consumption is about 500 megawatts. Since $t = 18$ represents 6 P.M., the graph shows that the power consumption at 6 P.M. is about 725 megawatts.

    (b) The power consumption is lowest between 3 A.M. and 4 A.M..

    (c) The power consumption is highest just before 12 noon.

71.

73. Answers will vary.

Exercises 2.2

1. (a) $h(-2) = 1; h(0) = -1; h(2) = 3; h(3) = 4.$
   (b) Domain: $[-3, 4]$. Range: $[-1, 4]$.

3. (a) $f(0) = 3 > \frac{1}{2} = g(0)$. So $f(0)$ is larger.
   (b) $f(-3) \approx -\frac{3}{2} < 2 = g(-3)$. So $g(-3)$ is larger.
   (c) For $x = -2$ and $x = 2$.

5. The curves in parts (a) and (c) are graphs of a function of x, by the vertical line test.

7. The given curve is the graph of a function of x. Domain: $[-3, 2]$. Range: $[-2, 2]$.

9. No, the given curve is not the graph of a function of x, by the vertical line test.

11. (a) $f(x) = x - 1$

(b) Domain: All real numbers.

Range: All real numbers

13. (a) $f(x) = x^2 - 4$

(b) Domain: All real numbers.

Range: $[-4, \infty)$

15. (a) $f(x) = \sqrt{16 - x^2}$

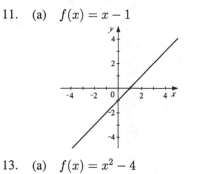

(b) We require $16 - x^2 \geq 0 \iff x^2 \leq 16 \iff |x| \leq 4 \iff -4 \leq x \leq 4$. Therefore, the domain is $[-4, 4]$.

Range: $f(4) = 0$ and $f(0) = 4$ so the range is $[0, 4]$.

17. (a) $f(x) = \sqrt{x-1}$

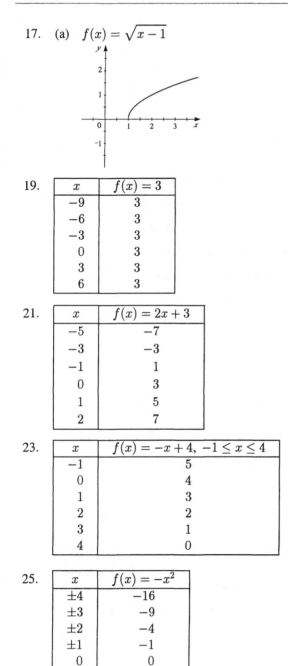

(b) We require $x - 1 \geq 0 \quad \Leftrightarrow \quad x \geq 1$.
Therefore, the domain is $[1, \infty)$.

Range: Since the square root is always positive the range is $[0, \infty)$.

19.

x	$f(x) = 3$
-9	3
-6	3
-3	3
0	3
3	3
6	3

21.

x	$f(x) = 2x + 3$
-5	-7
-3	-3
-1	1
0	3
1	5
2	7

23.

x	$f(x) = -x + 4,\ -1 \leq x \leq 4$
-1	5
0	4
1	3
2	2
3	1
4	0

25.

x	$f(x) = -x^2$
± 4	-16
± 3	-9
± 2	-4
± 1	-1
0	0

27.

x	$g(x) = x^3 - 8$
-2	-16
-1	-9
0	-8
1	-7
2	0
3	19

29.

x	$g(x) = \sqrt{-x}$
-9	3
-5	2.236
-4	2
-2	1.414
-1	1
0	0

31.

x	$F(x) = \frac{1}{x}$
-5	-0.2
-1	-1
-0.1	-10
0.1	10
1	1
5	0.2

33.

x	$H(x) = |2x|$
± 5	10
± 4	8
± 3	6
± 2	4
± 1	2
0	0

35.

x	$G(x) = |x| + x$
-5	0
-2	0
0	0
1	2
2	4
5	10

37.

x	$f(x) = \lvert 2x - 2 \rvert$
-5	12
-2	8
0	2
1	0
2	2
5	8

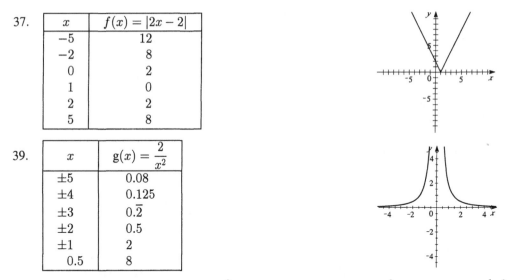

39.

x	$g(x) = \dfrac{2}{x^2}$
± 5	0.08
± 4	0.125
± 3	$0.\overline{2}$
± 2	0.5
± 1	2
0.5	8

41. Solving for y in terms of x gives: $x^2 + 2y = 4 \quad \Leftrightarrow \quad 2y = 4 - x^2 \quad \Leftrightarrow \quad y = 2 - \frac{1}{2}x^2$. This defines y as a function of x.

43. Solving for y in terms of x gives: $x = y^2 \quad \Leftrightarrow \quad y = \pm\sqrt{x}$. The last equation gives two values of y for a given value of x. Thus, this equation does not define y as a function of x.

45. Solving for y in terms of x gives: $x + y^2 = 9 \quad \Leftrightarrow \quad y^2 = 9 - x \quad \Leftrightarrow \quad y = \pm\sqrt{9 - x}$. The last equation gives two values of y for a given value of x. Thus, this equation does not define y as a function of x.

47. Solving for y in terms of x gives: $x^2 y + y = 1 \quad \Leftrightarrow \quad y(x^2 + 1) = 1 \quad \Leftrightarrow \quad y = \dfrac{1}{x^2 + 1}$. This defines y as a function of x.

49. Solving for y in terms of x gives: $2\lvert x \rvert + y = 0 \quad \Leftrightarrow \quad y = -2\lvert x \rvert$. This defines y as a function of x.

51. Solving for y in terms of x gives: $x = y^3 \quad \Leftrightarrow \quad y = \sqrt[3]{x}$. This defines y as a function of x.

53. (a) $f(x) = x^2 + c$, for $c = 0, 2, 4$, and 6.   (b) $f(x) = x^2 + c$, for $c = 0, -2, -4$, and -6.

       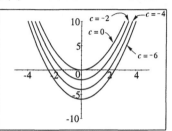

(c) The graphs in part (a) are obtained by shifting the graph of $f(x) = x^2$ upward c units, $c > 0$. The graphs in part (b) are obtained by shifting the graph of $f(x) = x^2$ downward c units.

55. (a) $f(x) = (x - c)^3$, for $c = 0, 2, 4$, and 6. (b) $f(x) = (x - c)^3$, for $c = 0, -2, -4$, and -6.

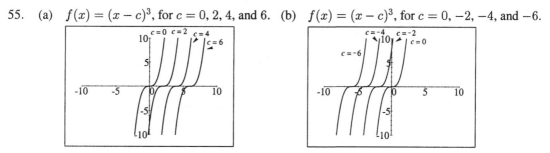

(c) The graphs in part (a) are obtained by shifting the graph of $f(x) = x^3$ to the right c units, $c > 0$. The graphs in part (b) are obtained by shifting the graph of $f(x) = x^3$ to the left $|c|$ units, $c < 0$.

57. (a) $f(x) = x^c$, for $c = \frac{1}{2}, \frac{1}{4}$, and $\frac{1}{6}$.   (b) $f(x) = x^c$, for $c = 1, \frac{1}{3}$, and $\frac{1}{5}$.

(c) Graphs of even roots are similar to $y = \sqrt{x}$, graphs of odd roots are similar to $y = \sqrt[3]{x}$. As c increases, the graph of $y = \sqrt[c]{x}$ becomes steeper near $x = 0$ and flatter when $x > 1$.

59. $f(x) = \begin{cases} 0 & \text{if } x < 2 \\ 1 & \text{if } x \geq 2 \end{cases}$ 61. $f(x) = \begin{cases} 3 & \text{if } x < 2 \\ x - 1 & \text{if } x \geq 2 \end{cases}$

63. $f(x) = \begin{cases} x & \text{if } x \leq 0 \\ x + 1 & \text{if } x > 0 \end{cases}$ 65. $f(x) = \begin{cases} -1 & \text{if } x < -1 \\ 1 & \text{if } -1 \leq x \leq 1 \\ -1 & \text{if } x > 1 \end{cases}$

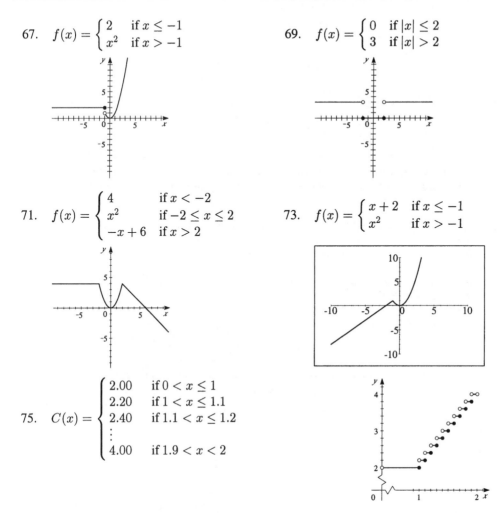

67. $f(x) = \begin{cases} 2 & \text{if } x \leq -1 \\ x^2 & \text{if } x > -1 \end{cases}$

69. $f(x) = \begin{cases} 0 & \text{if } |x| \leq 2 \\ 3 & \text{if } |x| > 2 \end{cases}$

71. $f(x) = \begin{cases} 4 & \text{if } x < -2 \\ x^2 & \text{if } -2 \leq x \leq 2 \\ -x+6 & \text{if } x > 2 \end{cases}$

73. $f(x) = \begin{cases} x+2 & \text{if } x \leq -1 \\ x^2 & \text{if } x > -1 \end{cases}$

75. $C(x) = \begin{cases} 2.00 & \text{if } 0 < x \leq 1 \\ 2.20 & \text{if } 1 < x \leq 1.1 \\ 2.40 & \text{if } 1.1 < x \leq 1.2 \\ \vdots \\ 4.00 & \text{if } 1.9 < x < 2 \end{cases}$

77. The slope of the line segment joining the points $(-2, 1)$ and $(4, -6)$ is $m = \frac{-6-1}{4-(-2)} = -\frac{7}{6}$. Using the point-slope form, we have $y - 1 = -\frac{7}{6}(x+2) \iff y = -\frac{7}{6}x - \frac{7}{3} + 1 \iff y = -\frac{7}{6}x - \frac{4}{3}$. Thus the function is $f(x) = -\frac{7}{6}x - \frac{4}{3}$ for $-2 \leq x \leq 4$.

79. The parabola has equation $x + (y-1)^2 = 0 \iff (y-1)^2 = -x \implies y - 1 = \pm\sqrt{-x}$. Since we seek the bottom half of the parabola, we choose $y - 1 = -\sqrt{-x} \iff y = 1 - \sqrt{-x}$. So the function is $f(x) = 1 - \sqrt{-x}, x \leq 0$.

81. The graph of $x = y^2$ is not the graph of a function because both $(1, 1)$ and $(-1, 1)$ satisfy the equation $x = y^2$. The graph of $x = y^3$ is the graph of a function because $x = y^3 \iff x^{1/3} = y$. If n is even, then both $(1, 1)$ and $(-1, 1)$ satisfies the equation $x = y^n$, so the graph of $x = y^n$ is not the graph of a function. When n is odd, $y = x^{1/n}$ is defined for all real numbers, and since $y = x^{1/n} \iff x = y^n$, the graph of $x = y^n$ is the graph of a function.

83. $f(x) = [\![x]\!]$ $g(x) = [\![2x]\!]$ $h(x) = [\![3x]\!]$

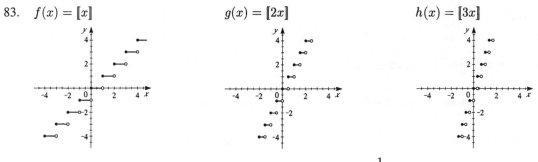

The graph of $k(x) = [\![nx]\!]$ is a step function whose steps are each $\dfrac{1}{n}$ wide.

Exercises 2.3

1. $T = kx$, where k is constant.

3. $v = \dfrac{k}{z}$, where k is constant.

5. $y = \dfrac{ks}{t}$, where k is constant.

7. $z = k\sqrt{y}$, where k is constant.

9. $V = klwh$, where k is constant.

11. $R = \dfrac{ki}{Pt}$, where k is constant.

13. Since y is directly proportional to x, $y = kx$. Since $y = 42$ when $x = 6$, we have $42 = k(6)$ $\Leftrightarrow$ $k = 7$. So $y = 7x$.

15. Since M varies directly as x and inversely as y, $M = \dfrac{kx}{y}$. Since $M = 5$ when $x = 2$ and $y = 6$, we have $5 = \dfrac{k(2)}{6}$ $\Leftrightarrow$ $k = 15$. Therefore $M = \dfrac{15x}{y}$.

17. Since W is inversely proportional to the square of r, $W = \dfrac{k}{r^2}$. Since $W = 10$ when $r = 6$, we have $10 = \dfrac{k}{(6)^2}$ $\Leftrightarrow$ $k = 360$. So $W = \dfrac{360}{r^2}$.

19. Since C is jointly proportional to l, w, and h, we have $C = klwh$. Since $C = 128$ when $l = w = h = 2$, we have $128 = k(2)(2)(2)$ $\Leftrightarrow$ $128 = 8k$ $\Leftrightarrow$ $k = 16$. Therefore, $C = 16lwh$.

21. Since s is inversely proportional to the square root of t, we have $s = \dfrac{k}{\sqrt{t}}$. Since $s = 100$ when $t = 25$, we have $100 = \dfrac{k}{\sqrt{25}}$ $\Leftrightarrow$ $100 = \dfrac{k}{5}$ $\Leftrightarrow$ $k = 500$. So $s = \dfrac{500}{\sqrt{t}}$.

23. (a) The force F needed is $F = kx$.

   (b) Since $F = 40$ when $x = 5$, we have $40 = k(5)$ $\Leftrightarrow$ $k = 8$.

   (c) From part (b), we have $F = 8x$. Substituting $x = 4$ into $F = 8x$ gives $F = 8(4) = 32$ N.

25. (a) $C = kpm$.

   (b) Since $C = 60,000$ when $p = 120$ and $m = 4000$, we get $60000 = k(120)(4000)$ $\Leftrightarrow$ $k = \frac{1}{8}$. So $C = \frac{1}{8}pm$.

   (c) Substituting $p = 92$ and $m = 5000$, we get $C = \frac{1}{8}(92)(5000) = \$57,500$.

27. (a) $R = \dfrac{kL}{d^2}$.

   (b) Since $R = 140$ when $L = 1.2$ and $d = 0.005$, we get $140 = \dfrac{k(1.2)}{(0.005)^2}$ $\Leftrightarrow$ $k = \frac{7}{2400} = 0.002916\overline{6}$.

   (c) Substituting $L = 3$ and $d = 0.008$, we have $R = \dfrac{7}{2400} \cdot \dfrac{3}{(0.008)^2} = \dfrac{4375}{32} \approx 137\ \Omega$.

29. Let C be the cost and A be the area of the sheet of gold. Since C is proportional to A, $C = kA$. When $C = 75$, $A = 15 \cdot 20 = 300$, so $75 = k300$ $\Leftrightarrow$ $k = \frac{1}{4}$. So $C = \frac{1}{4}A$. When $A = 3 \cdot 5 = 15$, we have $C = \frac{1}{4}(15) = \$3.75$.

31. Let V be the value of a building lot on Galiano Island, A the area of the lot, and q the quantity of the water produced. Since V is jointly proportional to the area and water quantity, we have $V = kAq$. When $A = 200 \cdot 300 = 60{,}000$ and $q = 10$, we have $V = \$48{,}000$, so $48{,}000 = k(60{,}000)(10)$ $\Leftrightarrow$ $k = 0.08$. Thus $V = 0.08Aq$. Now when $A = 400 \cdot 400 = 160{,}000$ and $q = 4$, the value is $V = 0.08(160{,}000)(4) = \$51{,}200$.

33. (a) Since f is inversely proportional to L, we have $f = \dfrac{k}{L}$, where k is a positive cpnstant.

    (b) If we replace L by $2L$ we have $\dfrac{k}{(2L)} = \frac{1}{2} \cdot \dfrac{k}{L} = \frac{1}{2} \cdot f$. So the frequency of the vibration is cut in half.

35. Examples include radioactive decay and exponential growth in biology.

Exercises 2.4

1. Average rate of change $= \dfrac{f(3) - f(2)}{3 - 2} = \dfrac{[3(3) - 2] - [3(2) - 2]}{1} = 7 - 4 = 3.$

3. Average rate of change $= \dfrac{h(4) - h(-1)}{4 - (-1)} = \dfrac{[4^2 + 2(4)] - [(-1)^2 + 2(-1)]}{5} = \dfrac{24 - (-1)}{5} = 5.$

5. Average rate of change $= \dfrac{f(10) - f(0)}{10 - 0} = \dfrac{[10^3 - 4(10^2)] - [0^3 - 4(0^2)]}{10 - 0} = \dfrac{600 - 0}{10} = 60.$

7. Average rate of change $= \dfrac{f(2 + h) - f(2)}{(2 + h) - 2} = \dfrac{[3(2 + h)^2] - [3(2^2)]}{h} = \dfrac{12 + 12h + 3h^2 - 12}{h}$

    $= \dfrac{12h + 3h^2}{h} = \dfrac{h(12 + 3h)}{h} = 12 + 3h.$

9. Average rate of change $= \dfrac{g(1) - g(a)}{1 - a} = \dfrac{\frac{1}{1} - \frac{1}{a}}{1 - a} \cdot \dfrac{a}{a} = \dfrac{a - 1}{a(1 - a)} = \dfrac{-1(1 - a)}{a(1 - a)} = \dfrac{-1}{a}.$

11. Average rate of change $= \dfrac{f(a + h) - f(a)}{(a + h) - a} = \dfrac{\frac{2}{a + h} - \frac{2}{a}}{h} \cdot \dfrac{a(a + h)}{a(a + h)} = \dfrac{2a - 2(a + h)}{ah(a + h)}$

    $= \dfrac{-2h}{ah(a + h)} = \dfrac{-2}{a(a + h)}.$

13. (a) Average rate of change $= \dfrac{f(a + h) - f(a)}{(a + h) - a} = \dfrac{\left[\frac{1}{2}(a + h) + 3\right] - \left[\frac{1}{2}a + 3\right]}{h}$

        $= \dfrac{\frac{1}{2}a + \frac{1}{2}h + 3 - \frac{1}{2}a - 3}{h} = \dfrac{\frac{1}{2}h}{h} = \dfrac{1}{2}.$

    (b) The slope of the line $f(x) = \frac{1}{2}x + 3$ is $\frac{1}{2}$, which is also the average rate of change.

15. We use the points $(1, 3)$ and $(4, 5)$, so the average rate of change $= \frac{5-3}{4-1} = \frac{2}{3}.$

17. We use the points $(0, 6)$ and $(5, 2)$, so the average rate of change $= \frac{2-6}{5-0} = \frac{-4}{5}.$

19. (a) Average rate of change of population $= \frac{1,591 - 856}{1994 - 1991} = \frac{735}{3} = 245$ persons/yr.

    (b) Average rate of change of population $= \frac{826 - 1,483}{1997 - 1995} = \frac{-657}{2} = -328.5$ persons/yr.

    (c) The population was increasing from 1990 to 1994.

    (d) The population was decreasing from 1994 to 1999.

21. (a) Average rate of change of sales $= \frac{584 - 512}{1999 - 1989} = \frac{72}{10} = 7.2$ units/yr.

    (b) Average rate of change of sales $= \frac{520 - 512}{1990 - 1989} = \frac{8}{1} = 8$ units/yr.

    (c) Average rate of change of sales $= \frac{410 - 520}{1992 - 1990} = \frac{-110}{2} = -55$ units/yr.

(d)

Year	CD players sold	Change in sales from previous year
1989	512	−
1990	520	8
1991	413	−107
1992	410	−3
1993	468	58
1994	510	42
1995	590	80
1996	607	17
1997	732	125
1998	612	−120
1999	584	−28

Sales *increased* most quickly between 1996 and 1997. Sales *decreased* most quickly between 1997 and 1998.

23. The function is increasing on $[-1, 1]$ and $[2, 4]$. It is decreasing on $[1, 2]$.

25. The function is increasing on $[-2, -1]$ and $[1, 2]$. It is decreasing on $[-3, -2]$, $[-1, 1]$, and $[2, 3]$.

27. (a) $f(x) = x^{2/5}$ is graphed in the viewing rectangle $[-10, 10]$ by $[-5, 5]$.

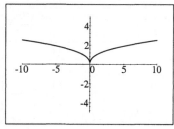

  (b) The function is increasing on $[0, \infty)$. It is decreasing on $(-\infty, 0]$.

29. (a) $f(x) = x^2 - 5x$ is graphed in the viewing rectangle $[-2, 7]$ by $[-10, 10]$.

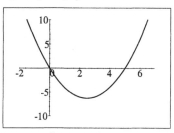

  (b) The function is increasing on $[2.5, \infty)$. It is decreasing on $(-\infty, 2.5]$.

31. (a) $f(x) = 2x^3 - 3x^2 - 12x$ is graphed in the viewing rectangle $[-3, 5]$ by $[-25, 20]$.

  (b) The function is increasing on $(-\infty, -1]$ and $[2, \infty)$. It is decreasing on $[-1, 2]$.

33. (a) $f(x) = x^3 + 2x^2 - x - 2$ is graphed in the viewing rectangle $[-5, 5]$ by $[-3, 3]$.

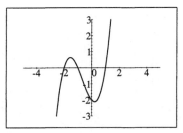

(b) The function is increasing on $(-\infty, -1.55]$ and $[0.22, \infty)$. It is decreasing on $[-1.55, 0.22]$.

35. (a)

Time (s)	Average speed (ft/s)
0-2	17
2-4	18
4-6	63
6-8	147
8-10	237

The average speed is increasing, so the car is accelerating. From the shape of the graph, we see that the slope continues to get steeper.

(b)

Time (s)	Average speed (ft/s)
30-32	263
32-34	144
34-36	91
36-38	74
38-40	48

The average speed is decreasing, so the car is decelerating. From the shape of the graph, we see that the slope continues to get flatter.

Exercises 2.5

1. (a) Shift the graph of $y = f(x)$ downward 3 units.
   (b) Shift the graph of $y = f(x)$ to the right 3 units.

3. (a) Stretch the graph of $y = f(x)$ vertically by a factor of 3.
   (b) Shrink the graph of $y = f(x)$ vertically by a factor of $\frac{1}{3}$.

5. (a) Reflect the graph of $y = f(x)$ about the x-axis, and stretch vertically by a factor of 2.
   (b) Reflect the graph of $y = f(x)$ about the x-axis, and shrink vertically by a factor of $\frac{1}{2}$.

7. (a) Shift the graph of $y = f(x)$ to the right 4 units, and then upward $\frac{3}{4}$ of a unit.
   (b) Shift the graph of $y = f(x)$ to the left 4 units, and then downward $\frac{3}{4}$ of a unit.

9. (a) Shrink the graph of $y = f(x)$ horizontally by a factor of $\frac{1}{4}$.
   (b) Stretch the graph of $y = f(x)$ horizontally by a factor of 4.

11. (a) $y = f(x - 2)$ (b) $y = f(x) - 2$ (c) $y = 2f(x)$

(d) $y = -f(x) + 3$ (e) $y = f(-x)$ (f) $y = \frac{1}{2}f(x - 1)$

13. (a) $f(x) = \dfrac{1}{x}$

(b) (i) $y = -\dfrac{1}{x}$. Reflect the graph of f about the x-axis.

(ii) $y = \dfrac{1}{x-1}$. Shift the graph of f to the right 1 unit.

(iii) $y = \dfrac{2}{x+2}$. Shift the graph of f to the left 2 units and stretch vertically by a factor of 2.

(iv) $y = 1 + \dfrac{1}{x-3}$. Shift the graph of f to the right 3 units and upward 1 unit.

15. (a) The graph of $g(x) = (x+2)^2$ is obtained by shifting the graph of $f(x)$ to the left 2 units.

(b) The graph of $g(x) = x^2 + 2$ is obtained by shifting the graph of $f(x)$ upward 2 units.

17. (a) The graph of $g(x) = 2\sqrt{x}$ is obtained by stretching the graph of $f(x)$ vertically by a factor of 2.

(b) The graph of $g(x) = \frac{1}{2}\sqrt{x-2}$ is obtained by shifting the graph of $f(x)$ to the right 2 units, and then shrinking the graph vertically by a factor of $\frac{1}{2}$.

19. $y = f(x-2) + 3$. When $f(x) = x^2$, we get $y = (x-2)^2 + 3 = x^2 - 4x + 4 + 3 = x^2 - 4x + 7$.

21. $y = -5f(x+3)$. When $f(x) = \sqrt{x}$, we get $y = -5\sqrt{x+3}$

23. $y = 0.1f\left(x - \frac{1}{2}\right) - 2$. When $f(x) = |x|$, we get $y = 0.1\left|x - \frac{1}{2}\right| - 2$

25. $f(x) = (x-2)^2$. Shift the graph of $y = x^2$ to the right 2 units.

27. $f(x) = -(x+1)^2$. Shift the graph of $y = x^2$ to the left 1 unit, then reflect about the x-axis.

29. $f(x) = x^3 + 2$. **Shift the graph of**
     $y = x^3$ **upward 2 units.**

31. $y = 1 + \sqrt{x}$. **Shift the graph of** $y = \sqrt{x}$
     upward 1 unit.

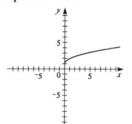

33. $y = \frac{1}{2}\sqrt{x + 4} - 3$. **Shift the graph of**
     $y = \sqrt{x}$ **to the left 4 units, shrink**
     vertically by a factor of $\frac{1}{2}$, **and then**
     shift it downward 3 units.

35. $y = 5 + (x + 3)^2$. **Shift the graph of**
     $y = x^2$ **to the left 3 units, then upward**
     5 units.

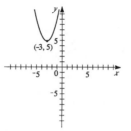

37. $y = |x| - 1$. **Shift the graph of** $y = |x|$
     downward 1 unit.

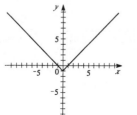

39. $y = |x + 2| + 2$. **Shift the graph of** $y = |x|$
     to the left 2 units and upward 2 units.

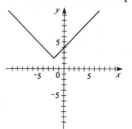

41.

For part (b), shift the graph in (a) to the left 5
units; for part (c), shift the graph in (a) to the
left 5 units, and stretch it vertically by a factor
of 2; for part (d), shift the graph in (a) to the
left 5 units, stretch it vertically by a factor of
2, and then shift it upward 4 units.

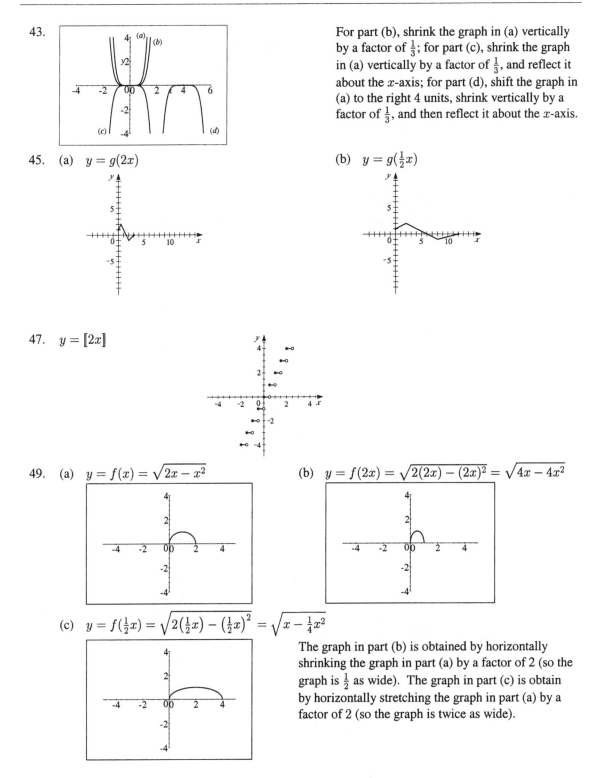

43.

For part (b), shrink the graph in (a) vertically by a factor of $\frac{1}{3}$; for part (c), shrink the graph in (a) vertically by a factor of $\frac{1}{3}$, and reflect it about the x-axis; for part (d), shift the graph in (a) to the right 4 units, shrink vertically by a factor of $\frac{1}{3}$, and then reflect it about the x-axis.

45. (a) $y = g(2x)$

(b) $y = g(\frac{1}{2}x)$

47. $y = [\![2x]\!]$

49. (a) $y = f(x) = \sqrt{2x - x^2}$

(b) $y = f(2x) = \sqrt{2(2x) - (2x)^2} = \sqrt{4x - 4x^2}$

(c) $y = f(\frac{1}{2}x) = \sqrt{2(\frac{1}{2}x) - (\frac{1}{2}x)^2} = \sqrt{x - \frac{1}{4}x^2}$

The graph in part (b) is obtained by horizontally shrinking the graph in part (a) by a factor of 2 (so the graph is $\frac{1}{2}$ as wide). The graph in part (c) is obtain by horizontally stretching the graph in part (a) by a factor of 2 (so the graph is twice as wide).

51. $f(-x) = (-x)^{-2} = x^{-2} = f(x)$. Thus $f(x)$
is even.

53. $f(-x) = (-x)^2 + (-x) = x^2 - x$. Thus
$f(-x) \neq f(x)$. Also, $f(-x) \neq -f(x)$, so
$f(x)$ is neither odd nor even.

55. $f(-x) = (-x)^3 - (-x) = -x^3 + x$
$= -(x^3 - x) = -f(x)$. Thus $f(x)$ is odd.

57. $f(-x) = 1 - \sqrt[3]{(-x)} = 1 + \sqrt[3]{x}$. Thus
$f(-x) \neq f(x)$. Also $f(-x) \neq -f(x)$, so
$f(x)$ is neither odd nor even.

59. Since $f(x) = x^2 - 4 < 0$, for $-2 < x < 2$, the graph of $y = g(x)$ is found by sketching the graph of
$y = f(x)$ for $x \leq -2$ and $x \geq 2$, then reflecting about the x-axis the part of the graph of $y = f(x)$
for $-2 < x < 2$.

61.   (a) $f(x) = 4x - x^2$ (b) $f(x) = |4x - x^2|$

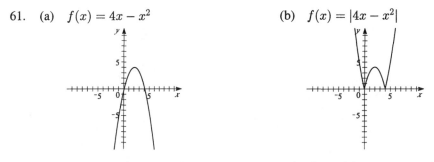

63. f even implies $f(-x) = f(x)$; g even implies $g(-x) = g(x)$; f odd implies $f(-x) = -f(x)$; and g odd implies $g(-x) = -g(x)$

If f and g are both even, then $(f + g)(-x) = f(-x) + g(-x) = f(x) + g(x) = (f + g)(x)$ and $f + g$ is even.

If f and g are both odd, then $(f + g)(-x) = f(-x) + g(-x) = -f(x) - g(x) = -(f + g)(x)$ and $f + g$ is odd.

If f odd and g even, then $(f + g)(-x) = f(-x) + g(-x) = -f(x) + g(x)$, which is neither odd nor even.

65. $f(x) = x^n$ is even when n is an even integer and $f(x) = x^n$ is odd when n is an odd integer.

These names were chosen because polynomials with only terms with odd powers are odd functions, and polynomials with only terms with even powers are even functions.

Exercises 2.6

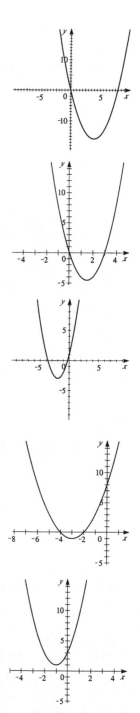

1. $y = x^2 - 8x$

    Vertex: $y = x^2 - 8x = x^2 - 8x + 16 - 16 = (x-4)^2 - 16$. Vertex is at $(4, -16)$.

    x-intercepts: $y = 0 \Rightarrow 0 = x^2 - 8x = x(x-8)$. So $x = 0$ or $x = 8$. The x-intercepts are at $x = 0$ and $x = 8$.

    y-intercepts: $x = 0 \Rightarrow y = 0$. The y-intercept is at $y = 0$.

3. $y = 2x^2 - 6x$

    Vertex: $y = 2x^2 - 6x = 2(x^2 - 3x) = 2\left[x^2 - 3x + \left(\frac{3}{2}\right)^2\right] - \frac{9}{2}$
    $= 2\left(x - \frac{3}{2}\right)^2 - \frac{9}{2}$. Vertex is at $\left(\frac{3}{2}, -\frac{9}{2}\right)$.

    x-intercepts: $y = 0 \Rightarrow 0 = 2x^2 - 6x = 2x(x-3) \Rightarrow x = 0$ or $x = 3$. The x-intercepts are at $x = 0$ and $x = 3$.

    y-intercepts: $x = 0 \Rightarrow y = 0$. The y-intercept is at $y = 0$.

5. $y = x^2 + 4x + 1$

    Vertex: $y = x^2 + 4x + 1 = x^2 + 4x + 4 - 4 + 1 = (x+2)^2 - 3$. Vertex is at $(-2, -3)$.

    x-intercepts: $y = 0 \Rightarrow 0 = x^2 + 4x + 1$. Using the quadratic formula, $x = \frac{-4 \pm \sqrt{12}}{2} = \frac{-4 \pm 2\sqrt{3}}{2} = -2 \pm \sqrt{3}$. The x-intercepts are at $x = -2 - \sqrt{3}$ and $x = -2 + \sqrt{3}$.

    y-intercepts: $x = 0 \Rightarrow y = 1$. The y-intercept is at $y = 1$.

7. $y = x^2 + 6x + 8$

    Vertex: $y = x^2 + 6x + 8 = (x^2 + 6x) + 8 = (x^2 + 6x + 9) + 8 - 9$
    $= (x+3)^2 - 1$. Vertex is at $(-3, -1)$.

    x-intercepts: $y = 0 \Rightarrow 0 = x^2 + 6x + 8(x+2)(x+4) \Rightarrow x = -2$ or $x = -4$. The x-intercepts are at $x = -2$ and $x = -4$.

    y-intercepts: $x = 0 \Rightarrow y = 8$. The y-intercept is at $y = 8$.

9. $y = 2x^2 + 4x + 3$

    Vertex: $y = 2x^2 + 4x + 3 = 2(x^2 + 2x) + 3$
    $= 2(x^2 + 2x + 1) + 3 - 2 = 2(x+1)^2 + 1$. Vertex is at $(-1, 1)$.

    x-intercepts: $y = 0 \Rightarrow 0 = 2x^2 + 4x + 3 = 2(x+1)^2 + 1 \Leftrightarrow 2(x+1)^2 = -1$. Since this last equation has no real solution, there are no x-intercepts.

    y-intercepts: $x = 0 \Rightarrow y = 3$. The y-intercept is at $y = 3$.

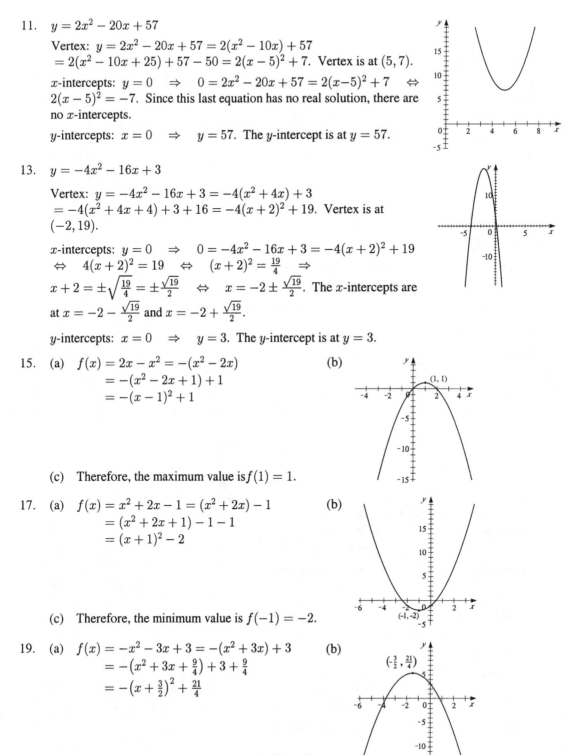

11. $y = 2x^2 - 20x + 57$

Vertex: $y = 2x^2 - 20x + 57 = 2(x^2 - 10x) + 57$
$= 2(x^2 - 10x + 25) + 57 - 50 = 2(x-5)^2 + 7$. Vertex is at $(5, 7)$.

x-intercepts: $y = 0 \Rightarrow 0 = 2x^2 - 20x + 57 = 2(x-5)^2 + 7 \Leftrightarrow$
$2(x - 5)^2 = -7$. Since this last equation has no real solution, there are
no x-intercepts.

y-intercepts: $x = 0 \Rightarrow y = 57$. The y-intercept is at $y = 57$.

13. $y = -4x^2 - 16x + 3$

Vertex: $y = -4x^2 - 16x + 3 = -4(x^2 + 4x) + 3$
$= -4(x^2 + 4x + 4) + 3 + 16 = -4(x+2)^2 + 19$. Vertex is at
$(-2, 19)$.

x-intercepts: $y = 0 \Rightarrow 0 = -4x^2 - 16x + 3 = -4(x+2)^2 + 19$
$\Leftrightarrow 4(x+2)^2 = 19 \Leftrightarrow (x+2)^2 = \frac{19}{4} \Rightarrow$
$x + 2 = \pm\sqrt{\frac{19}{4}} = \pm\frac{\sqrt{19}}{2} \Leftrightarrow x = -2 \pm \frac{\sqrt{19}}{2}$. The x-intercepts are
at $x = -2 - \frac{\sqrt{19}}{2}$ and $x = -2 + \frac{\sqrt{19}}{2}$.

y-intercepts: $x = 0 \Rightarrow y = 3$. The y-intercept is at $y = 3$.

15. (a) $f(x) = 2x - x^2 = -(x^2 - 2x)$
$= -(x^2 - 2x + 1) + 1$
$= -(x - 1)^2 + 1$

  (b)

  (c) Therefore, the maximum value is $f(1) = 1$.

17. (a) $f(x) = x^2 + 2x - 1 = (x^2 + 2x) - 1$
$= (x^2 + 2x + 1) - 1 - 1$
$= (x + 1)^2 - 2$

  (b)

  (c) Therefore, the minimum value is $f(-1) = -2$.

19. (a) $f(x) = -x^2 - 3x + 3 = -(x^2 + 3x) + 3$
$= -\left(x^2 + 3x + \frac{9}{4}\right) + 3 + \frac{9}{4}$
$= -\left(x + \frac{3}{2}\right)^2 + \frac{21}{4}$

  (b)

  (c) Therefore, the maximum value is $f\left(-\frac{3}{2}\right) = \frac{21}{4}$.

21. (a) $g(x) = 3x^2 - 12x + 13 = 3(x^2 - 4x) + 13$ (b)
$$= 3(x^2 - 4x + 4) + 13 - 12$$
$$= 3(x - 2)^2 + 1$$

(c) Therefore, the minimum value is $g(2) = 1$.

23. (a) $h(x) = 1 - x - x^2 = -(x^2 + x) + 1$ (b)
$$= -\left(x^2 + x + \tfrac{1}{4}\right) + 1 + \tfrac{1}{4}$$
$$= -\left(x + \tfrac{1}{2}\right)^2 + \tfrac{5}{4}$$

(c) Therefore, the maximum value is $h\left(-\tfrac{1}{2}\right) = \tfrac{5}{4}$.

25. $f(x) = x^2 + x + 1 = (x^2 + x) + 1 = \left(x^2 + x + \tfrac{1}{4}\right) + 1 + \tfrac{1}{4} = \left(x + \tfrac{1}{2}\right)^2 + \tfrac{3}{4}$.
Therefore, the minimum value is $f\left(-\tfrac{1}{2}\right) = \tfrac{3}{4}$.

27. $f(t) = 100 - 49t - 7t^2 = -7(t^2 + 7t) + 100 = -7\left(t^2 + 7t + \tfrac{49}{4}\right) + 100 + \tfrac{343}{4}$
$$= -7\left(t + \tfrac{7}{2}\right)^2 + \tfrac{743}{4}.$$
Therefore, the maximum value is $f\left(-\tfrac{7}{2}\right) = \tfrac{743}{4}$.

29. $f(s) = s^2 - 1.2s + 16 = (s^2 - 1.2s) + 16 = (s^2 - 1.2s + 0.36) + 16 - 0.36$
$$= (s - 0.6)^2 + 15.64.$$
Therefore, the minimum value is $f(0.6) = 15.64$.

31. $h(x) = \tfrac{1}{2}x^2 + 2x - 6 = \tfrac{1}{2}(x^2 + 4x) - 6 = \tfrac{1}{2}(x^2 + 4x + 4) - 6 - 2 = \tfrac{1}{2}(x + 2)^2 - 8$.
Therefore, the minimum value is $h(-2) = -8$.

33. $f(x) = 3 - x - \tfrac{1}{2}x^2 = -\tfrac{1}{2}(x^2 + 2x) + 3 = -\tfrac{1}{2}(x^2 + 2x + 1) + 3 + \tfrac{1}{2} = -\tfrac{1}{2}(x + 1) + \tfrac{7}{2}$.
Therefore, the maximum value is $f(-1) = \tfrac{7}{2}$.

35. Since the vertex is at $(1, -2)$, the function is of the form $f(x) = a(x - 1)^2 - 2$. Substituting the point $(4, 16)$, we get $16 = a(4 - 1)^2 - 2$ $\Leftrightarrow$ $16 = 9a - 2$ $\Leftrightarrow$ $9a = 18$ $\Leftrightarrow$ $a = 2$. So the function is $f(x) = 2(x - 1)^2 - 2 = 2x^2 - 4x$.

37. $f(x) = -x^2 + 4x - 3 = -(x^2 - 4x) - 3 = -(x^2 - 4x + 4) - 3 + 4 = -(x - 2)^2 + 1$. So the domain of $f(x)$ is $(-\infty, \infty)$. Since $f(x)$ has a maximum value of 1, the range is $(-\infty, 1]$.

39. $y = f(t) = 40t - 16t^2 = -16\left(t^2 - \tfrac{5}{2}\right) = -16\left[t^2 - \tfrac{5}{2}t + \left(\tfrac{5}{4}\right)^2\right] + 16\left(\tfrac{5}{4}\right)^2 = -16\left(t - \tfrac{5}{4}\right)^2 + 25$.
Thus the maximum height attained by the ball is $f\left(\tfrac{5}{4}\right) = 25$ feet.

41. $R(x) = 80x - 0.4x^2 = -0.4(x^2 - 200x) = -0.4(x^2 - 200x + 10,000) + 4,000$
$$= -0.4(x - 100)^2 + 4,000.$$
So revenue is maximized at $\$4,000$ when 100 units are sold.

43. $E(n) = \frac{2}{3}n - \frac{1}{90}n^2 = -\frac{1}{90}(n^2 - 60n) = -\frac{1}{90}(n^2 - 60n + 900) + 10 = -\frac{1}{90}(n - 30)^2 + 10$. Since
     the maximum of the function occurs when $n = 30$, the viewer should watch the commercial 30 times
     for maximum effectiveness.

45. (a) $f(x) = x^2 + 1.79x - 3.21$ is shown in the viewing
          rectangle on the right. The minimum value is
          $f(x) \approx -4.01$.

     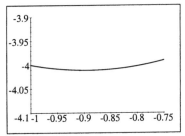

     (b) $f(x) = x^2 + 1.79x - 3.21$
          $= \left[x^2 + 1.79x + \left(\frac{1.79}{2}\right)^2\right] - 3.21 - \left(\frac{1.79}{2}\right)^2$
          $= (x + 0.895)^2 - 4.011025$

          Therefore, the exact minimum of $f(x)$ is -4.011025.

47. In the viewing rectangle on the right, we see that
     $f(x) = x^3 - x$ has a local minimum and a local maximum.
     Smaller x and y ranges (shown in the viewing rectangles
     below) show that $f(x)$ has a local maximum of ≈ 0.38 when
     $x \approx -0.58$ and a local minimum of ≈ -0.38 when $x \approx 0.58$.

49. In the viewing rectangle on the right, we see that
     $g(x) = x^4 - 2x^3 - 11x^2$ has two local minimums and a
     local maximum. The local maximum is $g(x) = 0$ when
     $x = 0$. Smaller x and y ranges (shown in the viewing
     rectangles below) show that local minima are $g(x) \approx -13.61$
     when $x \approx -1.71$ and $g(x) \approx -73.32$ when $x \approx 3.21$.

     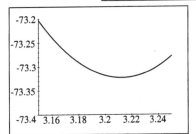

51. In the first viewing rectangle below, we see that $U(x) = x\sqrt{6-x}$ only has a local maximum.
     Smaller x and y ranges in the second viewing rectangle below show that $U(x)$ has a local maximum
     of ≈ 5.66 when $x \approx 4.00$.

53. In the viewing rectangle on the right, we see that
     $V(x) = \dfrac{1-x^2}{x^3}$ has a local minimum and a local maximum.
     Smaller x and y ranges (shown in the viewing rectangles
     below) show that $V(x)$ has a local maximum of ≈ 0.38 when
     $x \approx -1.73$ and a local minimum of ≈ -0.38 when $x \approx 1.73$.

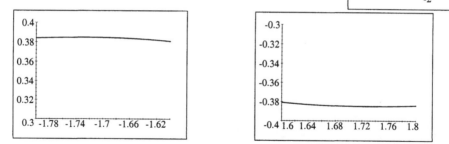

55. In the first viewing rectangle below, we see the general location of the minimum of
     $E(v) = 2.73v^3 \dfrac{10}{v-5}$. In the second viewing rectangle, we isolate the minimum, and from this
     graph, we see that energy is minimized when $v \approx 7.5$ mi/h.

57. In the first viewing rectangle on the next page, we see the general location of the minimum of
     $V = 999.87 - 0.06426T + 0.0085043T^2 - 0.0000679T^3$ is around $T = 4$. In the second viewing
     rectangle, we isolate the minimum, and from this graph, we see that the minimum volume of 1 kg of
     water occurs at $T \approx 3.96°$ C.

59. $f(x) = 3 + 4x^2 - x^4$. Substituting $t = x^2$, we have $f(\sqrt{t}) = 3 + 4t - t^2 = -(t^2 - 4t) + 3$
     $= -(t^2 - 4t + 4) + 3 + 4 = -(t - 2)^2 + 7$. Therefore, the function $f(\sqrt{t}) = f(x)$ has a
     maximum value of 7.

61. (a) If $x = a$ is a local maximum of $f(x)$ then $f(a) \geq f(x) \geq 0$ for all x around $x = a$. So
          $[g(a)]^2 \geq [g(x)]^2$ and thus $g(a) \geq g(x)$. Similarly, if $x = b$ is a local minimum of $f(x$, then
          $f(x) \geq f(b) \geq 0$, for all x around $x = b$. So $[g(x)]^2 \geq [g(b)]^2$ and thus $g(x) \geq g(b)$.

     (b) Using the distance formula, $g(x) = \sqrt{(x-3)^2 + (x^2 - 0)^2} = \sqrt{x^4 + x^2 - 6x + 9}$.

     (c) Let $f(x) = x^4 + x^2 - 6x + 9$. In the viewing rectangle we see that $f(x)$ has a minimum at
          $x = 1$. Thus $g(x)$ also has a minimum at $x = 1$ and this minimum value is
          $g(1) = \sqrt{1^4 + 1^2 - 6(1) + 9} = \sqrt{5}$.

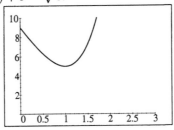

Exercises 2.7

1. Let w be the width of the building lot. Then the length of the lot is $3w$. So the area of the building lot is $A(w) = 3w^2$, $w > 0$.

3. Let w be the width of the base of the rectangle. Then the height of the rectangle is $\frac{1}{2}w$. Thus the volume of the box is given by the function $V(w) = \frac{1}{2}w^3$, $w > 0$.

5. Let P be the perimeter of the rectangle and y be the length of the other side. Since $P = 2x + 2y$ and the perimeter is 20, we have $2x + 2y = 20 \quad \Leftrightarrow \quad x + y = 10 \quad \Leftrightarrow \quad y = 10 - x$. Since area is $A = xy$, substituting gives $A(x) = x(10 - x) = 10x - x^2$, and since A must be positive, the domain is $0 < x < 10$.

7. Let h be the height of an altitude of the equilateral triangle whose side has length x, as shown in the diagram. Thus the area is given by $A = \frac{1}{2}xh$. By the Pythagorean Theorem, $h^2 + \left(\frac{1}{2}x\right)^2 = x^2 \quad \Leftrightarrow \quad h^2 + \frac{1}{4}x^2 = x^2 \quad \Leftrightarrow \quad h^2 = \frac{3}{4}x^2 \quad \Leftrightarrow$ $h = \frac{\sqrt{3}}{2}x$. Substituting into the area of a triangle, we get $A(x) = \frac{1}{2}xh = \frac{1}{2}x\left(\frac{\sqrt{3}}{2}x\right) = \frac{\sqrt{3}}{4}x^2$, $x > 0$.

9. We solve for r in the formula for the area of a circle. This gives $A = \pi r^2 \quad \Leftrightarrow \quad r^2 = \frac{A}{\pi} \quad \Rightarrow$ $r = \sqrt{\frac{A}{\pi}}$, so the model is $r(A) = \sqrt{\frac{A}{\pi}}$, $A > 0$.

11. Let h be the height of the box in feet. The volume of the box is $V = 60$. Then $x^2h = 60 \quad \Leftrightarrow$ $h = \dfrac{60}{x^2}$. The surface area, S, of the box is sum of the area of the 4 sides and the area of the base and top. Thus $S = 4xh + 2x^2 = 4x\left(\dfrac{60}{x^2}\right) + 2x^2 = \dfrac{240}{x} + 2x^2$, so the model is $S(x) = \dfrac{240}{x} + 2x^2$, $x > 0$.

13. Let d_1 be the distance traveled south by the first ship and d_2 be the distance traveled east by the second ship. Since the first ship travels south for t hours at 5 mi/h, so $d_1 = 15t$ and, similarly, $d_2 = 20t$. Since the ships are traveling at right angles to each other, we can apply the Pythagorean Theorem to get $D^2 = d_1^2 + d_2^2 = (15t)^2 + (20t)^2 = 225t^2 + 400t^2 = 625t^2$. $D(t) = 25t$, $t \geq 0$.

15. Let b be the length of the base, l be the length of the equal sides, and h be the height in centimeters. Since the perimeter is 8, $2l + b = 8 \quad \Leftrightarrow \quad 2l = 8 - b$ $\Leftrightarrow \quad l = \frac{1}{2}(8 - b)$. By the Pythagorean Theorem, $h^2 + \left(\frac{1}{2}b\right)^2 = l^2 \quad \Leftrightarrow$ $h = \sqrt{l^2 - \frac{1}{4}b^2}$. Therefore the area of the triangle is

$A = \frac{1}{2} \cdot b \cdot h = \frac{1}{2} \cdot b\sqrt{l^2 - \frac{1}{4}b^2} = \frac{b}{2}\sqrt{\frac{1}{4}(8 - b)^2 - \frac{1}{4}b^2}$

$= \frac{b}{4}\sqrt{64 - 16b + b^2 - b^2} = \frac{b}{4}\sqrt{64 - 16b} = \frac{b}{4} \cdot 4\sqrt{4 - b} = b\sqrt{4 - b}$,

so the model is $A(b) = b\sqrt{4 - b}$, $0 < b < 4$.

17. Let w be the length of the rectangle. By the Pythagorean Theorem, $\left(\frac{1}{2}w\right)^2 + h^2 = 10^2$ $\Leftrightarrow$

$\dfrac{w^2}{4} + h^2 = 10^2$ $\Leftrightarrow$ $w^2 = 4(100 - h^2)$ $\Leftrightarrow$ $w = 2\sqrt{100 - h^2}$ (since $w > 0$). Therefore, the

area of the rectangle is $A = wh = 2h\sqrt{100 - h^2}$, so the model is $A(h) = 2h\sqrt{100 - h^2}$,
$0 < h < 10$.

19. (a) We complete the table.

First number	Second number	Product
1	18	18
2	17	34
3	16	48
4	15	60
5	14	70
6	13	78
7	12	84
8	11	88
9	10	90
10	9	90
11	8	88

From the table we conclude that the numbers is still increasing, the numbers whose product is a maximum should both be 9.5.

(b) Let x be one number: then $19 - x$ is the other number, and so the product, p, is
$p(x) = x(19 - x) = 19x - x^2$.

(c) $p(x) = 19x - x^2 = -(x^2 - 19x) = -\left[x^2 - 19x + \left(\frac{19}{2}\right)^2\right] + \left(\frac{19}{2}\right)^2 = -(x - 9.5)^2 + 90.25$.
So the product is maximized when the numbers are both 9.5.

21. Let x and y be the two numbers. Since their sum is -24, we have $x + y = -24$ $\Leftrightarrow$
$y = -x - 24$. The product of the two numbers is $P = xy = x(-x - 24) = -x^2 - 24x$, which we
wish to maximize. So $P = -x^2 - 24x = -(x^2 + 24x) = -(x^2 + 24x + 144) + 144$
$= -(x + 12)^2 + 144$. Thus the maximum product is 144, and it occurs when $x = -12$ and
$y = -(-12) - 24 = -12$. Thus the two numbers are -12 and -12.

23. (a) Let x be the width of the field (in feet) and l be the length of the field (in feet). Since the
farmer has 2400 ft of fencing we must have $2x + l = 2400$.

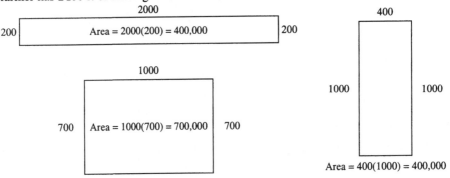

Width	Length	Area
200	2000	400,000
300	1800	540,000
400	1600	640,000
500	1400	700,000
600	1200	720,000
700	1000	700,000
800	800	640,000

It appears that the feild of largest area is about 600 ft. × 1200 ft.

(b) Let x be the width of the field (in feet) and l be the length of the field (in feet). Since the farmer has 2400 ft of fencing we must have $2x + l = 2400 \quad \Leftrightarrow \quad l = 2400 - 2x$. The area of the fenced-in field is given by
$$A(x) = l \cdot x = (2400 - 2x)x = -2x^2 + 2400x = -2(x^2 - 1200x).$$

(c) The area is $A(x) = -2(x^2 - 1200x + 600^2) + 2(600^2) = -2(x - 600)^2 + 720000$. So the maximum area occurs when $x = 600$ feet and $l = 2400 - 2(600) = 1200$ feet.

25. (a) Let x be the length of the fence along the road. If the area is 1200, we have $1200 = x \cdot$ width, so the width of the garden is $\dfrac{1200}{x}$. Then the cost of the fence is given by the function
$$C(x) = 5(x) + 3\left[x + 2 \cdot \frac{1200}{x}\right] = 8x + \frac{7200}{x}.$$

(b) We graph the function $y = C(x)$ in the viewing rectangle $[0, 75] \times [0, 800]$. From this we get the cost is minimized when $x = 30$ ft. Then the width is $\dfrac{1200}{30} = 40$ ft. So the length is 30 ft and the width is 40 ft.

(c) We graph the function $y = C(x)$ and $y = 600$ in the viewing rectangle $[10, 65] \times [450, 650]$. From this we get that the cost is at most $600 when $15 \leq x \leq 60$. So the range of lengths he can fence along the road is 15 feet to 60 feet.

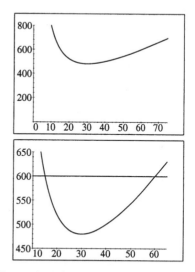

27. (a) Let p be the price of the ticket. So $10 - p$ is the differnce in ticket price and therefore the number of tickets sold is $27000 + 3000(10 - p) = 57000 - 3000p$. Thus the revenue is $R(p) = p(57000 - 3000p) = 57000p - 3000p^2$.

(b) $R(p) = 0 = p(57000 - 3000p)$. So $p = 0$ or $= \frac{57000}{3000} = 19$. So at $19 no one will come.

(c) We comple the square. $R(p) = 57000p - 3000p^2 = -3000(p^2 - 19p)$
$= -3000\left(p^2 - 19p + \frac{19^2}{4}\right) + 270750 = -3000\left(p - \frac{19}{2}\right)^2 + 270750$. The revenue is maximized when $p = \frac{19}{2}$, and so the price should be set at $9.50.

29.   (a)   Let h be the height in feet of the straight portion of the window. The circumference of the
            semicircle is $C = \frac{1}{2}\pi x$. Since the perimeter of the window is 30 feet, we have
            $x + 2h + \frac{1}{2}\pi x = 30$. Solving for h, we get $2h = 30 - x - \frac{1}{2}\pi x \quad \Leftrightarrow \quad h = 15 - \frac{1}{2}x - \frac{1}{4}\pi x$.
            The area of the window is
            $A(x) = xh + \frac{1}{2}\pi\left(\frac{1}{2}x\right)^2 = x\left(15 - \frac{1}{2}x - \frac{1}{4}\pi x\right) + \frac{1}{8}\pi x^2 = 15x - \frac{1}{2}x^2 - \frac{1}{8}\pi x^2.$

      (b) $A(x) = 15x - \frac{1}{2}x^2 - \frac{1}{8}\pi x^2 = 15x - \frac{1}{8}(\pi + 4)x^2 = -\frac{1}{8}(\pi + 4)\left[x^2 - \frac{120}{\pi+4}x\right]$
            $= -\frac{1}{8}(\pi + 4)\left[x^2 - \frac{120}{\pi+4}x + \left(\frac{60}{\pi+4}\right)^2\right] + \frac{450}{\pi+4} = -\frac{1}{8}(\pi + 4)\left(x - \frac{60}{\pi+4}\right)^2 + \frac{450}{\pi+4}$. The area is
            maximized when $x = \frac{60}{\pi+4} \approx 8.40$, and hence $h \approx 15 - \frac{1}{2}(8.40) - \frac{1}{4}\pi(8.40) \approx 4.20.$

31.   (a)   Let x be the length of one side of the base and let h be the height of the box in feet. Since the
            volume of the box is $V = x^2 h = 12$, we have $x^2 h = 12 \quad \Leftrightarrow \quad h = \dfrac{12}{x^2}$. The surface area, A,
            of the box is sum of the area of the 4 sides and the area of the base. Thus the surface area of
            the box is given by the formula $A(x) = 4xh + x^2 = 4x\left(\dfrac{12}{x^2}\right) + x^2 = \dfrac{48}{x} + x^2, x > 0.$

      (b)   The function $y = A(x)$ is shown in the first viewing rectangle below. In the second viewing
            rectangle, we isolate the minimum, and we see that the amount of material is minimized when x
            (the length and width) is 2.88 ft. Then the height is $h = \dfrac{12}{x^2} \approx 1.44$ ft.

33.   (a)   Let w be the width of the pen and l be the length in meters. We use the area to establish a
            relationship between w and l. Since the area is 100 m^2, we have $l \cdot w = 100 \quad \Leftrightarrow \quad l = \dfrac{100}{w}$.
            So the amount of fencing used is $F = 2l + 2w = 2\left(\dfrac{100}{w}\right) + 2w = \dfrac{200 + 2w^2}{w}.$

      (b)   Using a graphing device, we first graph F in the viewing rectangle, $[0, 40]$ by $[0, 100]$, and
            locate the approximate location of the minimum value. In the second viewing rectangle, $[8, 12]$
            by $[39, 41]$, we see that the minimum value of F occurs when $w = 10$. Therefore the pen
            should be a square with side 10 m.

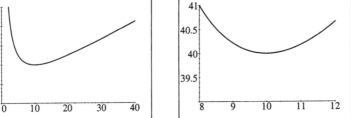

35. (a) Let x be the distance from point B to C, in miles. Then the distance from A to C is $\sqrt{x^2 + 25}$, and the energy used in flying from A to C then C to D is $f(x) = 14\sqrt{x^2 + 25} + 10(12 - x)$.

   (b) By using a graphing device, the energy expenditure is minimized when the distance from B to C is about 5.1 miles.

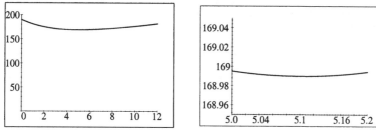

Exercises 2.8

1. $f(x) = x^2$ has domain $(-\infty, \infty)$. $g(x) = x + 2$ has domain $(-\infty, \infty)$. The intersection of the domains of f and g is $(-\infty, \infty)$.

   $(f + g)(x) = (x^2) + (x + 2) = x^2 + x + 2$, and the domain is $(-\infty, \infty)$.

   $(f - g)(x) = (x^2) - (x + 2) = x^2 - x - 2$, and the domain is $(-\infty, \infty)$.

   $(fg)(x) = (x^2)(x + 2) = x^3 + 2x^2$, and the domain is $(-\infty, \infty)$.

   $\left(\dfrac{f}{g}\right)(x) = \dfrac{x^2}{x + 2}$, and the domain is $\{\, x \mid x \neq -2 \,\}$.

3. $f(x) = \sqrt{1 + x^2}$, has domain $(-\infty, \infty)$. $g(x) = \sqrt{1 - x}$, has domain $(-\infty, 1]$. The intersection of the domains of f and g is $(-\infty, 1]$.

   $(f + g)(x) = \sqrt{1 + x^2} + \sqrt{1 - x}$, and the domain is $(-\infty, 1]$.

   $(f - g)(x) = \sqrt{1 + x^2} - \sqrt{1 - x}$, and the domain is $(-\infty, 1]$.

   $(fg)(x) = \sqrt{1 + x^2} \cdot \sqrt{1 - x} = \sqrt{1 - x + x^2 - x^3}$, and the domain is $(-\infty, 1]$.

   $\left(\dfrac{f}{g}\right)(x) = \dfrac{\sqrt{1 + x^2}}{\sqrt{1 - x}} = \sqrt{\dfrac{1 + x^2}{1 - x}}$, and the domain is $(-\infty, 1)$.

5. $f(x) = \dfrac{2}{x}$, has domain $x \neq 0$. $g(x) = -\dfrac{2}{x + 4}$, has domain $x \neq -4$. The intersection of the domains of f and g is $x \neq 0, -4$, in interval notation, this is $(-\infty, -4) \cup (-4, 0) \cup (0, \infty)$.

   $(f + g)(x) = \dfrac{2}{x} + \left(-\dfrac{2}{x + 4}\right) = \dfrac{2}{x} - \dfrac{2}{x + 4} = \dfrac{8}{x(x + 4)}$, and the domain is $(-\infty, -4) \cup (-4, 0) \cup (0, \infty)$.

   $(f - g)(x) = \dfrac{2}{x} - \left(-\dfrac{2}{x + 4}\right) = \dfrac{2}{x} + \dfrac{2}{x + 4} = \dfrac{4x + 8}{x(x + 4)}$, and the domain is $(-\infty, -4) \cup (-4, 0) \cup (0, \infty)$.

   $(fg)(x) = \dfrac{2}{x} \cdot \left(-\dfrac{2}{x + 4}\right) = -\dfrac{4}{x(x + 4)}$, and the domain is $(-\infty, -4) \cup (-4, 0) \cup (0, \infty)$.

   $\left(\dfrac{f}{g}\right)(x) = \dfrac{\dfrac{2}{x}}{-\dfrac{2}{x + 4}} = -\dfrac{x + 4}{x}$, and the domain is $(-\infty, -4) \cup (-4, 0) \cup (0, \infty)$.

7. $f(x) = \sqrt{x} + \sqrt{1 - x}$. The domain of $\sqrt{x}$ is $[0, \infty]]$, and the domain of $\sqrt{1 - x}$ is $(-\infty, 1]$. Thus the domain is $(-\infty, 1] \cap [0, \infty) = [0, 1]$.

9. $h(x) = (x + 1)^2 (2x - 8)^{1/4}$. Since $1/4$ is an even root, $2x - 8 \geq 0 \quad \Leftrightarrow \quad x \geq 4$. So the domain is $[4, \infty)$.

11.

13.

15.

17. (a) $f(g(0)) = f(2 - (0)^2) = f(2) = 3(2) - 5 = 1$

(b) $g(f(0)) = g(3(0) - 5) = g(-5) = 2 - (-5)^2 = -23$

19. (a) $(f \circ g)(-2) = f(g(-2)) = f(2 - (-2)^2) = f(-2) = 3(-2) - 5 = -11$

(b) $(g \circ f)(-2) = g(f(-2)) = g(3(-2) - 5) = g(-11) = 2 - (-11)^2 = -119$

21. (a) $(f \circ g)(x) = f(g(x)) = f(2 - x^2) = 3(2 - x^2) - 5 = 6 - 3x^2 - 5 = 1 - 3x^2$

(b) $(g \circ f)(x) = g(f(x)) = g(3x - 5) = 2 - (3x - 5)^2 = 2 - (9x^2 - 30x + 25)$
$= -9x^2 + 30x - 23$

23. $f(g(2)) = f(5) = 4$

25. $(g \circ f)(4) = g(f(4)) = g(2) = 5$

27. $(g \circ g)(-2) = g(g(-2)) = g(1) = 4$

29. $f(x) = 2x + 3$, has domain $(-\infty, \infty)$; $g(x) = 4x - 1$, has domain $(-\infty, \infty)$.
$(f \circ g)(x) = f(4x - 1) = 2(4x - 1) + 3 = 8x + 1$, and the domain is $(-\infty, \infty)$.
$(g \circ f)(x) = g(2x + 3) = 4(2x + 3) - 1 = 8x + 11$, and the domain is $(-\infty, \infty)$.
$(f \circ f)(x) = f(2x + 3) = 2(2x + 3) + 3 = 4x + 9$, and the domain is $(-\infty, \infty)$.
$(g \circ g)(x) = g(4x - 1) = 4(4x - 1) - 1 = 16x - 5$, and the domain is $(-\infty, \infty)$.

31. $f(x) = x^2$, has domain $(-\infty, \infty)$; $g(x) = x + 1$, has domain $(-\infty, \infty)$.
$(f \circ g)(x) = f(x + 1) = (x + 1)^2 = x^2 + 2x + 1$, and the domain is $(-\infty, \infty)$.
$(g \circ f)(x) = g(x^2) = (x^2) + 1 = x^2 + 1$, and the domain is $(-\infty, \infty)$.
$(f \circ f)(x) = f(x^2) = (x^2)^2 = x^4$, and the domain is $(-\infty, \infty)$.
$(g \circ g)(x) = g(x + 1) = (x + 1) + 1 = x + 2$, and the domain is $(-\infty, \infty)$.

33. $f(x) = \dfrac{1}{x}$, has domain $\{x \mid x \neq 0\}$; $g(x) = 2x + 4$, has domain $(-\infty, \infty)$.

$(f \circ g)(x) = f(2x + 4) = \dfrac{1}{2x + 4}$. $(f \circ g)(x)$ is defined for $2x + 4 \neq 0 \quad \Leftrightarrow \quad x \neq -2$. So the domain is $\{x \mid x \neq -2\} = (-\infty, -2) \cup (-2, \infty)$.

$(g \circ f)(x) = g\left(\dfrac{1}{x}\right) = 2\left(\dfrac{1}{x}\right) + 4 = \dfrac{2}{x} + 4$, the domain is $\{x \mid x \neq 0\} = (-\infty, 0) \cup (0, \infty)$.

$(f \circ f)(x) = f\left(\dfrac{1}{x}\right) = \dfrac{1}{\left(\dfrac{1}{x}\right)} = x$. $(f \circ f)(x)$ is defined whenever both $f(x)$ and $f(f(x))$ are defined; that is, whenever $\{x \mid x \neq 0\} = (-\infty, 0) \cup (0, \infty)$.

$(g \circ g)(x) = g(2x + 4) = 2(2x + 4) + 4 = 4x + 8 + 4 = 4x + 12$, and the domain is $(-\infty, \infty)$.

35. $f(x) = |x|$, has domain $(-\infty, \infty)$; $g(x) = 2x + 3$, has domain $(-\infty, \infty)$

$(f \circ g)(x) = f(2x + 4) = |2x + 3|$, and the domain is $(-\infty, \infty)$.

$(g \circ f)(x) = g(|x|) = 2|x| + 3$, and the domain is $(-\infty, \infty)$.

$(f \circ f)(x) = f(|x|) = ||x|| = |x|$, and the domain is $(-\infty, \infty)$.

$(g \circ g)(x) = g(2x + 3) = 2(2x + 3) + 3 = 4x + 6 + 3 = 4x + 9$. Domain is $(-\infty, \infty)$.

37. $f(x) = \dfrac{x}{x + 1}$, has domain $\{x \mid x \neq -1\}$; $g(x) = 2x - 1$, has domain $(-\infty, \infty)$

$(f \circ g)(x) = f(2x - 1) = \dfrac{2x - 1}{(2x - 1) + 1} = \dfrac{2x - 1}{2x}$, and the domain is $\{x \mid x \neq 0\} = (-\infty, 0) \cup (0, \infty)$.

$(g \circ f)(x) = g\left(\dfrac{x}{x + 1}\right) = 2\left(\dfrac{x}{x + 1}\right) - 1 = \dfrac{2x}{x + 1} - 1$, and the domain is $\{x \mid x \neq -1\} = (-\infty, -1) \cup (-1, \infty)$

$(f \circ f)(x) = f\left(\dfrac{x}{x + 1}\right) = \dfrac{\dfrac{x}{x + 1}}{\dfrac{x}{x + 1} + 1} = \dfrac{x + 1}{x} \cdot \dfrac{x + 1}{x + 1} = \dfrac{x}{x + x + 1} = \dfrac{x}{2x + 1}$. $(f \circ f)(x)$ is defined whenever both $f(x)$ and $f(f(x))$ are defined; that is, whenever $\{x \mid x \neq -1\}$ and $2x + 1 \neq 0 \quad \Rightarrow$ $\{x \mid x \neq -\frac{1}{2}\}$ which is $(-\infty, -1) \cup (-1, -\frac{1}{2}) \cup (-\frac{1}{2}, \infty)$.

$(g \circ g)(x) = g(2x - 1) = 2(2x - 1) - 1 = 4x - 2 - 1 = 4x - 3$, and the domain is $(-\infty, \infty)$.

39. $f(x) = \sqrt[3]{x}$, has domain $(-\infty, \infty)$; $g(x) = \sqrt[4]{x}$, has domain $[0, \infty)$.

$(f \circ g)(x) = f(\sqrt[4]{x}) = \sqrt[3]{\sqrt[4]{x}} = \sqrt[12]{x}$. $(f \circ g)(x)$ is defined whenever both $g(x)$ and $f(g(x))$ are defined. Since $f(x)$ has no restriction, the domain is $[0, \infty)$.

$(g \circ f)(x) = g(\sqrt[3]{x}) = \sqrt[4]{\sqrt[3]{x}} = \sqrt[12]{x}$. $(g \circ f)(x)$ is defined whenever both $f(x)$ and $g(f(x))$ are defined; that is, whenever $x \geq 0$. So the domain is $[0, \infty)$.

$(f \circ f)(x) = f(\sqrt[3]{x}) = \sqrt[3]{\sqrt[3]{x}} = \sqrt[9]{x}$. $(f \circ f)(x)$ is defined whenever both $f(x)$ and $f(f(x))$ are defined. Since $f(x)$ is defined everywhere, the domain is $(-\infty, \infty)$.

$(g \circ g)(x) = g(\sqrt[4]{x}) = \sqrt[4]{\sqrt[4]{x}} = \sqrt[16]{x}$. $(g \circ g)(x)$ is defined whenever both $g(x)$ and $g(g(x))$ are defined; that is, whenever $x \geq 0$. So the domain is $[0, \infty)$.

41. $(f \circ g \circ h)(x) = f(g(h(x))) = f(g(x-1)) = f(\sqrt{x-1}) = \sqrt{x-1} - 1$

43. $(f \circ g \circ h)(x) = f(g(h(x))) = f(g(\sqrt{x})) = f(\sqrt{x} - 5) = (\sqrt{x} - 5)^4 + 1$

45. $F(x) = (x-9)^5$. Let $f(x) = x^5$ and $g(x) = x - 9$, then $F(x) = (f \circ g)(x)$.

47. $G(x) = \dfrac{x^2}{x^2 + 4}$. Let $f(x) = \dfrac{x}{x+4}$ and $g(x) = x^2$, then $G(x) = (f \circ g)(x)$.

49. $H(x) = |1 - x^3|$. Let $f(x) = |x|$ and $g(x) = 1 - x^3$, then $H(x) = (f \circ g)(x)$.

For Exercises 51 and 53 there are several possible solutions, only one of which is shown.

51. $F(x) = \dfrac{1}{x^2 + 1}$. Let $f(x) = \dfrac{1}{x}$, $g(x) = x + 1$, and $h(x) = x^2$, then $F(x) = (f \circ g \circ h)(x)$.

53. $G(x) = (4 + \sqrt[3]{x})^9$. Let $f(x) = x^9$, $g(x) = 4 + x$, and $h(x) = \sqrt[3]{x}$, then $G(x) = (f \circ g \circ h)(x)$.

55. Let r be the radius of the circular ripple in centimeters. Since the ripple travels at a speed of 60 cm/s, the distance traveled in t seconds is the radius, so $r = 60t$. Therefore, the area of the circle can be written as $A(t) = \pi r^2 = \pi(60t)^2 = 3600\pi t^2$ cm^2.

57. Let r be the radius of the spherical balloon in centimeters. Since the radius is increasing at a rate of 2 cm/s, the radius is $r = 2t$ after t seconds. Therefore, the surface areae of the balloon can be written as $S = 4\pi r^2 = 4\pi(2t)^2 = 4\pi(4t^2) = 16\pi t^2$.

59. (a) $f(x) = 0.90x$

     (b) $g(x) = x - 100$

     (c) $f \circ g = f(x - 100) = 0.90(x - 100) = 0.90x - 90$. $f \circ g$ represents applying the $100 coupon, then the 10% discount.

          $g \circ f = g(0.90x) = 0.90x - 100$. $g \circ f$ represents applying the 10% discount, then the $100 coupon.

          So applying the 10% discount, then the $100 coupon gives the lower price.

61. $A(x) = 1.05x$. $(A \circ A)(x) = A(A(x)) = A(1.05x) = 1.05(1.05x) = (1.05)^2 x$.
     $(A \circ A \circ A)(x) = A(A \circ A(x)) = A((1.05)^2 x) = 1.05[(1.05)^2 x] = (1.05)^3 x$.
     $(A \circ A \circ A \circ A)(x) = A(A \circ A \circ A(x)) = A((1.05)^3 x) = 1.05[(1.05)^3 x] = (1.05)^4 x$. A represents the amount in the account after 1 year; $A \circ A$ represents the amount in the account after 2 years; $A \circ A \circ A$ represents the amount in the account after 3 years; and $A \circ A \circ A \circ A$ represents the amount in the account after 4 years. We can see that if we compose n copies of A, we get $(1.05)^n x$.

63. $g(x) = 2x + 1$ and $h(x) = 4x^2 + 4x + 7$

     Method 1: Notice that $(2x + 1)^2 = 4x^2 + 4x + 1$. We see that adding 6 to this quantity gives $(2x + 1)^2 + 6 = 4x^2 + 4x + 1 + 6 = 4x^2 + 4x + 7$, which is $h(x)$. So let $f(x) = x^2 + 6$, and we have $(f \circ g)(x) = (2x + 1)^2 + 6 = h(x)$.

     Method 2: Since $g(x)$ is linear and $h(x)$ is a second degree polynomial, $f(x)$ must be a second degree polynomial, that is, $f(x) = ax^2 + bx + c$ for some a, b, and c. Thus $f(g(x)) = f(2x + 1) = a(2x + 1)^2 + b(2x + 1) + c$ $\Leftrightarrow$

$4ax^2 + 4ax + a + 2bx + b + c = 4ax^2 + (4a + 2b)x + (a + b + c) = 4x^2 + 4x + 7$. Comparing this with $f(g(x))$, we have $4a = 4$ (the x^2 coefficients), $4a + 2b = 4$ (the x coefficients), and $a + b + c = 7$ (the constant terms) $\Leftrightarrow$ $a = 1$ and $2a + b = 2$ and $a + b + c = 7$ $\Leftrightarrow$ $a = 1$, $b = 0, c = 6$. Thus $f(x) = x^2 + 6$.

$f(x) = 3x + 5$ and $h(x) = 3x^2 + 3x + 2$

Note since $f(x)$ is linear and $h(x)$ is quadratic, $g(x)$ must also be quadratic. We can then use trial and error to find $g(x)$. Another method is the following: We wish to find g so that $(f \circ g)(x) = h(x)$. Thus $f(g(x)) = 3x^2 + 3x + 2$ $\Leftrightarrow$ $3(g(x)) + 5 = 3x^2 + 3x + 2$ $\Leftrightarrow$ $3(g(x)) = 3x^2 + 3x - 3$ $\Leftrightarrow$ $g(x) = x^2 + x - 1$.

Exercises 2.9

1. By the Horizontal Line Test, f is not one-to-one.

3. By the Horizontal Line Test, f is one-to-one.

5. By the Horizontal Line Test, f is not one-to-one.

7. $f(x) = 7x - 3$. If $x_1 \neq x_2$, then $7x_1 \neq 7x_2$ and $7x_1 - 3 \neq 7x_2 - 3$. So f is a one-to-one function.

9. $g(x) = \sqrt{x}$. If $x_1 \neq x_2$, then $\sqrt{x_1} \neq \sqrt{x_2}$ because two different numbers cannot have the same square root. Therefore, g is a one-to-one function.

11. $h(x) = x^3 + 1$. If $x_1 \neq x_2$, then $x_1^3 \neq x_2^3$ and $x_1^3 + 1 \neq x_2^3 + 1$. So f is a one-to-one function.

13. $f(x) = x^4 + 5$. Every nonzero number and its negative have the same fourth power. For example, $(-1)^4 = 1 = (1)^4$, so $f(-1) = f(1)$. Thus f is not a one-to-one function.

15. $f(x) = \dfrac{1}{x^2}$. Every nonzero number and its negative have the same square. For example, $\frac{1}{(-1)^2} = 1 = \frac{1}{(1)^2}$, so $f(-1) = f(1)$. Thus f is not a one-to-one function.

17. (a) $f(2) = 7$. Since f is one-to-one, $f^{-1}(7) = 2$.
     (b) $f^{-1}(3) = -1$. Since f is one-to-one, $f(-1) = 3$.

19. $f(x) = 5 - 2x$. Since f is one-to-one and $f(1) = 5 - 2(1) = 3$, then $f^{-1}(3) = 1$. (Find 1 by solving the equation $5 - 2x = 3$.)

21. $f(g(x)) = f(x - 3) = (x - 3) + 3 = x$, for all x.
     $g(f(x)) = g(x + 3) = (x + 3) - 3 = x$, for all x. Thus f and g are inverses of each other.

23. $f(g(x)) = f\left(\dfrac{x + 5}{2}\right) = 2\left(\dfrac{x + 5}{2}\right) - 5 = x + 5 - 5 = x$, for all x.

     $g(f(x)) = g(2x - 5) = \dfrac{(2x - 5) + 5}{2} = x$, for all x. Thus f and g are inverses of each other.

25. $f(g(x)) = f\left(\dfrac{1}{x}\right) = \dfrac{1}{1/x} = x$, for all x. Since $f(x) = g(x)$, we also have $g(f(x)) = x$. Thus f and g are inverses of each other.

27. $f(g(x)) = f(\sqrt{x + 4}) = \left(\sqrt{x + 4}\right)^2 - 4 = x + 4 - 4 = x$, for all $x \geq -4$.
     $g(f(x)) = g(x^2 - 4) = \sqrt{(x^2 - 4) + 4} = \sqrt{x^2} = x$, for all $x \geq 0$. Thus f and g are inverses of each other.

29. $f(g(x)) = f\left(\dfrac{1}{x} + 1\right) = \dfrac{1}{\left(\dfrac{1}{x} + 1\right) - 1} = x$, for all $x \neq 0$.

     $g(f(x)) = g\left(\dfrac{1}{x - 1}\right) = \dfrac{1}{\left(\dfrac{1}{x - 1}\right)} + 1 = (x - 1) + 1 = x$, for all $x \neq 1$. Thus f and g are inverses of each other.

31. $f(x) = 2x + 1$. $y = 2x + 1$ $\Leftrightarrow$ $2x = y - 1$ $\Leftrightarrow$ $x = \frac{1}{2}(y - 1)$. So $f^{-1}(x) = \frac{1}{2}(x - 1)$.

33. $f(x) = 4x + 7$. $y = 4x + 7$ $\Leftrightarrow$ $4x = y - 7$ $\Leftrightarrow$ $x = \frac{1}{4}(y - 7)$. So $f^{-1}(x) = \frac{1}{4}(x - 7)$.

35. $f(x) = \dfrac{x}{2}$. $y = \dfrac{x}{2}$ $\Leftrightarrow$ $x = 2y$. So $f^{-1}(x) = 2x$.

37. $f(x) = \dfrac{1}{x + 2}$. $y = \dfrac{1}{x + 2}$ $\Leftrightarrow$ $x + 2 = \dfrac{1}{y}$ $\Leftrightarrow$ $x = \dfrac{1}{y} - 2$. So $f^{-1}(x) = \dfrac{1}{x} - 2$.

39. $f(x) = \dfrac{1 + 3x}{5 - 2x}$. $y = \dfrac{1 + 3x}{5 - 2x}$ $\Leftrightarrow$ $y(5 - 2x) = 1 + 3x$ $\Leftrightarrow$ $5y - 2xy = 1 + 3x$ $\Leftrightarrow$

$3x + 2xy = 5y - 1$ $\Leftrightarrow$ $x(3 + 2y) = 5y - 1$ $\Leftrightarrow$ $x = \dfrac{5y - 1}{2y + 3}$. So $f^{-1}(x) = \dfrac{5x - 1}{2x + 3}$.

41. $f(x) = \sqrt{2 + 5x}, x \geq -\frac{2}{5}$. $y = \sqrt{2 + 5x}, y \geq 0$ $\Leftrightarrow$ $y^2 = 2 + 5x$ $\Leftrightarrow$ $5x = y^2 - 2$ $\Leftrightarrow$
$x = \frac{1}{5}(y^2 - 2)$ and $y \geq 0$. So $f^{-1}(x) = \frac{1}{5}(x^2 - 2), x \geq 0$.

43. $f(x) = 4 - x^2$, $x \geq 0$. $y = 4 - x^2$ $\Leftrightarrow$ $x^2 = 4 - y$ $\Leftrightarrow$ $x = \sqrt{4 - y}$. So
$f^{-1}(x) = \sqrt{4 - x}$. Note: $x \geq 0$ $\Rightarrow$ $f(x) \leq 4$.

45. $f(x) = 4 + \sqrt[3]{x}$. $y = 4 + \sqrt[3]{x}$ $\Leftrightarrow$ $\sqrt[3]{x} = y - 4$ $\Leftrightarrow$ $x = (y - 4)^3$. So $f^{-1}(x) = (x - 4)^3$.

47. $f(x) = 1 + \sqrt{1 + x}$. $y = 1 + \sqrt{1 + x}, y \geq 1$ $\Leftrightarrow$ $\sqrt{1 + x} = y - 1$ $\Leftrightarrow$ $1 + x = (y - 1)^2$
$\Leftrightarrow$ $x = (y - 1)^2 - 1 = y^2 - 2y$. So $f^{-1}(x) = x^2 - 2x, x \geq 1$.

49. $f(x) = x^4$, $x \geq 0$. $y = x^4, y \geq 0$ $\Leftrightarrow$ $x = \sqrt[4]{y}$. So $f^{-1}(x) = \sqrt[4]{x}, x \geq 0$.

51.   (a)   (b)

(c) $f(x) = 3x - 6$. $y = 3x - 6$ $\Leftrightarrow$ $3x = y + 6$ $\Leftrightarrow$ $x = \frac{1}{3}(y + 6)$. So
$f^{-1}(x) = \frac{1}{3}(x + 6)$.

53.   (a)   (b)

(c) $f(x) = \sqrt{x + 1}$, $x \geq -1$. $y = \sqrt{x + 1}, y \geq 0$ $\Leftrightarrow$ $y^2 = x + 1$ $\Leftrightarrow$ $x = y^2 - 1$ and
$y \geq 0$. So $f^{-1}(x) = x^2 - 1, x \geq 0$.

55. $f(x) = x^3 - x$. Using a graphing device and the Horizontal Line Test, we see that f is not a one-to-one function. For example, $f(0) = 0 = f(-1)$.

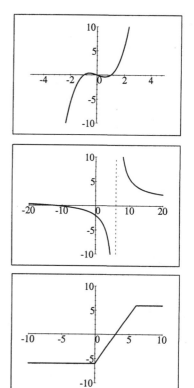

57. $f(x) = \dfrac{x + 12}{x - 6}$. Using a graphing device and the Horizontal Line Test, we see that f is a one-to-one function.

59. $f(x) = |x| - |x - 6|$. Using a graphing device and the Horizontal Line Test, we see that f is not a one-to-one function. For example $f(0) = -6 = f(-2)$.

61. If we restrict the domain of $f(x)$ to $[0, \infty)$, then $y = 4 - x^2 \quad \Leftrightarrow \quad x^2 = 4 - y \quad \Rightarrow$ $x = \sqrt{4 - y}$ (since $x \geq 0$, we take the positive square root). So $f^{-1}(x) = \sqrt{4 - x}$. If we restrict the domain of $f(x)$ to $(-\infty, 0]$, then $y = 4 - x^2 \quad \Leftrightarrow \quad x^2 = 4 - y \quad \Rightarrow$ $x = -\sqrt{4 - y}$ (since $x \leq 0$, we take the negative square root). So $f^{-1}(x) = -\sqrt{4 - x}$.

63. If we restrict the domain of $h(x)$ to $[-2, \infty)$, then $y = (x + 2)^2 \quad \Rightarrow \quad x + 2 = \sqrt{y}$ (since $x \geq -2$, we take the positive square root) $\quad \Leftrightarrow \quad x = -2 + \sqrt{y}$. So $h^{-1}(x) = -2 + \sqrt{x}$. If we restrict the domain of $h(x)$ to $(-\infty, -2]$, then $y = (x + 2)^2 \quad \Rightarrow \quad x + 2 = -\sqrt{y}$ (since $x \leq -2$, we take the negative square root) $\quad \Leftrightarrow \quad x = -2 - \sqrt{y}$. So $h^{-1}(x) = -2 - \sqrt{x}$.

65.

67. (a) $f(x) = 500 + 80x$.

(b) $f(x) = 500 + 80x$. $y = 500 + 80x$ $\Leftrightarrow$ $80x = y - 500$ $\Leftrightarrow$ $x = \dfrac{y - 500}{80}$. So

$f^{-1}(x) = \dfrac{x - 500}{80}$. f^{-1} represents the number of hours of investigation the investigate spends

on a case for x dollars.

(c) $f^{-1}(1220) = \dfrac{1220 - 500}{80} = \dfrac{720}{80} = 9$. The investigator spent 9 hours investigating this case.

69. (a) $v(r) = 18500(0.25 - r^2)$. $y = 18500(0.25 - r^2)$ $\Leftrightarrow$ $y = 4625 - 18500r^2$ $\Leftrightarrow$

$18500r^2 = 4625 - y$ $\Leftrightarrow$ $r^2 = \dfrac{4625 - y}{18500}$ $\Rightarrow$ $r = \pm\sqrt{\dfrac{4625 - y}{18500}}$. Since r represents a

measure $r \geq 0$, so $v^{-1}(r) = \sqrt{\dfrac{4625 - r}{18500}}$. v^{-1}represents the raduis in the vien that has the

velocity v.

(b) $v^{-1}(30) = \sqrt{\dfrac{4625 - 30}{18500}} \approx 0.498$ cm. The velocity is 30 at 0.05 cm from the center of the

artery or vein.

71. (a) $F(C) = \frac{9}{5}C + 32$. $y = \frac{9}{5}C + 32$ $\Leftrightarrow$ $\frac{9}{5}C = y - 32$ $\Leftrightarrow$ $C = \frac{5}{9}(y - 32)$. So

$F^{-1}(C) = \frac{5}{9}(C - 32)$. F^{-1} represents the Celsius temperature that corresponds to the

Fahrenheit temperature of F.

(b) $F^{-1}(86) = \frac{5}{9}(86 - 32) = \frac{5}{9}(54) = 30$. So 86° Fahrenheit is the same as 30° Celsius.

73. (a) $f(x) = \begin{cases} 0.1x, & \text{if } 0 \leq x \leq 20{,}000 \\ 2000 + 0.2(x - 20{,}000), & \text{if } x > 20{,}000 \end{cases}$

(b) We will find the inverse of each peice of the function f.

$f_1(x) = 0.1x$. $y = 0.1x$ $\Leftrightarrow$ $x = 10y$. So $f_1^{-1}(x) = 10x$.

$f_2(x) = 2000 + 0.2(x - 20{,}000) = 0.2x - 2000$. $y = 0.2x - 2000$ $\Leftrightarrow$ $0.2x = y + 2000$

$\Leftrightarrow$ $x = 5y + 10{,}000$. So $f_2^{-1}(x) = 5x + 10{,}000$.

Since $f(0) = 0$ and $f(20{,}000) = 2000$ we have $f^{-1}(x) = \begin{cases} 10x, & \text{if } 0 \leq x \leq 2000 \\ 5x + 10{,}000 & \text{if } x > 2000 \end{cases}$.

It respresnts the taxpayer's income.

(c) $f^{-1}(10{,}000) = 5(10{,}000) + 10{,}000 = 60{,}000$. The required income is \$60,000.

75. $f(x) = 7 + 2x$. $y = 7 + 2x$ $\Leftrightarrow$ $2x = y - 7$ $\Leftrightarrow$ $x = \dfrac{y - 7}{2}$. So $f^{-1}(x) = \dfrac{x - 7}{2}$. f^{-1} is

the number of toppings on a pizza that costs x dollars.

77. (a) $f(x) = \dfrac{2x + 1}{5}$ is "multiply by 2, add 1, and then divide by 5". So the reverse is "multiply by

5, subtract 1 , and then divide by 2" or $f^{-1}(x) = \dfrac{5x - 1}{2}$. Check:

$$f \circ f^{-1}(x) = f\left(\frac{5x-1}{2}\right)$$

$$= \frac{2\left(\dfrac{5x-1}{2}\right)+1}{5}$$

$$= \frac{5x-1+1}{5} = \frac{5x}{5} = x$$

$$f^{-1} \circ f(x) = f\left(\frac{2x+1}{5}\right)$$

$$= \frac{5\left(\dfrac{2x+1}{5}\right)-1}{2}$$

$$= \frac{2x+1-1}{2} = \frac{2x}{2} = x$$

(b) $f(x) = 3 - \dfrac{1}{x} = \dfrac{-1}{x} + 3$ is "take the negative reciprocal and add 3". Since the reverse of "take the negative reciprocal" is "take the negative reciprocal ", $f^{-1}(x)$ is "subtract 3 and take the negative reciprocal ", that is, $f^{-1}(x) = \dfrac{-1}{x-3}$. Check:

$$f \circ f^{-1}(x) = f\left(\frac{-1}{x-3}\right)$$

$$= 3 - \frac{1}{\dfrac{-1}{x-3}}$$

$$= 3 - \left(1 \cdot \frac{x-3}{-1}\right)$$

$$= 3 + x - 3 = x$$

$$f^{-1} \circ f(x) = f\left(3 - \frac{1}{x}\right)$$

$$= \frac{-1}{\left(3 - \dfrac{1}{x}\right) - 3}$$

$$= \frac{-1}{-\dfrac{1}{x}} = -1 \cdot \frac{x}{-1} = x$$

(c) $f(x) = \sqrt{x^3 + 2}$ is "cube, add 2, and then take the square root 3". So the reverse is "square, subtract 2, then take cube root " or $f^{-1}(x) = \sqrt[3]{x^2 - 2}$. Domain for $f(x)$ is $[-\sqrt[3]{2},\ \infty)$; domain for $f^{-1}(x)$ is $[0,\ \infty)$. Check:

$$f \circ f^{-1}(x) = f\left(\sqrt[3]{x^2 - 2}\right)$$

$$= \sqrt{\left(\sqrt[3]{x^2 - 2}\right)^3 + 2}$$

$$= \sqrt{x^2 - 2 + 2}$$

$$= \sqrt{x^2} = x \text{ (for the domains)}$$

$$f^{-1} \circ f(x) = f\left(\sqrt{x^3 + 2}\right)$$

$$= \sqrt[3]{\left(\sqrt{x^3 + 2}\right)^2 - 2}$$

$$= \sqrt[3]{x^3 + 2 - 2}$$

$$= \sqrt[3]{x^3} = x \text{ (for the domains)}$$

No; in a function like $f(x) = 3x - 2$, the variable occurs only once and it easy to see how to reverse these operations step by step. But in $f(x) = \dfrac{3x-2}{x+7}$, you apply two different operations to the variable x and then find the quotient of each of these values, so it is not possible to reverse the operations step by step.

79. (a) We find $g^{-1}(x)$: $y = 2x + 1 \quad \Leftrightarrow \quad 2x = y - 1 \quad \Leftrightarrow \quad x = \frac{1}{2}(y-1)$. So $g^{-1}(x) = \frac{1}{2}(x-1)$. Thus

$$f(x) = h \circ g^{-1}(x) = h\left(\tfrac{1}{2}(x-1)\right) = 4\left[\tfrac{1}{2}(x-1)\right]^2 + 4\left[\tfrac{1}{2}(x-1)\right] + 7$$
$$= x^2 - 2x + 1 + 2x - 2 + 7 = x^2 + 6.$$

(b) $f \circ g = h \quad \Leftrightarrow \quad f^{-1} \circ f \circ g = f^{-1} \circ h \quad \Leftrightarrow \quad I \circ g = f^{-1} \circ h \quad \Leftrightarrow \quad g = f^{-1} \circ h$. Note that we compose with f^{-1} on the left on each side of the equation. We find f^{-1}: $y = 3x + 5$ $\Leftrightarrow \quad 3x = y - 5 \quad \Leftrightarrow \quad x = \frac{1}{3}(y-5)$. So $f^{-1}(x) = \frac{1}{3}(x-5)$. Thus

$$g(x) = f^{-1} \circ h(x) = f^{-1}(3x^2 + 3x + 2) = \tfrac{1}{3}[(3x^2 + 3x + 2) - 5]$$
$$= \tfrac{1}{3}[3x^2 + 3x - 3] = x^2 + x - 1.$$

Review Exercises for Chapter 2

1. $f(x) = x^3 + 2x - 4$; $f(0) = (0)^3 + 2(0) - 4 = -4$; $f(2) = (2)^3 + 2(2) - 4 = 8$;
    $f(-2) = (-2)^3 + 2(-2) - 4 = -16$; $f(a) = (a)^3 + 2(a) - 4 = a^3 + 2a - 4$;
    $f(-a) = (-a)^3 + 2(-a) - 4 = -a^3 - 2a - 4$;
    $f(x+1) = (x+1)^3 + 2(x+1) - 4 = x^3 + 3x^2 + 3x + 1 + 2x + 2 - 4 = x^3 + 3x^2 + 5x - 1$;
    $f(2x) = (2x)^3 + 2(2x) - 4 = 8x^3 + 4x - 4$;
    $2f(x) - 2 = 2(x^3 + 2x - 4) - 2 = 2x^3 + 4x - 8 - 2 = 2x^3 + 4x - 10$.

3. (a) $f(-2) = -1$. $f(2) = 2$.

    (b) The domain of f is $[-4, 5]$.

    (c) The range of f is $[-4, 4]$.

    (d) f is increasing on $[-4, -2]$ and $[-1, 4]$; f is decreasing on $[-2, -1]$ and $[4, 5]$.

    (e) f is not a one-to-one, for example, $f(-2) = -1 = f(0)$. There are many more examples.

5. Domain: We must have $x + 3 \geq 0 \quad \Leftrightarrow \quad x \geq -3$. In interval notation, the domain is $[-3, \infty)$.
    Range: For x in the domain of f, we have $x \geq -3 \quad \Leftrightarrow \quad x + 3 \geq 0 \quad \Leftrightarrow \quad \sqrt{x+3} \geq 0 \quad \Leftrightarrow$
    $f(x) \geq 0$. So the range is $[0, \infty)$.

7. $f(x) = 7x + 15$. The domain is all real numbers, $(-\infty, \infty)$.

9. $f(x) = \sqrt{x + 4}$. We require $x + 4 \geq 0 \quad \Leftrightarrow \quad x \geq -4$. Thus the domain is $[-4, \infty)$.

11. $f(x) = \frac{1}{x} + \frac{1}{x+1} + \frac{1}{x+2}$. The denominators cannot equal 0, therefore the domain is
    $\{x \mid x \neq 0, -1, -2\}$.

13. $h(x) = \sqrt{4 - x} + \sqrt{x^2 - 1}$. We require the expression inside the radicals be nonnegative. So
    $4 - x \geq 0 \quad \Leftrightarrow \quad 4 \geq x$; also $x^2 - 1 \geq 0 \quad \Leftrightarrow \quad (x-1)(x+1) \geq 0$. Using the methods from
    Chapter 2, we have:

Interval	$(-\infty, -1)$	$(-1, 1)$	$(1, \infty)$
Sign of $x - 1$	$-$	$-$	$+$
Sign of $x + 1$	$-$	$+$	$+$
Sign of $(x-1)(x+1)$	$+$	$-$	$+$

Thus the domain is $(-\infty, 4] \cap \{ (-\infty, -1] \cup [1, \infty) \} = (-\infty, -1] \cup [1, 4]$.

15. $f(x) = 1 - 2x$ 17. $f(t) = 1 - \frac{1}{2}t^2$

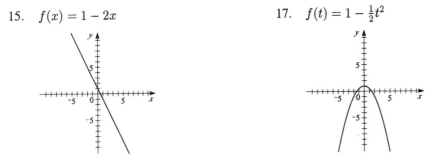

19. $f(x) = x^2 - 6x + 6$

21. $y = 1 - \sqrt{x}$

23. $y = \frac{1}{2}x^3$

25. $h(x) = \sqrt[3]{x}$

27. $g(x) = \frac{1}{x^2}$

29. $f(x) = \begin{cases} 1 - x & \text{if } x < 0 \\ 1 & \text{if } x \geq 0 \end{cases}$

31. $f4(x) = \begin{cases} x + 6 & \text{if } x < -2 \\ x^2 & \text{if } x \geq -2 \end{cases}$

33. $f(x) = 6x^3 - 15x^2 + 4x - 1$

(i) $[-2, 2]$ by $[-2, 2]$

(ii) $[-8, 8]$ by $[-8, 8]$

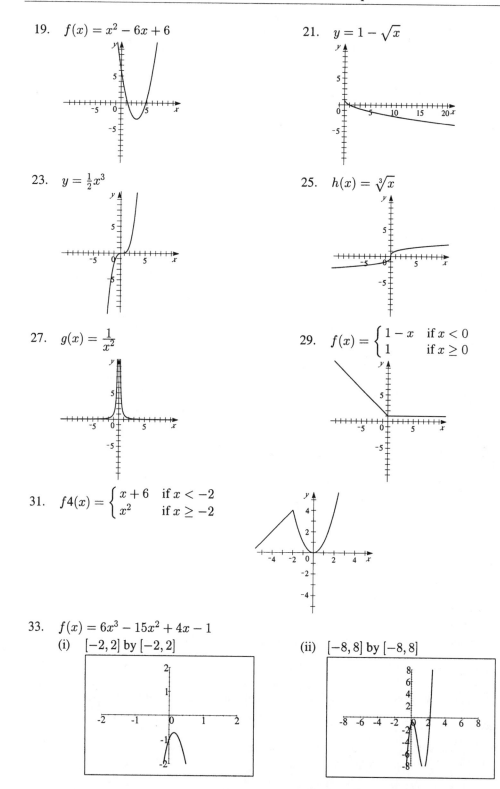

(iii) $[-4, 4]$ by $[-12, 12]$ (iv) $[-100, 100]$ by $[-100, 100]$

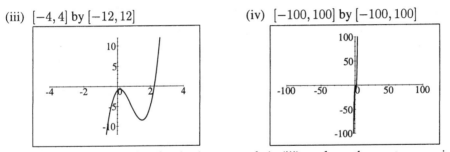

From the graphs, we see that the viewing rectangle in (iii) produces the most appropriate graph.

35. $f(x) = x^2 + 25x + 173$
$= (x^2 + 25x + \frac{625}{4}) + 173 - \frac{625}{4} = (x + \frac{25}{2})^2 + \frac{67}{4}$.
We use the viewing rectangle $[-30, 0]$ by $[0, 40]$.

37. $y = \dfrac{x}{\sqrt{x^2 + 16}}$. Since $\sqrt{x^2 + 16} \geq \sqrt{x^2} = |x|$, it

follows that y should behave like $\dfrac{x}{|x|}$. Thus we use the

viewing rectangle $[-20, 20]$ by $[-2, 2]$.

39. $f(x) = \sqrt{x^3 - 4x + 1}$. The domain consists of all x
where $x^3 - 4x + 1 \geq 0$. Using a graphing device, the
domain is approximately $[-2.1, 0.2] \cup [1.9, \infty)$.

41. Since M varies directly as z we have $M = kz$. Substituting $M = 120$ when $z = 15$, we find
$120 = k(15) \quad \Leftrightarrow \quad k = 8$. Therefore, $M = 8z$.

43. (a) The intensity I varies inversely as the square of the distance d, so $I = \dfrac{k}{d^2}$.

    (b) Substituting $I = 1000$ when $d = 8$, we get $1000 = \frac{k}{(8)^2} \quad \Leftrightarrow \quad k = 64,000$.

    (c) From parts (a) and (b), we have $I = \dfrac{64000}{d^2}$. Substituting $d = 20$, we get $I = \dfrac{64000}{(20)^2} = 160$

    candles.

45. Let v be the terminal velocity of the parachutist in mi/h and w be his weight in pounds. Since the
terminal velocity is directly proportional to the square root of the weight, we have $v = k\sqrt{w}$.

Substituting $v = 9$ when $w = 160$, we solve for k. This gives $9 = k\sqrt{160}$ $\Leftrightarrow$ $k = \frac{9}{\sqrt{160}} \approx 0.712$. Thus $v = 0.712\sqrt{w}$. When $w = 240$, the terminal velocity is $v = 0.712\sqrt{240} \approx 11$ mi/h.

47. Average rate of change $= \dfrac{f(2) - f(0)}{2 - 0} = \dfrac{[(2)^2 + 3(2)] - [0^2 + 3(0)]}{2} = \dfrac{4 + 6 - 0}{2} = 5.$

49. Average rate of change $= \dfrac{f(3 + h) - f(3)}{(3 + h) - 3} = \dfrac{\left[\frac{1}{3+h}\right] - \left[\frac{1}{3}\right]}{h} \cdot \dfrac{3(3 + h)}{3(3 + h)} = \dfrac{3 - (3 + h)}{3h(3 + h)}$

  $= \dfrac{-h}{3h(3 + h)} = \dfrac{-1}{3(3 + h)}.$

51. $f(x) = x^3 - 4x^2$ is graphed in the viewing rectangle $[-5, 5]$ by $[-20, 10]$. $f(x)$ is increasing on $(-\infty, 0]$ and $[2.67, \infty)$. It is decreasing on $[0, 2.67]$

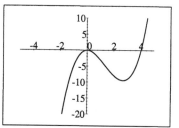

53. (a) $y = f(x) + 8$. Shift the graph of $f(x)$ upward 8 units.

  (b) $y = f(x + 8)$. Shift the graph of $f(x)$ to the left 8 units.

  (c) $y = 1 + 2f(x)$. Stretch the graph of $f(x)$ vertically by a factor of 2, then shift it upward 1 unit.

  (d) $y = f(x - 2) - 2$. Shift the graph of $f(x)$ to the right 2 units, then downward 2 units.

  (e) $y = f(-x)$. Reflect the graph of $f(x)$ about the y-axis.

  (f) $y = -f(-x)$. Reflect the graph of $f(x)$ first about the y-axis, then reflect about the x-axis.

  (g) $y = -f(x)$. Reflect the graph of $f(x)$ about the x-axis.

  (h) $y = f^{-1}(x)$. Reflect the graph of $f(x)$ about the line $y = x$.

55. (a) $f(x) = 2x^5 - 3x^2 + 2$.

  $f(-x) = 2(-x)^5 - 3(-x)^2 + 2 = -2x^5 - 3x^2 + 2$. Since $f(x) \neq f(-x)$, f is not even. $-f(x) = -2x^5 + 3x^2 - 2$. Since $-f(x) \neq f(-x)$, f is not odd.

  (b) $f(x) = x^3 - x^7$.

  $f(-x) = (-x)^3 - (-x)^7 = -(x^3 - x^7) = -f(x)$, hence f is odd.

  (c) $f(x) = \dfrac{1 - x^2}{1 + x^2}$. $f(-x) = \dfrac{1 - (-x)^2}{1 + (-x)^2} = \dfrac{1 - x^2}{1 + x^2} = f(x)$. Since $f(x) = f(-x)$, f is even.

  (d) $f(x) = \dfrac{1}{x + 2}$. $f(-x) = \dfrac{1}{(-x) + 2} = \dfrac{1}{2 - x}$. $-f(x) = -\dfrac{1}{x + 2}$. Since $f(x) \neq f(-x)$, f is not even, and since $f(-x) \neq -f(x)$, f is not odd.

57. $f(x) = x^2 + 4x + 1 = (x^2 + 4x + 4) + 1 - 4 = (x + 2)^2 - 3$

59. $g(x) = 2x^2 + 4x - 5 = 2(x^2 + 2x) - 5 = 2(x^2 + 2x + 1) - 5 - 2 = 2(x + 1)^2 - 7$. So the minimum value is $g(-1) = -7$.

61. $h(t) = -16t^2 + 48t + 32 = -16(t^2 - 3t) + 32 = -16(t^2 - 3t + \frac{9}{4}) + 32 + 36$
     $= -16(t^2 - 3t + \frac{9}{4}) + 68 = -16(t - \frac{3}{2})^2 + 68$
     The stone reaches a maximum height of 68 feet.

63. $f(x) = 3.3 + 1.6x - 2.5x^3$. In the first
     viewing rectangle, $[-2, 2]$ by $[-4, 8]$, we see
     that $f(x)$ has a local maximum and a local
     minimum.

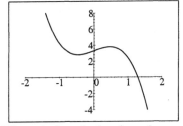

     In the next viewing rectangle, $[0.4, 0.5]$ by $[3.78, 3.80]$, we isolate the local maximum value as
     approximately 3.79 when $x \approx 0.46$. In the last viewing rectangle, $[-0.5, -0.4]$ by $[2.80, 2.82]$, we
     isolate the local minimum value as 2.81 when $x \approx -0.46$.

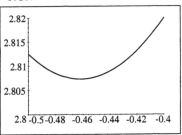

65. The sales of air conditioners will start to increase
     in May as it get hot, peaking in July and decreasing
     afterwards.

67. Let x be the width of the rectangle in cm and h be the height of the
     rectangle. If we orient the triangle on the xy-plane with the center of
     the base at the origin, then the coordinates of the vertices are $(-5, 0)$,
     $(5, 0)$, and $(0, 5\sqrt{3})$ (applying the Pythagorean Theorem). The point
     $\left(\frac{1}{2}x, h\right)$ must lie on the line segment joining the points $(5, 0)$ and
     $(0, 5\sqrt{3})$. This line segment has slope $-\sqrt{3}$ and y-intercept $5\sqrt{3}$ and
     so the equation is $y = -\sqrt{3}x + 5\sqrt{3}$. Thus
     $h = -\sqrt{3}\left(\frac{1}{2}x\right) + 5\sqrt{3} = \frac{-\sqrt{3}}{2}x + 5\sqrt{3} = \sqrt{3}\left(5 - \frac{x}{2}\right).$

     (a) The area of the rectangle is $A = xh = x \cdot \sqrt{3}(5 - \frac{x}{2}) = \sqrt{3}\,x\left(5 - \frac{x}{2}\right).$

     (b) $A = \sqrt{3}x\left(5 - \frac{x}{2}\right) = -\frac{\sqrt{3}}{2}(x^2 - 10x) = -\frac{\sqrt{3}}{2}(x^2 - 10x + 25) + \frac{25\sqrt{3}}{2}$
          $= -\frac{\sqrt{3}}{2}(x - 5)^2 + \frac{25\sqrt{3}}{2}.$ Therefore the area is maximum when $x = 5$ and by substitution

$h = \sqrt{3}(5 - \frac{5}{2}) = \frac{5\sqrt{3}}{2}$. Hence the dimensions of the rectangle with the largest area are 5 cm by $\frac{5\sqrt{3}}{2}$ cm.

69. $f(x) = x^2 - 3x + 2$ and $g(x) = 4 - 3x$.

  (a) $(f + g)(x) = (x^2 - 3x + 2) + (4 - 3x) = x^2 - 6x + 6$

  (b) $(f - g)(x) = (x^2 - 3x + 2) - (4 - 3x) = x^2 - 2$

  (c) $(fg)(x) = (x^2 - 3x + 2)(4 - 3x) = 4x^2 - 12x + 8 - 3x^3 + 9x^2 - 6x$
  $= -3x^3 + 13x^2 - 18x + 8$

  (d) $\left(\frac{f}{g}\right)(x) = \dfrac{x^2 - 3x + 2}{4 - 3x},\ x \neq \dfrac{4}{3}$

  (e) $(f \circ g)(x) = f(4 - 3x) = (4 - 3x)^2 - 3(4 - 3x) + 2 = 16 - 24x + 9x^2 - 12 + 9x + 2$
  $= 9x^2 - 15x + 6$

  (f) $(g \circ f)(x) = g(x^2 - 3x + 2) = 4 - 3(x^2 - 3x + 2) = -3x^2 + 9x - 2$

71. $f(x) = 3x - 1$ and $g(x) = 2x - x^2$.

  $(f \circ g)(x) = f(2x - x^2) = 3(2x - x^2) - 1 = -3x^2 + 6x - 1$, and the domain is $(-\infty, \infty)$.

  $(g \circ f)(x) = g(3x - 1) = 2(3x - 1) - (3x - 1)^2 = 6x - 2 - 9x^2 + 6x - 1 = -9x^2 + 12x - 3$, and the domain is $(-\infty, \infty)$

  $(f \circ f)(x) = f(3x - 1) = 3(3x - 1) - 1 = 9x - 4$, and the domain is $(-\infty, \infty)$.

  $(g \circ g)(x) = g(2x - x^2) = 2(2x - x^2) - (2x - x^2)^2 = 4x - 2x^2 - 4x^2 + 4x^3 - x^4$

  $= -x^4 + 4x^3 - 6x^2 + 4x$, and domain is $(-\infty, \infty)$.

73. $f(x) = \sqrt{1 - x}$, $g(x) = 1 - x^2$ and $h(x) = 1 + \sqrt{x}$.

  $(f \circ g \circ h)(x) = f(g(h(x))) = f\big(g(1 + \sqrt{x})\big) = f\left(1 - \left(1 + \sqrt{x}\right)^2\right) = f(1 - (1 + 2\sqrt{x} + x) =$
  $f(-x - 2\sqrt{x}) = \sqrt{1 - (-x - 2\sqrt{x})} = \sqrt{1 + 2\sqrt{x} + x} = \sqrt{(1 + \sqrt{x})^2} = 1 + \sqrt{x}$

75. $f(x) = 3 + x^3$. If $x_1 \neq x_2$, then $x_1^3 \neq x_2^3$ (unequal numbers have unequal cubes), and therefore $3 + x_1^3 \neq 3 + x_2^3$. Thus f is a one-to-one function.

77. $h(x) = \dfrac{1}{x^4}$. Since the fourth powers of a number and its negative are equal, h is not one-to-one. For example, $h(-1) = \dfrac{1}{(-1)^4} = 1$ and $h(1) = \dfrac{1}{(1)^4} = 1$, so $h(-1) = h(1)$.

79. $p(x) = 3.3 + 1.6x - 2.5x^3$. Using a graphing device and the Horizontal Line Test, we see that p is not a one-to-one function.

81. $f(x) = 3x - 2 \iff y = 3x - 2 \iff 3x = y + 2 \iff x = \frac{1}{3}(y + 2)$. So
     $f^{-1}(x) = \frac{1}{3}(x + 2)$.

83. $f(x) = (x + 1)^3 \iff y = (x + 1)^3 \iff x + 1 = \sqrt[3]{y} \iff x = -1 + \sqrt[3]{y}$. So
     $f^{-1}(x) = -1 + \sqrt[3]{x}$.

85. $f(x) = x^2 - 4,\ x \geq 0$.

     (a)   (b)
     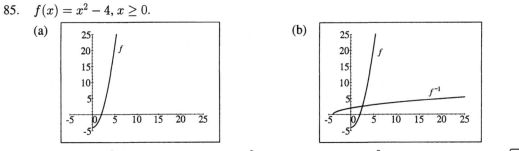

     (c) $f(x) = x^2 - 4,\ x \geq 0 \iff y = x^2 - 4,\ y \geq -4 \iff x^2 = y + 4 \iff x = \sqrt{y + 4}$.
     So $f^{-1}(x) = \sqrt{x + 4},\ x \geq -4$.

Chapter 2 Test

1. By the Vertical Line Test, figures (a) and (b) are graphs of functions. By the Horizontal Line Test, only figure (a) is the graph of a one-to-one function.

2. (a) $f(4) = \frac{\sqrt{4}}{4-1} = \frac{2}{3}$; $f(6) = \frac{\sqrt{6}}{6-1} = \frac{\sqrt{6}}{5}$; $f(a+1) = \frac{\sqrt{a+1}}{(a+1)-1} = \frac{\sqrt{a+1}}{a}$.

    (b) $f(x) = \frac{\sqrt{x}}{x-1}$. Our restrictions are that the input to the radical is nonnegative, and the denominator must not be equal to zero. Thus $x \geq 0$ and $x \neq 1$. In interval notation, the domain is $[0, 1) \cup (1, \infty)$.

3. (a) $M = k\dfrac{wh^2}{L}$.

    (b) Substituting $w = 4$, $h = 6$, $L = 12$, and $M = 4800$, we have $4800 = k\frac{(4)(6^2)}{12}$ $\Leftrightarrow$ $k = 400$. Thus $M = 400\dfrac{wh^2}{L}$.

    (c) Now if $L = 10$, $w = 3$, and $h = 10$, then $M = 400\frac{(3)(10^2)}{10} = 12,000$. So the beam can support $12,000$ pounds.

4. Average rate of change $= \dfrac{f(2+h) - f(2)}{(2+h) - 2} = \dfrac{[(2+h)^2 + 3(2+h)] - [2^2 + 3(2)]}{h}$
    $$= \frac{4 + 4h + h^2 + 6 + 3h - 4 - 6}{h} = \frac{7h + h^2}{h} = \frac{h(7+h)}{h} = 7 + h.$$

5. (a) $f(x) = x^3$

    (b) $g(x) = (x-1)^3 - 2$. To obtain the graph of g, shift the graph of f to the right 1 unit and downward 2 units.

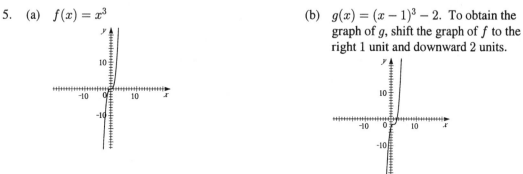

6. (a) $y = f(x-3) + 2$. Shift the graph of $f(x)$ to the right 3 units, then shift the graph upward 2 units.

    (b) $y = f(-x)$. Reflect the graph of $f(x)$ about the y-axis.

7. (a) $f(x) = 2x^2 - 8x + 13$
          $= 2(x^2 - 4x) + 13$
          $= 2(x^2 - 4x + 4) + 13 - 8$
          $= 2(x - 2)^2 + 5.$

    (b)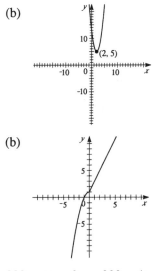

    (c) Since $f(x) = 2(x - 2)^2 + 5$ in standard form
         the minimum value of f is $f(2) = 5$.

8. (a) $f(-2) = 1 - (-2)^2 = 1 - 4 = -3$
         (since $-2 \leq 0$).

         $f(1) = 2(1) + 1 = 2 + 1 = 3$ (since
         $1 > 0$).

    (b)

9. (a) Since 800 ft of fencing are available, $4x + 2y = 800 \iff 2y = 800 - 4x \iff$
         $y = 400 - 2x$. Thus the area of the pens is $A = xy = x(400 - 2x) = 400x - 2x^2$.

    (b) $A = 400x - 2x^2 = -2(x^2 - 200x) = -2(x^2 - 200x + 100^2) + 20000$
         $= -2(x - 100)^2 + 20000$. So, when $x = 100$ ft the total area will be maximized.

10. $f(x) = x^2 + 2x - 1$; $g(x) = 2x - 3$.
    (a) $(f \circ g)(x) = f(g(x)) = f(2x - 3) = (2x - 3)^2 + 2(2x - 3) - 1$
         $= 4x^2 - 12x + 9 + 4x - 6 - 1 = 4x^2 - 8x + 2$
    (b) $(g \circ f)(x) = g(f(x)) = g(x^2 + 2x - 1) = 2(x^2 + 2x - 1) - 3 = 2x^2 + 4x - 2 - 3$
         $= 2x^2 + 4x - 5$
    (c) $f(g(2)) = f(1) = (1)^2 + 2(1) - 1 = 2.$ (We have used the fact that $g(2) = 2(2) - 3 = 1$.)
    (d) $g(f(2)) = g(7) = 2(7) - 3 = 11.$ (We have used the fact that $f(2) = 2^2 + 2(2) - 1 = 7$.)
    (e) $(g \circ g \circ g)(x) = g(g(g(x))) = g(g(2x - 3)) = g(4x - 9) = 2(4x - 9) - 3 = 8x - 18 - 3$
         $= 8x - 21.$ (We have used the fact that $g(2x - 3) = 2(2x - 3) - 3 = 4x - 6 - 3 = 4x - 9$.)

11. (a) $f(x) = \sqrt{3 - x}, x \leq 3 \iff$
         $y = \sqrt{3 - x} \iff y^2 = 3 - x \iff$
         $x = 3 - y^2$. Thus $f^{-1}(x) = 3 - x^2$,
         $x \geq 0$.

    (b) $f(x) = \sqrt{3 - x}, x \leq 3$ and
         $f^{-1}(x) = 3 - x^2, x \geq 0$

         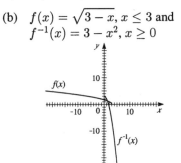

12. (a) The domain of f is $[0, 6]$, and
          the range of f is $[1, 7]$.

     (b)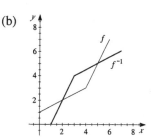

     (c) Average rate of change $= \dfrac{f(6) - f(2)}{6 - 2} = \dfrac{7 - 2}{4} = \dfrac{5}{4}$.

13. (a) $f(x) = 3x^4 - 14x^2 + 5x - 3$. The
          graph is shown in the viewing rectangle
          $[-10, 10]$ by $[-30, 10]$.

     (b) No, by the Horizontal Line Test.

     (c) The local minimum is approximately
          -27.18 when $x \approx -1.61$. Shown is the
          viewing rectangle $[-1.65, -1.55]$ by
          $[-27.5, -27]$.

          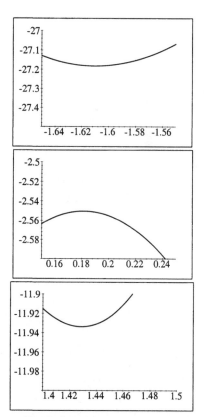

          The local maximum is approximately
          -2.55 when $x \approx 0.18$. Shown is the
          viewing rectangle $[0.15, 0.25]$ by
          $[-2.6, -2.5]$.

          The local minimum is approximately
          -11.93 when $x \approx 1.43$. Shown is the
          viewing rectangle $[1.4, 1.5]$ by
          $[-12, -11.9]$.

     (d) Using the graph in part (a) and the local minimum, -27.18, found in part (c), we see that the
          range is $[-27.18, \infty)$

(e)   Using the information from part (c) and the graph in part (a), $f(x)$ is increasing on the intervals $[-1.61, 0.18]$ and $[1.43, \infty)$ and decreasing on the intervals $(-\infty, -1.61]$ and $[0.18, 1.43]$.

Principles of Modeling

1. (a)

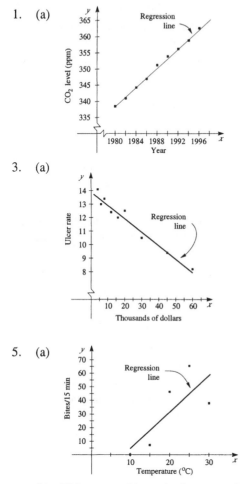

(b) Using a graphing calculator, we obtain
    the regression line $y = 1.5125x - 2656.4$.

(c) Using $x = 1998$ in the equation
    $y = 1.5125x - 2656.4$, we get
    $y \approx 365.6$ ppm CO_2. This value is close
    to the observed value of 366.7 ppm CO_2.

3. (a)

(b) Using a graphing calculator, we obtain the
    regression line $y = -0.0995x + 13.9$,
    where x is measured in thousands of
    dollars.

(c) Using the regression line equation,
    $y = -0.0995x + 13.9$, we get an estimated
    $y = 11.4$ ulcers per 100 population when
    $x = \$25,000$.

(d) Again using $y = -0.0995x + 13.9$, we get
    an estimated $y = 5.8$ ulcers per 100
    population when $x = \$80,000$.

5. (a)

(b) Using a graphing calculator, we obtain the regression line for the temperature-bite data
    $y = 2.6768x - 22.19$, and for the wind speed-bite data $y = -3.5336x + 46.73$.

(c) The correlation coefficient for the temperature-bite data is $r = 0.77$, so a linear model is not
    appropriate. The correlation coefficient for the wind-bite data is $r = -0.89$, so a linear model
    is more suitable in this case.

7. (a)

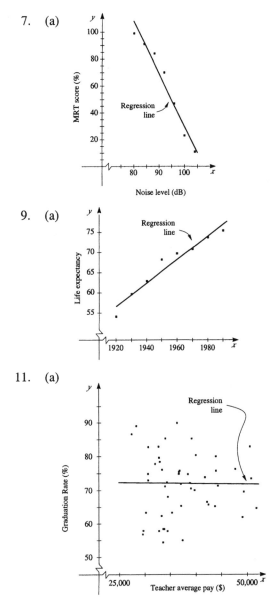

(b) Using a graphing calculator, we obtain
$y = -3.9018x + 419.7$.

(c) The correlation coefficient is $r = -0.98$,
so linear model is appropriate for x
between 80 dB and 104 dB.

(d) Substituting $x = 94$ into the regression
equation, we get
$y = -3.9018(94) + 419.7 \approx 53$. So
the intelligibility is about 53%.

9. (a)

(b) Using a graphing calculator, we obtain
$y = 0.29083x - 501.8$.

(c) We use $x = 2000$ in the equation
$y = 0.29083x - 501.8$, to get $y = 79.9$,
that is, a life expectancy of 79.9 years.

11. (a)

(b) Using a graphing calculator, we obtain
$y = -0.000012x + 72.0$

(c) The correlation coefficient is
$r = -0.00812$, so there is very little
correlation. It appears that teachers' salaries
do not affect graduation rates.

13. The students should find a fairly strong correlation between shoe size and height.

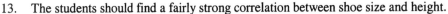

Chapter Three

Exercises 3.1

1. $P(x) = x^3 - 27$

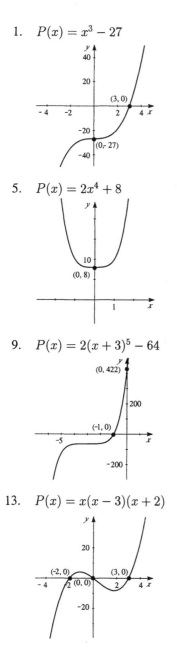

3. $P(x) = -(x+2)^3$

5. $P(x) = 2x^4 + 8$

7. $P(x) = -(x-1)^4 + 16$

9. $P(x) = 2(x+3)^5 - 64$

11. $P(x) = (x-1)(x+2)$

13. $P(x) = x(x-3)(x+2)$

15. $P(x) = (x-3)(x+2)(3x-2)$

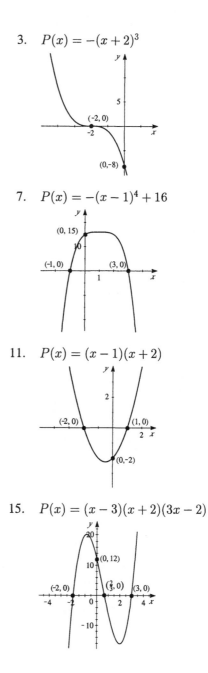

17. $P(x) = (x - 1)^2(x - 3)$

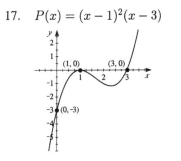

19. $P(x) = \frac{1}{12}(x + 2)^2(x - 3)^2$

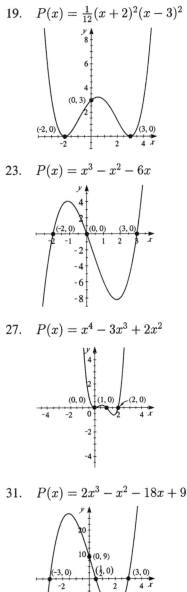

21. $P(x) = x^3(x + 2)(x - 3)^2$

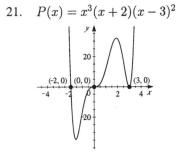

23. $P(x) = x^3 - x^2 - 6x$

25. $P(x) = -x^3 + x^2 + 12x$

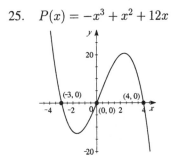

27. $P(x) = x^4 - 3x^3 + 2x^2$

29. $P(x) = x^3 + x^2 - x - 1$

31. $P(x) = 2x^3 - x^2 - 18x + 9$

33. $P(x) = x^4 - 2x^3 - 8x + 16$

35. $P(x) = x^4 - 3x^2 - 4$

37. III   39. V   41. VI

43. $P(x) = 3x^3 - x^2 + 5x + 1$; $Q(x) = 3x^3$.
    Since P has odd degree and positive leading coefficient, it has the following end behavior:
    $y \to \infty$ as $x \to \infty$ and $y \to -\infty$ as $x \to -\infty$.

On the large viewing rectangle, the graphs of P and Q look almost the same.

On the small viewing rectangle, the graphs of P and Q have different intercepts.

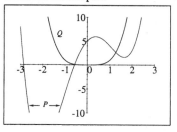

45. $P(x) = x^4 - 7x^2 + 5x + 5$; $Q(x) = x^4$.
    Since P has even degree and positive leading coefficient, it has the following end behavior:
    $y \to \infty$ as $x \to \infty$ and $y \to \infty$ as $x \to -\infty$.

On the large viewing rectangle, the graphs of P and Q look almost the same.

On the small viewing rectangle, the graphs of P and Q look very different and have different intercepts..

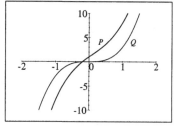

47. $P(x) = x^{11} - 9x^9$; $Q(x) = x^{11}$.
    Since P has odd degree and positive leading coefficient, it has the following end behavior:
    $y \to \infty$ as $x \to \infty$ and $y \to -\infty$ as $x \to -\infty$.

On the large viewing rectangle, the graphs of P and Q look like they have the same end behavior.

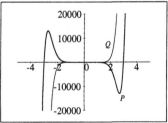

On the small viewing rectangle, the graphs of P and Q look very different and seem to have different end behavior.

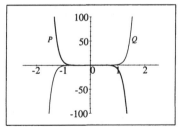

49. $y = -x^2 + 8x$, $[-4, 12]$ by $[-50, 30|$.
    y-intercept: 0
    Local maximum: $(4, 16)$

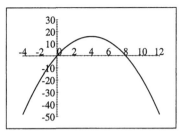

51. $y = x^3 - 12x + 9$, $[-5, 5]$ by $[-30, 30]$.
    Local maximum: $(-2, 25)$
    Local minimum: $(2, -7)$

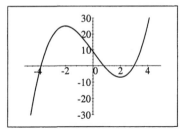

53. $y = x^4 + 4x^3$, $[-5, 5]$ by $[-30, 30]$.
    Local minimum: $(-3, -27)$

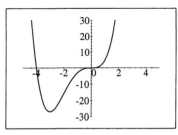

55. $y = 3x^5 - 5x^3 + 3$, $[-3, 3]$ by $[-5, 10]$.
    Local maximum: $(-1, 5)$
    Local minimum: $(1, 1)$

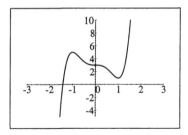

57. $y = -2x^2 + 3x + 5.$

One local maximum at $(0.75, 6.13)$.

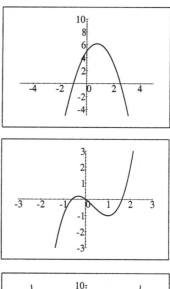

59. $y = x^3 - x^2 - x.$

One local maximum at $(-0.33, 0.19)$ and one local minimum at $(1.00, -1.00)$.

61. $y = x^4 - 5x^2 + 4.$

One local maximum at $(0, 4)$ and two local minima at $(-1.58, -2.25)$ and $(1.58, -2.25)$.

63. $y = (x - 2)^5 + 32.$

No extrema.

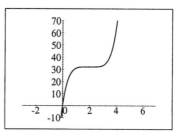

65. $y = x^8 - 3x^4 + x.$

One local maximum at $(0.44, 0.33)$ and two local minima at $(1.09, -1.15)$ and $(-1.12, -3.36)$.

67. $P(x) = cx^3$; $c = 1, 2, 5$, and $\frac{1}{2}$. Increasing the value of c stretches the graph vertically.

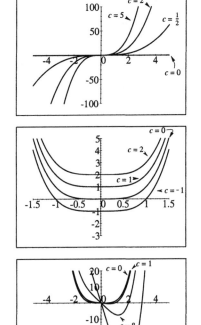

69. $P(x) = x^4 + c$; $c = -1, 0, 1$, and 2.
Increasing the value of c moves the graph up.

71. $P(x) = x^4 - cx$; $c = 0, 1, 8$, and 27.
Increasing the value of c causes a deeper dip in the graph, in the fourth quadrant, and moves the positive x-intercept to the right.

73. (a)

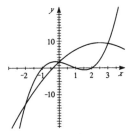

   (b) The two graphs appear to intersect at 3 points.

   (c) $x^3 - 2x^2 - x + 2 = -x^2 + 5x + 2$ $\Leftrightarrow$ $x^3 - x^2 - 6x = 0$ $\Leftrightarrow$ $x(x^2 - x - 6) = 0$
       $\Leftrightarrow$ $x(x-3)(x+2) = 0$. Then either $x = 0$, $x = 3$, or $x = -2$. If $x = 0$, then $y = 2$; if
       $x = 3$ then $y = 8$; if $x = -2$, then $y = -12$. Hence the points where the two graphs intersect
       are $(0, 2)$, $(3, 8)$, and $(-2, -12)$.

75. (a) Since f and g are odd, $f(-x) = -f(x)$ and $g(-x) = -g(x)$. Therefore,
       $(f + g)(-x) = f(-x) + g(-x) = -f(x) - g(x) = -[f(x) + g(x)] = -(f + g)(x)$, and so
       the function $f + g$ is also odd.

   (b) Since f and g are even, $f(-x) = f(x)$ and $g(-x) = g(x)$. Therefore,
       $(f + g)(-x) = f(-x) + g(-x) = f(x) + g(x) = (f + g)(x)$, and so the function $f + g$ is
       also even.

(c) Since f is odd and g is even, $f(-x) = -f(x)$ and $g(-x) = g(x)$. Therefore, $(f + g)(-x) = f(-x) + g(-x) = -f(x) + g(x) \neq -[f(x) + g(x)]$ (since $g(x) \neq -g(x)$ if x is a point for which $g(x) \neq 0$), and so the function $f + g$ is not odd. Also, $-f(x) + g(x) \neq f(x) + g(x)$ (for a similar reason), and so the function $f + g$ is not even. Thus, $f + g$ is neither even nor odd.

(d) Let $P(x)$ be a polynomial containing only odd powers of x. Then each term of $P(x)$ can be written as Cx^{2n+1}, for some constant C and integer n. Since $C(-x)^{2n+1} = -Cx^{2n+1}$, each term of $P(x)$ is an odd function. Thus by part (a), $P(x)$ is an odd function.

(e) Let $P(x)$ be a polynomial containing only even powers of x. Then each term of $P(x)$ can be written as Cx^{2n}, for some constant C and integer n. Since $C(-x)^{2n} = Cx^{2n}$, each term of $P(x)$ is an even function. Thus by part (b), $P(x)$ is an even function.

(f) Since $P(x)$ contains both even and odd powers of x, we can write it in the form $P(x) = R(x) + Q(x)$, where $R(x)$ contains all the even-powered terms in $P(x)$ and $Q(x)$ contains all the odd. By part (d), $Q(x)$ is an odd function, and by part (e), $R(x)$ is an even function. Thus, since neither $Q(x)$ nor $R(x)$ are constantly 0 (by assumption), by part (c), $P(x) = R(x) + Q(x)$ is neither even nor odd.

(g) $P(x) = x^5 + 6x^3 - x^2 - 2x + 5 = (x^5 + 6x^3 - 2x) + (-x^2 + 5) = P_O(x) + P_E(x)$ where $P_O(x) = x^5 + 6x^3 - 2x$ and $P_E(x) = -x^2 + 5$. Since $P_O(x)$ contains only odd powers of x, it is an odd function, and since $P_E(x)$ contains only even powers of x, it is an even function.

77. (a) Let h = height of the box. Then the total length of all 12 edges is $8x + 4h = 144$ in. Thus, $8x + 4h = 144 \iff 2x + h = 36 \iff h = 36 - 2x$. The volume of the box is equal to (area of base) $\times$ (height) $= (x^2) \times (36 - 2x) = -2x^3 + 36x^2$. Therefore, the volume of the box is $V(x) = -2x^3 + 36x^2 = 2x^2(18 - x)$.

(b) Since the length of the base is x, we must have $x > 0$. Likewise, the height must be positive so $36 - 2x > 0 \iff x < 18$. Putting these together, we get that the domain of V is $0 < x < 18$.

(c) Using the domain from part (b), we graph V in the viewing rectangle $[0, 18]$ by $[0, 2000]$. The maximum volume is $V = 1728 \text{ in}^3$ when $x = 12$ in.

79. $P(t) = 120t - 0.4t^4 + 1000$

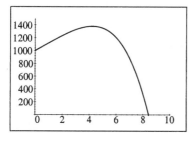

(a) A maximum population of approximately 1380 is attained after 4.22 months.

(b) The rabbit population disappears after approximately 8.42 months.

81. (a) From the graph,
          $P(x) = x^3 - 4x = x(x-2)(x+2)$ has
          three x-intercepts and two local extrema.

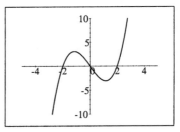

     (b) From the graph,
          $Q(x) = x^3 + 4x = x(x^2 + 4)$ has
          one x-intercept and no local extrema.

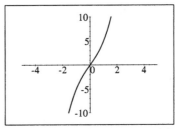

     (c) For the x-intercepts of $P(x) = x^3 - ax$, we solve $x^3 - ax = 0$. Then we have $x(x^2 - a) = 0$
          $\Leftrightarrow$ $x = 0$ or $x^2 = a$. If $x^2 = a$, then $x = \pm\sqrt{a}$. So P has 3 x-intercepts. Since
          $P(x) = x(x^2 - a) = x(x + \sqrt{a})(x - \sqrt{a})$, by part (c) of problem 67, P has 2 local extrema.
          For the x-intercepts of $Q(x) = x^3 + ax$, we solve $x^3 + ax = 0$. Then we have $x(x^2 + a) = 0$
          $\Leftrightarrow$ $x = 0$ or $x^2 = -a$. The equation $x^2 = -a$ has no real solutions because $a > 0$. So Q
          has 1 x-intercept. We now show that Q is always increasing and hence has no extrema. If
          $x_1 < x_2$, then $ax_1 < ax_2$ (because $a > 0$) and $x_1^3 < x_2^3$. So we have $x_1^3 + ax_1 < x_2^3 + ax_2$, and
          hence $Q(x_1) < Q(x_2)$. Thus Q is increasing, that is, its graph always rises, and so it has no
          local extrema.

83. Since the polynomial shown has five zeros, it has at least five factors, and so the degree of the
     polynomial is greater than or equal to 5.

85. No, it is not possible. Clearly a polynomial must have a local minimum between any two local
     maxima.

Exercises 3.2

1.
$$\begin{array}{r} x\ +1 \\ x+3\overline{\smash{\big)}\ x^2+4x-8} \\ \underline{x^2+3x} \\ x-8 \\ \underline{x+3} \\ -11 \end{array}$$

Thus the quotient is $x+1$ and the remainder is -11.

3.
$$\begin{array}{r} x^2\ +4x\ +22 \\ x-4\overline{\smash{\big)}\ x^3+0x^2\ +6x+\ 5} \\ \underline{x^3-4x^2} \\ 4x^2\ +6x \\ \underline{4x^2-16x} \\ 22x+\ 5 \\ \underline{22x-88} \\ 93 \end{array}$$

Thus the quotient is $x^2-4x+22$ and the remainder is 93.

5.
$$\begin{array}{r} x\ +2 \\ x^2-2x+2\overline{\smash{\big)}\ x^3+0x^2+6x+3} \\ \underline{x^3-2x^2+2x} \\ 2x^2+4x+3 \\ \underline{2x^2-4x+4} \\ 8x-1 \end{array}$$

Thus the quotient is $x+2$, and the remainder is $8x-1$.

7.
$$\begin{array}{r} 3x\ +1 \\ 2x^2+0x+5\overline{\smash{\big)}\ 6x^3+2x^2+22x+0} \\ \underline{6x^3\qquad\ +15x} \\ 2x^2\ +7x+0 \\ \underline{2x^2\qquad\ +5} \\ 7x-5 \end{array}$$

Thus the quotient is $3x+1$, and the remainder is $7x-5$.

9.
$$\begin{array}{r} x^4\qquad\qquad +1 \\ x^2+1\overline{\smash{\big)}\ x^6+0x^5+x^4+0x^3+x^2+0x+1} \\ \underline{x^6\qquad+x^4} \\ 0\qquad+x^2\qquad+1 \\ \underline{x^2\qquad+1} \\ 0 \end{array}$$

Thus the quotient is x^4+1, and the remainder is 0.

11. The synthetic division table for this problem takes the following form.

$$\begin{array}{r|rrr} 3 & 1 & -5 & 4 \\ & & 3 & -6 \\ \hline & 1 & -2 & -2 \end{array}$$

Thus the quotient is $x-2$, and the remainder is -2.

13. The synthetic division table for this problem takes the following form.

$$6 \,\big|\; \begin{array}{ccc} 3 & 5 & 0 \\ & 18 & 138 \\ \hline 3 & 23 & 138 \end{array}$$

Thus the quotient is $3x + 23$, and the remainder is 138.

15. Since $x + 2 = x - (-2)$, the synthetic division table for this problem takes the following form.

$$-2 \,\big|\; \begin{array}{cccc} 1 & 2 & 2 & 1 \\ & -2 & 0 & -4 \\ \hline 1 & 0 & 2 & -3 \end{array}$$

Thus the quotient is $x^2 + 2$, and the remainder is -3.

17. Since $x + 3 = x - (-3)$ and $x^3 - 8x + 2 = x^3 + 0x^2 - 8x + 2$, the synthetic division table for this problem takes the following form.

$$-3 \,\big|\; \begin{array}{cccc} 1 & 0 & -8 & 2 \\ & -3 & 9 & -3 \\ \hline 1 & -3 & 1 & -1 \end{array}$$

Thus the quotient is $x^2 - 3x + 1$, and the remainder is -1.

19. Since $x^5 + 3x^3 - 6 = x^5 + 0x^4 + 3x^3 + 0x^2 + 0x - 6$, the synthetic division table for this problem takes the following form.

$$1 \,\big|\; \begin{array}{cccccc} 1 & 0 & 3 & 0 & 0 & -6 \\ & 1 & 1 & 4 & 4 & 4 \\ \hline 1 & 1 & 4 & 4 & 4 & -2 \end{array}$$

Thus the quotient is $x^4 + x^3 + 4x^2 + 4x + 4$, and the remainder is -2.

21. The synthetic division table for this problem takes the following form.

$$\tfrac{1}{2} \,\big|\; \begin{array}{cccc} 2 & 3 & -2 & 1 \\ & 1 & 2 & 0 \\ \hline 2 & 4 & 0 & 1 \end{array}$$

Thus the quotient is $2x^2 + 4x$, and the remainder is 1.

23. Since $x^3 - 27 = x^3 + 0x^2 + 0x - 27$, the synthetic division table for this problem takes the following form.

$$3 \,\big|\; \begin{array}{cccc} 1 & 0 & 0 & -27 \\ & 3 & 9 & 27 \\ \hline 1 & 3 & 9 & 0 \end{array}$$

Thus the quotient is $x^2 + 3x + 9$, and the remainder is 0.

25. $P(x) = 4x^2 + 12x + 5$, $c = -1$

$$-1 \,\big|\; \begin{array}{ccc} 4 & 12 & 5 \\ & -4 & -8 \\ \hline 4 & 8 & -3 \end{array}$$

Therefore by the Remainder Theorem, $P(-1) = -3$.

27. $P(x) = x^3 + 3x^2 - 7x + 6$, $c = 2$

$$2 \,\big|\; \begin{array}{cccc} 1 & 3 & -7 & 6 \\ & 2 & 10 & 6 \\ \hline 1 & 5 & 3 & 12 \end{array}$$

Therefore by the Remainder Theorem, $P(2) = 12$.

29. $P(x) = x^3 + 2x^2 - 7$, $c = -2$

$$-2 \,\big|\; \begin{array}{cccc} 1 & 2 & 0 & -7 \\ & -2 & 0 & 0 \\ \hline 1 & 0 & 0 & -7 \end{array}$$

Therefore by the Remainder Theorem, $P(-2) = -7$.

31. $P(x) = 5x^4 + 30x^3 - 40x^2 + 36x + 14, c = -7$

$$\begin{array}{r|rrrrr} -7 & 5 & 30 & -40 & 36 & 14 \\ & & -35 & 35 & 35 & -497 \\ \hline & 5 & -5 & -5 & 71 & -483 \end{array}$$ Therefore by the Remainder Theorem, $P(-7) = -483$.

33. $P(x) = x^7 - 3x^2 - 1 = x^7 + 0x^6 + 0x^5 + 0x^4 + 0x^3 - 3x^2 + 0x - 1, c = 3$

$$\begin{array}{r|rrrrrrrr} 3 & 1 & 0 & 0 & 0 & 0 & -3 & 0 & -1 \\ & & 3 & 9 & 27 & 81 & 243 & 720 & 2160 \\ \hline & 1 & 3 & 9 & 27 & 81 & 240 & 720 & 2159 \end{array}$$ Therefore by the Remainder Theorem, $P(3) = 2159$.

35. $P(x) = 3x^3 + 4x^2 - 2x + 1, c = \frac{2}{3}$

$$\begin{array}{r|rrrr} \frac{2}{3} & 3 & 4 & -2 & 1 \\ & & 2 & 4 & \frac{4}{3} \\ \hline & 3 & 6 & 2 & \frac{7}{3} \end{array}$$ Therefore by the Remainder Theorem, $P\left(\frac{2}{3}\right) = \frac{7}{3}$.

37. $P(x) = x^3 + 2x^2 - 3x - 8, c = 0.1$

$$\begin{array}{r|rrrr} 0.1 & 1 & 2 & -3 & -8 \\ & & 0.1 & 0.21 & -0.279 \\ \hline & 1 & 2.1 & -2.79 & -8.279 \end{array}$$ Therefore by the Remainder Theorem, $P(0.1) = -8.279$.

39. $P(x) = x^3 - 3x^2 + 3x - 1, c = 1$

$$\begin{array}{r|rrrr} 1 & 1 & -3 & 3 & -1 \\ & & 1 & -2 & 1 \\ \hline & 1 & -2 & 1 & 0 \end{array}$$ Since the remainder is 0, $x - 1$ is a factor.

41. $P(x) = 2x^3 + 7x^2 + 6x - 5, c = \frac{1}{2}$

$$\begin{array}{r|rrrr} \frac{1}{2} & 2 & 7 & 6 & -5 \\ & & 1 & 4 & 5 \\ \hline & 2 & 8 & 10 & 0 \end{array}$$ Since the remainder is 0, $x - \frac{1}{2}$ is a factor.

43. $P(x) = x^3 - x^2 - 11x + 15, c = 3$

$$\begin{array}{r|rrrr} 3 & 1 & -1 & -11 & 15 \\ & & 3 & 6 & -15 \\ \hline & 1 & 2 & -5 & 0 \end{array}$$

Since the remainder is 0, we know that 3 is a zero $x^3 - x^2 - 11x + 15 = (x - 3)(x^2 + 2x - 5)$.
Now $x^2 + 2x - 5 = 0$ when $x = \dfrac{-2 \pm \sqrt{2^2 + 4(1)(5)}}{2} = -1 \pm \sqrt{6}$. Hence, the zeros are $-1 - \sqrt{6}, -1 + \sqrt{6}$, and 3.

45.   Since the zeros are $x = -1$, $x = 1$, and $x = 3$, the factors are $x + 1$, $x - 1$, and $x - 3$. Thus $P(x) = (x + 1)(x - 1)(x - 3) = x^3 - 3x^2 - x + 3$.

47.   Since the zeros are $x = -1$, $x = 1$, $x = 3$, and $x = 5$, the factors are $x + 1$, $x - 1$, $x - 3$, and $x - 5$. Thus $P(x) = (x + 1)(x - 1)(x - 3)(x - 5) = x^4 - 8x^3 + 14x^2 + 8x - 15$.

49.   Since the zeros of the polynomial are 1, -2, and 3, it follows that $P(x) = C(x - 1)(x + 2)(x - 3)$ $= C(x^3 - 2x^2 - 5x + 6) = Cx^3 - 2Cx^2 - 5Cx + 6C$. Since the coefficient of x^2 is to be 3, $-2C = 3$ so $C = -\frac{3}{2}$. Therefore, $P(x) = -\frac{3}{2}(x^3 - 2x^2 - 5x + 6) = -\frac{3}{2}x^3 + 3x^2 + \frac{15}{2}x - 9$ is the polynomial.

51. (A) By the Remainder Theorem the remainder when $P(x) = 6x^{1000} - 17x^{562} + 12x + 26$ is divided by $x + 1$ is
$$P(-1) = 6(-1)^{1000} - 17(-1)^{562} + 12(-1) + 26 = 6 - 17 - 12 + 26 = 3.$$

(B) If $x - 1$ is a factor of $Q(x) = x^{567} - 3x^{400} + x^9 + 2$, then $Q(1)$ must equal 0.
$Q(1) = (1)^{567} - 3(1)^{400} + (1)^9 + 2 = 1 - 3 + 1 + 2 = 1 \neq 0$, so $x - 1$ is not a factor.

Exercises 3.3

1. $P(x) = x^3 - 4x^2 + 3$ has possible rational zeros ± 1 and ± 3.

3. $R(x) = 2x^5 + 3x^3 + 4x^2 - 8$ has possible rational zeros $\pm 1, \pm 2, \pm 4, \pm 8, \pm\frac{1}{2}$.

5. $P(x) = x^3 + 3x^2 - 4$. The possible rational zeros are $\pm 1, \pm 2, \pm 4$. $P(x)$ has 1 variation in sign and hence 1 positive real zero. $P(-x) = -x^3 + 3x^2 - 4$ has 2 variations in sign and hence 0 or 2 negative real zeros.

$$\begin{array}{r|rrrr} 1 & 1 & 3 & 0 & -4 \\ & & 1 & 4 & 4 \\ \hline & 1 & 4 & 4 & 0 \end{array} \Rightarrow \quad x = 1 \text{ is a zero.}$$

$P(x) = x^3 + 3x^2 - 4 = (x-1)(x^2 + 4x + 4) = (x-1)(x+2)^2$. Therefore, the zeros are $x = -2, 1$.

7. $P(x) = x^3 - 3x - 2$. The possible rational zeros are $\pm 1, \pm 2$. $P(x)$ has 1 variation in sign and hence 1 positive real zero. $P(-x) = -x^3 + 3x - 2$ has 2 variations in sign and hence 0 or 2 negative real zeros.

$$\begin{array}{r|rrrr} 1 & 1 & 0 & -3 & -2 \\ & & 1 & 1 & -2 \\ \hline & 1 & 1 & -2 & -4 \end{array} \Rightarrow \quad x = 1 \text{ is not a zero.}$$

$$\begin{array}{r|rrrr} 2 & 1 & 0 & -3 & -2 \\ & & 2 & 4 & 2 \\ \hline & 1 & 2 & 1 & 0 \end{array} \Rightarrow \quad x = 2 \text{ is a zero.}$$

$P(x) = x^3 - 3x - 2 = (x-2)(x^2 + 2x + 1) = (x-2)(x+1)^2$. Therefore, the zeros are $x = 2, -1$.

9. $P(x) = x^3 - 6x^2 + 12x - 8$. The possible rational zeros are $\pm 1, \pm 2, \pm 4, \pm 8$. $P(x)$ has 3 variations in sign and hence 1 or 3 positive real zeros. $P(-x) = -x^3 - 6x^2 - 12x - 8$ has no variations in sign and hence 0 negative real zeros.

$$\begin{array}{r|rrrr} 1 & 1 & -6 & 12 & -8 \\ & & 1 & -5 & 7 \\ \hline & 1 & -5 & 7 & -1 \end{array} \Rightarrow \quad x = 1 \text{ is not a zero.}$$

$$\begin{array}{r|rrrr} 2 & 1 & -6 & 12 & -8 \\ & & 2 & -8 & 8 \\ \hline & 1 & -4 & 4 & 0 \end{array} \Rightarrow \quad x = 2 \text{ is a zero.}$$

$P(x) = x^3 - 6x^2 + 12x - 8 = (x-2)(x^2 - 4x + 4) = (x-2)^3$. Therefore, the zero is $x = 2$.

11. $P(x) = x^3 - 4x^2 + x + 6$. The possible rational zeros are $\pm 1, \pm 2, \pm 3, \pm 6$. $P(x)$ has 2 variations in sign and hence 0 or 2 positive real zeros. $P(-x) = -x^3 - 4x^2 - x + 6$ has 1 variation in sign and hence 1 negative real zeros.

$$\begin{array}{r|rrrr} -1 & 1 & -4 & 1 & 6 \\ & & -1 & 5 & -6 \\ \hline & 1 & -5 & 6 & 0 \end{array} \Rightarrow \quad x + 1 \text{ is a factor.}$$

So $P(x) = x^3 - 4x^2 + x + 6 = (x+1)(x^2 - 5x + 6) = (x+1)(x-3)(x-2)$. Therefore, the zeros are $x = -1, 2, 3$.

13. $P(x) = x^3 + 3x^2 + 6x + 4$. The possible rational zeros are $\pm 1, \pm 2, \pm 4$. $P(x)$ has no variation in sign and hence no positive real zeros. $P(-x) = -x^3 + 3x^2 - 6x + 4$ has 3 variations in sign and hence 1 or 3 negative real zeros.

$$
\begin{array}{r|rrrr}
-1 & 1 & 3 & 6 & 4 \\
   &   & -1 & -2 & -4 \\
\hline
   & 1 & 2 & 4 & 0
\end{array}
\quad \Rightarrow \quad x + 1 \text{ is a factor.}
$$

So $P(x) = x^3 + 3x^2 + 6x + 4 = (x + 1)(x^2 + 2x + 4)$. Now, $Q(x) = x^2 + 2x + 4$ has no real zeros, since the discriminant of this quadratic is $b^2 - 4ac = (2)^2 - 4(1)(4) = -12 < 0$. Thus, the only real zero is $x = -1$.

15. Method #1: $P(x) = x^4 - 5x^2 + 4$. The possible rational zeros are $\pm 1, \pm 2, \pm 4$. $P(x)$ has 1 variation in sign and hence 1 positive real zero. $P(-x) = x^4 - 5x^2 + 4$ has 2 variations in sign and hence 0 or 2 negative real zeros.

$$
\begin{array}{r|rrrrr}
1 & 1 & 0 & -5 & 0 & 4 \\
  &   & 1 & 1 & -4 & -4 \\
\hline
  & 1 & 1 & -4 & -4 & 0
\end{array}
\quad \Rightarrow \quad x = 1 \text{ is a zero.}
$$

Thus $P(x) = x^4 - 5x^2 + 4 = (x - 1)(x^3 + x^2 - 4x - 4)$. Continuing with the quotient we have:

$$
\begin{array}{r|rrrr}
-1 & 1 & 1 & -4 & -4 \\
   &   & -1 & 0 & 4 \\
\hline
   & 1 & 0 & -4 & 0
\end{array}
\quad \Rightarrow \quad x = -1 \text{ is a zero.}
$$

$P(x) = x^4 - 5x^2 + 4 = (x - 1)(x + 1)(x^2 - 4) = (x - 1)(x + 1)(x - 2)(x + 2)$. Therefore, the zeros are $x = \pm 1, \pm 2$.

Method #2: Substituting $u = x^2$, the polynomial becomes $P(u) = u^2 - 5u + 4$, which factors: $u^2 - 5u + 4 = (u - 1)(u - 4) = (x^2 - 1)(x^2 - 4)$, so either $x^2 = 1$ or $x^2 = 4$. If $x^2 = 1$, then $x = \pm 1$; if $x^2 = 4$, then $x = \pm 2$. Therefore, the zeros are $x = \pm 1, \pm 2$.

17. $P(x) = x^4 + 6x^3 + 7x^2 - 6x - 8$. The possible rational zeros are $\pm 1, \pm 2, \pm 4, \pm 8$. $P(x)$ has 1 variation in sign and hence 1 positive real zero. $P(-x) = x^4 - 6x^3 + 7x^2 + 6x - 8$ has 3 variations in sign and hence 1 or 3 negative real zeros.

$$
\begin{array}{r|rrrrr}
1 & 1 & 6 & 7 & -6 & -8 \\
  &   & 1 & 7 & 14 & 8 \\
\hline
  & 1 & 7 & 14 & 8 & 0
\end{array}
\quad \Rightarrow \quad x = 1 \text{ is a zero, and there are no other positive zeros.}
$$

Thus $P(x) = x^4 + 6x^3 + 7x^2 - 6x - 8 = (x - 1)(x^3 + 7x^2 + 14x + 8)$. Continuing by factoring the quotient, we have:

$$
\begin{array}{r|rrrr}
-1 & 1 & 7 & 14 & 8 \\
   &   & -1 & -6 & -8 \\
\hline
   & 1 & 6 & 8 & 0
\end{array}
\quad \Rightarrow \quad x = -1 \text{ is a zero.}
$$

So $P(x) = x^4 + 6x^3 + 7x^2 - 6x - 8 = (x - 1)(x + 1)(x^2 + 6x + 8)$
$= (x - 1)(x + 1)(x + 2)(x + 4)$. Therefore, the zeros are $x = -4, -2, \pm 1$.

19. $P(x) = 4x^4 - 25x^2 + 36$ has possible rational zeros $\pm 1, \pm 2, \pm 3, \pm 4, \pm 6, \pm 9, \pm 12, \pm 18, \pm 36,$ $\pm \frac{1}{2}, \pm \frac{1}{4}, \pm \frac{3}{2}, \pm \frac{3}{4}, \pm \frac{9}{2}, \pm \frac{9}{4}$. Since $P(x)$ has 2 variations in sign, there are 0 or 2 positive real zeros. Since $P(-x) = 4x^4 - 25x^2 + 36$ has 2 variations in sign, there are 0 or 2 negative real zeros.

$$
\begin{array}{r|rrrrr}
1 & 4 & 0 & -25 & 0 & 36 \\
  &   & 4 & 4 & -21 & -21 \\
\hline
  & 4 & 4 & -21 & -21 & 15 \\
\end{array}
$$

$$
\begin{array}{r|rrrrr}
2 & 4 & 0 & -25 & 0 & 36 \\
  &   & 8 & 16 & -18 & -36 \\
\hline
  & 4 & 8 & -9 & -18 & 0 \\
\end{array}
\Rightarrow \quad x = 2 \text{ is a zero.}
$$

$P(x) = (x - 2)(4x^3 + 8x^2 - 9x - 18)$

$$
\begin{array}{r|rrrr}
2 & 4 & 8 & -9 & -18 \\
  &   & 8 & 32 & 46 \\
\hline
  & 4 & 16 & 23 & 28 \\
\end{array}
\Rightarrow \quad \text{all positive, } x = 2 \text{ is an upper bound.}
$$

$$
\begin{array}{r|rrrr}
\frac{1}{2} & 4 & 8 & -9 & -18 \\
  &   & 2 & 5 & -2 \\
\hline
  & 4 & 10 & -4 & -20 \\
\end{array}
\qquad
\begin{array}{r|rrrr}
\frac{1}{4} & 4 & 8 & -9 & -18 \\
  &   & 1 & \frac{9}{4} & -\frac{27}{16} \\
\hline
  & 4 & 9 & -\frac{27}{4} & -\frac{315}{16} \\
\end{array}
$$

$$
\begin{array}{r|rrrr}
\frac{3}{2} & 4 & 8 & -9 & -18 \\
  &   & 6 & 21 & 18 \\
\hline
  & 4 & 14 & 12 & 0 \\
\end{array}
\Rightarrow \quad x = \frac{3}{2} \text{ is a zero.}
$$

$P(x) = (x - 2)(2x - 3)(2x^2 + 7x + 6) = (x - 2)(2x - 3)(2x + 3)(x + 2)$. Therefore, the zeros are $x = \pm 2, \pm \frac{3}{2}$.

Note: Since $P(x)$ has only even terms, factoring by substitution also works. Let $x^2 = u$; then $P(u) = 4u^2 - 25u + 36 = (u - 4)(4u - 9) = (x^2 - 4)(4x^2 - 9)$, which yields the same results.

21. $P(x) = x^4 + 8x^3 + 24x^2 + 32x + 16$. The possible rational zeros are $\pm 1, \pm 2, \pm 4, \pm 8, \pm 16$. $P(x)$ has no variations in sign and hence no positive real zero. $P(-x) = x^4 - 8x^3 + 24x^2 - 32x + 16$ has 4 variations in sign and hence 0 or 2 or 4 negative real zeros.

$$
\begin{array}{r|rrrrr}
-1 & 1 & 8 & 24 & 32 & 16 \\
  &   & -1 & -7 & -17 & -15 \\
\hline
  & 1 & 7 & 17 & 15 & 1 \\
\end{array}
\Rightarrow \quad x = -1 \text{ is not a zero.}
$$

$$
\begin{array}{r|rrrrr}
-2 & 1 & 8 & 24 & 32 & 16 \\
  &   & -2 & -12 & -24 & -16 \\
\hline
  & 1 & 6 & 12 & 8 & 0 \\
\end{array}
\Rightarrow \quad x = -2 \text{ is a zero.}
$$

Thus $P(x) = x^4 + 8x^3 + 24x^2 + 32x + 16 = (x + 2)(x^3 + 6x^2 + 12x + 8)$. Continuing by factoring the quotient, we have:

$$
\begin{array}{r|rrrr}
-2 & 1 & 6 & 12 & 8 \\
  &   & -2 & -8 & -8 \\
\hline
  & 1 & 4 & 4 & 0 \\
\end{array}
\Rightarrow \quad x = -2 \text{ is a zero.}
$$

Thus $P(x) = (x + 2)^2(x^2 + 4x + 4) = (x + 2)^4$. Therefore, the zero is $x = -2$

23. Factoring by grouping can be applied to this exercise. $4x^3 + 4x^2 - x - 1 = 4x^2(x + 1) - (x + 1)$ $= (x + 1)(4x^2 - 1) = (x + 1)(2x + 1)(2x - 1)$. Therefore, the zeros are $x = -1, \pm \frac{1}{2}$.

25. $P(x) = 4x^3 - 7x + 3$. The possible rational zeros are $\pm 1, \pm 3, \pm \frac{1}{2}, \pm \frac{3}{2}, \pm \frac{1}{4}, \pm \frac{3}{4}$. Since $P(x)$ has 2 variations in sign, there are 0 or 2 positive zeros. Since $P(-x) = -4x^3 + 7x + 3$ has 1 variation in sign, there is 1 negative zero.

$$\frac{1}{2} \begin{array}{|rrrr} 4 & 0 & -7 & 3 \\ & 2 & 1 & -3 \\ \hline 4 & 2 & -6 & 0 \end{array} \quad \Rightarrow \quad x = \tfrac{1}{2} \text{ is a zero.}$$

$P(x) = (x - \tfrac{1}{2})(4x^2 + 2x - 6) = (2x - 1)(2x^2 + x - 3) = (2x - 1)(x - 1)(2x + 3) = 0.$ Thus, the zeros are $x = -\tfrac{3}{2}, \tfrac{1}{2}, 1$.

27. $P(x) = 2x^4 - 7x^3 + 3x^2 + 8x - 4$. The possible rational zeros are ± 1, ± 2, ± 4, $\pm \tfrac{1}{2}$. $P(x)$ has 3 variations in sign and hence 1 or 3 positive real zeros. $P(-x) = 2x^4 + 7x^3 + 3x^2 - 8x - 4$ has 1 variation in sign and hence 1 negative real zero.

$$1 \begin{array}{|rrrrr} 2 & -7 & 3 & 8 & -4 \\ & 2 & -5 & -2 & 6 \\ \hline 2 & -5 & -2 & 6 & 2 \end{array} \quad \Rightarrow \quad x = 1 \text{ is not a zero.}$$

$$\frac{1}{2} \begin{array}{|rrrrr} 2 & -7 & 3 & 8 & -4 \\ & 1 & -3 & 0 & 4 \\ \hline 2 & -6 & 0 & 8 & 0 \end{array} \quad \Rightarrow \quad x = \tfrac{1}{2} \text{ is a zero.}$$

Thus $P(x) = 2x^4 - 7x^3 + 3x^2 + 8x - 4 = (x - \tfrac{1}{2})(2x^3 - 6x^2 + 8)$. Continuing by factoring the quotient, we have:

$$2 \begin{array}{|rrrr} 2 & -6 & 0 & 8 \\ & 4 & -4 & -8 \\ \hline 2 & -2 & -4 & 0 \end{array} \quad \Rightarrow \quad x = 2 \text{ is a zero.}$$

So $P(x) = (x - \tfrac{1}{2})(x - 2)(2x^2 - 2x - 4) = 2(x - \tfrac{1}{2})(x - 2)(x^2 - x - 2)$
$= 2(x - \tfrac{1}{2})(x - 2)^2(x + 1)$. Thus, the zeros are $x = \tfrac{1}{2}$, 2, -1.

29. $P(x) = x^5 + 3x^4 - 9x^3 - 31x^2 + 36$. The possible rational zeros are ± 1, ± 2, ± 3, ± 4, ± 6, ± 8, ± 9, ± 12, ± 18. $P(x)$ has 2 variations in sign and hence 0 or 2 positive real zeros. $P(-x) = -x^5 + 3x^4 + 9x^3 - 31x^2 + 36$ has 3 variations in sign and hence 1 or 3 negative real zeros.

$$1 \begin{array}{|rrrrrr} 1 & 3 & -9 & -31 & 0 & 36 \\ & 1 & 4 & -5 & -36 & -36 \\ \hline 1 & 4 & -5 & -36 & -36 & 0 \end{array} \quad \Rightarrow \quad x = 1 \text{ is a zero.}$$

So $P(x) = x^5 + 3x^4 - 9x^3 - 31x^2 + 36 = (x - 1)(x^4 + 4x^3 - 5x^2 - 36x - 36)$. Continuing by factoring the quotient, we have:

$$1 \begin{array}{|rrrrr} 1 & 4 & -5 & -36 & -36 \\ & 1 & 5 & 0 & -36 \\ \hline 1 & 1 & 0 & -36 & -72 \end{array} \qquad 2 \begin{array}{|rrrrr} 1 & 4 & -5 & -36 & -36 \\ & 2 & 12 & 14 & -44 \\ \hline 1 & 6 & 7 & -22 & -80 \end{array}$$

$$3 \begin{array}{|rrrrr} 1 & 4 & -5 & -36 & -36 \\ & 3 & 21 & 48 & 36 \\ \hline 1 & 7 & 16 & 12 & 0 \end{array} \quad \Rightarrow \quad x = 3 \text{ is a zero.}$$

So $P(x) = (x - 1)(x - 3)(x^3 + 7x^2 + 16x + 12)$. Since we have 2 positive zeros, there are no more positive zeros, so we continue by factoring the quotient with possible negative zeros.

$$-1 \begin{array}{|rrrr} 1 & 7 & 16 & 12 \\ & -1 & -6 & -10 \\ \hline 1 & 6 & 10 & 2 \end{array} \qquad -2 \begin{array}{|rrrr} 1 & 7 & 16 & 12 \\ & -2 & -10 & -12 \\ \hline 1 & 5 & 6 & 0 \end{array} \quad \Rightarrow \quad x = -2 \text{ is a zero.}$$

Then $P(x) = (x-1)(x-3)(x+2)(x^2+5x+6) = (x-1)(x-3)(x+2)^2(x+3)$. Thus, the zeros are $x = 1, 3, -2, -3$.

31. $P(x) = 3x^5 - 14x^4 - 14x^3 + 36x^2 + 43x + 10$ has possible rational zeros $\pm 1, \pm 2, \pm 5, \pm 10, \pm\frac{1}{3}, \pm\frac{2}{3}, \pm\frac{5}{3}, \pm\frac{10}{3}$. Since $P(x)$ has 2 variations in sign, there are 0 or 2 positive real zeros. Since $P(-x) = -3x^5 - 14x^4 + 14x^3 + 36x^2 - 43x + 10$ has 3 variations in sign, there are 1 or 3 negative real zeros.

$$\begin{array}{r|rrrrrr} 1 & 3 & -14 & -14 & 36 & 43 & 10 \\ & & 3 & -11 & -25 & 11 & 54 \\ \hline & 3 & -11 & -25 & 11 & 54 & 64 \end{array}$$

$$\begin{array}{r|rrrrrr} 2 & 3 & -14 & -14 & 36 & 43 & 10 \\ & & 6 & -16 & -60 & -48 & -10 \\ \hline & 3 & -8 & -30 & -24 & -5 & 0 \end{array} \Rightarrow \quad x = 2 \text{ is a zero.}$$

$P(x) = (x-2)(3x^4 - 8x^3 - 30x^2 - 24x - 5)$

$$\begin{array}{r|rrrrr} 2 & 3 & -8 & -30 & -24 & -5 \\ & & 6 & -4 & -68 & -184 \\ \hline & 3 & -2 & -34 & -92 & -189 \end{array}$$

$$\begin{array}{r|rrrrr} 5 & 3 & -8 & -30 & -24 & -5 \\ & & 15 & 35 & 25 & 5 \\ \hline & 3 & 7 & 5 & 1 & 0 \end{array} \Rightarrow \quad x = 5 \text{ is a zero.}$$

$P(x) = (x-2)(x-5)(3x^3 + 7x^2 + 5x + 1)$

Since $3x^3 + 7x^2 + 5x + 1$ has no change in signs, there are no more positive zeros.

$$\begin{array}{r|rrrr} -1 & 3 & 7 & 5 & 1 \\ & & -3 & -4 & -1 \\ \hline & 3 & 4 & 1 & 0 \end{array} \Rightarrow \quad x = -1 \text{ is a zero.}$$

$P(x) = (x-2)(x-5)(x+1)(3x^2 + 4x + 1) = (x-2)(x-5)(x+1)(x+1)(3x+1)$.
Therefore, the zeros are $x = -1, -\frac{1}{3}, 2, 5$.

33. $P(x) = x^3 + 4x^2 + 3x - 2$. The possible rational zeros are $\pm 1, \pm 2$. $P(x)$ has 1 variation in sign and hence 1 positive real zero. $P(-x) = -x^3 + 4x^2 - 3x - 2$ has 2 variations in sign and hence 0 or 2 negative real zeros.

$$\begin{array}{r|rrrr} 1 & 1 & 4 & 3 & -2 \\ & & 1 & 5 & 8 \\ \hline & 1 & 5 & 8 & 6 \end{array} \Rightarrow \quad x = 1 \text{ is an upper bound.}$$

$$\begin{array}{r|rrrr} -1 & 1 & 4 & 3 & -2 \\ & & -1 & -3 & 0 \\ \hline & 1 & 3 & 0 & -2 \end{array} \qquad \begin{array}{r|rrrr} -2 & 1 & 4 & 3 & -2 \\ & & -2 & -4 & 2 \\ \hline & 1 & 2 & -1 & 0 \end{array} \Rightarrow \quad x = -2 \text{ is a zero.}$$

So $P(x) = (x+2)(x^2 + 2x - 1)$. Using the quadratic formula on the second factor, we have:
$x = \dfrac{-2 \pm \sqrt{2^2 - 4(1)(-1)}}{2(1)} = \dfrac{-2 \pm \sqrt{8}}{2} = \dfrac{-2 \pm 2\sqrt{2}}{2} = -1 \pm \sqrt{2}$. Therefore, the zeros are $x = -2, -1 + \sqrt{2}, -1 - \sqrt{2}$.

35. $P(x) = x^4 - 6x^3 + 4x^2 + 15x + 4$. The possible rational zeros are $\pm 1, \pm 2, \pm 4$. $P(x)$ has 2 variations in sign and hence 0 or 2 positive real zeros. $P(-x) = x^4 + 6x^3 + 4x^2 - 15x + 4$ has 2 variations in sign and hence 0 or 2 negative real zeros.

$$1 \begin{array}{|rrrrr} 1 & -6 & 4 & 15 & 4 \\ & 1 & -5 & -1 & 14 \\ \hline 1 & -5 & -1 & 14 & 18 \end{array} \qquad 2 \begin{array}{|rrrrr} 1 & -6 & 4 & 15 & 4 \\ & 2 & -8 & -8 & 14 \\ \hline 1 & -4 & -4 & 7 & 18 \end{array}$$

$$4 \begin{array}{|rrrrr} 1 & -6 & 4 & 15 & 4 \\ & 4 & -8 & -16 & -4 \\ \hline 1 & -2 & -4 & -1 & 0 \end{array} \Rightarrow \quad x = 4 \text{ is a zero.}$$

So $P(x) = (x - 4)(x^3 - 2x^2 - 4x - 1)$. Continuing by factoring the quotient, we have:

$$4 \begin{array}{|rrrr} 1 & -2 & -4 & -1 \\ & 4 & 8 & 16 \\ \hline 1 & 2 & 4 & 15 \end{array} \Rightarrow \quad x = 4 \text{ is an upper bound.}$$

$$-1 \begin{array}{|rrrr} 1 & -2 & -4 & -1 \\ & -1 & 3 & 1 \\ \hline 1 & -3 & -1 & 0 \end{array} \Rightarrow \quad x = -1 \text{ is a zero.}$$

So $P(x) = (x - 4)(x + 1)(x^2 - 3x - 1)$. Using the quadratic formula on the third factor, we have:
$$x = \frac{-(-3) \pm \sqrt{(-3)^2 - 4(1)(-1)}}{2(1)} = \frac{3 \pm \sqrt{13}}{2}. \text{ Therefore, the zeros are } x = 4, -1, \frac{3 \pm \sqrt{13}}{2}.$$

37. $P(x) = x^4 - 7x^3 + 14x^2 - 3x - 9$. The possible rational zeros are $\pm 1, \pm 3, \pm 9$. $P(x)$ has 3 variations in sign and hence 1 or 3 positive real zeros. $P(-x) = x^4 + 7x^3 + 14x^2 + 3x - 4$ has 1 variation in sign and hence 1 negative real zero.

$$1 \begin{array}{|rrrrr} 1 & -7 & 14 & -3 & -9 \\ & 1 & -6 & 8 & 5 \\ \hline 1 & -6 & 8 & 5 & 4 \end{array} \qquad 3 \begin{array}{|rrrrr} 1 & -7 & 14 & -3 & -9 \\ & 3 & -12 & 6 & 9 \\ \hline 1 & -4 & 2 & 3 & 0 \end{array} \Rightarrow \quad x = 3 \text{ is a zero.}$$

So $P(x) = (x - 3)(x^3 - 4x^2 + 2x + 3)$. Since the constant term of the second term is 3, ± 9 are no longer possible zeros. Continuing by factoring the quotient, we have:

$$3 \begin{array}{|rrrr} 1 & -4 & 2 & 3 \\ & 3 & -3 & -3 \\ \hline 1 & -1 & -1 & 0 \end{array} \Rightarrow \quad x = 3 \text{ is a zero again.}$$

So $P(x) = (x - 3)^2(x^2 - x - 1)$. Using the quadratic formula on the second factor, we have:
$$x = \frac{-(-1) \pm \sqrt{(-1)^2 - 4(1)(-1)}}{2(1)} = \frac{1 \pm \sqrt{5}}{2}. \text{ Therefore, the zeros are } x = 3, \frac{1 \pm \sqrt{5}}{2}.$$

39. $P(x) = 4x^3 - 6x^2 + 1$. The possible rational zeros are $\pm 1, \pm \frac{1}{2}, \pm \frac{1}{4}$. $P(x)$ has 2 variations in sign and hence 0 or 2 positive real zeros. $P(-x) = -4x^3 - 6x^2 + 1$ has 1 variation in sign and hence 1 negative real zero.

$$1 \begin{array}{|rrrr} 4 & -6 & 0 & 1 \\ & 4 & -2 & -2 \\ \hline 4 & -2 & -2 & -1 \end{array} \qquad \tfrac{1}{2} \begin{array}{|rrrr} 4 & -6 & 0 & 1 \\ & 2 & -2 & -1 \\ \hline 4 & -4 & -2 & 0 \end{array} \Rightarrow \quad x = \tfrac{1}{2} \text{ is a zero.}$$

So $P(x) = \left(x - \frac{1}{2}\right)(4x^2 - 4x - 2)$. Using the quadratic formula on the second factor, we have:
$$x = \frac{-(-4) \pm \sqrt{(-4)^2 - 4(4)(-2)}}{2(4)} = \frac{4 \pm \sqrt{48}}{8} = \frac{4 \pm 4\sqrt{3}}{8} = \frac{1 \pm \sqrt{3}}{2}. \text{ Therefore, the zeros}$$
are $x = \frac{1}{2}, \frac{1 \pm \sqrt{3}}{2}$.

41. $P(x) = 2x^4 + 15x^3 + 17x^2 + 3x - 1$. The possible rational zeros are $\pm 1, \pm\frac{1}{2}$. $P(x)$ has 1 variation in sign and hence 1 positive real zero. $P(-x) = 2x^4 - 15x^3 + 17x^2 - 3x - 1$ has 3 variations in sign and hence 1 or 3 negative real zeros.

$$\begin{array}{r|rrrrr} \frac{1}{2} & 2 & 15 & 17 & 3 & -1 \\ & & 1 & 8 & \frac{25}{2} & \frac{31}{4} \\ \hline & 2 & 16 & 25 & \frac{31}{2} & \frac{27}{4} \end{array} \Rightarrow \quad x = \tfrac{1}{2} \text{ is an upper bound.}$$

$$\begin{array}{r|rrrrr} -\frac{1}{2} & 2 & 15 & 17 & 3 & -1 \\ & & -1 & -7 & -5 & 1 \\ \hline & 2 & 14 & 10 & -2 & 0 \end{array} \Rightarrow \quad x = -\tfrac{1}{2} \text{ is a zero.}$$

So $P(x) = \left(x + \frac{1}{2}\right)(2x^3 + 14x^2 + 10x - 2) = 2\left(x + \frac{1}{2}\right)(x^3 + 7x^2 + 5x - 1)$.

$$\begin{array}{r|rrrr} -1 & 1 & 7 & 5 & -1 \\ & & -1 & -6 & 1 \\ \hline & 1 & 6 & -1 & 0 \end{array} \Rightarrow \quad x = -1 \text{ is a zero.}$$

So $P(x) = \left(x + \frac{1}{2}\right)(2x^3 + 14x^2 + 10x - 2) = 2\left(x + \frac{1}{2}\right)(x + 1)(x^2 + 6x - 1)$

Using the quadratic formula on the third factor, we have: $x = \dfrac{-(6) \pm \sqrt{(6)^2 - 4(1)(-1)}}{2(1)}$

$= \frac{-6 \pm \sqrt{40}}{2} = \frac{-6 \pm 2\sqrt{10}}{2} = -3 \pm \sqrt{10}$. Therefore, the zeros are $x = -1, -\frac{1}{2}, -3 \pm \sqrt{10}$.

43. (a) $P(x) = x^3 - 3x^2 - 4x + 12$ has possible rational zeros $\pm 1, \pm 2, \pm 3, \pm 4, \pm 6, \pm 12$.

$$\begin{array}{r|rrrr} 1 & 1 & -3 & -4 & 12 \\ & & 1 & -2 & -6 \\ \hline & 1 & -2 & -6 & 6 \end{array} \qquad \begin{array}{r|rrrr} 2 & 1 & -3 & -4 & 12 \\ & & 2 & -2 & -12 \\ \hline & 1 & -1 & -6 & 0 \end{array} \Rightarrow \quad x = 2 \text{ is a zero.}$$

So $P(x) = (x - 2)(x^2 - x - 6) = (x - 2)(x + 2)(x - 3)$. The real zeros of P are $-2, 2, 3$.

(b)

45. (a) $P(x) = -x^3 + 2x^2 + 15x - 36$ has possible rational zeros $\pm 1, \pm 2, \pm 3, \pm 4, \pm 6, \pm 9, \pm 12, \pm 18$.

$$\begin{array}{r|rrrr} 1 & -1 & 2 & 15 & -36 \\ & & -1 & 1 & 16 \\ \hline & -1 & 1 & 16 & -20 \end{array} \qquad \begin{array}{r|rrrr} 2 & -1 & 2 & 15 & -36 \\ & & -2 & 0 & 30 \\ \hline & -1 & 0 & 15 & -6 \end{array}$$

$$\begin{array}{r|rrrr} 3 & -1 & 2 & 15 & -36 \\ & & -3 & -3 & -36 \\ \hline & -1 & -1 & 12 & 0 \end{array} \Rightarrow \quad x = 3 \text{ is a zero.}$$

So $P(x) = (x - 3)(-x^2 - x + 12) = (x - 3)(-x + 3)(x + 4) = -(x - 3)^2(x + 4)$. The real zeros of P are -4, 3.

(b)

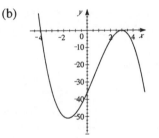

47. (a) $P(x) = x^4 - 5x^3 + 6x^2 + 4x - 8$ has possible rational zeros $\pm 1, \pm 2, \pm 4, \pm 8$.

$$
\begin{array}{r|rrrrr}
1 & 1 & -5 & 6 & 4 & -8 \\
  &   & 1 & -4 & 2 & 6 \\
\hline
  & 1 & -4 & 2 & 6 & -2 \\
\end{array}
\qquad
\begin{array}{r|rrrrr}
2 & 1 & -5 & 6 & 4 & -8 \\
  &   & 2 & -6 & 0 & 8 \\
\hline
  & 1 & -3 & 0 & 4 & 0 \\
\end{array}
\;\Rightarrow\; x = 2 \text{ is a zero.}
$$

So $P(x) = (x-2)(x^3 - 3x^2 + 4)$, and the possible rational zeros are restricted to $-1, \pm 2,$ ± 4.

$$
\begin{array}{r|rrrr}
2 & 1 & -3 & 0 & 4 \\
  &   & 2 & -2 & -4 \\
\hline
  & 1 & -1 & -2 & 0 \\
\end{array}
\;\Rightarrow\; x = 2 \text{ is a zero again.}
$$

$P(x) = (x-2)^2(x^2 - x - 2) = (x-2)^2(x-2)(x+1) = (x-2)^3(x+1)$. So the real zeros of P are -1 and 2.

(b)

49. (a) $P(x) = x^5 - x^4 - 5x^3 + x^2 + 8x + 4$ has possible rational zeros $\pm 1, \pm 2, \pm 4$.

$$
\begin{array}{r|rrrrrr}
1 & 1 & -1 & -5 & 1 & 8 & 4 \\
  &   & 1 & 0 & -5 & -4 & 4 \\
\hline
  & 1 & 0 & -5 & -4 & 4 & 8 \\
\end{array}
$$

$$
\begin{array}{r|rrrrrr}
2 & 1 & -1 & -5 & 1 & 8 & 4 \\
  &   & 2 & 2 & -6 & -10 & -4 \\
\hline
  & 1 & 1 & -3 & -5 & -2 & 0 \\
\end{array}
\;\Rightarrow\; x = 2 \text{ is a zero.}
$$

So $P(x) = (x-2)(x^4 + x^3 - 3x^2 - 5x - 2)$, and the possible rational zeros are restricted to $-1, \pm 2$.

$$
\begin{array}{r|rrrrr}
2 & 1 & 1 & -3 & -5 & -2 \\
  &   & 2 & 6 & 6 & 2 \\
\hline
  & 1 & 3 & 3 & 1 & 0 \\
\end{array}
\;\Rightarrow\; x = 2 \text{ is a zero again.}
$$

So $P(x) = (x-2)^2(x^3 + 3x^2 + 3x + 1)$, and the possible rational zeros are restricted to -1.

$$
\begin{array}{r|rrrr}
-1 & 1 & 3 & 3 & 1 \\
   &   & -1 & -2 & -1 \\
\hline
   & 1 & 2 & 1 & 0 \\
\end{array}
\;\Rightarrow\; x = -1 \text{ is a zero.}
$$

So $P(x) = (x-2)^2(x+1)(x^2+2x+1) = (x-2)^2(x+1)^3$., and the real zeros of P are -1 and 2.

(b)

51. $P(x) = x^3 - x^2 - x - 3$. Since $P(x)$ has 1 variation in sign, P has 1 positive real zero. Since $P(-x) = -x^3 - x^2 + x - 3$ has 2 variations in sign, P has 2 or 0 negative real zeros. Thus, P has 1 or 3 real zeros.

53. $P(x) = 2x^6 + 5x^4 - x^3 - 5x - 1$. Since $P(x)$ has 1 variation in sign, P has 1 positive real zero. Since $P(-x) = 2x^6 + 5x^4 + x^3 + 5x - 1$ has 1 variation in sign, P has 1 negative real zero. Therefore, P has 2 real zeros.

55. $P(x) = x^5 + 4x^3 - x^2 + 6x$. Since $P(x)$ has 2 variations in sign, P has 2 or 0 positive real zeros. Since $P(-x) = -x^5 - 4x^3 - x^2 - 6x$ has 0 variations in sign, P has 0 negative real zeros. Therefore, P has a total of 1 or 3 real zeros (since $x = 0$ is a zero, but is neither positive nor negative).

57. $P(x) = 2x^3 + 5x^2 + x - 2$; $a = -3, b = 1$

$$
\begin{array}{r|rrrr}
-3 & 2 & 5 & 1 & -2 \\
   &   & -6 & 3 & -12 \\
\hline
   & 2 & -1 & 4 & -14
\end{array}
$$
alternating signs $\Rightarrow$ lower bound.

$$
\begin{array}{r|rrrr}
1 & 2 & 5 & 1 & -2 \\
  &   & 2 & 7 & 8 \\
\hline
  & 2 & 7 & 8 & 6
\end{array}
$$
all non-negative $\Rightarrow$ upper bound.

Therefore $a = -3, b = 1$ are lower and upper bounds, respectively.

59. $P(x) = 8x^3 + 10x^2 - 39x + 9$; $a = -3, b = 2$

$$
\begin{array}{r|rrrr}
-3 & 8 & 10 & -39 & 9 \\
   &   & -24 & 42 & -9 \\
\hline
   & 8 & -14 & 3 & 0
\end{array}
$$
alternating signs $\Rightarrow$ lower bound.

$$
\begin{array}{r|rrrr}
2 & 8 & 10 & -39 & 9 \\
  &   & 16 & 52 & 26 \\
\hline
  & 8 & 26 & 13 & 35
\end{array}
$$
all non-negative $\Rightarrow$ upper bound.

Therefore $a = -3, b = 2$ are lower and upper bounds, respectively. Note that $x = -3$ is also a zero.

There are many possible solutions to Exercises 61 and 63 since we are only asked to find 'an upper bound' and 'a lower bound'.

61. $P(x) = x^3 - 3x^2 + 4$ and use the Upper and Lower Bounds Theorem:

$$
\begin{array}{r|rrrr}
-1 & 1 & -3 & 0 & 4 \\
   &   & -1 & 4 & -4 \\
\hline
   & 1 & -4 & 4 & 0
\end{array}
$$
alternating signs $\Rightarrow$ lower bound.

$$\begin{array}{r|rrrr} 3 & 1 & -3 & 0 & 4 \\ & & 3 & 0 & 0 \\ \hline & 1 & 0 & 0 & 4 \end{array}$$ all non-negative $\Rightarrow$ upper bound.

Therefore -1 is a lower bound (and a zero) and 3 is an upper bound.

63. $P(x) = x^4 - 2x^3 + x^2 - 9x + 2.$

$$\begin{array}{r|rrrrr} 1 & 1 & -2 & 1 & -9 & 2 \\ & & 1 & -1 & 0 & -9 \\ \hline & 1 & -1 & 0 & -9 & -7 \end{array} \qquad \begin{array}{r|rrrrr} 2 & 1 & -2 & 1 & -9 & 2 \\ & & 2 & 0 & 2 & -14 \\ \hline & 1 & 0 & 1 & -7 & -12 \end{array}$$

$$\begin{array}{r|rrrrr} 3 & 1 & -2 & 1 & -9 & 2 \\ & & 3 & 3 & 12 & 9 \\ \hline & 1 & 1 & 4 & 3 & 11 \end{array} \qquad \text{all positive} \quad \Rightarrow \quad \text{upper bound.}$$

$$\begin{array}{r|rrrrr} -1 & 1 & -2 & 1 & -9 & 2 \\ & & -1 & 3 & -4 & 13 \\ \hline & 1 & -3 & 4 & -13 & 15 \end{array} \qquad \text{alternating signs} \quad \Rightarrow \quad \text{lower bound.}$$

Therefore -1 is a lower bound and 3 is an upper bound.

65. $P(x) = 2x^4 + 3x^3 - 4x^2 - 3x + 2.$

$$\begin{array}{r|rrrrr} 1 & 2 & 3 & -4 & -3 & 2 \\ & & 2 & 5 & 1 & -2 \\ \hline & 2 & 5 & 1 & -2 & 0 \end{array} \Rightarrow \quad x = 1 \text{ is a zero.}$$

$P(x) = (x-1)(2x^3 + 5x^2 + x - 2)$

$$\begin{array}{r|rrrr} -1 & 2 & 5 & 1 & -2 \\ & & -2 & -3 & 2 \\ \hline & 2 & 3 & -2 & 0 \end{array} \Rightarrow \quad x = -1 \text{ is a zero.}$$

$P(x) = (x-1)(x+1)(2x^2 + 3x - 2) = (x-1)(x+1)(2x-1)(x+2)$. Therefore, the zeros are $x = -2, \frac{1}{2}, \pm 1$.

67.   <u>Method #1</u>: $P(x) = 4x^4 - 21x^2 + 5$ has 2 variations in sign, so by Descartes' rule of signs there are either 2 or 0 positive zeros. If we replace x with $(-x)$, the function does not change, so there are either 2 or 0 negative zeros. Possible rational zeros are $\pm 1, \pm \frac{1}{2}, \pm \frac{1}{4}, \pm 5, \pm \frac{5}{2}, \pm \frac{5}{4}$. By inspection, ± 1 and ± 5 are not zeros, so we must look for non-integer solutions:

$$\begin{array}{r|rrrrr} \frac{1}{2} & 4 & 0 & -21 & 0 & 5 \\ & & 2 & 1 & -10 & -5 \\ \hline & 4 & 2 & -20 & -10 & 0 \end{array} \Rightarrow \quad x = \frac{1}{2} \text{ is a zero.}$$

$P(x) = \left(x - \frac{1}{2}\right)(4x^3 + 2x^2 - 20x - 10)$, continuing with the quotient, we have:

$$\begin{array}{r|rrrr} -\frac{1}{2} & 4 & 2 & -20 & -10 \\ & & -2 & 0 & 10 \\ \hline & 4 & 0 & -20 & 0 \end{array} \Rightarrow \quad x = -\frac{1}{2} \text{ is a zero.}$$

$P(x) = \left(x - \frac{1}{2}\right)\left(x + \frac{1}{2}\right)(4x^2 - 20) = 0$. If $4x^2 - 20 = 0$, then $x = \pm\sqrt{5}$. Thus the zeros are $x = \pm\frac{1}{2}, \pm\sqrt{5}$.

<u>Method #2</u>: Substituting $u = x^2$, the equation becomes $4u^2 - 21u + 5 = 0$, which factors: $4u^2 - 21u + 5 = (4u - 1)(u - 5) = (4x^2 - 1)(x^2 - 5)$. Then either we have $x^2 = 5$, so that $x = \pm\sqrt{5}$, or we have $x^2 = \frac{1}{4}$, so that $x = \pm\sqrt{\frac{1}{4}} = \pm\frac{1}{2}$. Thus the zeros are $x = \pm\frac{1}{2}, \pm\sqrt{5}$.

69. $P(x) = x^5 - 7x^4 + 9x^3 + 23x^2 - 50x + 24$. The possible rational zeros are $\pm1, \pm2, \pm3, \pm4, \pm6,$ $\pm8, \pm12, \pm24$. $P(x)$ has 4 variations in sign and hence 0, 2, or 4 positive real zeros. $P(-x) = -x^5 - 7x^4 - 9x^3 + 23x^2 + 50x + 24$ has 1 variation in sign, and hence 1 negative real zero.

$$
\begin{array}{r|rrrrrr}
1 & 1 & -7 & 9 & 23 & -50 & 24 \\
  &   & 1 & -6 & 3 & 26 & -24 \\
\hline
  & 1 & -6 & 3 & 26 & -24 & 0
\end{array}
\Rightarrow \quad x = 1 \text{ is a zero.}
$$

$P(x) = (x-1)(x^4 - 6x^3 + 3x^2 + 26x - 24)$; continuing with the quotient, we try 1 again.

$$
\begin{array}{r|rrrrr}
1 & 1 & -6 & 3 & 26 & -24 \\
  &   & 1 & -5 & -2 & 24 \\
\hline
  & 1 & -5 & -2 & 24 & 0
\end{array}
\Rightarrow \quad x = 1 \text{ is a zero again.}
$$

$P(x) = (x-1)^2(x^3 - 5x^2 - 2x + 24)$; continuing with the quotient, we start by trying 1 again.

$$
\begin{array}{r|rrrr}
1 & 1 & -5 & -2 & 24 \\
  &   & 1 & -4 & -6 \\
\hline
  & 1 & -4 & -6 & 18
\end{array}
\qquad
\begin{array}{r|rrrr}
2 & 1 & -5 & -2 & 24 \\
  &   & 2 & -6 & -16 \\
\hline
  & 1 & -3 & -8 & 8
\end{array}
$$

$$
\begin{array}{r|rrrr}
3 & 1 & -5 & -2 & 24 \\
  &   & 3 & -6 & -24 \\
\hline
  & 1 & -2 & -8 & 0
\end{array}
\Rightarrow \quad x = 3 \text{ is a zero.}
$$

$P(x) = (x-1)^2(x-3)(x^2 - 2x - 8) = (x-1)^2(x-3)(x-4)(x+2)$. Therefore, the zeros are $x = -2, 1, 3, 4$.

71. $P(x) = x^3 - x - 2$. The only possible rational zeros of $P(x)$ are ±1 and ±2.

$$
\begin{array}{r|rrrr}
1 & 1 & 0 & -1 & -2 \\
  &   & 1 & 1 & 0 \\
\hline
  & 1 & 1 & 0 & -2
\end{array}
\qquad
\begin{array}{r|rrrr}
2 & 1 & 0 & -1 & -2 \\
  &   & 2 & 4 & 6 \\
\hline
  & 1 & 2 & 3 & 4
\end{array}
\qquad
\begin{array}{r|rrrr}
-1 & 1 & 0 & -1 & -2 \\
   &   & -1 & 1 & 0 \\
\hline
   & 1 & -1 & 0 & -2
\end{array}
$$

Since the row that contains -1 alternates between non-negative and non-positive, -1 is a lower bound and there is no need to try -2. Therefore, $P(x)$ does not have any rational zeros.

73. $P(x) = 3x^3 - x^2 - 6x + 12$ has possible rational zeros $\pm1, \pm2, \pm3, \pm4, \pm6, \pm12, \pm\frac{1}{3}, \pm\frac{2}{3}, \pm\frac{4}{3}$.

$$
\begin{array}{r|rrrr}
 & 3 & -1 & -6 & 12 \\
\hline
1 & 3 & 2 & -4 & 8 \\
2 & 3 & 5 & 4 & 20 \\
\frac{1}{3} & 3 & 0 & -6 & 10 \\
\frac{2}{3} & 3 & 1 & -\frac{16}{3} & \frac{76}{9} \\
\frac{4}{3} & 3 & 3 & -2 & \frac{28}{3} \\
-1 & 3 & -4 & -2 & 14 \\
-2 & 3 & -7 & 8 & -4 \\
-\frac{1}{3} & 3 & -2 & -\frac{16}{3} & \frac{124}{9} \\
-\frac{2}{3} & 3 & -3 & -4 & \frac{44}{3} \\
-\frac{4}{3} & 3 & -5 & \frac{2}{3} & \frac{100}{9}
\end{array}
$$

all positive $\Rightarrow x = 2$ is an upper bound (row for 2)

alternating signs $\Rightarrow x = -2$ is a lower bound (row for -2)

Therefore, there are no rational zeros.

75. $P(x) = x^3 - 3x^2 - 4x + 12$; $[-4, 4]$ by $[-15, 15]$.
     The possible rational zeros are $\pm 1, \pm 2, \pm 3, \pm 4, \pm 6, \pm 12$.
     By observing the graph of P, the rational zeros are
     $x = -2, 2, 3$.

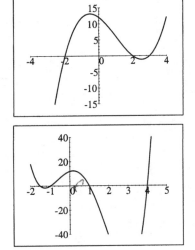

77. $P(x) = 2x^4 - 5x^3 - 14x^2 + 5x + 12$; $[-2, 5]$ by $[-40, 40]$.
     The possible rational zeros are $\pm 1, \pm 2, \pm 3, \pm 4, \pm 6$,
     $\pm 12, \pm \frac{1}{2}, \pm \frac{3}{2}$.
     By observing the graph of P, the zeros are $x = -\frac{3}{2}, -1, 1, 4$.

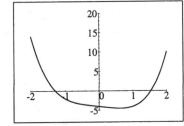

79. $x^4 - x - 4 = 0$. Possible rational solutions are $\pm 1, \pm 2, \pm 4$.

$$
\begin{array}{c|ccccc}
1 & 1 & 0 & 0 & -1 & -4 \\
  &   & 1 & 1 & 1 & 0 \\
\hline
  & 1 & 1 & 1 & 0 & -4
\end{array}
$$

$$
\begin{array}{c|ccccc}
2 & 1 & 0 & 0 & -1 & -4 \\
  &   & 2 & 4 & 8 & 14 \\
\hline
  & 1 & 2 & 4 & 7 & 10
\end{array}
\quad \Rightarrow \quad x = 2
$$
is an upper bound.

$$
\begin{array}{c|ccccc}
-1 & 1 & 0 & 0 & -1 & -4 \\
   &   & -1 & 1 & -1 & 2 \\
\hline
   & 1 & -1 & 1 & -2 & -2
\end{array}
$$

$$
\begin{array}{c|ccccc}
-2 & 1 & 0 & 0 & -1 & -4 \\
   &   & -2 & 4 & -8 & 18 \\
\hline
   & 1 & -2 & 4 & -9 & 14
\end{array}
\quad \Rightarrow \quad x = -2
$$
is a lower bound.

Therefore, we graph the function in the viewing rectangle
$[-2, 2]$ by $[-5, 20]$ and see there are two solutions.

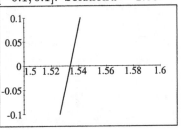

Viewing rectangle: $[-1.3, -1.25]$
by $[-0.1, 0.1]$. Solution $x \approx -1.28$.

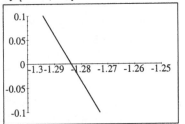

Viewing rectangle: $[1.5.1.6]$ by
$[-0.1, 0.1]$. Solution $x \approx 1.53$.

Thus the solutions are $x \approx -1.28. \ 1.53$.

81. $4.00x^4 + 4.00x^3 - 10.96x^2 - 5.88x + 9.09 = 0.$

$$
\begin{array}{r|rrrrr}
1 & 4 & 4 & -10.96 & -5.88 & 9.09 \\
  &   & 4 & 8 & -2.96 & -8.84 \\
\hline
  & 4 & 8 & -2.96 & -8.84 & 0.25 \\
2 & 4 & 4 & -10.96 & -5.88 & 9.09 \\
  &   & 8 & 24 & 26.08 & 40.40 \\
\hline
  & 4 & 12 & 13.04 & 20.2 & 49.49 \\
-2 & 4 & 4 & -10.96 & -5.88 & 9.09 \\
  &   & -8 & 8 & 5.92 & -0.08 \\
\hline
  & 4 & -4 & -2.96 & 0.04 & 9.01 \\
-3 & 4 & 4 & -10.96 & -5.88 & 9.09 \\
  &   & -12 & 24 & -39.12 & 135 \\
\hline
  & 4 & -8 & 13.04 & -45 & 144.09 \\
\end{array}
$$

$\Rightarrow \quad x = 2$ is an upper bound.

$\Rightarrow \quad x = -3$ is a lower bound.

Therefore, we graph the function in the viewing rectangle $[-3, 2]$ by $[-10, 40]$. There appear to be two solutions.

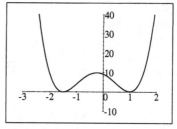

Viewing rectangle: $[-1.6, -1.4]$ by $[-0.1, 0.1]$. Solution $x \approx -1.50$.

Viewing rectangle: $[0.8, 1.2]$ by $[0, 1]$. The graph comes close but does not go through the x-axis. Thus there is no solution here.

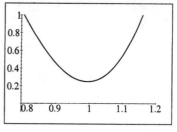

Therefore, the only solution is $x \approx -1.50$.

83. Let $r =$ the radius of the silo. The volume of the hemispherical roof is $\frac{1}{2}\left(\frac{4}{3}\pi r^3\right) = \frac{2}{3}\pi r^3$. The volume of the cylindrical section is $\pi(r^2)(30) = 30\pi r^2$. Because the total volume of the silo is 15000 ft^3, we get the following equation: $\frac{2}{3}\pi r^3 + 30\pi r^2 = 15000 \quad \Leftrightarrow$ $\frac{2}{3}\pi r^3 + 30\pi r^2 - 15000 = 0 \quad \Leftrightarrow \quad \pi r^3 + 45\pi r^2 - 22500 = 0.$ Using a graphing device, we first graph the polynomial in the viewing rectangle $[0, 15]$ by $[-10000, 10000]$. The solution, $r \approx 11.28$ ft., is shown in the viewing rectangle $[11.2, 11.4]$ by $[-1, 1]$.

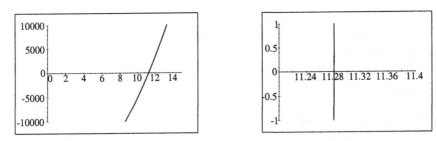

85. $h(t) = 11.60t - 12.41t^2 + 6.20t^3 - 1.58t^4 + 0.20t^5 - 0.01t^6$ is shown in the viewing rectangle
     $[0, 10]$ by $[0, 6]$.

(a) It started to snow again.

(b) No, $h(t) \leq 4$.

(c) The function $h(t)$ is shown in the
     viewing rectangle $[6, 6.5]$ by $[0, 0.5]$.
     The x-intercept of the function is a little
     less than 6.5, which means that the snow
     melted just before midnight on Saturday
     night.

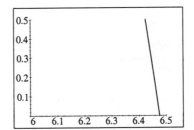

87. Let $r =$ the radius of the cone and cylinder. Let $h =$ the height of the cone. Since the height and
     diameter are equal, we get $h = 2r$. So the volume of the cylinder is $V_1 = \pi r^2 \cdot (cylinder\ height)$
     $= 20\pi r^2$, and the volume of the cone is $V_2 = \frac{1}{3}\pi r^2 h = \frac{1}{3}\pi r^2 (2r) = \frac{2}{3}\pi r^3$. Since the total volume
     is $\frac{500\pi}{3}$, it follows that $\frac{2}{3}\pi r^3 + 20\pi r^2 = \frac{500\pi}{3}$ $\Leftrightarrow$ $r^3 + 30r^2 - 250 = 0$. By Descartes' Rule of
     Signs, there is 1 positive zero.

r	$r^3 + 30r^2 - 250$
1	-219
2	-122
3	47
2.7	-11.617
2.8	7.152
2.765	1.440932999

Therefore, the radius should be 2.76 m (correct to two decimals).

89. Let b be the width of the base, and let l be the length of the box. Then the length plus girth is
     $l + 4b = 108$, and the volume is $V = lb^2 = 2200$. Solving the first equation for l and substituting
     this value into the second equation yields $l = 108 - 4b$ $\Rightarrow V = (108 - 4b)b^2 = 2200$ $\Leftrightarrow$
     $4b^3 - 108b^2 + 2200 = 0$ $\Leftrightarrow$ $4(b^3 - 27b^2 + 550) = 0$. Now $P(b) = b^3 - 27b^2 + 550$ has two

variations in sign, so there are 0 or 2 positive real zeros. We also observe that since $l > 0$, $b < 27$, so $b = 27$ is an upper bound. Thus the possible positive rational real zeros are 1, 2, 3, 10, 11, 22, 25.

$$
\begin{array}{r|rrrr}
1 & 1 & -27 & 0 & 550 \\
  &   & 1 & -26 & -26 \\
\hline
  & 1 & -26 & -26 & 524
\end{array}
\qquad
\begin{array}{r|rrrr}
2 & 1 & -27 & 0 & 550 \\
  &   & 2 & -50 & -100 \\
\hline
  & 1 & -25 & -50 & 450
\end{array}
$$

$$
\begin{array}{r|rrrr}
5 & 1 & -27 & 0 & 550 \\
  &   & 5 & -110 & -550 \\
\hline
  & 1 & -22 & -110 & 0
\end{array}
\qquad \Rightarrow \quad b = 5 \text{ is a zero.}
$$

$P(b) = (b - 5)(b^2 - 22b - 110)$. The other zeros are $b = \dfrac{22 \pm \sqrt{484 - 4(1)(-110)}}{2}$

$= \dfrac{22 \pm \sqrt{924}}{2} = \dfrac{22 \pm 30.397}{2}$. The positive answer from this factor is $b \approx 26.20$. Thus we have two possible solutions, $b = 5$ or $b \approx 26.20$. If $b = 5$, then $l = 108 - 4(5) = 88$; if $b \approx 26.20$, then $l = 108 - 4(26.20) = 3.20$. Thus the length of the box is either 88 in. or 3.20 in.

91. Suppose $-b$ is a negative lower bound for the real zeros of $P(x)$. Then clearly b is an upper bound for $P_1(x) = P(-x)$. Thus, as in Exercise 90, we can write $P_1(x) = (x - b) \cdot Q(x) + r$, where $r > 0$ and the coefficients of Q are all non-negative, and
$P(x) = P_1(-x) = (-x - b) \cdot Q(-x) + r = (x + b) \cdot [-Q(-x)] + r$. Since the coefficients of $Q(x)$ are all non-negative, the coefficients of $-Q(-x)$ will be alternately non-positive and non-negative, which proves the second part of the Upper and Lower Bounds Theorem.

93. (a) An odd degree polynomial must have a real zero. The end behavior of such a polynomial requires that the graph of the polynomial heads off in opposite directions as $x \to \infty$ and $x \to -\infty$. Thus the graph must cross the x-axis.

(b) There are many possibilities one of which is $P(x) = x^4 + 1$.

(c) $P(x) = x(x - \sqrt{2})(x + \sqrt{2}) = x^3 - 2x$.

(d) $P(x) = (x - \sqrt{2})(x + \sqrt{2})(x - \sqrt{3})(x + \sqrt{3}) = x^4 - 5x^2 + 6$.

If a polynomial with integer coefficients has no real zeroes, then the polynomial must have even degree.

95. (a) Using the cubic formula:

$$
x = \sqrt[3]{\dfrac{-2}{2} + \sqrt{\dfrac{2^2}{4} + \dfrac{(-3)^3}{27}}} + \sqrt[3]{\dfrac{-2}{2} - \sqrt{\dfrac{2^2}{4} + \dfrac{(-3)^3}{27}}} = \sqrt[3]{-1} + \sqrt[3]{-1} = -1 - 1 = -2.
$$

$$
\begin{array}{r|rrrr}
-2 & 1 & 0 & -3 & 2 \\
   &   & -2 & 4 & -2 \\
\hline
   & 1 & -2 & 1 & 0
\end{array}
$$

So $(x + 2)(x^2 - 2x + 1) = (x + 2)(x - 1)^2 = 0 \quad \Rightarrow \quad x = -2, 1$.

Using the methods from this section, we have
$$
\begin{array}{r|rrrr}
1 & 1 & 0 & -3 & 2 \\
  &   & 1 & 1 & -2 \\
\hline
  & 1 & 1 & -2 & 0
\end{array}
$$

So $x^3 - 3x + 2 = (x - 1)(x^2 + x - 2) = (x - 1)^2(x + 2) = 0 \quad \Leftrightarrow \quad x = -2, 1$.

Since this factors easily, the factoring method was easier.

(b) Using the cubic formula:

$$x = \sqrt[3]{\frac{-(-54)}{2} + \sqrt{\frac{(-54)^2}{4} + \frac{(-27)^3}{27}}} + \sqrt[3]{\frac{-(-54)}{2} - \sqrt{\frac{(-54)^2}{4} + \frac{(-27)^3}{27}}}$$

$$= \sqrt[3]{\frac{54}{2} + \sqrt{27^2 - 27^2}} + \sqrt[3]{\frac{54}{2} - \sqrt{27^2 - 27^2}} = \sqrt[3]{27} + \sqrt[3]{27} = 3 + 3 = 6.$$

$$
\begin{array}{r|rrrr}
6 & 1 & 0 & -27 & -54 \\
  &   & 6 & 36 & 54 \\
\hline
  & 1 & 6 & 9 & 0
\end{array}
$$

$x^3 - 27x - 54 = (x - 6)(x^2 + 6x + 9) = (x - 6)(x + 3)^2 = 0 \quad \Rightarrow \quad x = -3, 6.$

Using methods from this section,

$$
\begin{array}{r|rrrr}
-1 & 1 & 0 & -27 & -54 \\
   &   & -1 & 1 & 26 \\
\hline
   & 1 & -1 & -26 & -28
\end{array}
\qquad
\begin{array}{r|rrrr}
-2 & 1 & 0 & -27 & -54 \\
   &   & -2 & 4 & 46 \\
\hline
   & 1 & -2 & -23 & -8
\end{array}
$$

$$
\begin{array}{r|rrrr}
-3 & 1 & 0 & -27 & -54 \\
   &   & -3 & 9 & 54 \\
\hline
   & 1 & -3 & -18 & 0
\end{array}
$$

So $x^3 - 27x - 54 = = (x + 3)(x^2 - 3x - 18) = (x - 6)(x + 3)^2 = 0 \quad \Leftrightarrow \quad x = -3, 6.$
Since this factors easily, the factoring method was easier.

(c) Using the cubic formula:

$$x = \sqrt[3]{\frac{-4}{2} + \sqrt{\frac{4^2}{4} + \frac{3^3}{27}}} + \sqrt[3]{\frac{-4}{2} - \sqrt{\frac{4^2}{4} + \frac{3^3}{27}}}$$

$$= \sqrt[3]{-2 + \sqrt{4 + 1}} + \sqrt[3]{-2 - \sqrt{4 + 1}} = \sqrt[3]{-2 + \sqrt{5}} + \sqrt[3]{-2 - \sqrt{5}}.$$

From the graphing calculator, we see that $P(x) = x^3 + 3x + 4$ has one zero.

Using methods from this section, $P(x)$ has possible rational zeros $\pm 1, \pm 2, \pm 4.$

$$
\begin{array}{r|rrrr}
1 & 1 & 0 & 3 & 4 \\
  &   & 1 & 1 & 4 \\
\hline
  & 1 & 1 & 4 & 4
\end{array}
\quad \Rightarrow \quad \text{1 is an upper bound.}
$$

$$
\begin{array}{r|rrrr}
-1 & 1 & 0 & 3 & 4 \\
   &   & -1 & 1 & -4 \\
\hline
   & 1 & -1 & 4 & 0
\end{array}
\quad \Rightarrow x = -1 \text{ is a zero.}
$$

$P(x) = x^3 + 3x + 4 = (x + 1)(x^2 - x + 4).$ Using the quadratic formula we have:

$$x = \frac{-(-1) \pm \sqrt{(-1)^2 - 4(1)(4)}}{2} = \frac{1 \pm \sqrt{-15}}{2} \text{ which is not a real number.}$$

Since it is not easy to see that $\sqrt[3]{-2 + \sqrt{5}} + \sqrt[3]{-2 - \sqrt{5}} = -1$, we see that the factoring method was *much* easier.

Exercises 3.4

1. $5 - 7\,i$: real part 5, imaginary part -7.

3. $\dfrac{-2 - 5\,i}{3} = -\frac{2}{3} - \frac{5}{3}\,i$: real part $-\frac{2}{3}$, imaginary part $-\frac{5}{3}$.

5. 3: real part 3, imaginary part 0.

7. $-\frac{2}{3}\,i$: real part 0, imaginary part $-\frac{2}{3}$.

9. $\sqrt{3} + \sqrt{-4} = \sqrt{3} + 2\,i$: real part $\sqrt{3}$, imaginary part 2.

11. $(2 - 5\,i) + (3 + 4\,i) = (2 + 3) + (-5 + 4)\,i = 5 - i$.

13. $(-6 + 6\,i) + (9 - i) = (-6 + 9) + (6 - 1)\,i = 3 + 5\,i$.

15. $(7 - \frac{1}{2}\,i) - (5 + \frac{3}{2}\,i) = (7 - 5) + (-\frac{1}{2} - \frac{3}{2})\,i = 2 - 2\,i$.

17. $(-12 + 8\,i) - (7 + 4\,i) = -12 + 8\,i - 7 - 4\,i = (-12 - 7) + (8 - 4)\,i = -19 + 4\,i$.

19. $4(-1 + 2\,i) = -4 + 8\,i$.

21. $(7 - i)(4 + 2\,i) = 28 + 14\,i - 4\,i - 2\,i^2 = (28 + 2) + (14 - 4)\,i = 30 + 10\,i$.

23. $(3 - 4\,i)(5 - 12\,i) = 15 - 36\,i - 20\,i + 48\,i^2 = (15 - 48) + (-36 - 20)\,i = -33 - 56\,i$.

25. $(6 + 5\,i)(2 - 3\,i) = 12 - 18\,i + 10\,i - 15\,i^2 = (12 + 15) + (-18 + 10)\,i = 27 - 8\,i$.

27. $\dfrac{1}{i} = \dfrac{1}{i} \cdot \dfrac{i}{i} = \dfrac{i}{i^2} = \dfrac{i}{-1} = -i$.

29. $\dfrac{2 - 3\,i}{1 - 2\,i} = \dfrac{2 - 3\,i}{1 - 2\,i} \cdot \dfrac{1 + 2\,i}{1 + 2\,i} = \dfrac{2 + 4\,i - 3\,i - 6\,i^2}{1 - 4\,i^2} = \dfrac{(2 + 6) + (4 - 3)\,i}{1 + 4} = \dfrac{8 + i}{5}$ or $\dfrac{8}{5} + \dfrac{1}{5}\,i$.

31. $\dfrac{26 + 39\,i}{2 - 3\,i} = \dfrac{26 + 39\,i}{2 - 3\,i} \cdot \dfrac{2 + 3\,i}{2 + 3\,i} = \dfrac{52 + 78\,i + 78\,i + 117\,i^2}{4 - 9\,i^2} = \dfrac{(52 - 117) + (78 + 78)\,i}{4 + 9} = $
    $\dfrac{-65 + 156\,i}{13} = \dfrac{13(-5 + 12\,i)}{13} = -5 + 12\,i$.

33. $\dfrac{10\,i}{1 - 2\,i} = \dfrac{10\,i}{1 - 2\,i} \cdot \dfrac{1 + 2\,i}{1 + 2\,i} = \dfrac{10\,i + 20\,i^2}{1 - 4\,i^2} = \dfrac{-20 + 10\,i}{1 + 4} = \dfrac{5(-4 + 2\,i)}{5} = -4 + 2\,i$.

35. $\dfrac{4 + 6\,i}{3\,i} = \dfrac{4 + 6\,i}{3\,i} \cdot \dfrac{i}{i} = \dfrac{4\,i + 6\,i^2}{3\,i^2} = \dfrac{-6 + 4\,i}{-3} = \dfrac{-6}{-3} + \dfrac{4}{-3}\,i = 2 - \dfrac{4}{3}\,i$.

37. $\dfrac{1}{1 + i} - \dfrac{1}{1 - i} = \dfrac{1}{1 + i} \cdot \dfrac{1 - i}{1 - i} - \dfrac{1}{1 - i} \cdot \dfrac{1 + i}{1 + i} = \dfrac{1 - i}{1 - i^2} - \dfrac{1 + i}{1 - i^2} = \dfrac{1 - i}{2} + \dfrac{-1 - i}{2} = -i$.

39. $i^3 = i^2 \cdot i = -1 \cdot i = -i$.

41. $i^{100} = \left(i^4\right)^{25} = (1)^{25} = 1$.

43. $\sqrt{-25} = 5\,i$.

45. $\sqrt{-3}\,\sqrt{-12} = i\sqrt{3} \cdot 2i\sqrt{3} = 6\,i^2 = -6$.

47. $\left(3 - \sqrt{-5}\right)\left(1 + \sqrt{-1}\right) = \left(3 - i\sqrt{5}\right)(1 + i) = 3 + 3i - i\sqrt{5} - i^2\sqrt{5} = $
    $\left(3 + \sqrt{5}\right) + \left(3 - \sqrt{5}\right)i.$

49. $\dfrac{2 + \sqrt{-8}}{1 + \sqrt{-2}} = \dfrac{2 + 2i\sqrt{2}}{1 + i\sqrt{2}} = \dfrac{2 + 2i\sqrt{2}}{1 + i\sqrt{2}} \cdot \dfrac{1 - i\sqrt{2}}{1 - i\sqrt{2}} = \dfrac{2 - 2i\sqrt{2} + 2i\sqrt{2} - 4i^2}{1 - 2i^2} = $
    $\dfrac{(2 + 4) + (-2\sqrt{2} + 2\sqrt{2})\,i}{1 + 2} = \dfrac{6}{3} = 2.$

51. $\dfrac{\sqrt{-36}}{\sqrt{-2}\sqrt{-9}} = \dfrac{6\,i}{i\sqrt{2} \cdot 3\,i} = \dfrac{2}{i\sqrt{2}} \cdot \dfrac{i\sqrt{2}}{i\sqrt{2}} = \dfrac{2i\sqrt{2}}{2\,i^2} = \dfrac{i\sqrt{2}}{-1} = -i\sqrt{2}.$

53. $x^2 + 9 = 0 \quad \Leftrightarrow \quad x^2 = -9 \quad \Rightarrow \quad x = \pm 3\,i.$

55. $x^2 - 4x + 5 = 0 \quad \Rightarrow \quad x = \dfrac{-(-4) \pm \sqrt{(-4)^2 - 4(1)(5)}}{2(1)} = \dfrac{4 \pm \sqrt{16 - 20}}{2} = \dfrac{4 \pm \sqrt{-4}}{2}$
    $= \dfrac{4 \pm 2\,i}{2} = 2 \pm i.$

57. $x^2 + x + 1 = 0 \quad \Rightarrow \quad x = \dfrac{-(1) \pm \sqrt{(1)^2 - 4(1)(1)}}{2(1)} = \dfrac{-1 \pm \sqrt{1 - 4}}{2} = \dfrac{-1 \pm \sqrt{-3}}{2} = $
    $\dfrac{-1 \pm i\sqrt{3}}{2} = -\dfrac{1}{2} \pm \dfrac{i\sqrt{3}}{2}.$

59. $2x^2 - 2x + 1 = 0 \quad \Rightarrow \quad x = \dfrac{-(-2) \pm \sqrt{(-2)^2 - 4(2)(1)}}{2(2)} = \dfrac{2 \pm \sqrt{4 - 8}}{4} = \dfrac{2 \pm \sqrt{-4}}{4} = $
    $\dfrac{2 \pm 2\,i}{4} = \dfrac{1}{2} \pm \dfrac{1}{2}\,i.$

61. $t + 3 + \dfrac{3}{t} = 0 \quad \Leftrightarrow \quad t^2 + 3t + 3 = 0 \quad \Rightarrow \quad t = \dfrac{-(3) \pm \sqrt{(3)^2 - 4(1)(3)}}{2(1)} = \dfrac{-3 \pm \sqrt{9 - 12}}{2}$
    $= \dfrac{-3 \pm \sqrt{-3}}{2} = \dfrac{-3 \pm i\sqrt{3}}{2} = -\dfrac{3}{2} \pm \dfrac{i\sqrt{3}}{2}.$

63. $6x^2 + 12x + 7 = 0 \quad \Rightarrow \quad x = \dfrac{-(12) \pm \sqrt{(12)^2 - 4(6)(7)}}{2(6)} = \dfrac{-12 \pm \sqrt{144 - 168}}{12} = $
    $\dfrac{-12 \pm \sqrt{-24}}{12} = \dfrac{-12 \pm 2i\sqrt{6}}{12} = \dfrac{-12}{12} \pm \dfrac{2i\sqrt{6}}{12} = -1 \pm \dfrac{i\sqrt{6}}{6}.$

65. $\frac{1}{2}x^2 - x + 5 = 0 \quad \Rightarrow \quad x = \dfrac{-(-1) \pm \sqrt{(-1)^2 - 4(\frac{1}{2})(5)}}{2(\frac{1}{2})} = \dfrac{1 \pm \sqrt{1 - 10}}{1} = 1 \pm \sqrt{-9} = $
    $1 \pm 3i.$

67. LHS $= \overline{z} + \overline{w} = \overline{(a + b\,i)} + \overline{(c + d\,i)} = a - b\,i + c - d\,i = (a + c) + (-b - d)i = $
    $(a + c) - (b + d)i.$
    RHS $= \overline{z + w} = \overline{(a + b\,i) + (c + d\,i)} = \overline{(a + c) + (b + d)\,i} = (a + c) - (b + d)i.$

Since LHS $=$ RHS, this proves the statement.

69. LHS $= (\bar{z})^2 = \left(\overline{(a + b\,i)}\right)^2 = (a - bi)^2 = a^2 - 2ab\,i + b^2\,i^2 = (a^2 - b^2) - 2ab\,i.$

RHS $= \overline{z^2} = \overline{(a + b\,i)^2} = \overline{a^2 + 2ab\,i + b^2\,i^2} = \overline{(a^2 - b^2) + 2ab\,i} = (a^2 - b^2) - 2ab\,i.$

Since LHS $=$ RHS, this proves the statement.

71. $z + \bar{z} = (a + b\,i) + \overline{(a + b\,i)} = a + b\,i + a - b\,i = 2a$, which is a real number.

73. $z \cdot \bar{z} = (a + b\,i) \cdot \overline{(a + b\,i)} = (a + b\,i) \cdot (a - b\,i) = a^2 - b^2i^2 = a^2 + b^2$, which is a real number.

75. Using the quadratic formula, the solutions to the equation are $x = \dfrac{-b \pm \sqrt{b^2 - 4ac}}{2a}$. Since both solutions are imaginary, we have $b^2 - 4ac < 0 \quad \Leftrightarrow \quad 4ac - b^2 > 0$, so the solutions are $x = \dfrac{-b}{2a} \pm \dfrac{\sqrt{4ac - b^2}}{2a}\,i$, where $\sqrt{4ac - b^2}$ is a real number. Thus the solutions are complex conjugates of each other.

Exercises 3.5

1. $x^3 + 8 = 0 \quad \Leftrightarrow \quad (x+2)(x^2 - 2x + 4) = 0.$ So $x = -2$ or $x^2 - 2x + 4 = 0.$ If
    $x^2 - 2x + 4 = 0$ then $x = \dfrac{-(-2) \pm \sqrt{(-2)^2 - 4(1)(4)}}{2} = \dfrac{2 \pm \sqrt{-12}}{2} = \dfrac{2 \pm 2i\sqrt{3}}{2} = 1 \pm i\sqrt{3}.$
    Therefore, the solutions are $x = -2, 1 \pm i\sqrt{3}.$

3. $x^3 - 2x^2 + 2x = 0 \quad \Leftrightarrow \quad x(x^2 - 2x + 2) = 0.$ So $x = 0$ or $x^2 - 2x + 2 = 0.$ If
    $x^2 - 2x + 2 = 0$ then $x = \frac{-(-2) \pm \sqrt{(-2)^2 - 4(1)(2)}}{2} = \frac{2 \pm \sqrt{-4}}{2} = \frac{2 \pm 2i}{2} = 1 \pm i.$ Therefore, the solutions
    are $x = 0, 1 \pm i.$

5. $x^4 + 2x^2 + 1 = 0 \quad \Leftrightarrow \quad (x^2 + 1)^2 = 0 \quad \Leftrightarrow \quad x^2 + 1 = 0 \quad \Leftrightarrow \quad x^2 = -1 \quad \Leftrightarrow \quad x = \pm i$

7. $x^4 - 16 = 0 \quad \Leftrightarrow \quad 0 = (x^2 - 4)(x^2 + 4) = (x-2)(x+2)(x^2+4).$ So $x = \pm 2$ or $x^2 + 4 = 0.$
    If $x^2 + 4 = 0$ then $x^2 = -4 \quad \Rightarrow \quad x = \pm 2i.$ Therefore the four solutions are $x = \pm 2, \pm 2i.$

9. $x^6 - 1 = 0 \quad \Leftrightarrow \quad 0 = (x^3 - 1)(x^3 + 1) = (x-1)(x^2 + x + 1)(x+1)(x^2 - x + 1).$ Clearly,
    $x = \pm 1$ are solutions. If $x^2 + x + 1 = 0,$ then $x = \frac{-1 \pm \sqrt{1-4(1)(1)}}{2} = \frac{-1 \pm \sqrt{-3}}{2} = -\frac{1}{2} \pm \frac{\sqrt{-3}}{2}$ so
    $x = -\frac{1}{2} \pm \frac{\sqrt{3}}{2}i.$ If $x^2 - x + 1 = 0,$ then $x = \frac{1 \pm \sqrt{1-4(1)(1)}}{2} = \frac{1 \pm \sqrt{-3}}{2} = \frac{1}{2} \pm \frac{\sqrt{-3}}{2} = \frac{1}{2} \pm \frac{\sqrt{3}}{2}i.$
    Therefore, the solutions are $x = \pm 1, -\frac{1}{2} \pm \frac{\sqrt{3}}{2}i, \frac{1}{2} \pm \frac{\sqrt{3}}{2}i.$

11. $P(x) = x^2 + 25 = (x - 5i)(x + 5i).$ The zeros of P are $5i$ and $-5i,$ both multiplicity 1.

13. $Q(x) = x^2 + 2x + 2.$ Using the quadratic formula $x = \frac{-(2) \pm \sqrt{(2)^2 - 4(1)(2)}}{2(1)} = \frac{-2 \pm \sqrt{-4}}{2}$
    $= \frac{-2 \pm 2i}{2} = -1 \pm i.$ So $Q(x) = (x + 1 - i)(x + 1 + i).$ The zeros of Q are $-1 - i$ (multiplicity 1)
    and $-1 + i$ (multiplicity 1).

15. $P(x) = x^3 + 4x = x(x^2 + 4) = x(x - 2i)(x + 2i).$ The zeros of P are $0, 2i,$ and $-2i$ (all
    multiplicity 1).

17. $Q(x) = x^4 - 1 = (x^2 - 1)(x^2 + 1) = (x-1)(x+1)(x^2+1) = (x-1)(x+1)(x-i)(x+i).$
    The zeros of Q are $1, -1, i,$ and $-i$ (all multiplicity 1).

19. $P(x) = 16x^4 - 81 = (4x^2 - 9)(4x^2 + 9) = (2x-3)(2x+3)(2x-3i)(2x+3i).$ The zeros of P
    are $\frac{3}{2}, -\frac{3}{2}, \frac{3}{2}i,$ and $-\frac{3}{2}i$ (all multiplicity 1).

21. $P(x) = x^3 + x^2 + 9x + 9 = x^2(x+1) + 9(x+1) = (x+1)(x^2+9) = (x+1)(x-3i)(x+3i).$
    The zeros of P are $-1, 3i,$ and $-3i$ (all multiplicity 1).

23. $Q(x) = x^4 + 2x^2 + 1 = (x^2 + 1)^2 = (x-i)^2(x+i)^2.$ The zeros of Q are i and $-i$ (both
    multiplicity 2).

25. $P(x) = x^4 + 3x^2 - 4 = (x^2 - 1)(x^2 + 4) = (x-1)(x+1)(x-2i)(x+2i).$ The zeros of P are
    $1, -1, 2i,$ and $-2i$ (all multiplicity 1).

27. $P(x) = x^5 + 6x^3 + 9x = x(x^4 + 6x^2 + 9) = x(x^2 + 3)^2 = x(x - \sqrt{3}i)^2(x + \sqrt{3}i)^2.$ The zeros
    of P are 0 (multiplicity 1), $\sqrt{3}i$ (multiplicity 2), and $-\sqrt{3}i$ (multiplicity 2).

29. Since $1 + i$ and $1 - i$ are conjugates, the factorization of the polynomial must be
$P(x) = a(x - [1 + i])(x - [1 - i]) = a(x^2 - 2x + 2)$. If we let $a = 1$, we get
$P(x) = x^2 - 2x + 2$.

31. Since $2i$ and $-2i$ are conjugates, the factorization of the polynomial must be
$Q(x) = b(x - 3)(x - 2i)(x + 2i) = b(x - 3)(x^2 + 4) = b(x^3 - 3x^2 + 4x - 12)$. If we let $b = 1$,
we get $Q(x) = x^3 - 3x^2 + 4x - 12$.

33. Since i is a zero, by the Conjugate Roots Theorem, $-i$ is also a zero. So the factorization of the
polynomial must be $P(x) = a(x - 2)(x - i)(x + i) = a(x^3 - 2x^2 + x - 2)$. If we let $a = 1$, we
get $P(x) = x^3 - 2x^2 + x - 2$.

35. Since the zeros are $1 - 2i$ and 1 (with multiplicity two), by the Conjugate Roots Theorem, the other
zero is $1 + 2i$. So a factorization is
$$R(x) = c(x - [1 - 2i])(x - [1 + 2i])(x - 1)^2 = c([x - 1] + 2i)([x - 1] - 2i)(x - 1)^2$$
$$= c([x - 1]^2 - [2i]^2)(x^2 - 2x + 1) = c(x^2 - 2x + 1 + 4)(x^2 - 2x + 1)$$
$$= c(x^2 - 2x + 5)(x^2 - 2x + 1) = c(x^4 - 2x^3 + x^2 - 2x^3 + 4x^2 - 2x + 5x^2 - 10x + 5)$$
$$= c(x^4 - 4x^3 + 10x^2 - 12x + 5). \text{ If we let } c = 1 \text{ we get } R(x) = x^4 - 4x^3 + 10x^2 - 12x + 5.$$

37. Since the zeros are i and $1 + i$, by the Conjugate Roots Theorem, the other zeros are $-i$ and $1 - i$.
So a factorization is
$$T(x) = C(x - i)(x + i)(x - [1 + i])(x - [1 - i]) = C(x^2 - i^2)([x - 1] - i)([x - 1] + i)$$
$$= C(x^2 + 1)(x^2 - 2x + 1 - i^2) = C(x^2 + 1)(x^2 - 2x + 2) = C(x^4 - 2x^3 + 2x^2 + x^2 - 2x + 2)$$
$$= C(x^4 - 2x^3 + 3x^2 - 2x + 2) = Cx^4 - 2Cx^3 + 3Cx^2 - 2Cx + 2C.$$
Since the constant coefficient is 12, it follows that $2C = 12 \quad \Leftrightarrow \quad C = 6$, and so
$T(x) = 6(x^4 - 2x^3 + 3x^2 - 2x + 2) = 6x^4 - 12x^3 + 18x^2 - 12x + 12$.

39. $P(x) = x^3 + 2x^2 + 4x + 8 = x^2(x + 2) + 4(x + 2) = (x + 2)(x^2 + 4)$
$= (x + 2)(x - 2i)(x + 2i)$. Thus the zeros are -2 and $\pm 2i$.

41. $P(x) = x^3 - 2x^2 + 2x - 1$. By inspection, $P(1) = 1 - 2 + 2 - 1 = 0$, and hence $x = 1$ is a zero.

1	1	-2	2	-1
		1	-1	1
	1	-1	1	0

Thus $P(x) = (x - 1)(x^2 - x + 1)$. So $x = 1$ or $x^2 - x + 1 = 0$.

Using the quadratic formula, we have $x = \dfrac{1 \pm \sqrt{1 - 4(1)(1)}}{2} = \dfrac{1 \pm i\sqrt{3}}{2}$. Hence, the zeros are 1
and $\dfrac{1 \pm i\sqrt{3}}{2}$.

43. $P(x) = x^3 - 3x^2 + 3x - 2$.

2	1	-3	3	-2
		2	-2	2
	1	-1	1	0

Thus $P(x) = (x - 2)(x^2 - x + 1)$. So $x = 2$ or $x^2 - x + 1 = 0$

Using the quadratic formula we have $x = \dfrac{1 \pm \sqrt{1 - 4(1)(1)}}{2} = \dfrac{1 \pm i\sqrt{3}}{2}$. Hence, the zeros are 2,
and $\frac{1 \pm i\sqrt{3}}{2}$

45. $P(x) = 2x^3 + 7x^2 + 12x + 9$ has possible rational zeros $\pm 1, \pm 3, \pm 9, \pm\frac{1}{2}, \pm\frac{3}{2}, \pm\frac{9}{2}$. Since all
coefficients are positive, there are no positive real zeros.

$$\begin{array}{r|rrrr} -1 & 2 & 7 & 12 & 9 \\ & & -2 & -5 & -7 \\ \hline & 2 & 5 & 7 & 2 \end{array} \qquad \begin{array}{r|rrrr} -2 & 2 & 7 & 12 & 9 \\ & & -4 & -6 & -12 \\ \hline & 2 & 3 & 6 & -3 \end{array}$$

There is a zero between -1 and -2.

$$\begin{array}{r|rrrr} -\frac{3}{2} & 2 & 7 & 12 & 9 \\ & & -3 & -6 & -9 \\ \hline & 2 & 4 & 6 & 0 \end{array} \quad \Rightarrow \quad x = -\frac{3}{2} \text{ is a zero.}$$

$P(x) = \left(x + \frac{3}{2}\right)(2x^2 + 4x + 6) = 2\left(x + \frac{3}{2}\right)(x^2 + 2x + 3)$. Now $x^2 + 2x + 3$ has zeros

$$x = \frac{-2 \pm \sqrt{4 - 4(3)(1)}}{2} = \frac{-2 \pm 2\sqrt{-2}}{2} = -1 \pm i\sqrt{2}. \text{ Hence, the zeros are } -\frac{3}{2} \text{ and}$$

$-1 \pm i\sqrt{2}$.

47. $P(x) = x^4 + x^3 + 7x^2 + 9x - 18$. Since $P(x)$ has one change in sign, we are guaranteed a positive zero, and since $P(-x) = x^4 - x^3 + 7x^2 - 9x - 18$, there are 1 or 3 negative zeros.

$$\begin{array}{r|rrrrr} 1 & 1 & 1 & 7 & 9 & -18 \\ & & 1 & 2 & 9 & 18 \\ \hline & 1 & 2 & 9 & 18 & 0 \end{array} \quad \Rightarrow \quad \text{Therefore, } P(x) = (x - 1)(x^3 + 2x^2 + 9x + 18).$$

Continuing with the quotient, we try negative zeros.

$$\begin{array}{r|rrrr} -1 & 1 & 2 & 9 & 18 \\ & & -1 & -1 & -8 \\ \hline & 1 & 1 & 8 & 10 \end{array}$$

$$\begin{array}{r|rrrr} -2 & 1 & 2 & 9 & 18 \\ & & -2 & 0 & -18 \\ \hline & 1 & 0 & 9 & 0 \end{array}$$

$P(x) = (x - 1)(x + 2)(x^2 + 9) = (x - 1)(x + 2)(x - 3i)(x + 3i)$. Therefore, the zeros are 1, -2, and $\pm 3i$.

49. We see a pattern and utilize it to factor by grouping. This gives
$$P(x) = x^5 - x^4 + 7x^3 - 7x^2 + 12x - 12 = x^4(x - 1) + 7x^2(x - 1) + 12(x - 1)$$
$$= (x - 1)(x^4 + 7x^2 + 12) = (x - 1)(x^2 + 3)(x^2 + 4)$$
$$= (x - 1)(x - i\sqrt{3})(x + i\sqrt{3})(x - 2i)(x + 2i). \text{ Therefore, the zeros are } 1, \pm i\sqrt{3}, \text{ and } \pm 2i.$$

51. $P(x) = x^4 - 6x^3 + 13x^2 - 24x + 36$ has possible rational zeros $\pm 1, \pm 2, \pm 3, \pm 4, \pm 6, \pm 9, \pm 12,$ ± 18. $P(x)$ has 4 variations in signs and $P(-x)$ has no variation in signs.

$$\begin{array}{r|rrrrr} 1 & 1 & -6 & 13 & -24 & 36 \\ & & 1 & -5 & 8 & -16 \\ \hline & 1 & -5 & 8 & -16 & 20 \end{array} \qquad \begin{array}{r|rrrrr} 2 & 1 & -6 & 13 & -24 & 36 \\ & & 2 & -8 & 10 & -28 \\ \hline & 1 & -4 & 5 & -14 & 8 \end{array}$$

$$\begin{array}{r|rrrrr} 3 & 1 & -6 & 13 & -24 & 36 \\ & & 3 & -9 & 12 & -36 \\ \hline & 1 & -3 & 4 & -12 & 0 \end{array} \quad \Rightarrow \quad x = 3 \text{ is a zero.}$$

Continuing:

$$\begin{array}{r|rrrr} 3 & 1 & -3 & 4 & -12 \\ & & 3 & 0 & 12 \\ \hline & 1 & 0 & 4 & 0 \end{array} \quad \Rightarrow \quad x = 3 \text{ is a zero.}$$

$P(x) = (x-3)^2(x^2+4) = (x-3)^2(x-2i)(x+2i)$. Therefore, the zeros are 3 (multiplicity 2) and $\pm 2i$.

53. $P(x) = x^5 - 3x^4 + 12x^3 - 28x^2 + 27x - 9$ has possible rational zeros $\pm 1, \pm 3, \pm 9$. $P(x)$ has 4 variations in sign and $P(-x)$ has 1 variation in sign.

$$
\begin{array}{r|rrrrrr}
1 & 1 & -3 & 12 & -28 & 27 & -9 \\
  &   & 1 & -2 & 10 & -18 & 9 \\
\hline
  & 1 & -2 & 10 & -18 & 9 & 0
\end{array}
\Rightarrow \quad x = 1 \text{ is a zero.}
$$

$$
\begin{array}{r|rrrrr}
1 & 1 & -2 & 10 & -18 & 9 \\
  &   & 1 & -1 & 9 & -9 \\
\hline
  & 1 & -1 & 9 & -9 & 0
\end{array}
\Rightarrow \quad x = 1 \text{ is a zero.}
$$

$$
\begin{array}{r|rrrr}
1 & 1 & -1 & 9 & -9 \\
  &   & 1 & 0 & 9 \\
\hline
  & 1 & 0 & 9 & 0
\end{array}
\Rightarrow \quad x = 1 \text{ is a zero.}
$$

$P(x) = (x-1)^3(x^2+9) = (x-1)^3(x-3i)(x+3i)$. Therefore, the zeros are 1 (multiplicity 3) and $\pm 3i$.

55. (a) $P(x) = x^3 - 5x^2 + 4x - 20 = x^2(x-5) + 4(x-5) = (x-5)(x^2+4)$.

   (b) $P(x) = (x-5)(x-2i)(x+2i)$.

57. (a) $P(x) = x^4 + 8x^2 - 9 = (x^2-1)(x^2+9) = (x-1)(x+1)(x^2+9)$.

   (b) $P(x) = (x-1)(x+1)(x-3i)(x+3i)$.

59. (a) $P(x) = x^6 - 64 = (x^3-8)(x^3+8) = (x-2)(x^2+2x+4)(x+2)(x^2-2x+4)$.

   (b) $P(x) = (x-2)(x+2)(x+1-i\sqrt{3})(x+1+i\sqrt{3})(x-1-i\sqrt{3})(x-1+i\sqrt{3})$.

61. (a) $x^4 - 2x^3 - 11x^2 + 12x = x(x^3 - 2x^2 - 11x + 12) = 0$. We first find the bounds for our viewing rectangle.

$$
\begin{array}{r|rrrr}
 & 1 & -2 & -11 & 12 \\
5 & 1 & 3 & 4 & 32 \\
-4 & 1 & -6 & 13 & -50
\end{array}
\begin{array}{l}
\Rightarrow \quad x = 5 \text{ is an upper bound.} \\
\Rightarrow \quad x = -4 \text{ is a lower bound.}
\end{array}
$$

The viewing rectangle $[-4, 5]$ by $[-50, 10]$ shows that $P(x) = x^4 - 2x^3 - 11x^2 + 12x$ has 4 real solutions. Since this matches the degree of $P(x)$, $P(x)$ has no imaginary solutions.

   (b) $x^4 - 2x^3 - 11x^2 + 12x - 5 = 0$. We use the same bounds for our viewing rectangle, $[-4, 5]$ by $[-50, 10]$, and see that $R(x) = x^4 - 2x^3 - 11x^2 + 12x - 5$ has 2 real solutions. Since the degree of $R(x)$ is 4, $R(x)$ must have 2 imaginary solutions.

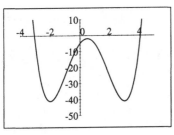

(c) $x^4 - 2x^3 - 11x^2 + 12x + 40 = 0$. We use the same bounds for our viewing rectangle, $[-4, 5]$ by $[-10, 50]$, and see that $T(x) = x^4 - 2x^3 - 11x^2 + 12x + 40$ has no real solutions. Since the degree of $T(x)$ is 4, $T(x)$ must have 4 imaginary solutions.

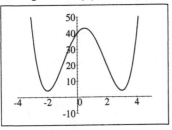

63. (a) $P(x) = x^2 - (1 + i)x + (2 + 2i)$. So
$P(2i) = (2i)^2 - (1 + i)(2i) + 2 + 2i = -4 - 2i + 2 + 2 + 2i = 0$, and
$P(1 - i) = (1 - i)^2 - (1 + i)(1 - i) + (2 + 2i) = 1 - 2i - 1 - 1 - 1 + 2 + 2i = 0$.
Therefore, $2i$ and $1 - i$ are solutions of the equation $x^2 - (1 + i)x + (2 + 2i) = 0$. However,
$P(-2i) = (-2i)^2 - (1 + i)(-2i) + 2 + 2i = -4 + 2i - 2 + 2 + 2i = -4 + 4i$, and
$P(1 + i) = (1 + i)^2 - (1 + i)(1 + i) + 2 + 2i = 2 + 2i$. Since, $P(-2i) \neq 0$ and
$P(1 + i) \neq 0$, $-2i$ and $1 + i$ are not solutions.

(b) This does not violate the Conjugate Roots Theorem because the coefficients of the polynomial $P(x)$ are not all real.

65. Since P has real coefficients, the imaginary zeros come in pairs: $a \pm bi$ (by the Conjugate Roots Theorem), where $b \neq 0$. Thus there must be an even number of imaginary zeros. Since P is of odd degree, it has an odd number of zeros (counting multiplicity). It follows that P has at least one real zero.

Exercises 3.6

1. $r(x) = \dfrac{x-2}{x+3}$. When $x = 0$, we have $r(0) = -\frac{2}{3}$, so the y-intercept is $-\frac{2}{3}$. The numerator is 0 when $x = 2$, so the x-intercept is 2.

3. $t(x) = \dfrac{x^2 - x - 2}{x - 6}$. When $x = 0$, we have $t(0) = \frac{-2}{-6} = \frac{1}{3}$, so the y-intercept is $\frac{1}{3}$. The numerator is 0 when $x^2 - x - 2 = (x-2)(x+1) = 0$ or when $x = 2$ or $x = -1$, so the x-intercepts are 2 and -1.

5. $r(x) = \dfrac{x^2 - 9}{x^2}$. Since 0 is not in the domain of $r(x)$, there is no y-intercept. The numerator is 0 when $x^2 - 9 = (x-3)(x+3) = 0$ or when $x = \pm 3$, so the x-intercepts are ± 3.

7. From the graph, the x-intercept is 3, the y-intercept is 3, the vertical asymptote is $x = 2$, and the horizontal asymptote is $y = 2$.

9. $r(x) = \dfrac{3}{x+2}$. There is a vertical asymptote where $x + 2 = 0 \quad \Leftrightarrow \quad x = -2$. We have

$$r(x) = \frac{3}{x+2} = \frac{\dfrac{3}{x}}{1 + \dfrac{2}{x}} \to 0 \text{ as } x \to \pm\infty,$$ so the horizontal asymptote is $y = 0$.

11. $t(x) = \dfrac{x^2}{x^2 - x - 6} = \dfrac{x^2}{(x-3)(x+2)} = \dfrac{1}{1 - \dfrac{1}{x} - \dfrac{6}{x^2}} \to 1 \text{ as } x \to \pm\infty$. Hence, the horizontal asymptote is $y = 1$. The vertical asymptotes occur when $(x-3)(x+2) = 0 \quad \Leftrightarrow \quad x = 3$ or $x = -2$, and so the vertical asymptotes are $x = 3$ and $x = -2$.

13. $s(x) = \dfrac{6}{x^2 + 2}$. There is no vertical asymptote since $x^2 + 2$ is never 0. Since

$$s(x) = \frac{6}{x^2 + 2} = \frac{\dfrac{6}{x^2}}{1 + \dfrac{2}{x^2}} \to 0 \text{ as } x \to \pm\infty,$$ the horizontal asymptote is $y = 0$.

15. $r(x) = \dfrac{6x - 2}{x^2 + 5x - 6}$. A vertical asymptote occurs when $x^2 + 5x - 6 = (x+6)(x-1) = 0 \quad \Leftrightarrow \quad x = 1$ or $x = -6$. Because the degree of the denominator is greater than the degree of the numerator, the horizontal asymptote is $y = 0$.

17. $y = \dfrac{x^2 + 2}{x - 1}$. A vertical asymptote occurs when $x - 1 = 0 \quad \Leftrightarrow \quad x = 1$. There are no horizontal asymptotes because the degree of the numerator is greater than the degree of the denominator.

In exercises 19-23, let $f(x) = \dfrac{1}{x}$.

19. $r(x) = \dfrac{1}{x-1} = f(x-1)$.

From this form we see that the graph of r is obtained from the graph of f by shifting 1 unit to the right. Thus r has vertical asymptote $x = 1$ and horizontal asymptote $y = 0$.

21. $s(x) = \dfrac{3}{x+1} = 3\left(\dfrac{1}{x+1}\right) = 3f(x+1)$.

From this form we see that the graph of s is obtained from the graph of f by shifting 1 unit to the left and stretching vertically by a factor of 3. Thus s has vertical asymptote $x = -1$ and horizontal asymptote $y = 0$.

23. $t(x) = \dfrac{2x-3}{x-2} = 2 + \dfrac{1}{x-2} = f(x-2) + 2$ (see long division below).

From this form we see that the graph of t is obtained from the graph of f by shifting 2 units to the right and 2 units vertically. Thus t has vertical asymptote $x = 2$ and horizontal asymptote $y = 2$.

25. $y = \dfrac{4x-4}{x+2}$. When $x = 0$, $y = -2$, so the y-intercept is -2. When $y = 0$, $4x - 4 = 0$ $\Leftrightarrow$ $x = 1$, so the x-intercept is 1. Since the degree of the numerator and denominator are the same the horizontal asymptote is $y = \frac{4}{1} = 4$. A vertical asymptote occurs when $x = -2$.

as $x \rightarrow$	-2^{+}	-2^{-}
sign of $y = \frac{4x-4}{x+2}$	$\frac{(-)}{(+)}$	$\frac{(-)}{(-)}$
$y \quad \rightarrow$	$-\infty$	∞

27. $s(x) = \dfrac{4-3x}{x+7}$. When $x = 0$, $y = \frac{4}{7}$, so the y-intercept is $\frac{4}{7}$. The x-intercepts occur when $y = 0$ $\Leftrightarrow$ $4 - 3x = 0$ $\Leftrightarrow$ $x = \frac{4}{3}$. A vertical asymptote occurs when $x = -7$. Since the degree of the numerator and denominator are the same the horizontal asymptote is $y = \frac{-3}{1} = -3$.

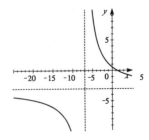

29. $r(x) = \dfrac{18}{(x-3)^2}$. When $x = 0$, $y = \frac{18}{9} = 2$, and so the y-intercept is

2. Since the numerator can never be zero, there is no x-intercept. There is a vertical asymptote when $x - 3 = 0 \quad \Leftrightarrow \quad x = 3$, and because the degree of the asymptote is $y = 0$.

31. $s(x) = \dfrac{4x - 8}{(x-4)(x+1)}$. When $x = 0$, $y = \frac{-8}{(-4)(1)} = 2$, so the

y-intercept is 2. When $y = 0$, $4x + 8 = 0 \quad \Leftrightarrow \quad x = -2$, so the x-intercept is -2. The vertical asymptotes are $x = -1$ and $x = 4$, and because the degree of the numerator is less than the degree of the denominator, the horizontal asymptote is $y = 0$.

33. $s(x) = \dfrac{6}{x^2 - 5x - 6}$. When $x = 0$, $y = \frac{6}{-6} = -1$, so the y-intercept

is -1. Since the numerator is never zero, there is no x-intercept. The vertical asymptotes occur when $x^2 - 5x - 6 = (x+1)(x-3) \quad \Leftrightarrow \quad x = -1$ and $x = 3$, and because the degree of the numerator is less less than the degree of the denominator, the horizontal asymptote is $y = 0$.

35. $t(x) = \dfrac{3x + 6}{x^2 + 2x - 8}$. When $x = 0$, $y = \frac{6}{-8} = -\frac{3}{4}$, so the y-intercept

y-intercept is $-\frac{3}{4}$. When $y = 0$, $3x + 6 = 0 \quad \Leftrightarrow \quad x = -2$, so the x-intercept is -2. The vertical asymptotes occur when $x^2 + 2x - 8 = (x-2)(x+4) = 0 \quad \Leftrightarrow \quad x = 2$ and $x = -4$. Since the degree of the numerator is less than the degree of the denominator, the horizontal asymptote is $y = 0$.

37. $r(x) = \dfrac{(x-1)(x+2)}{(x+1)(x-3)}$. When $x = 0$, $y = \frac{2}{3}$, so the y-intercept is $\frac{2}{3}$.

When $y = 0$, $(x-1)(x+2) = 0 \quad \Rightarrow \quad x = -2, 1$, so, the x-intercepts are -2 and 1. The vertical asymptotes are $x = -1$ and $x = 3$, and because the degree of the numerator and denominator are the same the horizontal asymptote is $y = \frac{1}{1} = 1$.

39. $r(x) = \dfrac{x^2 - 2x + 1}{x^2 + 2x + 1} = \dfrac{(x-1)^2}{(x+1)^2} = \left(\dfrac{x-1}{x+1}\right)^2$. When $x = 0$, $y = 1$,
so the y-intercept is 1. When $y = 0$, $x = 1$, so the x-intercept is 1. A
vertical asymptote occurs at $x + 1 = 0 \quad \Leftrightarrow \quad x = -1$. Because the
degree of the numerator and denominator are the same the horizontal
asymptote is $y = \frac{1}{1} = 1$.

41. $r(x) = \dfrac{2x^2 + 10x - 12}{x^2 + x - 6} = \dfrac{2(x-1)(x+6)}{(x-2)(x+3)}$. When $x = 0$,
$y = \frac{2(-1)(6)}{(-2)(3)} = 2$, so the y-intercept is 2. When $y = 0$,
$2(x-1)(x+6) = 0 \quad \Rightarrow \quad x = -6, 1$, so the x-intercepts are -6
and 1. Vertical asymptotes occur when $(x-2)(x+3) = 0 \quad \Leftrightarrow$
$x = -3$ or $x = 2$. Because the degree of the numerator and
denominator are the same the horizontal asymptote is $y = \frac{2}{1} = 2$.

43. $y = \dfrac{x^2 - x - 6}{x^2 + 3x} = \dfrac{(x-3)(x+2)}{x(x+3)}$. The x-intercept occurs when $y = 0$
$\Leftrightarrow \quad (x-3)(x+2) = 0 \quad \Rightarrow \quad x = -2, 3$, so the x-intercepts are
-2 and 3. There is no y-intercept because y is undefined when $x = 0$.
The vertical asymptotes are $x = 0$ and $x = -3$. Because the degree of
the numerator and denominator are the same, the horizontal asymptotes
is $y = \frac{1}{1} = 1$.

45. $r(x) = \dfrac{3x^2 + 6}{x^2 - 2x - 3} = \dfrac{3(x^2 + 2)}{(x-3)(x+1)}$. When $x = 0$, $y = -2$, so
the y-intercept is -2. Since the numerator can never equal zero, there
is -2. Since the numerator can never equal zero, there is no x-intercept.
Vertical asymptotes occur when $x = -1, 3$. Because the degree of
the numerator and denominator are the same, the horizontal
asymptote is.$y = \frac{3}{1} = 3$.

47. $s(x) = \dfrac{x^2 - 2x + 1}{x^3 - 3x^2} = \dfrac{(x-1)^2}{x^2(x-3)}$. Since $x = 0$ is not in the domain
of $s(x)$, there is no y-intercept. The x-intercept occurs when $y = 0$
$\Leftrightarrow \quad x^2 - 2x + 1 = (x-1)^2 = 0 \quad \Rightarrow \quad x = 1$, so the x-intercept
is 1. Vertical asymptotes occur when $x = -1, 3$. Since the degree of
the numerator is less than the degree of the denominator, the horizontal
asymptote is $y = 0$.

49. $r(x) = \dfrac{x^2}{x-2}$. When $x = 0$, $y = 0$, so the graph passes through the
origin. There is a vertical asymptote when $x - 2 = 0 \iff x = 2$,
with $y \to \infty$ as $x \to 2^+$, and $y \to -\infty$ as $x \to 2^-$. Because the
degree of the numerator is greater than the degree of the denominator,
there is no horizontal asymptotes. By using long division, we see
that $y = x + 2 + \dfrac{4}{x-2}$, so $y = x + 2$ is a slant asymptote.

51. $r(x) = \dfrac{x^2 - 2x - 8}{x} = \dfrac{(x-4)(x+2)}{x}$. The vertical asymptote is
$x = 0$, thus, there is no y-intercept. If $y = 0$, then $(x-4)(x+2) = 0$
$\Rightarrow x = -2, 4$, so the x-intercepts are -2 and 4. Because the degree
f the numerator is greater than the degree of the denominator, there
are no horizontal asymptotes. By using long division, we see that
$y = x - 2 - \dfrac{8}{x}$, so $y = x - 2$ is a slant asymptote.

53. $r(x) = \dfrac{x^2 + 5x + 4}{x - 3} = \dfrac{(x+4)(x+1)}{x - 3}$. When $x = 0$, $y = -\frac{4}{3}$, so the
y-intercept is $-\frac{4}{3}$. When $y = 0$, $(x+4)(x+1) = 0 \iff x = -4$,
-1, so the two x-intercepts are -4 and -1. A vertical asymptote
occurs when $x = 3$, with $y \to \infty$ as $x \to 3^+$, and $y \to -\infty$
as $x \to 3^-$. Using long division, we see that $y = x + 8 + \dfrac{28}{x - 3}$,
so $y = x + 8$ is a slant asymptote.

55. $r(x) = \dfrac{x^3 + x^2}{x^2 - 4} = \dfrac{x^2(x+1)}{(x-2)(x+2)}$. When $x = 0$, $y = 0$, so the
graph passes through the origin. Moreover, when $y = 0$, we have
$x^2(x+1) = 0 \Rightarrow x = 0, -1$, so the x-intercepts are 0 and -1.
Vertical asymptotes occur when $x = \pm 2$, and because the degree of
the numerator is greater than the degree of the dominator there are
no horizontal asymptotes. Using long division, we see that
$y = x + 1 + \dfrac{4x + 4}{x^2 - 4}$, so $y = x + 1$ is a slant asymptote.

as $x \to$	-2^-	-2^+	2^-	2^+
sign of $y = \dfrac{x^2(x+1)}{(x-2)(x+2)}$	$\dfrac{(+)(-)}{(-)(-)}$	$\dfrac{(+)(-)}{(-)(+)}$	$\dfrac{(+)(+)}{(-)(+)}$	$\dfrac{(+)(+)}{(+)(+)}$
$y \to$	$-\infty$	∞	$-\infty$	∞

57. $f(x) = \dfrac{2x^2 + 6x + 6}{x + 3}$, $g(x) = 2x$. Vertical asymptote: $x = -3$.
$[-10, 5]$ by $[-20, 10]$ Graph of f. $[-20, 20]$ by $[-50, 50]$ Graph of f and g.

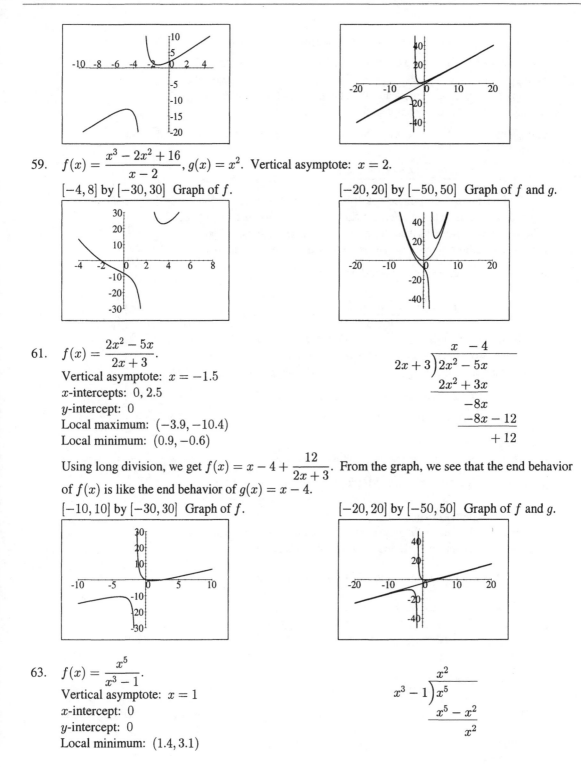

59. $f(x) = \dfrac{x^3 - 2x^2 + 16}{x - 2}$, $g(x) = x^2$. Vertical asymptote: $x = 2$.

$[-4, 8]$ by $[-30, 30]$ Graph of f. $[-20, 20]$ by $[-50, 50]$ Graph of f and g.

61. $f(x) = \dfrac{2x^2 - 5x}{2x + 3}$.

Vertical asymptote: $x = -1.5$
x-intercepts: $0, 2.5$
y-intercept: 0
Local maximum: $(-3.9, -10.4)$
Local minimum: $(0.9, -0.6)$

$$
\begin{array}{r}
x \quad -4 \\
2x + 3 \overline{)\; 2x^2 - 5x } \\
\underline{2x^2 + 3x } \\
-8x \\
\underline{-8x - 12} \\
+12
\end{array}
$$

Using long division, we get $f(x) = x - 4 + \dfrac{12}{2x + 3}$. From the graph, we see that the end behavior
of $f(x)$ is like the end behavior of $g(x) = x - 4$.

$[-10, 10]$ by $[-30, 30]$ Graph of f. $[-20, 20]$ by $[-50, 50]$ Graph of f and g.

63. $f(x) = \dfrac{x^5}{x^3 - 1}$.

Vertical asymptote: $x = 1$
x-intercept: 0
y-intercept: 0
Local minimum: $(1.4, 3.1)$

$$
\begin{array}{r}
x^2 \\
x^3 - 1 \overline{)\; x^5 } \\
\underline{x^5 - x^2} \\
x^2
\end{array}
$$

Thus $y = x^2 + \dfrac{x^2}{x^3 - 1}$. From the graph we see that the end behavior of $f(x)$ is like the end behavior of $g(x) = x^2$.

$[-5, 5]$ by $[-10, 10]$ Graph of f.

$[-10, 10]$ by $[-10, 10]$ Graph of f and g.

65. $f(x) = \dfrac{x^4 - 3x^3 + 6}{x - 3}$.

Vertical asymptote: $x = 3$
x-intercept: $1.6,\ 2.7$
y-intercept: -2
Local maximum: $(-0.4, -1.8),\ (2.4, 3.8)$
Local minimum: $(0.6, -2.3),\ (3.4, 54.3)$

$$x - 3 \,)\overline{\begin{array}{l} x^3 \\ x^4 - 3x^3 + 6 \\ \underline{x^4 - 3x^3} \\ 6 \end{array}}$$

Thus $y = x^3 + \dfrac{6}{x - 3}$. From the graph we see that the end behavior of $f(x)$ is like the end behavior of $g(x) = x^3$.

$[-10, 10]$ by $[-20, 100]$ Graph of f.

$[-10, 10]$ by $[-20, 100]$ Graph of f and g.

67. (a)

(b) $p(t) = \dfrac{3000t}{t + 1} = 3000 - \dfrac{3000}{t + 1}$.
So as $t \to \infty$, we have $p(t) \to 3000$.

69.   [0, 20] by [0, 3]

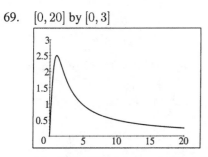

(a)   The highest concentration of drug is 2.50 mg/L, and it is reached 1 hour after the drug is administered.

(b)   The concentration of the drug in the bloodstream goes to 0.

(c)   From the first viewing rectangle, we see that an approximate solution is near $t = 15$. Thus we graph $y = \dfrac{5t}{t^2 + 1}$ and $y = 0.3$ in the viewing rectangle $[14, 18]$ by $[0, 0.5]$. So it takes about 16.61 hours for the concentration to drop below 0.3 mg/L.

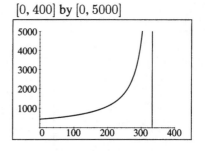

71. $P(v) = P_0 \left(\dfrac{s_0}{s_0 - v} \right) \quad \Rightarrow$

$P(v) = 440 \left(\dfrac{332}{332 - v} \right)$

If the speed of the train approaches the speed of sound, the pitch of the whistle becomes very large. This would be experienced as a "sonic boom"— an effect seldom heard with trains.

[0, 400] by [0, 5000]

73.   Vertical asymptote $x = 3$: $p(x) = \dfrac{1}{x - 3}$

Vertical asymptote $x = 3$ and horizontal asymptote $y = 2$: $r(x) = \dfrac{2x}{x - 3}$.

Vertical asymptotes $x = 1$ and $x = -1$, horizontal asymptote 0, and x-intercept 4: $q(x) = \dfrac{x - 4}{(x - 1)(x + 1)}$.

Of course, other answers are possible.

75. (a) $r(x) = \dfrac{3x^2 - 3x - 6}{x - 2} = \dfrac{3(x-2)(x+1)}{x-2} = 3(x+1)$,

for $x \neq 2$. Therefore, $r(x) = 3x + 3$, $x \neq 2$. Since $3(2) + 3 = 9$, the graph is the line $y = 3x + 3$ with the point $(2, 9)$ removed.

(b) $s(x) = \dfrac{x^2 + x - 20}{x + 5} = \dfrac{(x-4)(x+5)}{x+5} = x - 4$, for

$x \neq -5$. Therefore, $s(x) = x - 4$, $x \neq -5$. Since $(-5) - 4 = -9$, the graph is the line $y = x - 4$ with the point $(-5, -9)$ removed.

$t(x) = \dfrac{2x^2 - x - 1}{x - 1} = \dfrac{(2x+1)(x-1)}{x-1} = 2x + 1$, for

$x \neq 1$. Therefore, $t(x) = 2x + 1$, $x \neq 1$. Since $2(1) + 1 = 3$, the graph is the line $y = 2x + 1$ with the point $(1, 3)$ removed.

$u(x) = \dfrac{x - 2}{x^2 - 2x} = \dfrac{x - 2}{x(x - 2)} = \dfrac{1}{x}$, for $x \neq 2$.

Therefore, $u(x) = \dfrac{1}{x}$, $x \neq 2$. When $x = 2$, $\dfrac{1}{x} = \dfrac{1}{2}$,

the graph is the curve $y = \dfrac{1}{x}$ with the point $(2, \frac{1}{2})$ removed.

Review Exercises for Chapter 3

1. $P(x) = x^3 + 27$

3. $P(x) = -(x-2)^4$

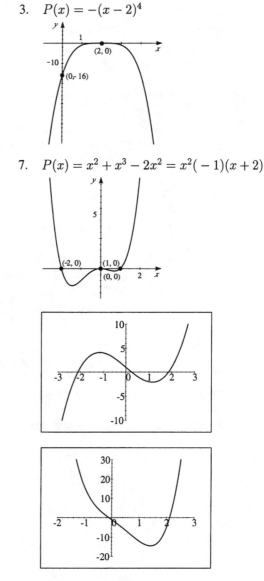

5. $P(x) = x^3 - 16x = x(x-4)(x+4)$

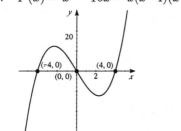

7. $P(x) = x^2 + x^3 - 2x^2 = x^2(-1)(x+2)$

9. $P(x) = x^3 - 4x + 1$.
    x-intercepts: $-2.1, 0.3$, and 1.9.
    y-intercept: 1
    Local maximum is $(-1.2, 4.1)$.
    Local minimum is $(1.2, -2.1)$.
    $y \to \infty$ as $x \to \infty$;
    $y \to -\infty$ as $x \to -\infty$

11. $P(x) = 3x^4 - 4x^3 - 10x - 1$.
    x-intercept: -0.1 and 2.1.
    y-intercept: -1
    local minimum: $(1.4, -14.5)$
    There is no local maximum.
    $y \to \infty$ as $x \to \pm\infty$.

13. (a) Use the Pythagorean Theorem and solving for y^2 we have, $x^2 + y^2 = 10^2$ $\Leftrightarrow$ $y^2 = 100 - x^2$. Subsituting we get $S = 13.8x(100 - x^2) = 1380x - 13.8x^3$.

    (b) Domain is $[0, 10]$.

(c)

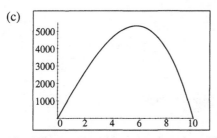

(d)   The strongest beam is when the width is 5.7 inches.

15. $\dfrac{x^2 - 3x + 5}{x - 2}$

$$2 \;\big|\; \begin{array}{ccc} 1 & -3 & 5 \\ & 2 & -2 \\ \hline 1 & -1 & 3 \end{array}$$

Using synthetic division, we see that $Q(x) = x - 1$ and $R(x) = 3$.

17. $\dfrac{x^3 - x^2 + 11x + 2}{x - 4}$

$$4 \;\big|\; \begin{array}{cccc} 1 & -1 & 11 & 2 \\ & 4 & 12 & 92 \\ \hline 1 & 3 & 23 & 94 \end{array}$$

Using synthetic division, we see that $Q(x) = x^2 + 3x + 23$ and $R(x) = 94$.

19. $\dfrac{x^4 - 8x^2 + 2x + 7}{x + 5}$

$$-5 \;\big|\; \begin{array}{ccccc} 1 & 0 & -8 & 2 & 7 \\ & -5 & 25 & -85 & 415 \\ \hline 1 & -5 & 17 & -83 & 422 \end{array}$$

Using synthetic division, we see that $Q(x) = x^3 - 5x^2 + 17x - 83$ and $R(x) = 422$.

21. $\dfrac{2x^3 + x^2 - 8x + 15}{x^2 + 2x - 1}$

$$\require{enclose}\begin{array}{r} 2x \quad - 3 \\ x^2 + 2x - 1 \enclose{longdiv}{\,2x^3 \;+ x^2 - 8x + 15} \\ \underline{2x^3 + 4x^2 - 2x } \\ -3x^2 - 6x + 15 \\ \underline{-3x^2 - 6x \;+ 3} \\ 12 \end{array}$$

Therefore, $Q(x) = 2x - 3$, and $R(x) = 12$.

23. $P(x) = 2x^3 - 9x^2 - 7x + 13$; find $P(5)$.

$$5 \;\big|\; \begin{array}{cccc} 2 & -9 & -7 & 13 \\ & 10 & 5 & -10 \\ \hline 2 & 1 & -2 & 3 \end{array}$$ Therefore, $P(5) = 3$.

25. $\frac{1}{2}$ is a zero of $P(x) = 2x^4 + x^3 - 5x^2 + 10x - 4$ if $P\left(\frac{1}{2}\right) = 0$.

$$
\begin{array}{r|rrrrr}
\tfrac{1}{2} & 2 & 1 & -5 & 10 & -4 \\
  &   & 1 & 1 & -2 & 4 \\
\hline
  & 2 & 2 & -4 & 8 & 0
\end{array}
$$

Since $P\!\left(\tfrac{1}{2}\right) = 0$, $\tfrac{1}{2}$ is a zero of the polynomial.

27. $P(x) = x^{500} + 6x^{201} - x^2 - 2x + 4$. The remainder from dividing $P(x)$ by $x - 1$ is
$P(1) = (1)^{500} + 6(1)^{201} - (1)^2 - 2(1) + 4 = 8$.

29. (a) $x^5 - 6x^3 - x^2 + 2x + 18 = 0$ has possible rational zeros $\pm 1, \pm 2, \pm 3, \pm 6, \pm 9, \pm 18$.

  (b) Since $P(x)$ has 2 variations in sign, there are either 0 or 2 positive real zeros. Since
  $P(-x) = -x^5 + 6x^3 - x^2 - 2x + 18$ has 3 variations in sign, there are 1 or 3 negative real
  zeros.

31. $(2 - 3\,i) + (1 + 4\,i) = (2 + 1) + (-3 + 4)\,i = 3 + i$.

33. $(2 + i)(3 - 2\,i) = 6 - 4\,i + 3\,i - 2\,i^2 = 6 - i + 2 = 8 - i$.

35. $\dfrac{4 + 2i}{2 - i} = \dfrac{4 + 2i}{2 - i} \cdot \dfrac{2 + i}{2 + i} = \dfrac{8 + 8i + 2i^2}{4 - i^2} = \dfrac{8 + 8i - 2}{4 + 1} = \dfrac{6 + 8i}{5} = \tfrac{6}{5} + \tfrac{8}{5}\,i$.

37. $i^{25} = i^{24}\,i = (i^4)^6\,i = (1)^6\,i = i$.

39. $(1 - \sqrt{-1}\,)(1 + \sqrt{-1}\,) = (1 - i)(1 + i) = 1 + i - i - i^2 = 1 + 1 = 2$.

41. Since the zeros are $-\tfrac{1}{2}$, 2, and 3, a factorization is $P(x) = C\!\left(x + \tfrac{1}{2}\right)(x - 2)(x - 3)$
  $= \tfrac{C}{2}(2x + 1)(x^2 - 5x + 6) = \tfrac{C}{2}(2x^3 - 10x^2 + 12x + x^2 - 5x + 6) = \tfrac{C}{2}(2x^3 - 9x^2 + 7x + 6)$.
  Since the constant coefficient is 12, $\tfrac{C}{2}(6) = 12 \quad \Leftrightarrow \quad C = 4$, and so the polynomial is
  $P(x) = 4x^3 - 18x^2 + 14x + 12$.

43. No, there is no polynomial of degree 4 with integer coefficients that has zeros i, $2i$, $3i$ and $4i$. Since
  the imaginary zeros of polynomial equations with real coefficients come in complex conjugate pairs,
  there would have to be 8 zeros, which is impossible for a polynomial of degree 4.

45. $P(x) = x^3 - 3x^2 - 13x + 15$ has possible rational zeros $\pm 1, \pm 3, \pm 5, \pm 15$.

$$
\begin{array}{r|rrrr}
1 & 1 & -3 & -13 & 15 \\
  &   & 1 & -2 & -15 \\
\hline
  & 1 & -2 & -15 & 0
\end{array}
\quad \Rightarrow \quad x = 1 \text{ is a zero.}
$$

So $P(x) = x^3 - 3x^2 - 13x + 15 = (x - 1)(x^2 - 2x - 15) = (x - 1)(x - 5)(x + 3)$. Therefore,
the zeros are -3, 1, and 5.

47. $P(x) = x^4 + 6x^3 + 17x^2 + 28x + 20$ has possible rational zeros $\pm 1, \pm 2, \pm 4, \pm 5, \pm 10, \pm 20$.
  Since all of the coefficients are positive, there are no positive real zeros.

$$
\begin{array}{r|rrrrr}
-1 & 1 & 6 & 17 & 28 & 20 \\
   &   & -1 & -5 & -12 & -16 \\
\hline
   & 1 & 5 & 12 & 16 & 4 \\
-2 & 1 & 6 & 17 & 28 & 20 \\
   &   & -2 & -8 & -18 & -20 \\
\hline
   & 1 & 4 & 9 & 10 & 0
\end{array}
\quad \Rightarrow \quad x = -2 \text{ is a zero.}
$$

$P(x) = x^4 + 6x^3 + 17x^2 + 28x + 20 = (x + 2)(x^3 + 4x^2 + 9x + 10)$. Continuing with the
quotient, we have

$$\begin{array}{r|rrrr} -2 & 1 & 4 & 9 & 10 \\ & & -2 & -4 & -10 \\ \hline & 1 & 2 & 5 & 0 \end{array} \Rightarrow \quad x = -2 \text{ is a zero.}$$

Thus $P(x) = x^4 + 6x^3 + 17x^2 + 28x + 20 = (x+2)^2(x^2 + 2x + 5)$. Now $x^2 + 2x + 5 = 0$ when $x = \frac{-2 \pm \sqrt{4 - 4(5)(1)}}{2} = \frac{-2 \pm 4i}{2} = -1 \pm 2i$. Thus, the zeros are -2 (multiplicity 2) and $-1 \pm 2i$.

49. $P(x) = x^5 - 3x^4 - x^3 + 11x^2 - 12x + 4$ has possible rational zeros $\pm 1, \pm 2, \pm 4$.

$$\begin{array}{r|rrrrrr} 1 & 1 & -3 & -1 & 11 & -12 & 4 \\ & & 1 & -2 & -3 & 8 & -4 \\ \hline & 1 & -2 & -3 & 8 & -4 & 0 \end{array} \Rightarrow \quad x = 1 \text{ is a zero.}$$

$P(x) = x^5 - 3x^4 - x^3 + 11x^2 - 12x + 4 = (x-1)(x^4 - 2x^3 - 3x^2 + 8x - 4)$. Continuing with the quotient, we have

$$\begin{array}{r|rrrrr} 1 & 1 & -2 & -3 & 8 & -4 \\ & & 1 & -1 & -4 & 4 \\ \hline & 1 & -1 & -4 & 4 & 0 \end{array} \Rightarrow \quad x = 1 \text{ is a zero.}$$

So $x^5 - 3x^4 - x^3 + 11x^2 - 12x + 4 = (x-1)^2(x^3 - x^2 - 4x + 4) = (x-1)^3(x^2 - 4)$
$= (x-1)^3(x-2)(x+2)$. Therefore, the zeros are 1 (multiplicity 3), -2, and 2.

51. $P(x) = x^6 - 64 = (x^3 - 8)(x^3 + 8) = (x-2)(x^2 + 2x + 4)(x+2)(x^2 - 2x + 4)$. Now using the quadratic formula to find the zeros of $x^2 + 2x + 4$, we have
$x = \frac{-2 \pm \sqrt{4 - 4(4)(1)}}{2} = \frac{-2 \pm 2\sqrt{3}i}{2} = -1 \pm \sqrt{3}i$, and using the quadratic formula to find the zeros of
$x^2 - 2x + 4$, we have $x = \frac{2 \pm \sqrt{4 - 4(4)(1)}}{2} = \frac{2 \pm 2\sqrt{3}i}{2} = 1 \pm \sqrt{3}i$. Therefore, the zeros are 2, -2,
$1 \pm \sqrt{3}i$, and $-1 \pm \sqrt{3}i$.

53. $P(x) = 6x^4 - 18x^3 + 6x^2 - 30x + 36 = 6(x^4 - 3x^3 + x^2 - 5x + 6)$ has possible rational zeros $\pm 1, \pm 2, \pm 3, \pm 6$.

$$\begin{array}{r|rrrrr} 1 & 6 & -18 & 6 & -30 & 36 \\ & & 6 & -12 & -6 & -36 \\ \hline & 6 & -12 & -6 & -36 & 0 \end{array} \Rightarrow \quad x = 1 \text{ is a zero.}$$

So $P(x) = 6x^4 - 18x^3 + 6x^2 - 30x + 36 = (x-1)(6x^3 - 12x^2 - 6x - 36)$
$= 6(x-1)(x^3 - 2x^2 - x - 6)$. Continuing with the quotient we have

$$\begin{array}{r|rrrr} 1 & 1 & -2 & -1 & -6 \\ & & 1 & -1 & -2 \\ \hline & 1 & -1 & -2 & -8 \end{array}$$

$$\begin{array}{r|rrrr} 2 & 1 & -2 & -1 & -6 \\ & & 2 & 0 & -2 \\ \hline & 1 & 0 & -1 & -8 \end{array}$$

$$\begin{array}{r|rrrr} 3 & 1 & -2 & -1 & -6 \\ & & 3 & 3 & 6 \\ \hline & 1 & 1 & 2 & 0 \end{array} \Rightarrow \quad x = 3 \text{ is a zero.}$$

So, $P(x) = 6x^4 - 18x^3 + 6x^2 - 30x + 36 = 6(x-1)(x-3)(x^2 + x + 2)$. Now, $x^2 + x + 2 = 0$
when $x = \frac{-1 \pm \sqrt{1 - 4(1)(2)}}{2} = \frac{-1 \pm \sqrt{7}i}{2}$, and so the zeros are 1, 3, and $\frac{-1 \pm \sqrt{7}i}{2}$.

55. $2x^2 = 5x + 3 \quad \Leftrightarrow \quad 2x^2 - 5x - 3 = 0$.
The solutions are $x = -0.5, 3$.

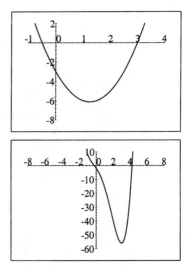

57. $x^4 - 3x^3 - 3x^2 - 9x - 2 = 0$ has solutions
$x \approx -0.24, 4.24$.

59. $r(x) = \dfrac{3x - 12}{x + 1}$. When $x = 0$, we have $r(0) = \frac{-12}{1} = -12$, so the
y-intercept is -12. Since $y = 0$, when $3x - 12 = 0 \quad \Leftrightarrow \quad x = 4$,
the x-intercept is 4. The vertical asymptote is $x = -1$. Because the
degree of the denominator and numerator are the same, the
horizontal asymptote is $y = \frac{3}{1} = 3$.

61. $r(x) = \dfrac{x - 2}{x^2 - 2x - 8} = \dfrac{x - 2}{(x + 2)(x - 4)}$. When $x = 0$, we have
$r(0) = \frac{-2}{-8} = \frac{1}{4}$, so the y-intercept is $\frac{1}{4}$. When $y = 0$, we have
$x - 2 = 0 \quad \Leftrightarrow \quad x = 2$, so the x-intercepts is 2. The vertical
asymptotes occur when $x = -2$ and $x = 4$. The horizontal
than the degree of the numerator.

63. $r(x) = \dfrac{x^2 - 9}{2x^2 + 1} = \dfrac{(x + 3)(x - 3)}{2x^2 + 1}$. When $x = 0$, we have
$r(0) = \frac{-9}{1}$, so the y-intercept is -9. When $y = 0$, we have
$x^2 - 9 = 0 \quad \Leftrightarrow \quad x = \pm 3$ so the x-intercepts are -3 and 3. Since
$2x^2 + 1 > 0$, the denominator is never zero so there are no vertical
asymptotes. The horizontal asymptote is at $y = \frac{1}{2}$ because the
degree of the denominator and numerator are the same.

65. $r(x) = \dfrac{x-3}{2x+6}$.

From the graph we see that

x-intercept: 3

y-intercept: -0.5

Vertical asymptote: $x = -3$

Horizontal asymptote: $y = 0.5$

No local extrema.

67. $r(x) = \dfrac{x^3 + 8}{x^2 - x - 2}$.

From the graph we see that

x-intercept: -2

y-intercept: -4

Vertical asymptote: $x = -1, x = 2$

Horizontal asymptote is $y = 0.5$.

Local maximum is $(0.425, -3.599)$.

Local minimum is $(4.216, 7.175)$.

By using long division, we see that $f(x) = x + 1 + \dfrac{10 - x}{x^2 - x - 2}$, so f has a slant asymptote $y = x + 1$.

69. The graphs $y = x^4 + x^2 + 24x$ and $y = 6x^3 + 20$ intersect when $x^4 + x^2 + 24x = 6x^3 + 20 \Leftrightarrow$ $x^4 - 6x^3 + x^2 + 24x - 20 = 0$. The possible rational zeros are $\pm 1, \pm 2, \pm 4, \pm 5, \pm 10, \pm 20$.

$$
\begin{array}{r|rrrrr}
1 & 1 & -6 & 1 & 24 & -20 \\
  &   & 1 & -5 & -4 & 20 \\
\hline
  & 1 & -5 & -4 & 20 & 0
\end{array} \Rightarrow \quad x = 1 \text{ is a zero.}
$$

So $x^4 - 6x^3 + x^2 + 24x - 20 = (x - 1)(x^3 - 5x^2 - 4x + 20) = 0$. Continuing with the quotient:

$$
\begin{array}{r|rrrr}
1 & 1 & -5 & -4 & 20 \\
  &   & 1 & -4 & -8 \\
\hline
  & 1 & -4 & -8 & 12
\end{array}
\qquad
\begin{array}{r|rrrr}
2 & 1 & -5 & -4 & 20 \\
  &   & 2 & -6 & -20 \\
\hline
  & 1 & -3 & -10 & 0
\end{array} \Rightarrow \quad x = 2 \text{ is a zero.}
$$

So $x^4 - 6x^3 + x^2 + 24x - 20 = (x - 1)(x - 2)(x^2 - 3x - 10)$ $= (x - 1)(x - 2)(x - 5)(x + 2) = 0$. Hence, the points of intersection are $(1, 26)$, $(2, 68)$, $(5, 770)$, and $(-2, -28)$.

Chapter 3 Test

1. $f(x) = (x+1)^3 + 8$
$= [(x+1) + 2][(x+1)^2 - 2(x+1) + 4]$
$\qquad\qquad\qquad$ Sum of cubes.
$= (x+3)(x^2 + 2x + 1 - 2x - 2 + 4)$
$= (x+3)(x^2 + 3)$

2. (a)

$$
\begin{array}{r|rrrrr}
2 & 1 & 0 & -4 & 2 & 5 \\
  &   & 2 & 4 & 0 & 4 \\
\hline
  & 1 & 2 & 0 & 2 & 9 \\
\end{array}
$$

Therefore, quotient is $Q(x) = x^3 + 2x^2 + 2$, and the remainder is $R(x) = 9$.

(b)
$$
\begin{array}{r}
x^3 + 2x^2 \qquad + \tfrac{1}{2} \\
2x^2 - 1 \overline{\smash{)}\, 2x^5 + 4x^4 - x^3 - \;\; x^2 + 0x + 7} \\
\underline{2x^5 \qquad\qquad -x^3} \\
4x^4 \qquad\quad - x^2 \\
\underline{4x^4 \qquad\quad - 2x^2} \\
x^2 \qquad +7 \\
\underline{x^2 \qquad -\tfrac{1}{2}} \\
7\tfrac{1}{2} \text{ or } \tfrac{15}{2}
\end{array}
$$

Therefore, quotient is $Q(x) = x^3 + 2x^2 + \tfrac{1}{2}$, and the remainder is $R(x) = \tfrac{15}{2}$.

3. (a) Possible rational zeros are: $\pm 1, \pm 3, \pm\tfrac{1}{2}, \pm\tfrac{3}{2}$.

   (b)
$$
\begin{array}{r|rrrr}
-1 & 2 & -5 & -4 & 3 \\
   &   & -2 & 7 & -3 \\
\hline
   & 2 & -7 & 3 & 0 \\
\end{array}
\quad\Rightarrow\quad x = -1 \text{ is a zero.}
$$

$P(x) = (x+1)(2x^2 - 7x + 3) = (x+1)(2x-1)(x-3) = 2(x-1)(x-\tfrac{1}{2})(x-3)$

   (c) The zeros of P are $x = 1, 3, \tfrac{1}{2}$.

   (d)

4. (a) $(6 - 2i) - (7 - \tfrac{1}{2}i) = 6 - 2i - 7 + \tfrac{1}{2}i = (6 - 7) + (-2 + \tfrac{1}{2})i = -1 - \tfrac{3}{2}i.$

   (b) $(1+i)(3 - 2i) = 3 - 2i + 3i - 2i^2 = 3 + i + 2 = 5 + i.$

(c) $\dfrac{5+10\,i}{3-4\,i} = \dfrac{5+10\,i}{3-4\,i} \cdot \dfrac{3+4\,i}{3+4\,i} = \dfrac{15+50\,i+40\,i^2}{9-16\,i^2} = \dfrac{15+50\,i-40}{9+16} = \dfrac{-25+50\,i}{25}$
$= -1+2\,i.$

(d) $i^{50} = i^{48}\,i^2 = (i^4)^{12}\,(-1) = (1)^{12}(-1) = -1.$

(e) $(2-\sqrt{-2})(\sqrt{8}+\sqrt{-4}) = (2-\sqrt{2}\,i)(2\sqrt{2}+2\,i) = 4\sqrt{2}+4\,i-4\,i-2\sqrt{2}\,i^2$
$= 4\sqrt{2}+2\sqrt{2} = 6\sqrt{2}.$

5. $P(x) = x^3 - x^2 - 4x - 6.$ Possible rational zeros are: $\pm1, \pm2, \pm3, \pm6.$

$$
\begin{array}{r|rrrr}
1 & 1 & -1 & -4 & -6 \\
  &   & 1 & 0 & -4 \\
\hline
  & 1 & 0 & -4 & -10
\end{array}
\qquad
\begin{array}{r|rrrr}
2 & 1 & -1 & -4 & -6 \\
  &   & 2 & 2 & -4 \\
\hline
  & 1 & 1 & -2 & -10
\end{array}
$$

$$
\begin{array}{r|rrrr}
3 & 1 & -1 & -4 & -6 \\
  &   & 3 & 6 & 6 \\
\hline
  & 1 & 2 & 2 & 0
\end{array}
\quad \Rightarrow \quad x = 3 \text{ is a zero.}
$$

So $P(x) = (x-3)(x^2+2x+2).$ Using the quadratic formula on the second factor, we have
$x = \dfrac{-2 \pm \sqrt{2^2 - 4(1)(2)}}{2(1)} = \dfrac{-2 \pm \sqrt{-4}}{2} = \dfrac{-2 \pm 2\sqrt{-1}}{2} = -1 \pm i.$ So zeros of $P(x)$ are 3,
$-1-i,$ and $-1+i.$

6. $P(x) = x^4 - 2x^3 + 5x^2 - 8x + 4.$ The possible rational zeros of P are: $\pm1, \pm2,$ and $\pm4.$ Since
there are four changes in sign, P has 4, 2, or 0 positive real zeros.

$$
\begin{array}{r|rrrrr}
1 & 1 & -2 & 5 & -8 & 4 \\
  &   & 1 & -1 & 4 & -4 \\
\hline
  & 1 & -1 & 4 & -4 & 0
\end{array}
$$

So $P(x) = (x-1)(x^3 - x^2 + 4x - 4).$ Factoring the second factor by grouping we have:
$P(x) = (x-1)[x^2(x-1) + 4(x-1)] = (x-1)(x^2+4)(x-1) = (x-1)^2(x-2i)(x+2i).$

7. Since $3i$ is a zero of $P(x)$, $-3i$ is also a zero of $P(x)$. And since -1 is a zero of multiplicity 2,
$P(x) = (x+1)^2(x-3i)(x+3i) = (x^2+2x+1)(x^2+9) = x^4 + 2x^3 + 10x^2 + 18x + 9.$

8. $P(x) = 2x^4 - 7x^3 + x^2 - 18x + 3.$

(a) Since $P(x)$ has 4 variations in sign, $P(x)$ can have 4, 2, or 0 positive real zeros. Since
$P(-x) = 2x^4 + 7x^3 + x^2 + 18x + 3$ has no variations in sign, there are no negative real zeros.

(b)
$$
\begin{array}{r|rrrrr}
4 & 2 & -7 & 1 & -18 & 3 \\
  &   & 8 & 4 & 20 & 8 \\
\hline
  & 2 & 1 & 5 &   2 & 11
\end{array}
$$

Since the last row contains no negative entries, 4 is an upper bound for the real zeros of $P(x)$.

$$
\begin{array}{r|rrrrr}
-1 & 2 & -7 & 1 & -18 & 3 \\
   &   & -1 & 9 & -10 & 28 \\
\hline
   & 2 & -9 & 10 & -28 & 31
\end{array}
$$

Since the last row alternates in sign, -1 is a lower bound for the real zeros of $P(x)$.

(c) Using the upper and lower limit from part b, we graph $P(x)$ in the viewing rectangle $[-1, 4]$ by $[-1, 1]$. The two real zeros are 0.17 and 3.93.

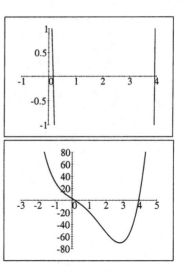

(d) Local minimum $(2.8, -70.3)$.

9. $r(x) = \dfrac{2x - 1}{x^2 - x - 2}$, $s(x) = \dfrac{x^3 + 27}{x^2 + 4}$, $t(x) = \dfrac{x^3 - 9x}{x + 2}$ and $u(x) = \dfrac{x^2 + x - 6}{x^2 - 25}$.

(a) $r(x)$ has the horizontal asymptote $y = 0$ because the degree of the denominator is greater than the degree of the numerator. $u(x)$ has the horizontal asymptote $y = \frac{1}{1} = 1$ because the degree of the numerator and the denominator are the same.

(b) The degree of the numerator of $s(x)$ is one more than the degree of the denominator, so $s(x)$ has a slant asymptote.

(c) The denominator of $s(x)$ is never 0, so $s(x)$ has no vertical asymptotes.

(d) $u(x) = \dfrac{x^2 + x - 6}{x^2 - 25} = \dfrac{(x + 3)(x - 2)}{(x - 5)(x + 5)}$. When $x = 0$, we have $u(x) = \dfrac{-6}{-25} = \dfrac{6}{25}$, so the y-intercept is $y = \frac{6}{25}$. When $y = 0$, we have $x = -3$ or $x = 2$, so the x-intercepts are -3 and 2. The vertical asymptotes are $x = -5$ and $x = 5$. The horizontal asymptote occurs at $y = \frac{1}{1} = 1$ because the degree of the denominator and numerator are the same.

(e)

$$\begin{array}{r} x^2 \ -2x \ -5 \\ x+2 \overline{\smash{\big)}\ x^3 + 0x^2 - 9x \ +0} \\ \underline{x^3 + 2x^2} \\ -2x^2 - 9x \\ \underline{-2x^2 - 4x} \\ -5x \ +0 \\ \underline{-5x - 10} \\ -10 \end{array}$$

Thus $P(x) = x^2 - 2x - 5$ and $t(x) = \dfrac{x^3 - 9x}{x + 2}$ have the same end behavior.

Focus on Problem Solving

1. The network is not traversable, since there are more than two vertices of odd order.

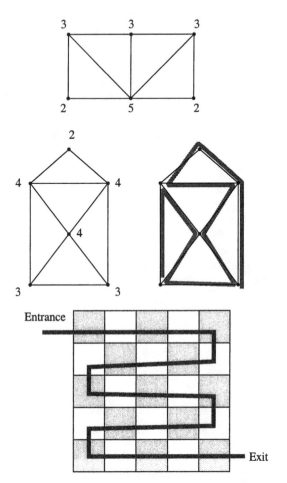

3. Since there are exactly two vertices of odd order, the network is traversable. Any path that traverses this network must start at one odd vertex and end at the other. For example, we may choose the path shown.

5. The diagram shows that a museum tour is possible if there are 5 rooms to a side. For an $n \times n$ museum, where n is an <u>odd</u> number, a similar right-left path works. If n is <u>even</u>, an argument similar to the one in the text (WBWB$\cdots$WB) shows that such a tour is impossible.

7. Consider the line joining B to A. Each time we cross the curve we move from outside to inside or from inside to outside. So we count the number of crossings in going from B to A along the line segment. B is clearly outside the curve, so if the number n of crossings is odd, A is inside; if n is even, A is outside. In the case illustrated, $n = 5$, so A is inside.

9. The equation will have four roots, so let the other root be k. Then
$x^4 + ax^2 + bx + c = (x - 1)(x - 2)(x - 3)(x - k)$. The coefficient of x^3 on the right will be $-1 - 2 - 3 - k = -6 - k$. But this must equal the coefficient of x^3 on the left which is 0. Therefore $k = -6$. Equating constant coefficients gives $c = (-1)(-2)(-3)(-k)$
$= (-1)(-2)(-3)(6) = -36$.

11. Color the grid as a checkerboard, that is, with squares alternating black and white. Now each domino covers two squares, one black and one white. For the dominoes to cover the grid without overlapping, an equal number of black and white squares must be on the grid. However, the grid has 32 of one color and 30 of the other color. Therefore, it is impossible to cover the grid without overlapping the dominoes.

13. $f_0(x) = \dfrac{1}{1-x}$ and $f_{n+1} = f_0 \circ f_n$ for $n = 0, 1, 2, \ldots$

$f_1(x) = f_0\left(\dfrac{1}{1-x}\right) = \dfrac{1}{1 - \frac{1}{1-x}} = \dfrac{1-x}{1(1-x)-1} = \dfrac{1-x}{-x} = \dfrac{x-1}{x}$,

$f_2(x) = f_0\left(\dfrac{x-1}{x}\right) = \dfrac{1}{1 - \left(\frac{x-1}{x}\right)} = \dfrac{x}{x-(x-1)} = x$,

$f_3(x) = f_0(x) \quad \Rightarrow \quad f_4(x) = f_1(x) \quad \Rightarrow \quad f_5(x) = f_2(x) \quad \Rightarrow \quad f_6(x) = f_3(x) = f_0(x).$

Thus $f_n(x) = \begin{cases} f_0(x) & \text{if } n = 3m \\ f_1(x) & \text{if } n = 3m+1 \\ f_2(x) & \text{if } n = 3m+2 \end{cases}$ for any natural number m.

Since $100 = 3 \cdot 33 + 1$, $f_{100}(x) = f_1(x)$ and $f_{100}(3) = f_1(3) = \frac{3-1}{3} = \frac{2}{3}$.

15. $f(x) = x - [\![x]\!]$

17. (a) Let $n, n+1, n+2$, and $n+3$ be four consecutive integers. Thus,
$n(n+1)(n+2)(n+3)+1 = n^4 + 6n^3 + 11n^2 + 6n + 1$. To show that this is a perfect square, we start by looking at some cases of n. For $n = 1$, we have
$n(n+1)(n+2)(n+3)+1 = 1 \cdot 2 \cdot 3 \cdot 4 + 1 = 25 = 5^2$, and for $n = 2$, we have
$n(n+1)(n+2)(n+3)+1 = 2 \cdot 3 \cdot 4 \cdot 5 + 1 = 121 = 11^2$. We next need to find a relation between n and the perfect square. After some experimentation we find that $5 = (1)(4)+1$, and $11 = (2)(5)+1$. Thus the perfect square is $[n(n+3)+1]^2 = (n^2 + 3n + 1)^2$
$= n^4 + 6n^3 + 11n^2 + 6n + 1$. Putting these together we can check that
$n(n+1)(n+2)(n+3)+1 = (n^2 + 3n + 1)^2.$

     (b) Let $n, n+1$, and $n+2$ be three consecutive integers. Then the product of three consecutive integers plus the middle is $n(n+1)(n+2) + (n+1) = n^3 + 3n^2 + 2n + n + 1$
$= n^3 + 3n^2 + 3n + 1 = (n+1)^3.$

19. We follow the hint and put the original rectangle in the coordinate plane which has been tiled in a checkerboard pattern of black and white squares, each $\frac{1}{2}$ unit by $\frac{1}{2}$ unit. Since each of the smaller rectangles has at least one side of integer length, the area of each of the smaller rectangles is composed of equal amounts of black and white. So when we add all the smaller rectangles, the total area is composed of equal amounts of black and white. Thus the original rectangle is composed of equal amounts of black and white, so at least one side of the original rectangle must have integer length.

Chapter Four
Exercises 4.1

1. $f(x) = 2^x$

x	y
-4	$\frac{1}{16}$
-2	$\frac{1}{4}$
0	1
2	4
4	16

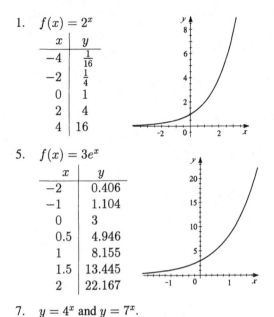

3. $f(x) = \left(\frac{1}{3}\right)^x$

x	y
-2	9
-1	3
0	1
1	$\frac{1}{3}$
2	$\frac{1}{9}$

5. $f(x) = 3e^x$

x	y
-2	0.406
-1	1.104
0	3
0.5	4.946
1	8.155
1.5	13.445
2	22.167

7. $y = 4^x$ and $y = 7^x$.

9. From the graph, $f(2) = a^2 = 9$, so $a = 3$. Thus $f(x) = 3^x$.

11. From the graph, $f(2) = a^2 = \frac{1}{16}$, so $a = \frac{1}{4}$. Thus $f(x) = \left(\frac{1}{4}\right)^x$.

13. III   15. I   17. II

19. $f(x) = -3^x$

The graph of f is obtained by reflecting the graph of $y = 3^x$ about the x-axis.

Domain: $(-\infty, \infty)$

Range: $(-\infty, 0)$

Asymptote: $y = 0$

21. $g(x) = 2^x - 3$

The graph of g is obtained by shifting the graph of $y = 2^x$ downward 3 units.

Domain: $(-\infty, \infty)$

Range: $(-3, \infty)$

Asymptote: $y = -3$

23. $h(x) = 4 + \left(\frac{1}{2}\right)^x$

The graph of h is obtained by shifting the graph of $y = \left(\frac{1}{2}\right)^x$ upward 4 units.

Domain: $(-\infty, \infty)$

Range: $(4, \infty)$

Asymptote: $y = 4$

25. $f(x) = 10^{x+3}$

The graph of f is obtained by shifting the graph of $y = 10^x$ to the left 3 units.

Domain: $(-\infty, \infty)$

Range: $(0, \infty)$

Asymptote: $y = 0$

27. $y = -e^x$

The graph of $y = -e^x$ is obtained from the graph of $y = e^x$ by reflecting it about the x-axis.

Domain: $(-\infty, \infty)$

Range: $(-\infty, 0)$

Asymptote: $y = 0$

29. $y = e^{-x} - 1$

The graph of $y = e^{-x} - 1$ is obtained from the graph of $y = e^x$ by reflecting it about the y-axis then shifting downward 1 unit.

Domain: $(-\infty, \infty)$

Range: $(-1, \infty)$

Asymptote: $y = -1$

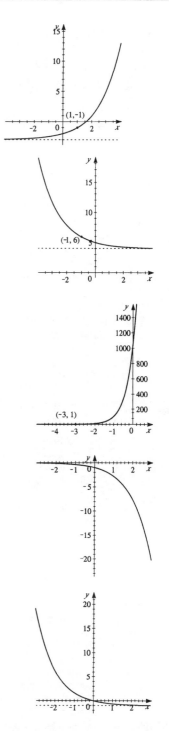

184

31. $y = e^{x-2}$

The graph of $y = e^{x-2}$ is obtained from the graph of $y = e^x$ by shifting it to the right 2 units.

Domain: $(-\infty, \infty)$

Range: $(0, \infty)$

Asymptote: $y = 0$

33. Using the points $(0, 3)$ and $(2, 12)$, we have $f(0) = Ca^0 = 3 \Leftrightarrow C = 3$. We also have $f(2) = 3a^2 = 12 \Leftrightarrow a^2 = 4 \Leftrightarrow a = 2$ (recall that for an exponential function $f(x) = a^x$ we require $a > 0$). Thus $f(x) = 3 \cdot 2^x$.

35. (a)

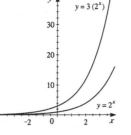

(b) Since $g(x) = 3(2^x) = 3f(x)$ and $f(x) > 0$, the height of the graph of $g(x)$ is always three times the height of the graph of $f(x) = 2^x$, so the graph of g is steeper than the graph of f.

37. $f(x) = 10^x$, so $\dfrac{f(x+h) - f(x)}{h} = \dfrac{10^{x+h} - 10^x}{h} = \dfrac{10^x \cdot 10^h - 10^x}{h} = 10^x \dfrac{10^h - 1}{h}$.

39. (a) From the graphs in (i) - (iii) below, we see that the graph of f ultimately increases much more quickly than the graph of g.

(i) $[0, 5]$ by $[0, 20]$ (ii) $[0, 25]$ by $[0, 10^7]$

(iii) $[0, 50]$ by $[0, 10^8]$

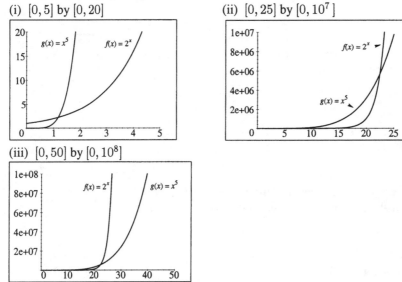

(b) From the graphs in parts (i) and (ii), we see that the approximate solutions are $x \approx 1.2$ and $x \approx 22.4$.

41.

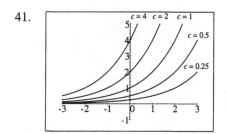

The larger the value of c, the more rapidly the graph of $f(x) = c\,2^x$ increases. Also, some students might notice that the graphs are just shifted horizontally 1 unit. This is because of our choice of c; each c in this exercise is of the form 2^k. So $f(x) = 2^k \cdot 2^x = 2^{x+k}$.

43. $m(t) = 13\,e^{-0.015t}$

(a) $m(0) = 13$ kg.

(b) $m(45) = 13\,e^{-0.015(45)} = 13\,e^{-0.675} = 6.619$ kg. Thus the mass of the radioactive substance after 45 days is about 7 kg.

45. $v(t) = 80(1 - e^{-0.2t})$

(a) $v(0) = 80(1 - e^0) = 80(1 - 1) = 0$.

(b) $v(5) = 80(1 - e^{-0.2(5)}) \approx 80(0.632) = 50.57$ ft/s. So the velocity after 5 s is about 51 ft/s.
$v(10) = 80(1 - e^{-0.2(10)}) \approx 80(0.865) = 69.2$ ft/s. So the velocity after 10 s is about 69 ft/s.

(c)

(d)   The terminal velocity is 80 ft/s.

47.   (a)   Substituting $n_0 = 50$ and $t = 12$, we have $n(12) = \dfrac{300}{0.05 + \left(\frac{300}{50} - 0.05\right)e^{-0.55(12)}} \approx 5164$.

(b)

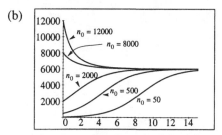

(c)   The population approaches a size of 6000 rabbits.

49. $P = 10{,}000$, $r = 0.10$, and $n = 2$. So $A(t) = 10{,}000\left(1 + \frac{0.10}{2}\right)^{2t} = 10{,}000 \cdot 1.05^{2t}$.

(a) $A(5) = 10{,}000 \cdot 1.05^{10} \approx 16{,}288.95$, and so the value of the investment is \$16,288.95.

(b) $A(10) = 10{,}000 \cdot 1.05^{20} \approx 26{,}532.98$, and so the value of the investment is \$26,532.98.

(c) $A(15) = 10{,}000 \cdot 1.05^{30} \approx 43{,}219.42$, and so the value of the investment is \$43,219.42.

51. $P = 3000$ and $r = 0.09$. Then we have $A(t) = 3000\left(1 + \dfrac{0.09}{n}\right)^{nt}$, and so

$$A(5) = 3000\left(1 + \frac{0.09}{n}\right)^{5n}.$$

   (a) If $n = 1$, $A(5) = 3000\left(1 + \frac{0.09}{1}\right)^{5} = 3000 \cdot 1.09^5 \approx \$4{,}615.87$.

   (b) If $n = 2$, $A(5) = 3000\left(1 + \frac{0.09}{2}\right)^{10} = 3000 \cdot 1.045^{10} \approx \$4{,}658.91$.

   (c) If $n = 12$, $A(5) = 3000\left(1 + \frac{0.09}{12}\right)^{60} = 3000 \cdot 1.0075^{60} \approx \$4{,}697.04$.

   (d) If $n = 52$, $A(5) = 3000\left(1 + \frac{0.09}{52}\right)^{260} \approx \$4{,}703.11$.

   ·(e) If $n = 365$, $A(5) = 3000\left(1 + \frac{0.09}{365}\right)^{1825} \approx \$4{,}704.68$.

   (f) If $n = 24 \cdot 365 = 8760$, $A(5) = 3000\left(1 + \frac{0.09}{8760}\right)^{43800} \approx \$4{,}704.93$.

   (g) If interest is compounded continuously, $A(5) = 3000 \cdot e^{0.45} \approx \$4{,}704.94$.

53. We find the effective rate, with $P = 1$, and $t = 1$. So $A = \left(1 + \frac{r}{n}\right)^{n}$

   (i) $n = 2, r = 0.085$; $A(2) = \left(1 + \frac{0.085}{2}\right)^{2} = (1.0425)^2 \approx 1.0868$.

   (ii) $n = 4, r = 0.0825$; $A(4) = \left(1 + \frac{0.0825}{4}\right)^{4} = (1.020625)^4 \approx 1.0851$.

   (iii) continuous compounding, $r = 0.08$; $A(1) = e^{0.08} \approx 1.0833$.

   Since (i) is larger than the others, the best investment is the one at 8.5% compounded semiannually.

55. (a) We must solve for P in the equation $10000 = P\left(1 + \frac{0.09}{2}\right)^{2(3)} = P(1.045)^6$ $\Leftrightarrow$
       $10000 = 1.3023P$ $\Leftrightarrow$ $P = 7678.96$. Thus the present value is \$7,678.96.

   (b) We must solve for P in the equation $100000 = P\left(1 + \frac{0.08}{12}\right)^{12(5)} = P(1.00667)^{60}$ $\Leftrightarrow$
       $100000 = 1.4898P$ $\Leftrightarrow$ $P = \$67{,}121.04$.

57.

59. $\cosh(-x) = \dfrac{e^{-x} + e^{-(-x)}}{2} = \dfrac{e^{-x} + e^{x}}{2} = \dfrac{e^{x} + e^{-x}}{2} = \cosh(x)$.

61. $[\cosh(x)]^2 - [\sinh(x)]^2 = \left(\dfrac{e^x + e^{-x}}{2}\right)^2 - \left(\dfrac{e^x - e^{-x}}{2}\right)^2$

   $= \frac{1}{4}(e^{2x} + 2 + e^{-2x}) - \frac{1}{4}(e^{2x} - 2 + e^{-2x}) = \frac{2}{4} + \frac{2}{4} = 1$.

63.

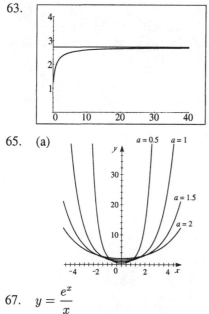

Note from the graph, that $y = \left(1 + \frac{1}{x}\right)^x$ approaches e as x get large.

65. (a)

(b) As a increases the curve $y = \dfrac{a}{2}\left(e^{x/a} + e^{-x/a}\right)$ flattens out and the y intercept increases.

67. $y = \dfrac{e^x}{x}$

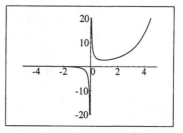

Vertical Asymptote: $x = 0$

Horizontal Asymptote: $y = 0$, left side only.

As $x \rightarrow -\infty, y \rightarrow 0$, and as $x \rightarrow \infty$,

$y \rightarrow \infty$.

69. $g(x) = e^x + e^{-3x}$

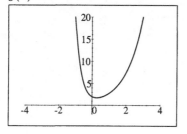

The graph of $g(x)$ is shown in the viewing rectangle $[-4, 4]$ by $[0, 20]$. From the graph, we see that there is a local minimum ≈ 1.75 when $x \approx 0.27$.

71. $y = xe^x$

(a) From the graph, we see that the function $f(x) = x\,e^x$ is *in*creasing on $(-\infty, 1]$ and decreasing on $[1, \infty)$.

(b) From the graph, we see that the range is approximately $(-\infty, 0.37)$.

73. Since $f(40) = 2^{40} = 1099511627776$, it would take a sheet of paper 4 inches by 1099511627776 inches. Since there are 12 inches in every foot and 5,280 feet in ever mile, 1099511627776 inches ≈ 1.74 million miles. So the dimensions of the sheet of paper required are 4 inches by about 1.74 million miles.

Exercises 4.2

1. (a) $5^2 = 25$ (b) $5^0 = 1$

3. (a) $8^{1/3} = 2$ (b) $2^{-3} = \frac{1}{8}$

5. (a) $e^x = 5$ (b) $e^5 = y$

7. (a) $\log_5 125 = 3$ (b) $\log_{10} 0.0001 = -4$

9. (a) $\log_8 \frac{1}{8} = -1$ (b) $\log_2\left(\frac{1}{8}\right) = -3$

11. (a) $\ln 2 = x$ (b) $\ln y = 3$

13. (a) $\log_3 3 = 1$ (b) $\log_3 1 = \log_3 3^0 = 0$
    (c) $\log_3 3^2 = 2$

15. (a) $\log_6 36 = \log_6 6^2 = 2$ (b) $\log_9 81 = \log_9 9^2 = 2$
    (c) $\log_7 7^{10} = 10$

17. (a) $\log_3\left(\frac{1}{27}\right) = \log_3 3^{-3} = -3$ (b) $\log_{10}\sqrt{10} = \log_{10} 10^{1/2} = \frac{1}{2}$
    (c) $\log_5 0.2 = \log_5\left(\frac{1}{5}\right) = \log_5 5^{-1} = -1$

19. (a) $2^{\log_2 37} = 37$ (b) $3^{\log_3 8} = 8$
    (c) $e^{\ln\sqrt{5}} = \sqrt{5}$

21. (a) $\log_8 0.25 = \log_8 8^{-2/3} = -\frac{2}{3}$ (b) $\ln e^4 = 4$
    (c) $\ln\left(\frac{1}{e}\right) = \ln e^{-1} = -1$

23. (a) $\log_2 x = 5 \quad\Leftrightarrow\quad x = 2^5 = 32$ (b) $x = \log_2 16 = \log_2 2^4 = 4$

25. (a) $x = \log_3 243 = \log_3 3^5 = 5$ (b) $\log_3 x = 3 \quad\Leftrightarrow\quad x = 3^3 = 27$

27. (a) $\log_{10} x = 2 \quad\Leftrightarrow\quad x = 10^2 = 100$ (b) $\log_5 x = 2 \quad\Leftrightarrow\quad x = 5^2 = 25$

29. (a) $\log_x 16 = 4 \quad\Leftrightarrow\quad x^4 = 16 \quad\Leftrightarrow\quad x = 2$
    (b) $\log_x 8 = \frac{3}{2} \quad\Leftrightarrow\quad x^{3/2} = 8 \quad\Leftrightarrow\quad x = 8^{2/3} = 4$

31. (a) $\log 2 \approx 0.3010$ (b) $\log 35.2 \approx 1.5465$
    (c) $\log\left(\frac{2}{3}\right) \approx -0.1761$

33. (a) $\ln 5 \approx 1.6094$ (b) $\ln 25.3 \approx 3.2308$
    (c) $\ln\left(1 + \sqrt{3}\right) \approx 1.0051$

35. Since the point $(5, 1)$ is on the graph, we have $1 = \log_a 5 \quad\Leftrightarrow\quad a^1 = 5$. Thus the function is $y = \log_5 x$.

37. Since the point $\left(3, \frac{1}{2}\right)$ is on the graph, we have $\frac{1}{2} = \log_a 3 \quad\Leftrightarrow\quad a^{1/2} = 3 \quad\Leftrightarrow\quad a = 9$. Thus the function is $y = \log_9 x$.

39. II   **41.** III   **43.** VI

45. The graph of $y = \log_4 x$ is obtained from the graph of $y = 4^x$ by reflecting it about the line $y = x$.

47. $f(x) = \log_2(x - 4)$

The graph of f is obtained from the graph of $y = \log_2 x$ by shifting it to the right 4 units.

Domain: $(4, \infty)$

Range: $(-\infty, \infty)$

Vertical asymptote: $x = 4$

49. $g(x) = \log_5(-x)$

The graph of g is obtained from the graph of $y = \log_5 x$ by reflecting it about the y-axis.

Domain: $(-\infty, 0)$

Range: $(-\infty, \infty)$

Vertical asymptote: $x = 0$

51. $y = 2 + \log_3 x$

The graph of $y = 2 + \log_3 x$ is obtained from the graph of $y = \log_3 x$ by shifting it upward 2 units.

Domain: $(0, \infty)$

Range: $(-\infty, \infty)$

Vertical asymptote: $x = 0$

53. $y = 1 - \log_{10} x$

The graph of $y = 1 - \log_{10} x$ is obtained from the graph of $y = \log_{10} x$ by reflecting it about the x-axis, and then shifting it upward 1 unit.

Domain: $(0, \infty)$

Range: $(-\infty, \infty)$

Vertical asymptote: $x = 0$

55. $y = |\ln x|$

Note that $y = \begin{cases} \ln x & x \geq 1 \\ -\ln x & 0 < x < 1. \end{cases}$

The graph of $y = |\ln x|$ is obtained from the graph of $y = \ln x$ by reflecting the part of the graph for $0 < x < 1$ about the x-axis.

Domain: $(0, \infty)$

Range: $[0, \infty)$

Vertical asymptote: $x = 0$

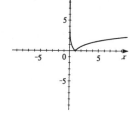

57. $f(x) = \log_{10}(x + 3)$. We require that $x + 3 > 0$ $\Leftrightarrow$ $x > -3$, so the domain is $(-3, \infty)$.

59. $g(x) = \log_3(x^2 - 1)$. We require that $x^2 - 1 > 0$ $\Leftrightarrow$ $x^2 > 1$ $\Rightarrow$ $x < -1$ or $x > 1$, so the domain is $(-\infty, -1) \cup (1, \infty)$.

61. $h(x) = \ln x + \ln(2 - x)$. We require that $x > 0$ and $2 - x > 0$ $\Leftrightarrow$ $x > 0$ and $x < 2$ $\Leftrightarrow$ $0 < x < 2$, so the domain is $(0, 2)$.

63. $y = \log_{10}(1 - x^2)$

Domain: $(-1, 1)$

Vertical asymptote: $x = -1$ and $x = 1$

Local maximum $y = 0$ at $x = 0$

65. $y = x + \ln x$

Domain: $(0, \infty)$

Vertical asymptote: $x = 0$

No local extrema.

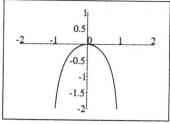

67. $y = \dfrac{\ln x}{x}$

Domain: $(0, \infty)$

Vertical asymptote: $x = 0$

Horizontal asymptote: $y = 0$

Local maximum $y \approx 0.37$ at $x \approx 2.72$

69. The graph of $g(x) = \sqrt{x}$ grows faster than the graph of $f(x) = \ln x$.

71. (a)

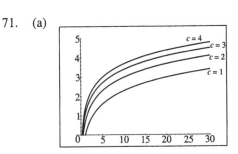

(b) Notice that $f(x) = \log(cx) = \log c + \log x$, so as c increases, the graph of $f(x) = \log(cx)$ is shifted upward $\log c$ units.

73. (a) $f(x) = \log_2(\log_{10}x)$. Since the domain of $\log_2 x$ is the positive real numbers, we have: $\log_{10}x > 0 \Leftrightarrow x > 10^0 = 1$. Thus the domain of $f(x)$ is $(1, \infty)$.

(b) $y = \log_2(\log_{10}x) \Leftrightarrow 2^y = \log_{10}x \Leftrightarrow 10^{2^y} = x$. Thus $f^{-1}(x) = 10^{2^x}$.

75. (a) $f(x) = \dfrac{2^x}{1+2^x}$. $y = \dfrac{2^x}{1+2^x} \Leftrightarrow y + y\,2^x = 2^x \Leftrightarrow y = 2^x - y\,2^x = 2^x(1-y) \Leftrightarrow$

$2^x = \dfrac{y}{1-y} \Leftrightarrow x = \log_2\left(\dfrac{y}{1-y}\right)$. Thus $f^{-1}(x) = \log_2\left(\dfrac{x}{1-x}\right)$.

(b) $\dfrac{x}{1-x} > 0$. Solving this using the methods from Chapter 2, we start with the endpoints of the potential intervals, 0 and 1.

Interval	$(-\infty, 0)$	$(0, 1)$	$(1, \infty)$
Sign of x	$-$	$+$	$+$
Sign of $1 - x$	$+$	$+$	$-$
Sign of $\dfrac{x}{1-x}$	$-$	$+$	$-$

Thus the domain of $f^{-1}(x)$ is $(0, 1)$.

77. $\log(\log 10^{100}) = \log 100 = 2$

$\log(\log(\log 10^{\text{googol}})) = \log(\log(\text{googol})) = \log(\log 10^{100}) = \log(100) = 2$

79. The numbers between 1000 and 9999 (inclusive) each have 4 digits, while $\log 1000 = 3$ and $\log 10{,}000 = 4$. Since $[\![\log x]\!] = 3$ for all integers x where $1000 \le x < 10000$, the number of digits is $[\![\log x]\!] + 1$. Likewise, if x is an integer where $10^{n-1} \le x < 10^n$, then x would have n digits and $[\![\log x]\!] = n - 1$. Since $[\![\log x]\!] = n - 1 \Leftrightarrow n = [\![\log x]\!] + 1$, the number of digits in x is $[\![\log x]\!] + 1$.

Exercises 4.3

1. $\log_2 2x = \log_2 2 + \log_2 x = 1 + \log_2 x$

3. $\log_2[x(x-1)] = \log_2 x + \log_2(x-1)$

5. $\log 6^{10} = 10\log 6$

7. $\log_2(AB^2) = \log_2 A + \log_2 B^2 = \log_2 A + 2\log_2 B$

9. $\log_3(x\sqrt{y}) = \log_3 x + \log_3\sqrt{y} = \log_3 x + \frac{1}{2}\log_3 y$

11. $\log_5\sqrt[3]{x^2+1} = \frac{1}{3}\log_5(x^2+1)$

13. $\ln\sqrt{ab} = \frac{1}{2}\ln ab = \frac{1}{2}(\ln a + \ln b)$

15. $\log\left(\dfrac{x^3 y^4}{z^6}\right) = \log(x^3 y^4) - \log z^6 = 3\log x + 4\log y - 6\log z$

17. $\log_2\left(\dfrac{x(x^2+1)}{\sqrt{x^2-1}}\right) = \log_2 x + \log_2(x^2+1) - \dfrac{1}{2}\log_2(x^2-1)$

19. $\ln\left(x\sqrt{\dfrac{y}{z}}\right) = \ln x + \dfrac{1}{2}\ln\left(\dfrac{y}{z}\right) = \ln x + \dfrac{1}{2}(\ln y - \ln z)$

21. $\log\sqrt[4]{x^2+y^2} = \frac{1}{4}\log(x^2+y^2)$

23. $\log\sqrt{\dfrac{x^2+4}{(x^2+1)(x^3-7)^2}} = \frac{1}{2}\log\dfrac{x^2+4}{(x^2+1)(x^3-7)^2} = \frac{1}{2}[\log(x^2+4) - \log(x^2+1)(x^3-7)^2]$

$= \frac{1}{2}[\log(x^2+4) - \log(x^2+1) - 2\log(x^3-7)]$

25. $\ln\dfrac{x^3\sqrt{x-1}}{3x+4} = \ln\left(x^3\sqrt{x-1}\right) - \ln(3x+4) = 3\ln x + \frac{1}{2}\ln(x-1) - \ln(3x+4)$

27. $\log_5\sqrt{125} = \log_5 5^{3/2} = \frac{3}{2}$

29. $\log 2 + \log 5 = \log 10 = 1$

31. $\log_4 192 - \log_4 3 = \log_4\frac{192}{3} = \log_4 64 = \log_4 4^3 = 3$

33. $\ln 6 - \ln 15 + \ln 20 = \ln\frac{6}{15} + \ln 20 = \ln(\frac{2}{5}\cdot 20) = \ln 8$

35. $10^{2\log 4} = (10^{\log 4})^2 = 4^2 = 16$

37. $\log(\log 1000^{10,000}) = \log(10,000\log 1000) = (\log 10,000) + \log(\log 10^3) = \log 10^4 + \log(3\log 10)$
$= 4\log 10 + \log 3 + \log(\log 10) = 4 + \log 3 + \log 1 = 4 + \log 3$

39. $\log_3 5 + 5\log_3 2 = \log_3 5 + \log_3 2^5 = \log_3(5\cdot 2^5) = \log_3 160$

41. $\log_2 A + \log_2 B - 2\log_2 C = \log_2(AB) - \log_2(C^2) = \log_2\left(\dfrac{AB}{C^2}\right)$

43. $4\log x - \frac{1}{3}\log(x^2+1) + 2\log(x-1) = \log x^4 - \log\sqrt[3]{x^2+1} + \log(x-1)^2$

$$= \log\left(\frac{x^4}{\sqrt[3]{x^2+1}}\right) + \log(x-1)^2 = \log\left(\frac{x^4(x-1)^2}{\sqrt[3]{x^2+1}}\right)$$

45. $\ln 5 + 2\ln x + 3\ln(x^2+5) = \ln(5x^2) + \ln(x^2+5)^3 = \ln[5x^2(x^2+5)^3]$

47. $\frac{1}{3}\log(2x+1) + \frac{1}{2}[\log(x-4) - \log(x^4-x^2-1)] =$

$$\log\sqrt[3]{2x+1} + \frac{1}{2}\log\frac{x-4}{x^4-x^2-1} = \log\left(\sqrt[3]{2x+1} \cdot \sqrt{\frac{x-4}{x^4-x^2-1}}\right)$$

49. $\log_2 5 = \frac{\log 5}{\log 2} \approx 2.321928$

51. $\log_3 16 = \frac{\log 16}{\log 3} \approx 2.523719$

53. $\log_7 2.61 = \frac{\log 2.61}{\log 7} \approx 0.493008$

55. $\log_4 125 = \frac{\log 125}{\log 4} \approx 3.482892$

57. $\log_3 x = \frac{\log_e x}{\log_e 3} = \frac{\ln x}{\ln 3} = \frac{1}{\ln 3}\ln x.$

The graph of $y = \frac{1}{\ln 3}\ln x$ is shown in the
viewing rectangle $[-1, 4]$ by $[-3, 2]$.

59. $\log e = \frac{\ln e}{\ln 10} = \frac{1}{\ln 10}$

61. $-\ln(x - \sqrt{x^2-1}) = \ln\left(\frac{1}{x-\sqrt{x^2-1}}\right) = \ln\left(\frac{1}{x-\sqrt{x^2-1}} \cdot \frac{x+\sqrt{x^2-1}}{x+\sqrt{x^2-1}}\right)$

$$= \ln\left(\frac{x+\sqrt{x^2-1}}{x^2-(x^2-1)}\right) = \ln\left(x + \sqrt{x^2-1}\right)$$

63. The error is on the first line: $\log 0.1 < 0$, so $2\log 0.1 < \log 0.1$.

Exercises 4.4

1. $e^x = 16$ $\Leftrightarrow$ $\ln e^x = \ln 16$ $\Leftrightarrow$ $x \ln e = \ln 16$ $\Leftrightarrow$ $x = 2.7726$

3. $10^{2x} = 5$ $\Leftrightarrow$ $\log 10^{2x} = \log 5$ $\Leftrightarrow$ $2x \log 10 = \log 5$ $\Leftrightarrow$ $2x = \log 5$ $\Leftrightarrow$
    $x = \frac{1}{2} \log 5 = 0.3495$

5. $2^{1-x} = 3$ $\Leftrightarrow$ $\log 2^{1-x} = \log 3$ $\Leftrightarrow$ $(1-x) \log 2 = \log 3$ $\Leftrightarrow$ $1 - x = \frac{\log 3}{\log 2}$ $\Leftrightarrow$
    $x = 1 - \frac{\log 3}{\log 2} \approx -0.5850$

7. $3e^x = 10$ $\Leftrightarrow$ $e^x = \frac{10}{3}$ $\Leftrightarrow$ $x = \ln\left(\frac{10}{3}\right) \approx 1.2040$

9. $e^{1-4x} = 2$ $\Leftrightarrow$ $1 - 4x = \ln 2$ $\Leftrightarrow$ $-4x = -1 + \ln 2$ $\Leftrightarrow$ $x = \frac{1 - \ln 2}{4} = 0.0767$

11. $4 + 3^{5x} = 8$ $\Leftrightarrow$ $3^{5x} = 4$ $\Leftrightarrow$ $\log 3^{5x} = \log 4$ $\Leftrightarrow$ $5x \log 3 = \log 4$ $\Leftrightarrow$ $5x = \frac{\log 4}{\log 3}$
    $\Leftrightarrow$ $x = \frac{\log 4}{5 \log 3} \approx 0.2524$

13. $8^{0.4x} = 5$ $\Leftrightarrow$ $\log 8^{0.4x} = \log 5$ $\Leftrightarrow$ $0.4x \log 8 = \log 5$ $\Leftrightarrow$ $0.4x = \frac{\log 5}{\log 8}$ $\Leftrightarrow$
    $x = \frac{\log 5}{0.4 \log 8} \approx 1.9349$

15. $5^{-x/100} = 2$ $\Leftrightarrow$ $\log 5^{-x/100} = \log 2$ $\Leftrightarrow$ $-\frac{x}{100} \log 5 = \log 2$ $\Leftrightarrow$
    $x = -\frac{100 \log 2}{\log 5} \approx -43.0677$

17. $e^{2x+1} = 200$ $\Leftrightarrow$ $2x + 1 = \ln 200$ $\Leftrightarrow$ $2x = -1 + \ln 200$ $\Leftrightarrow$ $x = \frac{-1 + \ln 200}{2} \approx 2.1492$

19. $5^x = 4^{x+1}$ $\Leftrightarrow$ $\log 5^x = \log 4^{x+1}$ $\Leftrightarrow$ $x \log 5 = (x+1)\log 4 = x \log 4 + \log 4$ $\Leftrightarrow$
    $x \log 5 - x \log 4 = \log 4$ $\Leftrightarrow$ $x(\log 5 - \log 4) = \log 4$ $\Leftrightarrow$ $x = \frac{\log 4}{\log 5 - \log 4} \approx 6.2126$

21. $2^{3x+1} = 3^{x-2}$ $\Leftrightarrow$ $\log 2^{3x+1} = \log 3^{x-2}$ $\Leftrightarrow$ $(3x+1)\log 2 = (x-2)\log 3$ $\Leftrightarrow$
    $3x \log 2 + \log 2 = x \log 3 - 2 \log 3$ $\Leftrightarrow$ $3x \log 2 - x \log 3 = -\log 2 - 2 \log 3$ $\Leftrightarrow$
    $x(3 \log 2 - \log 3) = -(\log 2 + 2 \log 3)$ $\Leftrightarrow$ $s = -\frac{\log 2 + 2\log 3}{3 \log 2 - \log 3} \approx -2.9469$

23. $\dfrac{50}{1 + e^{-x}} = 4$ $\Leftrightarrow$ $50 = 4 + 4e^{-x}$ $\Leftrightarrow$ $46 = 4e^{-x}$ $\Leftrightarrow$ $11.5 = e^{-x}$ $\Leftrightarrow$ $\ln 11.5 = -x$
    $\Leftrightarrow$ $x = -\ln 11.5 \approx -2.4423$

25. $100(1.04)^{2t} = 300$ $\Leftrightarrow$ $1.04^{2t} = 3$ $\Leftrightarrow$ $\log 1.04^{2t} = \log 3$ $\Leftrightarrow$ $2t \log 1.04 = \log 3$ $\Leftrightarrow$
    $t = \frac{\log 3}{2 \log 1.04} \approx 14.0055$

27. $x^2 2^x - 2^x = 0$ $\Leftrightarrow$ $2^x(x^2 - 1) = 0$ $\Rightarrow$ $2^x = 0$ (never) or $x^2 - 1 = 0$. If $x^2 - 1 = 0$, then
    $x^2 = 1$ $\Rightarrow$ $x = \pm 1$. So the only solutions are $x = \pm 1$.

29. $4x^3 e^{-3x} - 3x^4 e^{-3x} = 0$ $\Leftrightarrow$ $x^3 e^{-3x}(4 - 3x) = 0$ $\Rightarrow$ $x = 0$ or $e^{-3x} = 0$ (never) or
    $4 - 3x = 0$. If $4 - 3x = 0$, then $3x = 4$ $\Leftrightarrow$ $x = \frac{4}{3}$. So the solutions are $x = 0$ and $x = \frac{4}{3}$.

31. $e^{2x} - 3e^x + 2 = 0$ $\Leftrightarrow$ $(e^x - 1)(e^x - 2) = 0$ $\Rightarrow$ $e^x - 1 = 0$ or $e^x - 2 = 0$. If $e^x - 1 = 0$,
    then $e^x = 1$ $\Leftrightarrow$ $x = \ln 1 = 0$. If $e^x - 2 = 0$, then $e^x = 2$ $\Leftrightarrow$ $x = \ln 2 \approx 0.6931$. So the
    solutions are $x = 0$ and $x \approx 0.6931$.

33. $e^{4x} + 4e^{2x} - 21 = 0$ $\Leftrightarrow$ $(e^{2x} + 7)(e^{2x} - 3) = 0$ $\Rightarrow$ $e^{2x} = -7$ or $e^{2x} = 3$. Now $e^{2x} = -7$
    has no solution, since $e^{2x} > 0$ for all x. But we <u>can</u> solve $e^{2x} = 3$ $\Leftrightarrow$ $2x = \ln 3$ $\Leftrightarrow$
    $x = \frac{1}{2}\ln 3 \approx 0.5493$. So the only solution is $x \approx 0.5493$.

35. $\ln x = 10$ $\Leftrightarrow$ $x = e^{10} \approx 22026$

37. $\log x = -2$ $\Leftrightarrow$ $x = 10^{-2} = 0.01$

39. $\log(3x + 5) = 2$ $\Leftrightarrow$ $3x + 5 = 10^2 = 100$ $\Leftrightarrow$ $3x = 95$ $\Leftrightarrow$ $x = \frac{95}{3} \approx 31.6667$

41. $2 - \ln(3 - x) = 0$ $\Leftrightarrow$ $2 = \ln(3 - x)$ $\Leftrightarrow$ $e^2 = 3 - x$ $\Leftrightarrow$ $x = 3 - e^2 \approx -4.3891$

43. $\log_2 3 + \log_2 x = \log_2 5 + \log_2(x - 2)$ $\Leftrightarrow$ $\log_2(3x) = \log_2(5x - 10)$ $\Leftrightarrow$ $3x = 5x - 10$
    $\Leftrightarrow$ $2x = 10$ $\Leftrightarrow$ $x = 5$

45. $\log x + \log(x - 1) = \log(4x)$ $\Leftrightarrow$ $\log[x(x - 1)] = \log(4x)$ $\Leftrightarrow$ $x^2 - x = 4x$ $\Leftrightarrow$
    $x^2 - 5x = 0$ $\Leftrightarrow$ $x(x - 5) = 0$ $\Rightarrow$ $x = 0$ or $x = 5$. So the *possible* solutions are $x = 0$ and
    $x = 5$. However, when $x = 0$, $\log x$ is undefined. Thus the only solution is $x = 5$.

47. $\log_5(x + 1) - \log_5(x - 1) = 2$ $\Leftrightarrow$ $\log_5\left(\dfrac{x + 1}{x - 1}\right) = 2$ $\Leftrightarrow$ $\dfrac{x + 1}{x - 1} = 5^2$ $\Leftrightarrow$
    $x + 1 = 25x - 25$ $\Leftrightarrow$ $24x = 26$ $\Leftrightarrow$ $x = \frac{13}{12}$

49. $\log_9(x - 5) + \log_9(x + 3) = 1$ $\Leftrightarrow$ $\log_9[(x - 5)(x + 3)] = 1$ $\Leftrightarrow$ $(x - 5)(x + 3) = 9^1$
    $\Leftrightarrow$ $x^2 - 2x - 24 = 0$ $\Leftrightarrow$ $(x - 6)(x + 4) = 0$ $\Rightarrow$ $x = 6$ or-4. However, $x = -4$ is
    inadmissible, so $x = 6$ is the only solution.

51. $\log(x + 3) = \log x + \log 3$ $\Leftrightarrow$ $\log(x + 3) = \log(3x)$ $\Leftrightarrow$ $x + 3 = 3x$ $\Leftrightarrow$ $2x = 3$ $\Leftrightarrow$
    $x = \frac{3}{2}$

53. $2^{2/\log_5 x} = \frac{1}{16}$ $\Leftrightarrow$ $\log_2 2^{2/\log_5 x} = \log_2\left(\frac{1}{16}\right)$ $\Leftrightarrow$ $\dfrac{2}{\log_5 x} = -4$ $\Leftrightarrow$ $\log_5 x = -\frac{1}{2}$ $\Leftrightarrow$
    $x = 5^{-1/2} = \frac{1}{\sqrt{5}} \approx 0.4472$

55. (a) $A(3) = 5000\left(1 + \frac{0.085}{4}\right)^{4(3)} = 5000(1.02125^{12}) = 6435.09$. Thus the amount after 3 years is
    $6,435.09.

    (b) $10000 = 5000\left(1 + \frac{0.085}{4}\right)^{4t} = 5000(1.02125^{4t})$ $\Leftrightarrow$ $2 = 1.02125^{4t}$ $\Leftrightarrow$
    $\log 2 = 4t\log 1.02125$ $\Leftrightarrow$ $t = \frac{\log 2}{4\log 1.02125} \approx 8.24$ years. Thus the investment will double in
    about 8.24 years.

57. $8000 = 5000\left(1 + \frac{0.075}{4}\right)^{4t} = 5000(1.01875^{4t})$ $\Leftrightarrow$ $1.6 = 1.01875^{4t}$ $\Leftrightarrow$
    $\log 1.6 = 4t\log 1.01875$ $\Leftrightarrow$ $t = \frac{\log 1.6}{4\log 1.01875} \approx 6.3253$ years. The investment will increase to
    $8000 in approximately 6 years and 4 months.

59. $2 = e^{0.085t}$ $\Leftrightarrow$ $\ln 2 = 0.085t$ $\Leftrightarrow$ $t = \frac{\ln 2}{0.085} \approx 8.15$ years. Thus the investment will double in
    about 8.15 years.

61. $r_{\text{eff}} = \left(1 + \frac{r}{n}\right)^n - 1$. Here $r = 0.08$ and $n = 12$, so $r_{\text{eff}} = \left(1 + \frac{0.08}{12}\right)^{12} - 1 = (1.0066667)^{12} - 1$
    $= 8.30\%$.

63. $15e^{-0.087t} = 5$ $\Leftrightarrow$ $e^{-0.087t} = \frac{1}{3}$ $\Leftrightarrow$ $-0.087t = \ln\left(\frac{1}{3}\right) = -\ln 3$ $\Leftrightarrow$ $t = \frac{\ln 3}{0.087} \approx 12.6277$.
So only 5 grams remain after approximately 13 days.

65. (a) $P(3) = \dfrac{10}{1 + 4e^{-0.8(3)}} = 7.337$ So there are approximately 7340 fish after 3 years.

    (b) We solve for t. $\dfrac{10}{1 + 4e^{-0.8t}} = 5$ $\Leftrightarrow$ $1 + 4e^{-0.8t} = \dfrac{10}{5} = 2$ $\Leftrightarrow$ $4e^{-0.8t} = 1$ $\Leftrightarrow$
    $e^{-0.8t} = 0.25$ $\Leftrightarrow$ $-0.8t = \ln 0.25$ $\Leftrightarrow$ $t = \frac{\ln 0.25}{-0.8} = 1.73$. So the population will reach
    5000 fish in about 1 year and 9 months.

67. (a) $I = \frac{60}{13}\left(1 - e^{-13t/5}\right)$ $\Leftrightarrow$ $\frac{13}{60}I = 1 - e^{-13t/5}$ $\Leftrightarrow$ $e^{-13t/5} = 1 - \frac{13}{60}I$ $\Leftrightarrow$
    $-\frac{13}{5}t = \ln\left(1 - \frac{13}{60}I\right)$ $\Leftrightarrow$ $t = -\frac{5}{13}\ln\left(1 - \frac{13}{60}I\right)$.

    (b) Substituting $I = 2$, we have $t = -\frac{5}{13}\ln\left[1 - \frac{13}{60}(2)\right] \approx 0.218$ seconds.

69. $\ln x = 3 - x$ $\Leftrightarrow$ $\ln x + x - 3 = 0$. Let
$f(x) = \ln x + x - 3$. We need to solve the equation
$f(x) = 0$. From the graph of f, we get $x \approx 2.21$.

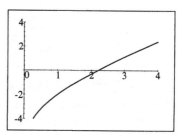

71. $x^3 - x = \log_{10}(x + 1)$ $\Leftrightarrow$ $x^3 - x - \log_{10}(x + 1) = 0$.
Let $f(x) = x^3 - x - \log_{10}(x + 1)$. We need to solve the
equation $f(x) = 0$. From the graph of f, we get $x = 0$
or $x \approx 1.14$.

73. $e^x = -x$ $\Leftrightarrow$ $e^x + x = 0$. Let $f(x) = e^x + x$. We need to
solve the equation $f(x) = 0$. From the graph of f, we get
$x \approx -0.57$.

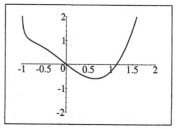

75. $4^{-x} = \sqrt{x}$ $\Leftrightarrow$ $4^{-x} - \sqrt{x} = 0$. Let $f(x) = 4^{-x} - \sqrt{x}$.
We need to solve the equation $f(x) = 0$. From the graph of f,
we get $x \approx 0.36$.

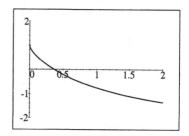

77. $\log(x-2) + \log(9-x) < 1$ $\Leftrightarrow$ $\log[(x-2)(9-x)] < 1$ $\Leftrightarrow$ $\log(-x^2 + 11x - 18) < 1$ $\Rightarrow$ $-x^2 + 11x - 18 < 10^1$ $\Leftrightarrow$ $0 < x^2 - 11x + 28$ $\Leftrightarrow$ $0 < (x-7)(x-4)$. Also, since the domain of a logarithm is positive we must have $0 < -x^2 + 11x - 18$ $\Leftrightarrow$ $0 < (x-2)(9-x)$. Using the methods from Chapter 3 with the endpoints 2, 4, 7, 9 for the intervals, we have:

Interval	$(-\infty, 2)$	$(2, 4)$	$(4, 7)$	$(7, 9)$	$(9, \infty)$
Sign of $x - 7$	$-$	$-$	$-$	$+$	$+$
Sign of $x - 4$	$-$	$-$	$+$	$+$	$+$
Sign of $x - 2$	$-$	$+$	$+$	$+$	$+$
Sign of $9 - x$	$+$	$+$	$+$	$+$	$-$
Sign of $(x-7)(x-4)$	$+$	$+$	$-$	$+$	$+$
Sign of $(x-2)(9-x)$	$-$	$+$	$+$	$+$	$-$

Thus the solution is $(2, 4) \cup (7, 9)$.

79. $2 < 10^x < 5$ $\Leftrightarrow$ $\log 2 < x < \log 5$ $\Leftrightarrow$ $0.3010 < x < 0.6990$. Hence the solution to the inequality is approximately the interval $(0.3010, 0.6990)$.

81. Since $x - 1 > 0$ $\Leftrightarrow$ $x > 1$, we can take the log of both sides of the equation $(x-1)^{\log(x-1)} = 100(x-1)$. Then we have $\log[(x-1)^{\log(x-1)}] = \log[100(x-1)]$ $\Leftrightarrow$ $[\log(x-1)][\log(x-1)] = 2 + \log(x-1)$ $\Leftrightarrow$ $[\log(x-1)]^2 - \log(x-1) - 2 = 0$ $\Leftrightarrow$ $[\log(x-1) + 1][\log(x-1) - 2] = 0$ $\Rightarrow$

$$\log(x-1) + 1 = 0 \qquad \text{or} \qquad \log(x-1) - 2 = 0$$
$$\log(x-1) = -1 \qquad\qquad\qquad \log(x-1) = 2$$
$$x - 1 = \tfrac{1}{10} \qquad\qquad\qquad\qquad x - 1 = 10^2$$
$$x = \tfrac{11}{10} \qquad\qquad\qquad\qquad\qquad x = 101$$

The solutions are $x = 1.1$ or $x = 101$.

83. $4^x - 2^{x+1} = 3$ $\Leftrightarrow$ $2^{2x} - 2 \cdot 2^x = 3$ $\Leftrightarrow$ $(2^x)^2 - 2 \cdot 2^x - 3 = 0$ $\Leftrightarrow$ $(2^x - 3)(2^x + 1) = 0$ $\Leftrightarrow$ $2^x = 3$ or $2^x = -1$. Since $2^x > 0$ for all x, $2^x = -1$ has no solution, but $2^x = 3$ $\Leftrightarrow$ $x \log 2 = \log 3$ $\Leftrightarrow$ $x = \frac{\log 3}{\log 2} \approx 1.58$. So the only solution is $x \approx 1.58$.

85. Notice that $\log\left(x^{1/\log x}\right) = \dfrac{1}{\log x} \log x = 1$, so $x^{1/\log x} = 10^1$ for all $x > 0$. So $x^{1/\log x} = 5$ has no solution, and $x^{1/\log x} = k$ has a solution only when $k = 10$. This is verified by the graph of $f(x) = x^{1/\log x}$.

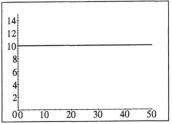

Exercises 4.5

1. (a) $n(0) = 500$.

    (b) The relative growth rate is $0.45 = 45\%$.

    (c) $n(3) = 500e^{0.45(3)} \approx 1929$.

    (d) $10000 = 500\,e^{0.45t} \quad \Leftrightarrow \quad 20 = e^{0.45t} \quad \Leftrightarrow \quad 0.45t = \ln 20 \quad \Leftrightarrow \quad t = \frac{\ln 20}{0.45} \approx 6.66$ hours, or 6 hours 40 minutes.

3. (a) $r = 0.08$ and $n(0) = 18000$. Thus the population is given by the formula $n(t) = 18000\,e^{0.08t}$.

    (b) $t = 2008 - 2000 = 8$. Then we have $n(8) = 18000\,e^{0.08(8)} = 18000\,e^{0.64} \approx 34{,}137$. Thus there should be 34,137 foxes in the region by the year 2008.

    (c)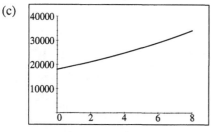

5. (a) $n(t) = 112000e^{0.04t}$.

    (b) $t = 2000 - 1994 = 6$ and $n(6) = 112000\,e^{0.04(6)} \approx 142380$. The projected population is about 142,000.

    (c) $200000 = 112000\,e^{0.04t} \quad \Leftrightarrow \quad \frac{25}{14} = e^{0.04t} \quad \Leftrightarrow \quad 0.04t = \ln\!\left(\frac{25}{14}\right) \quad \Leftrightarrow$

    $t = 25\ln\!\left(\frac{25}{14}\right) \approx 14.5$. Since $1994 + 14.5 = 2008.5$, the population will reach 200,000 during the year 2008.

7. (a) The deer population in 1996 was 20,000.

    (b) Using the model $n(t) = 20000\,e^{rt}$ and the point $(4, 31000)$, we have $31000 = 20000\,e^{4r} \quad \Leftrightarrow \quad 1.55 = e^{4r} \quad \Leftrightarrow \quad 4r = \ln 1.55 \quad \Leftrightarrow \quad r = \frac{1}{4}\ln 1.55 \approx 0.1096$. Thus $n(t) = 20000\,e^{0.1096t}$

    (c) $n(8) = 20000\,e^{0.1096(8)} \approx 48218$, so the projected deer population in 2004 is about 48,000.

    (d) $100000 = 20000\,e^{0.1096t} \quad \Leftrightarrow \quad 5 = e^{0.1096t} \quad \Leftrightarrow \quad 0.1096t = \ln 5 \quad \Leftrightarrow \quad t = \frac{\ln 5}{0.1096}$
    ≈ 14.63. Since $1996 + 14.63 = 2010.63$, the deer population will reach 100,000 during the year 2010.

9. (a) Using the formula $n(t) = n_0\,e^{rt}$ with $n_0 = 8600$ and $n(1) = 10000$, we solve for r, giving $10000 = n(1) = 8600\,e^r \quad \Leftrightarrow \quad \frac{50}{43} = e^r \quad \Leftrightarrow \quad r = \ln\!\left(\frac{50}{43}\right) \approx 0.1508$. Thus $n(t) = 8600\,e^{0.1508\,t}$.

    (b) $n(2) = 8600\,e^{0.1508(2)} \approx 11627$. Thus the number of bacteria after two hours is about 11,600.

    (c) $17200 = 8600e^{0.1508\,t} \quad \Leftrightarrow \quad 2 = e^{0.1508\,t} \quad \Leftrightarrow \quad 0.1508t = \ln 2 \quad \Leftrightarrow \quad t = \frac{\ln 2}{0.1508} \approx 4.596$.
    Thus the number of bacteria will double in about 4.6 hours.

11. (a) $2n_0 = n_0 e^{0.02t}$ $\Leftrightarrow$ $2 = e^{0.02t}$ $\Leftrightarrow$ $0.02t = \ln 2$ $\Leftrightarrow$ $t = 50 \ln 2 \approx 34.65$. So we have $t = 1995 + 34.65 = 2029.65$, and hence at the current growth rate the population will double by the year 2029.

    (b) $3n_0 = n_0 e^{0.02t}$ $\Leftrightarrow$ $3 = e^{0.02t}$ $\Leftrightarrow$ $0.02t = \ln 3$ $\Leftrightarrow$ $t = 50 \ln 3 \approx 54.93$. So we have $t = 1995 + 54.93 = 2049.93$, and hence at the current growth rate the population will triple by the year 2049.

13. $n(t) = n_0 e^{2t}$. When $n_0 = 1$, the critical level is $n(24) = e^{2(24)} = e^{48}$. We solve the equation $e^{48} = n_0 e^{2t}$, where $n_0 = 10$. This gives $e^{48} = 10 e^{2t}$ $\Leftrightarrow$ $48 = \ln 10 + 2t$ $\Leftrightarrow$ $2t = 48 - \ln 10$ $\Leftrightarrow$ $t = \frac{1}{2}(48 - \ln 10) \approx 22.85$ hours.

15. (a) Using $m(t) = m_0 e^{-rt}$ with $m_0 = 10$ and $h = 30$, we have $r = \dfrac{\ln 2}{h} = \dfrac{\ln 2}{30} \approx 0.023$. Thus $m(t) = 10e^{-0.023t}$.

    (b) $m(80) = 10e^{-0.023(80)} \approx 1.6$ grams.

    (c) $2 = 10e^{-0.023t}$ $\Leftrightarrow$ $\frac{1}{5} = e^{-0.023t}$ $\Leftrightarrow$ $\ln\left(\frac{1}{5}\right) = -0.023t$ $\Leftrightarrow$ $t = \frac{-\ln 5}{-0.023} \approx 70$ years.

17. By the formula in the text, $m(t) = m_0 e^{-rt}$ where $r = \frac{\ln 2}{h}$, so $m(t) = 50e^{-\frac{\ln 2}{28} \cdot t}$. We need to solve for t in the equation $32 = 50e^{-\frac{\ln 2}{28}t}$. This gives $e^{-\frac{\ln 2}{28}t} = \dfrac{32}{50}$ $\Leftrightarrow$ $-\dfrac{\ln 2}{28}t = \ln\left(\dfrac{32}{50}\right)$ $\Leftrightarrow$ $t = -\frac{28}{\ln 2} \cdot \ln\left(\frac{32}{50}\right) \approx 18.03$, so it takes about 18 years.

19. By the formula for radioactive decay, we have $m(t) = m_0 e^{-rt}$, where $r = \frac{\ln 2}{h}$, in other words $m(t) = m_0 e^{-\frac{\ln 2}{h} \cdot t}$. In this exercise we have to solve for h in the equation $200 = 250e^{-\frac{\ln 2}{h} \cdot 48}$ $\Leftrightarrow$ $0.8 = e^{-\frac{\ln 2}{h} \cdot 48}$ $\Leftrightarrow$ $\ln(0.8) = -\frac{\ln 2}{h} \cdot 48$ $\Leftrightarrow$ $h = -\frac{\ln 2}{\ln 0.8} \cdot 48 \approx 149.1$ hours. So the half-life is approximately 149 hours.

21. By the formula in the text, $m(t) = m_0 e^{-\frac{\ln 2}{h} \cdot t}$, so we have $0.65 = 1 \cdot e^{-\frac{\ln 2}{5730} \cdot t}$ $\Leftrightarrow$ $\ln(0.65) = -\dfrac{\ln 2}{5730}t$ $\Leftrightarrow$ $t = -\dfrac{5730 \ln 0.65}{\ln 2} \approx 3561$. Thus the artifact is about 3560 years old.

23. (a) $T(0) = 65 + 145\, e^{-0.05(0)} = 65 + 145 = 210°\text{F}$.

    (b) $T(10) = 65 + 145\, e^{-0.05(10)} \approx 152.9$. Thus the temperature after 10 minutes is about 153°F.

    (c) $100 = 65 + 145\, e^{-0.05t}$ $\Leftrightarrow$ $35 = 145\, e^{-0.05t}$ $\Leftrightarrow$ $0.2414 = e^{-0.05t}$ $\Leftrightarrow$ $\ln 0.2414 = -0.05t$ $\Leftrightarrow$ $t = -\dfrac{\ln 0.2414}{0.05} \approx 28.4$. Thus the temperature will be 100°F in about 28 minutes.

25. Using Newton's Law of Cooling, $T(t) = T_s + D_0\, e^{-kt}$ with $T_s = 75$ and $D_0 = 185 - 75 = 110$. So $T(t) = 75 + 110\, e^{-kt}$.

    (a) Since $T(30) = 150$, we have $T(30) = 75 + 110\, e^{-30k} = 150$ $\Leftrightarrow$ $110\, e^{-30k} = 75$ $\Leftrightarrow$ $e^{-30k} = \frac{15}{22}$ $\Leftrightarrow$ $-30k = \ln\left(\frac{15}{22}\right)$ $\Leftrightarrow$ $k = -\frac{1}{30} \ln\left(\frac{15}{22}\right)$. Thus we have $T(45) = 75 + 110\, e^{(45/30) \ln(15/22)} \approx 136.9$, and so the temperature of the turkey after 45 minutes is about 137° F.

(b) The temperature will be $100°\,F$ when $75 + 110\,e^{(t/30)\ln(15/22)} = 100$ $\Leftrightarrow$

$e^{(t/30)\ln(15/22)} = \frac{25}{110} = \frac{5}{22}$ $\Leftrightarrow$ $\left(\frac{t}{30}\right)\ln\left(\frac{15}{22}\right) = \ln\left(\frac{5}{22}\right)$ $\Leftrightarrow$ $t = 30\dfrac{\ln\left(\frac{5}{22}\right)}{\ln\left(\frac{15}{22}\right)} \approx 116.1$. So the

temperature will be $100°\,F$ after 116 minutes.

27. (a) $\text{pH} = -\log[\text{H}^+] = -\log(5.0 \times 10^{-3}) \approx 2.3$

    (b) $\text{pH} = -\log[\text{H}^+] = -\log(3.2 \times 10^{-4}) \approx 3.5$

    (c) $\text{pH} = -\log[\text{H}^+] = -\log(5.0 \times 10^{-9}) \approx 8.3$

29. (a) $\text{pH} = -\log[\text{H}^+] = 3.0$ $\Leftrightarrow$ $[\text{H}^+] = 10^{-3}\ \text{M}$

    (b) $\text{pH} = -\log[\text{H}^+] = 6.5$ $\Leftrightarrow$ $[\text{H}^+] = 10^{-6.5} \approx 3.2 \times 10^{-7}\ \text{M}$

31. $4.0 \times 10^{-7} \le [\text{H}^+] \le 1.6 \times 10^{-5}$ $\Leftrightarrow$ $\log(4.0 \times 10^{-7}) \le \log[\text{H}^+] \le \log(1.6 \times 10^{-5})$ $\Leftrightarrow$ $-\log(4.0 \times 10^{-7}) \ge \text{pH} \ge -\log(1.6 \times 10^{-5})$ $\Leftrightarrow$ $6.4 \ge \text{pH} \ge 4.8$. Therefore the range of pH readings for cheese is approximately 4.8 to 6.4.

33. Let I_0 be the intensity of the smaller earthquake and I_1 the intensity of the larger earthquake. Then $I_1 = 20\,I_0$. Notice that $M_0 = \log\left(\frac{I_0}{S}\right) = \log I_0 - \log S$ and $M_1 = \log\left(\frac{I_1}{S}\right) = \log\left(\frac{20\,I_0}{S}\right)$ $= \log 20 + \log I_0 - \log S$. Then $M_1 - M_0 = \log 20 + \log I_0 - \log S - \log I_0 + \log S = \log 20 \approx 1.3$. Therefore the magnitude is 1.3 times larger.

35. Let the subscript A represent the Alaska earthquake and SF represent the San Francisco earthquake. Then $M_A = \log\left(\frac{I_A}{S}\right) = 8.6$ $\Leftrightarrow$ $I_A = S \cdot 10^{8.6}$; also, $M_{SF} = \log\left(\frac{I_{SF}}{S}\right) = 8.3$ $\Leftrightarrow$ $I_{SF} = S \cdot 10^{8.6}$. So $\dfrac{I_A}{I_{SF}} = \dfrac{S \cdot 10^{8.6}}{S \cdot 10^{8.3}} = 10^{0.3} \approx 1.995$, and hence the Alaskan earthquake was roughly twice as intense as the San Francisco earthquake.

37. Let the subscript MC represent the Mexico City earthquake, and T represent the Tangshan earthquake. We have $\dfrac{I_T}{I_{MC}} = 1.26$ $\Leftrightarrow$ $\log 1.26 = \log\dfrac{I_T}{I_{MC}} = \log\dfrac{I_T/S}{I_{MC}/S} = \log\dfrac{I_T}{S} - \log\dfrac{I_{MC}}{S}$ $= M_T - M_{MC}$. Therefore $M_T = M_{MC} + \log 1.26 \approx 8.1 + 0.1 = 8.2$. Thus the magnitude of the Tangshan earthquake was roughly 8.2.

39. $98 = 10\log\left(\frac{I}{10^{-12}}\right)$ $\Leftrightarrow$ $\log(I \cdot 10^{12}) = 9.8$ $\Leftrightarrow$ $\log I = 9.8 - \log 10^{12} = -2.2$ $\Leftrightarrow$ $I = 10^{-2.2} \approx 6.3 \times 10^{-3}$. So the intensity was 6.3×10^{-3} watts/m^2.

41. (a) $\beta_1 = 10\log\left(\dfrac{I_1}{I_0}\right)$ and $I_1 = \dfrac{k}{d_1^2}$ $\Leftrightarrow$ $\beta_1 = 10\log\left(\dfrac{k}{d_1^2 I_0}\right) = 10\left[\log\left(\dfrac{k}{I_0}\right) - 2\log d_1\right]$

$= 10\log\left(\dfrac{k}{I_0}\right) - 20\log d_1$. Similarly, $\beta_2 = 10\log\left(\dfrac{k}{I_0}\right) - 20\log d_2$. Substituting the

expression for β_1, gives $\beta_2 = 10\log\left(\dfrac{k}{I_0}\right) - 20\log d_1 + 20\log d_1 - 20\log d_2$

$= \beta_1 + 20\log d_1 - 20\log d_2 = \beta_1 + 20\log\left(\dfrac{d_1}{d_2}\right)$.

    (b) $\beta_1 = 120$, $d_1 = 2$, and $d_2 = 10$. Then $\beta_2 = \beta_1 + 20\log\left(\dfrac{d_1}{d_2}\right) = 120 + 20\log\left(\dfrac{2}{10}\right)$ $= 120 + 20\log 0.2 \approx 106$, and so the intensity level at 10 m is approximately 106 dB.

Review Exercises for Chapter 4

1. $f(x) = 3^{-x}$.
    Domain: $(-\infty, \infty)$
    Range: $(0, \infty)$
    Asymptote: $y = 0$.

3. $y = 5 - 10^x$.
    Domain: $(-\infty, \infty)$
    Range: $(-\infty, 5)$
    Asymptote: $y = 5$.

5. $f(x) = \log_3(x - 1)$.
    Domain: $(1, \infty)$
    Range: $(-\infty, \infty)$
    Asymptote: $x = 1$.

7. $y = 2 - \log_2 x$.
    Domain: $(0, \infty)$
    Range: $(-\infty, \infty)$
    Asymptote: $x = 0$.

9. $F(x) = e^x - 1$.
    Domain: $(-\infty, \infty)$
    Range: $(-1, \infty)$
    Asymptote: $y = -1$.

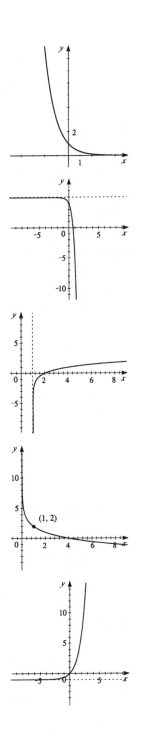

11. $y = 2\ln x$.
    Domain: $(0, \infty)$
    Range: $(-\infty, \infty)$
    Asymptote: $x = 0$.

13. $f(x) = 10^{x^2} + \log(1 - 2x)$. Since $\log u$ is defined only for $u > 0$, we require $1 - 2x > 0$ $\Leftrightarrow$ $-2x > -1$ $\Leftrightarrow$ $x < \frac{1}{2}$, and so the domain is $\left(-\infty, \frac{1}{2}\right)$.

15. $h(x) = \ln(x^2 - 4)$. We must have $x^2 - 4 > 0$ (since $\ln y$ is defined only for $y > 0$) $\Leftrightarrow$ $x^2 - 4 > 0$ $\Leftrightarrow$ $(x-2)(x+2) > 0$. The endpoints of the intervals are -2 and 2.

Interval	$(-\infty, -2)$	$(-2, 2)$	$(2, \infty)$
Sign of $x - 2$	$-$	$-$	$+$
Sign of $x + 2$	$-$	$+$	$+$
Sign of $(x-2)(x+2)$	$+$	$-$	$+$

Thus the domain is $(-\infty, -2) \cup (2, \infty)$.

17. $\log_2 1024 = 10$ $\Leftrightarrow$ $2^{10} = 1024$

19. $\log x = y$ $\Leftrightarrow$ $10^y = x$

21. $2^6 = 64$ $\Leftrightarrow$ $\log_2 64 = 6$

23. $10^x = 74$ $\Leftrightarrow$ $\log_{10} 74 = x$ $\Leftrightarrow$ $\log 74 = x$

25. $\log_2 128 = \log_2(2^7) = 7$

27. $10^{\log 45} = 45$

29. $\ln(e^6) = 6$

31. $\log_3 \frac{1}{27} = \log_3 3^{-3} = -3$

33. $\log_5 \sqrt{5} = \log_5 5^{1/2} = \frac{1}{2}$

35. $\log 25 + \log 4 = \log(25 \cdot 4) = \log 10^2 = 2$

37. $\log_2(16^{23}) = \log_2(2^4)^{23} = \log_2 2^{92} = 92$

39. $\log_8 6 - \log_8 3 + \log_8 2 = \log_8\left(\frac{6}{3} \cdot 2\right) = \log_8 4 = \log_8 8^{2/3} = \frac{2}{3}$

41. $\log(AB^2C^3) = \log A + 2\log B + 3\log C$

43. $\ln\sqrt{\dfrac{x^2 - 1}{x^2 + 1}} = \frac{1}{2}\ln\left(\dfrac{x^2 - 1}{x^2 + 1}\right) = \frac{1}{2}[\ln(x^2 - 1) - \ln(x^2 + 1)]$

45. $\log_5\left(\dfrac{x^2(1 - 5x)^{3/2}}{\sqrt{x^3 - x}}\right) = \log_5 x^2(1 - 5x)^{3/2} - \log_5\sqrt{x(x^2 - 1)}$

    $= 2\log_5 x + \frac{3}{2}\log_5(1 - 5x) - \frac{1}{2}\log_5(x^3 - x)$

47. $\log 6 + 4\log 2 = \log 6 + \log 2^4 = \log(6 \cdot 2^4) = \log 96$

49. $\frac{3}{2}\log_2(x - y) - 2\log_2(x^2 + y^2) = \log_2(x - y)^{3/2} - \log_2(x^2 + y^2)^2 = \log_2\left(\dfrac{(x - y)^{3/2}}{(x^2 + y^2)^2}\right)$

51. $\log(x - 2) + \log(x + 2) - \frac{1}{2}\log(x^2 + 4) = \log[(x - 2)(x + 2)] - \log\sqrt{x^2 + 4} =$
     $\log\left(\dfrac{x^2 - 4}{\sqrt{x^2 + 4}}\right)$

53. $\log_2(1 - x) = 4 \quad \Leftrightarrow \quad 1 - x = 2^4 \quad \Leftrightarrow \quad x = 1 - 2^4 = -15$

55. $5^{5-3x} = 26 \quad \Leftrightarrow \quad \log_5 26 = 5 - 3x \quad \Leftrightarrow \quad 3x = 5 - \log_5 26 \quad \Leftrightarrow \quad x = \frac{1}{3}(5 - \log_5 26) \approx 0.99$

57. $e^{3x/4} = 10 \quad \Leftrightarrow \quad \ln e^{3x/4} = \ln 10 \quad \Leftrightarrow \quad \frac{3x}{4} = \ln 10 \quad \Leftrightarrow \quad x = \frac{4}{3}\ln 10 \approx 3.07$

59. $\log x + \log(x + 1) = \log 12 \quad \Leftrightarrow \quad \log[x(x + 1)] = \log 12 \quad \Leftrightarrow \quad x(x + 1) = 12 \quad \Leftrightarrow$
     $x^2 + x - 12 = 0 \quad \Leftrightarrow \quad (x + 4)(x - 3) = 0 \quad \Rightarrow \quad x = 3 \text{ or } -4.$ Because $\log x$ and $\log(x + 1)$
     are undefined at $x = -4$, it follows that $x = 3$ is the only solution.

61. $x^2 e^{2x} + 2x\, e^{2x} = 8\, e^{2x} \quad \Leftrightarrow \quad e^{2x}(x^2 + 2x - 8) = 0 \quad \Leftrightarrow \quad x^2 + 2x - 8 = 0 \text{ (since } e^{2x} > 0 \text{ for}$
     all x) $\quad \Leftrightarrow \quad (x + 4)(x - 2) = 0 \quad \Leftrightarrow \quad x = 2, -4$

63. $5^{-2x/3} = 0.63 \quad \Leftrightarrow \quad \dfrac{-2x}{3}\log 5 = \log 0.63 \quad \Leftrightarrow \quad x = -\dfrac{3\log 0.63}{2\log 5} \approx 0.430618$

65. $5^{2x+1} = 3^{4x-1} \quad \Leftrightarrow \quad (2x + 1)\log 5 = (4x - 1)\log 3 \quad \Leftrightarrow \quad 2x\log 5 + \log 5 = 4x\log 3 - \log 3$
     $\Leftrightarrow \quad x(2\log 5 - 4\log 3) = -\log 3 - \log 5 \quad \Leftrightarrow \quad x = \dfrac{\log 3 + \log 5}{4\log 3 - 2\log 5} \approx 2.303600$

67. $y = e^{x/(x+2)}$.
     Vertical Asymptote: $x = -2$
     Horizontal Asymptote: $y = 2.72$
     No maximum or minimum.

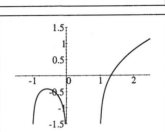

69. $y = \log(x^3 - x)$.
     Vertical Asymptotes: $x = -1$, $x = 0$, $x = 1$
     Horizontal Asymptote: none
     Local maximum ≈ -0.41 when $x \approx -0.58$

71. $3 \log x = 6 - 2x$.

We graph $y = 3 \log x$ and $y = 6 - 2x$ in the same viewing rectangle. The solution occurs where the two graphs intersect. From the graphs, we see that the solution is $x \approx 2.42$.

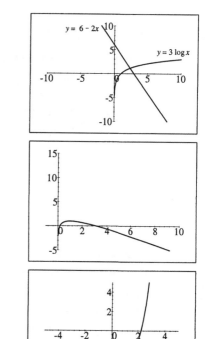

73. $\ln x > x - 2$. We graph the function $f(x) = \ln x - x + 2$, and we see that the graph lies above the x-axis for $0.16 < x < 3.15$. So the approximate solution of the given inequality is $0.16 < x < 3.15$.

75. $f(x) = e^x - 3e^{-x} - 4x$.

We graph the function $f(x)$, and we see that the function is increasing on $(-\infty, 0]$ and $[1.10, \infty)$ and that it is decreasing on $[0, 1.10]$.

77. $\log_4 15 = \frac{\log 15}{\log 4} = 1.953445$

79. Notice that $\log_4 258 > \log_4 256 = \log_4 4^4 = 4$ and so $\log_4 258 > 4$. Also $\log_5 620 < \log_5 625 = \log_5 5^4 = 4$ and so $\log_5 620 < 4$. Then $\log_4 258 > 4 > \log_5 620$ and so $\log_4 258$ is larger.

81. $P = 12{,}000$, $r = 0.10$, and $t = 3$. Then $A = P\left(1 + \frac{r}{n}\right)^{nt}$.

(a) For $n = 2$, $A = 12{,}000\left(1 + \frac{0.10}{2}\right)^{2(3)} = 12{,}000(1.05^6) \approx \$16{,}081.15$.

(b) For $n = 12$, $A = 12{,}000\left(1 + \frac{0.10}{12}\right)^{12(3)} \approx \$16{,}178.18$.

(c) For $n = 365$, $A = 12{,}000\left(1 + \frac{0.10}{365}\right)^{365(3)} \approx \$16{,}197.64$.

(d) For $n = \infty$, $A = P\,e^{rt} = 12{,}000\,e^{0.10(3)} \approx \$16{,}198.31$.

83. (a) Using the model $n(t) = n_0\,e^{rt}$, with $n_0 = 30$ and $r = 0.15$, we have the formula
$$n(t) = 30\,e^{0.15t}.$$

(b) $n(4) = 30\,e^{0.15(4)} \approx 55$.

(c) $500 = 30\,e^{0.15t} \iff \frac{50}{3} = e^{0.15t} \iff 0.15t = \ln\!\left(\frac{50}{3}\right) \iff t = \frac{1}{0.15}\ln\!\left(\frac{50}{3}\right) \approx 18.76$.
So the stray cat population will reach 500 in about 19 years.

85. (a) From the formula for radioactive decay, we have $m(t) = 10e^{-rt}$, where $r = -\dfrac{\ln 2}{2.7 \times 10^5}$. So

    after 1000 years the amount remaining is $m(1000) = 10 \cdot e^{-\frac{\ln 2}{2.7 \times 10^5} \cdot 1000} = 10e^{-\frac{\ln 2}{2.7 \times 10^2}}$

    $= 10e^{-\frac{\ln 2}{270}} \approx 9.97$. Therefore the amount remaining is about 9.97 mg.

    (b) We solve for t in the equation $7 = 10e^{-\frac{\ln 2}{2.7 \times 10^5} \cdot t}$. We have $7 = 10\, e^{-\frac{\ln 2}{2.7 \times 10^5} \cdot t}$ $\Leftrightarrow$

    $0.7 = e^{-\frac{\ln 2}{2.7 \times 10^5} \cdot t}$ $\Leftrightarrow$ $\ln 0.7 = -\dfrac{\ln 2}{2.7 \times 10^5} \cdot t$ $\Leftrightarrow$

    $t = -\dfrac{\ln 0.7}{\ln 2} \cdot 2.7 \times 10^5 \approx 138{,}934.75$. Thus it takes about 139,000 years.

87. (a) From the formula for radioactive decay, $r = \dfrac{\ln 2}{1590} \approx 0.0004359$ and $n(t) = 150 \cdot e^{-0.0004359\, t}$.

    (b) $n(1000) = 150 \cdot e^{-0.0004359 \cdot 1000} \approx 97.00$, and so the amount remaining is about 97.00 mg.

    (c) Find t so that $50 = 150 \cdot e^{-0.0004359\, t}$. We have $50 = 150 \cdot e^{-0.0004359\, t}$ $\Leftrightarrow$ $\frac{1}{3} = e^{-0.0004359\, t}$

    $\Leftrightarrow$ $t = -\frac{1}{0.0004359} \ln\left(\frac{1}{3}\right) \approx 2520$. Thus only 50 mg remain after about 2520 years.

89. (a) Using $n_0 = 1500$ and $n(5) = 3200$ in the formula $n(t) = n_0\, e^{rt}$, we have
    $3200 = n(5) = 1500\, e^{5r}$ $\Leftrightarrow$ $e^{5r} = \frac{32}{15}$ $\Leftrightarrow$ $5r = \ln\left(\frac{32}{15}\right)$ $\Leftrightarrow$ $r = \frac{1}{5}$
    $\ln\left(\frac{32}{15}\right) \approx 0.1515$. Thus $n(t) = 1500 \cdot e^{0.1515t}$.

    (b) We have $t = 1999 - 1988 = 11$ so $n(11) = 1500e^{0.1515 \cdot 11} \approx 7940$. Thus in 1999 the bird
    population should be about 7940 birds.

91. $[H^+] = 1.3 \times 10^{-8}$ M. Then pH $= -\log[H^+] = -\log(1.3 \times 10^{-8}) \approx 7.9$, and so fresh egg whites
    are basic.

93. Let I_0 be the intensity of the smaller earthquake and I_1 be the intensity of the larger earthquake.
    Then $I_1 = 35\, I_0$. Since $M = \log\left(\frac{I}{S}\right)$, we have $M_0 = \log\left(\frac{I_0}{S}\right) = 6.5$ and $M_1 = \log\left(\frac{I_1}{S}\right)$
    $= \log\left(\frac{35\, I_0}{S}\right) = \log 35 + \log\left(\frac{I_0}{S}\right) = \log 35 + M_0 = \log 35 + 6.5 \approx 8.04$. So the magnitude on the
    Richter scale of the larger earthquake is approximately 8.0.

Chapter 4 Test

1. $y = 2^x$ and $y = \log_2 x$.

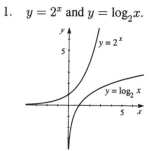

2. $f(x) = \log(x + 2)$.
    Domain: $(-2, \infty)$
    Range: $(-\infty, \infty)$
    Vertical asymptote: $x = -2$.

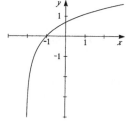

3. (a) $\log_5 \sqrt{125} = \log_5 (5^3)^{\frac{1}{2}} = \log_5 5^{3/2} = \frac{3}{2}$

    (b) $\log_2 56 - \log_2 7 = \log_2 \left(\frac{56}{7}\right) = \log_2 8 = \log_2 2^3 = 3$

    (c) $\log_8 4 = \log_8 8^{2/3} = \frac{2}{3}$

    (d) $\log_6 4 + \log_6 9 = \log_6 (4 \cdot 9) = \log_6 6^2 = 2$

4. $\log \sqrt{\dfrac{x+2}{x^4(x^2+4)}} = \frac{1}{2} \log \left(\dfrac{x+2}{x^4(x^2+4)}\right) = \frac{1}{2} \left[\log(x+2) - (4\log x + \log(x^2+4))\right]$

    $= \frac{1}{2}\log(x+2) - 2\log x - \frac{1}{2}\log(x^2+4)$

5. $\ln x - 2\ln(x^2+1) + \frac{1}{2}\ln(3-x^4) = \ln\left(x\sqrt{3-x^4}\right) - \ln(x^2+1)^2 = \ln\left(\dfrac{x\sqrt{3-x^4}}{(x^2+1)^2}\right)$

6. (a) $2^{x-1} = 10 \quad \Leftrightarrow \quad \log 2^{x-1} = \log 10 = 1 \quad \Leftrightarrow \quad (x-1)\log 2 = 1 \quad \Leftrightarrow \quad x - 1 = \frac{1}{\log 2}$
         $\Leftrightarrow \quad x = 1 + \frac{1}{\log 2} \approx 4.32$

    (b) $5\ln(3-x) = 4 \quad \Leftrightarrow \quad \ln(3-x) = \frac{4}{5} \quad \Leftrightarrow \quad e^{\ln(3-x)} = e^{4/5} \quad \Leftrightarrow \quad 3 - x = e^{4/5} \quad \Leftrightarrow$
         $x = 3 - e^{4/5} \approx 0.77$

    (c) $10^{x+3} = 6^{2x} \quad \Leftrightarrow \quad \log 10^{x+3} = \log 6^{2x} \quad \Leftrightarrow \quad x + 3 = 2x\log 6 \quad \Leftrightarrow \quad 2x\log 6 - x = 3$
         $\Leftrightarrow \quad x(2\log 6 - 1) = 3 \quad \Leftrightarrow \quad x = \dfrac{3}{2\log 6 - 1} \approx 5.39$

    (d) $\log_2(x+2) + \log_2(x-1) = 2 \quad \Leftrightarrow \quad \log_2((x+2)(x-1)) = 2 \quad \Leftrightarrow \quad x^2 + x - 2 = 2^2$
         $\Leftrightarrow \quad x^2 + x - 6 = 0 \quad \Leftrightarrow \quad (x+3)(x-2) = 0 \quad \Rightarrow \quad x = -3 \text{ or } x = 2.$ However, both
         logarithms are undefined at $x = -3$, so the only solution is $x = 2$.

7. (a) From the formula for population growth, we have $8000 = 1000e^{r \cdot 1}$ $\Leftrightarrow$ $8 = e^r$ $\Leftrightarrow$
        $r = \ln 8 \approx 2.07944$. Thus $n(t) = 1000e^{2.07944\,t}$.

    (b) $n(1.5) = 1000e^{2.07944(1.5)} \approx 22{,}627$

    (c) $15000 = 1000e^{2.07944\,t}$ $\Leftrightarrow$ $15 = e^{2.07944\,t}$ $\Leftrightarrow$ $\ln 15 = 2.07944t$ $\Leftrightarrow$
        $t = \frac{\ln 15}{2.07944} \approx 1.3$. Thus the population will reach 15,000 after approximately 1.3 hours.

    (d)

8. (a) $A(t) = 12{,}000\left(1 + \dfrac{0.056}{12}\right)^{12t}$, where t is in years.

    (b) $A(t) = 12{,}000\left(1 + \dfrac{0.056}{365}\right)^{365t}$. So $A(3) = 12{,}000\left(1 + \dfrac{0.056}{365}\right)^{365(3)} = \$14{,}195.06$.

    (c) $A(t) = 12{,}000\left(1 + \dfrac{0.056}{2}\right)^{2t} = 12{,}000(1.028)^{2t}$. So $20{,}000 = 12{,}000(1.028)^{2t}$ $\Leftrightarrow$
        $1.6667 = 1.028^{2t}$ $\Leftrightarrow$ $\ln 1.6667 = \ln 1.028^{2t}$ $\Leftrightarrow$ $\ln 1.6667 = 2t \ln 1.028$ $\Leftrightarrow$
        $t = \frac{\ln 1.6667}{2 \ln 1.028} \approx 9.25$ years.

9. $f(x) = \dfrac{e^x}{x^3}$

    (a)

    (b) Vertical asymptote: $x = 0$; Horizontal
        asymptote: $y = 0$.

    (c) Local minimum ≈ 0.74 when $x \approx 3.00$

    (d) Range $\approx (-\infty, 0) \cup [0.74, \infty)$

    (e) $\dfrac{e^x}{x^3} = 2x + 1$.

        We see that the graphs intersect at
        $x \approx -0.85, 0.96,$ and 9.92.

Focus on Modeling

1. (a)

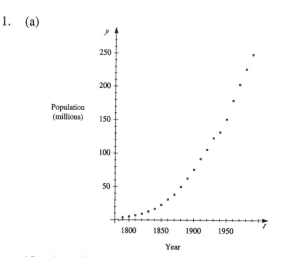

(b) Using a graphing calculator, we obtain the model $y = ab^t$, where $a = 4.041807 \times 10^{-16}$ and $b = 1.021003194$, and y is the population (in millions) in the year t.

(c) Substituting $t = 2000$ into the model of part (b), we get $y = ab^{2000} \approx 457.9$ million.

(d) According to the model, the population in 1965 should have been about $y = ab^{1965} \approx 221.2$ million.

(e) The values given by the model are clearly much too large. This means that an exponential model is NOT appropriate for these data.

3. (a) Yes.

(b)

Year	Health Expenditures (billions of dollars)	
t	E	$\ln E$
1960	27.1	3.29953
1970	74.3	4.30811
1980	251.1	5.52585
1985	434.5	6.07420
1987	506.2	6.22693
1989	623.9	6.43599
1990	696.6	6.54621
1991	755.8	6.62778
1992	820.3	6.70967
1993	884.2	6.78468

Yes, the scatter plot appears to be linear.

(c) Let T be the number of years elapsed since 1960. Then $\ln E = 3.3016 + 0.10769T$.

(d) $E = e^{3.3016 + 0.10769T} = 27.156\, e^{0.10769\,T}$ (where $T = t - 1960$).

(e) When $t = 1996$, then $T = 36$, so the estimated 1996 health-care expenditures are $27.156\, e^{0.10769 \cdot (36)} = 1310.9$ billion dollars.

5. (a) Let t be the number of years elapsed since 1970, and let y be the number of millions of tons of
         lead emissions in year t. Using a graphing calculator, we obtain the exponential model
         $y = ab^t$, where $a = 301.813054$ and $b = 0.819745$.

    (b) Using a graphing calculator, we obtain the fourth-degree polynomial model
         $y = at^4 + bt^3 + ct^2 + dt + e$, where $a = -0.002430$, $b = 0.135159$, $c = -2.014322$,
         $d = -4.055294$, and $e = 199.092227$.

    (c) The exponential model is shown as a
         solid curve and the polynomial model as
         a dotted curve in the graph to the right.
         From the graph, the polynomial model
         appears to fit the data better.

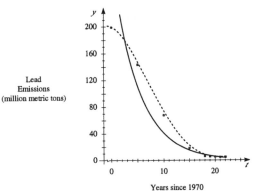

Lead
Emissions
(million metric tons)

Years since 1970

    (d) Exponential model: 1972 $(t = 2)$ $y = 202.8$
                              1982 $(t = 12)$ $y = 27.8$

         Polynomial model: 1972 $y = 184.0$
                              1982 $y = 43.5$

7. (a)

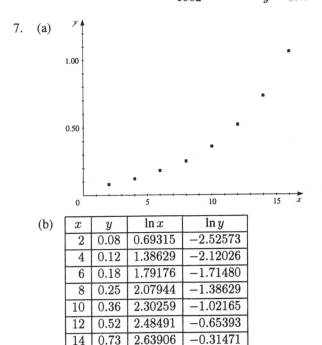

    (b)

x	y	$\ln x$	$\ln y$
2	0.08	0.69315	-2.52573
4	0.12	1.38629	-2.12026
6	0.18	1.79176	-1.71480
8	0.25	2.07944	-1.38629
10	0.36	2.30259	-1.02165
12	0.52	2.48491	-0.65393
14	0.73	2.63906	-0.31471
16	1.06	2.77259	0.05827

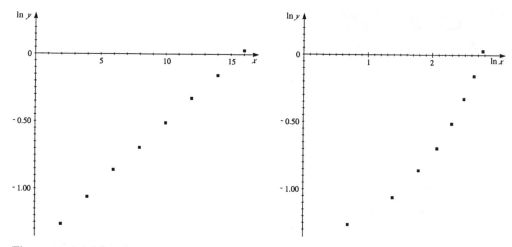

(c)   The exponential function.

(d) $y = a \cdot b^x$ where $a = 0.057697$ and $b = 1.200236$.

9.   (a)   Using the LnReg command on a TI-83 we get $y = a + b \ln x$ where $a = -7154.888128$ and $b = 1061.006551$.

     (b)   Using the model $C = -7154.888128 + (1061.006551)\ln 2005 \approx 912$ metric tons.

Chapter Five
Exercises 5.1

1. Since $\left(\frac{3}{5}\right)^2 + \left(\frac{4}{5}\right)^2 = \frac{9}{25} + \frac{16}{25} = 1$, $P\left(\frac{3}{5}, \frac{4}{5}\right)$ lies on the unit circle.

3. Since $\left(-\frac{2}{3}\right)^2 + \left(-\frac{\sqrt{5}}{3}\right)^2 = \frac{4}{9} + \frac{5}{9} = 1$, $P\left(-\frac{2}{3}, -\frac{\sqrt{5}}{3}\right)$ lies on the unit circle.

5. $\left(\frac{4}{5}\right)^2 + y^2 = 1$ $\Leftrightarrow$ $y^2 = 1 - \frac{16}{25}$ $\Leftrightarrow$ $y^2 = \frac{9}{25}$ $\Leftrightarrow$ $y = \pm\frac{3}{5}$. Since $P(x, y)$ is in quadrant I, y is positive, so the point is $P\left(\frac{4}{5}, \frac{3}{5}\right)$.

7. $x^2 + \left(\frac{2}{3}\right)^2 = 1$ $\Leftrightarrow$ $x^2 = 1 - \frac{4}{9}$ $\Leftrightarrow$ $x^2 = \frac{5}{9}$ $\Leftrightarrow$ $x = \pm\frac{\sqrt{5}}{3}$. Since x is negative, the point is $P\left(-\frac{\sqrt{5}}{3}, \frac{2}{3}\right)$.

9. $\left(-\frac{\sqrt{2}}{3}\right)^2 + y^2 = 1$ $\Leftrightarrow$ $y^2 = 1 - \frac{2}{9}$ $\Leftrightarrow$ $y^2 = \frac{7}{9}$ $\Leftrightarrow$ $y = \pm\frac{\sqrt{7}}{3}$. Since $P(x, y)$ is in quadrant III, y is negative; thus the point is $P\left(-\frac{\sqrt{2}}{3}, -\frac{\sqrt{7}}{3}\right)$.

11.

t	Terminal Point		t	Terminal Point
0	$(1, 0)$		π	$(-1, 0)$
$\frac{\pi}{4}$	$\left(\frac{\sqrt{2}}{2}, \frac{\sqrt{2}}{2}\right)$		$\frac{5\pi}{4}$	$\left(-\frac{\sqrt{2}}{2}, -\frac{\sqrt{2}}{2}\right)$
$\frac{\pi}{2}$	$(0, 1)$		$\frac{3\pi}{2}$	$(0, -1)$
$\frac{3\pi}{4}$	$\left(-\frac{\sqrt{2}}{2}, \frac{\sqrt{2}}{2}\right)$		$\frac{7\pi}{4}$	$\left(\frac{\sqrt{2}}{2}, -\frac{\sqrt{2}}{2}\right)$
π	$(-1, 0)$		2π	$(1, 0)$

13. $P(x, y) = (0, 1)$

15. $P(x, y) = \left(-\frac{\sqrt{3}}{2}, \frac{1}{2}\right)$

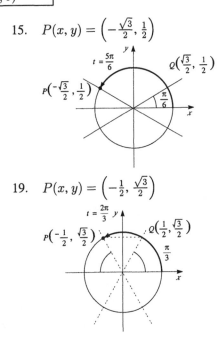

17. $P(x, y) = \left(\frac{1}{2}, -\frac{\sqrt{3}}{2}\right)$

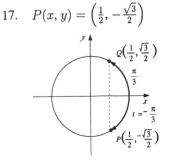

19. $P(x, y) = \left(-\frac{1}{2}, \frac{\sqrt{3}}{2}\right)$

21. $P(x, y) = \left(-\frac{\sqrt{2}}{2}, -\frac{\sqrt{2}}{2}\right)$

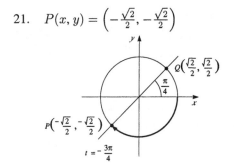

23. Let $Q(x, y) = \left(\frac{3}{5}, \frac{4}{5}\right)$ be the terminal point determined by t.

   (a) $\pi - t$ determines the point $P(-x, y) = \left(-\frac{3}{5}, \frac{4}{5}\right)$

   (b) $-t$ determines the point $P(x, -y) = \left(\frac{3}{5}, -\frac{4}{5}\right)$

   (c) $\pi + t$ determines the point $P(-x, -y) = \left(-\frac{3}{5}, -\frac{4}{5}\right)$

   (d) $2\pi + t$ determines the point $P(x, y) = \left(\frac{3}{5}, \frac{4}{5}\right)$

25. (a) $\overline{t} = \frac{5\pi}{4} - \pi = \frac{\pi}{4}$ (b) $\overline{t} = \frac{7\pi}{3} - 2\pi = \frac{\pi}{3}$

    (c) $\overline{t} = \frac{4\pi}{3} - \pi = \frac{\pi}{3}$ (d) $\overline{t} = \frac{\pi}{6}$

27. (a)   Since $-\frac{11\pi}{5}$ is coterminal with $-\frac{11\pi}{5} + 2\pi = -\frac{\pi}{5}$, we have $\overline{t} = -\left(-\frac{\pi}{5}\right) = \frac{\pi}{5}$

   (b) $\overline{t} = \frac{13\pi}{6} - 2\pi = \frac{\pi}{6}$ (c) $\overline{t} = \frac{7\pi}{3} - 2\pi = \frac{\pi}{3}$ (d) $\overline{t} = \pi - \frac{5\pi}{6} = \frac{\pi}{6}$

29. (a) $\overline{t} = \pi - \frac{2\pi}{3} = \frac{\pi}{3}$ (b) $P\left(-\frac{1}{2}, \frac{\sqrt{3}}{2}\right)$

31. (a) $\overline{t} = \pi - \frac{3\pi}{4} = \frac{\pi}{4}$ (b) $P\left(-\frac{\sqrt{2}}{2}, \frac{\sqrt{2}}{2}\right)$

33. (a) $\overline{t} = \pi - \frac{2\pi}{3} = \frac{\pi}{3}$ (b) $P\left(-\frac{1}{2}, -\frac{\sqrt{3}}{2}\right)$

35. (a) $\overline{t} = \frac{13\pi}{4} - 3\pi = \frac{\pi}{4}$ (b) $P\left(-\frac{\sqrt{2}}{2}, -\frac{\sqrt{2}}{2}\right)$

37. (a) $\overline{t} = \frac{7\pi}{6} - \pi = \frac{\pi}{6}$ (b) $P\left(-\frac{\sqrt{3}}{2}, -\frac{1}{2}\right)$

39. (a) $\overline{t} = 4\pi - \frac{11\pi}{3} = \frac{\pi}{3}$ (b) $P\left(\frac{1}{2}, \frac{\sqrt{3}}{2}\right)$

41. (a) $\overline{t} = \frac{16\pi}{3} - 5\pi = \frac{\pi}{3}$ (b) $P\left(-\frac{1}{2}, -\frac{\sqrt{3}}{2}\right)$

43. $t = 1 \quad \Rightarrow \quad (0.5, 0.8)$

45. $t = -1.1 \quad \Rightarrow \quad (0.5, -0.9)$

47. The distances PQ and PR are equal because they both subtend arcs of length $\frac{\pi}{3}$. Since $P(x, y)$ is a point on the unit circle, $x^2 + y^2 = 1$. Now, $d(P, Q) = \sqrt{(x - x)^2 + (y - (-y))^2} = 2y$ and $d(R, S) = \sqrt{(x - 0)^2 + (y - 1)^2} = \sqrt{x^2 + y^2 - 2y + 1} = \sqrt{2 - 2y}$ (using the fact that $x^2 + y^2 = 1$). Setting these equal gives $2y = \sqrt{2 - 2y} \quad \Rightarrow \quad 4y^2 = 2 - 2y \quad \Leftrightarrow$

$4y^2 + 2y - 2 = 0 \quad \Leftrightarrow \quad 2(2y - 1)(y + 1) = 0$. So $y = -1$ or $y = \frac{1}{2}$. Since P is in quadrant I, $y = \frac{1}{2}$ is the only viable solution. Again using $x^2 + y^2 = 1$ we have $x^2 + \left(\frac{1}{2}\right)^2 = 1 \quad \Leftrightarrow \quad x^2 = \frac{3}{4}$ $\Rightarrow \quad x = \pm\frac{\sqrt{3}}{2}$. Again, since P is in quadrant I the coordinates must be $\left(\frac{\sqrt{3}}{2}, \frac{1}{2}\right)$.

Exercises 5.2

1.

t	$\sin t$	$\cos t$
0	0	1
$\frac{\pi}{4}$	$\frac{\sqrt{2}}{2}$	$\frac{\sqrt{2}}{2}$
$\frac{\pi}{2}$	1	0
$\frac{3\pi}{4}$	$\frac{\sqrt{2}}{2}$	$-\frac{\sqrt{2}}{2}$
π	0	-1
$\frac{5\pi}{4}$	$-\frac{\sqrt{2}}{2}$	$-\frac{\sqrt{2}}{2}$
$\frac{3\pi}{2}$	-1	0
$\frac{7\pi}{4}$	$-\frac{\sqrt{2}}{2}$	$\frac{\sqrt{2}}{2}$
2π	0	1

3. (a) $\sin\left(-\frac{\pi}{3}\right) = -\frac{\sqrt{3}}{2}$ (b) $\cos\left(-\frac{\pi}{3}\right) = \frac{1}{2}$

5. (a) $\cos\pi = -1$ (b) $\cos(-\pi) = -1$

7. (a) $\sin\frac{\pi}{2} = 1$ (b) $\sin\frac{3\pi}{2} = -1$

9. (a) $\cos\frac{\pi}{2} = 0$ (b) $\cos\frac{5\pi}{2} = 0$

11. (a) $\cos\frac{7\pi}{3} = \frac{1}{2}$ (b) $\sec\frac{7\pi}{3} = 2$

13. (a) $\cos\frac{\pi}{3} = \frac{1}{2}$ (b) $\cos\left(-\frac{\pi}{3}\right) = \frac{1}{2}$

15. (a) $\tan\frac{\pi}{6} = \frac{1}{\sqrt{3}} = \frac{\sqrt{3}}{3}$ (b) $\tan\left(-\frac{\pi}{6}\right) = -\frac{1}{\sqrt{3}} = -\frac{\sqrt{3}}{3}$

17. (a) $\sec\frac{11\pi}{3} = \sec\frac{5\pi}{3} = 2$ (b) $\csc\frac{11\pi}{3} = \csc\frac{5\pi}{3} = -\frac{2}{\sqrt{3}} = -\frac{2\sqrt{3}}{3}$

19. (a) $\sin\frac{9\pi}{4} = \sin\frac{\pi}{4} = \frac{1}{\sqrt{2}} = \frac{\sqrt{2}}{2}$ (b) $\csc\frac{9\pi}{4} = \csc\frac{\pi}{4} = \sqrt{2}$

21. (a) $\tan\left(-\frac{\pi}{4}\right) = -1$ (b) $\cot\left(-\frac{\pi}{4}\right) = -1$

23. $t = 0 \Rightarrow \sin t = 0, \cos t = 1, \tan t = 0, \sec t = 1, \csc t$ and $\cot t$ are undefined.

25. $t = \pi \Rightarrow \sin t = 0, \cos t = -1, \tan t = 0, \sec t = -1, \csc t$ and $\cot t$ are undefined.

27. $\left(\frac{3}{5}\right)^2 + \left(\frac{4}{5}\right)^2 = \frac{9}{25} + \frac{16}{25} = 1$. So $\sin t = \frac{4}{5}, \cos t = \frac{3}{5}$, and $\tan t = \frac{\frac{4}{5}}{\frac{3}{5}} = \frac{4}{3}$.

29. $\left(\frac{\sqrt{5}}{4}\right)^2 + \left(-\frac{\sqrt{11}}{4}\right)^2 = \frac{5}{16} + \frac{11}{16} = 1$. So $\sin t = -\frac{\sqrt{11}}{4}, \cos t = \frac{\sqrt{5}}{4}$, and $\tan$
$t = \frac{-\frac{\sqrt{11}}{4}}{\frac{\sqrt{5}}{4}} = -\frac{\sqrt{11}}{\sqrt{5}} = -\frac{\sqrt{55}}{5}$.

31. $\left(\frac{40}{41}\right)^2 + \left(\frac{9}{41}\right)^2 = \frac{1600}{1681} + \frac{81}{1681} = 1$. So $\sin t = \frac{9}{41}, \cos t = \frac{40}{41}$, and $\tan t = \frac{\frac{9}{41}}{\frac{40}{41}} = \frac{9}{40}$.

33. $\left(-\frac{5}{13}\right)^2 + \left(-\frac{12}{13}\right)^2 = \frac{25}{169} + \frac{144}{169} = 1$. So $\sin t = -\frac{12}{13}$, $\cos t = -\frac{5}{13}$, and $\tan t \frac{-\frac{12}{13}}{-\frac{5}{13}} = \frac{12}{5}$.

35. (a) 0.8   (b) 0.84147

37. (a) 0.9   (b) 0.93204

39. (a) 1.0   (b) 1.02964

41. (a) −0.6   (b) −0.57482

43. $\sin t \cdot \cos t$. Since $\sin t$ is positive in quadrant II and $\cos t$ is negative in quadrant II, their product is negative.

45. $\dfrac{\tan t \cdot \sin t}{\cot t} = \tan t \cdot \dfrac{1}{\cot t} \cdot \sin t = \tan t \cdot \tan t \cdot \sin t = \tan^2 t \cdot \sin t$. Since $\tan^2 t$ is always positive and $\sin t$ is negative in quadrant III, the expression is negative in quadrant III.

47. quadrant II   49. quadrant II

51. $\sin t = \sqrt{1 - \cos^2 t}$ 53. $\tan t = \dfrac{\sin t}{\cos t} = \dfrac{\sin t}{\sqrt{1 - \sin^2 t}}$

55. $\sec t = -\sqrt{1 + \tan^2 t}$ 57. $\tan t = \sqrt{\sec^2 t - 1}$

59. $\tan^2 t = \dfrac{\sin^2 t}{\cos^2 t} = \dfrac{\sin^2 t}{1 - \sin^2 t}$

61. $\sin t = \frac{3}{5}$ and t is in quadrant II, so the terminal point determined by t is $P\left(x, \frac{3}{5}\right)$. Since P is on the unit circle $x^2 + \left(\frac{3}{5}\right)^2 = 1$. Solving for x gives $x = \pm\sqrt{1 - \frac{9}{25}} = \pm\sqrt{\frac{16}{25}} = \pm\frac{4}{5}$. Since t is in quadrant III, $x = -\frac{4}{5}$. Thus the terminal point is $P\left(-\frac{4}{5}, \frac{3}{5}\right)$. Thus, $\cos t = -\frac{4}{5}$, $\tan t = -\frac{3}{4}$, $\csc t = \frac{5}{3}$, $\sec t = -\frac{5}{4}$, $\cot t = -\frac{4}{3}$.

63. $\sec t = 3$ and t lies in quadrant IV. Thus, $\cos t = \frac{1}{3}$ and the terminal point determined by t is $P\left(\frac{1}{3}, y\right)$. Since P is on the unit circle $\left(\frac{1}{3}\right)^2 + y^2 = 1$. Solving for y gives $y = \pm\sqrt{1 - \frac{1}{9}}$ $= \pm\sqrt{\frac{8}{9}} = \pm\frac{2\sqrt{2}}{3}$. Since t is in quadrant IV, $y = -\frac{2\sqrt{2}}{3}$. Thus the terminal point is $P\left(\frac{1}{3}, -\frac{2\sqrt{2}}{3}\right)$. Therefore, $\sin t = -\frac{2\sqrt{2}}{3}$, $\cos t = \frac{1}{3}$, $\tan t = -2\sqrt{2}$, $\csc t = -\frac{3}{2\sqrt{2}} = -\frac{3\sqrt{2}}{4}$, $\cot t = -\frac{1}{2\sqrt{2}} = -\frac{\sqrt{2}}{4}$.

65. $\tan t = -\frac{3}{4}$ and $\cos t > 0$, so t is in quadrant IV. Since $\sec^2 t = \tan^2 t + 1$ we have $\sec^2 t = \left(-\frac{3}{4}\right)^2 + 1 = \frac{9}{16} + 1 = \frac{25}{16}$. Thus $\sec t = \pm\sqrt{\frac{25}{16}} = \pm\frac{5}{4}$. Since $\cos t > 0$, we have $\cos t = \dfrac{1}{\sec t} = \dfrac{1}{\frac{5}{4}} = \frac{4}{5}$. Let $P\left(\frac{4}{5}, y\right)$. Since $\tan t \cdot \cos t = \sin t$ we have $\sin t = \left(-\frac{3}{4}\right)\left(\frac{4}{5}\right) = -\frac{3}{5}$. Thus, the terminal point determined by t is $P\left(\frac{4}{5}, -\frac{3}{5}\right)$, and so $\sin t = -\frac{3}{5}$, $\cos t = \frac{4}{5}$, $\csc t = -\frac{5}{3}$, $\sec t = \frac{5}{4}$, $\cot t = -\frac{4}{3}$.

67. $\sin t = -\frac{1}{4}$, $\sec t < 0$, so t is in quadrant III. So the terminal point determined by t is $P\left(x, -\frac{1}{4}\right)$. Since P is on the unit circle $x^2 + \left(-\frac{1}{4}\right)^2 = 1$. Solving for x gives $x = \pm\sqrt{1 - \frac{1}{16}} = \pm\sqrt{\frac{15}{16}}$ $= \pm\frac{\sqrt{15}}{4}$. Since t is in quadrant III, $x = -\frac{\sqrt{15}}{4}$. Thus, the terminal point determined by t is

$P\left(-\frac{\sqrt{15}}{4}, -\frac{1}{4}\right)$, and so $\cos t = -\frac{\sqrt{15}}{4}$, $\tan t = \frac{1}{\sqrt{15}} = \frac{\sqrt{15}}{15}$, $\csc t = -4$, $\sec t = -\frac{4}{\sqrt{15}} = -\frac{4\sqrt{15}}{15}$,
$\cot t = \sqrt{15}$.

69. $f(-x) = (-x)^2 \sin(-x) = -x^2 \sin x = -f(x)$ so f is odd.

71. $f(-x) = \sin(-x)\cos(-x) = -\sin x \cos x = -f(x)$ so f is odd.

73. $f(-x) = |-x| \cos(-x) = |x| \cos x = f(x)$ so f is even.

75. $f(-x) = (-x)^3 + \cos(-x) = -x^3 + \cos x$ which is neither $f(x)$ nor $-f(x)$, so f is neither even nor odd.

77. Notice that if $P(t) = (x, y)$, then $P(t + \pi) = (-x, -y)$. Thus,

   (a) $\sin(t + \pi) = -y$, and $\sin t = y$. Therefore, $\sin(t + \pi) = -\sin t$.

   (b) $\cos(t + \pi) = -x$, and $\cos t = x$. Therefore, $\cos(t + \pi) = -\cos t$.

   (c) $\tan(t + \pi) = \dfrac{\sin(t + \pi)}{\cos(t + \pi)} = \dfrac{-y}{-x} = \dfrac{y}{x} = \dfrac{\sin t}{\cos t} = \tan t$.

Exercises 5.3

1. $y = 1 + \sin x$

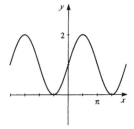

3. $y = 1 - \cos x$

5. $y = -2 \sin x$

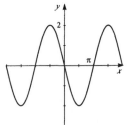

7. $y = 4 - 2 \cos x$

9. $y = |\cos x|$

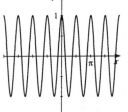

11. $y = \cos 4x$
    amplitude $= 1$, period $= \frac{\pi}{2}$

13. $y = 3 \sin 3x$
    amplitude $= 3$, period $= \frac{2\pi}{3}$

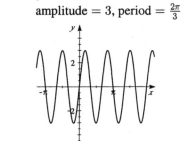

15. $y = 10 \sin \frac{1}{2}x$
     amplitude $= 10$, period $= 4\pi$

17. $y = -\cos \frac{1}{3}x$
     amplitude $= 1$, period $= 6\pi$

19. $y = 3 \cos 3\pi x$
     amplitude $= 3$, period $= \frac{2}{3}$

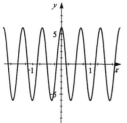

21. $y = \cos(x - \frac{\pi}{2})$
     amplitude $= 1$, period $= 2\pi$,
     phase shift $= \frac{\pi}{2}$

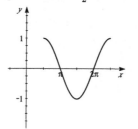

23. $y = -2 \sin\left(x - \frac{\pi}{6}\right)$
     amplitude $= 2$, period $= 2\pi$,
     phase shift $= \frac{\pi}{6}$

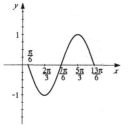

25. $y = 5 \cos(3x - \frac{\pi}{4}) = 5 \cos 3(x - \frac{\pi}{12})$
     amplitude $= 5$, period $= \frac{2\pi}{3}$,
     phase shift $= \frac{\pi}{12}$

27. $y = 2 \sin\left(\frac{2}{3}x - \frac{\pi}{6}\right) = 2 \sin \frac{2}{3}\left(x - \frac{\pi}{4}\right)$
     amplitude $= 2$, period $= 3\pi$,
     phase shift $= \frac{\pi}{4}$

29. $y = 3 \cos \pi(x + \frac{1}{2})$
     amplitude $= 3$, period $= 2$,
     phase shift $= -\frac{1}{2}$

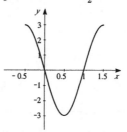

31. $y = -\frac{1}{2}\cos(2x - \frac{\pi}{3}) = -\frac{1}{2}\cos 2(x - \frac{\pi}{6})$

amplitude $= \frac{1}{2}$, period $= \pi$,

phase shift $= \frac{\pi}{6}$

33. $y = \sin(3x + \pi) = \sin 3(x + \frac{\pi}{3})$

amplitude $= 1$, period $= \frac{2\pi}{3}$,

phase shift $= -\frac{\pi}{3}$

35. (a) amplitude $= a = 4$, period $= \frac{2\pi}{k} = 2\pi$, phase shift $= b = 0$

(b) $y = a \sin k(x - b) = 4 \sin x$

37. (a) amplitude $= a = 3$, period $= \frac{2\pi}{k} = 4\pi$, phase shift $= b = 0$

(b) $y = 3 \sin \frac{1}{2}x$

39. (a) amplitude $= a = \frac{1}{2}$, period $= \frac{2\pi}{k} = \pi$, phase shift $= b = -\frac{\pi}{3}$

(b) $y = -\frac{1}{2}\cos 2\left(x + \frac{\pi}{3}\right)$

41. $f(x) = \cos 100x$,

$[-0.1, 0.1]$ by $[-1.5, 1.5]$

43. $f(x) = \sin \frac{x}{40}$,

$[-250, 250]$ by $[-1.5, 1.5]$

45. $y = \tan 25x$, $[-0.2, 0.2]$ by $[-3, 3]$

47. $y = e^{\sin 20x}$, $[-0.5, 0.5]$ by $[0, 3]$

49. (a) The period of the wave is $\dfrac{2\pi}{\pi/10} = 20$ seconds.

(b) Since $h(0) = 3$ and $h(10) = -3$, the wave height is $3 - (-3) = 6$ feet.

51. (a) The period of p is $\frac{2\pi}{160\pi} = \frac{1}{80}$ minute.

(b) Since each period represents a heart beat, there are 80 heart beats per minute.

(c)

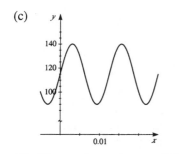

(d)   The maximum (or systolic) is $115 + 25 = 140$ and the minimum (or diastolic) is $115 - 25 = 90$. The read would be $140/90$ which higher than normal.

53. $f(x) = x$, $g(x) = \sin x$, $[-6.28, \ 6.28]$ by $[-7, \ 7]$

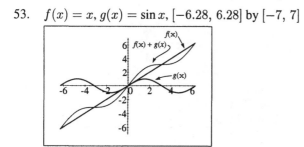

55. $y = x^2$, $y = -x^2$, $y = x^2 \sin x$

$y = x^2 \sin x$ is a sine curve that lies between the graphs of $y = x^2$ and $y = -x^2$.

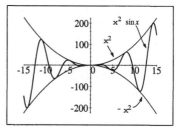

57. $y = e^x$, $y = -e^x$, $y = e^x \sin 5\pi x$

$y = e^x \sin 5\pi x$ is a sine curve that lies between the graphs of $y = e^x$ and $y = -e^x$.

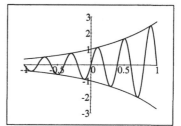

59. $y = \cos 3\pi x$, $y = -\cos 3\pi x$,
$y = \cos 3\pi x \cos 21\pi x$

$y = \cos 3\pi x \cos 21\pi x$ is a cosine curve that lies between the graphs of $y = \cos 3\pi x$ and $y = -\cos 3\pi x$.

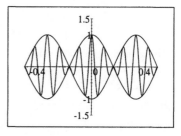

61. $y = \sin x + \sin 2x$. The period is 2π, so we
     graph the function over one period, $(-\pi, \pi)$.
     Maximum value 1.76 when $x \approx 0.94 + 2n\pi$,
     minimum value -1.76 when
     $x \approx -0.94 + 2n\pi$, for $n = 0, \pm1, \pm2, \ldots$.

63. $y = 2\sin x + \sin^2 x$. he period is 2π, so we
     graph the function over one period, $(-\pi, \pi)$.
     Maximum value 3.00 when $x \approx 1.57 + 2n\pi$,
     minimum value -1.00 when
     $x \approx -1.57 + 2n\pi$, for $n = 0, \pm1, \pm2, \ldots$.

65. $\cos x = 0.4, \ x \in [0, \pi]$

     $x \approx 1.16$

67. $\csc x = 3, \ x \in [0, \pi]$

     $x \approx 0.34, 2.80$

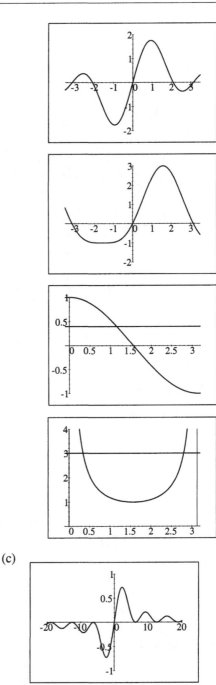

69. $f(x) = \dfrac{1 - \cos x}{x}$ (c)

     (a) Since $f(-x) = \dfrac{1 - \cos(-x)}{-x}$
          $= \dfrac{1 - \cos x}{-x} = -f(x)$, the function is
          odd.

     (b) The x-intercepts occur when
          $1 - \cos x = 0 \quad \Leftrightarrow \quad \cos x = 1 \quad \Leftrightarrow$
          $x = 0, \pm2\pi, \pm4\pi, \pm6\pi, \ldots$

     (d) As $x \to \pm\infty, f(x) \to 0$.

     (e) As $x \to 0, f(x) \to 0$.

71. (a) Periodic, period is 2.

(b) Not periodic. $f(2.5) \neq f(4.5)$.

(c) Not periodic, graph of the function on the interval $[-2, 0]$ is different from graph of the function on the interval $[0, 2]$.

(d) Periodic, period is 3.

73. From the graph we see that the amplitude is 5 and the period is 2π. In Exercise 75 in Section 8.2, we proved the reduction formulas $\sin(x + \pi) = -\sin x$. So starting with $y = -5\sin x$ we may also represent the curve by:

$y = -5\sin(x - b)$ where $b = 2n\pi$, where n is an integer;

$y = 5\sin(x - b)$ where $b = (2n + 1)\pi$, where n is an integer;

We also proved the identity $\cos(x + \pi) = -\cos x$. So starting with $y = -5\cos\left(x - \frac{\pi}{2}\right)$ we may also represent the curve by:

$y = -5\cos(x - b)$ where $b = \frac{\pi}{2} + 2n\pi$, where n is an integer;

$y = 5\cos(x - b)$ where $b = \frac{\pi}{2} + (2n + 1)\pi$, where n is an integer.

Exercises 5.4

1. $y = 4\tan x$, period $= \pi$

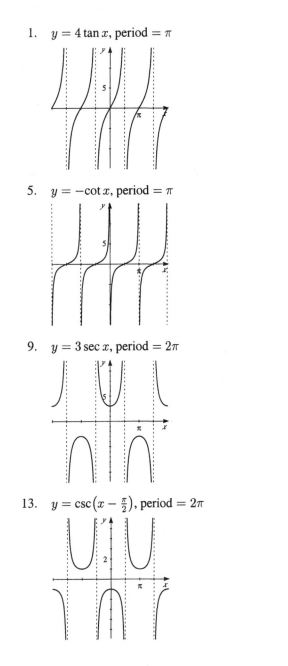

3. $y = -\frac{1}{2}\tan x$, period $= \pi$

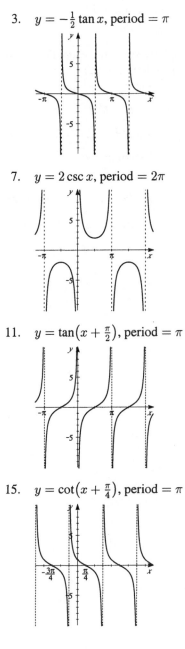

5. $y = -\cot x$, period $= \pi$

7. $y = 2\csc x$, period $= 2\pi$

9. $y = 3\sec x$, period $= 2\pi$

11. $y = \tan\left(x + \frac{\pi}{2}\right)$, period $= \pi$

13. $y = \csc\left(x - \frac{\pi}{2}\right)$, period $= 2\pi$

15. $y = \cot\left(x + \frac{\pi}{4}\right)$, period $= \pi$

17. $y = \frac{1}{2}\sec\left(x - \frac{\pi}{6}\right)$, period $= 2\pi$

19. $y = \tan 2x$, period $= \frac{\pi}{2}$

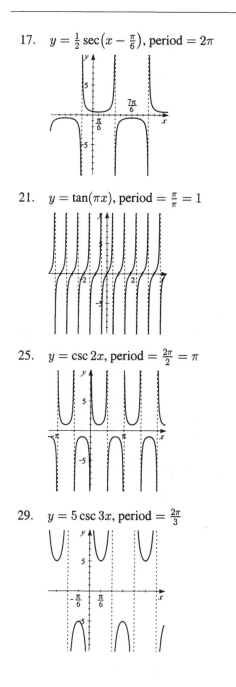

21. $y = \tan(\pi x)$, period $= \frac{\pi}{\pi} = 1$

23. $y = \sec 2x$, period $= \frac{2\pi}{2} = \pi$

25. $y = \csc 2x$, period $= \frac{2\pi}{2} = \pi$

27. $y = 2\tan 3x$, period $= \frac{\pi}{3}$

29. $y = 5\csc 3x$, period $= \frac{2\pi}{3}$

31. $y = \tan 2\left(x + \frac{\pi}{2}\right)$, period $= \frac{\pi}{2}$

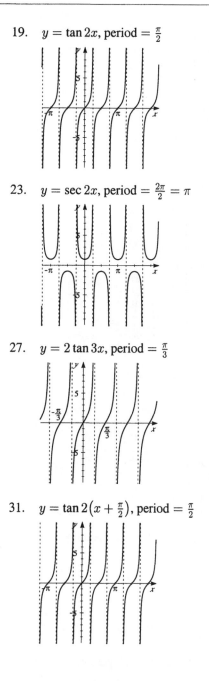

33. $y = \tan 2(x - \pi) = \tan 2x$, period $= \frac{\pi}{2}$ 35. $y = \cot\left(2x - \frac{\pi}{2}\right) = \cot 2\left(x - \frac{\pi}{4}\right)$, period $= \frac{\pi}{2}$

37. $y = 2\csc\left(\pi x - \frac{\pi}{3}\right) = 2\csc\pi\left(x - \frac{1}{3}\right)$,   39. $y = 5\sec\left(3x - \frac{\pi}{2}\right) = 5\sec 3\left(x - \frac{\pi}{6}\right)$,
    period $= \frac{2\pi}{\pi} = 2$ period $= \frac{2\pi}{3}$

41. $y = \tan\left(\frac{2}{3}x - \frac{\pi}{6}\right) = \tan\frac{2}{3}\left(x - \frac{\pi}{4}\right)$,   43. $y = 3\sec\pi\left(x + \frac{1}{2}\right)$, period $= \frac{2\pi}{\pi} = 2$

    period $= \dfrac{\pi}{\left(\frac{2}{3}\right)} = \dfrac{3\pi}{2}$

45. $y = -2\tan\left(2x - \frac{\pi}{3}\right) = -2\tan 2\left(x - \frac{\pi}{6}\right)$,
    period $= \frac{\pi}{2}$

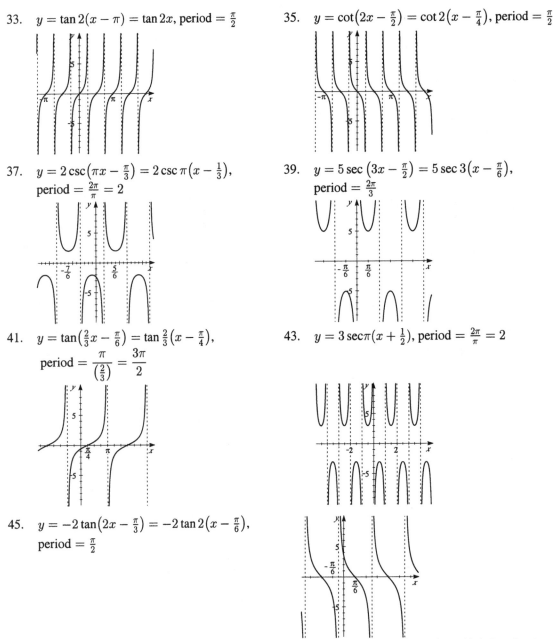

47. (a) If f is periodic with period p, then by the definition of a period, $f(x + p) = f(x)$ for all x in
        the domain of f. Therefore, $\dfrac{1}{f(x + p)} = \dfrac{1}{f(x)}$ for all $f(x) \neq 0$. Thus, $\dfrac{1}{f}$ is also periodic
        with period p.

    (b) Since $\sin x$ has period 2π, it follows from part (a) that $\csc x = \dfrac{1}{\sin x}$ also has period 2π.
        Similarly, since $\cos x$ has period 2π, we conclude $\sec x = \dfrac{1}{\cos x}$ also has period 2π.

Review Exercises for Chapter 5

1.　(a)　Since $\left(-\frac{\sqrt{3}}{2}\right)^2 + \left(\frac{1}{2}\right)^2 = \frac{3}{4} + \frac{1}{4} = 1$, the point $P\left(-\frac{\sqrt{3}}{2}, \frac{1}{2}\right)$ lies on the unit circle.

　　(b)　$\sin t = \frac{1}{2}, \cos t = -\frac{\sqrt{3}}{2}, \tan t = \dfrac{\frac{1}{2}}{-\frac{\sqrt{3}}{2}} = -\frac{\sqrt{3}}{3}$.

3.　$t = \frac{2\pi}{3}$
　　(a)　$\bar{t} = \pi - \frac{2\pi}{3} = \frac{\pi}{3}$
　　(b)　$P\left(-\frac{1}{2}, \frac{\sqrt{3}}{2}\right)$
　　(c)　$\sin t = \frac{\sqrt{3}}{2}, \cos t = -\frac{1}{2}, \tan t = -\sqrt{3}, \csc t = \frac{2\sqrt{3}}{3}, \sec t = -2$, and $\cot t = -\frac{\sqrt{3}}{3}$.

5.　$t = -\frac{11\pi}{4}$
　　(a)　$\bar{t} = 3\pi + \left(-\frac{11\pi}{4}\right) = \frac{\pi}{4}$
　　(b)　$P\left(-\frac{\sqrt{2}}{2}, -\frac{\sqrt{2}}{2}\right)$
　　(c)　$\sin t = -\frac{\sqrt{2}}{2}, \cos t = -\frac{\sqrt{2}}{2}, \tan t = 1, \csc t = -\sqrt{2}, \sec t = -\sqrt{2}, \cot t = 1$.

7.　(a)　$\sin \frac{3\pi}{4} = \sin \frac{\pi}{4} = \frac{\sqrt{2}}{2}$　　　　　(b)　$\cos \frac{3\pi}{4} = -\cos \frac{\pi}{4} = -\frac{\sqrt{2}}{2}$

9.　(a)　$\sin 1.1 \approx 0.89121$　　　　　　　　(b)　$\cos 1.1 \approx 0.45360$

11.　(a)　$\cos \frac{9\pi}{2} = \cos \frac{\pi}{2} = 0$　　　　　　(b)　$\sec \frac{9\pi}{2}$ is undefined

13.　(a)　$\tan \frac{5\pi}{2}$ is undefined　　　　　　(b)　$\cot \frac{5\pi}{2} = \cot \frac{\pi}{2} = 0$

15.　(a)　$\tan \frac{5\pi}{6} = -\frac{\sqrt{3}}{3}$　　　　　　　(b)　$\cot \frac{5\pi}{6} \approx -\sqrt{3}$

17.　$\dfrac{\tan t}{\cos t} = \dfrac{\frac{\sin t}{\cos t}}{\cos t} = \dfrac{\sin t}{\cos^2 t} = \dfrac{\sin t}{1 - \sin^2 t}$

19.　$\tan t = \dfrac{\sin t}{\cos t} = \dfrac{\sin t}{\pm\sqrt{1 - \sin^2 t}} = \dfrac{\sin t}{\sqrt{1 - \sin^2 t}}$　(since t is in quadrant IV, $\cos t$ is positive)

21.　$\sin t = \frac{5}{13}, \cos t = -\frac{12}{13}$. Then $\tan t = \dfrac{\frac{5}{13}}{-\frac{12}{13}} = -\frac{5}{12}, \csc t = \frac{13}{5}, \sec t = -\frac{13}{12}$, and $\cot t = -\frac{12}{5}$.

23.　$\cot t = -\frac{1}{2}, \csc t = \frac{\sqrt{5}}{2}$. Since $\csc t = \dfrac{1}{\sin t}$, we know $\sin t = \frac{2}{\sqrt{5}} = \frac{2\sqrt{5}}{5}$. Now $\cot t = \dfrac{\cos t}{\sin t}$, so
　　$\cos t = \sin t \cdot \cot t = \frac{2\sqrt{5}}{5} \cdot \left(-\frac{1}{2}\right) = -\frac{\sqrt{5}}{5}$, and $\tan t = \dfrac{1}{\left(-\frac{1}{2}\right)} = -2$ while
　　$\sec t = \dfrac{1}{\cos t} = \dfrac{1}{\left(-\frac{\sqrt{5}}{5}\right)} = -\frac{5}{\sqrt{5}} = -\sqrt{5}$.

25.　$\tan t = \frac{1}{4}, t$ is in quadrant III　$\Rightarrow$　$\sec t + \cot t = -\sqrt{\tan^2 t + 1} + \dfrac{1}{\tan t} = -\sqrt{\left(\frac{1}{4}\right)^2 + 1} + 4$
　　$= -\sqrt{\frac{17}{16}} + 4 = 4 - \frac{\sqrt{17}}{4} = \frac{16 - \sqrt{17}}{4}$

27. $\cos t = \frac{3}{5}$, t is in quadrant I $\Rightarrow$ $\tan t + \sec t = \dfrac{\sin t}{\cos t} + \dfrac{1}{\cos t} = \dfrac{\sqrt{1 - \cos^2 t}}{\cos t} + \dfrac{1}{\cos t}$

$$= \dfrac{\sqrt{1 - \left(\frac{3}{5}\right)^2}}{\frac{3}{5}} + \dfrac{5}{3} = \dfrac{\sqrt{\frac{16}{25}}}{\frac{3}{5}} + \dfrac{5}{3} = \dfrac{4}{5} \cdot \dfrac{5}{3} + \dfrac{5}{3} = \dfrac{9}{3} = 3$$

29. $y = 10 \cos \frac{1}{2}x$

(a) amplitude $= 10$, period $= \dfrac{2\pi}{\left(\frac{1}{2}\right)} = 4\pi$,   (b)

phase shift $= 0$

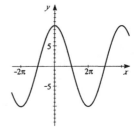

31. $y = -\sin \frac{1}{2}x$

(a) amplitude $= 1$, period $= \dfrac{2\pi}{\left(\frac{1}{2}\right)} = 4\pi$,   (b)

phase shift $= 0$

33. $y = 3\sin(2x - 2) = 3\sin 2(x - 1)$

(a) amplitude $= 3$, period $= \frac{2\pi}{2} = \pi$,   (b)

phase shift $= 1$

35. $y = -\cos\left(\frac{\pi}{2}x + \frac{\pi}{6}\right) = -\cos \frac{\pi}{2}\left(x + \frac{1}{3}\right)$

(a) amplitude $= 1$, period $= \dfrac{2\pi}{\left(\frac{\pi}{2}\right)} = 4$,   (b)

phase shift $= -\frac{1}{3}$

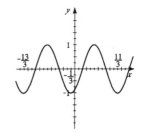

37. From the graph we see that the amplitude is 5, the period is $\frac{\pi}{2}$, and there is no phase shift. Therefore, the function is $y = 5\sin 4x$.

39.   From the graph we see that the amplitude is $\frac{1}{2}$, the period is 1, and there is a phase shift of $-\frac{1}{3}$.
      Therefore, the function is $y = \frac{1}{2}\sin 2\pi(x + \frac{1}{3})$.

41. $y = 3\tan x$, period $= \pi$

43. $y = 2\cot\left(x - \frac{\pi}{2}\right)$, period $= \pi$

45. $y = 4\csc(2x + \pi) = 4\csc 2(x + \frac{\pi}{2})$,

      period $= \frac{2\pi}{2} = \pi$

47. $y = \tan\left(\frac{1}{2}x - \frac{\pi}{8}\right) = \tan\frac{1}{2}(x - \frac{\pi}{4})$,

      period $= \dfrac{\pi}{\left(\frac{1}{2}\right)} = 2\pi$

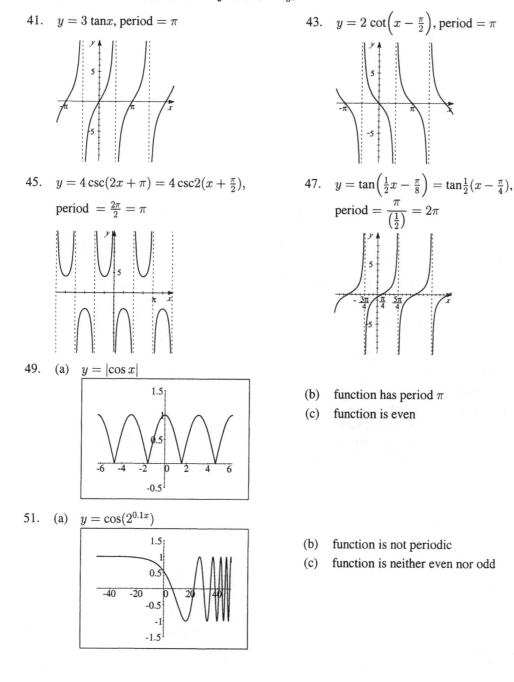

49.   (a) $y = |\cos x|$

      (b)   function has period π
      (c)   function is even

51.   (a) $y = \cos(2^{0.1x})$

      (b)   function is not periodic
      (c)   function is neither even nor odd

53. (a) $y = e^{-|x|}\cos 3x$

(b) function is not periodic

(c) function is even

55. $y = x$, $y = -x$, $y = x\sin x$

$y = x\sin x$ is a sine function whose graph lies between those of $y = x$ and $y = -x$.

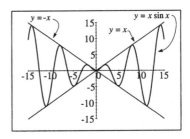

57. $y = x$, $y = \sin 4x$, $y = x + \sin 4x$

$y = x + \sin 4x$ is the sum of the two functions $y = x$ and $y = \sin 4x$.

59. $y = \cos x + \sin 2x$

Since the period is 2π, we graph over the interval $-\pi$ to π. The maximum value is 1.76 when $x \approx 0.63 \pm 2n\pi$, the minimum value is -1.76 when $x \approx 2.51 \pm 2n\pi$, n an integer.

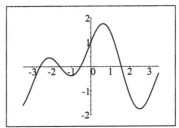

61. We want to find solutions to $\sin x = 0.3$ in the interval $[0, 2\pi]$, so we plot the functions $y = \sin x$ and $y = 0.3$ and look for their intersection. We see that $x \approx 0.305$ or $x \approx 2.837$.

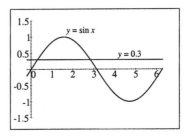

63. $f(x) = \dfrac{\sin^2 x}{x}$

(a) The function is odd.

(b) The graph intersects the x-axis at $x = 0$, $\pm\pi$, $\pm 2\pi$, $\pm 3\pi$, ...

(c)

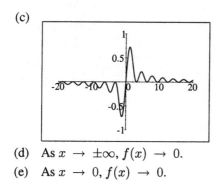

(d)   As $x \rightarrow \pm\infty$, $f(x) \rightarrow 0$.

(e)   As $x \rightarrow 0$, $f(x) \rightarrow 0$.

Chapter 5 Test

1. Since $P(x, y)$ lies on the unit circle, $x^2 + y^2 = 1 \implies y = \pm \sqrt{1 - \left(\frac{\sqrt{11}}{6}\right)^2} = \pm\sqrt{\frac{25}{36}} = \pm\frac{5}{6}$. But $P(x, y)$ lies in the fourth quadrant. Therefore y is negative $\implies y = -\frac{5}{6}$.

2. Since P is on the unit circle, $x^2 + y^2 = 1 \iff x^2 = 1 - y^2$. Thus, $x^2 = 1 - \left(\frac{4}{5}\right)^2 = \frac{9}{25}$, and so $x = \pm\frac{3}{5}$. From the diagram, x is clearly negative $\implies x = -\frac{3}{5}$. Therefore, P is the point $\left(-\frac{3}{5}, \frac{4}{5}\right)$.

    (a) $\sin t = \frac{4}{5}$.   (b) $\cos t = -\frac{3}{5}$.

    (c) $\tan t = \dfrac{\frac{4}{5}}{-\frac{3}{5}} = -\frac{4}{3}$.   (d) $\sec(t) = -\frac{5}{3}$.

3. (a) $\sin \frac{7\pi}{6} = -0.5$.   (b) $\cos \frac{13\pi}{4} = -\frac{\sqrt{2}}{2}$.

    (c) $\tan\left(-\frac{5\pi}{3}\right) = \sqrt{3}$.   (d) $\csc\left(\frac{3\pi}{2}\right) = -1$.

4. $\tan t = \dfrac{\sin t}{\cos t} = \dfrac{\sin t}{\pm\sqrt{1 - \sin^2 t}}$. But t is in quadrant II $\implies \cos t$ is negative, so we choose the negative square root. Thus, $\tan t = \dfrac{\sin t}{-\sqrt{1 - \sin^2 t}}$.

5. $\cos t = -\frac{8}{17}$, t in quadrant III $\implies \tan t \cdot \cot t + \csc t = 1 + \dfrac{1}{-\sqrt{1 - \cos^2 t}}$ (since t in quadrant III) $= 1 - \dfrac{1}{-\sqrt{1 - \frac{64}{289}}} = 1 - \dfrac{1}{\frac{15}{17}} = -\frac{2}{15}$.

6. $y = -5\cos 4x$
    (a) amplitude $= 5$, period $= \frac{2\pi}{4} = \frac{\pi}{2}$, no phase shift.   (b)

7. $y = 2\sin\left(\frac{1}{2}x - \frac{\pi}{6}\right) = \sin\frac{1}{2}\left(x - \frac{\pi}{3}\right)$
    (a) amplitude $= 2$, period $= \dfrac{2\pi}{\left(\frac{1}{2}\right)} = 4\pi$,   (b)

    phase shift $= \frac{\pi}{3}$.

8. $y = -\csc 2x$, period $= \frac{2\pi}{2} = \pi$ 9. $y = \tan 2\left(x - \frac{\pi}{4}\right)$, period $= \frac{\pi}{2}$

10. From the graph we see that the amplitude is 2 and the phase shift is $-\frac{\pi}{3}$. Also, the period is π so
    $\frac{2\pi}{k} = \pi$ $\Rightarrow$ $k = \frac{2\pi}{\pi} = 2$. Thus, the function is $y = 2\sin 2(x + \frac{\pi}{3})$.

11. $y = \dfrac{\cos x}{1 + x^2}$

    (a)

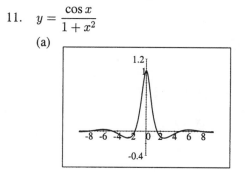

    (b) function is even
    (c) minimum value -0.11 when $x \approx \pm 2.54$, maximum
         value 1 when $x = 0$.

Focus on Modeling

1. $y = 2\sin 3t$.
    (a) amplitude $= 2$, period $= \frac{2\pi}{3}$,

    $\text{frequency} = \dfrac{1}{\text{period}} = \frac{3}{2\pi}$.

    (b)

3. $y = -0.25\cos(1.5t - \frac{\pi}{3}) = -0.25\cos(\frac{3}{2}t - \frac{\pi}{3}) = -0.25\cos\frac{3}{2}(t - \frac{2\pi}{9})$
    (a) amplitude $= 0.25$, period $= \dfrac{2\pi}{\left(\frac{3}{2}\right)} = \frac{4\pi}{3}$,

    $\text{frequency} = \dfrac{1}{\text{period}} = \frac{3}{4\pi}$.

    (b)

5. $y = 0.2\cos 20\pi t + 8$
    (a) frequency $= \dfrac{20\pi}{2\pi} = 10$ cycles/min

    (b)

    (c) Since
    $y = 0.2\cos 20\pi t + 8 \le 0.2(1) + 8 = 8.2$
    and when $t = 0$, $y = 8.2$, the maximum
    displacement is 8.2 ft.

7. (a) When $t = 0, \pi, 2\pi, \ldots$ we have $\cos 2t = 1$ so y is maximized at $y = 8900$.
    (b) The length of time between successive periods of maximum population is the length of a period
    which is $\frac{2\pi}{2} = \pi \approx 3.14$ years.

9. The graph resembles a sine wave with an amplitude of 5, a period of $\frac{2}{5}$, and no phase shift.
    Therefore, $a = 5$, $\dfrac{2\pi}{\omega} = \frac{2}{5}$ $\Leftrightarrow$ $\omega = 5\pi$, and the formula is $d(t) = 5\sin 5\pi t$.

11. $a = 21$, $f = \frac{1}{12}$ cycle/hour $\Rightarrow$ $\dfrac{\omega}{2\pi} = \frac{1}{12}$ $\Leftrightarrow$ $\omega = \frac{\pi}{6}$. So, $y = 21\sin(\frac{\pi}{6}t)$ (assuming the tide
     is at mean level and rising when $t = 0$).

13. Since the mass travels from its highest point (compressed spring) to its lowest point in $\frac{1}{2}$ s, it completes half a period in $\frac{1}{2}$ s. So, $\frac{1}{2}$(one period) $= \frac{1}{2}$ s $\Rightarrow$ $\frac{1}{2} \cdot \dfrac{2\pi}{\omega} = \frac{1}{2}$ $\Leftrightarrow$ $\omega = 2\pi$. Also, $a = 5$. So $y = 5\cos 2\pi t$.

15. Since the ferris wheel has a radius of $10\,\mathrm{m}$ and the bottom of the wheel is $1\,\mathrm{m}$ above the ground, the minimum height is $1\,\mathrm{m}$ and the maximum height is $21\,\mathrm{m}$. Then $a = 10$ and $\dfrac{2\pi}{\omega} = 20$ sec $\Leftrightarrow$ $\omega = \frac{\pi}{10}$, and so $y = 11 + 10\sin\left(\frac{\pi}{10}t\right)$, where t is in seconds.

17. $a = 0.2$, $\dfrac{2\pi}{\omega} = 10$ $\Leftrightarrow$ $\omega = \frac{\pi}{5}$. Then $y = 3.8 + 0.2\sin\left(\frac{\pi}{5}t\right)$.

19. $E_0 = 155$, $\dfrac{\omega}{2\pi} = 60$ $\Leftrightarrow$ $\omega = 120\pi$. Thus $E(t) = E_0 \cos \omega t = 155\cos 120\pi t$.

21. (a) The maximum voltage is the amplitude, that is, $V_{\max} = a = 45$ V.

    (b) From the graph we see that 4 cycles are completed every 0.1 seconds, or equivalently, 40 cycles are completed every second, so $f = 40$.

    (c) The number of revolutions per second of the armature is the frequency, that is, $\dfrac{\omega}{2\pi} = f = 40$.

    (d) $a = 45$, $f = \dfrac{\omega}{2\pi} = 40$ $\Leftrightarrow$ $\omega = 80\pi$. Then $V(t) = 45\cos 80\pi t$.

23. (a)

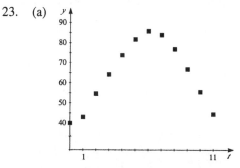

    (b) Let t be the time (in months) from January. We find a function of the form
    $y = a\cos\omega(t - c) + b$, where y is temperature in °F.
    $a = \frac{1}{2}$(maximum value − minimum value) $= \frac{1}{2}(85.8 - 40) = 22.9$.
    Period $= 2$(July − Jan.) $= 2(6 - 0) = 12$ and so $\omega = \frac{2\pi}{12} \approx 0.52$.
    $b = \frac{1}{2}$(maximum value + minimum value) $= \frac{1}{2}(85.8 + 40) = 62.9$.

Since the maximum value occurs in July, $c = 6$. Thus the function is
$y = 22.9 \cos 0.52(t - 6) + 62.9$.

(c)

(d) Using the `SinReg` command on the TI-83 we find that for the function $y = a \sin(bt + c) + d$, where $a = 23.4$, $b = 0.48$, $c = -1.36$, and $d = 62.2$. Thus we get the model
$y = 23.4 \sin(0.48t - 1.36) + 62.2$.

25. (a)

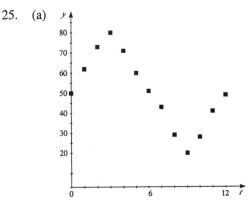

(b) Let t be the time years. We find a function of the form $y = a \sin \omega(t - c) + b$, where y is the owl population.

$a = \frac{1}{2}$(maximum value − minimum value) $= \frac{1}{2}(80 - 20) = 30$.

Period $= 2(9 - 3) = 12$ and so $\omega = \frac{2\pi}{12} \approx 0.52$.

$b = \frac{1}{2}$(maximum value + minimum value) $= \frac{1}{2}(80 + 20) = 50$.

Since the values start at the middle we have $c = 0$. Thus the function is $y = 30 \sin 0.52t + 50$.

(c)

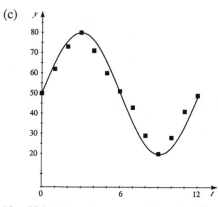

(d) Using the `SinReg` command on the TI--83 we find that for the function $y = a \sin(bt + c) + d$, where $a = 25.8$, $b = 0.52$, $c = -0.02$, and $d = 50.6$. Thus we get the model $y = 25.8 \sin(0.52t - 0.02) + 50.6$.

27. $k = 1$, $c = 0.9$, and $\dfrac{\omega}{2\pi} = \frac{1}{2}$ $\Leftrightarrow$ $\omega = \pi$. Since $f(0) = 0$, $f(t) = e^{-0.9t} \sin \pi t$.

29. $\dfrac{ke^{-ct}}{ke^{-c(t+3)}} = 4$ $\Leftrightarrow$ $e^{-ct+c(t+3)} = 4$ $\Leftrightarrow$ $e^{3c} = 4$ $\Leftrightarrow$ $3c = \ln 4$ $\Leftrightarrow$ $c = \frac{1}{3} \ln 4 \approx 0.46$.

Chapter Six
Exercises 6.1

1. $36° = 36° \cdot \frac{\pi}{180°}$ rad $= \frac{\pi}{5}$ rad ≈ 0.628 rad

3. $-480° = -480° \cdot \frac{\pi}{180°}$ rad $= \frac{-8\pi}{3}$ rad ≈ -8.378 rad

5. $60° = 60° \cdot \frac{\pi}{180°}$ rad $= \frac{\pi}{3}$ rad ≈ 1.047 rad

7. $-135° = -135° \cdot \frac{\pi}{180°}$ rad $= \frac{-3\pi}{4}$ rad ≈ -2.356 rad

9. $\frac{3\pi}{4} = \frac{3\pi}{4} \cdot \frac{180°}{\pi} = 135°$

11. $\frac{5\pi}{6} = \frac{5\pi}{6} \cdot \frac{180°}{\pi} = 150°$

13. $-1.5 = -1.5 \cdot \frac{180°}{\pi} = \frac{-270°}{\pi} \approx -85.9°$

15. $-\frac{\pi}{12} = -\frac{\pi}{12} \cdot \frac{180°}{\pi} = -15°$

17. $50°$ is coterminal with: $50° + 360° = 410°$, $50° + 720° = 770°$, $50° - 360° = -310°$, $50° - 720° = -670°$.

19. $\frac{3\pi}{4}$ is coterminal with: $\frac{3\pi}{4} + 2\pi = \frac{11\pi}{4}$, $\frac{3\pi}{4} + 4\pi = \frac{19\pi}{4}$, $\frac{3\pi}{4} - 2\pi = -\frac{5\pi}{4}$, $\frac{3\pi}{4} - 4\pi = -\frac{13\pi}{4}$.

21. $-\frac{\pi}{4}$ is coterminal with: $-\frac{\pi}{4} + 2\pi = \frac{7\pi}{4}$, $-\frac{\pi}{4} + 4\pi = \frac{15\pi}{4}$, $-\frac{\pi}{4} - 2\pi = -\frac{9\pi}{4}$, $-\frac{\pi}{4} - 4\pi = -\frac{17\pi}{4}$

23. Since $430° - 70° = 360°$, the angles are coterminal.

25. Since $\frac{17\pi}{6} - \frac{5\pi}{6} = \frac{12\pi}{6} = 2\pi$; the angles are coterminal.

27. Since $875° - 155° = 720° = 2 \times 360°$, the angles are coterminal.

29. Since $733° - 2 \cdot 360° = 13°$, the angles $733°$ and $13°$ are coterminal.

31. Since $1110° - 3 \cdot 360° = 30°$, the angles $1110°$ and $30°$ are coterminal.

33. Since $-800° + 3 \cdot 360° = 280°$, the angles $-800°$ and $280°$ are coterminal.

35. Since $\frac{17\pi}{6} - 2\pi = \frac{5\pi}{6}$, the angles $\frac{17\pi}{6}$ and $\frac{5\pi}{6}$ are coterminal.

37. Since $87\pi - 43 \cdot 2\pi = \pi$, the angles 87π and π are coterminal.

39. Since $\frac{17\pi}{4} - 2 \cdot 2\pi = \frac{\pi}{4}$, the angles $\frac{17\pi}{4}$ and $\frac{\pi}{4}$ are coterminal.

41. Using the formula $s = \theta r$, the length of the arc is $s = \left(220 \cdot \frac{\pi}{180}\right) \cdot 5 = \frac{55\pi}{9} \approx 19.2$.

43. Solving for r we have $r = \frac{s}{\theta}$, so the radius of the circle is $r = \frac{8}{2} = 4$.

45. Using the formula $s = \theta r$, the length of the arc is $s = 2 \cdot 2 = 4$ mi.

47. Solving for θ we have $\theta = \frac{s}{r}$, so the measure of the central angle is $\theta = \frac{100}{50} = 2$ rad. Converting to degrees we have $\theta = 2 \cdot \frac{180°}{\pi} \approx 114.6°$

49. Solving for r we have $r = \frac{s}{\theta}$, so the radius of the circle is $r = \frac{6}{\pi/6} = \frac{36}{\pi} \approx 11.46$ m.

51. We find the measure of the angle in degrees and then convert to radians. $\theta = 40.5° - 25.5° = 15°$ and $15 \cdot \frac{\pi}{180}$ rad $= \frac{\pi}{12}$ rad. Then using the formula $s = \theta r$, we have $s = \frac{\pi}{12} \cdot 3960 = 330\pi \approx 1036.725$ and so the distance between the two cities is roughly 1037 mi.

53. In one day, the earth travels $\frac{1}{365}$ of its orbit which is $\frac{2\pi}{365}$ rad. Then $s = \theta r = \frac{2\pi}{365} \cdot 93{,}000{,}000 \approx 1{,}600{,}911.3$ and so the distance traveled is approximately 1.6 million miles.

55. The central angle is 1 minute $= \frac{1}{60}° = \frac{1}{60} \cdot \frac{\pi}{180}$ rad $= \frac{\pi}{10{,}800}$ rad. Then $s = \theta r = \frac{\pi}{10{,}800} \cdot 3960$ ≈ 1.152 and so a nautical mile is approximately 1.15 mi.

57. $A = \frac{1}{2}r^2\theta = \frac{1}{2} \cdot 10^2 \cdot 1 = 50$ m^2

59. $\theta = 2$ rad, $A = 16$ m^2. Since $A = \frac{1}{2}r^2\theta$, we have $r = \sqrt{2A/\theta} = \sqrt{2 \cdot 16/2} = \sqrt{16} = 4$ m.

61. Since the area of the circle is 72 cm^2, the radius of the circle is $r = \sqrt{A/\pi} = \sqrt{72/\pi}$. Then the area of the sector is $A = \frac{1}{2}r^2\theta = \frac{1}{2} \cdot \frac{72}{\pi} \cdot \frac{\pi}{6} = 6$ cm^2.

63. $v = \dfrac{8 \cdot 2\pi \cdot 2}{15} = \dfrac{32\pi}{15} \approx 6.702$ ft/s.

65. (a) Angular speed: $\omega = \dfrac{1000 \cdot 2\pi \text{ rad}}{1 \text{ min}} = 2000\pi$ rad/min.

     (b) Linear speed: $v = \dfrac{1000 \cdot 2\pi \cdot (6/12)}{60} = \dfrac{50\pi}{3}$ ft/s ≈ 52.48 ft/s.

67. $v = \dfrac{600 \cdot 2\pi \cdot (11/12) \text{ ft}}{1 \text{ min}} \cdot \dfrac{1 \text{ mi}}{5280 \text{ ft}} \cdot \dfrac{60 \text{ min}}{1 \text{ hr}} = 12.5\pi$ mi/h ≈ 39.3 mi/h.

69. $v = \dfrac{100 \cdot 2\pi \cdot 0.20 \text{ m}}{60 \text{ sec}} = \frac{2\pi}{3} \approx 2.09$ m/s.

Exercises 6.2

1. $\sin\theta = \frac{4}{5}$, $\cos\theta = \frac{3}{5}$, $\tan\theta = \frac{4}{3}$, $\csc\theta = \frac{5}{4}$, $\sec\theta = \frac{5}{3}$, $\cot\theta = \frac{3}{4}$

3. The remaining side is obtained by the Pythagorean Theorem: $\sqrt{41^2 - 40^2} = \sqrt{81} = 9$. Then
    $\sin\theta = \frac{40}{41}$, $\cos\theta = \frac{9}{41}$, $\tan\theta = \frac{40}{9}$, $\csc\theta = \frac{41}{40}$, $\sec\theta = \frac{41}{9}$, $\cot\theta = \frac{9}{40}$

5. The remaining side is obtained by the Pythagorean Theorem: $\sqrt{3^2 + 2^2} = \sqrt{13}$. Then
    $\sin\theta = \frac{2}{\sqrt{13}} = \frac{2\sqrt{13}}{13}$, $\cos\theta = \frac{3}{\sqrt{13}} = \frac{3\sqrt{13}}{13}$, $\tan\theta = \frac{2}{3}$, $\csc\theta = \frac{\sqrt{13}}{2}$, $\sec\theta = \frac{\sqrt{13}}{3}$, $\cot\theta = \frac{3}{2}$

7. $c = \sqrt{5^2 + 3^2} = \sqrt{34}$
    (a) $\sin\alpha = \cos\beta = \frac{3}{\sqrt{34}} = \frac{3\sqrt{34}}{34}$
    (b) $\tan\alpha = \cot\beta = \frac{3}{5}$
    (c) $\sec\alpha = \csc\beta = \frac{\sqrt{34}}{5}$

9. Since $\sin 30° = \dfrac{x}{25}$, we have $x = 25\sin 30° = 25 \cdot \frac{1}{2} = \frac{25}{2}$.

11. Since $\sin 60° = \dfrac{x}{13}$, we have $x = 13\sin 60° = 13 \cdot \frac{\sqrt{3}}{2} = \frac{13\sqrt{3}}{2}$.

13. Since $\tan 36° = \dfrac{12}{x}$, we have $x = \frac{12}{\tan 36°} \approx 16.51658$.

15. $\dfrac{x}{28} = \cos\theta \quad\Leftrightarrow\quad x = 28\cos\theta$, and $\dfrac{y}{28} = \sin\theta \quad\Leftrightarrow\quad y = 28\sin\theta$

17. $\sin\theta = \frac{3}{5}$. Then the third side is
    $x = \sqrt{5^2 - 3^2} = 4$. The other five ratios are
    $\cos\theta = \frac{4}{5}$, $\tan\theta = \frac{3}{4}$, $\csc\theta = \frac{5}{3}$, $\sec\theta = \frac{5}{4}$,
    and $\cot\theta = \frac{4}{3}$.

19. $\cot\theta = 1$. Then the third side is
    $r = \sqrt{1^2 + 1^2} = \sqrt{2}$. The other five ratios
    are $\sin\theta = \frac{1}{\sqrt{2}} = \frac{\sqrt{2}}{2}$, $\cos\theta = \frac{1}{\sqrt{2}} = \frac{\sqrt{2}}{2}$,
    $\tan\theta = 1$, $\csc\theta = \sqrt{2}$, and $\sec\theta = \sqrt{2}$.

21. $\sec\theta = 7$. The third side is $y = \sqrt{7^2 - 2^2} = \sqrt{45} = 3\sqrt{5}$ The other five
    ratios are $\sin\theta = \frac{3\sqrt{5}}{7}$, $\cos\theta = \frac{2}{7}$, $\tan\theta = \frac{3\sqrt{5}}{2}$, $\csc\theta = \frac{7}{3\sqrt{5}} = \frac{7\sqrt{5}}{15}$,
    and $\cot\theta = \frac{2}{3\sqrt{5}} = \frac{2\sqrt{5}}{15}$.

23. $\sin\frac{\pi}{6} + \cos\frac{\pi}{6} = \frac{1}{2} + \frac{\sqrt{3}}{2} = \frac{1+\sqrt{3}}{2}$

25. $\sin 30° \cos 60° + \sin 60° \cos 30° = \frac{1}{2} \cdot \frac{1}{2} + \frac{\sqrt{3}}{2} \cdot \frac{\sqrt{3}}{2} = \frac{1}{4} + \frac{3}{4} = 1$

27. $(\cos 30°)^2 - (\sin 30°)^2 = \left(\frac{\sqrt{3}}{2}\right)^2 - \left(\frac{1}{2}\right)^2 = \frac{3}{4} - \frac{1}{4} = \frac{1}{2}$

29. This is an isosceles right triangle, so the
other leg $= 16 \tan 45° = 16$,
hypotenuse $= \frac{16}{\sin 45°} = 16\sqrt{2} \approx 22.63$, and

other angle $= 90° - 45° = 45°$

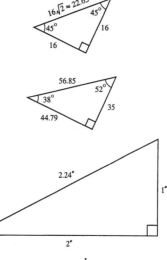

31. The other leg $= 35 \tan 52° = 44.79$,
hypotenuse $= \frac{35}{\cos 52°} = 56.85$, and
other angle $= 90° - 52° = 52°$.

33. $\sin\theta \approx \frac{1}{2.24} \approx 0.45.$ $\cos\theta \approx \frac{2}{2.24} \approx 0.89,$
$\tan\theta = \frac{1}{2},$ $\csc\theta \approx 2.24,$ $\sec\theta \approx \frac{2.24}{2} \approx 1.12,$
$\cot\theta \approx 2.00.$

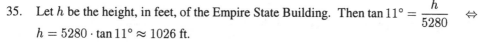

35. Let h be the height, in feet, of the Empire State Building. Then $\tan 11° = \dfrac{h}{5280}$ $\Leftrightarrow$
$h = 5280 \cdot \tan 11° \approx 1026$ ft.

37. (a) Let h be the distance, in miles, that the beam has diverged. Then $\tan 0.5° = \dfrac{h}{240{,}000}$ $\Leftrightarrow$
$h = 240{,}000 \cdot \tan 0.5° \approx 2100$ mi.

     (b) Since the deflection is about 2100 mi whereas the radius of the moon is about 1000 mi, the
beam will not strike the moon.

39. Let h represent the height, in feet, that the ladder reaches on the building. Then $\sin 72° = \dfrac{h}{20}$ $\Leftrightarrow$
$h = 20 \cdot \sin 72° \approx 19$ ft.

41. Let θ be the angle of elevation of the sun. Then $\tan\theta = \frac{96}{120} = 0.8$ $\Leftrightarrow$
$\theta = \tan^{-1} 0.8 \approx 0.675 \approx 38.7°$.

43. Let h be the height, in feet, of the kite above the ground. Then $\sin 50° = \dfrac{h}{450}$ $\Leftrightarrow$
$h = 450 \cdot \sin 50° \approx 345$ ft.

45. Let h_1 be the height of the window in feet and h_2 be the height from the window to the top of the
tower. Then $\tan 25° = \dfrac{h_1}{325}$ $\Leftrightarrow$ $h_1 = 325 \cdot \tan 25° \approx 152$ ft. Also, $\tan 39° = \dfrac{h_2}{325}$ $\Leftrightarrow$
$h_2 = 325 \cdot \tan 39° \approx 263$ ft. Therefore, the height of the window is approximately 152 ft and the
height of the tower is approximately $152 + 263 = 415$ ft.

47. Let d_1 be the distance, in feet, between a point directly below the plane and one car, and d_2 be the
distance, in feet, between the same point and the other car. Then $\tan 52° = \dfrac{d_1}{5150}$ $\Leftrightarrow$
$d_1 = 5150 \cdot \tan 52° \approx 6591.7$ ft. Also, $\tan 38° = \dfrac{d_2}{5150}$ $\Leftrightarrow$ $d_2 = 5150 \cdot \tan 38° \approx 4023.6$ ft.
So the distance between the two cars is now about 2570 ft.

49. Let x be the horizontal distance, in feet, between a point on the ground directly below the top of the mountain and the point on the plain closest to the mountain. Let h be the height, in feet, of the mountain. Then $\tan 35° = \dfrac{h}{x}$ and $\tan 32° = \dfrac{h}{x + 1000}$. So $h = x \tan 35° = (x + 1000)\tan 32°$

   $\Leftrightarrow \quad x = \dfrac{1000 \cdot \tan 32°}{\tan 35° - \tan 32°} \approx 8294.2$. Thus $h \approx 8294.2 \cdot \tan 35° \approx 5808$ ft.

51. Let d be the distance, in miles, from the earth to the sun. Then $\tan 89.95° = \dfrac{d}{240{,}000} \quad \Leftrightarrow$

   $d = 240{,}000 \cdot \tan 89.95° \approx 91.7$ million miles.

53. Let r represent the radius, in miles, of the earth. Then $\sin 60.276° = \dfrac{r}{r + 600} \quad \Leftrightarrow$

   $(r + 600)\sin 60.276° = r \quad \Leftrightarrow \quad 600 \cdot \sin 60.276° = r(1 - \sin 60.276°) \quad \Leftrightarrow$

   $r = \dfrac{600 \cdot \sin 60.276°}{1 - \sin 60.276°} \approx 3960.099$. So the radius of the earth is approximately 3960 mi.

55. $x = \dfrac{100}{\tan 60°} + \dfrac{100}{\tan 30°} \approx 230.9$

57. Let h be the length of the shared side. Then $\sin 60° = \dfrac{50}{h} \quad \Leftrightarrow \quad h = \dfrac{50}{\sin 60°} \approx 57.735 \quad \Leftrightarrow$

   $\sin 65° = \dfrac{h}{x} \quad \Leftrightarrow \quad x = \dfrac{h}{\sin 65°} \approx 63.7$

59. $\sin \theta = \dfrac{1}{a} \quad \Leftrightarrow \quad a = \sin \theta,\ \tan \theta = \dfrac{b}{1} \quad \Leftrightarrow \quad b = \tan \theta,\ \cos \theta = \dfrac{1}{c} \quad \Leftrightarrow \quad c = \sec \theta,\ \cos \theta = \dfrac{d}{1}$

   $\Leftrightarrow \quad d = \cos \theta$

Exercises 6.3

1. (a) $210°$: reference angle is $225° - 210° = 30°$

   (b) $300°$: reference angle is $360° - 300° = 60°$

   (c) $-120°$: reference angle is $180° - 120° = 60°$

3. (a) $\frac{9\pi}{4}$: reference angle is $\frac{9\pi}{4} - 2\pi = \frac{\pi}{4}$

   (b) $\frac{23\pi}{6}$: reference angle is $4\pi - \frac{23\pi}{6} = \frac{\pi}{6}$

   (c) $-\frac{\pi}{3}$: reference angle is $\frac{\pi}{3}$

5. (a) $\frac{11\pi}{5}$: reference angle is $\frac{11\pi}{5} - 2\pi = \frac{\pi}{5}$

   (b) $\frac{11}{5}$: reference angle is $\pi - 2.2 \approx 0.94$

   (c) $-\frac{4\pi}{7}$: reference angle is $\pi - \frac{4\pi}{7} = \frac{3\pi}{7}$

7. $\sin 150° = \sin 30° = \frac{1}{2}$

9. $\cos 135° = -\cos 45° = -\frac{1}{\sqrt{2}} = -\frac{\sqrt{2}}{2}$

11. $\tan(-60°) = -\tan 60° = -\sqrt{3}$

13. $\csc(-630°) = \csc 90° = \dfrac{1}{\sin 90°} = 1$

15. $\cos 570° = -\cos 30° = -\frac{\sqrt{3}}{2}$

17. $\tan 750° = \tan 30° = \frac{1}{\sqrt{3}} = \frac{\sqrt{3}}{3}$

19. $\sin\left(\frac{2\pi}{3}\right) = \sin\left(\frac{\pi}{3}\right) = \frac{\sqrt{3}}{2}$

21. $\sin\left(\frac{3\pi}{2}\right) = -\sin\left(\frac{\pi}{2}\right) = -1$

23. $\cos\left(-\frac{7\pi}{3}\right) = \cos\left(\frac{\pi}{3}\right) = \frac{1}{2}$

25. $\sec\left(\frac{17\pi}{3}\right) = \sec\left(\frac{\pi}{3}\right) = \dfrac{1}{\cos\left(\frac{\pi}{3}\right)} = 2$

27. $\cot\left(-\frac{\pi}{4}\right) = -\cot\left(\frac{\pi}{4}\right) = \frac{-1}{\tan\left(\frac{\pi}{4}\right)} = -1$

29. $\tan\left(\frac{5\pi}{2}\right) = \tan\left(\frac{\pi}{2}\right)$ which is undefined

31. Since $\sin\theta < 0$ and $\cos\theta < 0$, we have θ in quadrant III.

33. $\sec\theta > 0 \;\Rightarrow\; \cos\theta > 0$. Also $\tan\theta < 0 \;\Rightarrow\; \frac{\sin\theta}{\cos\theta} < 0 \;\Leftrightarrow\; \sin\theta < 0$ (since $\cos\theta > 0$). Since $\sin\theta < 0$ and $\cos\theta > 0$, we get θ is in quadrant IV.

35. $\sec^2\theta = 1 + \tan^2\theta \;\Leftrightarrow\; \tan^2\theta = \dfrac{1}{\cos^2\theta} - 1 \;\Leftrightarrow\; \tan\theta = \sqrt{\dfrac{1}{\cos^2\theta} - 1} = \sqrt{\dfrac{1 - \cos^2\theta}{\cos^2\theta}}$

    $= \dfrac{\sqrt{1 - \cos^2\theta}}{|\cos\theta|} = \dfrac{\sqrt{1 - \cos^2\theta}}{-\cos\theta}$ (since $\cos\theta < 0$ in quadrant III, $|\cos\theta| = -\cos\theta$). Thus

    $\tan\theta = -\dfrac{\sqrt{1 - \cos^2\theta}}{\cos\theta}$.

37. $\cos^2\theta + \sin^2\theta = 1 \;\Leftrightarrow\; \cos\theta = \sqrt{1 - \sin^2\theta}$ ($\cos\theta > 0$ in quadrant IV)

39. $\sec^2\theta = 1 + \tan^2\theta \;\Leftrightarrow\; \sec\theta = -\sqrt{1 + \tan^2\theta}$ ($\sec\theta < 0$ in quadrant II)

41. $\sin\theta = \frac{3}{5}$. Then $x = -\sqrt{5^2 - 3^2} = -\sqrt{16} = -4$, since θ in quadrant II. Thus, $\cos\theta = -\frac{4}{5}$, $\tan\theta = -\frac{3}{4}$, $\csc\theta = \frac{5}{3}$, $\sec\theta = -\frac{5}{4}$, $\cot\theta = -\frac{4}{3}$.

43. $\tan\theta = -\frac{3}{4}$. Then $r = \sqrt{3^2 + 4^2} = 5$, and so $\sin\theta = -\frac{3}{5}$, $\cos\theta = \frac{4}{5}$, $\csc\theta = -\frac{5}{3}$, $\sec\theta = \frac{5}{4}$,
     $\cot\theta = -\frac{4}{3}$.

45. $\csc\theta = 2$. Then $\sin\theta = \frac{1}{2}$ and $x = \sqrt{2^2 - 1^2} = \sqrt{3}$. So $\sin\theta = \frac{1}{2}$, $\cos\theta = \frac{\sqrt{3}}{2}$, $\tan\theta = \frac{1}{\sqrt{3}} = \frac{\sqrt{3}}{3}$,
     $\sec\theta = \frac{2}{\sqrt{3}} = \frac{2\sqrt{3}}{3}$, $\cot\theta = \sqrt{3}$.

47. $\cos\theta = -\frac{2}{7}$. Then $y = \sqrt{7^2 - 2^2} = \sqrt{45} = 3\sqrt{5}$, and so $\sin\theta = \frac{3\sqrt{5}}{7}$, $\tan\theta = -\frac{3\sqrt{5}}{2}$,
     $\csc\theta = \frac{7}{3\sqrt{5}} = \frac{7\sqrt{5}}{15}$, $\sec\theta = -\frac{7}{2}$, $\cot\theta = -\frac{2}{3\sqrt{5}} = -\frac{2\sqrt{5}}{15}$.

49. (a) $\sin 2\theta = \sin\left(2 \cdot \frac{\pi}{3}\right) = \sin\frac{2\pi}{3} = \sin\frac{\pi}{3} = \frac{\sqrt{3}}{2}$, while $2\sin\theta = 2\sin\frac{\pi}{3} = 2 \cdot \frac{\sqrt{3}}{2} = \sqrt{3}$.

     (b) $\sin\frac{1}{2}\theta = \sin\left(\frac{1}{2} \cdot \frac{\pi}{3}\right) = \sin\frac{\pi}{6} = \frac{1}{2}$, while $\dfrac{\sin\theta}{2} = \frac{1}{2} \cdot \sin\frac{\pi}{3} = \frac{1}{2} \cdot \frac{\sqrt{3}}{2} = \frac{\sqrt{3}}{4}$.

     (c) $\sin^2\theta = \left(\sin\frac{\pi}{3}\right)^2 = \left(\frac{\sqrt{3}}{2}\right)^2 = \frac{3}{4}$, while $\sin(\theta^2) = \sin\left(\frac{\pi}{3}\right)^2 = \sin\frac{\pi^2}{9} \approx 0.88967$.

51. $a = 10$, $b = 22$, and $\theta = 10°$. Then $A = \frac{1}{2}ab\sin\theta = \frac{1}{2} \cdot 10 \cdot 22 \cdot \sin 10° = 110\sin 10° \approx 19.1$

53. $A = 16$, $a = 5$, and $b = 7$. So $\sin\theta = \dfrac{2A}{ab} = \frac{2 \cdot 16}{5 \cdot 7} = \frac{32}{35}$ $\Leftrightarrow$ $\theta = \sin^{-1}\left(\frac{32}{35}\right) \approx 66.1°$.

55. (a) We label the lenghts L_1 and L_2 as shown in the figure on the
          right. Since $\sin\theta = \frac{9}{L_1}$ and $\cos\theta = \frac{6}{L_2}$, we have $L_1 = 9\csc\theta$
          and $L_2 = 6\sec\theta$. Thus $L(\theta) = L_1 + L_2 = 9\csc\theta + 6\sec\theta$.

     (b)

     (c) The minimum vaule of $L(\theta)$ is 21.07.

     (d) The minimum value of $L(\theta)$ is the shortest distance the pipe must pass through.

57. (a) From the figure in the text, we express *depth* and *width* in terms of θ. Since $\sin\theta = \dfrac{depth}{20}$ and
          $\cos\theta = \dfrac{width}{20}$ we have $depth = 20\sin\theta$ and $width = 20\cos\theta$. Thus the cross-section area of
          the beam is $A(\theta) = (depth)(width) = (20\cos\theta)(20\sin\theta) = 400\cos\theta\sin\theta$.

(b)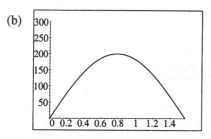

(c)   The dimensions of the beam with the largest cross-sectional area is the square beam, $10\sqrt{2}$ by $10\sqrt{2}$ (about 14.14 by 14.14).

59. $\sin^2\theta + \cos^2\theta = 1 \quad \Leftrightarrow \quad (\sin^2\theta + \cos^2\theta) \cdot \dfrac{1}{\cos^2\theta} = 1 \cdot \dfrac{1}{\cos^2\theta} \quad \Leftrightarrow \quad \tan^2\theta + 1 = \sec^2\theta$

61. $\sin 4° = 0.0697564737$ but $\sin 4 = -0.7568024953$. Your partner has found $\sin 4°$ instead of $\sin 4$ radians.

Exercises 6.4

1. $\angle C = 180° - 98.4° - 24.6° = 57°.$ $x = \dfrac{376 \cdot \sin 57°}{\sin 98.4°} \approx 318.75$

3. $\angle C = 180° - 52° - 70° = 58°.$ $x = \dfrac{26.7 \cdot \sin 52°}{\sin 58°} \approx 24.8$

5. $\sin C = \dfrac{36 \cdot \sin 120°}{45} \approx 0.693$ $\Leftrightarrow$ $\angle C \approx \sin^{-1} 0.693 \approx 44°.$

7. $\angle C = 180° - 46° - 20° = 114°.$ Then $a = \dfrac{65 \cdot \sin 46°}{\sin 114°} \approx 51$ and $b = \dfrac{65 \cdot \sin 20°}{\sin 114°} \approx 24.$

9. $\angle C = 180° - 50° - 68° = 62°.$ Then

$a = \dfrac{230 \cdot \sin 50°}{\sin 62°} \approx 200,$ and

$b = \dfrac{230 \cdot \sin 68°}{\sin 62°} \approx 242.$

11. $\angle B = 180° - 30° - 65° = 85°.$ Then

$a = \dfrac{10 \cdot \sin 30°}{\sin 85°} \approx 5.0,$ and

$c = \dfrac{10 \cdot \sin 65°}{\sin 85°} \approx 9.$

13. $\angle A = 180° - 51° - 29° = 100°.$ Then

$a = \dfrac{44 \cdot \sin 100°}{\sin 29°} \approx 89,$ and

$c = \dfrac{44 \cdot \sin 51°}{\sin 29°} \approx 71.$

15. Since $\angle A > 90°$ there is only one triangle. $\sin B = \dfrac{15 \cdot \sin 110°}{28} \approx 0.503$ $\Leftrightarrow$

$\angle B \approx \sin^{-1} 0.503 \approx 30°.$ Then $\angle C \approx 180° - 110° - 30° = 40°,$ and so $c = \dfrac{28 \cdot \sin 40°}{\sin 110°} \approx 19.$
Thus $\angle B \approx 30°,$ $\angle C \approx 40°,$ and $c \approx 19.$

17. $\angle A = 125°$ is the largest angle but since side a is not the longest side, there can be no such triangle.

19. $\sin C = \dfrac{30 \cdot \sin 25°}{25} \approx 0.507$ $\Leftrightarrow$ $\angle C_1 \approx \sin^{-1} 0.507 \approx 30.47°$ or
$\angle C_2 \approx 180° - 39.47° \approx 149.53°.$

If $\angle C_1 = 30.47°$, then $\angle A_1 \approx 180° - 25° - 30.47° = 124.53°$ and $a_1 = \dfrac{25 \cdot \sin 124.53°}{\sin 25°} \approx 48.73.$

If $\angle C_2 = 149.53°$, then $\angle A_2 \approx 180° - 25° - 149.53° = 5.47°$ and $a_2 = \dfrac{25 \cdot \sin 5.47°}{\sin 25°} \approx 5.64.$
Thus the two triangles are: $\angle A_1 \approx 125°,$ $\angle C_1 \approx 30°,$ and $a_1 \approx 49;$ or $\angle A_2 \approx 5°,$ $\angle C_2 \approx 150°,$ and $a_2 \approx 5.6.$

21. $\sin B = \dfrac{100 \cdot \sin 50°}{50} \approx 1.532$. Since $|\sin \theta| \le 1$ for all θ, there can be no such angle B, and thus no such triangle.

23. $\angle C = 180° - 82° - 52° = 46°$, so by the Law of Sines, $\dfrac{AC}{\sin 52°} = \dfrac{AB}{\sin 46°}$ $\Leftrightarrow$

$AC = \dfrac{AB \cdot \sin 52°}{\sin 46°}$, so substituting we have $AC = \dfrac{200 \cdot \sin 52°}{\sin 46°} \approx 219$ ft.

25. (a) Let a be the distance from satellite to the tracking station A in miles. Then the subtended angle at the satellite is $\angle C = 180° - 93° - 84.2° = 2.8°$, and so $a = \dfrac{50 \cdot \sin 84.2°}{\sin 2.8°} \approx 1018$ mi.

    (b) Let d be the distance above the ground in miles. Then $d = 1018.3 \cdot \sin 87° \approx 1017$ mi.

27. Let x be the length of the cable as shown in the figure on the right. Since $\alpha = 12°$, other angles in $\triangle ABC$ are $\beta = 90° + 58° = 148°$, and $\gamma = 180° - (12° + 148°) = 20°$.

    Thus, $\dfrac{x}{\sin 148°} = \dfrac{100}{\sin 20°}$ $\Leftrightarrow$

    $x = 100 \cdot \dfrac{\sin 148°}{\sin 20°} \approx 155$ ft.

29. (a) In $\triangle ABC$, $\angle B = 180° - \beta$, so $\angle C = 180° - \alpha - (180° - \beta) = \beta - \alpha$. By the Law of Sines, $\dfrac{BC}{\sin \alpha} = \dfrac{AB}{\sin(\beta - \alpha)}$ $\Rightarrow$ $BC = AB \cdot \dfrac{\sin \alpha}{\sin(\beta - \alpha)} = d \cdot \dfrac{\sin \alpha}{\sin(\beta - \alpha)}$.

    (b) From part (a) we know that $BC = d \cdot \dfrac{\sin \alpha}{\sin(\beta - \alpha)}$. But, $\sin \beta = \dfrac{h}{BC}$ $\Leftrightarrow$ $BC = \dfrac{h}{\sin \beta}$.

    Therefore, $BC = d \cdot \dfrac{\sin \alpha}{\sin(\beta - \alpha)} = \dfrac{h}{\sin \beta}$ $\Rightarrow$ $h = d \cdot \dfrac{\sin \alpha \cdot \sin \beta}{\sin(\beta - \alpha)}$.

    (c) $h = d \cdot \dfrac{\sin \alpha \cdot \sin \beta}{\sin(\beta - \alpha)} = 800 \cdot \dfrac{\sin 25° \sin 29°}{\sin 4°} \approx 800 \cdot \dfrac{0.20489}{0.06976} \approx 2350$ ft.

31. Label the diagram as shown to the right, and let the hill's angle of elevation be α. Then applying the Law of Sines to $\triangle ABC$,

    $\dfrac{\sin \beta}{120} = \dfrac{\sin 8°}{30}$ $\Leftrightarrow$ $\sin \beta = 4 \cdot \sin 8° \approx 0.55669$ $\Rightarrow$

    $\beta \approx \sin^{-1} 0.55669 \approx 33.8°$. But from $\triangle ABD$,

    $\angle BAD + \angle B = (\alpha + 8°) + \beta = 90°$, so

    $\alpha \approx 90° - 8° - 33.8° = 48.2°$

33. (a) $\sin B = \dfrac{20 \cdot \sin 40°}{15} \approx 0.857$ $\Leftrightarrow$ $\angle B_1 \approx \sin^{-1} 0.857 \approx 58.99°$ or

    $\angle B_2 \approx 180° - 58.99° \approx 121.01°$.

If $\angle B_1 = 30.47°$, then $\angle C_1 \approx 180° - 15° - 58.99° = 106.01°$ and

$$c_1 = \frac{15 \cdot \sin 106.01°}{\sin 40°} \approx 22.43.$$

If $\angle B_2 = 121.01°$, then $\angle C_2 \approx 180° - 15° - 121.01° = 43.99°$ and

$$c_2 = \frac{15 \cdot \sin 43.99}{\sin 40°} \approx 16.21. \text{ Thus there are two triangles.}$$

(b) By the area formula given in Section 7.3, $\dfrac{\text{Area of } \triangle ABC}{\text{Area of } \triangle A'B'C'} = \dfrac{\frac{1}{2}ab \cdot \sin C}{\frac{1}{2}ab \cdot \sin C'} = \dfrac{\sin C}{\sin C'}$, since a

and b are the same in both triangles.

35.

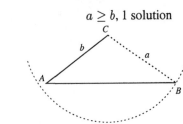

$a \geq b$, 1 solution

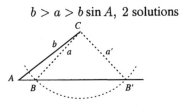

$b > a > b \sin A$, 2 solutions

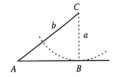

$a = b \sin A$, 1 solution

$a < b \sin A$, 0 solutions

$\angle A = 30°$, $b = 100$, $\sin A = \frac{1}{2}$. Using the criteria above,

If $a \geq b = 100$ then there is one triangle.

If $100 > a > 100 \sin 30° = 50$, then there are two possible triangles.

If $a = 50$, then there is one (right) triangle.

And if $a < 50$, then no triangles are possible.

Exercises 6.5

1. $x^2 = 21^2 + 42^2 - 2 \cdot 21 \cdot 42 \cdot \cos 39° = 441 + 1764 - 1764 \cos 39° \approx 834.115$ and so
   $x \approx \sqrt{834.115} \approx 28.9$.

3. $x^2 = 25^2 + 25^2 - 2 \cdot 25 \cdot 25 \cdot \cos 140° = 625 + 625 - 1250 \cos 140° \approx 2207.556$ and so
   $x \approx \sqrt{2207.556} \approx 47$.

5. $37.83^2 = 68.01^2 + 42.15^2 - 2 \cdot 68.01 \cdot 42.15 \cdot \cos\theta$. Then $\cos\theta = \frac{37.83^2 - 68.01^2 - 42.15^2}{-2 \cdot 68.01 \cdot 42.15} \approx 0.867$
   $\Leftrightarrow \quad \theta \approx \cos^{-1} 0.867 \approx 29.89°$.

7. $x^2 = 24^2 + 30^2 - 2 \cdot 24 \cdot 30 \cdot \cos 30° = 576 + 900 - 1440 \cos 30° \approx 228.923$ and so
   $x \approx \sqrt{228.923} \approx 15$.

9. $c^2 = 10^2 + 18^2 - 2 \cdot 10 \cdot 18 \cdot \cos 120° = 100 + 324 - 360 \cos 120° = 604$ and so
   $c \approx \sqrt{604} \approx 24.576$. Then $\sin A \approx \dfrac{18 \cdot \sin 120°}{24.576} \approx 0.634295 \quad \Leftrightarrow$
   $\angle A \approx \sin^{-1} 0.634295 \approx 39.4°$, and $\angle B \approx 180° - 120° - 39.4° = 20.6°$.

11. $c^2 = 3^2 + 4^2 - 2 \cdot 3 \cdot 4 \cdot \cos 53° = 9 + 16 - 24 \cos 53° \approx 10.556 \quad \Leftrightarrow \quad c \approx \sqrt{10.556} \approx 3.2$.
    Then $\sin B = \dfrac{4 \cdot \sin 53°}{3.25} \approx 0.983 \quad \Leftrightarrow \quad \angle B \approx \sin^{-1} 0.983 \approx 79°$ and
    $\angle A \approx 180° - 53° - 79° = 48°$.

13. $20^2 = 25^2 + 22^2 - 2 \cdot 25 \cdot 22 \cdot \cos A \quad \Leftrightarrow \quad \cos A = \dfrac{20^2 - 25^2 - 22^2}{-2 \cdot 25 \cdot 22} \approx 0.644 \quad \Leftrightarrow$
    $\angle A \approx \cos^{-1} 0.644 \approx 50°$. Then $\sin B \approx \dfrac{25 \cdot \sin 49.9°}{20} \approx 0.956 \quad \Leftrightarrow \quad \angle B \approx \sin^{-1} 0.956 \approx 73°$,
    and so $\angle C \approx 180° - 50° - 73° = 57°$.

15. $\sin C = \dfrac{162 \cdot \sin 40°}{125} \approx 0.833 \quad \Leftrightarrow \quad \angle C_1 \approx \sin^{-1} 0.833 \approx 56.4°$ or
    $\angle C_2 \approx 180° - 56.4° \approx 123.6°$.

    If $\underline{\angle C_1 \approx 56.4°}$, then $\angle A_1 \approx 180° - 40° - 56.4° = 83.6°$ and $a_1 = \dfrac{125 \cdot \sin 83.6°}{\sin 40°} \approx 193$

    If $\underline{\angle C_2 \approx 123.6°}$, then $\angle A_2 \approx 180° - 40° - 123.6° = 16.4°$ and $a_2 = \dfrac{125 \cdot \sin 16.4°}{\sin 40°} \approx 54.9$.

    Thus the two triangles are: $\angle A \approx 83.6°$, $\angle C \approx 56.4°$, and $a \approx 193$; or $\angle A \approx 16.4°$, $\angle C \approx 123.6°$,
    and $a \approx 55$.

17. $\sin B = \dfrac{65 \cdot \sin 55°}{50} \approx 1.065$. Since $|\sin\theta| \le 1$ for all θ, there is no such $\angle B$, and hence no such
    triangle.

19. $\angle B = 180° - 35° - 85° = 60°$. Then $x = \dfrac{3 \cdot \sin 35°}{\sin 60°} \approx 2$.

21. $x = \dfrac{50 \cdot \sin 30°}{\sin 100°} \approx 25.4$.

23. $b^2 = 110^2 + 130^2 - 2(110)(130) \cdot \cos 38° = 12{,}100 + 16{,}900 - 28{,}600 \cos 38° \approx 6462.892$ and so

$b \approx 80.4$. Therefore $\sin\theta \approx \dfrac{130 \cdot \sin 38°}{80.4} \approx 0.996 \quad \Leftrightarrow \quad \theta \approx 84.6°$

25. $x^2 = 38^2 + 48^2 - 2 \cdot 38 \cdot 48 \cdot \cos 30° = 1444 + 2304 - 3648\cos 30° \approx 588.739$ and so $x \approx 24.3$.

27. Let c be the distance across the lake, in miles. Then $c^2 = 2.82^2 + 3.56^2 - 2(2.82)(3.56) \cdot \cos 40.3°$
     $\approx 5.313 \quad \Leftrightarrow \quad c \approx 2.30$ mi.

29. In half an hour, the faster car travels 25 miles while the slower car travels 15 miles. The distance
     between them is given by the Law of Cosines: $d^2 = 25^2 + 15^2 - 2(25)(15) \cdot \cos 65° \quad \Rightarrow$
     $d = \sqrt{25^2 + 15^2 - 2(25)(15) \cdot \cos 65°} = 5\sqrt{25 + 9 - 30 \cdot \cos 65°} \approx 23.1$ mi.

31. The pilot travels a distance of $625 \times 1.5 = 937.5$ miles in her original direction and $625 \times 2 = 1250$
     miles in the new direction. Since she makes a course correction of $10°$ to the right, the included
     angle is $180° - 10° = 170°$. From the figure below, we use the Law of Cosines to get the
     expression $d^2 = 937.5^2 + 1250^2 - 2(937.5)(1250) \cdot \cos 170° \approx 4,749,549.42$, so $d \approx 2179$ miles.
     Thus, the pilot's distance from her original position is approximately 2179 miles.

33. (a) The angle subtended at Egg Island is $100°$. Thus using the Law
         of Cosines, the distance from Forrest Island to the fisherman's
         home port is
         $x^2 = 30^2 + 50^2 - 2 \cdot 30 \cdot 50 \cdot \cos 100°$
         $\quad = 900 + 2500 - 3000\cos 100° \approx 3920.945$
         and so $x \approx \sqrt{3920.945} \approx 62.62$ miles.

     (b) Let θ be the angle shown in the figure. Using the Law
         of Sines, $\sin\theta = \dfrac{50 \cdot \sin 100°}{62.62} \approx 0.7863 \quad \Leftrightarrow$
         $\theta \approx \sin^{-1} 0.7863 \approx 51.8°$. Then $\gamma = 90° - 20° - 51.8° = 18.2°$.
         Thus the bearing to his home port is S 18.2° E.

35. The largest angle is the one opposite the longest side; call this angle θ. Then by the Law of Cosines,
     $44^2 = 36^2 + 22^2 - 2(36)(22) \cdot \cos\theta \quad \Leftrightarrow \quad \cos\theta = \dfrac{36^2 + 22^2 - 44^2}{2(36)(22)} = -0.09848 \quad \Rightarrow$
     $\theta \approx \cos^{-1}(-0.09848) \approx 96°$.

37. Let d be the distance between the kites; then $d^2 \approx 380^2 + 420^2 - 2(380)(420) \cdot \cos 30° \quad \Rightarrow$
     $d \approx \sqrt{380^2 + 420^2 - 2(380)(420) \cdot \cos 30°} \approx 211$ ft.

39. Solution #1: From the figure on the right, we see that $\gamma = 106°$ and $\sin 74° = \dfrac{3400}{b}$

$\Leftrightarrow$ $b = \dfrac{3400}{\sin 74°} \approx 3537$. Thus, $x^2 = 800^2 + 3537^2 - 2(800)(3537) \cdot \cos 106°$

$\Rightarrow$ $x = \sqrt{800^2 + 3537^2 - 2(800)(3537) \cdot \cos 106°}$ $\Rightarrow$ $x \approx 3835$ ft.

Solution #2: Notice that $\tan 74° = \dfrac{3400}{a}$ $\Leftrightarrow$ $a = \dfrac{3400}{\tan 74°} \approx 974.9$.

By the Pythagorean theorem, $x^2 = (a + 800)^2 + 3400^2$. So,
$x = \sqrt{(974.9 + 800)^2 + 3400^2} \approx 3835$ ft.

41. Label the centers of the circles A, B, and C, as in the figure to the right. By

the Law of Cosines, $\cos A = \dfrac{AB^2 + AC^2 - BC^2}{2(AB)(AC)} = \dfrac{9^2 + 10^2 - 11^2}{2(9)(10)} = \dfrac{1}{3}$

$\Rightarrow$ $\angle A \approx 70.53°$. Now, by the Law of Sines,

$\dfrac{\sin 70.53°}{11} = \dfrac{\sin B}{AC} = \dfrac{\sin C}{AB}$. So $\sin B = \dfrac{10}{11} \cdot \sin 70.53° \approx 0.85710$

$\Rightarrow$ $B \approx \sin^{-1} 0.85710 \approx 58.99°$ and $\sin C = \dfrac{9}{11} \cdot \sin 70.53° \approx 0.77139$ $\Rightarrow$

$C \approx \sin^{-1} 0.77139 \approx 50.48°$. The area of $\triangle ABC$ is

$\dfrac{1}{2}(AB)(AC)\sin A = \dfrac{1}{2}(9)(10)(\sin 70.53°) \approx 42.426$. The area of sector A is given by

$S_A = \pi R^2 \cdot \dfrac{\theta}{360°} = \pi(4)^2 \cdot \dfrac{70.53°}{360°} \approx 9.848$. Similarly, the areas of sectors B and C are

$S_B \approx 12.870$, $S_C \approx 15.859$. Thus, the area enclosed between the circles is

$A = \triangle ABC - S_A - S_B - S_C$ $\Rightarrow$ $A \approx 42.426 - 9.848 - 12.870 - 15.859 \approx 3.85$ cm^2.

43. First notice that $\angle DBC = 180° - 20° - 95° = 65°$ and $\angle DAC = 180° - 60° - 45° = 75°$. From

$\triangle ACD$ we get $\dfrac{AC}{\sin 45°} = \dfrac{20}{\sin 75°}$ $\Leftrightarrow$ $AC = \dfrac{20\sin 45°}{\sin 75°} \approx 14.6°$. From $\triangle BCD$ we get

$\dfrac{BC}{\sin 95°} = \dfrac{20}{\sin 65°}$ $\Leftrightarrow$ $BC = \dfrac{20\sin 95°}{\sin 65°} \approx 22.0$. By applying the Law of Cosines to $\triangle ABC$

we get $(AB)^2 = (AC)^2 + (BC)^2 - 2(AC)(BC)\cos 40°$

$\approx (14.6)^2 + (22.0)^2 - 2 \cdot 14.6 \cdot 22.0 \cdot \cos 40° \approx 205$, so $AB \approx \sqrt{205} \approx 14.3$m. Therefore, the

distance between the points A and B is approximately 14.3 m.

45. By Heron's formula, $A = \sqrt{s(s-a)(s-b)(s-c)}$, where $s = \dfrac{a+b+c}{2} = \dfrac{112 + 148 + 190}{2}$

$= 225$. Thus, $A = \sqrt{225(225 - 112)(225 - 148)(225 - 190)} \approx 8277.7$ sq. ft. Since the land
value is \$20 per square foot, the value of the lot is approximately $8277.7 \times \$20 = \$165,554$.

47. Using the Law of Cosines, $b^2 = a^2 + c^2 - 2ac \cos B$ $\Leftrightarrow$
$(10.5)^2 = (13.2)^2 + (18.0)^2 - 2(13.2)(18.0) \cos B$ $\Leftrightarrow$ $-387.99 = -475.2 \cos B$ $\Leftrightarrow$
$\cos B \approx 0.816$ $\Leftrightarrow$ $B \approx 35.3°$. (The small difference in the two measurements is due to round
off error.) There is only one possible answer with the Law of Cosines because cosine is uniquely
defined between $0°$ and $180°$.

Review Exercises for Chapter 6

1. (a) $60° = 60 \cdot \frac{\pi}{180} = \frac{\pi}{3} \approx 1.05$ rad   (b) $330° = 330 \cdot \frac{\pi}{180} = \frac{11\pi}{6} \approx 5.76$ rad

   (c) $-135° = -135 \cdot \frac{\pi}{180} = -\frac{3\pi}{4} \approx -3.36$ rad

   (d) $-90° = -90 \cdot \frac{\pi}{180} = -\frac{\pi}{2} \approx -1.57$ rad

3. (a) $\frac{5\pi}{2}$ rad $= \frac{5\pi}{2} \cdot \frac{180}{\pi} = 450°$ (b) $-\frac{\pi}{6}$ rad $= -\frac{\pi}{6} \cdot \frac{180}{\pi} = -30°$

   (c) $\frac{9\pi}{4}$ rad $= \frac{9\pi}{4} \cdot \frac{180}{\pi} = 405°$ (d) 3.1 rad $= 3.1 \cdot \frac{180}{\pi} = \frac{558}{\pi} \approx 177.6°$

5. $r = 8$ m, $\theta = 1$ rad. Then $s = r\theta = 8 \cdot 1 = 8$ m.

7. $s = 100$ ft, $\theta = 70° = 70 \cdot \frac{\pi}{180} = \frac{7\pi}{18}$ rad. Then $r = \frac{s}{\theta} = 100 \cdot \frac{18}{7\pi} = \frac{1800}{7\pi} \approx 82$ ft.

9. $r = 3960$ miles, s $= 2450$ miles. Then $\theta = \dfrac{s}{r} = \frac{2450}{3960} \approx 0.619$ rad $= 0.619 \cdot \frac{\pi}{180}° \approx 35.448°$ and so the angle is approximately $35.4°$.

11. $A = \frac{1}{2}r^2\theta = \frac{1}{2}(200)^2\left(52° \times \frac{\pi}{180°}\right) \approx 18{,}151$ ft^2

13. Angular speed: $\omega = \dfrac{150 \cdot 2\pi \text{ rad}}{1 \text{ min}} = 300\pi$ rad/min. ≈ 942.5 rad/min.

    Linear speed: $v = \dfrac{150 \cdot 2\pi \cdot 8}{1} = 2400\pi$ in./min ≈ 7539.8 in./min.

15. $r = \sqrt{5^2 + 7^2} = \sqrt{74}$. Then $\sin\theta = \frac{5}{\sqrt{74}}$, $\cos\theta = \frac{7}{\sqrt{74}}$, $\tan\theta = \frac{5}{7}$, $\csc\theta = \frac{\sqrt{74}}{5}$, $\sec\theta = \frac{\sqrt{74}}{7}$, and $\cot\theta = \frac{7}{5}$.

17. $\dfrac{x}{5} = \cos 40°$ $\Leftrightarrow$ $x = 5\cos 40° \approx 3.83$, and $\dfrac{y}{5} = \sin 40°$ $\Leftrightarrow$ $y = 5 \sin 40° \approx 3.21$

19. $\dfrac{1}{x} = \sin 20°$ $\Leftrightarrow$ $x = \dfrac{1}{\sin 20°} \approx 2.92$, and $\dfrac{x}{y} = \cos 20°$ $\Leftrightarrow$ $y = \dfrac{x}{\cos 20°} \approx \dfrac{2.924}{0.9397} \approx 3.11$

21. $w = 3 \sin 20° \approx 1.026$,
    $v = 3 \cos 20° \approx 2.819$.

23. $\tan\theta = \dfrac{1}{a}$ $\Leftrightarrow$ $a = \dfrac{1}{\tan\theta} = \cot\theta$, $\sin\theta = \dfrac{1}{b}$ $\Leftrightarrow$ $b = \dfrac{1}{\sin\theta} = \csc\theta$

25. One side of the hexagon together with radial line segments through its endpoints forms a triangle with two sides of length 8 m and subtended angle $60°$. Let x be the length of one such side (in m). So by the Law of Cosines
    $$x^2 = 8^2 + 8^2 - 2 \cdot 8 \cdot 8 \cdot \cos 60° = 64 \quad \Leftrightarrow$$
    $x = 8$. Thus the perimeter of the hexagon is
    $6x = 6 \cdot 8 = 48$ m

27. Let r represent the radius, in miles, of the moon. Then $\tan \frac{\theta}{2} = \dfrac{r}{r + |AB|}$, $\theta = 0.518°$ $\Leftrightarrow$

$r = (r + 236{,}900) \cdot \tan 0.259°$ $\Leftrightarrow$ $r(1 - \tan 0.259°) = 236{,}900 \cdot \tan 0.259°$ $\Leftrightarrow$

$r = \dfrac{236{,}900 \cdot \tan 0.259°}{1 - \tan 0.259°} \approx 1076$ and so the radius of the moon is roughly 1076 miles.

29. $\sin 315° = -\sin 45° = -\dfrac{1}{\sqrt{2}} = -\dfrac{\sqrt{2}}{2}$

31. $\tan(-135°) = \tan 45° = 1$

33. $\cot\left(-\frac{22\pi}{3}\right) = \cot\left(\frac{2\pi}{3}\right) = \cot \frac{\pi}{3} = -\dfrac{1}{\sqrt{3}} = -\dfrac{\sqrt{3}}{3}$

35. $\cos 585° = \cos 225° = -\cos 45° = -\dfrac{1}{\sqrt{2}} = -\dfrac{\sqrt{2}}{2}$

37. $\csc \frac{8\pi}{3} = \csc \frac{2\pi}{3} = \csc \frac{\pi}{3} = \dfrac{2}{\sqrt{3}} = \dfrac{2\sqrt{3}}{3}$

39. $\cot(-390°) = \cot(-30°) = -\cot 30° = -\sqrt{3}$

41. $r = \sqrt{(-5)^2 + 12^2} = \sqrt{169} = 13$. Then $\sin\theta = \frac{12}{13}$, $\cos\theta = -\frac{5}{13}$, $\tan\theta = -\frac{12}{5}$, $\csc\theta = \frac{13}{12}$, $\sec\theta = -\frac{13}{5}$, and $\cot\theta = -\frac{5}{12}$.

43. $y - \sqrt{3}x + 1 = 0$ $\Leftrightarrow$ $y = \sqrt{3}x - 1$, so the slope of the line is $m = \sqrt{3}$. Then $\tan\theta = m = \sqrt{3}$ $\Leftrightarrow$ $\theta = 60°$.

45. $\sec^2\theta = 1 + \tan^2\theta$ $\Leftrightarrow$ $\tan^2\theta = \frac{1}{\cos^2\theta} - 1$ $\Leftrightarrow$ $\tan\theta = \sqrt{\frac{1}{\cos^2\theta} - 1} = \sqrt{\frac{1-\cos^2\theta}{\cos^2\theta}}$

$= \dfrac{\sqrt{1-\cos^2\theta}}{|\cos\theta|} = \dfrac{\sqrt{1-\cos^2\theta}}{-\cos\theta}$ (since $\cos\theta < 0$ in quadrant III, $|\cos\theta| = -\cos\theta$). Thus

$\tan\theta = -\dfrac{\sqrt{1-\cos^2\theta}}{\cos\theta}$.

47. $\tan^2\theta = \dfrac{\sin^2\theta}{\cos^2\theta} = \dfrac{\sin^2\theta}{1 - \sin^2\theta}$

49. $\tan\theta = \frac{\sqrt{7}}{3}$, $\sec\theta = \frac{4}{3}$. Then $\cos\theta = \frac{3}{4}$ and $\sin\theta = \tan\theta \cdot \cos\theta = \frac{\sqrt{7}}{4}$, $\csc\theta = \frac{4}{\sqrt{7}} = \frac{4\sqrt{7}}{7}$, and $\cot\theta = \frac{3}{\sqrt{7}} = \frac{3\sqrt{7}}{7}$.

51. $\sin\theta = \frac{3}{5}$. Since $\cos\theta < 0$, θ is in quadrant II. Thus, $x = -\sqrt{5^2 - 3^2} = -\sqrt{16} = -4$. Therefore, $\cos\theta = -\frac{4}{5}$, $\tan\theta = -\frac{3}{4}$, $\csc\theta = \frac{5}{3}$, $\sec\theta = -\frac{5}{4}$, $\cot\theta = -\frac{4}{3}$.

53. $\tan\theta = -\frac{1}{2}$. $\sec^2\theta = 1 + \tan^2\theta = 1 + \frac{1}{4} = \frac{5}{4}$ $\Leftrightarrow$ $\cos^2\theta = \frac{4}{5}$ $\Rightarrow$ $\cos\theta = -\sqrt{\frac{4}{5}} = -\frac{2}{\sqrt{5}}$

since $\cos\theta < 0$ in quadrant II. But $\tan\theta = \dfrac{\sin\theta}{\cos\theta} = -\frac{1}{2}$ $\Leftrightarrow$ $\sin\theta = -\frac{1}{2}\cos\theta$

$= -\frac{1}{2}\left(-\frac{2}{\sqrt{5}}\right) = \frac{1}{\sqrt{5}}$. Therefore, $\sin\theta + \cos\theta = \frac{1}{\sqrt{5}} + \left(-\frac{2}{\sqrt{5}}\right) = -\frac{1}{\sqrt{5}} = -\frac{\sqrt{5}}{5}$.

55. By the Pythagorean identity, $\sin^2\theta + \cos^2\theta = 1$ for any angle θ.

57. $\angle B = 180° - 30° - 80° = 70°$, and so by the Law of Sines, $x = \dfrac{10 \cdot \sin 30°}{\sin 70°} \approx 5.32$.

59. $x^2 = 100^2 + 210^2 - 2 \cdot 100 \cdot 210 \cdot \cos 40° \approx 21926.133$ $\Leftrightarrow$ $x \approx 148.07$

61. $\sin B = \dfrac{20 \cdot \sin 60°}{70} \approx 0.247$ $\Leftrightarrow$ $\angle B \approx \sin^{-1} 0.247 \approx 14.33°.$ Then

$\angle C \approx 180° - 60° - 14.33° = 105.67°$, and so $x \approx \dfrac{70 \cdot \sin 105.67°}{\sin 60°} \approx 77.82.$

63. After 2 hours the ships have traveled distances $d_1 = 40$ mi and $d_2 = 56$ mi. The subtended angle is $180° - 32° - 42° = 106°$. Let d be the distance between the two ships in miles. Then by the Law of Cosines $d^2 = 40^2 + 56^2 - 2(40)(56) \cdot \cos 106° \approx 5970.855$ $\Leftrightarrow$ $d \approx 77.3$ miles.

65. Let d be the distance, in miles, between the points A and B. Then by the Law of Cosines $d^2 = 3.2^2 + 5.6^2 - 2(3.2)(5.6) \cdot \cos 42° \approx 14.966$ $\Leftrightarrow$ $d \approx 3.9$ mi.

67. Let h represent the height, in m, of the cliff, and d the horizontal distance to the cliff. The third horizontal angle is $180° - 69.4° - 51.6° = 59°$ and so $d = \dfrac{200 \cdot \sin 51.6°}{\sin 59°} \approx 182.857.$ Then

$\tan 33.1° = \dfrac{h}{d}$ $\Leftrightarrow$ $h = d \tan 33.1° \approx 182.857 \tan 33.1° \approx 119.2$ m.

69. By Heron's formula, $A = \sqrt{s(s-a)(s-b)(s-c)}$, where $s = \dfrac{a+b+c}{2} = \dfrac{5+6+8}{2} = 9.5.$

Thus, $A = \sqrt{9.5(9.5-5)(9.5-6)(9.5-8)} \approx 14.98.$

Chapter 6 Test

1. $300° = 300 \cdot \frac{\pi}{180} = \frac{5\pi}{3}$ rad. $-18° = -18 \cdot \frac{\pi}{180} = -\frac{\pi}{10}$ rad.

2. $\frac{5\pi}{6}$ rad $= \frac{5\pi}{6} \cdot \frac{180}{\pi} = 150°$ 2.4 rad $= 2.4 \cdot \frac{180}{\pi} = \frac{432}{\pi} \approx 137.5°$

3. (a) Angular speed: $\omega = \dfrac{200 \cdot 2\pi \text{ rad}}{1 \text{ min}} = 400\pi$ rad/min.

    (b) Linear speed: $v = \dfrac{200 \cdot 2\pi \cdot 25}{1} = 10000\pi$ ft/min ≈ 31415.9.ft/min. $= 5.95$ ft/min.

4. (a) $\sin 405° = \sin 45° = \frac{1}{\sqrt{2}} = \frac{\sqrt{2}}{2}$ (b) $\tan(-150°) = \tan 30° = \frac{1}{\sqrt{3}} = \frac{\sqrt{3}}{3}$

    (c) $\sec \frac{5\pi}{3} = \sec \frac{\pi}{3} = 2$ (d) $\csc \frac{5\pi}{2} = \csc \frac{\pi}{2} = 1$

5. $r = \sqrt{3^2 + 2^2} = \sqrt{13}$. Then $\tan \theta + \sin \theta = \frac{2}{3} + \frac{2}{\sqrt{13}} = \frac{2(\sqrt{13}+3)}{3\sqrt{13}} = \frac{26+6\sqrt{13}}{39}$

6. $\sin \theta = \dfrac{a}{24}$ $\Leftrightarrow$ $a = 24 \sin \theta$. Also, $\cos \theta = \dfrac{b}{24}$ $\Leftrightarrow$ $b = 24 \cos \theta$.

7. $\cos \theta = -\frac{1}{3}$ and θ is in quadrant III, so $r = 3$, $x = -1$, and $y = -\sqrt{3^2 - 1^2} = -2\sqrt{2}$. Then
    $\tan \theta \cot \theta + \csc \theta = \tan \theta \cdot \dfrac{1}{\tan \theta} + \csc \theta = 1 - \dfrac{3}{2\sqrt{2}} = \dfrac{2\sqrt{2}-3}{2\sqrt{2}} = \dfrac{4-3\sqrt{2}}{4}$.

8. $\sin \theta = \frac{5}{13}$, $\tan \theta = -\frac{5}{12}$. Then $\sec \theta = \dfrac{1}{\cos \theta} = \dfrac{1}{\cos \theta} \cdot \dfrac{\sin \theta}{\sin \theta} = \tan \theta \cdot \dfrac{1}{\sin \theta} = -\frac{5}{12} \cdot \frac{13}{5} = -\frac{13}{12}$.

9. $\sec^2\theta = 1 + \tan^2\theta$ $\Leftrightarrow$ $\tan \theta = \pm\sqrt{\sec^2\theta - 1}$. Thus, $\tan\theta = -\sqrt{\sec^2\theta - 1}$ since $\tan \theta < 0$ in quadrant II.

10. $\tan 73° = \dfrac{h}{6}$ $\Rightarrow$ $h = 6 \tan 73° \approx 19.6$ ft.

11. By the Law of Cosines $x^2 = 10^2 + 12^2 - 2(10)(12) \cdot \cos 48° \approx 8.409$ $\Leftrightarrow$ $x \approx 9.1$

12. $\angle C = 180° - 52° - 69° = 59°$. Then by the Law of Sines $x = \dfrac{230 \cdot \sin 69°}{\sin 59°} \approx 250.5$

13. Let h be the height of the shorter altitude. Then $\tan 20° = \dfrac{h}{50}$ $\Leftrightarrow$ $h = 50 \tan 20°$ and
    $\tan 28° = \dfrac{x+h}{50}$ $\Leftrightarrow$ $x + h = 50 \tan 28°$ $\Leftrightarrow$ $x = 50 \tan 28° - h = 50 \tan 28° - 50 \tan 20°$
    ≈ 8.4.

14. Let $\angle A$ and $\angle X$ be the other angles in the triangle. Then $\sin A = \dfrac{15 \cdot \sin 108°}{28} \approx 0.509$ $\Leftrightarrow$
    $\angle A \approx 30.63°$. Then $\angle X \approx 180° - 108° - 30.63° \approx 41.37°$, and so $x \approx \dfrac{28 \cdot \sin 41.37°}{\sin 108°} \approx 19.5$

15. (a) $A(\text{sector}) = \frac{1}{2}r^2\theta = \frac{1}{2} \cdot 10^2 \cdot 72 \cdot \frac{\pi}{180} = 50 \cdot \frac{72\pi}{180}$

    $A(\text{triangle}) = \frac{1}{2}r \cdot r\sin \theta = \frac{1}{2} \cdot 10^2 \sin 72°$. Thus the area of the shaded region is

$A(\text{shaded}) = A(\text{sector}) - A(\text{triangle}) = 50\left(\frac{72\pi}{180} - \sin 72°\right) \approx 15.3\text{m}^2.$

(b) The shaded region is bounded by two pieces: one piece is part of the triangle, the other is part of the circle. The first part has length
$l = \sqrt{10^2 + 10^2 - 2(10)(10) \cdot \cos 72°} = 10\sqrt{2 - 2 \cdot \cos 72°}.$ The second has length
$s = 10 \cdot 72° \cdot \frac{\pi}{180°} = 4\pi.$ Thus, the perimeter of the shaded region is
$p = l + s = 10\sqrt{2 - 2\cos 72°} + 4\pi \approx 24.3 \text{ m}.$

16. (a) If θ is the angle opposite the longest side, then by the Laws of Cosines
$\cos\theta = \frac{9^2 + 13^2 - 20^2}{2(9)(20)} = -0.6410.$ Therefore, $\theta = \cos^{-1}(-0.6410) \approx 129.9°.$

(b) From question 16, $\theta = 130°$, so the area of the triangle is $\mathcal{A} = \frac{1}{2}(9)(13) \cdot \sin 130° \approx 44.9$
units^2. Another way to find the area is to use Heron's formula:
$\mathcal{A} = \sqrt{s(s-a)(s-b)(s-c)},$ where $s = \dfrac{a+b+c}{2} = \frac{9+13+20}{2} = 21.$ Thus,
$\mathcal{A} = \sqrt{21(21-20)(21-13)(21-9)} = \sqrt{2016} \approx 44.9 \text{ units}^2.$

17. Label the figure as shown to the right. Now
$\angle\beta = 85° - 75° = 10°$, so by the Law of
Sines, $\dfrac{x}{\sin 75°} = \dfrac{100}{\sin 10°} \quad \Leftrightarrow$

$x = 100 \cdot \dfrac{\sin 75°}{\sin 10°}.$ Since $\sin 85° = \dfrac{h}{x} \quad \Leftrightarrow$

$h = x \sin 85° = 100 \cdot \dfrac{\sin 75°}{\sin 10°} \sin 85° \approx 554.$

Focus on Problem Solving

1. Tetrahedron: faces are all triangles and three faces meet at each vertex. Thus $V = \dfrac{3F}{3} = F$ and
    $E = \dfrac{3F}{2}$. Substituting into Euler's formula we have $F - \dfrac{3F}{2} + F = 2 \quad \Leftrightarrow \quad \frac{1}{2}F = 2 \quad \Leftrightarrow$
    $F = 4$. So $V = 4$ and $E = \frac{12}{2} = 6$.

    Octahedron: faces are all triangles and four faces meet at each vertex. Thus $V = \dfrac{3F}{4}$ and $E = \dfrac{3F}{2}$.
    Substituting into Euler's formula we have $F - \dfrac{3F}{2} + \dfrac{3F}{4} = 2 \quad \Leftrightarrow \quad \frac{1}{4}F = 2 \quad \Leftrightarrow \quad F = 8$. So
    $V = \frac{24}{4} = 6$ and $E = \frac{24}{2} = 12$.

    Cube: faces are all rectangles and three faces meet at each vertex. Thus $V = \dfrac{4F}{3}$ and
    $E = \dfrac{4F}{2} = 2F$. Substituting into Euler's formula we have $F - 2F + \dfrac{4F}{3} = 2 \quad \Leftrightarrow \quad \frac{1}{3}F = 2$
    $\Leftrightarrow \quad F = 6$. So $V = \frac{24}{3} = 8$ and $E = 12$.

    Dodecahedron: faces are all pentagon and three faces meet at each vertex. Thus $V = \dfrac{5F}{3}$ and
    $E = \dfrac{5F}{2}$. Substituting into Euler's formula we have $F - \dfrac{5F}{2} + \dfrac{5F}{3} = 2 \quad \Leftrightarrow \quad \frac{1}{6}F = 2 \quad \Leftrightarrow$
    $F = 12$. So $V = \frac{60}{3} = 20$ and $E = \frac{60}{2} = 30$.

    Icosahedron: faces are all triangles and five faces meet at each vertex. Thus $V = \dfrac{3F}{5}$ and
    $E = \dfrac{3F}{2}$. Substituting into Euler's formula we have $F - \dfrac{3F}{2} + \dfrac{3F}{5} = 2 \quad \Leftrightarrow \quad \frac{1}{10}F = 2 \quad \Leftrightarrow$
    $F = 20$. So $V = \frac{60}{5} = 12$ and $E = \frac{60}{2} = 30$.

3. In order to tile the plane with regular polygons, a whole number of poly-
    gons must meet at each corner point (so the sum of the angles at each
    corner is 360°). Since the interior angle of a regular pentagon is 108°, it
    is impossible for a whole number of pentagons to meet at a corner
    (because 360° is not evenly divisible by 108°). The plane can be tiled
    with regular hexagons, as shown is the figure on the right. For $n \geq 7$, the
    interior angle of a regular n-gon is strictly between 120° and 180°, so it is
    impossible for a whole number of such n-gons to meet at a corner (because 360° is not evenly
    divisible by any such number). Thus it is only possible to tile the plane with equilateral triangles,
    squares, and regular hexagons.

5. The belt is tangent to the pulley at the point
    where the belt leaves the pulley. Thus the
    length of the belt between adjacent tangent
    points is the same as the length between the
    centers of the corresponding pulleys. The
    length of the belt around the pulleys can be
    pieced together to form a circle of radius 1.
    Thus the length of the belt is

    $L = P + 2\pi(1) = P + 2\pi$. (See the following
    figure.)

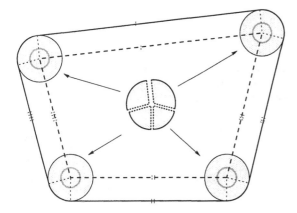

7.   The area we seek is the shaded region in the figure on the left. It consists of two sections (like that shown in the figure on the right) with the overlap being the parallelogram $ABCD$. Now $AB = AC = AD = CB = CA = CD = 1$ since all are radii. So $\triangle ABC$ and $\triangle ADC$ are equilateral triangles whose area are each $\frac{1}{2}bh = \frac{1}{2} \cdot 1 \cdot \cos 60° = \frac{\sqrt{3}}{4}$. Thus the area of parallelogram $ABCD$ is $\frac{\sqrt{3}}{2}$. Since $\angle BAD = \angle BCD = 120°$, the area of each sector is $\frac{1}{3}\pi$. Thus the area we seek is $2 \cdot \frac{1}{3}\pi - \frac{\sqrt{3}}{2} = \frac{4\pi - 3\sqrt{3}}{6} \approx 1.2$.

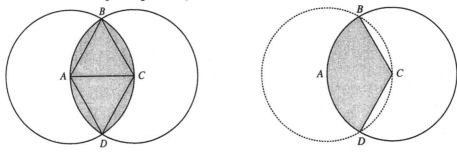

9.   We use the identity $\sin(2\pi - x) = -\sin x$ to deduce $\sin\left(\frac{\pi}{100}\right) = -\sin\left(\frac{199\pi}{100}\right)$, $\sin\left(\frac{2\pi}{100}\right) = -\sin\left(\frac{198\pi}{100}\right)$, ... , and in general, $\sin\left(\frac{k\pi}{100}\right) = -\sin\left(\frac{(200-k)\pi}{100}\right)$, for $k = 1, 2, \ldots, 199$. Thus the sum is $\sin\frac{\pi}{100} + \ldots + \sin\frac{199\pi}{100} = 0$.

11.   Imagine that the walls of the room are folded down as in the diagram. Notice that the diagram shows two points labeled B. So one of the straight lines from A to B gives the shortest path. If $a \leq b$ then the length of the shortest path is $\sqrt{(a+c)^2 + b^2}$ and if $a \geq b$, then the length of the shortest path is $\sqrt{a^2 + (b+c)^2}$.

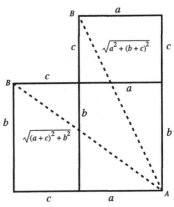

13. $x^2 + y^2 = 4z + 3$. We consider all possible cases for x and y even or odd.

Case 1: x, y are both odd. Since the square of an odd number is odd, and the sum of two odd numbers is even, the left hand side is even but the right hand side is odd. Thus the left hand side cannot equal the right hand side.

Case 2: x, y are both even. Since the square of an even number is even, and the sum of two even numbers is even, the left hand side is even but the right hand side is odd. Thus the left hand side cannot equal the right hand side.

Case 3: x odd and y even. Let $x = 2n + 1$ and let $y = 2m$ for some integers n and m. Then $(2n + 1)^2 + (2m)^2 = 4z + 3$ $\Leftrightarrow$ $4n^2 + 4n + 1 + 4m^2 = 4z + 3$ $\Leftrightarrow$ $4(n^2 + n + m^2) + 1 = 4z + 3$. However, when the left hand side is divided by 4 the remainder is 1, but when the right hand side is divided by 4 the remainder is 3. Thus the left hand side cannot equal the right hand side.

Case 4: x even and y odd. This is handled in the same way as case 3.

Thus there are no integer solutions to $x^2 + y^2 = 4z + 3$.

15. (a) $13 = 2^2 + 3^2$; $41 = 4^2 + 5^2$

(b) $(a^2 + b^2)(c^2 + d^2) = a^2c^2 + b^2d^2 + a^2d^2 + b^2c^2$
$$= a^2c^2 + 2abcd + b^2d^2 + a^2d^2 - 2abcd + b^2c^2$$
$$= (ac + bd)^2 + (ad - bc)^2$$

(c) We first factor $533 = 13 \cdot 41$.

Let $a = 2$, $b = 3$, $c = 4$, $d = 5$, then by the formula in part (b)
$533 = 13 \cdot 41 = (2^2 + 3^2)(4^2 + 5^2) = (2 \cdot 4 + 3 \cdot 5)^2 + (2 \cdot 5 - 3 \cdot 4)^2 = 23^2 + (-2)^2$
$= 23^2 + 2^2$. So $533 = 23^2 + 2^2$.

Let $a = 2$, $b = 3$, $c = 5$, $d = 4$, then by the formula in part (b)
$533 = 13 \cdot 41 = (2^2 + 3^2)(5^2 + 4^2) = (2 \cdot 5 + 3 \cdot 4)^2 + (2 \cdot 4 - 3 \cdot 5)^2 = 22^2 + (-7)^2$
$= 22^2 + 7^2$. So $533 = 22^2 + 7^2$.

17. Label the figures as shown. The unshaded area is c^2 in the first figure and $a^2 + b^2$ in the second figure. These unshaded areas are equal, since in each case they equal the area of the large square minus the areas of the four shaded triangles. Thus $a^2 + b^2 = c^2$. Finally, note that a, b, and c are the legs and hypotenuse of the shaded triangle.

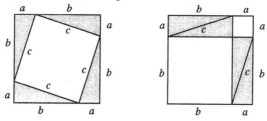

Chapter Seven
Exercises 7.1

1. $\sin t \cot t = \sin t \cdot \dfrac{\cos t}{\sin t} = \cos t$

3. $\tan x \csc x = \dfrac{\sin x}{\cos x} \cdot \dfrac{1}{\sin x} = \dfrac{1}{\cos x} = \sec x$

5. $\tan^2 x - \sec^2 x = \dfrac{\sin^2 x}{\cos^2 x} - \dfrac{1}{\cos^2 x} = \dfrac{\sin^2 x - 1}{\cos^2 x} = \dfrac{-\cos^2 x}{\cos^2 x} = -1$

7. $\sin u + \cot u \cos u = \sin u + \dfrac{\cos u}{\sin u} \cdot \cos u = \dfrac{\sin^2 u + \cos^2 u}{\sin u} = \dfrac{1}{\sin u} = \csc u$

9. $\dfrac{\sin x \sec x}{\tan x} = \dfrac{\sin x \cdot \dfrac{1}{\cos x}}{\dfrac{\cos x}{\sin x}} = 1$

11. $\dfrac{1 + \cos y}{1 + \sec y} = \dfrac{1 + \cos y}{1 + \dfrac{1}{\cos y}} = \dfrac{1 + \cos y}{\dfrac{\cos y + 1}{\cos y}} = \dfrac{1 + \cos y}{1} \cdot \dfrac{\cos y}{\cos y + 1} = \cos y$

13. $\dfrac{\sec^2 x - 1}{\sec^2 x} = \dfrac{\tan^2 x}{\sec^2 x} = \dfrac{\sin^2 x}{\cos^2 x} \cdot \cos^2 x = \sin^2 x$

    Alternative approach: $\dfrac{\sec^2 x - 1}{\sec^2 x} = 1 - \dfrac{1}{\sec^2 x} = 1 - \cos^2 x = \sin^2 x$

15. $\dfrac{1 + \csc x}{\cos x + \cot x} = \dfrac{1 + \dfrac{1}{\sin x}}{\cos x + \dfrac{\cos x}{\sin x}} = \dfrac{1 + \dfrac{1}{\sin x}}{\cos x + \dfrac{\cos x}{\sin x}} \cdot \dfrac{\sin x}{\sin x} = \dfrac{\sin x + 1}{\cos x(\sin x + 1)} = \dfrac{1}{\cos x} = \sec x$

17. $\dfrac{1 + \sin u}{\cos u} + \dfrac{\cos u}{1 + \sin u} = \dfrac{(1 + \sin u)^2 + \cos^2 u}{\cos u(1 + \sin u)} = \dfrac{1 + 2\sin u + \sin^2 u + \cos^2 u}{\cos u(1 + \sin u)} = \dfrac{1 + 2\sin u + 1}{\cos u(1 + \sin u)}$

    $= \dfrac{2 + 2\sin u}{\cos u(1 + \sin u)} = \dfrac{2(1 + \sin u)}{\cos u(1 + \sin u)} = \dfrac{2}{\cos u} = 2\sec u$

19. $\dfrac{2 + \tan^2 x}{\sec^2 x} - 1 = \dfrac{1 + 1 + \tan^2 x}{\sec^2 x} - 1 = \dfrac{1}{\sec^2 x} + \dfrac{1 + \tan^2 x}{\sec^2 x} - 1 = \dfrac{1}{\sec^2 x} + \dfrac{\sec^2 x}{\sec^2 x} - 1$

    $= \dfrac{1}{\sec^2 x} + 1 - 1 = \dfrac{1}{\sec^2 x} = \cos^2 x$

21. $\tan \theta + \cos(-\theta) + \tan(-\theta) = \tan \theta + \cos \theta - \tan \theta = \cos \theta$

23. $\dfrac{\sin \theta}{\tan \theta} = \dfrac{\sin \theta}{\dfrac{\sin \theta}{\cos \theta}} = \sin \theta \cdot \dfrac{\cos \theta}{\sin \theta} = \cos \theta$

25. $\dfrac{\cos u \sec u}{\tan u} = \cos u \dfrac{1}{\cos u} \cot u = \cot u$

27. $\dfrac{\tan y}{\csc y} = \dfrac{\sin y}{\cos y}\sin y = \dfrac{\sin^2 y}{\cos y} = \dfrac{1-\cos^2 y}{\cos y} = \sec y - \cos y$

29. $\sin B + \cos B \cot B = \sin B + \cos B \dfrac{\cos B}{\sin B} = \dfrac{\sin^2 B + \cos^2 B}{\sin B} = \dfrac{1}{\sin B} = \csc B$

31. $\cot(-\alpha)\cos(-\alpha) + \sin(-\alpha) = -\dfrac{\cos\alpha}{\sin\alpha}\cos\alpha - \sin\alpha = \dfrac{-\cos^2\alpha - \sin^2\alpha}{\sin\alpha} = \dfrac{-1}{\sin\alpha} = -\csc\alpha$

33. $\tan\theta + \cot\theta = \dfrac{\sin\theta}{\cos\theta} + \dfrac{\cos\theta}{\sin\theta} = \dfrac{\sin^2\theta + \cos^2\theta}{\cos\theta\sin\theta} = \dfrac{1}{\cos\theta\sin\theta} = \sec\theta\csc\theta$

35. $(1-\cos\beta)(1+\cos\beta) = 1 - \cos^2\beta = \sin^2\beta = \dfrac{1}{\csc^2\beta}$

37. $\dfrac{(\sin x + \cos x)^2}{\sin^2 x - \cos^2 x} = \dfrac{(\sin x + \cos x)^2}{(\sin x + \cos x)(\sin x - \cos x)} = \dfrac{\sin x + \cos x}{\sin x - \cos x}$

$= \dfrac{(\sin x + \cos x)(\sin x - \cos x)}{(\sin x - \cos x)(\sin x - \cos x)} = \dfrac{\sin^2 x - \cos^2 x}{(\sin x - \cos x)^2}$

39. $\dfrac{\sec t - \cos t}{\sec t} = \dfrac{\dfrac{1}{\cos t} - \cos t}{\dfrac{1}{\cos t}} = \dfrac{\dfrac{1}{\cos t} - \cos t}{\dfrac{1}{\cos t}}\cdot\dfrac{\cos t}{\cos t} = \dfrac{1-\cos^2 t}{1} = \sin^2 t$

41. $\dfrac{1}{1-\sin^2 y} = \dfrac{1}{\cos^2 y} = \sec^2 y = 1 + \tan^2 y$

43. $(\cot x - \csc x)(\cos x + 1) = \cot x\cos x + \cot x - \csc x\cos x - \csc x$

$= \dfrac{\cos^2 x}{\sin x} + \dfrac{\cos x}{\sin x} - \dfrac{\cos x}{\sin x} - \dfrac{1}{\sin x} = \dfrac{\cos^2 x - 1}{\sin x} = \dfrac{-\sin^2 x}{\sin x} = -\sin x$

45. $(1-\cos^2 x)(1+\cot^2 x) = \sin^2 x\left(1 + \dfrac{\cos^2 x}{\sin^2 x}\right) = \sin^2 x + \cos^2 x = 1$

47. $2\cos^2 x - 1 = 2(1-\sin^2 x) - 1 = 2 - 2\sin^2 x - 1 = 1 - 2\sin^2 x$

49. $\dfrac{1-\cos\alpha}{\sin\alpha} = \dfrac{1-\cos\alpha}{\sin\alpha}\cdot\dfrac{1+\cos\alpha}{1+\cos\alpha} = \dfrac{1-\cos^2\alpha}{\sin\alpha(1+\cos\alpha)} = \dfrac{\sin^2\alpha}{\sin\alpha(1+\cos\alpha)} = \dfrac{\sin\alpha}{1+\cos\alpha}$

51. $\dfrac{\sin x - 1}{\sin x + 1} = \dfrac{\sin x - 1}{\sin x + 1}\cdot\dfrac{\sin x + 1}{\sin x + 1} = \dfrac{\sin^2 x - 1}{(\sin x + 1)^2} = \dfrac{-\cos^2 x}{(\sin x + 1)^2}$

53. $\dfrac{(\sin t + \cos t)^2}{\sin t\cos t} = \dfrac{\sin^2 t + 2\sin t\cos t + \cos^2 t}{\sin t\cos t} = \dfrac{\sin^2 t + \cos^2 t}{\sin t\cos t} + \dfrac{2\sin t\cos t}{\sin t\cos t} = \dfrac{1}{\sin t\cos t} + 2$

$= 2 + \sec t\cos t$

55. $\dfrac{1+\tan^2 u}{1-\tan^2 u} = \dfrac{1 + \dfrac{\sin^2 u}{\cos^2 u}}{1 - \dfrac{\sin^2 u}{\cos^2 u}} = \dfrac{1 + \dfrac{\sin^2 u}{\cos^2 u}}{1 - \dfrac{\sin^2 u}{\cos^2 u}}\cdot\dfrac{\cos^2 u}{\cos^2 u} = \dfrac{\cos^2 u + \sin^2 u}{\cos^2 u - \sin^2 u} = \dfrac{1}{\cos^2 u - \sin^2 u}$

57. $\dfrac{\sec x}{\sec x - \tan x} = \dfrac{\sec x}{\sec x - \tan x}\cdot\dfrac{\sec x + \tan x}{\sec x + \tan x} = \dfrac{\sec x(\sec x + \tan x)}{\sec^2 x - \tan^2 x} = \dfrac{\sec x(\sec x + \tan x)}{1}$

$$= \sec x(\sec x + \tan x)$$

59. $\sec v - \tan v = (\sec v - \tan v) \cdot \dfrac{\sec v + \tan v}{\sec v + \tan v} = \dfrac{\sec^2 v - \tan^2 v}{\sec v + \tan v} = \dfrac{1}{\sec v + \tan v}$

61. $\dfrac{\sin x + \cos x}{\sec x + \csc x} = \dfrac{\sin x + \cos x}{\dfrac{1}{\cos x} + \dfrac{1}{\sin x}} = \dfrac{\sin x + \cos x}{\dfrac{\sin x + \cos x}{\cos x \sin x}} = (\sin x + \cos x)\dfrac{\cos x \sin x}{\sin x + \cos x} = \cos x \sin x$

63. $\dfrac{\csc x - \cot x}{\sec x - 1} = \dfrac{\dfrac{1}{\sin x} - \dfrac{\cos x}{\sin x}}{\dfrac{1}{\cos x} - 1} = \dfrac{\dfrac{1}{\sin x} - \dfrac{\cos x}{\sin x}}{\dfrac{1}{\cos x} - 1} \cdot \dfrac{\sin x \cos x}{\sin x \cos x} = \dfrac{\cos x(1 - \cos x)}{\sin x(1 - \cos x)} = \dfrac{\cos x}{\sin x} = \cot x$

65. $\tan^2 u - \sin^2 u = \dfrac{\sin^2 u}{\cos^2 u} - \dfrac{\sin^2 u \cos^2 u}{\cos^2 u} = \dfrac{\sin^2 u}{\cos^2 u}(1 - \cos^2 u) = \tan^2 u \sin^2 u$

67. $\sec^4 x - \tan^4 x = (\sec^2 x - \tan^2 x)(\sec^2 x + \tan^2 x) = 1\,(\sec^2 x + \tan^2 x) = \sec^2 x + \tan^2 x$

69. $\dfrac{\sin\theta - \csc\theta}{\cos\theta - \cot\theta} = \dfrac{\sin\theta - \dfrac{1}{\sin\theta}}{\cos\theta - \dfrac{\cos\theta}{\sin\theta}} = \dfrac{\dfrac{\sin^2\theta - 1}{\sin\theta}}{\dfrac{\cos\theta\sin\theta - \cos\theta}{\sin\theta}} = \dfrac{\cos^2\theta}{\cos\theta(\sin\theta - 1)} = \dfrac{\cos\theta}{\sin\theta - 1}$

71. $\dfrac{\cos^2 t + \tan^2 t - 1}{\sin^2 t} = \dfrac{-\sin^2 t + \tan^2 t}{\sin^2 t} = -1 + \dfrac{\sin^2 t}{\cos^2 t} \cdot \dfrac{1}{\sin^2 t} = -1 + \sec^2 t = \tan^2 t$

73. $\dfrac{1}{\sec x + \tan x} + \dfrac{1}{\sec x - \tan x} = \dfrac{\sec x - \tan x + \sec x + \tan x}{(\sec x + \tan x)(\sec x - \tan x)} = \dfrac{2\sec x}{\sec^2 x - \tan^2 x}$

$= \dfrac{2\sec x}{1} = 2\sec x$

75. $(\tan x + \cot x)^2 = \tan^2 x + 2\tan x \cot x + \cot^2 x = \tan^2 x + 2 + \cot^2 x = (\tan^2 x + 1) + (\cot^2 x + 1)$
$= \sec^2 x + \csc^2 x$

77. $\dfrac{\sec u - 1}{\sec u + 1} = \dfrac{\dfrac{1}{\cos u} - 1}{\dfrac{1}{\cos u} + 1} \cdot \dfrac{\cos u}{\cos u} = \dfrac{1 - \cos u}{1 + \cos u}$

79. $\dfrac{\sin^3 x + \cos^3 x}{\sin x + \cos x} = \dfrac{(\sin x + \cos x)(\sin^2 x - \sin x \cos x + \cos^2 x)}{\sin x + \cos x} = \sin^2 - \sin x \cos x + \cos^2 x$

$= 1 - \sin x \cos x$

81. $\dfrac{1 + \sin x}{1 - \sin x} = \dfrac{1 + \sin x}{1 - \sin x} \cdot \dfrac{1 + \sin x}{1 + \sin x} = \dfrac{(1 + \sin x)^2}{1 - \sin^2 x} = \dfrac{(1 + \sin x)^2}{\cos^2 x} = \left(\dfrac{1 + \sin x}{\cos x}\right)^2$

$= (\tan x + \sec x)^2$

83. $(\tan x + \cot x)^4 = \left(\dfrac{\sin x}{\cos x} + \dfrac{\cos x}{\sin x}\right)^4 = \left(\dfrac{\sin^2 x + \cos^2 x}{\sin x \cos x}\right)^4 = \left(\dfrac{1}{\sin x \cos x}\right)^4 = \sec^4 x \csc^4 x$

85. $x = \sin\theta$; then $\dfrac{x}{\sqrt{1 - x^2}} = \dfrac{\sin\theta}{\sqrt{1 - \sin^2\theta}} = \dfrac{\sin\theta}{\sqrt{\cos^2\theta}} = \dfrac{\sin\theta}{\cos\theta} = \tan\theta$ (since $\cos\theta \geq 0$ for
$0 \leq \theta \leq \frac{\pi}{2}$).

87. $x = \sec\theta$; then $\sqrt{x^2 - 1} = \sqrt{\sec^2\theta - 1} = \sqrt{(\tan^2\theta + 1) - 1} = \sqrt{\tan^2\theta} = \tan\theta$ (since $\tan\theta \geq 0$
for $0 \leq \theta < \frac{\pi}{2}$)

89. $x = 3\sin\theta$; then $\sqrt{9 - x^2} = \sqrt{9 - (3\sin\theta)^2} = \sqrt{9 - 9\sin^2\theta} = \sqrt{9(1 - \sin^2\theta)} = 3\sqrt{\cos^2\theta}$
$= 3\cos\theta$ (since $\cos\theta \geq 0$ for $0 \leq \theta < \frac{\pi}{2}$).

91. $f(x) = \cos^2 x - \sin^2 x$, $g(x) = 1 - 2\sin^2 x$. From the graph
this appears to be an identity.

<u>Proof:</u> $f(x) = \cos^2 x - \sin^2 x = \cos^2 x + \sin^2 x - 2\sin^2 x$

$= 1 - 2\sin^2 x = g(x)$. Since $f(x) = g(x)$ for all x, this is an
identity.

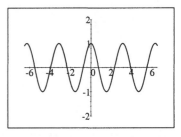

93. $f(x) = (\sin x + \cos x)^2$, $g(x) = 1$

From the graph this does not appear to be an identity. In order
to show this, we can set $x = \frac{\pi}{4}$. Then we have
$f(\frac{\pi}{4}) = \left(\frac{1}{\sqrt{2}} + \frac{1}{\sqrt{2}}\right)^2 = \left(\frac{2}{\sqrt{2}}\right)^2 = \left(\sqrt{2}\right)^2 = 2 \neq 1 = g(\frac{\pi}{4})$.
Since $f(\frac{\pi}{4}) \neq g(\frac{\pi}{4})$, this is not an identity.

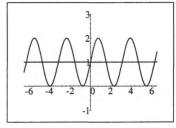

95. (a) Choose $x = \frac{\pi}{2}$. Then $\sin 2x = \sin\pi = 0$ whereas $2\sin x = 2\sin\frac{\pi}{2} = 2$.

(b) Choose $x = \frac{\pi}{4}$ and $y = \frac{\pi}{4}$. Then $\sin(x + y) = \sin\frac{\pi}{2} = 1$ whereas $\sin x + \sin y = \sin\frac{\pi}{4} + \sin\frac{\pi}{4}$
$= \frac{1}{\sqrt{2}} + \frac{1}{\sqrt{2}} = \frac{2}{\sqrt{2}}$. Since these are not equal, the equation is not an identity.

(c) Choose $\theta = \frac{\pi}{4}$. Then $\sec^2\theta + \csc^2\theta = (\sqrt{2})^2 + (\sqrt{2})^2 = 4 \neq 1$.

(d) Choose $x = \frac{\pi}{4}$. Then $\dfrac{1}{\sin x + \cos x} = \dfrac{1}{\sin\frac{\pi}{4} + \cos\frac{\pi}{4}} = \dfrac{1}{\frac{1}{\sqrt{2}} + \frac{1}{\sqrt{2}}} = \dfrac{1}{\sqrt{2}}$ whereas

$\csc x + \sec x = \csc\frac{\pi}{4} + \sec\frac{\pi}{4} = \sqrt{2} + \sqrt{2}$. Since these are not equal, the equation is not an
identity.

97. No. All this proves is that $f(x) = g(x)$ for x in the range of the viewing rectangle. It does not prove
that these functions are equal for all values of x. For example, let $f(x) = 1 - \dfrac{x^2}{2} + \dfrac{x^4}{24} - \dfrac{x^6}{720}$ and
$g(x) = \cos x$. In the first viewing rectangle the graphs of these two functions appear identical.
However, when the domain is expanded in the second viewing rectangle, you can see that these two
functions are not identical.

Exercises 7.2

1. $\cos 15° = \cos(60° - 45°) = \cos 60° \cos 45° + \sin 60° \sin 45° = \frac{1}{2} \cdot \frac{\sqrt{2}}{2} + \frac{\sqrt{3}}{2} \cdot \frac{\sqrt{2}}{2} = \frac{\sqrt{2}+\sqrt{6}}{4}$

3. $\sin 165° = \sin(45° + 120°) = \sin 45° \cos 120° + \cos 45° \sin 120° = \frac{\sqrt{2}}{2} \cdot \left(-\frac{1}{2}\right) + \frac{\sqrt{2}}{2} \cdot \frac{\sqrt{3}}{2}$
    $= \frac{-\sqrt{2}+\sqrt{6}}{4} = \frac{\sqrt{6}-\sqrt{2}}{4}$

5. $\tan 75° = \tan(45° + 30°) = \dfrac{\tan 45° + \tan 30°}{1 - \tan 45° \tan 30°} = \dfrac{1 + \frac{\sqrt{3}}{3}}{1 - 1 \cdot \frac{\sqrt{3}}{3}} = \dfrac{3+\sqrt{3}}{3-\sqrt{3}} = \dfrac{(3+\sqrt{3})^2}{6} = \dfrac{9+6\sqrt{3}+3}{6}$
    $= \frac{12+6\sqrt{3}}{6} = 2 + \sqrt{3}$

7. $\sin\left(\frac{19\pi}{12}\right) = -\sin\frac{7\pi}{12} = -\sin\left(\frac{\pi}{4} + \frac{\pi}{3}\right) = -\sin\frac{\pi}{4}\cos\frac{\pi}{3} + \cos\frac{\pi}{4}\sin\frac{\pi}{6} = -\frac{\sqrt{2}}{2} \cdot \frac{1}{2} + \frac{\sqrt{2}}{2} \cdot \frac{\sqrt{3}}{2} = \frac{\sqrt{6}-\sqrt{2}}{4}$

9. $\cos\left(-\frac{\pi}{12}\right) = \cos\frac{\pi}{12} = \cos\left(\frac{\pi}{4} - \frac{\pi}{6}\right) = \cos\frac{\pi}{4}\cos\frac{\pi}{6} + \sin\frac{\pi}{4}\sin\frac{\pi}{6} = \frac{\sqrt{2}}{2} \cdot \frac{\sqrt{3}}{2} + \frac{\sqrt{2}}{2} \cdot \frac{1}{2} = \frac{\sqrt{6}+\sqrt{2}}{4}$

11. $\sin 18° \cos 27° + \cos 18° \sin 27° = \sin(18° + 27°) = \sin 45° = \frac{1}{\sqrt{2}} = \frac{\sqrt{2}}{2}.$

13. $\cos\frac{3\pi}{7} \cos\frac{2\pi}{21} + \sin\frac{3\pi}{7} \sin\frac{2\pi}{21} = \cos\left(\frac{3\pi}{7} - \frac{2\pi}{21}\right) = \cos\left(\frac{9\pi-2\pi}{21}\right) = \cos\frac{\pi}{3} = \frac{1}{2}$

15. $\dfrac{\tan 73° - \tan 13°}{1 + \tan 73° \tan 13°} = \tan(73° - 13°) = \tan 60° = \sqrt{3}$

17. $\tan\left(\frac{\pi}{2} - u\right) = \dfrac{\sin\left(\frac{\pi}{2} - u\right)}{\cos\left(\frac{\pi}{2} - u\right)} = \dfrac{\sin\frac{\pi}{2}\cos u - \cos\frac{\pi}{2}\sin u}{\cos\frac{\pi}{2}\cos u + \sin\frac{\pi}{2}\sin u} = \dfrac{1 \cdot \cos u - 0 \cdot \sin u}{0 \cdot \cos u + 1 \cdot \sin u} = \dfrac{\cos u}{\sin u} = \cot u$

19. $\sec\left(\frac{\pi}{2} - u\right) = \dfrac{1}{\cos\left(\frac{\pi}{2} - u\right)} = \dfrac{1}{\cos\frac{\pi}{2}\cos u + \sin\frac{\pi}{2}\sin u} = \dfrac{1}{0 \cdot \cos u + 1 \cdot \sin u} = \dfrac{1}{\sin u} = \csc u$

21. $\sin\left(x - \frac{\pi}{2}\right) = \sin x \cos\frac{\pi}{2} - \cos x \sin\frac{\pi}{2} = 0 \cdot \sin x - 1 \cdot \cos x = -\cos x$

23. $\sin(x - \pi) = \sin x \cos \pi - \cos x \sin \pi = -1 \cdot \sin x - 0 \cdot \cos x = -\sin x$

25. $\tan(x - \pi) = \dfrac{\tan x - \tan \pi}{1 + \tan x \tan \pi} = \dfrac{\tan x - 0}{1 + \tan x \cdot 0} = \tan x$

27. $\cos\left(x + \frac{\pi}{6}\right) + \sin\left(x - \frac{\pi}{3}\right) = \cos x \cos\frac{\pi}{6} - \sin x \sin\frac{\pi}{6} + \sin x \cos\frac{\pi}{3} - \cos x \sin\frac{\pi}{3}$
    $= \frac{\sqrt{3}}{2}\cos x - \frac{1}{2}\sin x + \frac{1}{2}\sin x - \frac{\sqrt{3}}{2}\cos x = 0$

29. $\sin(x + y) - \sin(x - y) = \sin x \cos y + \cos x \sin y - (\sin x \cos y - \cos x \sin y) = 2\cos x \sin y$

31. $\cot(x - y) = \dfrac{1}{\tan(x - y)} = \dfrac{1 + \tan x \tan y}{\tan x - \tan y} = \dfrac{1 + \frac{1}{\cot x}\frac{1}{\cot y}}{\frac{1}{\cot x} - \frac{1}{\cot y}} \cdot \dfrac{\cot x \cot y}{\cot x \cot y} = \dfrac{\cot x \cot y + 1}{\cot y - \cot x}$

33. $\tan x - \tan y = \dfrac{\sin x}{\cos x} - \dfrac{\sin y}{\cos y} = \dfrac{\sin x \cos y - \cos x \sin y}{\cos x \cos y} = \dfrac{\sin(x - y)}{\cos x \cos y}$

35. $\dfrac{\sin(x + y) - \sin(x - y)}{\cos(x + y) + \cos(x - y)} = \dfrac{\sin x \cos y + \cos x \sin y - (\sin x \cos y - \cos x \sin y)}{\cos x \cos y - \sin x \sin y + \cos x \cos y + \sin x \sin y}$

$$= \frac{2\cos x \sin y}{2 \cos x \cos y} = \tan y$$

37. $\sin(x + y + z) = \sin[(x + y) + z] = \sin(x + y)\cos z + \cos(x + y)\sin z$

$\quad = \cos z \left[\sin x \cos y + \cos x \sin y\right] + \sin z \left[\cos x \cos y - \sin x \sin y\right]$

$\quad = \sin x \cos y \cos z + \cos x \sin y \cos z + \cos x \cos y \sin z - \sin x \sin y \sin z$

39. $k = \sqrt{A^2 + B^2} = \sqrt{\left(-\sqrt{3}\right)^2 + 1^2} = \sqrt{4} = 2.$ $\sin \phi = \frac{1}{2}$ and $\cos \phi = \frac{-\sqrt{3}}{2}$ $\Rightarrow$ $\phi = \frac{5\pi}{6}.$

$\quad$ Therefore, $-\sqrt{3}\sin x + \cos x = k\sin(x + \phi) = 2\sin(x + \frac{5\pi}{6}).$

41. $k = \sqrt{A^2 + B^2} = \sqrt{5^2 + (-5)^2} = \sqrt{50} = 5\sqrt{2}.$ $\sin \phi = \frac{-5}{5\sqrt{2}} = -\frac{1}{\sqrt{2}}$ and $\cos \phi = \frac{5}{5\sqrt{2}} = \frac{1}{\sqrt{2}}$

$\quad \Rightarrow$ $\phi = \frac{7\pi}{4}.$ Therefore, $5(\sin 2x - \cos 2x) = k\sin(2x + \phi) = 5\sqrt{2}\sin(2x + \frac{7\pi}{4}).$

43. (a) $f(x) = \sin x + \cos x$ $\Rightarrow$ $k = \sqrt{1^2 + 1^2} = \sqrt{2},$ and ϕ satisfies $\sin \phi = \cos \phi = \frac{1}{\sqrt{2}}$ $\Rightarrow$

$\quad\quad \phi = \frac{\pi}{4}.$ Thus, we can write $f(x) = k\sin(x + \phi) = \sqrt{2}\sin(x + \frac{\pi}{4}).$

$\quad$ (b) We see that this is a sine curve with

$\quad\quad$ amplitude $= \sqrt{2},$ period $= 2\pi,$ and phase shift $= -\frac{\pi}{4}..$

45. If $\beta - \alpha = \frac{\pi}{2},$ then $\beta = \alpha + \frac{\pi}{2}.$ Now if we let $y = x + \alpha,$ then $\sin(x + \alpha) + \cos(x + \alpha + \frac{\pi}{2})$

$\quad = \sin y + \cos(y + \frac{\pi}{2}) = \sin y + (-\sin y) = 0.$ Therefore, $\sin(x + \alpha) + \cos(x + \beta) = 0.$

47. Let $\angle A$ and $\angle B$ be the two angles shown in the diagram below. Then $180° = \gamma + A + B,$
$\quad 90° = \alpha + A,$ and $90° = \beta + B.$ Subtracting the second and third equation from the first we get

$$\begin{array}{ll}
180° = \gamma + A + B & \\
-90° = -\alpha - A & \\
-90° = -\beta - B & \\
\hline
0 = \gamma - \alpha - \beta & \Leftrightarrow \quad \alpha + \beta = \gamma.
\end{array}$$

$$\tan \gamma = \tan(\alpha + \beta) = \frac{\tan \alpha + \tan \beta}{1 - \tan \alpha \tan \beta} = \frac{\frac{4}{6} + \frac{3}{4}}{1 - \frac{4}{6} \cdot \frac{3}{4}} = \frac{\frac{8}{12} + \frac{9}{12}}{1 - \frac{1}{2}} = 2 \cdot \frac{17}{12} = \frac{17}{6}.$$

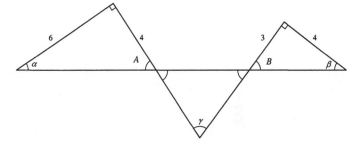

49. (a) $y = \sin^2\left(x + \frac{\pi}{4}\right) + \sin^2\left(x - \frac{\pi}{4}\right)$

From the graph we see that the value of y seems to always be equal to 1.

(b) $y = \sin^2\left(x + \frac{\pi}{4}\right) + \sin^2\left(x - \frac{\pi}{4}\right) = \left(\sin x \cos\frac{\pi}{4} + \cos x \sin\frac{\pi}{4}\right)^2 + \left(\sin x \cos\frac{\pi}{4} - \cos x \sin\frac{\pi}{4}\right)^2$

$= \left[\frac{1}{\sqrt{2}}(\sin x + \cos x)\right]^2 + \left[\frac{1}{\sqrt{2}}(\sin x - \cos x)\right]^2 = \frac{1}{2}[(\sin x + \cos x)^2 + (\sin x - \cos x)^2]$

$= \frac{1}{2}[(\sin^2 x + 2\sin x \cos x + \cos^2 x) + (\sin^2 x - 2\sin x \cos x + \cos^2 x)]$

$= \frac{1}{2}[(1 + 2\sin x \cos x) + (1 - 2\sin x \cos x)] = \frac{1}{2} \cdot 2 = 1$

51. (a) $y = f_1(t) + f_2(t) = 5\sin t + 5\cos t = 5(\sin t + \cos t)$

(b) $k = \sqrt{A^2 + B^2} = \sqrt{5^2 + 5^2} = 5\sqrt{2}$. Therefore, $\sin\phi = \frac{B}{\sqrt{A^2+B^2}} = \frac{5}{5\sqrt{2}} = \frac{1}{\sqrt{2}}$ and

$\cos\phi = \frac{A}{\sqrt{A^2+B^2}} = \frac{1}{\sqrt{2}}$. Thus, $\phi = \frac{\pi}{4}$.

53. $\tan(s + t) = \frac{\sin(s+t)}{\cos(s+t)} = \frac{\sin s \cos t + \cos s \sin t}{\cos s \cos t + \sin s \sin t} = \frac{\sin s \cos t + \cos s \sin t}{\cos s \cos t - \sin s \sin t} \cdot \frac{\dfrac{1}{\cos s \cos t}}{\dfrac{1}{\cos s \cos t}}$

$= \dfrac{\dfrac{\sin s}{\cos s} + \dfrac{\sin t}{\cos t}}{1 - \dfrac{\sin s}{\cos s} \cdot \dfrac{\sin t}{\cos t}} = \dfrac{\tan s + \tan t}{1 - \tan s \tan t}$

Exercises 7.3

1. $\sin x = \frac{5}{13}$, x in quadrant I $\Rightarrow$ $\cos x = \frac{12}{13}$ and $\tan x = \frac{5}{12}$.

   $\sin 2x = 2 \sin x \cos x = 2\left(\frac{5}{13}\right)\left(\frac{12}{13}\right) = \frac{120}{169}$

   $\cos 2x = \cos^2 x - \sin^2 x = \left(\frac{12}{13}\right)^2 - \left(\frac{5}{13}\right)^2 = \frac{144-25}{169} = \frac{119}{169}$

   $\tan 2x = \dfrac{\sin 2x}{\cos 2x} = \dfrac{\frac{120}{169}}{\frac{119}{169}} = \frac{120}{169} \cdot \frac{169}{119} = \frac{120}{119}$

3. $\cos x = \frac{4}{5}$. Then, $\sin x = -\frac{3}{5}$ ($\csc x < 0$) and $\tan x = -\frac{3}{4}$.

   $\sin 2x = 2 \sin x \cos x = 2(-\frac{3}{5}) \cdot \frac{4}{5} = -\frac{24}{25}$

   $\cos 2x = \cos^2 x - \sin^2 x = (\frac{4}{5})^2 - (-\frac{3}{5})^2 = \frac{16-9}{25} = \frac{7}{25}$

   $\tan 2x = \dfrac{\sin 2x}{\cos 2x} = \dfrac{-\frac{24}{25}}{\frac{7}{25}} = -\frac{24}{25} \cdot \frac{25}{7} = -\frac{24}{7}$

5. $\sin x = -\frac{3}{5}$. Then, $\cos x = -\frac{4}{5}$ and $\tan x = \frac{3}{4}$ (x is in quadrant III).

   $\sin 2x = 2 \sin x \cos x = 2(-\frac{3}{5})(-\frac{4}{5}) = \frac{24}{25}$

   $\cos 2x = \cos^2 x - \sin^2 x = (-\frac{4}{5})^2 - (-\frac{3}{5})^2 = \frac{16-9}{25} = \frac{7}{25}$

   $\tan 2x = \dfrac{\sin 2x}{\cos 2x} = \dfrac{\frac{24}{25}}{\frac{7}{25}} = \frac{24}{25} \cdot \frac{25}{7} = \frac{24}{7}$

7. $\tan x = -\frac{1}{3}$, $\cos x > 0$. So $\sin x < 0$. Thus, $\sin x = -\frac{1}{\sqrt{10}}$ and $\cos x = \frac{3}{\sqrt{10}}$.

   $\sin 2x = 2 \sin x \cos x = 2 \cdot \left(-\frac{1}{\sqrt{10}}\right)\left(\frac{3}{\sqrt{10}}\right) = -\frac{6}{10} = -\frac{3}{5}$

   $\cos 2x = \cos^2 x - \sin^2 x = \left(\frac{3}{\sqrt{10}}\right)^2 - \left(-\frac{1}{\sqrt{10}}\right)^2 = \frac{8}{10} = \frac{4}{5}$

   $\tan 2x = \dfrac{\sin 2x}{\cos 2x} = \dfrac{-\frac{3}{5}}{\frac{4}{5}} = -\frac{3}{5} \cdot \frac{5}{4} = -\frac{3}{4}$

9. $\sin^4 x = (\sin^2 x)^2 = \left(\dfrac{1 - \cos 2x}{2}\right)^2 = \frac{1}{4} - \frac{1}{2} \cos 2x + \frac{1}{4} \cos^2 2x$

   $= \frac{1}{4} - \frac{1}{2} \cos 2x + \frac{1}{4} \cdot \dfrac{1 + \cos 4x}{2} = \frac{1}{4} - \frac{1}{2} \cos 2x + \frac{1}{8} + \frac{1}{8} \cos 4x = \frac{3}{8} - \frac{1}{2} \cos 2x + \frac{1}{8} \cos 4x$

   $= \frac{1}{2}\left(\frac{3}{4} - \cos 2x + \frac{1}{4} \cos 4x\right)$

11. Since $\sin^4 x \cos^4 x = (\sin^2 x \cos^2 x)^2$ we can use the result of Example 4 to get

   $\sin^4 x \cos^4 x = \left(\frac{1}{8} - \frac{1}{8} \cos 4x\right)^2 = \frac{1}{64} - \frac{1}{32} \cos 4x + \frac{1}{64} \cos^2 4x$

   $= \frac{1}{64} - \frac{1}{32} \cos 4x + \frac{1}{64}\left(\dfrac{1 + \cos 8x}{2}\right) = \frac{1}{64} - \frac{1}{32} \cos 4x + \frac{1}{128} + \frac{1}{128} \cos 8x$

   $= \frac{3}{128} - \frac{1}{32} \cos 4x + \frac{1}{128} \cos 8x = \frac{1}{32}\left(\frac{3}{4} - \cos 4x + \frac{1}{4} \cos 8x\right)$

13.   We use the result of Example 4, to get $\cos^2 x \sin^4 x = (\sin^2 x \cos^2 x)\sin^2 x$

$$= \left(\tfrac{1}{8} - \tfrac{1}{8}\cos 4x\right) \cdot \left(\tfrac{1}{2} - \frac{\cos 2x}{2}\right) = \tfrac{1}{16} - \tfrac{1}{16}\cos 2x - \tfrac{1}{16}\cos 4x + \tfrac{1}{16}\cos 2x \cos 4x$$

15. $\sin 15^\circ = \sqrt{\tfrac{1}{2}(1 - \cos 30^\circ)} = \sqrt{\tfrac{1}{2}\left(1 - \tfrac{\sqrt{3}}{2}\right)} = \sqrt{\tfrac{1}{4}(2 - \sqrt{3})} = \tfrac{1}{2}\sqrt{2 - \sqrt{3}}$

17. $\cos 22.5^\circ = \sqrt{\tfrac{1}{2}(1 + \cos 45^\circ)} = \sqrt{\tfrac{1}{2}\left(1 + \tfrac{\sqrt{2}}{2}\right)} = \tfrac{1}{2}\sqrt{2 + \sqrt{2}}$

19. $\tan \tfrac{\pi}{8} = \dfrac{1 - \cos \tfrac{\pi}{4}}{\sin \tfrac{\pi}{4}} = \dfrac{1 - \tfrac{1}{\sqrt{2}}}{\tfrac{1}{\sqrt{2}}} = \sqrt{2} - 1$

21. $\sin \tfrac{\pi}{12} = \sqrt{\tfrac{1}{2}(1 - \cos \tfrac{\pi}{6})} = \sqrt{\tfrac{1}{2}(1 - \tfrac{\sqrt{3}}{2})} = \tfrac{1}{2}\sqrt{2 - \sqrt{3}}$

23.   (a) $2 \sin 18^\circ \cos 18^\circ = \sin 36^\circ$ (b) $2 \sin 3\theta \cos 3\theta = \sin 6\theta$

25.   (a) $\cos^2 34^\circ - \sin^2 34^\circ = \cos 68^\circ$ (b) $\cos^2 5\theta - \sin^2 5\theta = \cos 10\theta$

27.   (a) $\dfrac{\sin 8^\circ}{1 + \cos 8^\circ} = \tan \tfrac{8^\circ}{2} = \tan 4^\circ$ (b) $\dfrac{1 - \cos 4\theta}{\sin 4\theta} = \tan \tfrac{4\theta}{2} = \tan 2\theta$

29. $\sin x = \tfrac{3}{5}$. Since x is in quadrant I, $\cos x = \tfrac{4}{5}$ and $\dfrac{x}{2}$ is also in quadrant I. Thus

$$\sin \frac{x}{2} = \sqrt{\tfrac{1}{2}(1 - \cos x)} = \sqrt{\tfrac{1}{2}(1 - \tfrac{4}{5})} = \tfrac{1}{\sqrt{10}} = \tfrac{\sqrt{10}}{10}$$

$$\cos \frac{x}{2} = \sqrt{\tfrac{1}{2}(1 + \cos x)} = \sqrt{\tfrac{1}{2}(1 + \tfrac{4}{5})} = \tfrac{3}{\sqrt{10}} = \tfrac{3\sqrt{10}}{10}$$

$$\tan \frac{x}{2} = \frac{\sin \tfrac{x}{2}}{\cos \tfrac{x}{2}} = \tfrac{1}{\sqrt{10}} \cdot \tfrac{\sqrt{10}}{3} = \tfrac{1}{3}$$

31. $\csc x = 3$. Then, $\sin x = \tfrac{1}{3}$ and since x is in quadrant II, $\cos x = -\tfrac{2\sqrt{2}}{3}$. Since $90^\circ \le x \le 180^\circ$, we have $45^\circ \le \tfrac{x}{2} \le 90^\circ$ and so $\tfrac{x}{2}$ is in quadrant I. Thus

$$\sin \frac{x}{2} = \sqrt{\tfrac{1}{2}(1 - \cos x)} = \sqrt{\tfrac{1}{2}(1 + \tfrac{2\sqrt{2}}{3})} = \sqrt{\tfrac{1}{6}(3 + 2\sqrt{2})}$$

$$\cos \frac{x}{2} = \sqrt{\tfrac{1}{2}(1 + \cos x)} = \sqrt{\tfrac{1}{2}(1 - \tfrac{2\sqrt{2}}{3})} = \sqrt{\tfrac{1}{6}(3 - 2\sqrt{2})}$$

$$\tan \frac{x}{2} = \frac{\sin \tfrac{x}{2}}{\cos \tfrac{x}{2}} = \sqrt{\tfrac{3 + 2\sqrt{2}}{3 - 2\sqrt{2}}} = 3 + 2\sqrt{2}$$

33. $\sec x = \tfrac{3}{2}$. Then $\cos x = \tfrac{2}{3}$ and since x is in quadrant IV, $\sin x = -\tfrac{\sqrt{5}}{3}$. Since $270^\circ \le x \le 360^\circ$, we have $135^\circ \le \tfrac{x}{2} \le 180^\circ$ and so $\tfrac{x}{2}$ is in quadrant II. Thus

$$\sin \tfrac{x}{2} = \sqrt{\tfrac{1}{2}(1 - \cos x)} = \sqrt{\tfrac{1}{2}(1 - \tfrac{2}{3})} = \tfrac{1}{\sqrt{6}} = \tfrac{\sqrt{6}}{6}$$

$$\cos \tfrac{x}{2} = -\sqrt{\tfrac{1}{2}(1 + \cos x)} = -\sqrt{\tfrac{1}{2}(1 + \tfrac{2}{3})} = \tfrac{-\sqrt{5}}{\sqrt{6}} = -\tfrac{\sqrt{30}}{6}$$

$$\tan \tfrac{x}{2} = \frac{\sin \tfrac{x}{2}}{\cos \tfrac{x}{2}} = \tfrac{1}{\sqrt{6}} \cdot \tfrac{\sqrt{6}}{-\sqrt{5}} = -\tfrac{1}{\sqrt{5}} = -\tfrac{\sqrt{5}}{5}$$

35. $\sin 2x \cos 3x = \frac{1}{2}[\sin(2x + 3x) + \sin(2x - 3x)] = \frac{1}{2}(\sin 5x - \sin x)$

37. $\cos x \sin 4x = \frac{1}{2}[\sin(4x + x) + \sin(4x - x)] = \frac{1}{2}(\sin 5x + \sin 3x)$

39. $3\cos 4x \cos 7x = 3 \cdot \frac{1}{2}[\cos(4x + 7x) + \cos(4x - 7x)] = \frac{3}{2}(\cos 11x + \cos 3x)$

41. $\sin 5x + \sin 3x = 2\sin\left(\frac{5x+3x}{2}\right)\cos\left(\frac{5x-3x}{2}\right) = 2\sin 4x \cos x$

43. $\cos 4x - \cos 6x = -2\sin\left(\frac{4x+6x}{2}\right)\sin\left(\frac{4x-6x}{2}\right) = -2\sin 5x \sin(-x) = 2\sin 5x \sin x$

45. $\sin 2x - \sin 7x = 2\cos\left(\frac{2x+7x}{2}\right)\sin\left(\frac{2x-7x}{2}\right) = 2\cos\frac{9x}{2}\sin\frac{-5x}{2} = -2\cos\frac{9x}{2}\sin\frac{5x}{2}$

47. $2\sin 52.5° \sin 97.5° = 2 \cdot \frac{1}{2}[\cos(52.5° - 97.5°) - \cos(52.5° + 97.5°)] = \cos(-45°) - \cos 150°$

$= \cos 45° - \cos 150° = \frac{\sqrt{2}}{2} + \frac{\sqrt{3}}{2} = \frac{1}{2}(\sqrt{2} + \sqrt{3})$

49. $\cos 37.5° \sin 7.5° = \frac{1}{2}(\sin 45° - \sin 30°) = \frac{1}{2}\left(\frac{\sqrt{2}}{2} - \frac{1}{2}\right) = \frac{1}{4}(\sqrt{2} - 1)$

51. $\cos 255° - \cos 195° = -2\sin\left(\frac{255°+195°}{2}\right)\sin\left(\frac{255°-195°}{2}\right) = -2\sin 225° \sin 30° = -2\left(-\frac{\sqrt{2}}{2}\right)\frac{1}{2} = \frac{\sqrt{2}}{2}$

53. $\cos^2 5x - \sin^2 5x = \cos(2 \cdot 5x) = \cos 10x$

55. $(\sin x + \cos x)^2 = \sin^2 x + 2\sin x \cos x + \cos^2 x = 1 + 2\sin x \cos x = 1 + \sin 2x$

57. $\dfrac{\sin 4x}{\sin x} = \dfrac{(2\sin 2x \cos 2x)}{\sin x} = \dfrac{2(2\sin x \cos x)(\cos 2x)}{\sin x} = 4\cos x \cos 2x$

59. $\dfrac{2(\tan x - \cot x)}{\tan^2 x - \cot^2 x} = \dfrac{2(\tan x - \cot x)}{(\tan x + \cot x)(\tan x - \cot x)} = \dfrac{2}{\tan x + \cot x} = \dfrac{2}{\dfrac{\sin x}{\cos x} + \dfrac{\cos x}{\sin x}}$

$= \dfrac{2}{\dfrac{\sin x}{\cos x} + \dfrac{\cos x}{\sin x}} \cdot \dfrac{\sin x \cos x}{\sin x \cos x} = \dfrac{2\sin x \cos x}{\sin^2 x + \cos^2 x} = 2\sin x \cos x = \sin 2x$

61. $\tan 3x = \tan(2x + x) = \dfrac{\tan 2x + \tan x}{1 - \tan 2x \tan x} = \dfrac{\dfrac{2\tan x}{1 - \tan^2 x} + \tan x}{1 - \dfrac{2\tan x}{1 - \tan^2 x}\tan x} = \dfrac{2\tan x + \tan x(1 - \tan^2 x)}{1 - \tan^2 x - 2\tan x \tan x}$

$= \dfrac{3\tan x - \tan^3 x}{1 - 3\tan^2 x}$

63. $\cos^4 x - \sin^4 x = (\cos^2 x + \sin^2 x)(\cos^2 x - \sin^2 x) = \cos^2 x - \sin^2 x = \cos 2x$

65. $\dfrac{\sin x + \sin 5x}{\cos x + \cos 5x} = \dfrac{2\sin 3x \cos 2x}{2\cos 3x \cos 2x} = \dfrac{\sin 3x}{\cos 3x} = \tan 3x$

67. $\dfrac{\sin 10x}{\sin 9x + \sin x} = \dfrac{2\sin 5x \cos 5x}{2\sin 5x \cos 4x} = \dfrac{\cos 5x}{\cos 4x}$

69. $\dfrac{\sin x + \sin y}{\cos x + \cos y} = \dfrac{2\sin\left(\frac{x+y}{2}\right)\cos\left(\frac{x-y}{2}\right)}{2\cos\left(\frac{x+y}{2}\right)\cos\left(\frac{x-y}{2}\right)} = \dfrac{\sin\left(\frac{x+y}{2}\right)}{\cos\left(\frac{x+y}{2}\right)} = \tan\left(\frac{x+y}{2}\right)$

71. $\sin 45° + \sin 15° = 2\sin\left(\frac{45°+15°}{2}\right)\cos\left(\frac{45°-15°}{2}\right) = 2\sin 30° \cos 15° = 2 \cdot \frac{1}{2} \cdot \cos 15° = \cos 15°$

$= \sin(90° - 15°) = \sin 75°$ (applying the cofunction identity)

73. $\dfrac{\sin x + \sin 2x + \sin 3x + \sin 4x + \sin 5x}{\cos x + \cos 2x + \cos 3x + \cos 4x + \cos 5x} = \dfrac{(\sin x + \sin 5x) + (\sin 2x + \sin 4x) + \sin 3x}{(\cos x + \cos 5x) + (\cos 2x + \cos 4x) + \cos 3x}$

$= \dfrac{2\sin 3x \cos 2x + 2\sin 3x \cos x + \sin 3x}{2\cos 3x \cos 2x + 2\cos 3x \cos x + \cos 3x} = \dfrac{\sin 3x\,(2\cos 2x + 2\cos x + 1)}{\cos 3x(2\cos 2x + 2\cos x + 1)} = \tan 3x$

75. (a) $f(x) = \dfrac{\sin 3x}{\sin x} - \dfrac{\cos 3x}{\cos x}$

The function appears to have a constant value of 2 wherever it is defined.

(b) $f(x) = \dfrac{\sin 3x}{\sin x} - \dfrac{\cos 3x}{\cos x} = \dfrac{\sin 3x \cos x - \cos 3x \sin x}{\sin x \cos x} = \dfrac{\sin (3x - x)}{\sin x \cos x} = \dfrac{\sin 2x}{\sin x \cos x}$

$= \dfrac{2\sin x \cos x}{\sin x \cos x} = 2$ for all x for which the function is defined.

77. (a) $y = \sin 6x + \sin 7x$

(b) By a sum to product identity
$y = \sin 6x + \sin 7x$
$= 2\sin\left(\dfrac{6x + 7x}{2}\right)\cos\left(\dfrac{6x - 7x}{2}\right)$
$= 2\cdot\sin\left(\tfrac{13}{2}x\right)\cdot\cos\left(-\tfrac12 x\right)$
$= 2\sin\left(\tfrac{13}{2}x\right)\cos\left(\tfrac12 x\right).$

(c) $y = \sin 6x + \sin 7x$, with $y = 2\cos\left(\tfrac12 x\right)$ and $y = -2\cos\left(\tfrac12 x\right)$

The graph of $y = f(x)$ lies between the other two graphs.

79. (a) In both logs the length of the adjacent side is $20\cos\theta$ and the length of the opposite side is $20\sin\theta$. Thus the cross-sectional area of the beam is modeled by $A(\theta) = (20\cos\theta)(20\sin\theta)$
$= 400\sin\theta\cos\theta = 200(2\sin\theta\cos\theta) = 200\sin 2\theta.$

(b) The function $y = \sin u$ is maximized when $u = \tfrac{\pi}{2}$. So $2\theta = \tfrac{\pi}{2}$ $\Leftrightarrow$ $\theta = \tfrac{\pi}{4}$. Thus the maximum cross-sectional area is $A\left(\tfrac{\pi}{4}\right) = 200\sin 2\left(\tfrac{\pi}{4}\right) = 200.$

81. We first label the figure as shown on the right.
Because the sheet of paper is folded over
$\angle EAC = \angle CAB = \theta$. Thus
$\angle BCA = \angle ACE = 90° - \theta$. It follows that
$\angle ECD = 180° - \angle BCA - \angle ACE$
$= 180° - (90° - \theta) - (90° - \theta) = 2\theta$. Also, from the
figure we see that $BC = L\sin\theta$ and $CE = L\sin\theta$ so
$DC = EC\cos 2\theta = L\sin\theta\cos 2\theta$. Thus
$6 = DB = DC + CB = L\sin\theta\cos 2\theta + L\sin\theta$
$= L\sin\theta(1 + \cos 2\theta) = L\sin\theta \cdot 2\cos^2\theta$. So
$$L = \frac{6}{2\sin\theta\cos^2\theta} = \frac{3}{\sin\theta\cos^2\theta}.$$

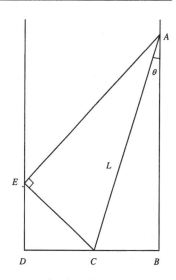

83. (a) $\cos 4x = \cos(2x + 2x) = 2\cos^2 2x - 1 = 2(2\cos^2 x - 1)^2 - 1 = 8\cos^4 x - 8\cos^2 x + 1$.
    Thus the desired polynomial is $P(t) = 8t^4 - 8t^2 + 1$.

    (b) $\cos 5x = \cos(4x+x) = \cos 4x\cos x - \sin 4x\sin x$
    $= \cos x(8\cos^4 x - 8\cos^2 x + 1) - 2\sin 2x\cos 2x\sin x$
    $= 8\cos^5 x - 8\cos^3 x + \cos x - 4\sin x\cos x(2\cos^2 x - 1)\sin x$ (from part (a))
    $= 8\cos^5 x - 8\cos^3 x + \cos x - 4\cos x(2\cos^2 x - 1)\sin^2 x$
    $= 8\cos^5 x - 8\cos^3 x + \cos x - 4\cos x(2\cos^2 x - 1)(1 - \cos^2 x)$
    $= 8\cos^5 x - 8\cos^3 x + \cos x + 8\cos^5 x - 12\cos^3 x + 4\cos x = 16\cos^5 x - 20\cos^3 x + 5\cos x$.
    Thus the desired polynomial is $P(t) = 16t^5 - 20t^3 + 5t$.

85. We find the area of $\triangle ABC$ in two different ways. First, let AB be the base and CD be the height.
Since $\angle BOC = 2\theta$ we see that $CD = \sin 2\theta$. So
$$Area = \tfrac{1}{2}(base)(height) = \tfrac{1}{2} \cdot 2 \cdot \sin 2\theta = \sin 2\theta.$$
On the other hand, in $\triangle ABC$ we see that $\angle C$ is a right angle. So, $BC = 2\sin\theta$ and $AC = 2\cos\theta$, and
$$Area = \tfrac{1}{2}(base)(height) = \tfrac{1}{2} \cdot (2\sin\theta)(2\cos\theta) = 2\sin\theta\cos\theta.$$
Comparing the two expressions for the area of $\triangle ABC$ we get $\sin 2\theta = 2\sin\theta\cos\theta$.

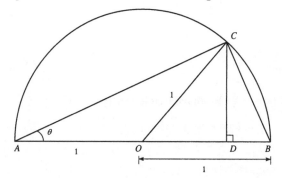

Note: The two facts from geometry used in this solution are given in the problem itself.

Exercises 7.4

1.   (a) $\sin^{-1}\frac{1}{2} = \frac{\pi}{6}$ (b) $\cos^{-1}\frac{1}{2} = \frac{\pi}{3}$ (c) $\cos^{-1}2$ is not defined.

3.   (a) $\sin^{-1}\frac{\sqrt{2}}{2} = \frac{\pi}{4}$ (b) $\cos^{-1}\frac{\sqrt{2}}{2} = \frac{\pi}{4}$ (c) $\sin^{-1}(-\frac{\sqrt{2}}{2}) = -\frac{\pi}{4}$

5.   (a) $\sin^{-1}1 = \frac{\pi}{2}$ (b) $\cos^{-1}1 = 0$ (c) $\cos^{-1}(-1) = \pi$

7.   (a) $\tan^{-1}\frac{\sqrt{3}}{3} = \frac{\pi}{6}$ (b) $\tan^{-1}(-\frac{\sqrt{3}}{3}) = -\frac{\pi}{6}$ (c) $\sin^{-1}(-2)$ is not defined.

9.   (a) $\sin^{-1}(0.13844) \approx 0.13889$ (b) $\cos^{-1}(-0.92761) \approx 2.75876$

11.   (a) $\tan^{-1}(1.23456 \approx 0.88998$ (b) $\sin^{-1}(1.23456)$ is not defined

13. $\sin(\sin^{-1}\frac{1}{4}) = \frac{1}{4}$ 15. $\tan(\tan^{-1}5) = 5$

17. $\cos^{-1}(\cos\frac{\pi}{3}) = \frac{\pi}{3}$ 19. $\sin^{-1}\left[\sin\left(-\frac{\pi}{6}\right)\right] = -\frac{\pi}{6}$

21. $\tan^{-1}(\tan\frac{2\pi}{3}) = \tan^{-1}\left[\tan(\frac{2\pi}{3} - \pi)\right] = \tan^{-1}(\tan\frac{-\pi}{3}) = -\frac{\pi}{3}$ (since $\frac{2\pi}{3} > \frac{\pi}{2}$)

23. $\tan(\sin^{-1}\frac{1}{2}) = \tan\frac{\pi}{6} = \frac{\sqrt{3}}{3}$ 25. $\cos(\sin^{-1}\frac{\sqrt{3}}{2}) = \cos\frac{\pi}{3} = \frac{1}{2}$

27. $\tan^{-1}(2\sin\frac{\pi}{3}) = \tan^{-1}(2 \cdot \frac{\sqrt{3}}{2}) = \tan^{-1}\sqrt{3} = \frac{\pi}{3}$

29.   Let $u = \cos^{-1}\frac{3}{5}$, so $\cos u = \frac{3}{5}$. Then from   31.   Let $u = \tan^{-1}\frac{12}{5}$, so $\tan u = \frac{12}{5}$. Then from
the triangle $\sin(\cos^{-1}\frac{3}{5}) = \sin u = \frac{4}{5}$.   the triangle $\sin(\tan^{-1}\frac{12}{5}) = \sin u = \frac{12}{13}$.

33.   Let $\theta = \sin^{-1}\frac{12}{13}$, so $\sin\theta = \frac{12}{13}$. Then from   35.   Let $u = \tan^{-1}2$, so $\tan u = 2$. Then from
the triangle $\sec(\sin^{-1}\frac{12}{13}) = \sec\theta = \frac{13}{5}$.   the triangle $\cos(\tan^{-1}2) = \cos u = \frac{1}{\sqrt{5}} = \frac{\sqrt{5}}{5}$.

37.   Let $u = \cos^{-1}\frac{3}{5}$, so $\cos u = \frac{3}{5}$. From the triangle $\sin u = \frac{4}{5}$ so

$$\sin(2\cos^{-1}\frac{3}{5}) = \sin(2u) = 2\sin u\cos u = 2 \cdot \frac{4}{5} \cdot \frac{3}{5} = \frac{24}{25}$$

39. Let $u = \cos^{-1}\frac{1}{2}$ and $v = \sin^{-1}\frac{1}{2}$, so $\cos u = \frac{1}{2}$ and $\sin v = \frac{1}{2}$. From the triangle
$\sin(\sin^{-1}\frac{1}{2} + \cos^{-1}\frac{1}{2}) = \sin(v + u) = \sin v \cos u + \cos v \sin u$
$= \frac{1}{2} \cdot \frac{1}{2} + \frac{\sqrt{3}}{2} \cdot \frac{\sqrt{3}}{2} = 1.$
Another solution: $\sin(\sin^{-1}\frac{1}{2} + \cos^{-1}\frac{1}{2}) = \sin(\frac{\pi}{6} + \frac{\pi}{3}) = \sin\frac{\pi}{2} = 1.$

41. Let $u = \sin^{-1}x$, so $\sin u = x$. From the triangle $\cos(\sin^{-1}x) = \cos u = \sqrt{1 - x^2}.$

43. Let $u = \sin^{-1}x$, so $\sin u = x$. From the triangle $\tan(\sin^{-1}x) = \tan u = \dfrac{x}{\sqrt{1 - x^2}}.$

45. Let $u = \tan^{-1}x$, so $\tan u = x$. From the triangle
$$\cos(2\tan^{-1}x) = \cos 2u - 1 = 2\cos^2 u - 1 = \frac{2}{1 + x^2} - 1 = \frac{1 - x^2}{1 + x^2}.$$

47. Let $u = \cos^{-1}x$ and $v = \sin^{-1}x$, so $\cos u = x$ and $\sin v = x$. From the triangle
$\cos(\cos^{-1}x + \sin^{-1}x) = \cos(\cos^{-1}x)\cos(\sin^{-1}x) - \sin(\cos^{-1}x)\sin(\sin^{-1}x)$
$= \cos u \cos v - \sin u \sin v = x\sqrt{1 - x^2} - x\sqrt{1 - x^2} = 0.$

49. (a) Solving $\tan\theta = \dfrac{h}{2}$ for h we have $h = 2\tan\theta$.

   (b) Solving $\tan\theta = \dfrac{h}{2}$ for θ we have $\theta = \tan^{-1}\left(\frac{h}{2}\right)$

51. (a) Solving $\sin\theta = \dfrac{h}{680}$ for θ we have $\theta = \sin^{-1}\left(\dfrac{h}{680}\right).$

   (b) Set $h = 500$ to get $\theta = \sin^{-1}\left(\frac{500}{680}\right) = 0.82610$ rad.

53. (a) $y = \sin^{-1}x + \cos^{-1}x$. Note the domain of both $\sin^{-1}x$ and $\cos^{-1}x$ is $[-1, 1]$.

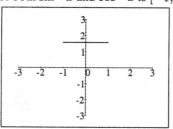

Conjecture: $y = \frac{\pi}{2}$ for $-1 \le x \le 1$.

   (b) To prove this conjecture, let $\sin^{-1}x = u$
$\Leftrightarrow \sin u = x, -\frac{\pi}{2} \le u \le \frac{\pi}{2}$. Using the cofunction identity $\sin u = \cos\left(\frac{\pi}{2} - u\right) = x$,
$\cos^{-1}x = \frac{\pi}{2} - u$. Therefore,
$\sin^{-1}x + \cos^{-1}x = u + \left(\frac{\pi}{2} - u\right) = \frac{\pi}{2}.$

55. (a) $\tan^{-1} x + \tan^{-1} 2x = \frac{\pi}{4}$

From the graph, $x \approx 0.28$

(b) To solve the equation exactly, we set $\tan^{-1} x + \tan^{-1} 2x = \frac{\pi}{4}$ $\Leftrightarrow$

$\tan^{-1} x = \frac{\pi}{4} - \tan^{-1} 2x$ $\Rightarrow$ $\tan(\tan^{-1} x) = \tan\left(\frac{\pi}{4} - \tan^{-1} 2x\right)$ $\Rightarrow$

$x = \dfrac{\tan\frac{\pi}{4} - \tan\left(\tan^{-1} 2x\right)}{1 + \tan\frac{\pi}{4} \cdot \tan\left(\tan^{-1} 2x\right)} = \dfrac{1 - 2x}{1 + (1)2x}$ $\Rightarrow$ $x(1 + 2x) = 1 - 2x$ $\Leftrightarrow$

$x + 2x^2 = 1 - 2x$. Thus, $2x^2 + 3x - 1 = 0$. We use the quadratic formula to solve for x:

$x = \dfrac{-3 \pm \sqrt{3^2 - 4(2)(-1)}}{2(2)} = \dfrac{-3 \pm \sqrt{17}}{4}$. Substituting into the original equation, we see that

$x = \dfrac{-3 - \sqrt{17}}{4}$ is not a solution, and so $x = \dfrac{-3 + \sqrt{17}}{4} \approx 0.28$ is the only root.

57. $f(x) = \sin(\sin^{-1} x) = x$

Domain: $[-1, 1]$

Range: $[-1, 1]$

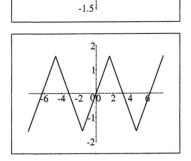

$g(x) = \sin^{-1}(\sin x)$

Domain: $[-\infty, \infty]$

Range: $[-\frac{\pi}{2}, \frac{\pi}{2}]$

Note $g(x) = x$ only for $x \in [-\frac{\pi}{2}, \frac{\pi}{2}]$

Exercises 7.5

1. $\sin x - 1 = 0 \quad \Leftrightarrow \quad \sin x = 1$. In the interval $[0, 2\pi)$ the only solution is $x = \frac{\pi}{2}$. Therefore, the solutions are $x = \frac{\pi}{2} + 2k\pi$, for any integer k.

3. $2\cos x - 1 = 0 \quad \Leftrightarrow \quad 2\cos x = 1 \quad \Leftrightarrow \quad \cos x = \frac{1}{2}$. In the interval $[0, 2\pi)$ the solutions are $x = \frac{\pi}{3}, \frac{5\pi}{3}$. Therefore, the solutions are $x = \frac{\pi}{3} + 2k\pi, \frac{5\pi}{3} + 2k\pi, k = 0, \pm 1, \pm 2, \ldots$.

5. $2\sin x + \sqrt{3} = 0 \quad \Leftrightarrow \quad 2\sin x = -\sqrt{3} \quad \Leftrightarrow \quad \sin x = -\frac{\sqrt{3}}{2}$. In the interval $[0, 2\pi)$ the solutions are $x = \frac{4\pi}{3}, \frac{5\pi}{3}$. Therefore, the solutions are $x = \frac{4\pi}{3} + 2k\pi, \frac{5\pi}{3} + 2k\pi, k = 0, \pm 1, \pm 2, \ldots$.

7. $4\cos^2 x - 1 = 0 \quad \Leftrightarrow \quad 4\cos^2 x = 1 \quad \Leftrightarrow \quad 4\cos^2 x = 1 \quad \Leftrightarrow \quad \cos^2 x = \frac{1}{4} \quad \Leftrightarrow$ $\cos x = \pm\frac{1}{2}$. In the interval $[0, 2\pi)$ the solutions are $x = \frac{\pi}{3}, \frac{2\pi}{3}, \frac{4\pi}{3}, \frac{5\pi}{3}$. So the solutions are $x = \frac{\pi}{3} + 2k\pi, \frac{2\pi}{3} + 2k\pi, \frac{4\pi}{3} + 2k\pi, \frac{5\pi}{3} + 2k\pi$ which can also be expressed as $x = \frac{\pi}{3} + k\pi, \frac{2\pi}{3} + k\pi$, $k = 0, \pm 1, \pm 2, \ldots$.

9. $\sec^2 x - 2 = 0 \quad \Leftrightarrow \quad \sec^2 x = 2 \quad \Leftrightarrow \quad \sec x = \pm\sqrt{2}$. In the interval $[0, 2\pi)$ the solutions are $x = \frac{\pi}{4}, \frac{3\pi}{4}, \frac{5\pi}{4}, \frac{7\pi}{4}$. So the solutions can be expressed as the odd multiples of $\frac{\pi}{4}$ which are $x = \frac{(2k+1)\pi}{4}, k = 0, \pm 1, \pm 2, \ldots$.

11. $\cos x (2\sin x + 1) = 0 \quad \Leftrightarrow \quad \cos x = 0$ or $2\sin x + 1 = 0 \quad \Leftrightarrow \quad \sin x = -\frac{1}{2}$. On $[0, 2\pi]$: $\cos x = 0 \quad \Leftrightarrow \quad x = \frac{\pi}{2}, \frac{3\pi}{2}$ and $\sin x = -\frac{1}{2} \quad \Leftrightarrow \quad x = \frac{7\pi}{6}, \frac{11\pi}{6}$. Thus the solutions are $x = \frac{\pi}{2} + k\pi, x = \frac{7\pi}{6} + 2k\pi, x = \frac{11\pi}{6} + 2k\pi, k = 0, \pm 1, \pm 2, \ldots$.

13. $(\tan x + \sqrt{3})(\cos x + 2) = 0 \quad \Leftrightarrow \quad \tan x + \sqrt{3} = 0$ or $\cos x + 2 = 0$. Since $|\cos x| \leq 1$ for all x, there is no solution for $\cos x + 2 = 0$. Hence, $\tan x + \sqrt{3} = 0 \quad \Leftrightarrow \quad \tan x = -\sqrt{3} \quad \Leftrightarrow$ $x = -\frac{\pi}{3}$ on $\left(-\frac{\pi}{2}, \frac{\pi}{2}\right)$. Thus the solutions are $x = -\frac{\pi}{3} + k\pi, k = 0, \pm 1, \pm 2, \ldots$.

15. $\cos x \sin x - 2\cos x = 0 \quad \Leftrightarrow \quad \cos x (\sin x - 2) = 0 \quad \Leftrightarrow \quad \cos x = 0$ or $\sin x - 2 = 0$. Since $|\sin x| \leq 1$ for all x, there is no solution for $\sin x - 2 = 0$. Hence, $\cos x = 0 \quad \Leftrightarrow \quad x = \frac{\pi}{2} + 2k\pi$, $\frac{3\pi}{2} + 2k\pi \quad \Leftrightarrow \quad x = \frac{\pi}{2} + k\pi, k = 0, \pm 1, \pm 2, \ldots$.

17. $4\cos^2 x - 4\cos x + 1 = 0 \quad \Leftrightarrow \quad (2\cos x - 1)^2 = 0 \quad \Leftrightarrow \quad 2\cos x - 1 = 0 \quad \Leftrightarrow \quad \cos x = \frac{1}{2}$ $\Leftrightarrow \quad x = \frac{\pi}{3} + 2k\pi, \frac{5\pi}{3} + 2k\pi, k = 0, \pm 1, \pm 2, \ldots$.

19. $\sin^2 x = 2\sin x + 3 \quad \Leftrightarrow \quad \sin^2 x - 2\sin x - 3 = 0 \quad \Leftrightarrow \quad (\sin x - 3)(\sin x + 1) = 0 \quad \Leftrightarrow$ $\sin x - 3 = 0$ or $\sin x + 1 = 0$. Since $|\sin x| \leq 1$ for all x, there is no solution for $\sin x - 3 = 0$. Hence $\sin x + 1 = 0 \quad \Leftrightarrow \quad \sin x = -1 \quad \Leftrightarrow \quad x = \frac{3\pi}{2} + 2k\pi, k = 0, \pm 1, \pm 2, \ldots$.

21. $\sin^2 x = 4 - 2\cos^2 x \quad \Leftrightarrow \quad \sin^2 x + \cos^2 x + \cos^2 x = 4 \quad \Leftrightarrow \quad 1 + \cos^2 x = 4 \quad \Leftrightarrow \quad \cos^2 x = 3$ Since $|\cos x| \leq 1$ for all x, it follows that $\cos^2 x \leq 1$ and so there are no solutions for $\cos^2 x = 3$.

23. $2\sin 3x + 1 = 0 \quad \Leftrightarrow \quad 2\sin 3x = -1 \quad \Leftrightarrow \quad \sin 3x = -\frac{1}{2}$. In the interval $[0, 6\pi)$ the solution are $3x = \frac{7\pi}{6}, \frac{11\pi}{6}, \frac{19\pi}{6}, \frac{23\pi}{6}, \frac{31\pi}{6}, \frac{35\pi}{6} \quad \Leftrightarrow \quad x = \frac{7\pi}{18}, \frac{11\pi}{18}, \frac{19\pi}{18}, \frac{23\pi}{18}, \frac{25\pi}{18}, \frac{29\pi}{18}$. So $x = \frac{7\pi}{18} + \frac{2k\pi}{3}$, $\frac{11\pi}{18} + \frac{2k\pi}{3}$, for any integer k.

25. $\sec 4x - 2 = 0 \quad \Leftrightarrow \quad \sec 4x = 2 \quad \Leftrightarrow \quad 4x = \frac{\pi}{3} + 2k\pi, \frac{5\pi}{3} + 2k\pi \quad \Leftrightarrow \quad x = \frac{\pi}{12} + \frac{1}{2}k\pi$, $\frac{5\pi}{12} + \frac{1}{2}k\pi$, for any integer k.

27. $\sqrt{3}\sin 2x = \cos 2x$ $\Leftrightarrow$ $\tan 2x = \frac{1}{\sqrt{3}}$ (if $\cos 2x \neq 0$) $\Leftrightarrow$ $2x = \frac{\pi}{6} + k\pi$ $\Leftrightarrow$
     $x = \frac{\pi}{12} + \frac{1}{2}k\pi$, for any integer k.

29. $\cos\frac{x}{2} - 1 = 0$ $\Leftrightarrow$ $\cos\frac{x}{2} = 1$ $\Leftrightarrow$ $\frac{x}{2} = 2k\pi$ $\Leftrightarrow$ $x = 4k\pi$, for any integer k.

31. $\tan\frac{x}{4} + \sqrt{3} = 0$ $\Leftrightarrow$ $\tan\frac{x}{4} = -\sqrt{3}$ $\Leftrightarrow$ $\frac{x}{4} = \frac{2\pi}{3} + k\pi$ $\Leftrightarrow$ $x = \frac{8\pi}{3} + 4k\pi$ for any integer
     k.

33. $\tan^5 x - 9\tan x = 0$ $\Leftrightarrow$ $\tan x(\tan^4 x - 9) = 0$ $\Leftrightarrow$ $\tan x = 0$ or $\tan^4 x = 9$ $\Leftrightarrow$ $\tan x = 0$
     or $\tan x = \pm\sqrt{3}$ $\Leftrightarrow$ $x = 0, \pi, \frac{\pi}{3}, \frac{2\pi}{3}, \frac{4\pi}{3}, \frac{5\pi}{3}$ in $[0, 2\pi)$. Thus $x = \frac{k\pi}{3}$, for any integer k.

35. $4\sin x\cos x + 2\sin x - 2\cos x - 1 = 0$ $\Leftrightarrow$ $(2\sin x - 1)(2\cos x + 1) = 0$ $\Leftrightarrow$
     $2\sin x - 1 = 0$ or $2\cos x + 1 = 0$ $\Leftrightarrow$ $\sin x = \frac{1}{2}$ or $\cos x = -\frac{1}{2}$ $\Leftrightarrow$ $x = \frac{\pi}{6}, \frac{5\pi}{6}, \frac{2\pi}{3}, \frac{4\pi}{3}$ in
     $[0, 2\pi)$. Thus $x = \frac{\pi}{6} + 2k\pi, \frac{5\pi}{6} + 2k\pi, \frac{2\pi}{3} + 2k\pi, \frac{4\pi}{3} + 2k\pi$, for any integer k.

37. $\cos^2 2x - \sin^2 2x = 0$ $\Leftrightarrow$ $(\cos 2x - \sin 2x)(\cos 2x + \sin 2x) = 0$ $\Leftrightarrow$ $\cos 2x = \pm\sin 2x$
     $\Leftrightarrow$ $\tan 2x = \pm 1$ $\Leftrightarrow$ $2x = \frac{\pi}{4}, \frac{3\pi}{4}, \frac{5\pi}{4}, \frac{7\pi}{4}, \frac{9\pi}{4}, \frac{11\pi}{4}, \frac{13\pi}{4}, \frac{15\pi}{4}$ in $[0, 4\pi)$ $\Leftrightarrow$ $x = \frac{\pi}{8}, \frac{3\pi}{8}, \frac{5\pi}{8},$
     $\frac{7\pi}{8}, \frac{9\pi}{8}, \frac{11\pi}{8}, \frac{13\pi}{8}, \frac{15\pi}{8}$ in $[0, 2\pi)$. So the solution can be expressed as the odd multiples of $\frac{\pi}{8}$ which are
     $x = \frac{\pi}{8} + \frac{k\pi}{4}$, for any integer k.

39. $2\cos 3x = 1$ $\Leftrightarrow$ $\cos 3x = \frac{1}{2}$ $\Rightarrow$ $3x = \frac{\pi}{3}, \frac{5\pi}{3}, \frac{7\pi}{3}, \frac{11\pi}{3}, \frac{13\pi}{3}, \frac{17\pi}{3}$ on $[0, 6\pi)$ $\Leftrightarrow$ $x = \frac{\pi}{9},$
     $\frac{5\pi}{9}, \frac{7\pi}{9}, \frac{11\pi}{9}, \frac{13\pi}{9}, \frac{17\pi}{9}$ on $[0, 2\pi)$.

41. $2\sin x\tan x - \tan x = 1 - 2\sin x$ $\Leftrightarrow$ $2\sin x\tan x - \tan x + 2\sin x - 1 = 0$ $\Leftrightarrow$
     $(2\sin x - 1)(\tan x + 1) = 0$ $\Leftrightarrow$ $2\sin x - 1 = 0$ or $\tan x + 1 = 0$ $\Leftrightarrow$ $\sin x = \frac{1}{2}$ or
     $\tan x = -1$ $\Leftrightarrow$ $x = \frac{\pi}{6}, \frac{5\pi}{6}$ or $x = \frac{3\pi}{4}, \frac{7\pi}{4}$. Thus, the solutions in $[0, 2\pi)$ are $\frac{\pi}{6}, \frac{3\pi}{4}, \frac{5\pi}{6}, \frac{7\pi}{4}$.

43. $\tan x - 3\cot x = 0$ $\Leftrightarrow$ $\dfrac{\sin x}{\cos x} - \dfrac{3\cos x}{\sin x} = 0$ $\Leftrightarrow$ $\dfrac{\sin^2 x - 3\cos^2 x}{\cos x\sin x} = 0$ $\Leftrightarrow$
     $\dfrac{\sin^2 x + \cos^2 x - 4\cos^2 x}{\cos x\sin x} = 0$ $\Leftrightarrow$ $\dfrac{1 - 4\cos^2 x}{\cos x\sin x} = 0$ $\Leftrightarrow$ $1 - 4\cos^2 x = 0$ $\Leftrightarrow$
     $4\cos^2 x = 1$ $\Leftrightarrow$ $\cos x = \pm\frac{1}{2}$ $\Leftrightarrow$ $x = \frac{\pi}{3}, \frac{2\pi}{3}, \frac{4\pi}{3}, \frac{5\pi}{3}$ in $[0, 2\pi)$.

45. $\tan 3x + 1 = \sec 3x$ $\Rightarrow$ $(\tan 3x + 1)^2 = \sec^2 3x$ $\Leftrightarrow$ $\tan^2 3x + 2\tan 3x + 1 = \sec^2 3x$ $\Leftrightarrow$
     $\sec^2 3x + 2\tan 3x = \sec^2 3x$ $\Leftrightarrow$ $2\tan 3x = 0$ $\Leftrightarrow$ $3x = 0, \pi, 2\pi, 3\pi, 4\pi, 5\pi$ in $[0, 6\pi)$
     $\Leftrightarrow$ $x = 0, \frac{\pi}{3}, \frac{2\pi}{3}, \pi, \frac{4\pi}{3}, \frac{5\pi}{3}$ in $[0, 2\pi)$. Since squaring both sides is an operation that can
     introduce extraneous solutions, we must check each of the possible solution in the original equation.
     We see that $x = \frac{\pi}{3}, \pi, \frac{5\pi}{3}$ are not solutions. Hence the only solutions are $x = 0, \frac{2\pi}{3}, \frac{4\pi}{3}$.

47. (a) Since the period of cosine is 2π the solutions are $x \approx 1.15928 + 2k\pi$ and $x \approx 5.12391 + 2k\pi$,
          for any integer k.

     (b) $\cos x = 0.4$ $\Rightarrow$ $x = \cos^{-1} 0.4 \approx 1.15928$. The other solution is
          $2\pi - \cos^{-1} 0.4 \approx 5.12391$.

49. (a) Since the period of secant is 2π the solutions are $x \approx 1.36943 \pm 2k\pi$ and $\approx 4.91375 \pm 2k\pi$,
          for any integer k.

     (b) $\sec x = 5$ $\Leftrightarrow$ $\cos x = \frac{1}{5}$ $\Rightarrow$ $x = \cos^{-1}\frac{1}{5} \approx 1.36944$. The other solution is
          $2\pi - \cos^{-1}\frac{1}{5} \approx 4.91375$.

51. (a) Since $\sin(\pi + x) = -\sin x$, we can express the general solutions as $x \approx 0.46365 + k\pi$ and $x \approx 2.67795 + k\pi$, for any integer k.

   (b) $5\sin^2 x - 1 = 0 \;\Rightarrow\; \sin^2 x = \frac{1}{5} \;\Rightarrow\; \sin x = \pm\frac{1}{\sqrt{5}}$. Now $\sin x = \frac{1}{\sqrt{5}} \;\Rightarrow\;$
   $x = \sin^{-1}\left(\frac{1}{\sqrt{5}}\right) \approx 0.46365$, and $x \approx \pi - 0.46365 \approx 2.67795$. Also, $\sin x = -\frac{1}{\sqrt{5}} \;\Rightarrow\;$
   $x = \sin^{-1}\left(-\frac{1}{\sqrt{5}}\right) \approx -0.46365$, so in the interval $[0, 2\pi)$ $x \approx \pi - (-0.46365) \approx 3.60524$ and
   $x \approx 2\pi - 0.46365 \approx 5.81954$

53. (a) Since the period for sine is 2π, the general solution is of the form $x \approx 0.33984 + 2k\pi$ and $x \approx 2.80176 + 2k\pi$, for any integer k.

   (b) $3\sin^2 x - 7\sin x + 2 = 0 \;\Rightarrow\; (3\sin x - 1)(\sin x - 2) = 0 \;\Rightarrow\; 3\sin x - 1 = 0$ or $\sin$
   $x - 2 = 0$. Since $|\sin x| \le 1$, $\sin x - 2 = 0$ has no solution. Thus $3\sin x - 1 = 0 \;\Rightarrow\;$
   $\sin x = \frac{1}{3} \;\Rightarrow\; x \approx 0.33984$ and $x \approx \pi - 0.33984 \approx 2.80176$.

55. $f(x) = 3\cos x + 1$; $g(x) = \cos x - 1$.
   $f(x) = g(x)$ when $3\cos x + 1 = \cos x - 1$
   $\Leftrightarrow\; 2\cos x = -2 \;\Leftrightarrow\; \cos x = -1 \;\Leftrightarrow$
   $x = \pi + 2k\pi = (2k + 1)\pi$. The points of
   intersection are $([2k + 1]\pi, -2)$, for any
   integer k.

57. $f(x) = \tan x$; $g(x) = \sqrt{3}$. $f(x) = g(x)$ when
   $\tan x = \sqrt{3} \;\Leftrightarrow\; x = \frac{\pi}{3} + k\pi$. The
   intersection points are $\left(\frac{\pi}{3} + k\pi, \sqrt{3}\right)$, for any
   integer k.

59. We substitute $v_0 = 2200$ and $R(\theta) = 5000$ and solve for θ. So $5000 = \dfrac{(2200)^2 \sin 2\theta}{32} \;\Leftrightarrow\;$
   $5000 = 151250 \sin 2\theta \;\Leftrightarrow\; \sin 2\theta = 0.03308 \;\Rightarrow\; 2\theta = 1.89442°$ or
   $2\theta = 180° - 1.89442° = 178.10558°$. If $2\theta = 1.89442°$ then $\theta = 0.94721°$ and if
   $2\theta = 178.10558°$ then $\theta = 89.05279$.

61. We substitute $\theta_1 = 70°$ and $v_1/v_2 = 1.33$ into Snell's Law to get: $\dfrac{\sin 70°}{\sin \theta_2} = 1.33 \;\Leftrightarrow$
   $\sin \theta_2 = \dfrac{\sin 70°}{1.33} = 0.7065 \;\Rightarrow\; \theta_2 \approx 44.95°$.

63. $\cos x \cos 3x - \sin x \sin 3x = 0 \;\Leftrightarrow\; \cos(x + 3x) = 0 \;\Leftrightarrow\; \cos 4x = 0 \;\Leftrightarrow\; 4x = \frac{\pi}{2}, \frac{3\pi}{2},$
   $\frac{5\pi}{2}, \frac{7\pi}{2}, \frac{9\pi}{2}, \frac{11\pi}{2}, \frac{13\pi}{2}, \frac{15\pi}{2}$ in $[0, 8\pi) \;\Leftrightarrow\; x = \frac{\pi}{8}, \frac{3\pi}{8}, \frac{5\pi}{8}, \frac{7\pi}{8}, \frac{9\pi}{8}, \frac{11\pi}{8}, \frac{13\pi}{8}, \frac{15\pi}{8}$ in $[0, 2\pi)$.

65. $\sin 2x \cos x + \cos 2x \sin x = \frac{\sqrt{3}}{2} \;\Leftrightarrow\; \sin(2x + x) = \frac{\sqrt{3}}{2} \;\Leftrightarrow\; \sin 3x = \frac{\sqrt{3}}{2} \;\Leftrightarrow\; 3x = \frac{\pi}{3},$
   $\frac{2\pi}{3}, \frac{7\pi}{3}, \frac{8\pi}{3}, \frac{13\pi}{3}, \frac{14\pi}{3}$ in $[0, 6\pi) \;\Leftrightarrow\; x = \frac{\pi}{9}, \frac{2\pi}{9}, \frac{7\pi}{9}, \frac{8\pi}{9}, \frac{13\pi}{9}, \frac{14\pi}{9}$ in $[0, 2\pi)$.

67. $\sin 2x + \cos x = 0$ $\Leftrightarrow$ $2\sin x \cos x + \cos x = 0$ $\Leftrightarrow$ $\cos x\,(2\sin x + 1) = 0$ $\Leftrightarrow$
     $\cos x = 0$ or $\sin x = -\frac{1}{2}$ $\Leftrightarrow$ $x = \frac{\pi}{2}, \frac{7\pi}{6}, \frac{3\pi}{2}, \frac{11\pi}{6}$.

69. $\cos 2x + \cos x = 2$ $\Leftrightarrow$ $2\cos^2 x - 1 + \cos x - 2 = 0$ $\Leftrightarrow$ $2\cos^2 x + \cos x - 3 = 0$
     $\Leftrightarrow$ $(2\cos x + 3)(\cos x - 1) = 0$ $\Leftrightarrow$ $2\cos x + 3 = 0$ or $\cos x - 1 = 0$ $\Leftrightarrow$
     $\cos x = -\frac{3}{2}$ (which is impossible) or $\cos x = 1$ $\Leftrightarrow$ $x = 0$ in $[0, 2\pi)$.

71. $\sin x + \sin 3x = 0$ $\Leftrightarrow$ $2\sin 2x \cos(-x) = 0$ $\Leftrightarrow$ $2\sin 2x \cos x = 0$ $\Leftrightarrow$ $\sin 2x = 0$ or
     $\cos x = 0$ $\Leftrightarrow$ $2x = k\pi$ or $x = \frac{k\pi}{2}$ $\Leftrightarrow$ $x = \frac{k\pi}{2}$, for any integer k.

73. $\cos 4x + \cos 2x = \cos x$ $\Leftrightarrow$ $2\cos 3x \cos x = \cos x$ $\Leftrightarrow$ $\cos x\,(2\cos 3x - 1) = 0$ $\Leftrightarrow$
     $\cos x = 0$ or $\cos 3x = \frac{1}{2}$ $\Leftrightarrow$ $x = \frac{\pi(2k+1)}{2}$ or $3x = \frac{\pi}{3} + 2k\pi, \frac{5\pi}{3} + 2k\pi, \frac{7\pi}{3} + 2k\pi, \frac{11\pi}{3} + 2k\pi,$
     $\frac{13\pi}{3} + 2k\pi, \frac{17\pi}{3} + 2k\pi$ $\Leftrightarrow$ $x = \frac{\pi(2k+1)}{2}, \frac{\pi}{9} + \frac{2k\pi}{3}, \frac{5\pi}{9} + \frac{2k\pi}{3}$.

75. $\sin 2x = x$ 77. $2^{\sin x} = x$

                                     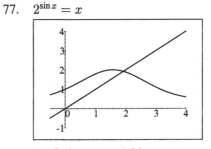

3 solutions: $x = 0$, $x \approx \pm 0.95$ 1 solution: $x \approx 1.92$

79. $\dfrac{\cos x}{1 + x^2} = x^2$

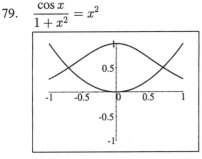

2 solutions: $x \approx \pm 0.71$

81.   "A" is a true statement. Every identity is an equation. The difference between an identity and an equation is that an identity is true for all values in the domain, whereas an equation may only be true for certain values in the domain and false for others.

Exercises 7.6

1. $4i.$ $|4i| = \sqrt{0^2 + 4^2} = 4$

3. $5 + 2i.$ $|5 + 2i| = \sqrt{5^2 + 2^2} = \sqrt{29}$

5. $\sqrt{3} + i.$ $\left|\sqrt{3} + i\right| = \sqrt{3 + 1} = 2$

7. $\dfrac{3 + 4i}{5}.$ $\left|\dfrac{3 + 4i}{5}\right| = \sqrt{\dfrac{9}{25} + \dfrac{16}{25}} = 1$

9. $z = 1 + i$
   $2z = 2 + 2i,$
   $-z = -1 - i,$
   $\tfrac{1}{2}z = \tfrac{1}{2} + \tfrac{1}{2}i$

11. $z = 8 + 2i$
    $\overline{z} = 8 - 2i$

13. $z_1 = 2 - i, z_2 = 2 + i.$
    Then $z_1 + z_2 = 2 - i + 2 + i = 4.$
    $z_1 z_2 = (2 - i)(2 + i) = 4 - i^2 = 5$

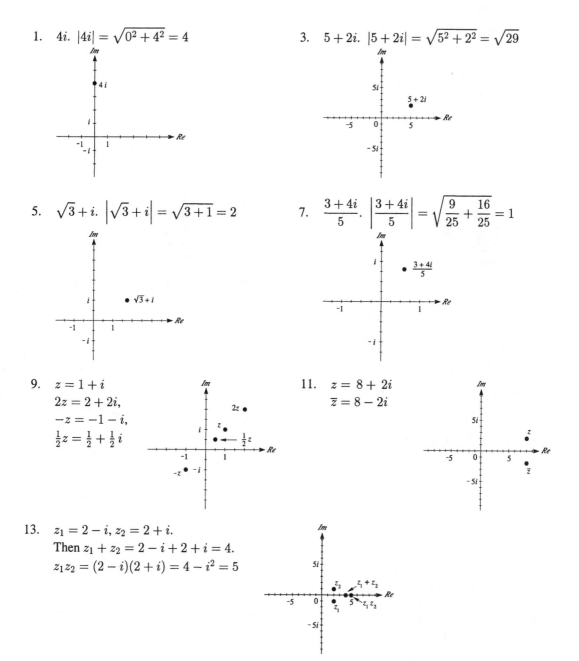

15. $\{z = a + bi \mid a \leq 0, b \geq 0\}$

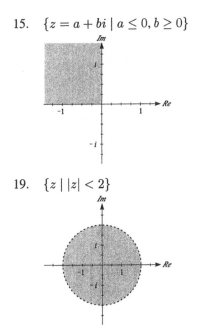

17. $\{z \mid |z| = 3\}$

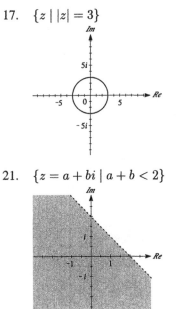

19. $\{z \mid |z| < 2\}$

21. $\{z = a + bi \mid a + b < 2\}$

23. $1 + i$. Then $\tan\theta = \frac{1}{1} = 1$ with θ in quadrant I $\Rightarrow$ $\theta = \frac{\pi}{4}$, and $r = \sqrt{1^2 + 1^2} = \sqrt{2}$. Hence, $1 + i = \sqrt{2}\left(\cos\frac{\pi}{4} + i\sin\frac{\pi}{4}\right)$.

25. $\sqrt{2} - \sqrt{2}\,i$. Then $\tan\theta = \frac{\sqrt{2}}{\sqrt{2}} = -1$ with θ in quadrant IV $\Rightarrow$ $\theta = \frac{7\pi}{4}$, and $r = \sqrt{2+2} = 2$. Hence, $\sqrt{2} - \sqrt{2}\,i = 2\left(\cos\frac{7\pi}{4} + i\sin\frac{7\pi}{4}\right)$.

27. $2\sqrt{3} - 2i$. Then $\tan\theta = \frac{-2}{2\sqrt{3}} = -\frac{1}{\sqrt{3}}$ with θ in quadrant IV $\Rightarrow$ $\theta = \frac{11\pi}{6}$, and $r = \sqrt{12+4} = 4$. Hence, $2\sqrt{3} - 2i = 4\left(\cos\frac{11\pi}{6} + i\sin\frac{11\pi}{6}\right)$.

29. $-3\,i$. Then $\theta = \frac{3\pi}{2}$, and $r = \sqrt{0+9} = 3$. Hence, $3\,i = 3\left(\cos\frac{3\pi}{2} + i\sin\frac{3\pi}{2}\right)$.

31. $5 + 5i$. Then $\tan\theta = \frac{5}{5} = 1$ with θ in quadrant I $\Rightarrow$ $\theta = \frac{\pi}{4}$, and $r = \sqrt{25+25} = 5\sqrt{2}$. Hence, $5 + 5i = 5\sqrt{2}\left(\cos\frac{\pi}{4} + i\sin\frac{\pi}{4}\right)$.

33. $4\sqrt{3} - 4i$. Then $\tan\theta = \frac{-4}{4\sqrt{3}} = -\frac{1}{\sqrt{3}}$ with θ in quadrant IV $\Rightarrow$ $\theta = \frac{11\pi}{6}$, and $r = \sqrt{48+16} = 8$. Hence, $4\sqrt{3} - 4i = 8\left(\cos\frac{11\pi}{6} + i\sin\frac{11\pi}{6}\right)$.

35. -20. Then $\theta = \pi$, and $r = 20$. Hence, $-20 = 20\left(\cos\pi + i\sin\pi\right)$.

37. $3 + 4i$. Then $\tan\theta = \frac{4}{3}$ with θ in quadrant I $\Rightarrow$ $\theta = \tan^{-1}\frac{4}{3}$, and $r = \sqrt{9+16} = 5$. Hence, $3 + 4i = 5\left[\cos\left(\tan^{-1}\frac{4}{3}\right) + i\sin\left(\tan^{-1}\frac{4}{3}\right)\right]$.

39. $3i\,(1 + i) = -3 + 3i$. Then $\tan\theta = \frac{3}{-3} = -1$ with θ in quadrant II $\Rightarrow$ $\theta = \frac{3\pi}{4}$, and $r = \sqrt{9+9} = 3\sqrt{2}$. Hence, $3i\,(1 + i) = 3\sqrt{2}\left(\cos\frac{3\pi}{4} + i\sin\frac{3\pi}{4}\right)$.

41. $4\left(\sqrt{3} + i\right) = 4\sqrt{3} + 4i$. Then $\tan\theta = \frac{4}{4\sqrt{3}} = \frac{1}{\sqrt{3}}$ with θ in quadrant I $\Rightarrow$ $\theta = \frac{\pi}{6}$, and $r = \sqrt{48+16} = 8$. Hence, $4\left(\sqrt{3} + i\right) = 8\left(\cos\frac{\pi}{6} + i\sin\frac{\pi}{6}\right)$.

43. $2+i$. Then $\tan\theta = \frac{1}{2}$ with θ in quadrant I $\Rightarrow$ $\theta = \tan^{-1}\frac{1}{2}$, and $r = \sqrt{4+1} = \sqrt{5}$. Hence, $2+i = \sqrt{5}\left[\cos(\tan^{-1}\frac{1}{2}) + i\sin(\tan^{-1}\frac{1}{2})\right]$.

45. $\sqrt{2}+\sqrt{2}i$. Then $\tan\theta = \frac{\sqrt{2}}{\sqrt{2}} = 1$ with θ in quadrant I $\Rightarrow$ $\theta = \frac{\pi}{4}$, and $r = \sqrt{2+2} = 2$.
    Hence, $2+\sqrt{2}i = 2\left(\cos\frac{\pi}{4} + i\sin\frac{\pi}{4}\right)$.

47. $z_1 = \cos\pi + i\sin\pi$, $z_2 = \cos\frac{\pi}{3} + i\sin\frac{\pi}{3}$
    $z_1 z_2 = \cos\left(\pi + \frac{\pi}{3}\right) + i\sin\left(\pi + \frac{\pi}{3}\right) = \cos\frac{4\pi}{3} + i\sin\frac{4\pi}{3}$
    $z_1/z_2 = \cos\left(\pi - \frac{\pi}{3}\right) + i\sin\left(\pi - \frac{\pi}{3}\right) = \cos\frac{2\pi}{3} + i\sin\frac{2\pi}{3}$

49. $z_1 = 3\left(\cos\frac{\pi}{6} + i\sin\frac{\pi}{6}\right)$, $z_2 = 5\left(\cos\frac{4\pi}{3} + i\sin\frac{4\pi}{3}\right)$
    $z_1 z_2 = 3\cdot 5\left[\cos\left(\frac{\pi}{6} + \frac{4\pi}{3}\right) + i\sin\left(\frac{\pi}{6} + \frac{4\pi}{3}\right)\right] = 15\left(\cos\frac{9\pi}{6} + i\sin\frac{9\pi}{6}\right) = 15\left(\cos\frac{3\pi}{2} + i\sin\frac{3\pi}{2}\right)$
    $z_1/z_2 = \frac{3}{5}\left[\cos\left(\frac{\pi}{6} - \frac{4\pi}{3}\right) + i\sin\left(\frac{\pi}{6} - \frac{4\pi}{3}\right)\right] = \frac{3}{5}\left[\cos\left(-\frac{7\pi}{6}\right) + i\sin\left(-\frac{7\pi}{6}\right)\right] = \frac{3}{5}\left[\cos\left(\frac{7\pi}{6}\right) - i\sin\left(\frac{7\pi}{6}\right)\right]$

51. $z_1 = 4\left(\cos 120° + i\sin 120°\right)$, $z_2 = 2\left(\cos 30° + i\sin 30°\right)$
    $z_1 z_2 = 4\cdot 2[\cos(120° + 30°) + i\sin(120° + 30°)] = 8(\cos 150° + i\sin 150°)$
    $z_1/z_2 = \frac{4}{2}\left[\cos\left(120° - 30°\right) + i\sin\left(120° - 30°\right)\right] = 2\left(\cos 90° + i\sin 90°\right)$

53. $z_1 = 4\left(\cos 200° + i\sin 200°\right)$, $z_2 = 25\left(\cos 150° + i\sin 150°\right)$
    $z_1 z_2 = 4\cdot 25[\cos(200° + 150°) + i\sin(200° + 150°)] = 100(\cos 350° + i\sin 350°)$
    $z_1/z_2 = \frac{4}{25}\left[\cos(200° - 150°) + i\sin(200° - 150°)\right] = \frac{4}{25}\left(\cos 50° + i\sin 50°\right)$

55. $z_1 = \sqrt{3}+i$. Then $\tan\theta_1 = \frac{1}{\sqrt{3}}$ with θ_1 in quadrant I $\Rightarrow$ $\theta_1 = \frac{\pi}{6}$, and $r_1 = \sqrt{3+1} = 2$.
    $z_2 = 1 + \sqrt{3}i$. Then $\tan\theta_2 = \sqrt{3}$ with θ_2 in quadrant I $\Rightarrow$ $\theta_2 = \frac{\pi}{3}$, and $r_1 = \sqrt{1+3} = 2$.
    Hence, $z_1 = 2\left(\cos\frac{\pi}{6} + i\sin\frac{\pi}{6}\right)$ and $z_2 = 2\left(\cos\frac{\pi}{3} + i\sin\frac{\pi}{3}\right)$.
    $z_1 z_2 = 2\cdot 2\left[\cos\left(\frac{\pi}{6} + \frac{\pi}{3}\right) + i\sin\left(\frac{\pi}{6} + \frac{\pi}{3}\right)\right] = 4\left(\cos\frac{\pi}{2} + i\sin\frac{\pi}{2}\right)$
    $z_1/z_2 = \frac{2}{2}\left[\cos\left(\frac{\pi}{6} - \frac{\pi}{3}\right) + i\sin\left(\frac{\pi}{6} - \frac{\pi}{3}\right)\right] = \cos\left(-\frac{\pi}{6}\right) + i\sin\left(-\frac{\pi}{6}\right) = \cos\frac{\pi}{6} - i\sin\frac{\pi}{6}$
    $1/z_1 = \frac{1}{2}\left[\cos\left(-\frac{\pi}{6}\right) + i\sin\left(-\frac{\pi}{6}\right)\right] = \frac{1}{2}\left(\cos\frac{\pi}{6} - i\sin\frac{\pi}{6}\right)$

57. $z_1 = 2\sqrt{3} - 2i$. Then $\tan\theta_1 = \frac{-2}{2\sqrt{3}} = -\frac{1}{\sqrt{3}}$ with θ_1 in quadrant IV $\Rightarrow$ $\theta_1 = \frac{11\pi}{6}$, and $r_1 = \sqrt{12+4} = 4$.
    $z_2 = -1 + i$. Then $\tan\theta_2 = -1$ with θ_2 in quadrant II $\Rightarrow$ $\theta_2 = \frac{3\pi}{4}$, and $r_2 = \sqrt{1+1} = \sqrt{2}$.
    Hence, $z_1 = 4\left(\cos\frac{11\pi}{6} + i\sin\frac{11\pi}{6}\right)$ and $z_2 = \sqrt{2}\left(\cos\frac{3\pi}{4} + i\sin\frac{3\pi}{4}\right)$.
    $z_1 z_2 = 4\cdot\sqrt{2}\left[\cos\left(\frac{11\pi}{6} + \frac{3\pi}{4}\right) + i\sin\left(\frac{11\pi}{6} + \frac{3\pi}{4}\right)\right] = 4\sqrt{2}\left(\cos\frac{7\pi}{12} + i\sin\frac{7\pi}{12}\right)$
    $z_1/z_2 = \frac{4}{\sqrt{2}}\left[\cos\left(\frac{11\pi}{6} - \frac{3\pi}{4}\right) + i\sin\left(\frac{11\pi}{6} - \frac{3\pi}{4}\right)\right] = 2\sqrt{2}\left(\cos\frac{13\pi}{12} + i\sin\frac{13\pi}{12}\right)$
    $1/z_1 = \frac{1}{4}\left(\cos\left(-\frac{11\pi}{6}\right) + i\sin\left(-\frac{11\pi}{6}\right)\right) = \frac{1}{4}\left(\cos\frac{11\pi}{6} - i\sin\frac{11\pi}{6}\right)$

59. $z_1 = 5 + 5i$. Then $\tan\theta_1 = \frac{5}{5} = 1$ with θ_1 in quadrant I $\Rightarrow$ $\theta_1 = \frac{\pi}{4}$, and $r_1 = \sqrt{25+25} = 5\sqrt{2}$.
    $z_2 = 4$. Then $\theta_2 = 0$, and $r_2 = 4$.

Hence, $z_1 = 5\sqrt{2}\left(\cos\frac{\pi}{4} + i\sin\frac{\pi}{4}\right)$ and $z_2 = 4\left(\cos 0 + i\sin 0\right)$.

$z_1 z_2 = 5\sqrt{2} \cdot 4\left[\cos(\frac{\pi}{4} + 0) + i\sin(\frac{\pi}{4} + 0)\right] = 20\sqrt{2}\left(\cos\frac{\pi}{4} + i\sin\frac{\pi}{4}\right)$

$z_1/z_2 = \frac{5\sqrt{2}}{4}\left(\cos\frac{\pi}{4} + i\sin\frac{\pi}{4}\right)$

$1/z_1 = \frac{1}{5\sqrt{2}}\left(\cos(-\frac{\pi}{4}) + i\sin(-\frac{\pi}{4})\right) = \frac{\sqrt{2}}{10}\left(\cos\frac{\pi}{4} - i\sin\frac{\pi}{4}\right)$

61. $z_1 = -20$. Then $\theta_1 = \pi$, and $r_1 = 20$.

$z_2 = \sqrt{3} + i$. Then $\tan\theta_2 = \frac{1}{\sqrt{3}}$ with θ_2 in quadrant I $\quad\Rightarrow\quad$ $\theta_2 = \frac{\pi}{6}$, and $r_2 = \sqrt{3+1} = 2$.

Hence, $z_1 = 20\left(\cos\pi + i\sin\pi\right)$ and $z_2 = 2\left(\cos\frac{\pi}{6} + i\sin\frac{\pi}{6}\right)$.

$z_1 z_2 = 20 \cdot 2\left[\cos(\pi + \frac{\pi}{6}) + i\sin(\pi + \frac{\pi}{6})\right] = 40\left(\cos\frac{7\pi}{6} + i\sin\frac{7\pi}{6}\right)$

$z_1/z_2 = \frac{20}{2}\left[\cos(\pi - \frac{\pi}{6}) + i\sin(\pi - \frac{\pi}{6})\right] = 10\left(\cos\frac{5\pi}{6} + i\sin\frac{5\pi}{6}\right)$

$1/z_1 = \frac{1}{20}\left[\cos(-\pi) + i\sin(-\pi)\right] = \frac{1}{20}\left(\cos\pi - i\sin\pi\right)$

63. From Exercise 1: $1 + i = \sqrt{2}\left(\cos\frac{\pi}{4} + i\sin\frac{\pi}{4}\right)$. Thus,

$(1 + i)^{20} = (\sqrt{2})^{20}\left(\cos 20(\frac{\pi}{4}) + i\sin 20(\frac{\pi}{4})\right) = (2^{1/2})^{20}\left(\cos 5\pi + i\sin 5\pi\right)$

$= 2^{10}(-1 + 0i) = -1024$

65. $r = \sqrt{12 + 4} = 4$ and $\tan\theta = \frac{2}{2\sqrt{3}} = \frac{1}{\sqrt{3}}$ $\quad\Rightarrow\quad$ $\theta = \frac{\pi}{6}$. Thus $2\sqrt{3} + 2i = 4\left(\cos\frac{\pi}{6} + i\sin\frac{\pi}{6}\right)$.

So, $(2\sqrt{3} + 2i)^5 = 4^5\left(\cos\frac{5\pi}{6} + i\sin\frac{5\pi}{6}\right) = 1024\left(-\frac{\sqrt{3}}{2} + \frac{1}{2}i\right) = 512\left(-\sqrt{3} + i\right)$

67. $r = \sqrt{\frac{1}{2} + \frac{1}{2}} = 1$ and $\tan\theta = 1$ $\quad\Rightarrow\quad$ $\theta = \frac{\pi}{4}$. Thus $\frac{\sqrt{2}}{2} + \frac{\sqrt{2}}{2}i = \cos\frac{\pi}{4} + i\sin\frac{\pi}{4}$. Therefore,

$(\frac{\sqrt{2}}{2} + \frac{\sqrt{2}}{2}i)^{12} = \cos 12(\frac{\pi}{4}) + i\sin 12(\frac{\pi}{4}) = \cos 3\pi + i\sin 3\pi = -1$

69. $r = \sqrt{4 + 4} = 4\sqrt{2}$ and $\tan\theta = -1$ with θ in quadrant IV $\quad\Rightarrow\quad$ $\theta = \frac{7\pi}{4}$. Thus

$2 - 2i = 2\sqrt{2}\left(\cos\frac{7\pi}{4} + i\sin\frac{7\pi}{4}\right)$. So, $(2 - 2i)^8 = (2\sqrt{2})^8\left(\cos 14\pi + i\sin 14\pi\right)$

$= 4096\left(1 - 0i\right) = 4096$

71. $r = \sqrt{1 + 1} = \sqrt{2}$ and $\tan\theta = 1$ with θ in quadrant III $\quad\Rightarrow\quad$ $\theta = \frac{5\pi}{4}$. Thus

$-1 - i = \sqrt{2}\left(\cos\frac{5\pi}{4} + i\sin\frac{5\pi}{4}\right)$. Thus, $(-1 - i)^7 = (\sqrt{2})^7\left(\cos\frac{35\pi}{4} + i\sin\frac{35\pi}{4}\right)$

$= 8\sqrt{2}\left(\cos\frac{3\pi}{4} + i\sin\frac{3\pi}{4}\right) = 8\sqrt{2}\left(\frac{1}{\sqrt{2}} - i\frac{1}{\sqrt{2}}\right) = 8\left(-1 + i\right)$

73. $r = \sqrt{12 + 4} = 4$ and $\tan\theta = \frac{2}{2\sqrt{3}} = \frac{1}{\sqrt{3}}$ $\quad\Rightarrow\quad$ $\theta = \frac{\pi}{6}$. Thus $2\sqrt{3} + 2i = 4\left(\cos\frac{\pi}{6} + i\sin\frac{\pi}{6}\right)$.

So, $(2\sqrt{3} + 2i)^{-5} = \left(\frac{1}{4}\right)^5\left(\cos\frac{-5\pi}{6} + i\sin\frac{-5\pi}{6}\right) = \frac{1}{1024}\left(-\frac{\sqrt{3}}{2} - \frac{1}{2}i\right) = \frac{1}{2048}\left(-\sqrt{3} - i\right)$

75. $r = \sqrt{48 + 16} = 8$ and $\tan\theta = \frac{4}{4\sqrt{3}} = \frac{1}{\sqrt{3}}$ $\quad\Rightarrow\quad$ $\theta = \frac{\pi}{6}$. Thus

$4\sqrt{3} + 4i = 8\left(\cos\frac{\pi}{6} + i\sin\frac{\pi}{6}\right)$. So,

$(4\sqrt{3} + 4i)^{1/2} = \sqrt{8}\left[\cos\left(\frac{\pi/6 + 2k\pi}{2}\right) + i\sin\left(\frac{\pi/6 + 2k\pi}{2}\right)\right]$, for $k = 0, 1$.

Thus the two roots are $w_0 = 2\sqrt{2}\left(\cos\frac{\pi}{12} + i\sin\frac{\pi}{12}\right)$ and

$w_1 = 2\sqrt{2}\left(\cos\frac{13\pi}{12} + i\sin\frac{13\pi}{12}\right)$

77. $-81i = 81\left(\cos\frac{3\pi}{2} + i\sin\frac{3\pi}{2}\right)$. Thus, $(-81i)^{1/4} = 81^{1/4}$
$\left[\cos\left(\frac{3\pi/2+2k\pi}{4}\right) + i\sin\left(\frac{3\pi/2+2k\pi}{4}\right)\right]$ for $k = 0, 1, 2, 3$. The four roots
are $w_0 = 3\left(\cos\frac{3\pi}{8} + i\sin\frac{3\pi}{8}\right)$, $w_1 = 3\left(\cos\frac{7\pi}{8} + i\sin\frac{7\pi}{8}\right)$,
$w_2 = 3\left(\cos\frac{11\pi}{8} + i\sin\frac{11\pi}{8}\right)$, and $w_3 = 3\left(\cos\frac{15\pi}{8} + i\sin\frac{15\pi}{8}\right)$

79. $1 = \cos 0 + i\sin 0$. Thus, $1^{1/8} = \cos\frac{2k\pi}{8} + i\sin\frac{2k\pi}{8}$, for $k = 0, 1, 2$,
3, 4, 5, 6, 7. So, the eight roots are $w_0 = \cos 0 + i\sin 0 = 1$,
$w_1 = \cos\frac{\pi}{4} + i\sin\frac{\pi}{4} = \frac{\sqrt{2}}{2} + i\frac{\sqrt{2}}{2}$, $w_2 = \cos\frac{\pi}{2} + i\sin\frac{\pi}{2} = i$,
$w_3 = \cos\frac{3\pi}{4} + i\sin\frac{3\pi}{4} = -\frac{\sqrt{2}}{2} + i\frac{\sqrt{2}}{2}$, $w_4 = \cos\pi + i\sin\pi = -1$,
$w_5 = \cos\frac{5\pi}{4} + i\sin\frac{5\pi}{4} = -\frac{\sqrt{2}}{2} - i\frac{\sqrt{2}}{2}$, $w_6 = \cos\frac{3\pi}{2} + i\sin\frac{3\pi}{2} = -i$,
and $w_7 = \cos\frac{7\pi}{4} + i\sin\frac{7\pi}{4} = \frac{\sqrt{2}}{2} - i\frac{\sqrt{2}}{2}$.

81. $i = \cos\frac{\pi}{2} + i\sin\frac{\pi}{2}$. So, $i^{1/3} = \cos\left(\frac{\pi/2+2k\pi}{3}\right) + i\sin\left(\frac{\pi/2+2k\pi}{3}\right)$ for
$k = 0, 1, 2$. Thus the three roots are $w_0 = \cos\frac{\pi}{6} + i\sin\frac{\pi}{6}$
$= \frac{\sqrt{3}}{2} + \frac{1}{2}i$, $w_1 = \cos\frac{5\pi}{6} + i\sin\frac{5\pi}{6} = -\frac{\sqrt{3}}{2} + \frac{1}{2}i$,
and $w_2 = \cos\frac{3\pi}{2} + i\sin\frac{3\pi}{2} = -i$.

83. $-1 = \cos\pi + i\sin\pi$. Then $(-1)^{1/4} = \cos\left(\frac{\pi+2k\pi}{4}\right) + i\sin\left(\frac{\pi+2k\pi}{4}\right)$ for
$k = 0, 1, 2, 3$. So, the four roots are
$w_0 = \cos\frac{\pi}{4} + i\sin\frac{\pi}{4} = \frac{\sqrt{2}}{2} + i\frac{\sqrt{2}}{2}$, $w_1 = \cos\frac{3\pi}{4} + i\sin\frac{3\pi}{4}$
$= -\frac{\sqrt{2}}{2} + i\frac{\sqrt{2}}{2}$, $w_2 = \cos\frac{5\pi}{4} + i\sin\frac{5\pi}{4} = -\frac{\sqrt{2}}{2} - i\frac{\sqrt{2}}{2}$, and
$w_3 = \cos\frac{7\pi}{4} + i\sin\frac{7\pi}{4} = \frac{\sqrt{2}}{2} - i\frac{\sqrt{2}}{2}$.

85. $z^4 + 1 = 0 \Leftrightarrow z = (-1)^{1/4} = \frac{\sqrt{2}}{2}(\pm1 \pm i)$ (from Exercise 59).

87. $z^3 - 4\sqrt{3} - 4i = 0 \Leftrightarrow z = (4\sqrt{3} + 4i)^{1/3}$. Since $4\sqrt{3} + 4i = 8\left(\cos\frac{\pi}{6} + i\sin\frac{\pi}{6}\right)$,
$\left(4\sqrt{3} + 4i\right)^{1/3} = 8^{1/3}\left[\cos\left(\frac{\pi/6+2k\pi}{3}\right) + i\sin\left(\frac{\pi/6+2k\pi}{3}\right)\right]$, for $k = 0, 1, 2$. Thus there are three roots
$z = 2\left(\cos\frac{\pi}{18} + i\sin\frac{\pi}{18}\right)$, $z = 2\left(\cos\frac{13\pi}{18} + i\sin\frac{13\pi}{8}\right)$, $z = 2\left(\cos\frac{25\pi}{18} + i\sin\frac{25\pi}{18}\right)$

89. $z^3 + 1 = -i \Rightarrow z = (-1-i)^{1/3}$. Since $-1-i = \sqrt{2}\left(\cos\frac{5\pi}{4} + i\sin\frac{5\pi}{4}\right)$,
$z = (-1-i)^{1/3} = 2^{1/6}\left[\cos\left(\frac{5\pi/4+2k\pi}{3}\right) + i\sin\left(\frac{5\pi/4+2k\pi}{3}\right)\right]$ for $k = 0, 1, 2$. Thus the three solutions to
this equation are $z = 2^{1/6}\left[\cos\frac{5\pi}{12} + i\sin\frac{5\pi}{12}\right]$, $2^{1/6}\left[\cos\frac{13\pi}{12} + i\sin\frac{13\pi}{12}\right]$, and $2^{1/6}\left[\cos\frac{21\pi}{12} + i\sin\frac{21\pi}{12}\right]$.

91. (a) $w = \cos\frac{2\pi}{n} + i\sin\frac{2\pi}{n}$ for a positive integer n. Then, $w^k = \cos\frac{2k\pi}{n} + i\sin\frac{2k\pi}{n}$. Now
$w^0 = \cos 0 + i\sin 0 = 1$ and for $k \neq 0$, $(w^k)^n = \cos 2k\pi + i\sin 2k\pi = 1$. So the nth roots of

1 are $\cos \frac{2k\pi}{n} + i \sin \frac{2k\pi}{n} = w^k$ for $k = 0, 1, 2, \ldots, n-1$. In other words, the nth roots of 1 are $w^0, w^1, w^2, w^3, \ldots, w^{n-1}$ or $1, w, w^2, w^3, \ldots, w^{n-1}$.

(b) For $k = 0, 1, \ldots, n-1$, we have $(sw^k)^n = s^n(w^k)^n = z \cdot 1 = z$, so sw^k are nth roots of z for $k = 0, 1, \ldots, n-1$.

93. The cube roots of 1 are $w^0 = 1$, $w^1 = \cos \frac{2\pi}{3} + i \sin \frac{2\pi}{3}$, $w^2 = \cos \frac{4\pi}{3} + i \sin \frac{4\pi}{3}$ so $w^0 \cdot w^1 \cdot w^2 = (1)\left(\cos \frac{2\pi}{3} + i \sin \frac{2\pi}{3}\right)\left(\cos \frac{4\pi}{3} + i \sin \frac{4\pi}{3}\right) = \cos 2\pi + i \sin 2\pi = 1$.

The fourth roots of 1 are $w^0 = 1$, $w^1 = i$, $w^2 = -1$, $w^3 = -i$. So the product of the four fourth roots of 1 is: $w^0 \cdot w^1 \cdot w^2 \cdot w^3 = (1) \cdot (i) \cdot (-1) \cdot (-i) = i^2 = -1$.

The fifth roots of 1 are $w^0 = 1$, $w^1 = \cos \frac{2\pi}{5} + i \sin \frac{2\pi}{5}$, $w^2 = \cos \frac{4\pi}{5} + i \sin \frac{4\pi}{5}$, $w^3 = \cos \frac{6\pi}{5} + i \sin \frac{6\pi}{5}$, $w^4 = \cos \frac{8\pi}{5} + i \sin \frac{8\pi}{5}$. So the product of the five fifth roots of 1 is: $1(\cos \frac{2\pi}{5} + i \sin \frac{2\pi}{5})(\cos \frac{4\pi}{5} + i \sin \frac{4\pi}{5})(\cos \frac{6\pi}{5} + i \sin \frac{6\pi}{5})(\cos \frac{8\pi}{5} + i \sin \frac{8\pi}{5}) = \cos 4\pi + i \sin 4\pi = 1$.

The sixth roots of 1 are $w^0 = 1$, $w^1 = \cos \frac{\pi}{3} + i \sin \frac{\pi}{3}$, $w^2 = \cos \frac{2\pi}{3} + i \sin \frac{2\pi}{3}$, $w^3 = -1$, $w^4 = \cos \frac{4\pi}{3} + i \sin \frac{4\pi}{3}$, $w^5 = \cos \frac{5\pi}{3} + i \sin \frac{5\pi}{3}$. So the product of the six sixth roots of 1 is: $1(\cos \frac{\pi}{3} + i \sin \frac{\pi}{3})(\cos \frac{2\pi}{3} + i \sin \frac{2\pi}{3})(-1)(\cos \frac{4\pi}{3} + i \sin \frac{4\pi}{3})(\cos \frac{5\pi}{3} + i \sin \frac{5\pi}{3})$
$= \cos 5\pi + i \sin 5\pi = -1$.

The eight roots of 1 are $w^0 = 1$, $w^1 = \cos \frac{\pi}{4} + i \sin \frac{\pi}{4}$, $w^2 = i$, $w^3 = \cos \frac{3\pi}{4} + i \sin \frac{3\pi}{4}$, $w^4 = -1$, $w^5 = \cos \frac{5\pi}{4} + i \sin \frac{5\pi}{4}$, $w^6 = -i$, $w^7 = \cos \frac{7\pi}{4} + i \sin \frac{7\pi}{4}$. So the product of the eight eighth roots of 1 is: $1\left(\cos \frac{\pi}{4} + i \sin \frac{\pi}{4}\right) i \left(\cos \frac{3\pi}{4} + i \sin \frac{3\pi}{4}\right)(-1)\left(\cos \frac{5\pi}{4} + i \sin \frac{5\pi}{4}\right)(-i)\left(\cos \frac{7\pi}{4} + i \sin \frac{7\pi}{4}\right)$
$= i^2 \cdot (\cos 2\pi + i \sin 2\pi) = -1$.

The product of the nth roots of 1 is -1 if n is even and 1 if n is odd.

Proof. This proof requires one fact that will be proved in Chapter 12: The sum of the first m integers is $\frac{m(m+1)}{2}$.

Let $w = \cos \frac{2\pi}{n} + i \sin \frac{2\pi}{n}$. Then, $w^k = \cos \frac{2k\pi}{n} + i \sin \frac{2k\pi}{n}$ for $k = 0, 1, 2, \ldots, n-1$. The argument of the product of the n roots of unity can be found by adding the arguments of each w^k. So the argument of the product is $\theta = 0 + \frac{2(1)\pi}{n} + \frac{2(2)\pi}{n} + \frac{2(3)\pi}{n} + \cdots + \frac{2(n-2)\pi}{n} + \frac{2(n-1)\pi}{n}$
$= \frac{2\pi}{n}[0 + 1 + 2 + 3 + \cdots + (n-2) + (n-1)]$. Since this is the sum of the first $n-1$ integers, this sum is $\frac{2\pi}{n} \cdot \frac{(n-1)(n)}{2} = (n-1)\pi$. Thus the product of the n roots of unity is $\cos[(n-1)\pi] + i \sin[(n-1)\pi] = -1$ if n is even and 1 if n is odd.

Exercises 7.7

1. $2\mathbf{u} = 2\langle -2, 3 \rangle = \langle -4, 6 \rangle$

3. $\mathbf{u} + \mathbf{v} = \langle -2, 3 \rangle + \langle 3, 4 \rangle$
    $= \langle -2 + 3, 3 + 4 \rangle = \langle 1, 7 \rangle$

5. $\mathbf{v} - 2\mathbf{u} = \langle 3, 4 \rangle - 2\langle -2, 3 \rangle$
    $= \langle 3 - 2(-2), 4 - 2(3) \rangle = \langle 7, -2 \rangle$

In Exercises 7 – 15, $\mathbf{v}$ represents the vector with initial point P and terminal point Q.

7. $P(2, 1), Q(5, 4).\ \mathbf{v} = \langle 5 - 2, 4 - 1 \rangle = \langle 3, 3 \rangle$

9. $P(1, 2), Q(4, 1).\ \mathbf{v} = \langle 4 - 1, 1 - 2 \rangle = \langle 3, -1 \rangle$

11. $P(3, 2), Q(8, 9).\ \mathbf{v} = \langle 8 - 3, 9 - 2 \rangle = \langle 5, 7 \rangle$

13. $P(5, 3), Q(1, 0).\ \mathbf{v} = \langle 1 - 5, 0 - 3 \rangle = \langle -4, -3 \rangle$

15. $P(-1, -1), Q(-1, 1).\ \mathbf{v} = \langle -1 - (-1), 1 - (-1) \rangle = \langle 0, 2 \rangle$

17. $\mathbf{u} = \langle 2, 7 \rangle, \mathbf{v} = \langle 3, 1 \rangle.\ 2\mathbf{u} = 2 \cdot \langle 2, 7 \rangle = \langle 4, 14 \rangle;\ -3\mathbf{v} = -3 \cdot \langle 3, 1 \rangle = \langle -9, -3 \rangle;$
    $\mathbf{u} + \mathbf{v} = \langle 2, 7 \rangle + \langle 3, 1 \rangle = \langle 5, 8 \rangle;\ 3\mathbf{u} - 4\mathbf{v} = \langle 6, 21 \rangle - \langle 12, 4 \rangle = \langle -6, 17 \rangle$

19. $\mathbf{u} = \langle 0, -1 \rangle, \mathbf{v} = \langle -2, 0 \rangle.\ 2\mathbf{u} = 2 \cdot \langle 0, -1 \rangle = \langle 0, -2 \rangle;\ -3\mathbf{v} = -3 \cdot \langle -2, 0 \rangle = \langle 6, 0 \rangle;$
    $\mathbf{u} + \mathbf{v} = \langle 0, -1 \rangle + \langle -2, 0 \rangle = \langle -2, -1 \rangle;\ 3\mathbf{u} - 4\mathbf{v} = \langle 0, -3 \rangle - \langle -8, 0 \rangle = \langle 8, -3 \rangle$

21. $\mathbf{u} = 2\mathbf{i}, \mathbf{v} = 3\mathbf{i} - 2\mathbf{j}.\ 2\mathbf{u} = 2 \cdot 2\mathbf{i} = 4\mathbf{i};\ -3\mathbf{v} = -3(3\mathbf{i} - 2\mathbf{j}) = -9\mathbf{i} + 6\mathbf{j};$
    $\mathbf{u} + \mathbf{v} = 2\mathbf{i} + 3\mathbf{i} - 2\mathbf{j} = 5\mathbf{i} - 2\mathbf{j};\ 3\mathbf{u} - 4\mathbf{v} = 3 \cdot 2\mathbf{i} - 4(3\mathbf{i} - 2\mathbf{j}) = -6\mathbf{i} + 8\mathbf{j}$

23. $\mathbf{u} = 2\mathbf{i} + \mathbf{j}, \mathbf{v} = 3\mathbf{i} - 2\mathbf{j}.$ Then $|\mathbf{u}| = \sqrt{2^2 + 1^2} = \sqrt{5};\ |\mathbf{v}| = \sqrt{3^2 + 2^2} = \sqrt{13};\ 2\mathbf{u} = 4\mathbf{i} + 2\mathbf{j};$
    $|2\mathbf{u}| = \sqrt{4^2 + 2^2} = 2\sqrt{5};\ \frac{1}{2}\mathbf{v} = \frac{3}{2}\mathbf{i} - \mathbf{j};\ |\frac{1}{2}\mathbf{v}| = \sqrt{\left(\frac{3}{2}\right)^2 + 1^2} = \frac{1}{2}\sqrt{13};\ \mathbf{u} + \mathbf{v} = 5\mathbf{i} - \mathbf{j};$
    $|\mathbf{u} + \mathbf{v}| = \sqrt{5^2 + 1^2} = \sqrt{26};\ \mathbf{u} - \mathbf{v} = 2\mathbf{i} + \mathbf{j} - 3\mathbf{i} + 2\mathbf{j} = -\mathbf{i} + 3\mathbf{j};$
    $|\mathbf{u} - \mathbf{v}| = \sqrt{1^2 + 3^2} = \sqrt{10};\ |\mathbf{u}| - |\mathbf{v}| = \sqrt{5} - \sqrt{13}$

25. $\mathbf{u} = \langle 10, -1 \rangle, \mathbf{v} = \langle -2, -2 \rangle.$ Then $|\mathbf{u}| = \sqrt{10^2 + 1^2} = \sqrt{101};\ |\mathbf{v}| = \sqrt{(-2)^2 + (-2)^2} = 2\sqrt{2};$
    $2\mathbf{u} = \langle 20, -2 \rangle;\ |2\mathbf{u}| = \sqrt{20^2 + 2^2} = \sqrt{404} = 2\sqrt{101};\ \frac{1}{2}\mathbf{v} = \langle -1, -1 \rangle;$

$|\frac{1}{2}\mathbf{v}| = \sqrt{(-1)^2 + (-1)^2} = \sqrt{2}; \ \mathbf{u} + \mathbf{v} = \langle 8, -3 \rangle; \ |\mathbf{u} + \mathbf{v}| = \sqrt{8^2 + 3^2} = \sqrt{73}; \ \mathbf{u} - \mathbf{v} = \langle 12, 1 \rangle;$
$|\mathbf{u} - \mathbf{v}| = \sqrt{12^2 + 1^2} = \sqrt{145}; \ |\mathbf{u}| - |\mathbf{v}| = \sqrt{101} - 2\sqrt{2}$

In Exercises 27 – 33, x represents the horizontal component and y the vertical component.

27. $|\mathbf{v}| = 40$, direction $\theta = 30°$. $x = 40 \cos 30° = 20\sqrt{3}$, $y = 40 \sin 30° = 20$. Thus,
$\mathbf{v} = x\mathbf{i} + y\mathbf{j} = 20\sqrt{3}\,\mathbf{i} + 20\mathbf{j}$

29. $|\mathbf{v}| = 1$, direction $\theta = 225°$. $x = \cos 225° = -\frac{1}{\sqrt{2}}$, $y = \sin 225° = -\frac{1}{\sqrt{2}}$. Thus,
$\mathbf{v} = x\mathbf{i} + y\mathbf{j} = -\frac{1}{\sqrt{2}}\mathbf{i} - \frac{1}{\sqrt{2}}\mathbf{j} = -\frac{\sqrt{2}}{2}\mathbf{i} - \frac{\sqrt{2}}{2}\mathbf{j}$

31. $|\mathbf{v}| = 4$, direction $\theta = 10°$. $x = 4\cos 10° \approx 3.94$, $y = 4\sin 10° \approx 0.69$. Thus,
$\mathbf{v} = x\mathbf{i} + y\mathbf{j} = (4\cos 10°)\mathbf{i} + (4\sin 10°)\mathbf{j} \approx 3.94\mathbf{i} + 0.69\mathbf{j}$

33. $|\mathbf{v}| = 30$, direction $\theta = 30°$. $x = 30\cos 30° = 30 \cdot \frac{\sqrt{3}}{2} \approx 25.98$, $y = 30\sin 30° = 15$. So, the
horizontal component of force is $15\sqrt{3}$ lb and the vertical component is -15 lb.

35. $\mathbf{v} = \langle 3, 4 \rangle$. The magnitude is $|\mathbf{v}| = \sqrt{3^2 + 4^2} = 5$. The direction is $\tan \theta = \frac{4}{3}$ $\Leftrightarrow$
$\theta = \tan^{-1}\left(\frac{4}{3}\right) \approx 53.13°$

37. $\mathbf{v} = \langle -12, 5 \rangle$. The magnitude is $|\mathbf{v}| = \sqrt{(-12)^2 + 5^2} = \sqrt{169} = 13$. The direction is θ where
$\tan \theta = -\frac{5}{12}$ with θ in quadrant II $\Leftrightarrow$ $\theta = \tan^{-1}\left(-\frac{5}{12}\right) \approx 157.38°$

39. $\mathbf{v} = \mathbf{i} + \sqrt{3}\,\mathbf{j}$. The magnitude is $|\mathbf{v}| = \sqrt{1^2 + (\sqrt{3})^2} = 2$. The direction is θ where $\tan \theta = \sqrt{3}$
with θ in quadrant I $\Leftrightarrow$ $\theta = \tan^{-1}\sqrt{3} = 60°$

41. The flow of the river can be represented by the vextor $\mathbf{v} = -3\mathbf{j}$ and the swimmer can be represented
by the vector $\mathbf{u} = 2\mathbf{i}$. Therefore the true velocity is $\mathbf{u} + \mathbf{v} = 2\mathbf{i} - 3\mathbf{j}$.

43. (a) The velocity of the wind is $\langle 0, 40 \rangle$.

(b) The velocity of the jet relative to the air is $\langle 425, 0 \rangle$.

(c) The true velocity of the jet is $\mathbf{v} = 425\,\mathbf{i} + 40\,\mathbf{j} = \langle 425, 40 \rangle$.

(d) The true speed of the jet is $|\mathbf{v}| = \sqrt{425^2 + 40^2} \approx 427$ mi/h, and the true direction is
$\theta = \tan^{-1}\left(\frac{40}{425}\right) \approx 5.4°$ $\Rightarrow$ θ is N 84.6° E.

45. If the direction of the plane is N 30° W, the airplane speed is $\mathbf{u} = \langle u_x, u_y \rangle$ where $u_x = -765 \cos 60°$
$= -382.5$, and $u_y = 765 \sin 60° \approx 662.51$. If the direction of the wind is N 30° E, the wind speed
is $\mathbf{w} = \langle w_x, w_y \rangle$ where $w_x = 55 \cos 60° = 27.5$, and $w_y = 55 \sin 60° \approx 47.63$. Thus, the actual
flight path is $\mathbf{v} = \mathbf{u} + \mathbf{w} = \langle -382.5 + 27.5, 662.51 + 47.63 \rangle = \langle -355, 710.14 \rangle$, and so the true
speed is $|\mathbf{v}| = \sqrt{355^2 + 710.14^2} \approx 794$ mi/h, and the true direction is $\theta = \tan^{-1}\left(\frac{710.14}{-355}\right) \approx 116.6°$
so θ is N 26.6° W.

47. (a) The velocity of the river is represented by the vector $\mathbf{r} = \langle 10, 0 \rangle$.

(b) Since the boater direction is 60° from the shore at 20 mi/h, the velocity of the boat is
represented by the vector $\mathbf{b} = \langle 20 \cos 60°, 20 \sin 60° \rangle \approx \langle 10, 17.32 \rangle$.

(c) $\mathbf{w} = \mathbf{r} + \mathbf{b} = \langle 10 + 10, 0 + 17.32 \rangle = \langle 20, 17.32 \rangle$

(d)   The true speed of the boat is $|\mathbf{w}| = \sqrt{20^2 + 17.32^2} \approx 26.5$ mi/h, and the true direction is
$\theta = \tan^{-1}\left(\frac{17.32}{20}\right) \approx 40.9° \approx$ N $49.1°$ E.

49.   (a)   Let $\mathbf{b} = \langle b_x, b_y \rangle$ represent the velocity of the boat relative to the water. Then
$\mathbf{b} = \langle 24\cos 18°, 24\sin 18° \rangle$.

(b)   Let $\mathbf{w} = \langle w_x, w_y \rangle$ represent the velocity of the water. Then $\mathbf{w} = \langle 0, w \rangle$ where w is the speed
of the water. So the true velocity of the boat is $\mathbf{b} + \mathbf{w} = \langle 24\cos 18°, 24\sin 18° - w \rangle$. For the
direction to be due east, we must have $24\sin 18° - w = 0 \quad \Leftrightarrow \quad w = 7.42$ mi/h. Therefore,
the true speed of the water is 7.4 mi/h. Since $\mathbf{b} + \mathbf{w} = \langle 24\cos 18°, 0 \rangle$, the true speed of the
boat is $|\mathbf{b} + \mathbf{w}| = 24\cos 18° \approx 22.8$ mi/h.

51. $\mathbf{F}_1 = \langle 2, 5 \rangle, \mathbf{F}_2 = \langle 3, -8 \rangle$.

(a)   Then $\mathbf{F}_1 + \mathbf{F}_2 = \langle 2 + 3, 5 - 8 \rangle = \langle 5, -3 \rangle$.

(b)   The additional force required is $\mathbf{F}_3 = \langle 0, 0 \rangle - \langle 5, -3 \rangle = \langle -5, 3 \rangle$.

53. $\mathbf{F}_1 = 4\mathbf{i} - \mathbf{j}, \mathbf{F}_2 = 3\mathbf{i} - 7\mathbf{j}, \mathbf{F}_3 = -8\mathbf{i} + 3\mathbf{j}$, and $\mathbf{F}_4 = \mathbf{i} + \mathbf{j}$.

(a)   Then $\mathbf{F}_1 + \mathbf{F}_2 + \mathbf{F}_3 + \mathbf{F}_4 = (4 + 3 - 8 + 1)\mathbf{i} + (-1 - 7 + 3 + 1)\mathbf{j} = 0\mathbf{i} - 4\mathbf{j}$.

(b)   The additional force required is $\mathbf{F}_5 = 0\mathbf{i} + 0\mathbf{j} - (0\mathbf{i} - 4\mathbf{j}) = 4\mathbf{j}$.

55. $\mathbf{F}_1 = \langle 10\cos 60°, 10\sin 60° \rangle = \langle 5, 5\sqrt{3} \rangle, \mathbf{F}_2 = \langle -8\cos 30°, 8\sin 30° \rangle = \langle -4\sqrt{3}, 4 \rangle$, and
$\mathbf{F}_3 = \langle -6\cos 20°, -6\sin 20° \rangle \approx \langle -5.638, -2.052 \rangle$.

(a) $\mathbf{F}_1 + \mathbf{F}_2 + \mathbf{F}_3 = \langle 5 - 4\sqrt{3} - 5.638, 5\sqrt{3} + 4 - 2.052 \rangle \approx \langle -7.57, 10.61 \rangle$.

(b)   The additional force required is $\mathbf{F}_4 = \langle 0, 0 \rangle - \langle -7.57, 10.61 \rangle = \langle 7.57, -10.61 \rangle$.

57.   From the figure we see that $\mathbf{T}_1 = -|\mathbf{T}_1|\cos 50°\,\mathbf{i} + |\mathbf{T}_1|\sin 50°\,\mathbf{j}$ and
$\mathbf{T}_2 = |\mathbf{T}_2|\cos 30°\,\mathbf{i} + |\mathbf{T}_2|\sin 30°\,\mathbf{j}$. Since $\mathbf{T}_1 + \mathbf{T}_2 = 100\mathbf{j}$ we get
$-|\mathbf{T}_1|\cos 50° + |\mathbf{T}_2|\cos 30° = 0$ and $|\mathbf{T}_1|\sin 50° + |\mathbf{T}_2|\sin 30° = 100$. From the first equation
$|\mathbf{T}_2| = |\mathbf{T}_1|\frac{\cos 50°}{\cos 30°}$ and substituting into the second equation gives

$|\mathbf{T}_1|\sin 50° + |\mathbf{T}_1|\frac{\cos 50° \sin 30°}{\cos 30°} = 100 \quad \Leftrightarrow \quad |\mathbf{T}_1|(\sin 50° \cos 30° + \cos 50° \sin 30°)$

$= 100\cos 30° \quad \Leftrightarrow \quad |\mathbf{T}_1|\sin(50° + 30°) = 100\cos 30° \quad \Leftrightarrow \quad |\mathbf{T}_1| = 100\frac{\cos 30°}{\sin 80°} \approx 87.9416$.

Similarly, solving for $|\mathbf{T}_1|$ in the first equation gives $|\mathbf{T}_1| = |\mathbf{T}_2|\frac{\cos 30°}{\cos 50°}$ and substituting gives

$|\mathbf{T}_2|\frac{\cos 30° \sin 50°}{\cos 50°} + |\mathbf{T}_2|\sin 30° = 100 \quad \Leftrightarrow$

$|\mathbf{T}_2|(\cos 30° \sin 50° + \cos 50° \sin 30°) = 100\cos 50° \quad \Leftrightarrow \quad |\mathbf{T}_2| = \frac{100\cos 50°}{\sin 80°} \approx 65.2704$. Thus

$\mathbf{T}_1 \approx (-87.9416\cos 50°)\mathbf{i} + (87.9416\sin 50°)\mathbf{j} \approx -56.5\mathbf{i} + 67.4\mathbf{j}$ and

$\mathbf{T}_2 \approx (65.2704\cos 30°)\mathbf{i} + (65.2704\sin 30°)\mathbf{j} \approx 56.5\mathbf{i} + 32.6\mathbf{j}$.

59.   When we add two (or more vectors) the resultant vector can be found by first placing the initial point
of the second vector at the terminal point of the first vector. The resultant vector can then found by
using the new terminal point of the second vector and the initial point of the first vector. When the n
vectors are placed head to tail in the plane so that they form a polygon, the initial point and the
terminal point are the same. Thus the sum of these n vectors is the zero vector.

Exercises 7.8

1. (a) $\mathbf{u} \cdot \mathbf{v} = \langle 2, 0 \rangle \cdot \langle 1, 1 \rangle = 2 + 0 = 2$

   (b) $\cos\theta = \dfrac{\mathbf{u} \cdot \mathbf{v}}{|\mathbf{u}|\,|\mathbf{v}|} = \dfrac{2}{2\cdot\sqrt{2}} = \dfrac{1}{\sqrt{2}} \;\Rightarrow\; \theta = 45°$

3. (a) $\mathbf{u} \cdot \mathbf{v} = \langle 2, 7 \rangle \cdot \langle 3, 1 \rangle = 6 + 7 = 13$

   (b) $\cos\theta = \dfrac{\mathbf{u} \cdot \mathbf{v}}{|\mathbf{u}|\,|\mathbf{v}|} = \dfrac{13}{\sqrt{53}\cdot\sqrt{10}} \;\Rightarrow\; \theta \approx 56°$

5. (a) $\mathbf{u} \cdot \mathbf{v} = \langle 3, -2 \rangle \cdot \langle 1, 2 \rangle = 3 + (-4) = -1$

   (b) $\cos\theta = \dfrac{\mathbf{u} \cdot \mathbf{v}}{|\mathbf{u}|\,|\mathbf{v}|} = \dfrac{-1}{\sqrt{13}\cdot\sqrt{5}} \;\Rightarrow\; \theta \approx 97°$

7. (a) $\mathbf{u} \cdot \mathbf{v} = \langle 0, -5 \rangle \cdot \langle -1, -\sqrt{3} \rangle = 0 + 5\sqrt{3} = 5\sqrt{3}$

   (b) $\cos\theta = \dfrac{\mathbf{u} \cdot \mathbf{v}}{|\mathbf{u}|\,|\mathbf{v}|} = \dfrac{5\sqrt{3}}{5\cdot2} = \dfrac{\sqrt{3}}{2} \;\Rightarrow\; \theta = 30°$

9. $\mathbf{u} \cdot \mathbf{v} = -12 + 12 = 0 \;\Rightarrow\;$ vectors are orthogonal

11. $\mathbf{u} \cdot \mathbf{v} = -8 + 12 = 4 \neq 0 \;\Rightarrow\;$ vectors are not orthogonal

13. $\mathbf{u} \cdot \mathbf{v} = -24 + 24 = 0 \;\Rightarrow\;$ vectors are orthogonal

15. $\mathbf{u} \cdot \mathbf{v} + \mathbf{u} \cdot \mathbf{w} = \langle 2, 1 \rangle \cdot \langle 1, -3 \rangle + \langle 2, 1 \rangle \cdot \langle 3, 4 \rangle = 2 - 3 + 6 + 4 = 9$

17. $(\mathbf{u} + \mathbf{v}) \cdot (\mathbf{u} - \mathbf{v}) = [\langle 2, 1 \rangle + \langle 1, -3 \rangle] \cdot [\langle 2, 1 \rangle - \langle 1, -3 \rangle] = \langle 3, -2 \rangle \cdot \langle 1, 4 \rangle = 3 - 8 = -5$

19. $x = \dfrac{\mathbf{u} \cdot \mathbf{v}}{|\mathbf{v}|} = \dfrac{12-24}{5} = -\dfrac{12}{5}$

21. $x = \dfrac{\mathbf{u} \cdot \mathbf{v}}{|\mathbf{v}|} = \dfrac{0-24}{1} = -24$

23. (a) $\mathbf{u}_1 = \text{proj}_{\mathbf{v}}\mathbf{u} = \left(\dfrac{\mathbf{u} \cdot \mathbf{v}}{|\mathbf{v}|^2}\right)\mathbf{v} = \left(\dfrac{\langle -2,4 \rangle \cdot \langle 1,1 \rangle}{1^2+1^2}\right)\langle 1, 1 \rangle = \langle 1, 1 \rangle.$

    (b) $\mathbf{u}_2 = \mathbf{u} - \mathbf{u}_1 = \langle -2, 4 \rangle - \langle 1, 1 \rangle = \langle -3, 3 \rangle$

25. (a) $\mathbf{u}_1 = \text{proj}_{\mathbf{v}}\mathbf{u} = \left(\dfrac{\mathbf{u} \cdot \mathbf{v}}{|\mathbf{v}|^2}\right)\mathbf{v} = \left(\dfrac{\langle 1,2 \rangle \cdot \langle 1,-3 \rangle}{1^2+(-3)^2}\right)\langle 1, -3 \rangle = -\dfrac{1}{2}\langle 1, -3 \rangle = \langle -\dfrac{1}{2}, \dfrac{3}{2} \rangle$

    (b) $\mathbf{u}_2 = \mathbf{u} - \mathbf{u}_1 = \langle 1, 2 \rangle - \langle -\dfrac{1}{2}, \dfrac{3}{2} \rangle = \langle \dfrac{3}{2}, \dfrac{1}{2} \rangle$

27. (a) $\mathbf{u}_1 = \text{proj}_{\mathbf{v}}\mathbf{u} = \left(\dfrac{\mathbf{u} \cdot \mathbf{v}}{|\mathbf{v}|^2}\right)\mathbf{v} = \left(\dfrac{\langle 2,9 \rangle \cdot \langle -3,4 \rangle}{(-3)^3+4^2}\right)\langle -3, 4 \rangle = \dfrac{6}{5}\langle -3, 4 \rangle = \langle -\dfrac{18}{5}, \dfrac{24}{5} \rangle$

    (b) $\mathbf{u}_2 = \mathbf{u} - \mathbf{u}_1 = \langle 2, 9 \rangle - \langle -\dfrac{18}{5}, \dfrac{24}{5} \rangle = \langle \dfrac{28}{5}, \dfrac{21}{5} \rangle$

29. $W = \mathbf{F} \cdot \mathbf{d} = \langle 4, -5 \rangle \cdot \langle 3, 8 \rangle = -28$

31. $W = \mathbf{F} \cdot \mathbf{d} = \langle 10, 3 \rangle \cdot \langle 4, -5 \rangle = 25$

33. $W = \mathbf{F} \cdot \mathbf{d} = \langle 4, -7 \rangle \cdot \langle 4, 0 \rangle = 16$ ft-lb

35. The distance vector is $\mathbf{D} = \langle 200, 0 \rangle$ and the force vector is $\mathbf{F} = \langle 50 \cos 30°, 50 \sin 30° \rangle$. Hence, the work done is $W = \mathbf{F} \cdot \mathbf{D} = \langle 200, 0 \rangle \cdot \langle 50 \cos 30°, 50 \sin 30° \rangle = 200 \cdot 50 \cos 30° \approx 8660$ ft-lb.

37. Since the weight of the car is 2755 lb, the force exerted perpendicular to the earth is 2755 lb. Resolving this into a force $\mathbf{u}$ perpendicular to the driveway gives $|\mathbf{u}| = 2766 \cos 65° \approx 1164$ lb. Thus, a force of about 1164 lb is required.

39. Since the force required parallel to the driveway is 80 lb and the weight of the package is 200 lb, it follows that $80 = 200 \sin \theta$, where θ is the angle of inclination of the plane. Then $\theta = \sin^{-1}\left(\frac{80}{200}\right) \approx 23.58°$, and so the angle of inclination is approximately 23.6°.

41. Let $\mathbf{u} = \langle u_1, u_2 \rangle$ and $\mathbf{v} = \langle v_1, v_2 \rangle$. Then
$\mathbf{u} \cdot \mathbf{v} = \langle u_1, u_2 \rangle \cdot \langle v_1, v_2 \rangle = u_1 v_1 + u_2 v_2 = v_1 u_1 + v_2 u_2 = \langle v_1, v_2 \rangle \cdot \langle u_1, u_2 \rangle = \mathbf{v} \cdot \mathbf{u}$

43. Let $\mathbf{u} = \langle u_1, u_2 \rangle$, $\mathbf{v} = \langle v_1, v_2 \rangle$, and $\mathbf{w} = \langle w_1, w_2 \rangle$. Then
$(\mathbf{u} + \mathbf{v}) \cdot \mathbf{w} = (\langle u_1, u_2 \rangle + \langle v_1, v_2 \rangle) \cdot \langle w_1, w_2 \rangle = \langle u_1 + v_1, u_2 + v_2 \rangle \cdot \langle w_1, w_2 \rangle$
$\qquad = u_1 w_1 + v_1 w_1 + u_2 w_2 + v_2 w_2 = u_1 w_1 + u_2 w_2 + v_1 w_1 + v_2 w_2$
$\qquad = \langle u_1, u_2 \rangle \cdot \langle w_1, w_2 \rangle + \langle v_1, v_2 \rangle \cdot \langle w_1, w_2 \rangle = \mathbf{u} \cdot \mathbf{w} + \mathbf{v} \cdot \mathbf{w}$

45. We use the definition that $\text{proj}_{\mathbf{v}}\mathbf{u} = \left(\dfrac{\mathbf{u} \cdot \mathbf{v}}{|\mathbf{v}|^2}\right)\mathbf{v}$. Then

$$\text{proj}_{\mathbf{v}}\mathbf{u} \cdot (\mathbf{u} - \text{proj}_{\mathbf{v}}\mathbf{u}) = \left(\frac{\mathbf{u} \cdot \mathbf{v}}{|\mathbf{v}|^2}\right)\mathbf{v} \cdot \left[\mathbf{u} - \left(\frac{\mathbf{u} \cdot \mathbf{v}}{|\mathbf{v}|^2}\right)\mathbf{v}\right]$$

$$= \left(\frac{\mathbf{u} \cdot \mathbf{v}}{|\mathbf{v}|^2}\right)(\mathbf{v} \cdot \mathbf{u}) - \left(\frac{\mathbf{u} \cdot \mathbf{v}}{|\mathbf{v}|^2}\right)\mathbf{v} \cdot \left(\frac{\mathbf{u} \cdot \mathbf{v}}{|\mathbf{v}|^2}\right)\mathbf{v}$$

$$= \frac{(\mathbf{u} \cdot \mathbf{v})^2}{|\mathbf{v}|^2} - \frac{(\mathbf{u} \cdot \mathbf{v})^2}{|\mathbf{v}|^4}|\mathbf{v}|^2 = \frac{(\mathbf{u} \cdot \mathbf{v})^2}{|\mathbf{v}|^2} - \frac{(\mathbf{u} \cdot \mathbf{v})^2}{|\mathbf{v}|^2} = 0.$$

Thus $\mathbf{u}$ and $\mathbf{u} - \text{proj}_{\mathbf{v}}\mathbf{u}$ are orthogonal.

Review Exercises for Chapter 7

1. $\sin\theta(\cot\theta + \tan\theta) = \sin\theta\left(\dfrac{\cos\theta}{\sin\theta} + \dfrac{\sin\theta}{\cos\theta}\right) = \cos\theta + \dfrac{\sin^2\theta}{\cos\theta} = \dfrac{\cos^2\theta + \sin^2\theta}{\cos\theta} = \dfrac{1}{\cos\theta} = \sec\theta$

3. $\cos^2 x \csc x - \csc x = (1 - \sin^2 x)\csc x - \csc x = \csc x - \sin^2 x \csc x - \csc x$

     $= -\sin^2 x \cdot \dfrac{1}{\sin x} = -\sin x$

5. $\dfrac{\cos^2 x - \tan^2 x}{\sin^2 x} = \dfrac{\cos^2 x}{\sin^2 x} - \dfrac{\tan^2 x}{\sin^2 x} = \cot^2 x - \dfrac{1}{\cos^2 x} = \cot^2 x - \sec^2 x$

7. $\dfrac{\cos^2 x}{1 - \sin x} = \dfrac{\cos x}{\dfrac{1}{\cos x}(1 - \sin x)} = \dfrac{\cos x}{\dfrac{1}{\cos x} - \dfrac{\sin x}{\cos x}} = \dfrac{\cos x}{\sec x - \tan x}$

9. $\sin^2 x \cot^2 x + \cos^2 x \tan^2 x = \sin^2 x \cdot \dfrac{\cos^2 x}{\sin^2 x} + \cos^2 x \cdot \dfrac{\sin^2 x}{\cos^2 x} = \cos^2 x + \sin^2 x = 1$

11. $\dfrac{\sin 2x}{1 + \cos 2x} = \dfrac{2\sin x \cos x}{1 + 2\cos^2 x - 1} = \dfrac{2\sin x \cos x}{2\cos^2 x} = \dfrac{2\sin x}{2\cos x} = \tan x$

13. $\tan\dfrac{x}{2} = \dfrac{1 - \cos x}{\sin x} = \dfrac{1}{\sin x} - \dfrac{\cos x}{\sin x} = \csc x - \cot x$

15. $\sin(x + y)\sin(x - y) = \tfrac{1}{2}\left[\cos((x+y)-(x-y)) - \cos((x+y)+(x-y))\right]$

     $= \tfrac{1}{2}(\cos 2y - \cos 2x) = \tfrac{1}{2}\left[1 - 2\sin^2 y - (1 - 2\sin^2 x)\right] = \tfrac{1}{2}(2\sin^2 x - 2\sin^2 y) = \sin^2 x - \sin^2 y$

17. $1 + \tan x \tan\dfrac{x}{2} = 1 + \dfrac{\sin x}{\cos x}\cdot\dfrac{1 - \cos x}{\sin x} = 1 + \dfrac{1 - \cos x}{\cos x} = 1 + \dfrac{1}{\cos x} - 1 = \dfrac{1}{\cos x} = \sec x$

19. $\left(\cos\tfrac{x}{2} - \sin\tfrac{x}{2}\right)^2 = \cos^2\tfrac{x}{2} - 2\sin\tfrac{x}{2}\cos\tfrac{x}{2} + \sin^2\tfrac{x}{2} = \sin^2\tfrac{x}{2} + \cos^2\tfrac{x}{2} - 2\sin\tfrac{x}{2}\cos\tfrac{x}{2}$

     $= 1 - \sin(2\cdot\tfrac{x}{2}) = 1 - \sin x$

21. $\dfrac{\sin 2x}{\sin x} - \dfrac{\cos 2x}{\cos x} = \dfrac{2\sin x \cos x}{\sin x} - \dfrac{2\cos^2 x - 1}{\cos x} = 2\cos x - 2\cos x + \dfrac{1}{\cos x} = \sec x$

23. $\tan(x + \tfrac{\pi}{4}) = \dfrac{\tan x + \tan\tfrac{\pi}{4}}{1 - \tan x \tan\tfrac{\pi}{4}} = \dfrac{1 + \tan x}{1 - \tan x}$

25.   (a) $f(x) = 1 - \left(\cos\tfrac{x}{2} - \sin\tfrac{x}{2}\right)^2$,

         $g(x) = \sin x$

     (b)   The graphs suggest that $f(x) = g(x)$ is an identity. To prove this, expand $f(x)$ and simplify, using the double-angle formula for sine:

$$f(x) = 1 - \left(\cos\tfrac{x}{2} - \sin\tfrac{x}{2}\right)^2$$

$$= 1 - \left[\cos^2\tfrac{x}{2} - 2\cos\tfrac{x}{2}\sin\tfrac{x}{2} + \sin^2\tfrac{x}{2}\right]$$

$$= 1 + 2\cos\tfrac{x}{2}\sin\tfrac{x}{2} - \left[\cos^2\tfrac{x}{2} + \sin^2\tfrac{x}{2}\right]$$

$$= 1 + \sin x - (1) = \sin x = g(x)$$

27. (a) $f(x) = \tan x \tan \frac{x}{2}$, $g(x) = \dfrac{1}{\cos x}$

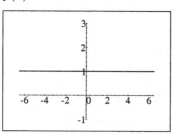

   (b) The graphs suggest that $f(x) \neq g(x)$ in general. For example, choose $x = \frac{\pi}{3}$ and evaluate:

$$f(\tfrac{\pi}{3}) = \tan \tfrac{\pi}{3} \tan \tfrac{\pi}{6} = \sqrt{3} \cdot \tfrac{1}{\sqrt{3}} = 1 \text{, whereas}$$

$$g(\tfrac{\pi}{3}) = \dfrac{1}{\tfrac{1}{2}} = 2 \text{, so } f(x) \neq g(x).$$

29. (a) $f(x) = 2 \sin^2 3x + \cos 6x$

   (b) The graph suggests that $f(x) = 1$ for all x. To prove this, we use the double angle formula to note that $\cos 6x = \cos[2(3x)] = 1 - 2 \sin^2 3x$,

   so $f(x) = 2 \sin^2 3x + (1 - 2 \sin^2 3x) = 1.$

31. $\cos x \sin x - \sin x = 0$ $\Leftrightarrow$ $\sin x (\cos x - 1) = 0$ $\Leftrightarrow$ $\sin x = 0$ or $\cos x = 1$ $\Leftrightarrow$
$x = 0$, π or $x = 0$. Therefore, the solutions are $x = 0$ and π.

33. $2 \sin^2 x - 5 \sin x + 2 = 0$ $\Leftrightarrow$ $(2 \sin x - 1)(\sin x - 2) = 0$ $\Leftrightarrow$ $\sin x = \frac{1}{2}$ or $\sin x = 2$ (which
is inadmissible) $\Leftrightarrow$ $x = \frac{\pi}{6}, \frac{5\pi}{6}$. Thus, the solutions in $[0, 2\pi)$ are $x = \frac{\pi}{6}$ and $\frac{5\pi}{6}$.

35. $2 \cos^2 x - 7 \cos x + 3 = 0$ $\Leftrightarrow$ $(2 \cos x - 1)(\cos x - 3) = 0$ $\Leftrightarrow$ $\cos x = \frac{1}{2}$ or $\cos x = 3$
(which is inadmissible) $\Leftrightarrow$ $x = \frac{\pi}{3}, \frac{5\pi}{3}$. Therefore, the solutions in $[0, 2\pi)$ are $x = \frac{\pi}{3}, \frac{5\pi}{3}$.

37. Note: $x = \pi$ is not a solution because then the denominator is zero. $\dfrac{1 - \cos x}{1 + \cos x} = 3$ $\Leftrightarrow$
$1 - \cos x = 3 + 3 \cos x$ $\Leftrightarrow$ $-4 \cos x = 2$ $\Leftrightarrow$ $\cos x = -\frac{1}{2}$ $\Leftrightarrow$ $x = \frac{2\pi}{3}, \frac{4\pi}{3}$ in $[0, 2\pi)$.

39. (factor by grouping) $\tan^3 x + \tan^2 x - 3 \tan x - 3 = 0$ $\Leftrightarrow$ $(\tan x + 1)(\tan^2 x - 3) = 0$ $\Leftrightarrow$
$\tan x = -1$ or $\tan x = \pm \sqrt{3}$ $\Leftrightarrow$ $x = \frac{3\pi}{4}, \frac{7\pi}{4}$ or $x = \frac{\pi}{3}, \frac{2\pi}{3}, \frac{4\pi}{3}, \frac{5\pi}{3}$. Therefore, the solutions in
$[0, 2\pi)$ are $x = \frac{\pi}{3}, \frac{2\pi}{3}, \frac{3\pi}{4}, \frac{4\pi}{3}, \frac{5\pi}{3}, \frac{7\pi}{4}$.

41. $\tan \frac{1}{2} x + 2 \sin 2x = \csc x$ $\Leftrightarrow$ $\dfrac{1 - \cos x}{\sin x} + 4 \sin x \cos x = \dfrac{1}{\sin x}$ $\Leftrightarrow$
$1 - \cos x + 4 \sin^2 x \cos x = 1$ $\Leftrightarrow$ $4 \sin^2 x \cos x - \cos x = 0$ $\Leftrightarrow$ $\cos x (4 \sin^2 x - 1) = 0$
$\Leftrightarrow$ $\cos x = 0$ or $\sin x = \pm \frac{1}{2}$ $\Leftrightarrow$ $x = \frac{\pi}{2}, \frac{3\pi}{2}$ or $x = \frac{\pi}{6}, \frac{5\pi}{6}, \frac{7\pi}{6}, \frac{11\pi}{6}$. Thus, the solutions in
$[0, 2\pi)$ are $x = \frac{\pi}{6}, \frac{\pi}{2}, \frac{5\pi}{6}, \frac{7\pi}{6}, \frac{3\pi}{2}, \frac{11\pi}{6}$.

43. $\tan x + \sec x = \sqrt{3}$ $\Leftrightarrow$ $\dfrac{\sin x}{\cos x} + \dfrac{1}{\cos x} = \sqrt{3}$ $\Leftrightarrow$ $\sin x + 1 = \sqrt{3} \cos x$ $\Leftrightarrow$
$\sqrt{3} \cos x - \sin x = 1$ $\Leftrightarrow$ $\frac{\sqrt{3}}{2} \cos x - \frac{1}{2} \sin x = \frac{1}{2}$ $\Leftrightarrow$ $\cos \frac{\pi}{6} \cos x - \sin \frac{\pi}{6} \sin x = \frac{1}{2}$ $\Leftrightarrow$
$\cos(x + \frac{\pi}{6}) = \frac{1}{2}$ $\Leftrightarrow$ $x + \frac{\pi}{6} = \frac{\pi}{3}, \frac{5\pi}{3}$ $\Leftrightarrow$ $x = \frac{\pi}{6}, \frac{3\pi}{2}$. However $x = \frac{3\pi}{2}$ is inadmissible
because $\sec \frac{3\pi}{2}$ is undefined. Thus, the only solution is in $[0, 2\pi)$ is $x = \frac{\pi}{6}$.

45. We graph $f(x) = \cos x$ and $g(x) = x^2 - 1$ in the viewing rectangle $[0, 6.5]$ by $[-2, 2]$. The two functions intersect at only one point, $x \approx 1.18$.

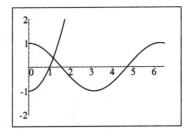

47. (a) $2000 = \dfrac{(400)^2 \sin\theta}{64} \quad\Leftrightarrow\quad \sin\theta = 0.8 \quad\Rightarrow\quad \theta = 53.1°.$

(b) $\dfrac{(400)^2 \sin\theta}{64} = 2500 \sin\theta \le 2500$. Therefore it is impossible for the projectile to reach a height of 3000 ft.

(c) The function $M(\theta) = 2500\sin\theta$ is maximized when $\sin\theta = 1$ so $\theta = 90°$. The projectile will travel the highest when it shoot straight up.

49. Since $15°$ is in quadrant I: $\cos 15° = \sqrt{\dfrac{1 + \cos 30°}{2}} = \sqrt{\dfrac{2+\sqrt3}{4}} = \dfrac12 \sqrt{2+\sqrt3}.$

51. $\tan\dfrac{\pi}{8} = \dfrac{1 - \cos\frac{\pi}{4}}{\sin\frac{\pi}{4}} = \dfrac{1 - \frac{1}{\sqrt2}}{\frac{1}{\sqrt2}} = \left(1 - \dfrac{1}{\sqrt2}\right)\sqrt2 = \sqrt2 - 1.$

53. $\sin 5° \cos 40° + \cos 5° \sin 40° = \sin(5° + 40°) = \sin 45° = \dfrac{1}{\sqrt2} = \dfrac{\sqrt2}{2}.$

55. $\cos^2\dfrac{\pi}{8} - \sin^2\dfrac{\pi}{8} = \cos\left(2\left(\dfrac{\pi}{8}\right)\right) = \cos\dfrac{\pi}{4} = \dfrac{1}{\sqrt2} = \dfrac{\sqrt2}{2}.$

57. $\cos 37.5° \cos 7.5° = \dfrac12 [\cos 45° + \cos 30°] = \dfrac12 \left[\dfrac{\sqrt2}{2} + \dfrac{\sqrt3}{2}\right] = \dfrac14 (\sqrt2 + \sqrt3)$. Note: We have used a product-to-sum identity.

In Exercises 59 – 63, x and y are in quadrant I, so we know that $\sec x = \dfrac32 \quad\Rightarrow\quad \cos x = \dfrac23$, so $\sin x = \dfrac{\sqrt5}{3}$ and $\tan x = \dfrac{\sqrt5}{2}$. Also, $\csc y = 3 \quad\Rightarrow\quad \sin y = \dfrac13$, and so $\cos y = \dfrac{2\sqrt2}{3}$, and $\tan y = \dfrac{1}{2\sqrt2} = \dfrac{\sqrt2}{4}.$

59. $\sin(x + y) = \sin x \cos y + \cos x \sin y = \dfrac{\sqrt5}{3} \cdot \dfrac{2\sqrt2}{3} + \dfrac23 \cdot \dfrac13 = \dfrac29 (1 + \sqrt{10}).$

61. $\tan(x + y) = \dfrac{\tan x + \tan y}{1 - \tan x \tan y} = \dfrac{\frac{\sqrt5}{2} + \frac{\sqrt2}{4}}{1 - \left(\frac{\sqrt5}{2}\right)\left(\frac{\sqrt2}{4}\right)} = \dfrac{\frac{\sqrt5}{2} + \frac{\sqrt2}{4}}{1 - \left(\frac{\sqrt5}{2}\right)\left(\frac{\sqrt2}{4}\right)} \cdot \dfrac88$

$= \dfrac{2(2\sqrt5 + \sqrt2)}{8 - \sqrt{10}} \cdot \dfrac{8 + \sqrt{10}}{8 + \sqrt{10}} = \dfrac23 \left(\sqrt2 + \sqrt5\right).$

63. $\cos\dfrac{y}{2} = \sqrt{\dfrac{1 + \cos y}{2}} = \sqrt{\dfrac{1 + \left(\frac{2\sqrt2}{3}\right)}{2}} = \sqrt{\dfrac{3 + 2\sqrt2}{6}}$ (since cosine is positive in quadrant I).

65. $\sin^{-1}\left(\dfrac{\sqrt3}{2}\right) = \dfrac{\pi}{3}.$

67. $\cos(\tan^{-1}\sqrt{3}) = \cos\frac{\pi}{3} = \frac{1}{2}$.

69. Let $u = \sin^{-1}\frac{2}{5}$ and so $\sin u = \frac{2}{5}$. Then from
the triangle $\tan(\sin^{-1}\frac{2}{5}) = \tan u = \frac{2}{\sqrt{21}}$.

71. $\cos(2\sin^{-1}\frac{1}{3}) = 1 - 2\sin^2(\sin^{-1}\frac{1}{3}) = 1 - 2\left(\frac{1}{3}\right)^2 = \frac{7}{9}$.

73. Let $\theta = \tan^{-1}x \quad \Leftrightarrow \quad \tan\theta = x$. Then from
the triangle on the right we have

$$\sin(\tan^{-1}x) = \sin\theta = \frac{x}{\sqrt{1+x^2}}$$

75. $\cos\theta = \frac{x}{3} \quad \Rightarrow \quad \theta = \cos^{-1}\left(\frac{x}{3}\right)$

77. (a) $\tan\theta = \dfrac{10}{x} \quad \Leftrightarrow \quad \theta = \tan^{-1}\left(\dfrac{10}{x}\right)$.

(b) $\theta = \tan^{-1}\left(\frac{10}{x}\right)$, for $x > 0$, is shown in the
viewing rectangle on the right. There is no
maximum value since the function is undefined
at 0. (But when $x = 0$, the driver no longer
can see the sign.)

79. (a)

(b) $4 + 4i$. Then $r = \sqrt{16 + 16} = 4\sqrt{2}$, and $\theta = \tan^{-1}\frac{4}{4} = \frac{\pi}{4}$ (in quadrant I).

(c) $4 + 4i = 4\sqrt{2}\left(\cos\frac{\pi}{4} + i\sin\frac{\pi}{4}\right)$.

81. (a)

(b) $5 + 3i$. Then $r = \sqrt{25 + 9} = \sqrt{34}$, and $\theta = \tan^{-1}\frac{3}{5}$.

(c) $5 + 3i = \sqrt{34}\,[\cos(\tan^{-1}\tfrac{3}{5}) + i\sin(\tan^{-1}\tfrac{3}{5})].$

83. (a)

(b) $-1 + i$. Then $r = \sqrt{1+1} = \sqrt{2}$, and $\tan\theta = \frac{1}{-1}$ with θ in quadrant II $\Leftrightarrow$ $\theta = \frac{3\pi}{4}$.

(c) $-1 + i = \sqrt{2}\left(\cos\frac{3\pi}{4} + i\sin\frac{3\pi}{4}\right)$.

85. $1 - \sqrt{3}i$ has $r = \sqrt{1+3} = 2$ and $\tan\theta = \frac{-\sqrt{3}}{1} = -\sqrt{3}$ with θ in quadrant III $\Leftrightarrow$ $\theta = \frac{5\pi}{3}$.

Therefore, $1 - \sqrt{3}i = 2\left(\cos\frac{5\pi}{3} + i\sin\frac{5\pi}{3}\right)$, and so $(1 - \sqrt{3}i)^4 = 2^4\left(\cos\frac{20\pi}{3} + i\sin\frac{20\pi}{3}\right)$

$= 16\left(\cos\frac{2\pi}{3} + i\sin\frac{2\pi}{3}\right) = 16\left(-\frac{1}{2} + i\frac{\sqrt{3}}{2}\right) = 8(-1 + i\sqrt{3}).$

87. $\sqrt{3} + i$ has $r = \sqrt{3+1} = 2$ and $\tan\theta = \frac{1}{\sqrt{3}}$ with θ in quadrant I $\Leftrightarrow$ $\theta = \frac{\pi}{6}$. Therefore,

$\sqrt{3} + i = 2\left(\cos\frac{\pi}{6} + i\sin\frac{\pi}{6}\right)$, and so $(\sqrt{3} + i)^{-4} = 2^{-4}\left(\cos\frac{-4\pi}{6} + i\sin\frac{-4\pi}{6}\right)$

$= \frac{1}{16}\left(\cos\frac{2\pi}{3} - i\sin\frac{2\pi}{3}\right) = \frac{1}{16}\left(-\frac{1}{2} - i\frac{\sqrt{3}}{2}\right) = \frac{1}{32}(-1 - i\sqrt{3}) = -\frac{1}{32}(1 + i\sqrt{3}).$

89. $-16i$ has $r = 16$ and $\theta = \frac{3\pi}{2}$. Thus, $-16i = 16\left(\cos\frac{3\pi}{2} + i\sin\frac{3\pi}{2}\right)$ and so

$(-16i)^{1/2} = 16^{1/2}\left[\cos\left(\frac{3\pi+4k\pi}{2}\right) + i\sin\left(\frac{3\pi+4k\pi}{2}\right)\right]$ for $k = 0, 1$. Thus the roots are

$w_0 = 4\left(\cos\frac{3\pi}{4} + i\sin\frac{3\pi}{4}\right) = 4\left(-\frac{1}{\sqrt{2}} + i\frac{1}{\sqrt{2}}\right) = 2\sqrt{2}(-1 + i)$ and

$w_1 = 4\left(\cos\frac{7\pi}{4} + i\sin\frac{7\pi}{4}\right) = 4\left(\frac{1}{\sqrt{2}} - i\frac{1}{\sqrt{2}}\right) = 2\sqrt{2}(1 - i).$

91. $1 = \cos 0 + i\sin 0$. Then, $1^{1/6} = 1\left(\cos\frac{2k\pi}{6} + i\sin\frac{2k\pi}{6}\right)$ for $k = 0, 1, 2, 3, 4, 5$. Thus the six roots

are $w_0 = 1(\cos 0 + i\sin 0) = 1$, $w_1 = 1\left(\cos\frac{\pi}{3} + i\sin\frac{\pi}{3}\right) = \frac{1}{2} + i\frac{\sqrt{3}}{2}$, $w_2 = 1\left(\cos\frac{2\pi}{3} + i\sin\frac{2\pi}{3}\right)$

$= -\frac{1}{2} + i\frac{\sqrt{3}}{2}$, $w_3 = 1(\cos\pi + i\sin\pi) = -1$, $w_4 = 1\left(\cos\frac{4\pi}{3} + i\sin\frac{4\pi}{3}\right) = -\frac{1}{2} - i\frac{\sqrt{3}}{2}$, and

$w_5 = 1\left(\cos\frac{5\pi}{3} + i\sin\frac{5\pi}{3}\right) = \frac{1}{2} - i\frac{\sqrt{3}}{2}.$

93. $\mathbf{u} = \langle -2, 3\rangle$ and $\mathbf{v} = \langle 8, 1\rangle$. Then $|\mathbf{u}| = \sqrt{(-2)^2 + 3^2} = \sqrt{13}$; $\mathbf{u} + \mathbf{v} = \langle -2 + 8, 3 + 1\rangle = \langle 6, 4\rangle$;

$\mathbf{u} - \mathbf{v} = \langle -2 - 8, 3 - 1\rangle = \langle -10, 2\rangle$; $2\mathbf{u} = \langle -4, 6\rangle$;

and $3\mathbf{u} - 2\mathbf{v} = \langle -6, 9\rangle - \langle 16, 2\rangle = \langle -6 - 16, 9 - 2\rangle = \langle -22, 7\rangle.$

95. $P(0, 3)$ and $Q(3, -1)$. $\mathbf{u} = \langle 3 - 0, -1 - 3\rangle = \langle 3, -4\rangle = 3\mathbf{i} - 4\mathbf{j}$

97. Let $Q(x, y)$ be the terminal point. Then $\langle x - 5,\ y - 6\rangle = \langle 5, -8\rangle$ $\Leftrightarrow$ $x - 5 = 5$ and

$y - 6 = -8$ $\Leftrightarrow$ $x = 10$ and $y = -2$. Therefore, the terminal point is $Q(10, -2)$.

99. (a) The resultant force $\mathbf{r}$ is the sum of the forces; to find this we first resolve the two vectors:

$\mathbf{v_1} = 2.0 \times 10^4$ lb N$50°$E $= \langle 2.0 \times 10^4 \cdot \cos 40°, 2.0 \times 10^4 \cdot \sin 40°\rangle \approx \langle 15321, 12856\rangle$, and

$\mathbf{v_2} = 3.4 \times 10^4$ lb S$75°$E $= \langle 3.4 \times 10^4 \cdot \cos(-15°), 3.4 \times 10^4 \cdot \sin(-15°)\rangle$

$\approx \langle 32841, -8800 \rangle$. Thus $\mathbf{r} = \mathbf{v}_1 + \mathbf{v}_2 \approx \langle 15321, 12856 \rangle + \langle 32841, -8800 \rangle$
$= \langle 48163, 4056 \rangle \approx \langle 4.82, 0.41 \rangle \times 10^4 = (4.82\,\mathbf{i} + 0.41\,\mathbf{j}) \times 10^4$.

(b) The magnitude is $|\mathbf{r}| = \sqrt{48163^2 + 4056^2} \approx 4.8 \times 10^4$ lb. We have $\theta \approx \tan^{-1}\left(\frac{4056}{48163}\right) \approx 4.8°$. Thus the direction of $\mathbf{r}$ is approximately N $85.2°$ E.

101. $\mathbf{u} = \langle 4, -3 \rangle$ and $\mathbf{v} = \langle 9, -8 \rangle$. Then $|\mathbf{u}| = \sqrt{(4)^2 + (-3)^2} = \sqrt{25} = 5$;
$\mathbf{u} \cdot \mathbf{u} = \langle 4, -3 \rangle \cdot \langle 4, -3 \rangle = (4)(4) + (-3)(-3) = 16 + 9 = 25$;
$\mathbf{u} \cdot \mathbf{v} = \langle 4, -3 \rangle \cdot \langle 9, -8 \rangle = (4)(9) + (-3)(-8) = 36 + 24 = 60$.

103. $\mathbf{u} = -2\mathbf{i} + 2\mathbf{j}$ and $\mathbf{v} = \mathbf{i} + \mathbf{j}$. Then $|\mathbf{u}| = \sqrt{(-2)^2 + (2)^2} = \sqrt{8} = 2\sqrt{2}$;
$\mathbf{u} \cdot \mathbf{u} = -2\mathbf{i} + 2\mathbf{j} \cdot -2\mathbf{i} + 2\mathbf{j} = (-2)(-2) + (2)(2) = 4 + 4 = 8$;
$\mathbf{u} \cdot \mathbf{v} = -2\mathbf{i} + 2\mathbf{j} \cdot \mathbf{i} + \mathbf{j} = (-2)(1) + (2)(1) = -2 + 2 = 0$.

105. $\mathbf{u} = \langle -4, 2 \rangle$ and $\mathbf{v} = \langle 3, 6 \rangle$. Since $\mathbf{u} \cdot \mathbf{v} = -12 + 12 = 0$, the vectors are orthogonal.

107. $\mathbf{u} = 2\mathbf{i} + \mathbf{j}$ and $\mathbf{v} = \mathbf{i} + 3\mathbf{j}$. Then $\cos\theta = \dfrac{\mathbf{u} \cdot \mathbf{v}}{|\mathbf{u}|\,|\mathbf{v}|} = \dfrac{2+3}{\sqrt{5}\sqrt{10}} = \dfrac{5}{5\sqrt{2}}$ Thus, $\theta = \cos^{-1}\dfrac{5}{5\sqrt{2}}$
$= \cos^{-1}\dfrac{1}{\sqrt{2}} = 45°$.

109. (a) $\mathbf{u} = \langle 3, 1 \rangle$ and $\mathbf{v} = \langle 6, -1 \rangle$. Then the component of $\mathbf{u}$ along $\mathbf{v}$ is
$\dfrac{\mathbf{u} \cdot \mathbf{v}}{|\mathbf{v}|} = \dfrac{\langle 3,1 \rangle \cdot \langle 6,-1 \rangle}{\sqrt{\langle 6,-1 \rangle \cdot \langle 6,-1 \rangle}} = \dfrac{18-1}{\sqrt{36+1}} = \dfrac{17}{\sqrt{37}}$.

(b) $\mathbf{u}_1 = \text{proj}_{\mathbf{v}}\mathbf{u} = \left(\dfrac{\mathbf{u} \cdot \mathbf{v}}{|\mathbf{v}|^2}\right)\mathbf{v} = \left(\dfrac{\langle 3,1 \rangle \cdot \langle 6,-1 \rangle}{6^2+(-1)^2}\right)\langle 6,-1 \rangle = \dfrac{17}{37}\langle 6,-1 \rangle = \langle \dfrac{102}{37}, -\dfrac{17}{37} \rangle$.

(c) $\mathbf{u}_2 = \mathbf{u} - \mathbf{u}_1 = \langle 3,1 \rangle - \langle \dfrac{102}{37}, -\dfrac{17}{37} \rangle = \langle \dfrac{9}{37}, \dfrac{54}{37} \rangle$.

111. The displacement is $\mathbf{D} = \langle 7-1, -1-1 \rangle = \langle 6, -2 \rangle$. Thus, $W = \mathbf{F} \cdot \mathbf{D} = \langle 2, 9 \rangle \cdot \langle 6, -2 \rangle = -6$.

Chapter 7 Test

1. (a) $\tan\theta\sin\theta + \cos\theta = \dfrac{\sin\theta}{\cos\theta}\sin\theta + \cos\theta = \dfrac{\sin^2\theta}{\cos\theta} + \dfrac{\cos^2\theta}{\cos\theta} = \dfrac{1}{\cos\theta} = \sec\theta$

   (b) $\dfrac{\tan x}{1-\cos x} = \dfrac{\tan x}{1-\cos x}\cdot\dfrac{1+\cos x}{1+\cos x} = \dfrac{\tan x\,(1+\cos x)}{1-\cos^2 x} = \dfrac{\dfrac{\sin x}{\cos x}\,(1+\cos x)}{\sin^2 x}$

   $= \dfrac{1}{\sin x}\cdot\dfrac{1+\cos x}{\cos x} = \csc x\,(1+\sec x)$

   (c) $\dfrac{2\tan x}{1+\tan^2 x} = \dfrac{2\tan x}{\sec^2 x} = \dfrac{2\sin x}{\cos x}\cdot\cos^2 x = 2\sin x\cos x = \sin 2x$

2. $\dfrac{x}{\sqrt{4-x^2}} = \dfrac{2\sin\theta}{\sqrt{4-(2\sin\theta)^2}} = \dfrac{2\sin\theta}{\sqrt{4-4\sin^2\theta}} = \dfrac{2\sin\theta}{2\sqrt{1-\sin^2\theta}} = \dfrac{\sin\theta}{\sqrt{\cos^2\theta}} = \dfrac{\sin\theta}{|\cos\theta|} = \dfrac{\sin\theta}{\cos\theta}$

   $= \tan\theta$ (because $\cos\theta > 0$ for $-\frac{\pi}{2} < \theta < \frac{\pi}{2}$).

3. (a) $\sin 8°\cos 22° + \cos 8°\sin 22° = \sin(8° + 22°) = \sin 30° = \frac{1}{2}$.

   (b) $\sin 75° = \sin(45° + 30°) = \sin 45°\cos 30° + \cos 45°\sin 30° = \frac{\sqrt{2}}{2}\cdot\frac{\sqrt{3}}{2} + \frac{\sqrt{2}}{2}\cdot\frac{1}{2}$

   $= \frac{1}{4}(\sqrt{6} + \sqrt{2})$

   (c) $\sin\frac{\pi}{12} = \sin\left(\frac{\pi/6}{2}\right) = \sqrt{\dfrac{1-\cos\frac{\pi}{6}}{2}} = \sqrt{\dfrac{1-\frac{\sqrt{3}}{2}}{2}} = \sqrt{\dfrac{2-\sqrt{3}}{4}} = \frac{1}{2}\sqrt{2-\sqrt{3}}$

4. From the triangles we have $\cos(\alpha + \beta) = \cos\alpha\cos\beta - \sin\alpha\sin\beta = \frac{2}{\sqrt{5}}\cdot\frac{\sqrt{5}}{3} - \frac{1}{\sqrt{5}}\cdot\frac{2}{3}$

   $= \frac{2\sqrt{5}-2}{3\sqrt{5}} = \frac{10-2\sqrt{5}}{15}$.

5. (a) $\sin 3x\cos 5x = \frac{1}{2}\left[\sin(3x + 5x) + \sin(3x - 5x)\right] = \frac{1}{2}\left(\sin 8x - \sin 2x\right)$

   (b) $\sin 2x - \sin 5x = 2\cos\left(\frac{2x+5x}{2}\right)\sin\left(\frac{2x-5x}{2}\right) = -2\cos\frac{7x}{2}\sin\frac{3x}{2}$

6. $\sin\theta = -\frac{4}{5}$. Since θ is in quadrant III, $\cos\theta = -\frac{3}{5}$. Then, $\tan\frac{\theta}{2} = \dfrac{1-\cos u}{\sin u} = \dfrac{1-(-3/5)}{-4/5}$

   $= -\dfrac{1+(3/5)}{4/5} = -\dfrac{5+3}{4} = -2$.

7. $y = \sin x$ has domain $(-\infty, \infty)$ and $y = \sin^{-1}x$ has domain $[-1, 1]$.

   $y = \sin x$ $y = \sin^{-1}x$

8. (a) $\tan\theta = \frac{x}{4} \quad\Rightarrow\quad \theta = \tan^{-1}\left(\frac{x}{4}\right)$

(b) $\cos\theta = \frac{3}{x}$ $\Rightarrow$ $\theta = \cos^{-1}\left(\frac{3}{x}\right)$

9. (a) $2\cos^2 x + 5\cos x + 2 = 0$ $\Leftrightarrow$ $(2\cos x + 1)(\cos x + 2) = 0$ $\Leftrightarrow$ $\cos x = -\frac{1}{2}$ or $\cos x = -2$ (which is impossible). So, in the interval $[0, 2\pi)$ the solutions are $x = \frac{2\pi}{3}, \frac{4\pi}{3}$.

(b) $\sin 2x - \cos x = 0$ $\Leftrightarrow$ $2\sin x \cos x - \cos x = 0$ $\Leftrightarrow$ $\cos x\,(2\sin x - 1) = 0$ $\Leftrightarrow$ $\cos x = 0$ or $\sin x = \frac{1}{2}$ $\Leftrightarrow$ $x = \frac{\pi}{2}, \frac{3\pi}{2}$ or $x = \frac{\pi}{6}, \frac{5\pi}{6}$. Therefore, the solutions in $[0, 2\pi)$ are $x = \frac{\pi}{6}, \frac{\pi}{2}, \frac{5\pi}{6}, \frac{3\pi}{2}$.

10. $5\cos 2x = 2$ $\Leftrightarrow$ $\cos 2x = \frac{2}{5}$ $\Leftrightarrow$ $2x = \cos^{-1} 0.4 \approx 1.159279$. The solution in $[0, 4\pi)$ are $2x \approx 1.159279,\ 2\pi - 1.159279,\ 2\pi + 1.159279,\ 4\pi - 1.159279$ $\Leftrightarrow$ $2x \approx 1.159279,$ $5.123906,\ 7.442465,\ 11.407091$ $\Leftrightarrow$ $x \approx 0.57964,\ 2.56195,\ 3.72123,\ 5.70355$ in $[0, 2\pi)$.

11. Let $u = \tan^{-1}\frac{9}{40}$ so $\tan u = \frac{9}{40}$. From the triangle $r = \sqrt{9^2 + 40^2} = 41$. So, $\cos(\tan^{-1}\frac{9}{40}) = \cos u = \frac{40}{41}$.

12. (a)

(b) $1 + \sqrt{3}\,i$ has $r = \sqrt{1 + 3} = 2$ and $\theta = \tan^{-1}(\sqrt{3}) = \frac{\pi}{3}$. So, in trigonometric form, $1 + \sqrt{3}\,i = 2\left(\cos\frac{\pi}{3} + i\sin\frac{\pi}{3}\right)$.

(b) $z = 1 + \sqrt{3}\,i = 2\left(\cos\frac{\pi}{3} + i\sin\frac{\pi}{3}\right)$ $\Rightarrow$ $z^9 = 2^9\left(\cos\frac{9\pi}{3} + i\sin\frac{9\pi}{3}\right)$ $= 512\,(\cos 3\pi + i\sin 3\pi) = 512\,(-1 + i\,(0)) = -512$.

13. $z_1 = 4\left(\cos\frac{7\pi}{12} + i\sin\frac{7\pi}{12}\right)$ and $z_2 = 2\left(\cos\frac{5\pi}{12} + i\sin\frac{5\pi}{12}\right)$.

Then $z_1 z_2 = 4 \cdot 2\left[\cos\left(\frac{7\pi + 5\pi}{12}\right) + i\sin\left(\frac{7\pi + 5\pi}{12}\right)\right] = 8\,(\cos\pi + i\sin\pi) = -8$, and

$z_1/z_2 = \frac{4}{2}\left[\cos\left(\frac{7\pi - 5\pi}{12}\right) + i\sin\left(\frac{7\pi - 5\pi}{12}\right)\right] = 2\left(\cos\frac{\pi}{6} + i\sin\frac{\pi}{6}\right) = 2\left(\frac{\sqrt{3}}{2} + \frac{1}{2}i\right) = \sqrt{3} + i$

14. $27i$ has $r = 27$ and $\theta = \frac{\pi}{2}$, so $27i = 27(\cos\frac{\pi}{2} + i\sin\frac{\pi}{2})$.

Thus, $(27i)^{1/3} = \sqrt[3]{27}\left[\cos\left(\frac{(\pi/2) + 2k\pi}{3}\right) + i\sin\left(\frac{(\pi/2) + 2k\pi}{3}\right)\right]$

$= 3\left[\cos\left(\frac{\pi + 4k\pi}{6}\right) + i\sin\left(\frac{\pi + 4k\pi}{6}\right)\right]$ for $k = 0, 1, 2$. Thus the three roots are $w_0 = 3\left(\cos\frac{\pi}{6} + i\sin\frac{\pi}{6}\right) = 3\left(\frac{\sqrt{3}}{2} + \frac{1}{2}i\right) = \frac{3}{2}(\sqrt{3} + i)$,

$w_1 = 3\left(\cos\frac{5\pi}{6} + i\sin\frac{5\pi}{6}\right) = 3\left(-\frac{\sqrt{3}}{2} + \frac{1}{2}i\right) = \frac{3}{2}(-\sqrt{3} + i)$, and

$w_2 = 3\left(\cos\frac{9\pi}{6} + i\sin\frac{9\pi}{6}\right) = -3\,i$.

15. (a) Initial point $P(3, -1)$ and terminal point $Q(-3, 9)$. Therefore, $\mathbf{u} = \langle -3 - 3, 9 - (-1)\rangle$ $= \langle -6, 10\rangle = -6\mathbf{i} + 10\mathbf{j}$.

(b) $\mathbf{u} = \langle -6, 10 \rangle \quad \Rightarrow \quad |\mathbf{u}| = \sqrt{(-6)^2 + 10^2} = \sqrt{4 \cdot (9 + 25)} = 2\sqrt{34}$

16. $\mathbf{u} = \langle 1, 3 \rangle$ and $\mathbf{v} = \langle -6, 2 \rangle$

   (a) $\mathbf{u} - 3\mathbf{v} = \langle 1, 3 \rangle - \langle -18, 6 \rangle = \langle 19, -3 \rangle$

   (b) $|\mathbf{u} + \mathbf{v}| = |\langle 1 - 6, 3 + 2 \rangle| = |\langle -5, 5 \rangle| = \sqrt{(-5)^2 + 5^2} = 5\sqrt{2}$

   (c) $\mathbf{u} \cdot \mathbf{v} = (1)(-6) + (3)(2) = -6 + 6 = 0$

   (d)   Since $\mathbf{u} \cdot \mathbf{v} = 0$, it is true that $\mathbf{u}$ and $\mathbf{v}$ are perpendicular.

17.   Let $\mathbf{r}$ represent the velocity of the river and $\mathbf{b}$ the velocity of the boat. Then, $\mathbf{r} = \langle 8, 0 \rangle$ and $\mathbf{b} = \langle 12\sin 30°, 12\cos 30° \rangle = \langle 6, 6\sqrt{3} \rangle$.

   (a)   The resultant (or true) velocity is $\mathbf{v} = \mathbf{r} + \mathbf{b} = \langle 14, 6\sqrt{3} \rangle = 14\mathbf{i} + 6\sqrt{3}\mathbf{j}$.

   (b) $|\mathbf{v}| = \sqrt{14^2 + \left(6\sqrt{3}\right)^2} = \sqrt{196 + 108} = \sqrt{304} \approx 17.44$ and

   $\theta = \tan^{-1}\left(\frac{6\sqrt{3}}{14}\right) = \tan^{-1}\left(\frac{3\sqrt{3}}{7}\right) \approx 36.6°$. Therefore, the true speed of the boat is approximately 17.4 mi/h and the true direction is approximately N 53.4° E.

18.   (a) $\cos\theta = \frac{\langle 3,2 \rangle \cdot \langle 5,-1 \rangle}{|\langle 3,2 \rangle| \, |\langle 5,-1 \rangle|} = \frac{15 - 2}{\sqrt{13}\sqrt{26}} = \frac{13}{13\sqrt{2}} = \frac{1}{\sqrt{2}} \quad \Rightarrow \quad \theta = \frac{\pi}{4} \text{ (rad)} = 45°.$

   (b)   The component of $\mathbf{u}$ along $\mathbf{v}$ is $\dfrac{\mathbf{u} \cdot \mathbf{v}}{|\mathbf{v}|} = \frac{\langle 3,2 \rangle \cdot \langle 5,-1 \rangle}{\sqrt{26}} = \frac{15 - 2}{\sqrt{26}} = \frac{13}{\sqrt{26}} = \frac{\sqrt{26}}{2}.$

   (c) $\text{proj}_{\mathbf{v}}\mathbf{u} = \left(\dfrac{\mathbf{u} \cdot \mathbf{v}}{|\mathbf{v}|^2}\right)\mathbf{v} = \left(\frac{\langle 3,2 \rangle \cdot \langle 5,-1 \rangle}{5^2 + (-1)^2}\right)\langle 5,-1 \rangle = \frac{13}{26}\langle 5,-1 \rangle = \frac{1}{2}\langle 5,-1 \rangle = \langle \frac{5}{2}, -\frac{1}{2} \rangle.$

19.   The displacement vector is $\mathbf{D} = \langle 7, -13 \rangle - \langle 2, 2 \rangle = \langle 5, -15 \rangle$. Therefore, the work done is $W = \mathbf{F} \cdot \mathbf{D} = \langle 3, -5 \rangle \cdot \langle 5, -15 \rangle = 15 + 75 = 90.$

Focus on Problem Solving

1. The solutions to the equation are the points of intersection of the graphs of the functions $y = \sin x$ and $y = \dfrac{x}{1{,}000{,}000}$. We first find the number of positive solutions. The graph of $y = \dfrac{x}{1{,}000{,}000}$ is a line with slope $m = \frac{1}{1{,}000{,}000}$. The graphs intersect at two points on each of the intervals $[0, 2\pi]$, $[2\pi, 4\pi]$, $[4\pi, 6\pi]$, ... This pattern continues as long as $\dfrac{x}{1{,}000{,}000} \le 1 \quad \Leftrightarrow \quad x \le 1{,}000{,}000$. So we need to know how many of the intervals described lie between 0 and $1{,}000{,}000$. Since $\frac{1{,}000{,}000}{2\pi} \approx 159{,}154.94$ and since the points of intersection always occur in the first half of the positive intervals described above, it follows that the graphs intersect $159{,}155 \cdot 2 = 318{,}310$ times. Thus the given equation has $318{,}310$ solutions for $x \ge 0$. Because of symmetry, it is clear that there are also $318{,}310$ solutions for $x \le 0$. Since $x = 0$ is a solution counted in both cases, the total number of solutions of the given equation is $318{,}310 + 318{,}310 - 1 = 636{,}619$.

3. By similar triangles, $\dfrac{|AQ|}{|QC|} = \dfrac{|AP|}{x}$. So $\dfrac{50}{10} = \dfrac{30}{x} \quad \Leftrightarrow$ $50x = 300 \quad \Leftrightarrow \quad x = 6$. Using the Pythagorean Theorem $y^2 + 6^2 = 10^2 \quad \Leftrightarrow \quad y = 8$ and so $|DE| = 16$ cm.

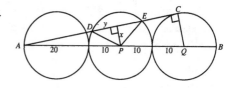

5. From Exercise 44 (b) in section 7.2, we know that $\tan\psi = \dfrac{m_2 - m_1}{1 + m_1 m_2}$, where ψ is the acute angle formed by two lines with slopes m_1 and m_2. In an equilateral triangle, all the angles are $60°$, so $\tan 60° = \sqrt{3} = \dfrac{m_2 - m_1}{1 + m_1 m_2}$. Suppose that the triangle's vertices are located at (x_1, y_1), (x_2, y_2), and (x_3, y_3). Then $m_1 = \dfrac{y_1 - y_3}{x_1 - x_3}$ and $m_2 = \dfrac{y_2 - y_3}{x_2 - x_3}$, that is, m_1 and m_2 are rational numbers (since coordinates at a lattice point are integers). Thus, $\dfrac{m_2 - m_1}{1 + m_1 m_2}$ is also rational; but this contradicts $\tan 60° = \sqrt{3}$. Therefore, it is impossible for all three vertices to be at lattice points.

7. $\sin 2\theta = a \quad \Leftrightarrow \quad 2\sin\theta\cos\theta = a$. Now, $(\sin\theta + \cos\theta)^2 = \sin^2\theta + 2\sin\theta\cos\theta + \cos^2\theta = 1 + 2\sin\theta\cos\theta = 1 + a$. Therefore $\sin\theta + \cos\theta = \sqrt{1+a}$.

9. (a) Label the diagram as shown. Applying the Law of Sines to $\triangle ABC$, we get $\dfrac{\sin B}{b} = \dfrac{\sin 60°}{c}$ or $\sin B = \dfrac{b\sin 60°}{c}$. Similarly, applying the Law of Sines to $\triangle BCD$ gives $\dfrac{\sin B}{r} = \dfrac{\sin 120°}{c + d}$ or $\sin B = \dfrac{r\sin 120°}{c + d}$. Since $\sin 120° = \sin 60°$,

we have: $\dfrac{b}{c} = \dfrac{r}{c + d} \quad \Leftrightarrow \quad \dfrac{b}{r} = \dfrac{c}{c + d}$ (*). Similarly, from $\triangle ADC$ and the Law of

Sines we have $\dfrac{\sin D}{b} = \dfrac{\sin 60°}{d}$ or $\sin D = \dfrac{b \sin 60°}{d}$, and from $\triangle BDC$ we have

$\dfrac{\sin D}{a} = \dfrac{\sin 120°}{c+d}$ or $\sin D = \dfrac{a \sin 120°}{c+d}$. Thus, $\dfrac{b \sin 60°}{d} = \dfrac{a \sin 120°}{c+d}$ or $\dfrac{b}{a} = \dfrac{d}{c+d}$.

Combining this with (*), we get $\dfrac{b}{r} + \dfrac{b}{a} = \dfrac{c}{c+d} + \dfrac{d}{c+d} = \dfrac{c+d}{c+d} = 1$. Solving for r,

we get $\dfrac{b}{r} = 1 - \dfrac{b}{a} = \dfrac{a-b}{a}$ $\Leftrightarrow$ $\dfrac{r}{b} = \dfrac{a}{a-b}$ $\Leftrightarrow$ $r = \dfrac{ab}{a-b}$.

(b) $r = \dfrac{4 \cdot 3}{4-3} = 12\text{ cm}$

(c) If $a = b$, then r is infinite, and so the face is a flat disk.

11. There are two possibilities: if $\sin x > 0$, then $|\sin x| = \sin x$, so $0 < x < \pi$ and the equation becomes $\sin x = \sin x + 2\cos x$ $\Leftrightarrow$ $2\cos x = 0$ $\Leftrightarrow$ $\cos x = 0$ $\Leftrightarrow$ $x = \frac{\pi}{2}, \frac{3\pi}{2}$. The second root is inadmissible since $\sin\frac{3\pi}{2} = -1 < 0$. Thus, if $\sin x > 0$ then $x = \frac{\pi}{2}$. On the other hand, if $\sin x < 0$, then $|\sin x| = -\sin x$, so $\pi < x < 2\pi$ and the equation becomes $-\sin x = \sin x + 2\cos x$ $\Leftrightarrow$ $2\sin x = -2\cos x$ $\Leftrightarrow$ $\tan x = -1$ $(\cos x \neq 0)$ $\Leftrightarrow$ $x = \frac{3\pi}{4}$, $\frac{7\pi}{4}$. Since $\sin\frac{3\pi}{4} = \frac{1}{\sqrt{2}} > 0$, the first root is inadmissible, and so $x = \frac{7\pi}{4}$. Thus the solutions are $\frac{\pi}{2}$ and $\frac{7\pi}{4}$.

13. Using the Change of Base formula we have
$(\log_2 3)(\log_3 4)(\log_4 5)\cdots(\log_{31} 32) = \dfrac{\log 3}{\log 2} \cdot \dfrac{\log 4}{\log 3} \cdot \dfrac{\log 5}{\log 4} \cdot \ldots \cdot \dfrac{\log 31}{\log 30} \cdot \dfrac{\log 32}{\log 31} = \dfrac{\log 32}{\log 2} = \log_2 32$
$= \log_2 2^5 = 5.$

Chapter Eight
Exercises 8.1

1. $\begin{cases} x - y = 2 \\ 2x + 3y = 9 \end{cases}$ Solving the first equation for x, we get $x = y + 2$ and substituting this into the second equation, gives $2(y+2) + 3y = 9 \Leftrightarrow 5y + 4 = 9 \Leftrightarrow 5y = 5 \Leftrightarrow y = 1$. Substituting for y we get $x = y + 2 = (1) + 2 = 3$. Thus the solution is $(3, 1)$.

3. $\begin{cases} y = x^2 \\ y = x + 12 \end{cases}$ Substituting $y = x^2$ into the second equation gives $x^2 = x + 12 \Leftrightarrow$ $0 = x^2 - x - 12 = (x-4)(x+3) \Rightarrow x = 4$ or $x = -3$. So since $y = x^2$, the solutions are $(-3, 9)$ and $(4, 16)$.

5. $\begin{cases} x^2 + y^2 = 8 \\ x + y = 0 \end{cases}$ Solving the second equation for y gives $y = -x$, and substituting this into the first equation gives $x^2 + (-x)^2 = 8 \Leftrightarrow 2x^2 = 8 \Leftrightarrow x = \pm 2$. So since $y = -x$, the solutions are $(2, -2)$ and $(-2, 2)$.

7. $\begin{cases} x + y^2 = 0 \\ 2x + 5y^2 = 75 \end{cases}$ Solving the first equation for x gives $x = -y^2$, and substituting this into the second equation gives $2(-y^2) + 5y^2 = 75 \Leftrightarrow 3y^2 = 75 \Leftrightarrow y^2 = 25 \Leftrightarrow y = \pm 5$. So since $x = -y^2$, the solutions are $(-25, -5)$ and $(-25, 5)$.

9. $\begin{cases} x + 2y = 5 \\ 2x + 3y = 8 \end{cases}$ Multiplying the first equation by 2 and the second by -1 gives the system $\begin{cases} 2x + 4y = 10 \\ -2x - 3y = -8 \end{cases}$. Adding, we get $y = 2$, and substituting into the first equation in the original system gives $x + 2(2) = 5 \Leftrightarrow x + 4 = 5 \Leftrightarrow x = 1$. The solution is $(1, 2)$.

11. $\begin{cases} x^2 - 2y = 1 \\ x^2 + 5y = 29 \end{cases}$ Subtracting the first equation from the second equation gives $7y = 28 \Rightarrow$ $y = 4$. Substituting $y = 4$ into the first equation of the original system gives $x^2 - 2(4) = 1 \Leftrightarrow$ $x^2 = 9 \Leftrightarrow x = \pm 3$. The solutions are $(3, 4)$ and $(-3, 4)$.

13. $\begin{cases} 3x^2 - y^2 = 11 \\ x^2 + 4y^2 = 8 \end{cases}$ Multiplying the first equation by 4 gives the system $\begin{cases} 12x^2 - 4y^2 = 44 \\ x^2 + 4y^2 = 8 \end{cases}$. Adding the equations gives $13x^2 = 52 \Leftrightarrow x = \pm 2$. Substituting into the first equation we get $3(4) - y^2 = 11 \Leftrightarrow y = \pm 1$. Thus, the solutions are $(2, 1)$, $(2, -1)$, $(-2, 1)$, and $(-2, -1)$.

15. $\begin{cases} x - y^2 + 3 = 0 \\ 2x^2 + y^2 - 4 = 0 \end{cases}$ Adding the two equations gives $2x^2 + x - 1 = 0$. Using the quadratic formula we have $x = \frac{-1 \pm \sqrt{1 - 4(2)(-1)}}{2(2)} = \frac{-1 \pm \sqrt{9}}{4} = \frac{-1 \pm 3}{4}$. So $x = \frac{-1-3}{4} = -1$ or $x = \frac{-1+3}{4} = \frac{1}{2}$. Subsituting $x = -1$ into the first equation gives $-1 - y^2 + 3 = 0 \Leftrightarrow y^2 = 2 \Leftrightarrow$ $y = \pm\sqrt{2}$. Subsituting $x = \frac{1}{2}$ into the first equation gives $\frac{1}{2} - y^2 + 3 = 0 \Leftrightarrow y^2 = \frac{7}{2} \Leftrightarrow$ $y = \pm\sqrt{\frac{7}{2}}$. Thus the solutions are $(-1, \pm\sqrt{2})$ and $(\frac{1}{2}, \pm\sqrt{\frac{7}{2}})$.

17. $\begin{cases} y + x^2 = 4x \\ y + 4x = 16 \end{cases}$ Subtracting the second equation from the first equation gives $x^2 - 4x = 4x - 16$
$\Leftrightarrow$ $x^2 - 8x + 16 = 0$ $\Leftrightarrow$ $(x-4)^2 = 0$ $\Leftrightarrow$ $x = 4$. Substituting this value for x into
either of the original equations gives $y = 0$. Therefore, the solution is $(4, 0)$.

19. $\begin{cases} x - 2y = 2 \\ y^2 - x^2 = 2x + 4 \end{cases}$ Now $x - 2y = 2$ $\Leftrightarrow$ $x = 2y + 2$. Substituting for x gives
$y^2 - x^2 = 2x + 4$ $\Leftrightarrow$ $y^2 - (2y+2)^2 = 2(2y+2) + 4$ $\Leftrightarrow$
$y^2 - 4y^2 - 8y - 4 = 4y + 4 + 4$ $\Leftrightarrow$ $y^2 + 4y + 4 = 0$ $\Leftrightarrow$ $(y+2)^2 = 0$ $\Leftrightarrow$ $y = -2$.
Since $x = 2y + 2$, we have $x = 2(-2) + 2 = -2$. Thus the solution is $(-2, -2)$.

21. $\begin{cases} x - y = 4 \\ xy = 12 \end{cases}$ Now $x - y = 4$ $\Leftrightarrow$ $x = 4 + y$. Substituting for x gives $xy = 12$ $\Leftrightarrow$
$(4 + y)y = 12$ $\Leftrightarrow$ $y^2 + 4y - 12 = 0$ $\Leftrightarrow$ $(y+6)(y-2) = 0$ $\Leftrightarrow$ $y = -6, y = 2$.
Since $x = 4 + y$, the solutions are $(-2, -6)$ and $(6, 2)$.

23. $\begin{cases} x^2 y = 16 \\ x^2 + 4y + 16 = 0 \end{cases}$ Now $x^2 y = 16$ $\Leftrightarrow$ $x^2 = \dfrac{16}{y}$. Substituting for x^2 gives
$\dfrac{16}{y} + 4y + 16 = 0$ $\Rightarrow$ $4y^2 + 16y + 16 = 0$ $\Leftrightarrow$ $y^2 + 4y + 4 = 0$ $\Leftrightarrow$ $(y+2)^2 = 0$
$\Leftrightarrow$ $y = -2$. Therefore, $x^2 = \frac{16}{-2} = -8$, which has no real solution, and so the system has no
solution.

25. $\begin{cases} x^2 + y^2 = 9 \\ x^2 - y^2 = 1 \end{cases}$ Adding the equations gives $2x^2 = 10$ $\Leftrightarrow$ $x^2 = 5$ $\Leftrightarrow$ $x = \pm\sqrt{5}$. Now
$x = \pm\sqrt{5}$ $\Rightarrow$ $y^2 = 9 - 5 = 4$ $\Leftrightarrow$ $y = \pm 2$, and so the solutions are $(\sqrt{5}, 2), (\sqrt{5}, -2)$,
$(-\sqrt{5}, 2)$, and $(-\sqrt{5}, -2)$.

27. $\begin{cases} 2x^2 - 8y^3 = 19 \\ 4x^2 + 16y^3 = 34 \end{cases}$ Multiplying the first equation by 2 gives the system $\begin{cases} 4x^2 - 16y^3 = 38 \\ 4x^2 + 16y^3 = 34 \end{cases}$
Adding the two equations gives $8x^2 = 72$ $\Leftrightarrow$ $x = \pm 3$, and then substituting into the first
equation we have $2(9) - 8y^3 = 19$ $\Leftrightarrow$ $y^3 = -\frac{1}{8}$ $\Leftrightarrow$ $y = -\frac{1}{2}$. Therefore, the solutions are
$(3, -\frac{1}{2})$ and $(-3, -\frac{1}{2})$.

29. $\begin{cases} \dfrac{2}{x} - \dfrac{3}{y} = 1 \\ -\dfrac{4}{x} + \dfrac{7}{y} = 1 \end{cases}$ If we let $u = \dfrac{1}{x}$ and $v = \dfrac{1}{y}$, the system is equivalent to $\begin{cases} 2u - 3v = 1 \\ -4u + 7v = 1 \end{cases}$.

Multiplying the first equation by 4 gives the system $\begin{cases} 4u - 6v = 2 \\ -4u + 7v = 1 \end{cases}$. Adding the equations gives
$v = 3$, and then substituting into the first equation gives $2u - 9 = 1$ $\Leftrightarrow$ $u = 5$. Thus, the
solution is $(\frac{1}{5}, \frac{1}{3})$.

31. $\begin{cases} y = 2x + 6 \\ y = -x + 5 \end{cases}$

The solution is $(-0.33, 5.33)$.

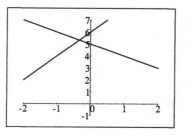

33. $\begin{cases} y = x^2 + 8x \\ y = 2x + 16 \end{cases}$

The solutions are $(-8, 0)$ and $(2, 20)$.

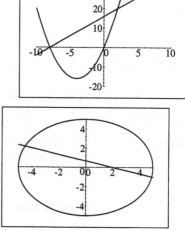

35. $\begin{cases} x^2 + y^2 = 25 \\ x + 3y = 2 \end{cases}$

$\Leftrightarrow \begin{cases} y = \pm\sqrt{25 - x^2} \\ y = -\frac{1}{3}x + \frac{2}{3} \end{cases}$

The solutions are $(-4.51, 2.17)$ and $(4.91, -0.97)$.

37. $\begin{cases} \frac{x^2}{9} + \frac{y^2}{18} = 1 \\ y = -x^2 + 6x - 2 \end{cases}$

$\Leftrightarrow \begin{cases} y = \pm\sqrt{18 - 2x^2} \\ y = -x^2 + 6x - 2 \end{cases}$

The solutions are $(1.23, 3.87)$ and $(-0.35, -4.21)$.

39. $\begin{cases} x^4 + 16y^4 = 32 \\ x^2 + 2x + y = 0 \end{cases}$

$\Leftrightarrow \begin{cases} y = \pm\dfrac{\sqrt[4]{32 - x^4}}{2} \\ y = -x^2 - 2x \end{cases}$

The solutions are $(-2.30, -0.70)$ and $(0.48, -1.19)$.

41. Let w and l be the lengths of the sides, in cm. Then we have the system $\begin{cases} lw = 180 \\ 2l + 2w = 54 \end{cases}$.

We solve the second equation for w giving, $w = 27 - l$, and substitute into the first equation to get
$l(27 - l) = 180 \quad \Leftrightarrow \quad l^2 - 27l + 180 = 0 \quad \Leftrightarrow \quad (l - 15)(l - 12) = 0 \quad \Rightarrow \quad l = 15 \text{ or } l = 12$.
If $l = 15$, then $w = 27 - 15 = 12$, and if $l = 12$, then $w = 27 - 12 = 15$. Therefore, the dimensions of the rectangle are 12 cm by 15 cm.

43. Let l and w be the length and width, respectively, of the rectangle. Then, the system of equations is
$\begin{cases} 2l + 2w = 70 \\ \sqrt{l^2 + w^2} = 25 \end{cases}$. Solving the first equation for l, we have $l = 35 - w$, and substituting into the

second yields $\sqrt{l^2 + w^2} = 25 \Leftrightarrow l^2 + w^2 = 625 \Leftrightarrow (35 - w)^2 + w^2 = 625 \Leftrightarrow$
$1225 - 70w + w^2 + w^2 = 625 \Leftrightarrow 2w^2 - 70w + 600 = 0 \Leftrightarrow (w - 15)(w - 20) = 0$
$\Rightarrow w = 15$ or $w = 20$. So the dimensions of the rectangle are 15 by 20.

45. At the points where the rocket path and the hillside meet, we have $\begin{cases} y = \frac{1}{2}x \\ y = -x^2 + 401x \end{cases}$. Substituting

for y in the second equation gives $\frac{1}{2}x = -x^2 + 401x \Leftrightarrow x^2 - \frac{801}{2}x = 0 \Leftrightarrow$
$x\left(x - \frac{801}{2}\right) = 0 \Rightarrow x = 0, x = \frac{801}{2}$. When $x = 0$, the rocket has not left the pad. When
$x = \frac{801}{2}$, then $y = \frac{1}{2}\left(\frac{801}{2}\right) = \frac{801}{4}$. So the rocket lands at the point $\left(\frac{801}{2}, \frac{801}{4}\right)$. The distance from the
base of the hill is $\sqrt{\left(\frac{801}{2}\right)^2 + \left(\frac{801}{4}\right)^2} \approx 447.77$ meters.

47. $\begin{cases} x^2 + y^2 = 25 \\ x^2 - 3x + y^2 + y = 30 \end{cases}$ Subtracting the two equations, we get $3x - y = 25 - 30 \Leftrightarrow$
$y = 3x + 5$. Since this is the equation of a line, and since any point satisfying both the original
equations must satisfy this equation, this must be the line that contains the points of intersection.
Thus the equation of the line passing through the intersection points is $y = 3x + 5$. (Notice, we did
not have to find the points of intersection to determine the equation of the line that contains them.)

49. $\begin{cases} x^2 + xy = 1 \\ xy + y^2 = 3 \end{cases}$ Adding the equations gives

$x^2 + xy + xy + y^2 = 4 \Leftrightarrow x^2 + 2xy + y^2 = 4 \Leftrightarrow (x + y)^2 = 4 \Rightarrow x + y = \pm 2$. If
$x + y = 2$, then from the first equation we get $x(x + y) = 1 \Rightarrow x \cdot 2 = 1 \Rightarrow x = \frac{1}{2}$, and so
$y = 2 - \frac{1}{2} = \frac{3}{2}$. If $x + y = -2$, then from the first equation we get $x(x + y) = 1 \Rightarrow$
$x \cdot (-2) = 1 \Rightarrow x = -\frac{1}{2}$, and so $y = -2 - \left(-\frac{1}{2}\right) = -\frac{3}{2}$. Thus the solutions are $\left(\frac{1}{2}, \frac{3}{2}\right)$ and
$\left(-\frac{1}{2}, -\frac{3}{2}\right)$.

51. $\begin{cases} \log x + \log y = \frac{3}{2} \\ 2\log x - \log y = 0 \end{cases}$ Adding the two equations gives $3\log x = \frac{3}{2} \Leftrightarrow \log x = \frac{1}{2} \Leftrightarrow$

$x = \sqrt{10}$. Substituting into the second equation we get $2\log 10^{1/2} - \log y = 0 \Leftrightarrow \log$
$10 - \log y = 0 \Leftrightarrow \log y = 1 \Leftrightarrow y = 10$. Thus the solution is $\left(\sqrt{10}, 10\right)$.

53. The point P is at an intersection of the circle of radius 26 centered at
A $(22, 32)$ and the circle of radius 20 centered at B $(28, 20)$. We have
the system $\begin{cases} (x - 22)^2 + (y - 32)^2 = 26^2 \\ (x - 28)^2 + (y - 20)^2 = 20^2 \end{cases} \Leftrightarrow$
$\begin{cases} x^2 - 44x + 484 + y^2 - 64y + 1024 = 676 \\ x^2 - 56x + 784 + y^2 - 40y + 400 = 400 \end{cases} \Leftrightarrow$
$\begin{cases} x^2 - 44x + y^2 - 64y = -832 \\ x^2 - 56x + y^2 - 40y = -784 \end{cases}$. Subtracting the two equations, we get

$12x - 24y = -48 \Leftrightarrow x - 2y = -4$, which is the equation of a line. Solving for x, we have
$x = 2y - 4$. Substituting into the first equation gives $(2y - 4)^2 - 44(2y - 4) + y^2 - 64y = -832$
$\Leftrightarrow 4y^2 - 16y + 16 - 88y + 176 + y^2 - 64y = -832 \Leftrightarrow 5y^2 - 168y + 192 = -832 \Leftrightarrow$

$5y^2 - 168y + 1024 = 0$. Using the quadratic formula, we have

$$y = \frac{168 \pm \sqrt{168^2 - 4(5)(1024)}}{2(5)} = \frac{168 \pm \sqrt{7744}}{10} = \frac{168 \pm 88}{10} \quad \Leftrightarrow \quad y = 8 \text{ or } y = 25.60.$$

Since the y coordinate of the point P must be less than that of point A, we have $y = 8$. Then $x = 2(8) - 4 = 12$. So the coordinates of P are $(12, 8)$.

To solve graphically, we must solve each equation for y. This gives $(x - 22)^2 + (y - 32)^2 = 26^2$ $\Leftrightarrow$ $(y - 32)^2 = 26^2 - (x - 22)^2$ $\Rightarrow$ $y - 32 = \pm\sqrt{676 - (x - 22)^2}$ $\Leftrightarrow$ $y = 32 \pm \sqrt{676 - (x - 22)^2}$. We use the function $y = 32 - \sqrt{676 - (x - 22)^2}$ because the intersection we at interested in is below the point A. Likewise, solving the second equation for y, we would get the function $y = 20 - \sqrt{400 - (x - 28)^2}$.

In a 3 dimensional situation, you would need the minimum of 3 satellites, since a point on the earth can be uniquely specified as the intersection of 3 spheres centered at the satellites.

Exercises 8.2

1. $\begin{cases} x + y = 4 \\ 2x - y = 2 \end{cases}$

   The solution is $x = 2$, $y = 2$.

3. $\begin{cases} 2x - 3y = 12 \\ -x + \frac{3}{2}y = 4 \end{cases}$

   No solution. The lines are parallel, so there is no intersection.

5. $\begin{cases} -x + \frac{1}{2}y = -5 \\ 2x - y = 10 \end{cases}$

   Infinite number of solutions.

7. $\begin{cases} x + y = 4 \\ -x + y = 0 \end{cases}$ Adding the two equations gives $2y = 4$ $\Leftrightarrow$ $y = 2$. Substituting for y in the first equation gives $x + 2 = 4$ $\Leftrightarrow$ $x = 2$. Hence, the solution is $(2, 2)$.

9. $\begin{cases} 2x - 3y = 9 \\ 4x + 3y = 9 \end{cases}$ Adding the two equations gives $6x = 18$ $\Leftrightarrow$ $x = 3$. Substituting for x in the second equation gives $4(3) + 3y = 9$ $\Leftrightarrow$ $12 + 3y = 9$ $\Leftrightarrow$ $3y = -3$ $\Leftrightarrow$ $x = -1$. Hence, the solution is $(3, -1)$.

11. $\begin{cases} x + 3y = 5 \\ 2x - y = 3 \end{cases}$ Solving the first equation for x gives $x = -3y + 5$. Substituting for x in the second equation gives $2(-3y + 5) - y = 3$ $\Leftrightarrow$ $-6y + 10 - y = 3$ $\Leftrightarrow$ $-7y = -7$ $\Leftrightarrow$ $y = 1$. Then $x = -3(1) + 5 = 2$. Hence, the solution is $(2, 1)$.

13. $-x + y = 2$ $\Leftrightarrow$ $y = x + 2$. Substituting for y into $4x - 3y = -3$ gives $4x - 3(x + 2) = -3$ $\Leftrightarrow$ $4x - 3x - 6 = -3$ $\Leftrightarrow$ $x = 3$, and so $y = (3) + 2 = 5$. Hence, the solution is $(3, 5)$.

15. $x + 2y = 7$ $\Leftrightarrow$ $x = 7 - 2y$. Substituting for x into $5x - y = 2$ gives $5(7 - 2y) - y = 2$ $\Leftrightarrow$ $35 - 10y - y = 2$ $\Leftrightarrow$ $-11y = -33$ $\Leftrightarrow$ $y = 3$, and so $x = 7 - 2(3) = 1$. Hence, the solution is $(1, 3)$.

17. $\frac{1}{2}x + \frac{1}{3}y = 2$ $\Leftrightarrow$ $x + \frac{2}{3}y = 4$ $\Leftrightarrow$ $x = 4 - \frac{2}{3}y$. Substituting for x into $\frac{1}{5}x - \frac{2}{3}y = 8$ gives
$\frac{1}{5}(4 - \frac{2}{3}y) - \frac{2}{3}y = 8$ $\Leftrightarrow$ $\frac{4}{5} - \frac{2}{15}y - \frac{10}{15}y = 8$ $\Leftrightarrow$ $12 - 2y - 10y = 120$ $\Leftrightarrow$ $y = -9$,
and so $x = 4 - \frac{2}{3}(-9) = 10$. Hence, the solution is $(10, -9)$.

19. Adding gives $3x + 2y = 8$
$$\underline{x - 2y = 0}$$
$$4x = 8 \quad \Leftrightarrow \quad x = 2.$$
So $x - 2y = (2) - 2y = 0$ $\Leftrightarrow$ $2y = 2$ $\Leftrightarrow$ $y = 1$. Thus, the solution is $(2, 1)$.

21. $\begin{cases} x + 4y = 8 \\ 3x + 12y = 2 \end{cases}$ Adding -3 times the first equation to the second equation gives
$$-3x - 12y = -24$$
$$\underline{3x + 12y = 2}$$
$$0 = -22, \text{ which is never true. Thus the system has no solution.}$$

23. $\begin{cases} 2x - 6y = 10 \\ -3x + 9y = -15 \end{cases}$ Adding 3 times the first equation to 2 times the second equation gives
$$6x - 18y = 30$$
$$\underline{-6x + 18y = -30}$$
$$0 = 0 \quad . \text{ Writing the equation in slope-intercept form, we have } 2x - 6y = 10 \quad \Leftrightarrow$$
$-6y = -2x + 10$ $\Leftrightarrow$ $y = \frac{1}{3}x - \frac{5}{3}$, so a solution is any pair of the form $\left(x, \frac{1}{3}x - \frac{5}{3}\right)$, where x is
any real number.

25. $\begin{cases} 6x + 4y = 12 \\ 9x + 6y = 18 \end{cases}$ Adding 3 times the first equation to -2 times the second equation gives
$$18x + 12y = 36$$
$$\underline{-18x - 12y = -36}$$
$$0 = 0 \quad . \text{ Writing the equation in slope-intercept form, we have } 6x + 4y = 12 \quad \Leftrightarrow$$
$4y = -6x + 12$ $\Leftrightarrow$ $y = -\frac{3}{2}x + 3$, so a solution is any pair of the form $\left(x, -\frac{3}{2}x + 3\right)$, where x
is any real number.

27. $\begin{cases} 8s - 3t = -3 \\ 5s - 2t = -1 \end{cases}$. Adding 2 times the first equation to 3 times the second equation gives
$$16s - 6t = -6$$
$$\underline{15s - 6t = -3}$$
$$s = -3. \text{ So } 8(-3) - 3t = -3 \quad \Leftrightarrow \quad -24 - 3t = -3 \quad \Leftrightarrow \quad t = -7. \text{ Thus, the solution}$$
is $(-3, -7)$.

29. $\begin{cases} \frac{1}{2}x + \frac{3}{5}y = 3 \\ \frac{5}{3}x + 2y = 10 \end{cases}$. Adding 10 times the first equation to -3 times the second equation gives
$$5x + 6y = 30$$
$$\underline{-5x - 6y = -30}$$
$$0 = 0 \quad . \text{ Writing the equation in slope-intercept form, we have } \frac{1}{2}x + \frac{3}{5}y = 3 \quad \Leftrightarrow$$
$\frac{3}{5}y = -\frac{1}{2}x + 3$ $\Leftrightarrow$ $y = -\frac{5}{6}x + 5$, so a solution is any pair of the form $\left(x, -\frac{5}{6}x + 5\right)$, where x is
any real number.

31. $x + y = 0$ $\times\,-1$ $-x - y = 0$
     $x + ay = 1$ $\times\,1$ $\Rightarrow$ $x + ay = 1$

$$\overline{ay - y = 1} \quad\Leftrightarrow\quad y(a-1) = 1 \quad\Leftrightarrow\quad y = \tfrac{1}{a-1}, a \neq 1.$$

So $x + \left(\tfrac{1}{a-1}\right) = 0$ $\Leftrightarrow$ $x = \tfrac{1}{1-a} = -\tfrac{1}{a-1}$. Thus the solution is $\left(-\tfrac{1}{a-1}, \tfrac{1}{a-1}\right)$.

33. $ax + by = 1$ $\times\,-b$ $-abx - b^2 y = -b$
     $bx + ay = 1$ $\times\,a$ $\Rightarrow$ $abx + a^2 y = a$

$$\overline{(a^2 - b^2)y = a - b} \quad\Leftrightarrow\quad y = \tfrac{a-b}{a^2-b^2} = \tfrac{1}{a+b}, a^2 - b^2 \neq 0.$$

So $ax + \tfrac{b}{a+b} = 1$ $\Leftrightarrow$ $ax = \tfrac{a}{a+b}$ $\Leftrightarrow$ $x = \tfrac{1}{a+b}$. Thus the solution is $\left(\tfrac{1}{a+b}, \tfrac{1}{a+b}\right)$.

35. Let the two numbers be x and y. This gives $x + y = 34$

$$\underline{x - y = 10}$$
$$2x = 44 \quad\Leftrightarrow\quad x = 22.$$

So $22 + y = 34$ $\Leftrightarrow$ $y = 12$. Therefore, the two numbers are 22 and 12.

37. Let d be the number of dimes and q be the number of quarters. This gives

$$d + q = 14 \qquad \times\,-1 \qquad\qquad -d - q = -14$$
$$0.10d + 0.25q = 2.75 \quad \times\,10 \;\Rightarrow\; \underline{d + 2.5q = 27.5}$$
$$1.5q = 13.5 \quad\Leftrightarrow\quad q = 9$$

So $d + (9) = 14$ $\Leftrightarrow$ $d = 5$. Thus the number of dimes is 5 and the number of quarters is 9.

39. Let x be the speed of the plane in still air and y be the speed of the wind. This gives

$$2x - 2y = 180 \qquad \times\,-6 \qquad 12x - 12y = 1080$$
$$1.2x + 1.2y = 180 \quad \times\,10 \;\Rightarrow\; \underline{12x + 12y = 1800}$$
$$24x = 2880 \quad\Leftrightarrow\quad x = 120.$$

So $2(120) - 2y = 180$ $\Leftrightarrow$ $-2y = -60$ $\Leftrightarrow$ $y = 30$. Therefore, the speed of the plane is 120 mi/h and the wind speed is 30 mi/h.

41. Let x be the cycling speed and y be the running speed. (Remember to divide by 60 to convert minutes to decimal hours.) We have

$$0.5x + 0.5y = 12.5 \times\,-2 \qquad\qquad -x - y = -25$$
$$0.75x + 0.2y = 16 \quad \times\,5 \;\Rightarrow\; \underline{3.75x + y = 80}$$
$$2.75x = 55 \quad\Leftrightarrow\quad x = 20.$$

So $20 + y = 25$ $\Leftrightarrow$ $y = 5$. Thus, the cycling speed is 20 mi/h and the running speed is 5 mi/h.

43. Let a be the grams of food A and b be the grams of food B. This gives

$$0.12a + 0.20b = 32 \qquad \times\,-250 \qquad -30a - 50b = -8000$$
$$100a + 50b = 22000 \qquad \times\,1 \;\Rightarrow\; \underline{100a + 50b = 22000}$$
$$70a = 14000 \quad\Leftrightarrow\quad a = 200.$$

So $0.12(200) + 0.20b = 32$ $\Leftrightarrow$ $0.20b = 8$ $\Leftrightarrow$ $b = 40$. Thus, she should use 200 grams of food A and 40 grams of food B.

45. Let x and y be the sulfuric acid concentrations in the first and second containers.

$$300x + 600y = 900(0.15) \qquad \times\,-1 \qquad -300x - 600y = -135$$
$$100x + 500y = 600(0.125) \qquad \times\,3 \;\Rightarrow\; \underline{300x + 1500y = 225}$$
$$900y = 90 \quad\Leftrightarrow\quad y = 0.10.$$

So $100x + 500(0.10) = 75$ $\Leftrightarrow$ $x = 0.25$. Thus, the concentrations of sulfuric acid are 25% in the first container and 10% in the second.

47. Let x be the amount he invests at 6% and let y be the amount he invests at 10%.
The ratio of the amounts invested gives $x = 2y$. Then the interest earned is $0.06x + 0.10y = 3520$ $\Leftrightarrow$ $6x + 10y = 352,000$. Substituting gives $6(2y) + 10y = 352,000$ $\Leftrightarrow$ $22y = 352,000$ $\Leftrightarrow$ $y = 16,000$. Then $x = 2(16,000) = 32,000$. Thus, he invests \$32,000 at 6% and \$16,000 at 10%.

49. Let x be the tens digit and y be the ones digit of the number.

$$
\begin{array}{lll}
x + y = 7 & \times 9 & 9x + 9y = 63 \\
10y + x = 27 + 10x + y & \times 1 \Rightarrow & 9x - 9y = -27 \\
\hline
& & 18x \quad\quad = 36 \quad \Leftrightarrow \quad x = 2.
\end{array}
$$

So $2 + y = 7$ $\Leftrightarrow$ $y = 5$. Thus, the number is 25.

51. $\begin{cases} 0.21x + 3.17y = 9.51 & l_1 \\ 2.35x - 1.17y = 5.89 & l_2 \end{cases}$

The solution is approximately $(3.87, 2.74)$.

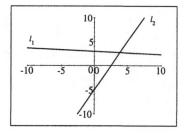

53. $\begin{cases} 2371x - 6552y = 13{,}591 & l_1 \\ 9815x + 992y = 618{,}555 & l_2 \end{cases}$

The solution is approximately $(61.00, 20.00)$.

55. $\displaystyle\sum_{k=1}^{n} x_k = 1 + 2 + 3 + 5 + 7 = 18$,

$\displaystyle\sum_{k=1}^{n} y_k = 3 + 5 + 6 + 6 + 9 = 29$,

$\displaystyle\sum_{k=1}^{n} x_k y_k = 1(3) + 2(5) + 3(6) + 5(6) + 7(9) = 124$,

$\displaystyle\sum_{k=1}^{n} x_k^2 = 1^2 + 2^2 + 3^2 + 5^2 + 7^2 = 88$, $n = 5$. Thus we get the system

$$
\begin{array}{lll}
\begin{cases} 18a + 5b = 29 \\ 88a + 18b = 124 \end{cases} & \begin{array}{l} \times -18 \\ \times 5 \end{array} & \begin{array}{l} -324a - 90b = -522 \\ 440a + 90b = 620 \end{array} \\
& & \hline \\
& & 116a \quad\quad = 98 \quad \Leftrightarrow \quad a \approx 0.845.
\end{array}
$$

Then $b = \frac{1}{5}[-18(0.845) + 29] \approx 2.758$. So, the regression line is $y = 0.845x + 2.758$.

Exercises 8.3

1. The equation $6x - \sqrt{3}y + \frac{1}{2}z = 0$ is linear.

3. The system $\begin{cases} xy - 3y + z = 5 \\ x - y^2 + 5z = 0 \\ 2x + yz = 3 \end{cases}$ is not a linear system, since the first equation contains a product of variables. In fact both the second and the third equation are not linear.

5. $\begin{cases} x - 2y + 4z = 3 \\ \quad y + 2z = 7 \\ \qquad z = 2 \end{cases}$ Substituting $z = 2$ into the second equation gives $y + 2(2) = 7 \quad \Leftrightarrow \quad y = 3$.

   Substituting $z = 2$ and $y = 3$ into the first equation gives $x - 2(3) + 4(2) = 3 \quad \Leftrightarrow \quad x = 1$. Thus the solution is $(1, 3, 2)$.

7. $\begin{cases} x + 2y + z = 7 \\ \quad -y + 3z = 9 \\ \qquad 2z = 6 \end{cases}$ Solving we get $2z = 6 \quad \Leftrightarrow \quad z = 3$. Substituting $z = 3$ into the second

   equation gives $-y + 3(3) = 9 \quad \Leftrightarrow \quad y = 0$. Substituting $z = 3$ and $y = 0$ into the first equation gives $x + 2(0) + 3 = 7 \quad \Leftrightarrow \quad x = 4$. Thus the solution is $(4, 0, 3)$.

9. $\begin{cases} 2x - y + 6z = 5 \\ \quad y + 4z = 0 \\ \qquad -2z = 1 \end{cases}$ Solving we get $-2z = 1 \quad \Leftrightarrow \quad z = -\frac{1}{2}$. Substituting $z = -\frac{1}{2}$ into the

   second equation gives $y + 4(-\frac{1}{2}) = 0 \quad \Leftrightarrow \quad y = 2$. Substituting $z = -\frac{1}{2}$ and $y = 2$ into the first equation gives $2x - (2) + 6(-\frac{1}{2}) = 5 \quad \Leftrightarrow \quad x = 5$. Thus the solution is $(5, 2, -\frac{1}{2})$.

11. $\begin{cases} x - 2y - z = 4 \\ x - y + 3z = 0 \\ 2x + y + z = 0 \end{cases}$ Using the first equation we subtract the first equation from the second equation.

   $\begin{array}{r} -x + 2y + z = -4 \\ x - y + 3z = 0 \\ \hline y + 4z = -4 \end{array}$ This gives the system

   $\begin{cases} x - 2y - z = 4 \\ \quad y + 4z = -4. \\ 2x + y + z = 0 \end{cases}$

   $\begin{cases} x - 2y - z = 4 \\ x - y + 3z = 0 \\ 2x + y + z = 0 \end{cases}$ Or using the third equation, we subtract $\frac{1}{2}$ times the third equation from the second equation.

   $\begin{array}{r} x - y + 3z = 0 \\ -x - \frac{1}{2}y - \frac{1}{2}z = 0 \\ \hline -\frac{3}{2}y + \frac{5}{2}z = 0 \end{array}$ This gives the

   system $\begin{cases} x - 2y - z = 4 \\ -\frac{3}{2}y + \frac{5}{2}z = 0. \\ 2x + y + z = 0 \end{cases}$

13. $\begin{cases} 2x - y + 3z = 2 \\ x + 2y - z = 4 \\ -4x + 5y + z = 10 \end{cases}$ Using the first equation we add 2 times the first equation to the third equation.

   $\begin{array}{r} 4x - 2y + 6z = 4 \\ -4x + 5y + z = 10 \\ \hline 3y + 7z = 14 \end{array}$ This gives the

   system $\begin{cases} 2x - y + 3z = 2 \\ x + 2y - z = 4 \,. \\ 3y + 7z = 14 \end{cases}$

$$\begin{cases} 2x - y + 3z = 2 \\ x + 2y - z = 4 \\ -4x + 5y + z = 10 \end{cases}$$ Or using the third equation, we add 4 times the second equation to the third equation.

$$\begin{array}{r} 4x + 8y - 4z = 16 \\ -4x + 5y + z = 10 \\ \hline 13y - 3z = 26 \end{array}$$ This gives

the system $\begin{cases} 2x - y + 3z = 2 \\ x + 2y - z = 4 \\ 13y - 3z = 26 \end{cases}$.

15. $\begin{cases} x + y + z = 4 \\ x + 3y + 3z = 10 \\ 2x + y - z = 3 \end{cases}$ Using the first equation we eliminate the x term from the second and the third equation.

$$\begin{array}{r} -x - y - z = -4 \\ x + 3y + 3z = 10 \\ \hline 2y + 2z = 6 \end{array}$$ and

$$\begin{array}{r} -2x - 2y - 2z = -8 \\ 2x + y - z = 3 \\ \hline -y - 3z = -5 \end{array} \quad \Leftrightarrow \quad y + 3z = 5$$

So we get the system $\begin{cases} x + y + z = 4 \\ 2y + 2z = 6. \\ y + 3z = 5 \end{cases}$ Which we can write as

$\begin{cases} x + y + z = 4 \\ y + 3z = 5 \\ 2y + 2z = 6 \end{cases}$ Eliminate the y term from the third equation,

$$\begin{array}{r} -2y - 6z = -10 \\ 2y + 2z = 6 \\ \hline -4z = -4 \end{array}$$ to get the system

$\begin{cases} x + y + z = 4 \\ y + 3z = 5 \\ -4z = -4 \end{cases}$

So $z = 1$ and $y + 3(1) = 8 \quad \Leftrightarrow \quad y = 2$. Then $x + 2 + 1 = 4 \quad \Leftrightarrow \quad x = 1$. So the solution is $(1, 2, 1)$.

17. $\begin{cases} x \quad\quad - 4z = 1 \\ 2x - y \quad - 6z = 4 \\ 2x + 3y - 2z = 8 \end{cases}$ Using the first equation we eliminate the x term from the second and the third equation.

$$\begin{array}{r} -2x \quad\quad + 8z = -2 \\ 2x - y - 6z = 4 \\ \hline -y + 2z = 2 \end{array}$$ and

$$\begin{array}{r} -2x \quad\quad + 8z = -2 \\ 2x + 3y - 2z = 8 \\ \hline 3y + 6z = 6 \end{array}$$ So we get the system

$\begin{cases} x \quad\quad - 4z = 1 \\ -y + 2z = 2 \\ 3y + 6z = 6 \end{cases}$ Eliminate the y term from the third equation,

$$\begin{array}{r} -3y + 6z = 6 \\ 3y + 6z = 6 \\ \hline 12z = 12 \end{array}$$

To get the system $\begin{cases} x \quad\quad - 4z = 1 \\ -y + 2z = 2 \\ 12z = 12 \end{cases}$. So $z = 1$ and $-y + 2(1) = 2 \quad \Leftrightarrow \quad y = 0$. Then $x - 4(1) = 1$

$\Leftrightarrow \quad x = 5$. So the solution is $(5, 0, 1)$.

19. $\begin{cases} 2x + 4y - z = 2 \\ x + 2y - 3z = -4 \\ 3x - y + z = 1 \end{cases}$ First rewrite as $\begin{cases} x + 2y - 3z = -4 \\ 2x + 4y - z = 2 \\ 3x - y + z = 1 \end{cases}$. Using the first equation we eliminate the x term from the second and the third equation.

$$\begin{array}{r} -2x - 4y + 6z = 8 \\ 2x + 4y - z = 2 \\ \hline 5z = 10 \end{array}$$ and

$$\begin{array}{r} -3x - 6y + 9z = 12 \\ 3x - y + z = 1 \\ \hline -7y + 10z = 13 \end{array}$$ So we get the system

$\begin{cases} x + 2y - 3z = -4 \\ 5z = 10 . \\ -7y + 10z = 13 \end{cases}$

which we can write as $\begin{cases} x + 2y - 3z = -4 \\ -7y + 10z = 13 . \\ 5z = 10 \end{cases}$ So $z = 2$ and $-7y + 10(2) = 13 \quad \Leftrightarrow \quad y = 1$. Then

$x + 2(1) - 3(2) = -4 \quad \Leftrightarrow \quad x = 0$. So the solution is $(0, 1, 2)$.

21. $\begin{cases} y - 2z = 0 \\ 2x + 3y \quad\; = 2 \\ -x - 2y + z = -1 \end{cases}$ First rewrite as $\begin{cases} -x - 2y + z = -1 \\ y - 2z = 0 \\ 2x + 3y \quad\; = 2 \end{cases}$. Using the first equation we eliminate the x term from the third equation.

$\begin{array}{r} -2x - 4y + 2z = -2 \\ 2x + 3y \qquad = 2 \\ \hline -y + 2z = 0 \end{array}$ So we get the system $\begin{cases} -x - 2y + z = -1 \\ y - 2z = 0 \\ -y + 2z = 0 \end{cases}$ Eliminate the y term from the third equation, $\begin{array}{r} y - 2z = 0 \\ -y + 2z = 0 \\ \hline 0 = 0 \end{array}$

to get the system $\begin{cases} -x - 2y + z = -1 \\ y - 2z = 0 \\ 0 = 0 \end{cases}$. The system is dependent, so when $z = t$ we solve for y to get

$y - 2t = 0 \quad\Leftrightarrow\quad y = 2t$. Then $-x - 2(2t) + t = -1 \quad\Leftrightarrow\quad -x - 3t = -1 \quad\Leftrightarrow\quad x = -3t + 1$. So the solution is $(-3t + 1, 2t, t)$.

23. $\begin{cases} x + 2y - z = 1 \\ 2x + 3y - 4z = -3 \\ 3x + 6y - 3z = 4 \end{cases}$ Using the first equation we eliminate the x term from the second and the third equation. $\begin{array}{r} -2x - 4y + 2z = -2 \\ 2x + 3y - 4z = -3 \\ \hline -y - 2z = -5 \end{array}$ and

$\begin{array}{r} -3x - 6y + 3z = -3 \\ 3x + 6y - 3z = 4 \\ \hline 0 = 1 \end{array}$ Since $0 = 1$ is false, this system is inconsistent.

25. $\begin{cases} 2x + 3y - z = 1 \\ x + 2y \quad\; = 3 \\ x + 3y + z = 4 \end{cases}$ First rewrite as $\begin{cases} x + 2y \quad\; = 3 \\ 2x + 3y - z = 1 \\ x + 3y + z = 4 \end{cases}$. Using the first equation we eliminate the x term from the second and the third equation.

$\begin{array}{r} -2x - 4y \quad\; = -6 \\ 2x + 3y - z = 1 \\ \hline -y - z = -5 \end{array}$ and $\begin{array}{r} -x - 2y \quad\; = -3 \\ x + 3y + z = 4 \\ \hline y + z = 1 \end{array}$ So we get the system $\begin{cases} x + 2y \quad\; = 3 \\ -y - z = -5 \\ y + z = 1 \end{cases}$.

Eliminate the y term from the third equation. $\begin{array}{r} -y - z = -5 \\ y + z = 1 \\ \hline 0 = -4 \end{array}$ Since $0 = -4$ is false, this system is inconsistent.

27. $\begin{cases} x + y - z = 0 \\ x + 2y - 3z = -3 \\ 2x + 3y - 4z = -3 \end{cases}$ Using the first equation we eliminate the x term from the second and the third equation. $\begin{array}{r} -x - y + z = 0 \\ x + 2y - 3z = -3 \\ \hline y - 2z = -3 \end{array}$ and

$\begin{array}{r} -2x - 2y - 2z = 0 \\ 2x + 3y - 4z = -3 \\ \hline y - 2z = -3 \end{array}$ So we get the system $\begin{cases} x + y - z = 0 \\ y - 2z = -3 \\ y - 2z = -3 \end{cases}$ Eliminate the y term from the third equation. $\begin{array}{r} -y + 2z = 3 \\ y - 2z = -3 \\ \hline 0 = 0 \end{array}$

So $z = t$ and $y - 2t = -3 \quad\Leftrightarrow\quad y = 2t - 3$. Then $x + (2t - 3) - t = 0 \quad\Leftrightarrow\quad x = -t + 3$. So the solution is $(-t + 3, 2t - 3, t)$.

29. $\begin{cases} x + 3y - 2z = 0 \\ 2x \quad\;\; + 4z = 4 \\ 4x + 6y \quad\; = 4 \end{cases}$ Using the first equation we eliminate the x term from the second and the third equation. $\begin{array}{r} -2x - 6y + 4z = 0 \\ 2x \quad\;\; + 4z = 4 \\ \hline -6y + 8z = 4 \end{array}$ and

$\begin{array}{r} -4x - 12y + 8z = 0 \\ 4x + 6y \quad\; = 4 \\ \hline -6y + 8z = 4 \end{array}$ So we get the system $\begin{cases} x + 3y - 2z = 0 \\ -6y + 8z = 4 \\ -6y + 8z = 4 \end{cases}$. Eliminate the y term from the third equation. $\begin{array}{r} 6y - 8z = -4 \\ -6y + 8z = 4 \\ \hline 0 = 0 \end{array}$

So $z = t$ and $-6y + 8t = 4 \quad\Leftrightarrow\quad -6y = -8t + 4 \quad\Leftrightarrow\quad y = \frac{4}{3}t - \frac{2}{3}$. Then

$x + 3\left(\frac{4}{3}t - \frac{2}{3}\right) - 2t = 0 \quad\Leftrightarrow\quad x = -2t + 2$. So the solution is $\left(-2t + 2, \frac{4}{3}t - \frac{2}{3}, t\right)$.

31.
$$\begin{cases} x & +z+2w = 6 \\ y - 2z & = -3 \\ x + 2y - z & = -2 \\ 2x + y + 3z - 2w = 0 \end{cases}$$

Using the first equation we eliminate the x term from the third and the fourth equation.

$$\begin{aligned} -x & - z - 2w = -6 \\ x + 2y - z & = -2 \\ \hline 2y - 2z - 2w = -8 \end{aligned}$$ and

$$\begin{aligned} -2x & - 2z - 4w = -12 \\ 2x + y + 3z - 2w = 0 \\ \hline y + z - 6w = -12 \end{aligned}$$

So we get the system

$$\begin{cases} x & +z+2w = 6 \\ y - 2z & = -3 \\ 2y - 2z - 2w = -8 \\ y + z - 6w = -12 \end{cases}.$$

Using the first equation we eliminate the y term from the third and the fourth equation.

$$\begin{aligned} -2y + 4z & = 6 \\ 2y - 2z - 2w = -8 \\ \hline 2z - 2w = -2 \end{aligned}$$ and

$$\begin{aligned} -y + 2z & = 3 \\ y + z - 6w = -12 \\ \hline 3z - 6w = -9 \end{aligned}$$

This gives us the system

$$\begin{cases} x & +z+2w = 6 \\ y - 2z & = -3 \\ 2z - 2w = -2 \\ 3z - 6w = -9 \end{cases}.$$

We divide the third equation by 2 to get this system .

$$\begin{cases} x & +z+2w = 6 \\ y - 2z & = -3 \\ z - 1w = -1 \\ 3z - 6w = -9 \end{cases}.$$

Eliminate the z term from the fourth equation,

$$\begin{aligned} -3z + 3w & = 3 \\ 3z - 6w = -9 \\ \hline -3w = -6 \end{aligned}$$ to get the system

$$\begin{cases} x & +z+2w = 6 \\ y - 2z & = -3 \\ z - w = -1 \\ -3w = -6 \end{cases}.$$

So $w = 2$ and $z - 2 = -1 \Leftrightarrow z = 1$. Then $y - 2(1) = -3 \Leftrightarrow y = -1$ and $x + 1 + 2(2) = 6 \Leftrightarrow x = 1$. Thus the solution is $(1, -1, 1, 2)$.

33. Quadratic containing the points $(-2, 3), (-1, 1), (1, 9)$:

Using the general form of a quadratic, $y = ax^2 + bx + c$, we substitute for x and y and solve for a, b, and c. This gives

$$\begin{array}{llll} (-2, 3) & a(-2)^2 + b(-2) + c = 3 & \Rightarrow & 4a - 2b + c = 3 \\ (-1, 1) & a(-1)^2 + b(-1) + c = 1 & \Rightarrow & a - b + c = 1 \\ (1, 9) & a(1)^2 + b(1) + c = 9 & \Rightarrow & a + b + c = 9 \end{array}$$

$\Rightarrow \begin{cases} a - b + c = 1 \\ a + b + c = 9. \\ 4a - 2b + c = 3 \end{cases}$

Using the first equation we eliminate the a term from the second and the third equation.

$$\begin{aligned} -a + b - c = -1 \\ a + b + c = 9 \\ \hline 2b = 8 \end{aligned}$$ and

$$\begin{aligned} -4a + 4b - 4c = -4 \\ 4a - 2b + c = 3 \\ \hline 2b - 3c = -1 \end{aligned}$$ So we get the system

$$\begin{cases} a - b + c = 1 \\ 2b = 8 \\ 2b - 3c = -1 \end{cases}.$$

Eliminate the b term from the third equation,

$$\begin{aligned} 2b = 8 \\ 2b - 3c = -1 \\ \hline -3c = -9 \end{aligned}$$ to get the system

$$\begin{cases} a - b + c = 1 \\ 2b = 8 \\ -3c = -9 \end{cases}.$$

So $c = 3$ and $b = 4$. Then $a - 4 + 3 = 1 \Leftrightarrow a = 2$. So the quadratic polynomial is $y = 2x^2 + 4x + 3$.

35. Quadratic containing the points $(-1, -10), (1, 0), (2, 15)$:

Using the general form of a quadratic, $y = ax^2 + bx + c$, we substitute for x and y and solve for a, b, and c. This gives

$$\begin{array}{llll} (-1, -10) & a(-1)^2 + b(-1) + c = -10 & \Rightarrow & a - b + c = -10 \\ (1, 0) & a(1)^2 + b(1) + c = 0 & \Rightarrow & a + b + c = 0 & \Rightarrow \\ (2, 15) & a(2)^2 + b(2) + c = 15 & \Rightarrow & 4a + 2b + c = 15 \end{array}$$

$$\begin{cases} a - b + c = -10 \\ a + b + c = 0 \\ 4a + 2b + c = 15 \end{cases}$$ Using the first equation we eliminate the a term from the second and the third equation. $\quad \begin{aligned} -a + b - c &= 10 \\ a + b + c &= 0 \\ \hline 2b \qquad &= 10 \end{aligned}$ and

$$\begin{aligned} -4a + 4b - 4c &= 40 \\ 4a + 2b + c &= 15 \\ \hline 6b - 3c &= 55 \end{aligned}$$ So we get the system $\begin{cases} a - b + c = -10 \\ \quad 2b \quad = 10 \\ \quad 6b - 3c = 55 \end{cases}$.

Eliminate the b term from the third equation, $\begin{aligned} -6b \qquad &= -30 \\ 6b - 3c &= 55 \\ \hline -3c &= 25 \end{aligned}$ to get the system $\begin{cases} a - b + c = -10 \\ \quad 2b \quad = 10 \\ \quad -3c = 25 \end{cases}$.

So $c = -\frac{25}{3}$ and $b = 5$. Then $a - 5 + \left(-\frac{25}{3}\right) = -10 \quad \Leftrightarrow \quad a = \frac{10}{3}$. So the quadratic polynomial is $y = \frac{10}{3}x^2 + 5x - \frac{25}{3}$.

37. Let x be the amount she invests at 4%, y be the amount she invests at 5%, and let z be the amount she invests at 6%. Modeling these we get the equations:

Total money $\qquad\qquad x + y + z = 100{,}000$
Annual income $\quad 0.04x + 0.05y + 0.06z = 0.051(100{,}000)$
Equal amounts $\qquad\qquad\qquad x = y$

$\Leftrightarrow \begin{cases} x + y + z = 100{,}000 \\ 4x + 5y + 6z = 510{,}000. \\ x - y = 0 \end{cases}$

Using the first equation we eliminate the x term from the second and the third equation. $\begin{aligned} -4x - 4y - 4z &= -400{,}000 \\ 4x + 5y + 6z &= 510{,}000 \\ \hline y + 2z &= 110{,}000 \end{aligned}$ and $\begin{aligned} -x - y - z &= -100{,}000 \\ x - y \qquad &= \qquad 0 \\ \hline -2y - z &= -100{,}000 \end{aligned}$

So we get the system $\begin{cases} x + y + z = 100{,}000 \\ y + 2z = 110{,}000 \\ -2y - z = -100{,}000 \end{cases}$. Eliminate the y term from the third equation. $\begin{aligned} 2y + 4z &= 220{,}000 \\ -2y - z &= -100{,}000 \\ \hline 3z &= 120{,}000 \end{aligned}$ Finally, we get the system

$$\begin{cases} x + y + z = 100{,}000 \\ y + 2z = 110{,}000 \\ 3z = 120{,}000 \end{cases}$$

So $z = 40{,}000$ and $y + 2(40{,}000) = 110{,}000 \quad \Leftrightarrow \quad y = 30{,}000$. Since $x = y$, $x = 30{,}000$. She must invest \$30,000 in short-term bonds, \$30,000 in intermediate-term bonds, and \$40,000 in long-term bonds.

39. Let a, b, and c be the ounce of Type A, Type B, and Type C pellets used. The requirements for the different vitamins gives the following system

$$\begin{cases} 2a + 3b + c = 9 \\ 3a + b + 3c = 14 \\ 8a + 5b + 7c = 32 \end{cases}$$ Using the first equation we eliminate the a term from the second and the third equation. $\begin{aligned} -6a - 9b - 3c &= -27 \\ 6a + 2b + 6c &= 28 \\ \hline -7b + 3c &= 1 \end{aligned}$ and

$$\begin{aligned} -8a - 12b - 4c &= -36 \\ 8a + 5b + 7c &= 32 \\ \hline -7b + 3c &= -4 \end{aligned}$$ So we get the system $\begin{cases} 2a + 3b + c = 9 \\ -7b + 3c = 1 \\ -7b + 3c = -4 \end{cases}$ Eliminate the b term from the third equation. $\begin{aligned} 7b - 3c &= -1 \\ -7b + 3c &= -4 \\ \hline 0 &= -5 \end{aligned}$

But $0 = -5$ is always false, so there is no solution.

41. (a) Quadratic containing the points $(-2, 10)$, $(1, -5)$, $(2, -6)$, $(4, -2)$:

Using the general form of a quadratic, $y = ax^2 + bx + c$, we substitute for x and y and solve for a, b, and c. This gives

$$(1, -5) \qquad a(1)^2 + b(1) + c = -5 \qquad \Rightarrow \qquad a + b + c = -5$$
$$(-2, 10) \quad a(-2)^2 + b(-2) + c = 10 \qquad \Rightarrow \qquad 4a - 2b + c = 10$$
$$(2, -6) \qquad a(2)^2 + b(2) + c = -6 \qquad \Rightarrow \qquad 4a + 2b + c = -6 \qquad \Rightarrow$$
$$(4, -2) \qquad a(4)^2 + b(4) + c = -2 \qquad \Rightarrow \qquad 16a + 4b + c = -2$$

$$\begin{cases} a + b + c = -5 \\ 4a - 2b + c = 10 \\ 4a + 2b + c = -6 \\ 16a + 4b + c = -2 \end{cases}$$
Using the first equation we eliminate the a terms from the other three equations.
$$\begin{array}{r} -4a - 4b - 4c = 20 \\ 4a - 2b + c = 10 \\ \hline -6b - 3c = 30 \end{array} ,$$

$$\begin{array}{r} -4a - 4b - 4c = 20 \\ 4a + 2b + c = -6 \\ \hline -2b - 3c = 14 \end{array} \text{ and}$$
$$\begin{array}{r} -16a - 16b - 16z = 80 \\ 16a + 4b + c = -2 \\ \hline -12b - 15c = 78 \end{array}$$
So we get the system
$$\begin{cases} a + b + c = -5 \\ -6b - 3c = 30 \\ -2b - 3c = 14 \\ -12b - 15c = 78 \end{cases}$$

To simplify we first divide the second and fourth equation by -3 to get
$$\begin{cases} a + b + c = -5 \\ 2b + c = -10 \\ -2b - 3c = 14 \\ 4b + 5c = -26 \end{cases}$$
Next eliminate the b terms from the third and fourth equation.
$$\begin{array}{r} 2b + c = -10 \\ -2b - 3c = 14 \\ \hline -2c = 4 \end{array} \text{ and}$$

$$\begin{array}{r} -4b - 2c = 20 \\ 4b + 5c = -26 \\ \hline 3c = -6 \end{array}$$
This results in the following system
$$\begin{cases} a + b + c = -5 \\ 2b + c = -10 \\ -2c = 4 \\ 3c = -6 \end{cases}$$

Each of the last two equations gives $c = -2$.
Back-substituting gives $2b + (-2) = -10 \quad \Leftrightarrow \quad b = -4$.
Back-substituting again gives $a + (-4) + (-2) = -5 \quad \Leftrightarrow \quad a = 1$.
The quadratic curve of exact fit is $y = x^2 - 4x - 2$.

(b) Use the QuadReg command (on the TI 83) we get the curve
$y = 1.13333333x^2 - 4.21333333x - 2.066666667$.

(c) Quadratic containing the points $(-2, 11)$, $(1, -6)$, $(2, -5)$, $(4, -1)$:

Using the general form of a quadratic, $y = ax^2 + bx + c$, we substitute for x and y and solve for a, b, and c. This gives

$(1, -6) \quad a(1)^2 + b(1) + c = -6 \quad \Rightarrow \quad a + b + c = -6$

$(2, -5) \quad a(2)^2 + b(2) + c = -5 \quad \Rightarrow \quad 4a + 2b + c = -5$

$(2, -5) \quad a(2)^2 + b(2) + c = -5 \quad \Rightarrow \quad 4a + 2b + c = -5 \qquad \Rightarrow$

$(4, -1) \quad a(4)^2 + b(4) + c = -1 \quad \Rightarrow \quad 16a + 4b + c = -1$

$$\begin{cases} a + b + c = -6 \\ 4a + 2b + c = -5 \\ 4a - 2b + c = 11 \\ 16a + 4b + c = -1 \end{cases}$$
Using the first equation we eliminate the a terms from the other three equations.
$$\begin{aligned} -4a - 4b - 4c &= 24 \\ 4a + 2b + c &= -5 \\ \hline -2b - 3c &= 19 \end{aligned} \quad ,$$

$$\begin{aligned} -4a - 4b - 4c &= 24 \\ 4a - 2b + c &= 11 \\ \hline -6b - 3c &= 35 \end{aligned} \quad \text{and} \quad \begin{aligned} -16a - 16b - 16z &= 96 \\ 16a + 4b + c &= -1 \\ \hline -12b - 15c &= 95 \end{aligned}$$
So we get the system
$$\begin{cases} a + b + c = -6 \\ -2b - 3c = 19 \\ -6b - 3c = 35 \\ -12b - 15c = 95 \end{cases}$$

Next eliminate the b terms from the third and fourth equation.
$$\begin{aligned} 6b + 9c &= -57 \\ -6b - 3c &= 35 \\ \hline 6c &= -22 \end{aligned} \quad \text{and} \quad \begin{aligned} 12b + 18c &= -114 \\ -12b - 15c &= 95 \\ \hline 3c &= -19 \end{aligned}$$
This results in the following system

$$\begin{cases} a + b + c = -6 \\ -2b - 3c = 19 \\ 6c = -22 \\ 3c = -19 \end{cases}$$

In this system we note that the second equation yields $c = -\frac{11}{3}$ while the fourth equation yields $c = -\frac{19}{3}$. Since both cannot be true, this system has no solution and as a result, there is no quadratic function that passes through all four points.

(d)

(e)   The curve of exact fit (when it exists) will contain all the points, while the curve of best fit might not contain any of the points but will always exists. For example we found both an exact curve and a curve of best fix for the points in part (a) but there was only curve of best fit for the points in part (c).

Exercises 8.4

1. (a) Yes, this matrix is in echelon form.

   (b) Yes, this matrix is in reduced echelon form.

   (c) $x = -3$
      $y = 5$

3. (a) Yes, this matrix is in echelon form.

   (b) No, this matrix is not in reduced echelon form, since the leading "one" in the second row does not have a zero above it.

   (c) $x + 2y + 8z = 0$
      $y + 3z = 2$
      $0 = 0$

5. (a) No, this matrix is not in echelon form, since the row of zeros is not at the bottom.

   (b) No, this matrix is not in reduced echelon form.

   (c) $x = 0$
      $0 = 0$
      $y + 5z = 1$

7. (a) Yes, this matrix is in echelon form.

   (b) Yes, this matrix is in reduced echelon form.

   (c) $x + y - w = 0$ Notice that this system does not have a solution.
      $z + 2w = 0$
      $0 = 1$
      $0 = 0$

9. $\begin{bmatrix} 1 & -2 & 1 & 1 \\ 0 & 1 & 2 & 5 \\ 1 & 1 & 3 & 8 \end{bmatrix}$ $\xrightarrow[R_3 - R_1 \to R_3]{}$ $\begin{bmatrix} 1 & -2 & 1 & 1 \\ 0 & 1 & 2 & 5 \\ 0 & 3 & 2 & 7 \end{bmatrix}$ $\xrightarrow[]{R_3 - 3R_2 \to R_3}$ $\begin{bmatrix} 1 & -2 & 1 & 1 \\ 0 & 1 & 2 & 5 \\ 0 & 0 & -4 & -8 \end{bmatrix}$

   Thus, $-4z = -8$ $\Leftrightarrow$ $z = 2; y + 2(2) = 5$ $\Leftrightarrow$ $y = 1;$ and $x - 2(1) + (2) = 1$ $\Leftrightarrow$
   $x = 1.$ Therefore, the solution is $(1, 1, 2).$

11. $\begin{bmatrix} 1 & 1 & 1 & 2 \\ 2 & -3 & 2 & 4 \\ 4 & 1 & -3 & 1 \end{bmatrix}$ $\xrightarrow[R_3 - 4R_1 \to R_3]{R_2 - 2R_1 \to R_2}$ $\begin{bmatrix} 1 & 1 & 1 & 2 \\ 0 & -5 & 0 & 0 \\ 0 & -3 & -7 & -7 \end{bmatrix}$ $\xrightarrow[]{R_3 - \frac{3}{5} R_2 \to R_3}$ $\begin{bmatrix} 1 & 1 & 1 & 2 \\ 0 & -5 & 0 & 0 \\ 0 & 0 & -7 & -7 \end{bmatrix}$

   Thus, $-7z = -7$ $\Leftrightarrow$ $z = 1; -5y = 0$ $\Leftrightarrow$ $y = 0;$ and $x + 0 + 1 = 2$ $\Leftrightarrow$ $x = 1.$
   Therefore, the solution is $(1, 0, 1).$

13. $\begin{bmatrix} 1 & 2 & -1 & -2 \\ 1 & 0 & 1 & 0 \\ 2 & -1 & -1 & -3 \end{bmatrix}$ $\xrightarrow[R_3 - 2R_1 \to R_3]{R_2 - R_1 \to R_2}$ $\begin{bmatrix} 1 & 2 & -1 & -2 \\ 0 & -2 & 2 & 2 \\ 0 & -5 & 1 & 1 \end{bmatrix}$ $\xrightarrow[]{-\frac{1}{2}R_2}$

   $\begin{bmatrix} 1 & 2 & -1 & -2 \\ 0 & 1 & 1 & 1 \\ 0 & -5 & 1 & 1 \end{bmatrix}$ $\xrightarrow[]{R_3 + 5R_2 \to R_3}$ $\begin{bmatrix} 1 & 2 & -1 & -2 \\ 0 & 1 & 1 & 1 \\ 0 & 0 & 6 & 6 \end{bmatrix}$

Thus, $6z = 6$ $\Leftrightarrow$ $z = 1; y + (1) = 1$ $\Leftrightarrow$ $y = 0$; and $x + 2(0) - (1) = -2$ $\Leftrightarrow$
$x = -1$. Therefore, the solution is $(-1, 0, 1)$.

15. $\begin{bmatrix} 1 & 2 & -1 & 9 \\ 2 & 0 & -1 & -2 \\ 3 & 5 & 2 & 22 \end{bmatrix}$ $\begin{array}{c} R_2 - 2R_1 \to R_2 \\ R_3 - 3R_1 \to R_3 \end{array}$ $\begin{bmatrix} 1 & 2 & -1 & 9 \\ 0 & -4 & 1 & -20 \\ 0 & -1 & 5 & -5 \end{bmatrix}$ $\xrightarrow{4R_3 - R_2 \to R_3}$

$\begin{bmatrix} 1 & 2 & -1 & 9 \\ 0 & -4 & 1 & -20 \\ 0 & 0 & 19 & 0 \end{bmatrix}$

Thus, $19x_3 = 0$ $\Leftrightarrow$ $x_3 = 0; -4x_2 = -20$ $\Leftrightarrow$ $x_2 = 5$; and $x_1 + 2(5) = 9$ $\Leftrightarrow$
$x_1 = -1$. Therefore, the solution is $(-1, 5, 0)$.

17. $\begin{bmatrix} 2 & -3 & -1 & 13 \\ -1 & 2 & -5 & 6 \\ 5 & -1 & -1 & 49 \end{bmatrix}$ $\begin{array}{c} 2R_2 + R_1 \to R_2 \\ 2R_3 - 5R_1 \to R_3 \end{array}$ $\begin{bmatrix} 2 & -3 & -1 & 13 \\ 0 & 1 & -11 & 25 \\ 0 & 13 & 3 & 33 \end{bmatrix}$ $\xrightarrow{R_3 - 13R_2 \to R_3}$

$\begin{bmatrix} 2 & -3 & -1 & 13 \\ 0 & 1 & -11 & 25 \\ 0 & 0 & 146 & -292 \end{bmatrix}$

Thus, $146z = -292$ $\Leftrightarrow$ $z = -2; y - 11(-2) = 25$ $\Leftrightarrow$ $y = 3$; and $2x - 3 \cdot 3 + 2 = 13$
$\Leftrightarrow$ $x = 10$. Therefore, the solution is $(10, 3, -2)$.

19. $\begin{bmatrix} 1 & 1 & 1 & 2 \\ 0 & 1 & -3 & 1 \\ 2 & 1 & 5 & 0 \end{bmatrix}$ $\xrightarrow{R_3 - 2R_1 \to R_3}$ $\begin{bmatrix} 1 & 1 & 1 & 2 \\ 0 & 1 & -3 & 1 \\ 0 & -1 & 3 & -4 \end{bmatrix}$ $\xrightarrow{R_3 + R_2 \to R_3}$ $\begin{bmatrix} 1 & 1 & 1 & 3 \\ 0 & 1 & -3 & 1 \\ 0 & 0 & 0 & -3 \end{bmatrix}$

The third row of the matrix states $0 = -3$, which is impossible. Hence, the system is inconsistent,
and there is no solution.

21. $\begin{bmatrix} 2 & -3 & -9 & -5 \\ 1 & 0 & 3 & 2 \\ -3 & 1 & -4 & -3 \end{bmatrix}$ $\xrightarrow{R_1 \leftrightarrow R_2}$ $\begin{bmatrix} 1 & 0 & 3 & 2 \\ 2 & -3 & -9 & -5 \\ -3 & 1 & -4 & -3 \end{bmatrix}$ $\begin{array}{c} R_2 - 2R_1 \to R_2 \\ R_3 + 3R_1 \to R_3 \end{array}$

$\begin{bmatrix} 1 & 0 & 3 & 2 \\ 0 & -3 & -15 & -9 \\ 0 & 1 & 5 & 3 \end{bmatrix}$ $\xrightarrow{-\frac{1}{3}R_2}$ $\begin{bmatrix} 1 & 0 & 3 & 2 \\ 0 & 1 & 5 & 3 \\ 0 & 1 & 5 & 3 \end{bmatrix}$ $\xrightarrow{R_3 - R_2 \to R_3}$

$\begin{bmatrix} 1 & 0 & 3 & 2 \\ 0 & 1 & 5 & 3 \\ 0 & 0 & 0 & 0 \end{bmatrix}$

Therefore, this system has infinitely many solutions, given by $x + 3t = 2$ $\Leftrightarrow$ $x = 2 - 3t$, and
$y + 5t = 3$ $\Leftrightarrow$ $y = 3 - 5t$. Hence, the solutions are $(2 - 3t, 3 - 5t, t)$, where t is any real
number.

23. $\begin{bmatrix} 1 & -1 & 3 & 3 \\ 4 & -8 & 32 & 24 \\ 2 & -3 & 11 & 4 \end{bmatrix}$ $\begin{array}{c} R_2 - 4R_1 \to R_2 \\ R_3 - 2R_1 \to R_3 \end{array}$ $\begin{bmatrix} 1 & -1 & 3 & 3 \\ 0 & -4 & 20 & 12 \\ 0 & -1 & 5 & -2 \end{bmatrix}$ $\begin{array}{c} -\frac{1}{4}R_2 \\ R_3 + R_2 \to R_3 \end{array}$

$\begin{bmatrix} 1 & -1 & 3 & 3 \\ 0 & 1 & -5 & -3 \\ 0 & 0 & 0 & -5 \end{bmatrix}$

The third row of the matrix states $0 = -5$, which is impossible. Hence, the system is inconsistent, and there is no solution.

25. $\begin{bmatrix} 1 & 4 & -2 & -3 \\ 2 & -1 & 5 & 12 \\ 8 & 5 & 11 & 30 \end{bmatrix}$ $\begin{array}{c} R_2-2R_1 \to R_2 \\ \hline R_3-8R_1 \to R_3 \end{array}$ $\begin{bmatrix} 1 & 4 & -2 & -3 \\ 0 & -9 & 9 & 18 \\ 0 & -27 & 27 & 54 \end{bmatrix}$ $\begin{array}{c} R_3-3R_2 \to R_3 \\ \hline \end{array}$

$\begin{bmatrix} 1 & 4 & -2 & -3 \\ 0 & -9 & 9 & 18 \\ 0 & 0 & 0 & 0 \end{bmatrix}$

Therefore, this system has infinitely many solutions, given by $-9y + 9t = 18 \quad \Leftrightarrow \quad y = -2+t$, and $x + 4(-2+t) - 2t = -3 \quad \Leftrightarrow \quad x = 5 - 2t$. Hence, the solutions are $(5 - 2t, -2 + t, t)$, where t is any real number.

27. $\begin{bmatrix} 2 & 1 & -2 & 12 \\ -1 & -\frac{1}{2} & 1 & -6 \\ 3 & \frac{3}{2} & -3 & 18 \end{bmatrix}$ $\begin{array}{c} R_1 \leftrightarrow R_2 \\ \hline -R_1 \end{array}$ $\begin{bmatrix} 1 & \frac{1}{2} & -1 & 6 \\ 2 & 1 & -2 & 12 \\ 3 & \frac{3}{2} & -3 & 18 \end{bmatrix}$ $\begin{array}{c} R_2-2R_1 \to R_2 \\ \hline R_3-3R_1 \to R_3 \end{array}$ $\begin{bmatrix} 1 & \frac{1}{2} & -1 & 6 \\ 0 & 0 & 0 & 0 \\ 0 & 0 & 0 & 0 \end{bmatrix}$

Therefore, this system has infinitely many solutions, given by $x + \frac{1}{2}s - t = 6 \quad \Leftrightarrow$ $x = 6 - \frac{1}{2}s + t$. Hence, the solutions are $(6 - \frac{1}{2}s + t, s, t)$, where s and t are any real numbers.

29. $\begin{bmatrix} 4 & -3 & 1 & -8 \\ -2 & 1 & -3 & -4 \\ 1 & -1 & 2 & 3 \end{bmatrix}$ $\begin{array}{c} R_1 \leftrightarrow R_3 \\ \hline \end{array}$ $\begin{bmatrix} 1 & -1 & 2 & 3 \\ -2 & 1 & -3 & -4 \\ 4 & -3 & 1 & -8 \end{bmatrix}$ $\begin{array}{c} R_2+2R_1 \to R_2 \\ \hline R_3-4R_1 \to R_3 \end{array}$

$\begin{bmatrix} 1 & -1 & 2 & 3 \\ 0 & -1 & 1 & 2 \\ 0 & 1 & -7 & -20 \end{bmatrix}$ $\begin{array}{c} -R_2 \\ \hline \end{array}$ $\begin{bmatrix} 1 & -1 & 2 & 3 \\ 0 & 1 & -1 & -2 \\ 0 & 1 & -7 & -20 \end{bmatrix}$ $\begin{array}{c} R_3-R_2 \to R_3 \\ \hline \end{array}$ $\begin{bmatrix} 1 & -1 & 2 & 3 \\ 0 & 1 & -1 & -2 \\ 0 & 0 & -6 & -18 \end{bmatrix}$

Therefore, $-6z = -18 \quad \Leftrightarrow \quad z = 3; y - (3) = -2 \quad \Leftrightarrow \quad y = 1;$ and $x - (1) + 2(3) = 3 \quad \Leftrightarrow$ $x = -2$. Hence, the solution is $(-2, 1, 3)$.

31. $\begin{bmatrix} 1 & 2 & -3 & -5 \\ -2 & -4 & -6 & 10 \\ 3 & 7 & -2 & -13 \end{bmatrix}$ $\begin{array}{c} R_2+2R_1 \to R_2 \\ \hline R_3-3R_1 \to R_3 \end{array}$ $\begin{bmatrix} 1 & 2 & -3 & -5 \\ 0 & 0 & -12 & 0 \\ 0 & 1 & 7 & 2 \end{bmatrix}$ $\begin{array}{c} R_2 \leftrightarrow R_3 \\ \hline \end{array}$

$\begin{bmatrix} 1 & 2 & -3 & -5 \\ 0 & 1 & 7 & 2 \\ 0 & 0 & -12 & 0 \end{bmatrix}$

Therefore, $-12z = 0 \quad \Leftrightarrow \quad z = 0; y + 7(0) = 2 \quad \Leftrightarrow \quad y = 2;$ and $x + 2(2) - 3(0) = -5$ $\Leftrightarrow \quad x = -9$. Hence, the solution is $(-9, 2, 0)$.

33. $\begin{bmatrix} -1 & 2 & 1 & -3 & 3 \\ 3 & -4 & 1 & 1 & 9 \\ -1 & -1 & 1 & 1 & 0 \\ 2 & 1 & 4 & -2 & 3 \end{bmatrix}$ $\begin{array}{c} -R_1 \\ \hline \end{array}$ $\begin{bmatrix} 1 & -2 & -1 & 3 & -3 \\ 3 & -4 & 1 & 1 & 9 \\ -1 & -1 & 1 & 1 & 0 \\ 2 & 1 & 4 & -2 & 3 \end{bmatrix}$

$\begin{array}{c} R_2-3R_1 \to R_2, \ R_3+R_1 \to R_3 \\ \hline R_4-2R_1 \to R_4 \end{array}$ $\begin{bmatrix} 1 & -2 & -1 & 3 & -3 \\ 0 & 2 & 4 & -8 & 18 \\ 0 & -3 & 0 & 4 & -3 \\ 0 & 5 & 6 & -8 & 9 \end{bmatrix}$ $\begin{array}{c} \frac{1}{2}R_2 \\ \hline \end{array}$

$$\begin{bmatrix} 1 & -2 & -1 & 3 & -3 \\ 0 & 1 & 2 & -4 & 9 \\ 0 & -3 & 0 & 4 & -3 \\ 0 & 5 & 6 & -8 & 9 \end{bmatrix} \quad \xrightarrow[R_4-5R_2\to R_4]{R_3+3R_2\to R_3} \quad \begin{bmatrix} 1 & -2 & -1 & 3 & -3 \\ 0 & 1 & 2 & -4 & 9 \\ 0 & 0 & 6 & -8 & 24 \\ 0 & 0 & -4 & 12 & -36 \end{bmatrix}$$

$$\xrightarrow{3R_4+2R_3\to R_4} \quad \begin{bmatrix} 1 & -2 & -1 & 3 & -3 \\ 0 & 1 & 2 & -4 & 9 \\ 0 & 0 & 6 & -8 & 24 \\ 0 & 0 & 0 & 20 & -60 \end{bmatrix}$$

Therefore, $20w = -60 \iff w = -3;\ 6z + 24 = 24 \iff z = 0.$ Then $y + 12 = 9 \iff y = -3$ and $x + 6 - 9 = -3 \iff x = 0.$ Hence, the solution is $(0, -3, 0, -3).$

35.
$$\begin{bmatrix} 1 & 1 & 2 & -1 & -2 \\ 0 & 3 & 1 & 2 & 2 \\ 1 & 1 & 0 & 3 & 2 \\ -3 & 0 & 1 & 2 & 5 \end{bmatrix} \quad \xrightarrow[R_4+3R_1\to R_4]{R_3-R_1\to R_3} \quad \begin{bmatrix} 1 & 1 & 2 & -1 & -2 \\ 0 & 3 & 1 & 2 & 2 \\ 0 & 0 & -2 & 4 & 4 \\ 0 & 3 & 7 & -1 & -1 \end{bmatrix} \quad \xrightarrow{R_4-R_2\to R_4}$$

$$\begin{bmatrix} 1 & 1 & 2 & -1 & -2 \\ 0 & 3 & 1 & 2 & 2 \\ 0 & 0 & -2 & 4 & 4 \\ 0 & 0 & 6 & -3 & -3 \end{bmatrix} \quad \xrightarrow{R_4+3R_3\to R_4} \quad \begin{bmatrix} 1 & 1 & 2 & -1 & -2 \\ 0 & 3 & 1 & 2 & 2 \\ 0 & 0 & -2 & 4 & 4 \\ 0 & 0 & 0 & 9 & 9 \end{bmatrix}$$

Therefore, $9w = 9 \iff w = 1;\ -2z + 4(1) = 4 \iff z = 0.$ Then $3y + (0) + 2(1) = 2 \iff y = 0$ and $x + (0) + 2(0) - (1) = -2 \iff x = -1.$ Hence, the solution is $(-1, 0, 0, 1).$

37.
$$\begin{bmatrix} 1 & 0 & 1 & 1 & 4 \\ 0 & 1 & -1 & 0 & -4 \\ 1 & -2 & 3 & 1 & 12 \\ 2 & 0 & -2 & 5 & -1 \end{bmatrix} \quad \xrightarrow[R_4-2R_1\to R_4]{R_3-R_1\to R_3} \quad \begin{bmatrix} 1 & 0 & 1 & 1 & 4 \\ 0 & 1 & -1 & 0 & -4 \\ 0 & -2 & 2 & 0 & 8 \\ 0 & 0 & -4 & 3 & -9 \end{bmatrix} \quad \xrightarrow{R_3+2R_2\to R_3}$$

$$\begin{bmatrix} 1 & 0 & 1 & 1 & 4 \\ 0 & 1 & -1 & 0 & -4 \\ 0 & 0 & 0 & 0 & 0 \\ 0 & 0 & -4 & 3 & -9 \end{bmatrix} \quad \xrightarrow{R_3\leftrightarrow -R_4} \quad \begin{bmatrix} 1 & 0 & 1 & 1 & 4 \\ 0 & 1 & -1 & 0 & -4 \\ 0 & 0 & 4 & -3 & 9 \\ 0 & 0 & 0 & 0 & 0 \end{bmatrix}$$

Therefore, $4z - 3t = 9 \iff 4z = 9 + 3t \iff z = \frac{9}{4} + \frac{3}{4}t.$ Then we have $y - \left(\frac{9}{4} + \frac{3}{4}t\right) = -4 \iff y = \frac{-7}{4} + \frac{3}{4}t$ and $x + \left(\frac{9}{4} + \frac{3}{4}t\right) + t = 4 \iff x = \frac{7}{4} - \frac{7}{4}t.$ Hence, the solutions are $\left(\frac{7}{4} - \frac{7}{4}t, \frac{-7}{4} + \frac{3}{4}t, \frac{9}{4} + \frac{3}{4}t, t\right)$, where t is any number.

39.
$$\begin{bmatrix} 1 & -1 & 0 & 1 & 0 \\ 3 & 0 & -1 & 2 & 0 \\ 1 & -4 & 1 & 2 & 0 \end{bmatrix} \quad \xrightarrow[R_3-R_1\to R_3]{R_2-3R_1\to R_2} \quad \begin{bmatrix} 1 & -1 & 0 & 1 & 0 \\ 0 & 3 & -1 & -1 & 0 \\ 0 & -3 & 1 & 1 & 0 \end{bmatrix} \quad \xrightarrow{R_3+R_2\to R_3}$$

$$\begin{bmatrix} 1 & -1 & 0 & 1 & 0 \\ 0 & 3 & -1 & -1 & 0 \\ 0 & 0 & 0 & 0 & 0 \end{bmatrix}$$

Therefore, the system has infinitely many solutions, given by $3y - s - t = 0 \iff y = \frac{1}{3}(s + t)$ and $x - \frac{1}{3}(s + t) + t = 0 \iff x = \frac{1}{3}(s - 2t).$ So the solutions are $\left(\frac{1}{3}[s - 2t], \frac{1}{3}[s + t], s, t\right)$, where s and t are any real numbers.

41. Let x, y, z represent the number of VitaMax, Vitron, and VitaPlus pills taken daily. The matrix representation for the system of equations is:

$$\begin{bmatrix} 5 & 10 & 15 & 50 \\ 15 & 20 & 0 & 50 \\ 10 & 10 & 10 & 50 \end{bmatrix} \xrightarrow[\frac{1}{5}R_3]{\frac{1}{5}R_1, \frac{1}{5}R_2} \begin{bmatrix} 1 & 2 & 3 & 10 \\ 3 & 4 & 0 & 10 \\ 2 & 2 & 2 & 10 \end{bmatrix} \xrightarrow[R_3-2R_1 \to R_3]{R_2-3R_1 \to R_2} \begin{bmatrix} 1 & 2 & 3 & 10 \\ 0 & -2 & -9 & -20 \\ 0 & -2 & -4 & -10 \end{bmatrix}$$

$$\xrightarrow{R_3-R_2 \to R_3} \begin{bmatrix} 1 & 2 & 3 & 10 \\ 0 & -2 & -9 & -20 \\ 0 & 0 & 5 & 10 \end{bmatrix}$$

Thus, $5z = 10 \iff z = 2$; $-2y - 18 = -20 \iff y = 1$; and $x + 2 + 6 = 10 \iff x = 2$. Hence, he should take 2 VitaMax, 1 Vitron, and 2 VitaPlus pills daily.

43. Let x, y, and z represent the distance, in miles, of the run, swim, and cycle parts of the race respectively. Then, since $time = \dfrac{distance}{speed}$, we get the following equations from the three contestants' race times:

$$\begin{cases} \left(\frac{x}{10}\right) + \left(\frac{y}{4}\right) + \left(\frac{z}{20}\right) = 2.5 \\ \left(\frac{x}{7.5}\right) + \left(\frac{y}{6}\right) + \left(\frac{z}{15}\right) = 3 \\ \left(\frac{x}{15}\right) + \left(\frac{y}{3}\right) + \left(\frac{z}{40}\right) = 1.75 \end{cases} \iff \begin{cases} 2x + 5y + z = 50 \\ 4x + 5y + 2z = 90 \\ 8x + 40y + 3z = 210 \end{cases},$$

which has the following matrix representation:

$$\begin{bmatrix} 2 & 5 & 1 & 50 \\ 4 & 5 & 2 & 90 \\ 8 & 40 & 3 & 210 \end{bmatrix} \xrightarrow[R_3-4R_1 \to R_3]{R_2-2R_1 \to R_2} \begin{bmatrix} 2 & 5 & 1 & 50 \\ 0 & -5 & 0 & -10 \\ 0 & 20 & -1 & 10 \end{bmatrix} \xrightarrow{R_3+4R_2 \to R_3}$$

$$\begin{bmatrix} 2 & 5 & 1 & 50 \\ 0 & -5 & 0 & -10 \\ 0 & 0 & -1 & -30 \end{bmatrix}.$$

Thus, $-z = -30 \iff z = 30$; $-5y = -10 \iff y = 2$; and $2x + 10 + 30 = 50 \iff x = 5$. So the race has a 5 mile run, 2 mile swim, and 30 mile cycle.

45. Let t be the number of tables produced, c the number of chairs, and a the number of armoires. Then, the system of equations is

$$\begin{cases} \frac{1}{2}t + c + a = 300 \\ \frac{1}{2}t + \frac{3}{2}c + a = 400 \\ t + \frac{3}{2}c + 2a = 590 \end{cases} \iff \begin{cases} t + 2c + 2a = 600 \\ t + 3c + 2a = 800 \\ 2t + 3c + 4a = 1180 \end{cases} \text{ and the matrix representation is:}$$

$$\begin{bmatrix} 1 & 2 & 2 & 600 \\ 1 & 3 & 2 & 800 \\ 2 & 3 & 4 & 1180 \end{bmatrix} \xrightarrow[R_3-2R_1 \to R_3]{R_2-R_1 \to R_2} \begin{bmatrix} 1 & 2 & 2 & 600 \\ 0 & 1 & 0 & 200 \\ 0 & -1 & 0 & -20 \end{bmatrix} \xrightarrow{R_3+R_2 \to R_3} \begin{bmatrix} 1 & 2 & 2 & 600 \\ 0 & 1 & 0 & 200 \\ 0 & 0 & 0 & 180 \end{bmatrix}.$$

The third row states $0 = 180$, which is impossible, and so the system is inconsistent. Therefore, it is impossible to use all of the available labor-hours.

49. Line containing the points $(0, 0)$, $(1, 12)$:

Using the general form of a line, $y = ax + b$, we substitute for x and y and solve for a and b. This gives $(0, 0)$ $0 = a(0) + b \quad \Rightarrow \quad b = 0$;

        $(1, 12) \quad 12 = a(1) + b \quad \Rightarrow \quad a = 12$.

Since $a = 12$ and $b = 0$, the equation of the line is $y = 12x$.

Quadratic containing the points $(0, 0)$, $(1, 12)$, $(3, 6)$:

Using the general form of a quadratic, $y = ax^2 + bx + c$, we substitute for x and y and solve for a, b, and c. This gives

$(0,0)$	$0 = a(0)^2 + b(0) + c$	$\Rightarrow$	$c = 0;$
$(1,12)$	$12 = a(1)^2 + b(1) + c$	$\Rightarrow$	$a + b = 12$ $\times -3$ $-3a - 3b = -36$
$(3,6)$	$6 = a(3)^2 + b(3) + c$	$\Rightarrow$	$9a + 3b = 6$ $\underline{9a + 3b = 6}$

$$6a = -30 \quad \Leftrightarrow$$

$a = -5$. So $a + b = 12 \quad \Leftrightarrow \quad b = 12 - a \quad \Rightarrow \quad b = 17$. Since $a = -5$, $b = 17$, and $c = 0$, the equation of the quadratic is $y = -5x^2 + 17x$.

Cubic containing the points $(0, 0)$, $(1, 12)$, $(2, 40)$, $(3, 6)$:

Using the general form of a cubic, $y = ax^3 + bx^2 + cx + d$, we substitute for x and y and solve for a, b, c, and d. This gives

$(0,0)$	$0 = a(0)^3 + b(0)^2 + c(0) + d$	$\Rightarrow$	$d = 0;$
$(1,12)$	$12 = a(1)^3 + b(1)^2 + c(1) + d$	$\Rightarrow$	$a + b + c + d = 12;$
$(2,40)$	$40 = a(2)^3 + b(2)^2 + c(2) + d$	$\Rightarrow$	$8a + 4b + 2c + d = 40;$
$(3,6)$	$6 = a(3)^3 + b(3)^2 + c(3) + d$	$\Rightarrow$	$27a + 9b + 3c + d = 6.$

Since $d = 0$ the system reduces to $\begin{cases} a + b + c = 12 \\ 8a + 4b + 2c = 40 \\ 27a + 9b + 3c = 6 \end{cases}$

$$\begin{bmatrix} 1 & 1 & 1 & 12 \\ 8 & 4 & 2 & 40 \\ 27 & 9 & 3 & 6 \end{bmatrix} \begin{array}{c} R_2 - 8R_1 \to R_2 \\ R_3 - 27R_1 \to R_3 \end{array} \begin{bmatrix} 1 & 1 & 1 & 12 \\ 0 & -4 & -6 & -56 \\ 0 & -18 & -24 & -318 \end{bmatrix} \begin{array}{c} -\frac{1}{2}R_2 \\ -\frac{1}{6}R_3 \end{array}$$

$$\begin{bmatrix} 1 & 1 & 1 & 12 \\ 0 & 2 & 3 & 28 \\ 0 & 3 & 4 & 53 \end{bmatrix} \xrightarrow{2R_3 - 3R_2 \to R_3} \begin{bmatrix} 1 & 1 & 1 & 12 \\ 0 & 2 & 3 & 28 \\ 0 & 0 & -1 & 22 \end{bmatrix}$$

So $c = -22$ and back-substituting we have $2b + 3(-22) = 28 \quad \Leftrightarrow \quad b = 47$ and $a + 47 + (-22) = 0 \quad \Leftrightarrow \quad a = -13$. So the cubic is $y = -13x^3 + 47x^2 - 22x$

Fourth-degree polynomial containing the points $(0, 0)$, $(1, 12)$, $(2, 40)$, $(3, 6)$, $(-1, -14)$:

Using the general form of a fourth-degree polynomial, $y = ax^4 + bx^3 + cx^2 + dx + e$, we substitute for x and y and solve for a, b, c, d and d. This gives

$(0,0)$	$0 = a(0)^4 + b(0)^3 + c(0)^2 + d(0) + e \quad \Rightarrow \quad e = 0$
$(1,12)$	$12 = a(1)^4 + b(1)^3 + c(1)^2 + d(1) + e$
$(2,40)$	$40 = a(2)^4 + b(2)^3 + c(2)^2 + d(2) + e$
$(3,6)$	$6 = a(3)^4 + b(3)^3 + c(3)^2 + d(3) + e$
$(-1,-14)$	$-14 = a(-1)^4 + b(-1)^3 + c(-1)^2 + d(-1) + e$

Since the first equation is $e = 0$, we eliminate e from the other equations to get the following system:

$$\begin{cases} a + b + c + d = 12 \\ 16a + 8b + 4c + 2d = 40 \\ 81a + 27b + 9c + 3d = 6 \\ a - b + c - d = -14 \end{cases}$$

$$\begin{bmatrix} 1 & 1 & 1 & 1 & 12 \\ 16 & 8 & 4 & 2 & 40 \\ 81 & 27 & 9 & 3 & 6 \\ 1 & -1 & 1 & -1 & -14 \end{bmatrix} \xrightarrow[\substack{R_2-16R_1 \to R_2,\ R_3-81R_1 \to R_3 \\ R_4-R_1 \to R_4}]{} \begin{bmatrix} 1 & 1 & 1 & 1 & 12 \\ 0 & -8 & -12 & -14 & -152 \\ 0 & -54 & -72 & -78 & -966 \\ 0 & -2 & 0 & -2 & -26 \end{bmatrix}$$

$$\xrightarrow[\substack{-\frac{1}{2}R_4 \to R_2 \\ R_2 \to R_3, R_3 \to R_4}]{} \begin{bmatrix} 1 & 1 & 1 & 1 & 12 \\ 0 & 1 & 0 & 1 & 13 \\ 0 & -8 & -12 & -14 & -152 \\ 0 & -54 & -72 & -78 & -966 \end{bmatrix} \xrightarrow[\substack{R_3+8R_2 \to R_3 \\ R_4+54R_2 \to R_4}]{} \begin{bmatrix} 1 & 1 & 1 & 1 & 12 \\ 0 & 1 & 0 & 1 & 13 \\ 0 & 0 & -12 & -6 & -48 \\ 0 & 0 & -72 & -24 & -264 \end{bmatrix}$$

$$\xrightarrow[R_4-6R_3 \to R_4]{} \begin{matrix} 1 & 1 & 1 & 1 & 12 \\ 0 & 1 & 0 & 1 & 13 \\ 0 & 0 & -12 & -6 & -48 \\ 0 & 0 & 0 & 12 & 24 \end{matrix}$$

So $d = 2$. Then $-12c - 6(2) = -48 \iff c = 3$ and $b + 2 = 13 \iff b = 11$. Finally, $a + 11 + 3 + 2 = 12 \iff a = -4$. So the fourth-degree polynomial containing these points is $y = -4x^4 + 11x^3 + 3x^2 + 2x$.

Exercises 8.5

1. The matrices have different dimensions, they cannot be equal.

3. $\begin{bmatrix} 2 & 6 \\ -5 & 3 \end{bmatrix} + \begin{bmatrix} -1 & -3 \\ 6 & 2 \end{bmatrix} = \begin{bmatrix} 1 & 3 \\ 1 & 5 \end{bmatrix}$

5. $3 \begin{bmatrix} 1 & 2 \\ 4 & -1 \\ 1 & 0 \end{bmatrix} = \begin{bmatrix} 3 & 6 \\ 12 & -3 \\ 3 & 0 \end{bmatrix}$

7. $\begin{bmatrix} 2 & 6 \\ 1 & 3 \\ 2 & 4 \end{bmatrix} \begin{bmatrix} 1 & -2 \\ 3 & 6 \\ -2 & 0 \end{bmatrix}$ is undefined because these matrices have incompatible dimensions.

9. $\begin{bmatrix} 1 & 2 \\ -1 & 4 \end{bmatrix} \begin{bmatrix} 1 & -2 & 3 \\ 2 & 2 & -1 \end{bmatrix} = \begin{bmatrix} 5 & 2 & 1 \\ 7 & 10 & -7 \end{bmatrix}$

In Exercises 11– 31, the matrices A, B, C, D, E, F, and G are defined as follows:

$$A = \begin{bmatrix} 2 & -5 \\ 0 & 7 \end{bmatrix} \quad B = \begin{bmatrix} 3 & \frac{1}{2} & 5 \\ 1 & -1 & 3 \end{bmatrix} \quad C = \begin{bmatrix} 2 & -\frac{5}{2} & 0 \\ 0 & 2 & -3 \end{bmatrix} \quad D = [7 \quad 3]$$

$$E = \begin{bmatrix} 1 \\ 2 \\ 0 \end{bmatrix} \quad F = \begin{bmatrix} 1 & 0 & 0 \\ 0 & 1 & 0 \\ 0 & 0 & 1 \end{bmatrix} \quad G = \begin{bmatrix} 5 & -3 & 10 \\ 6 & 1 & 0 \\ -5 & 2 & 2 \end{bmatrix}$$

11. $B + C = \begin{bmatrix} 3 & \frac{1}{2} & 5 \\ 1 & -1 & 3 \end{bmatrix} + \begin{bmatrix} 2 & -\frac{5}{2} & 0 \\ 0 & 2 & -3 \end{bmatrix} = \begin{bmatrix} 5 & -2 & 5 \\ 1 & 1 & 0 \end{bmatrix}$

13. $C - B = \begin{bmatrix} 2 & -\frac{5}{2} & 0 \\ 0 & 2 & -3 \end{bmatrix} - \begin{bmatrix} 3 & \frac{1}{2} & 5 \\ 1 & -1 & 3 \end{bmatrix} = \begin{bmatrix} -1 & -3 & -5 \\ -1 & 3 & -6 \end{bmatrix}$

15. $3B + 2C = 3 \begin{bmatrix} 3 & \frac{1}{2} & 5 \\ 1 & -1 & 3 \end{bmatrix} + 2 \begin{bmatrix} 2 & -\frac{5}{2} & 0 \\ 0 & 2 & -3 \end{bmatrix} = \begin{bmatrix} 13 & -\frac{7}{2} & 15 \\ 3 & 1 & 3 \end{bmatrix}$

17. $2C - 6B = 2 \begin{bmatrix} 2 & -\frac{5}{2} & 0 \\ 0 & 2 & -3 \end{bmatrix} - 6 \begin{bmatrix} 3 & \frac{1}{2} & 5 \\ 1 & -1 & 3 \end{bmatrix} = \begin{bmatrix} -14 & -8 & -30 \\ -6 & 10 & -24 \end{bmatrix}$

19. AD is undefined because A (2×2) and D (1×2) have incompatible dimensions.

21. $BF = \begin{bmatrix} 3 & \frac{1}{2} & 5 \\ 1 & -1 & 3 \end{bmatrix} \begin{bmatrix} 1 & 0 & 0 \\ 0 & 1 & 0 \\ 0 & 0 & 1 \end{bmatrix} = \begin{bmatrix} 3 & \frac{1}{2} & 5 \\ 1 & -1 & 3 \end{bmatrix}$

23. $(DA)B = [7 \quad 3] \begin{bmatrix} 2 & -5 \\ 0 & 7 \end{bmatrix} \begin{bmatrix} 3 & \frac{1}{2} & 5 \\ 1 & -1 & 3 \end{bmatrix} = [14 \quad -14] \begin{bmatrix} 3 & \frac{1}{2} & 5 \\ 1 & -1 & 3 \end{bmatrix} = [28 \quad 21 \quad 28]$

25. $GE = \begin{bmatrix} 5 & -3 & 10 \\ 6 & 1 & 0 \\ -5 & 2 & 2 \end{bmatrix} \begin{bmatrix} 1 \\ 2 \\ 0 \end{bmatrix} = \begin{bmatrix} -1 \\ 8 \\ -1 \end{bmatrix}$

27. $A^3 = \begin{bmatrix} 2 & -5 \\ 0 & 7 \end{bmatrix} \begin{bmatrix} 2 & -5 \\ 0 & 7 \end{bmatrix} \begin{bmatrix} 2 & -5 \\ 0 & 7 \end{bmatrix} = \begin{bmatrix} 4 & -45 \\ 0 & 49 \end{bmatrix} \begin{bmatrix} 2 & -5 \\ 0 & 7 \end{bmatrix} = \begin{bmatrix} 8 & -335 \\ 0 & 343 \end{bmatrix}$

29. B^2 is undefined because the dimensions $(2 \times 3$ and $2 \times 3)$ are incompatible.

31. $BF + FE$ is undefined because the dimensions, $(2 \times 3) \cdot (3 \times 3) = (2 \times 3)$ and $(3 \times 3) \cdot (3 \times 1) = (3 \times 1)$, are incompatible.

33. $\begin{cases} 2x - 5y = 7 \\ 3x + 2y = 4 \end{cases}$ written as a matrix equation is $\begin{bmatrix} 2 & -5 \\ 3 & 2 \end{bmatrix} \begin{bmatrix} x \\ y \end{bmatrix} = \begin{bmatrix} 7 \\ 4 \end{bmatrix}$.

35. $\begin{cases} 3x_1 + 2x_2 - x_3 + x_4 = 0 \\ x_1 - x_3 = 5 \\ 3x_2 + x_3 - x_4 = 4 \end{cases}$ written as a matrix equation is $\begin{bmatrix} 3 & 2 & -1 & 1 \\ 1 & 0 & -1 & 0 \\ 0 & 3 & 1 & -1 \end{bmatrix} \begin{bmatrix} x_1 \\ x_2 \\ x_3 \\ x_4 \end{bmatrix} = \begin{bmatrix} 0 \\ 5 \\ 4 \end{bmatrix}$.

37. $\begin{bmatrix} x & 2y \\ 4 & 6 \end{bmatrix} = \begin{bmatrix} 2 & -2 \\ 2x & -6y \end{bmatrix}$. Thus we must solve the system $\begin{cases} x = 2 \\ 2y = -2 \\ 4 = 2x \\ 6 = -6y \end{cases}$ So $x = 2$ and $2y = -2$

   $\Leftrightarrow y = -1$. Since these values for x and y also satisfy the last two equations, the solution is $x = 2, y = -1$.

39. $\begin{bmatrix} 6 & x \\ 1 & 0 \end{bmatrix} \begin{bmatrix} y & 2 \\ -1 & 2 \end{bmatrix} = \begin{bmatrix} 6y - x & 12 + 2x \\ y & 2 \end{bmatrix} = \begin{bmatrix} 4 & 16 \\ 1 & 2 \end{bmatrix}$. Thus we must solve the system

   $\begin{cases} 6y - x = 4 \\ 12 + 2x = 16 \\ y = 1 \\ 2 = 2 \end{cases}$. So $y = 1$ and $12 + 2x = 16 \quad \Leftrightarrow \quad x = 2$. Since these values for x and y also satisfy the first two equations, the solution is $x = 2, y = 1$.

41. $2X - A = B \quad \Leftrightarrow \quad X = \frac{1}{2}(A + B) = \frac{1}{2}\left(\begin{bmatrix} 4 & 6 \\ 1 & 3 \end{bmatrix} + \begin{bmatrix} 2 & 5 \\ 3 & 7 \end{bmatrix} \right) = \frac{1}{2} \begin{bmatrix} 6 & 11 \\ 4 & 10 \end{bmatrix} = \begin{bmatrix} 3 & \frac{11}{2} \\ 2 & 5 \end{bmatrix}$.

43. $3X + B = C \quad \Leftrightarrow \quad 3X = C - B \quad \Leftrightarrow \quad X = \frac{1}{3}(C - B)$, which is undefined because the dimensions, (3×2) and (2×2), are incompatible.

45. (a) $BA = [\,\$0.90 \quad \$0.80 \quad \$1.10\,] \begin{bmatrix} 4000 & 1000 & 3500 \\ 400 & 300 & 200 \\ 700 & 500 & 9000 \end{bmatrix} = [\,\$4690 \quad \$1690 \quad \$13{,}210\,]$

   (b) The entries in the product matrix represent the total food sales in Santa Monica, Long Beach, and Anaheim respectively.

47. (a) $AB = [\,6 \quad 10 \quad 14 \quad 28\,] \begin{bmatrix} 2000 & 2500 \\ 3000 & 1500 \\ 2500 & 1000 \\ 1000 & 500 \end{bmatrix} = [\,105{,}000 \quad 58{,}000\,]$

   (b) That day they canned 105,000 ounces of tomato sauce and 58,000 ounces of tomato paste.

49. $A = \begin{bmatrix} 1 & 0 & 6 & -1 \\ 2 & \frac{1}{2} & 4 & 0 \end{bmatrix}$, $B = [\,1 \quad 7 \quad -9 \quad 2\,]$, and $C = \begin{bmatrix} 1 \\ 0 \\ -1 \\ -2 \end{bmatrix}$.

ABC is undefined because the dimensions of A (2×4) and B (1×4) are not compatible.

$ACB = \begin{bmatrix} -3 \\ -2 \end{bmatrix} [\,1 \quad 7 \quad -9 \quad 2\,] = \begin{bmatrix} -3 & -21 & 27 & -6 \\ -2 & -14 & 18 & -4 \end{bmatrix}$

BAC is undefined because the dimensions of B (1×4) and A (2×4) are not compatible.

BCA is undefined because the dimensions of C (4×1) and A (2×4) are not compatible.

CAB is undefined because the dimensions of C (4×1) and A (2×4) are not compatible.

CBA is undefined because the dimensions of B (1×4) and A (2×4) are not compatible.

51. No, from Exercise 36, $(A + B)^2 = (A + B)(A + B) = A^2 + AB + BA + B^2 \neq$
   $A^2 + 2AB + B^2$ unless $AB = BA$ which is, in general, not true, as we saw in Example 3.

53. $A = \begin{bmatrix} 1 & 1 \\ 1 & 1 \end{bmatrix}$;

$A^2 = \begin{bmatrix} 1 & 1 \\ 1 & 1 \end{bmatrix} \begin{bmatrix} 1 & 1 \\ 1 & 1 \end{bmatrix} = \begin{bmatrix} 2 & 2 \\ 2 & 2 \end{bmatrix}$;

$A^3 = A \cdot A^2 = \begin{bmatrix} 1 & 1 \\ 1 & 1 \end{bmatrix} \begin{bmatrix} 2 & 2 \\ 2 & 2 \end{bmatrix} = \begin{bmatrix} 4 & 4 \\ 4 & 4 \end{bmatrix}$;

$A^4 = A \cdot A^3 = \begin{bmatrix} 1 & 1 \\ 1 & 1 \end{bmatrix} \begin{bmatrix} 4 & 4 \\ 4 & 4 \end{bmatrix} = \begin{bmatrix} 8 & 8 \\ 8 & 8 \end{bmatrix}$.

From this pattern, we see that

$A^n = \begin{bmatrix} 2^{n-1} & 2^{n-1} \\ 2^{n-1} & 2^{n-1} \end{bmatrix}$.

55. (a) $\begin{bmatrix} 1 & 0 & 1 & 0 & 1 & 1 \\ 0 & 3 & 0 & 1 & 2 & 1 \\ 1 & 2 & 0 & 0 & 3 & 0 \\ 1 & 3 & 2 & 3 & 2 & 0 \\ 0 & 3 & 0 & 0 & 2 & 1 \\ 1 & 2 & 0 & 1 & 3 & 1 \end{bmatrix}$

(b) $\begin{bmatrix} 2 & 1 & 2 & 1 & 2 & 2 \\ 1 & 3 & 1 & 2 & 3 & 2 \\ 2 & 3 & 1 & 1 & 3 & 1 \\ 2 & 3 & 3 & 3 & 3 & 1 \\ 1 & 3 & 1 & 1 & 3 & 2 \\ 2 & 3 & 1 & 2 & 3 & 2 \end{bmatrix}$

(c)
$$\begin{bmatrix} 2 & 3 & 2 & 3 & 2 & 2 \\ 3 & 0 & 3 & 2 & 1 & 2 \\ 2 & 1 & 3 & 3 & 0 & 3 \\ 2 & 0 & 1 & 0 & 1 & 3 \\ 3 & 0 & 3 & 3 & 1 & 2 \\ 2 & 1 & 3 & 2 & 0 & 2 \end{bmatrix}$$

(d)
$$\begin{bmatrix} 3 & 3 & 3 & 3 & 3 & 3 \\ 3 & 0 & 3 & 3 & 0 & 3 \\ 3 & 0 & 3 & 3 & 0 & 3 \\ 3 & 0 & 0 & 0 & 0 & 3 \\ 3 & 0 & 3 & 3 & 0 & 3 \\ 3 & 0 & 3 & 3 & 0 & 3 \end{bmatrix}$$ which corresponds to this image

(e)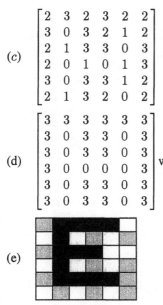

Exercises 8.6

1. $A = \begin{bmatrix} 4 & 1 \\ 7 & 2 \end{bmatrix}$; $B = \begin{bmatrix} 2 & -1 \\ -7 & 4 \end{bmatrix}$. $AB = \begin{bmatrix} 4 & 1 \\ 7 & 2 \end{bmatrix}\begin{bmatrix} 2 & -1 \\ -7 & 4 \end{bmatrix} = \begin{bmatrix} 1 & 0 \\ 0 & 1 \end{bmatrix}$ and

    $BA = \begin{bmatrix} 2 & -1 \\ -7 & 4 \end{bmatrix}\begin{bmatrix} 4 & 1 \\ 7 & 2 \end{bmatrix} = \begin{bmatrix} 1 & 0 \\ 0 & 1 \end{bmatrix}$.

3. $A = \begin{bmatrix} 1 & 3 & -1 \\ 1 & 4 & 0 \\ -1 & -3 & 2 \end{bmatrix}$; $B = \begin{bmatrix} 8 & -3 & 4 \\ -2 & 1 & -1 \\ 1 & 0 & 1 \end{bmatrix}$.

    $AB = \begin{bmatrix} 1 & 3 & -1 \\ 1 & 4 & 0 \\ -1 & -3 & 2 \end{bmatrix}\begin{bmatrix} 8 & -3 & 4 \\ -2 & 1 & -1 \\ 1 & 0 & 1 \end{bmatrix} = \begin{bmatrix} 1 & 0 & 0 \\ 0 & 1 & 0 \\ 0 & 0 & 1 \end{bmatrix}$ and

    $BA = \begin{bmatrix} 8 & -3 & 4 \\ -2 & 1 & -1 \\ 1 & 0 & 1 \end{bmatrix}\begin{bmatrix} 1 & 3 & -1 \\ 1 & 4 & 0 \\ -1 & -3 & 2 \end{bmatrix} = \begin{bmatrix} 1 & 0 & 0 \\ 0 & 1 & 0 \\ 0 & 0 & 1 \end{bmatrix}$

5. $A = \begin{bmatrix} 7 & 4 \\ 3 & 2 \end{bmatrix}$ $\Leftrightarrow$ $A^{-1} = \frac{1}{14-12}\begin{bmatrix} 2 & -4 \\ -3 & 7 \end{bmatrix} = \begin{bmatrix} 1 & -2 \\ -\frac{3}{2} & \frac{7}{2} \end{bmatrix}$.

    Then, $AA^{-1} = \begin{bmatrix} 7 & 4 \\ 3 & 2 \end{bmatrix}\begin{bmatrix} 1 & -2 \\ -\frac{3}{2} & \frac{7}{2} \end{bmatrix} = \begin{bmatrix} 1 & 0 \\ 0 & 1 \end{bmatrix}$,

    and $A^{-1}A = \begin{bmatrix} 1 & -2 \\ -\frac{3}{2} & \frac{7}{2} \end{bmatrix}\begin{bmatrix} 7 & 4 \\ 3 & 2 \end{bmatrix} = \begin{bmatrix} 1 & 0 \\ 0 & 1 \end{bmatrix}$.

7. $\begin{bmatrix} 5 & 3 \\ 3 & 2 \end{bmatrix}^{-1} = \frac{1}{10-9}\begin{bmatrix} 2 & -3 \\ -3 & 5 \end{bmatrix} = \begin{bmatrix} 2 & -3 \\ -3 & 5 \end{bmatrix}$

9. $\begin{bmatrix} 2 & 5 \\ -5 & -13 \end{bmatrix}^{-1} = \frac{1}{-26+25}\begin{bmatrix} -13 & -5 \\ 5 & 2 \end{bmatrix} = \begin{bmatrix} 13 & 5 \\ -5 & -2 \end{bmatrix}$

11. $\begin{bmatrix} 6 & -3 \\ -8 & 4 \end{bmatrix}^{-1} = \frac{1}{24-24}\begin{bmatrix} 4 & 3 \\ 8 & 6 \end{bmatrix}$, which is not defined, and so there is no inverse.

13. $\begin{bmatrix} 0.4 & -1.2 \\ 0.3 & 0.6 \end{bmatrix}^{-1} = \frac{1}{0.24+0.36}\begin{bmatrix} 0.6 & 1.2 \\ -0.3 & 0.4 \end{bmatrix} = \begin{bmatrix} 1 & 2 \\ -\frac{1}{2} & \frac{2}{3} \end{bmatrix}$

15. $\begin{bmatrix} 2 & 4 & 1 & 1 & 0 & 0 \\ -1 & 1 & -1 & 0 & 1 & 0 \\ 1 & 4 & 0 & 0 & 0 & 1 \end{bmatrix}$ $\xrightarrow[2R_3-R_1 \to R_3]{2R_2+R_1 \to R_2}$ $\begin{bmatrix} 2 & 4 & 1 & 1 & 0 & 0 \\ 0 & 6 & -1 & 1 & 2 & 0 \\ 0 & 4 & -1 & -1 & 0 & 2 \end{bmatrix}$

    $\xrightarrow[3R_1-2R_2 \to R_1]{3R_3-2R_2 \to R_3}$ $\begin{bmatrix} 6 & 0 & 5 & 1 & -4 & 0 \\ 0 & 6 & -1 & 1 & 2 & 0 \\ 0 & 0 & -1 & -5 & -4 & 6 \end{bmatrix}$ $\xrightarrow[R_2-R_3 \to R_2]{R_1+5R_3 \to R_1}$

    $\begin{bmatrix} 6 & 0 & 0 & -24 & -24 & 30 \\ 0 & 6 & 0 & 6 & 6 & -6 \\ 0 & 0 & -1 & -5 & -4 & 6 \end{bmatrix}$ $\xrightarrow[\frac{1}{6}R_2, \, -R_3]{\frac{1}{6}R_1}$ $\begin{bmatrix} 1 & 0 & 0 & -4 & -4 & 5 \\ 0 & 1 & 0 & 1 & 1 & -1 \\ 0 & 0 & 1 & 5 & 4 & -6 \end{bmatrix}$

Therefore, the inverse matrix is $\begin{bmatrix} -4 & -4 & 5 \\ 1 & 1 & -1 \\ 5 & 4 & -6 \end{bmatrix}.$

17. $\begin{bmatrix} 1 & 2 & 3 & 1 & 0 & 0 \\ 4 & 5 & -1 & 0 & 1 & 0 \\ 1 & -1 & -10 & 0 & 0 & 1 \end{bmatrix} \xrightarrow[\substack{R_2-4R_1 \to R_2 \\ R_3-R_1 \to R_3}]{} \begin{bmatrix} 1 & 2 & 3 & 1 & 0 & 0 \\ 0 & -3 & -13 & -4 & 1 & 0 \\ 0 & -3 & -13 & -1 & 0 & 1 \end{bmatrix}$

$\xrightarrow[R_3-R_2 \to R_3]{} \begin{bmatrix} 1 & 2 & 3 & 1 & 0 & 0 \\ 0 & -3 & -13 & -4 & 1 & 0 \\ 0 & 0 & 0 & 3 & -1 & 1 \end{bmatrix}$

Since the left half of the last row consists entirely of zeros, there is no inverse matrix.

19. $\begin{bmatrix} 0 & -2 & 2 & 1 & 0 & 0 \\ 3 & 1 & 3 & 0 & 1 & 0 \\ 1 & -2 & 3 & 0 & 0 & 1 \end{bmatrix} \xrightarrow[R_1 \leftrightarrow R_3]{} \begin{bmatrix} 1 & -2 & 3 & 0 & 0 & 1 \\ 3 & 1 & 3 & 0 & 1 & 0 \\ 0 & -2 & 2 & 1 & 0 & 0 \end{bmatrix} \xrightarrow[R_2-3R_1 \to R_2]{}$

$\begin{bmatrix} 1 & -2 & 3 & 0 & 0 & 1 \\ 0 & 7 & -6 & 0 & 1 & -3 \\ 0 & -2 & 2 & 1 & 0 & 0 \end{bmatrix} \xrightarrow[\substack{R_1-R_3 \to R_1 \\ R_2+3R_3 \to R_2}]{} \begin{bmatrix} 1 & 0 & 1 & -1 & 0 & 1 \\ 0 & 1 & 0 & 3 & 1 & -3 \\ 0 & -2 & 2 & 1 & 0 & 0 \end{bmatrix}$

$\xrightarrow[R_3+2R_2 \to R_3]{} \begin{bmatrix} 1 & 0 & 1 & -1 & 0 & 1 \\ 0 & 1 & 0 & 3 & 1 & -3 \\ 0 & 0 & 2 & 7 & 2 & -6 \end{bmatrix} \xrightarrow[\frac{1}{2}R_3]{} \begin{bmatrix} 1 & 0 & 1 & -1 & 0 & 1 \\ 0 & 1 & 0 & 3 & 1 & -3 \\ 0 & 0 & 1 & \frac{7}{2} & 1 & -3 \end{bmatrix}$

$\xrightarrow[R_1-R_3 \to R_1]{} \begin{bmatrix} 1 & 0 & 0 & -\frac{9}{2} & -1 & 4 \\ 0 & 1 & 0 & 3 & 1 & -3 \\ 0 & 0 & 1 & \frac{7}{2} & 1 & -3 \end{bmatrix}$

Therefore, the inverse matrix is $\begin{bmatrix} -\frac{9}{2} & -1 & 4 \\ 3 & 1 & -3 \\ \frac{7}{2} & 1 & -3 \end{bmatrix}.$

21. $\begin{bmatrix} 1 & 2 & 0 & 3 & 1 & 0 & 0 & 0 \\ 0 & 1 & 1 & 1 & 0 & 1 & 0 & 0 \\ 0 & 1 & 0 & 1 & 0 & 0 & 1 & 0 \\ 1 & 2 & 0 & 2 & 0 & 0 & 0 & 1 \end{bmatrix} \xrightarrow[\substack{R_3-R_2 \to R_3 \\ R_4-R_1 \to R_4}]{} \begin{bmatrix} 1 & 2 & 0 & 3 & 1 & 0 & 0 & 0 \\ 0 & 1 & 1 & 1 & 0 & 1 & 0 & 0 \\ 0 & 0 & -1 & 0 & 0 & -1 & 1 & 0 \\ 0 & 0 & 0 & -1 & -1 & 0 & 0 & 1 \end{bmatrix}$

$\xrightarrow[\substack{-R_3 \\ -R_4}]{} \begin{bmatrix} 1 & 2 & 0 & 3 & 1 & 0 & 0 & 0 \\ 0 & 1 & 1 & 1 & 0 & 1 & 0 & 0 \\ 0 & 0 & 1 & 0 & 0 & 1 & -1 & 0 \\ 0 & 0 & 0 & 1 & 1 & 0 & 0 & -1 \end{bmatrix} \xrightarrow[\substack{R_1-2R_2 \to R_1 \\ R_2-R_3 \to R_2}]{}$

$\begin{bmatrix} 1 & 0 & -2 & 1 & 1 & -2 & 0 & 0 \\ 0 & 1 & 0 & 1 & 0 & 0 & 1 & 0 \\ 0 & 0 & 1 & 0 & 0 & 1 & -1 & 0 \\ 0 & 0 & 0 & 1 & 1 & 0 & 0 & -1 \end{bmatrix} \xrightarrow[\substack{R_1+2R_3 \to R_1 \\ R_2-R_4 \to R_2}]{}$

$\begin{bmatrix} 1 & 0 & 0 & 1 & 1 & 0 & -2 & 0 \\ 0 & 1 & 0 & 0 & -1 & 0 & 1 & 1 \\ 0 & 0 & 1 & 0 & 0 & 1 & -1 & 0 \\ 0 & 0 & 0 & 1 & 1 & 0 & 0 & -1 \end{bmatrix} \xrightarrow[R_1 \to R_1-R_4]{} \begin{bmatrix} 1 & 0 & 0 & 0 & 0 & 0 & -2 & 1 \\ 0 & 1 & 0 & 0 & -1 & 0 & 1 & 1 \\ 0 & 0 & 1 & 0 & 0 & 1 & -1 & 0 \\ 0 & 0 & 0 & 1 & 1 & 0 & 0 & -1 \end{bmatrix}$

Therefore, the inverse matrix is $\begin{bmatrix} 0 & 0 & -2 & 1 \\ -1 & 0 & 1 & 1 \\ 0 & 1 & -1 & 0 \\ 1 & 0 & 0 & -1 \end{bmatrix}$.

23. $\begin{cases} 5x + 3y = 4 \\ 3x + 2y = 0 \end{cases}$ is equivalent to the matrix equation $\begin{bmatrix} 5 & 3 \\ 3 & 2 \end{bmatrix}\begin{bmatrix} x \\ y \end{bmatrix} = \begin{bmatrix} 4 \\ 0 \end{bmatrix}$.

Using the inverse from Exercise 3, $\begin{bmatrix} x \\ y \end{bmatrix} = \begin{bmatrix} 2 & -3 \\ -3 & 5 \end{bmatrix}\begin{bmatrix} 4 \\ 0 \end{bmatrix} = \begin{bmatrix} 8 \\ -12 \end{bmatrix}$.

Therefore, $x = 8$ and $y = -12$.

25. $\begin{cases} 2x + 5y = 2 \\ -5x - 13y = 20 \end{cases}$ is equivalent to the matrix equation $\begin{bmatrix} 2 & 5 \\ -5 & -13 \end{bmatrix}\begin{bmatrix} x \\ y \end{bmatrix} = \begin{bmatrix} 2 \\ 20 \end{bmatrix}$.

Using the inverse from Exercise 5, $\begin{bmatrix} x \\ y \end{bmatrix} = \begin{bmatrix} 13 & 5 \\ -5 & -2 \end{bmatrix}\begin{bmatrix} 2 \\ 20 \end{bmatrix} = \begin{bmatrix} 126 \\ -50 \end{bmatrix}$.

Therefore, $x = 126$ and $y = -50$.

27. $\begin{cases} 2x + 4y + z = 7 \\ -x + y - z = 0 \\ x + 4y = -2 \end{cases}$ is equivalent to the matrix equation $\begin{bmatrix} 2 & 4 & 1 \\ -1 & 1 & -1 \\ 1 & 4 & 0 \end{bmatrix}\begin{bmatrix} x \\ y \\ z \end{bmatrix} = \begin{bmatrix} 7 \\ 0 \\ -2 \end{bmatrix}$.

Using the inverse from Exercise 11, $\begin{bmatrix} x \\ y \\ z \end{bmatrix} = \begin{bmatrix} -4 & -4 & 5 \\ 1 & 1 & -1 \\ 5 & 4 & -6 \end{bmatrix}\begin{bmatrix} 7 \\ 0 \\ -2 \end{bmatrix} = \begin{bmatrix} -38 \\ 9 \\ 47 \end{bmatrix}$.

Therefore, $x = -38$, $y = 9$, and $z = 47$.

29. $\begin{cases} -2y + 2z = 12 \\ 3x + y + 3z = -2 \\ x - 2y + 3z = 8 \end{cases}$ is equivalent to the matrix equation $\begin{bmatrix} 0 & -2 & 2 \\ 3 & 1 & 3 \\ 1 & -2 & 3 \end{bmatrix}\begin{bmatrix} x \\ y \\ z \end{bmatrix} = \begin{bmatrix} 12 \\ -2 \\ 8 \end{bmatrix}$.

Using the inverse from Exercise 15, $\begin{bmatrix} x \\ y \\ z \end{bmatrix} = \begin{bmatrix} -\frac{9}{2} & -1 & 4 \\ 3 & 1 & -3 \\ \frac{7}{2} & 1 & -3 \end{bmatrix}\begin{bmatrix} 12 \\ -2 \\ 8 \end{bmatrix} = \begin{bmatrix} -20 \\ 10 \\ 16 \end{bmatrix}$.

Therefore, $x = -20$, $y = 10$, and $z = 16$.

31. Using the calculator you should get the result $(3, 2, 1)$.

33. Using the calculator you should get the result $(3, -2, 2)$.

35. Using the calculator you should get the result $(8, 1, 0, 3)$.

37. We have $\begin{bmatrix} 3 & -2 \\ -4 & 3 \end{bmatrix}^{-1} = \frac{1}{9-8}\begin{bmatrix} 3 & 2 \\ 4 & 3 \end{bmatrix} = \begin{bmatrix} 3 & 2 \\ 4 & 3 \end{bmatrix}$.

Hence, $\begin{bmatrix} x & y & z \\ u & v & w \end{bmatrix} = \begin{bmatrix} 3 & 2 \\ 4 & 3 \end{bmatrix}\begin{bmatrix} 1 & 0 & -1 \\ 2 & 1 & 3 \end{bmatrix} = \begin{bmatrix} 7 & 2 & 3 \\ 10 & 3 & 5 \end{bmatrix}$.

39. (a) $\begin{bmatrix} 3 & 1 & 3 & 1 & 0 & 0 \\ 4 & 2 & 4 & 0 & 1 & 0 \\ 3 & 2 & 4 & 0 & 0 & 1 \end{bmatrix}$ $\xrightarrow[\substack{R_3 - R_1 \to R_3 \\ R_1 \leftrightarrow R_2}]{}$ $\begin{bmatrix} 4 & 2 & 4 & 0 & 1 & 0 \\ 3 & 1 & 3 & 1 & 0 & 0 \\ 0 & 1 & 1 & -1 & 0 & 1 \end{bmatrix}$ $\xrightarrow[]{R_1 - R_2 \to R_1}$

$$\begin{bmatrix} 1 & 1 & 1 & -1 & 1 & 0 \\ 3 & 1 & 3 & 1 & 0 & 0 \\ 0 & 1 & 1 & -1 & 0 & 1 \end{bmatrix} \xrightarrow{R_2-3R_1 \to R_2} \begin{bmatrix} 1 & 1 & 1 & -1 & 1 & 0 \\ 0 & -2 & 0 & 4 & -3 & 0 \\ 0 & 1 & 1 & -1 & 0 & 1 \end{bmatrix} \xrightarrow[R_3-R_2 \to R_3]{R_1-R_2 \to R_1,\ -\frac{1}{2}R_2}$$

$$\begin{bmatrix} 1 & 0 & 1 & 1 & -\frac{1}{2} & 0 \\ 0 & 1 & 0 & -2 & \frac{3}{2} & 0 \\ 0 & 0 & 1 & 1 & -\frac{3}{2} & 1 \end{bmatrix} \xrightarrow{R_1-R_3 \to R_1} \begin{bmatrix} 1 & 0 & 0 & 0 & 1 & -1 \\ 0 & 1 & 0 & -2 & \frac{3}{2} & 0 \\ 0 & 0 & 1 & 1 & -\frac{3}{2} & 1 \end{bmatrix}$$

Therefore, the inverse of the matrix is $\begin{bmatrix} 0 & 1 & -1 \\ -2 & \frac{3}{2} & 0 \\ 1 & -\frac{3}{2} & 1 \end{bmatrix}$.

(b) $\begin{bmatrix} A \\ B \\ C \end{bmatrix} = \begin{bmatrix} 0 & 1 & -1 \\ -2 & \frac{3}{2} & 0 \\ 1 & -\frac{3}{2} & 1 \end{bmatrix} \begin{bmatrix} 10 \\ 14 \\ 13 \end{bmatrix} = \begin{bmatrix} 1 \\ 1 \\ 2 \end{bmatrix}$

Therefore, he should feed the rats 1 oz of A, 1 oz of B, and 2 oz of C.

(c) $\begin{bmatrix} A \\ B \\ C \end{bmatrix} = \begin{bmatrix} 0 & 1 & -1 \\ -2 & \frac{3}{2} & 0 \\ 1 & -\frac{3}{2} & 1 \end{bmatrix} \begin{bmatrix} 9 \\ 12 \\ 10 \end{bmatrix} = \begin{bmatrix} 2 \\ 0 \\ 1 \end{bmatrix}$

Therefore, he should feed the rats 2 oz of A, 0 oz of B, and 1 oz of C.

(d) $\begin{bmatrix} A \\ B \\ C \end{bmatrix} = \begin{bmatrix} 0 & 1 & -1 \\ -2 & \frac{3}{2} & 0 \\ 1 & -\frac{3}{2} & 1 \end{bmatrix} \begin{bmatrix} 2 \\ 4 \\ 11 \end{bmatrix} = \begin{bmatrix} -7 \\ 2 \\ 7 \end{bmatrix}$

Since $A < 0$, there is no combination of foods giving the required supply.

41. (a) $\begin{cases} x + y + 2z = 675 \\ 2x + y + z = 600 \\ x + 2y + z = 625 \end{cases}$

(b) $\begin{bmatrix} 1 & 1 & 2 \\ 2 & 1 & 1 \\ 1 & 2 & 1 \end{bmatrix} \begin{bmatrix} x \\ y \\ z \end{bmatrix} = \begin{bmatrix} 675 \\ 600 \\ 625 \end{bmatrix}$

(c) $\begin{bmatrix} 1 & 1 & 2 & 1 & 0 & 0 \\ 2 & 1 & 1 & 0 & 1 & 0 \\ 1 & 2 & 1 & 0 & 0 & 1 \end{bmatrix} \xrightarrow[R_3-R_1 \to R_3]{R_2-2R_1 \to R_2} \begin{bmatrix} 1 & 1 & 2 & 1 & 0 & 0 \\ 0 & -1 & -3 & -2 & 1 & 0 \\ 0 & 1 & -1 & -1 & 0 & 1 \end{bmatrix}$

$$\xrightarrow[R_3+R_2 \to R_3]{R_1+R_2 \to R_1} \begin{bmatrix} 1 & 0 & -1 & -1 & 1 & 0 \\ 0 & -1 & -3 & -2 & 1 & 0 \\ 0 & 0 & -4 & -3 & 1 & 1 \end{bmatrix} \xrightarrow[-\frac{1}{4}R_3]{-R_2}$$

$$\begin{bmatrix} 1 & 0 & -1 & -1 & 1 & 0 \\ 0 & 1 & 3 & 2 & -1 & 0 \\ 0 & 0 & 1 & \frac{3}{4} & -\frac{1}{4} & -\frac{1}{4} \end{bmatrix} \xrightarrow[R_2-3R_3 \to R_2]{R_1+R_3 \to R_1} \begin{bmatrix} 1 & 0 & 0 & -\frac{1}{4} & \frac{3}{4} & -\frac{1}{4} \\ 0 & 1 & 0 & -\frac{1}{4} & -\frac{1}{4} & \frac{3}{4} \\ 0 & 0 & 1 & \frac{3}{4} & -\frac{1}{4} & -\frac{1}{4} \end{bmatrix}$$

Therefore, the inverse of the matrix is $\begin{bmatrix} -\frac{1}{4} & \frac{3}{4} & -\frac{1}{4} \\ -\frac{1}{4} & -\frac{1}{4} & \frac{3}{4} \\ \frac{3}{4} & -\frac{1}{4} & -\frac{1}{4} \end{bmatrix}$ and

$$\begin{bmatrix} x \\ y \\ z \end{bmatrix} = \begin{bmatrix} -\frac{1}{4} & \frac{3}{4} & -\frac{1}{4} \\ -\frac{1}{4} & -\frac{1}{4} & \frac{3}{4} \\ \frac{3}{4} & -\frac{1}{4} & -\frac{1}{4} \end{bmatrix} \begin{bmatrix} 675 \\ 600 \\ 625 \end{bmatrix} = \begin{bmatrix} 125 \\ 150 \\ 200 \end{bmatrix}.$$

Thus he earns \$125 on a standard set, \$150 on a deluxe set, and \$200 on a leather-bound set.

43. $\begin{bmatrix} e^x & -e^{2x} \\ e^{2x} & e^{3x} \end{bmatrix}^{-1} = \frac{1}{e^{4x}+e^{4x}} \begin{bmatrix} e^{3x} & e^{2x} \\ -e^{2x} & e^x \end{bmatrix} = \frac{1}{2} \begin{bmatrix} e^{-x} & e^{-2x} \\ -e^{-2x} & e^{-3x} \end{bmatrix}$

45. $\begin{bmatrix} \cos\theta & \sin\theta \\ -\sin\theta & \cos\theta \end{bmatrix}^{-1} = \frac{1}{\cos^2\theta + \sin^2\theta} \begin{bmatrix} \cos\theta & -\sin\theta \\ \sin\theta & \cos\theta \end{bmatrix} = \begin{bmatrix} \cos\theta & -\sin\theta \\ \sin\theta & \cos\theta \end{bmatrix}$

47. No, consider the following counterexample: $A = \begin{bmatrix} 0 & 1 \\ 0 & 0 \end{bmatrix}$ and $B = \begin{bmatrix} 0 & 2 \\ 0 & 0 \end{bmatrix}$. Then, $AB = O$, but neither $A = O$ nor $B = O$.

There are infinitely many matrices for which $A^2 = O$. One example is $A = \begin{bmatrix} 0 & 1 \\ 0 & 0 \end{bmatrix}$. Then, $A^2 = O$, but $A \neq O$.

Exercises 8.7

1. The matrix $\begin{bmatrix} 2 & 0 \\ 0 & 3 \end{bmatrix}$ has determinant $|D| = (2)(3) - (0)(0) = 6$.

3. The matrix $\begin{bmatrix} 4 & 5 \\ 0 & -1 \end{bmatrix}$ has determinant $|D| = (4)(-1) - (5)(0) = -4$.

5. The matrix $\begin{bmatrix} 2 & 5 \end{bmatrix}$ does not have a determinant because the matrix is not square.

7. The matrix $\begin{bmatrix} \frac{1}{2} & \frac{1}{8} \\ 1 & \frac{1}{2} \end{bmatrix}$ has determinant $|D| = \frac{1}{2} \cdot \frac{1}{2} - 1 \cdot \frac{1}{8} = \frac{1}{4} - \frac{1}{8} = \frac{1}{8}$.

In Exercises 9 – 13, the matrix is $A = \begin{bmatrix} 1 & 0 & \frac{1}{2} \\ -3 & 5 & 2 \\ 0 & 0 & 4 \end{bmatrix}$.

9. $M_{11} = 5 \cdot 4 - 0 \cdot 2 = 20$, $A_{11} = (-1)^2 M_{11} = 20$

11. $M_{12} = -3 \cdot 4 - 0 \cdot 2 = -12$, $A_{12} = (-1)^3 M_{12} = 12$

13. $M_{23} = 1 \cdot 0 - 0 \cdot 0 = 0$, $A_{23} = (-1)^5 M_{23} = 0$

15. $M = \begin{bmatrix} 2 & 1 & 0 \\ 0 & -2 & 4 \\ 0 & 1 & -3 \end{bmatrix}$. Therefore, expanding by the first column, $|M| = 2 \begin{vmatrix} -2 & 4 \\ 1 & -3 \end{vmatrix}$
    $= 2(6 - 4) = 4$. Since $|M| \neq 0$, the matrix has an inverse.

17. $M = \begin{bmatrix} 1 & 3 & 7 \\ 2 & 0 & -1 \\ 0 & 2 & 6 \end{bmatrix}$. Therefore, expanding by the third row, $|M| = -2 \begin{vmatrix} 1 & 7 \\ 2 & -1 \end{vmatrix} + 6 \begin{vmatrix} 1 & 3 \\ 2 & 0 \end{vmatrix}$
    $= -2(-1 - 14) + 6(0 - 6) = 30 - 36 = -6$. Since $|M| \neq 0$, the matrix has an inverse.

19. $M = \begin{bmatrix} 30 & 0 & 20 \\ 0 & -10 & -20 \\ 40 & 0 & 10 \end{bmatrix}$. Therefore, expanding by the first row,

    $|M| = 30 \begin{vmatrix} -10 & -20 \\ 0 & 10 \end{vmatrix} + 20 \begin{vmatrix} 0 & -10 \\ 40 & 0 \end{vmatrix} = 30(-100 + 0) + 20(0 + 400)$
    $= -3000 + 8000 = 5000$, and so M^{-1} exists.

21. $M = \begin{bmatrix} 1 & 3 & 3 & 0 \\ 0 & 2 & 0 & 1 \\ -1 & 0 & 0 & 2 \\ 1 & 6 & 4 & 1 \end{bmatrix}$. Therefore, expanding by the third row,

$$|M| = -1 \begin{vmatrix} 3 & 3 & 0 \\ 2 & 0 & 1 \\ 6 & 4 & 1 \end{vmatrix} - 2 \begin{vmatrix} 1 & 3 & 3 \\ 0 & 2 & 0 \\ 1 & 6 & 4 \end{vmatrix} = 1 \begin{vmatrix} 3 & 3 \\ 6 & 4 \end{vmatrix} - 1 \begin{vmatrix} 3 & 3 \\ 2 & 0 \end{vmatrix} - 4 \begin{vmatrix} 1 & 3 \\ 1 & 4 \end{vmatrix} = -6 + 6 - 4 = -4,$$

and so M^{-1} exists.

23. $|M| = \begin{vmatrix} 0 & 0 & 4 & 6 \\ 2 & 1 & 1 & 3 \\ 2 & 1 & 2 & 3 \\ 3 & 0 & 1 & 7 \end{vmatrix} = \begin{vmatrix} 0 & 0 & 4 & 6 \\ 2 & 1 & 1 & 3 \\ 0 & 0 & 1 & 0 \\ 3 & 0 & 1 & 7 \end{vmatrix}$, by replacing R_3 with $R_3 - R_2$. Then, expanding by the

third row, $|M| = 1 \begin{vmatrix} 0 & 0 & 6 \\ 2 & 1 & 3 \\ 3 & 0 & 7 \end{vmatrix} = 6 \begin{vmatrix} 2 & 1 \\ 3 & 0 \end{vmatrix} = 6(2 \cdot 0 - 3 \cdot 1) = -18.$

25. $M = \begin{bmatrix} 1 & 2 & 3 & 4 & 5 \\ 0 & 2 & 4 & 6 & 8 \\ 0 & 0 & 3 & 6 & 9 \\ 0 & 0 & 0 & 4 & 8 \\ 0 & 0 & 0 & 0 & 5 \end{bmatrix}$. Then, expanding by the fifth row, $|M| = 5 \begin{vmatrix} 1 & 2 & 3 & 4 \\ 0 & 2 & 4 & 6 \\ 0 & 0 & 3 & 6 \\ 0 & 0 & 0 & 4 \end{vmatrix}$

$$= 5 \cdot 4 \begin{vmatrix} 1 & 2 & 3 \\ 0 & 2 & 4 \\ 0 & 0 & 3 \end{vmatrix} = 20 \cdot 3 \begin{vmatrix} 1 & 2 \\ 0 & 2 \end{vmatrix} = 60 \cdot 2 = 120.$$

27. $B = \begin{bmatrix} 4 & 1 & 0 \\ -2 & -1 & 1 \\ 4 & 0 & 3 \end{bmatrix}$

(a) $|B| = 2 \begin{vmatrix} 1 & 0 \\ 0 & 3 \end{vmatrix} - 1 \begin{vmatrix} 4 & 0 \\ 4 & 3 \end{vmatrix} - 1 \begin{vmatrix} 4 & 1 \\ 4 & 0 \end{vmatrix} = 6 - 12 + 4 = -2$

(b) $|B| = -1 \begin{vmatrix} 4 & 1 \\ 4 & 0 \end{vmatrix} + 3 \begin{vmatrix} 4 & 1 \\ -2 & -1 \end{vmatrix} = 4 - 6 = -2$

(c) Yes, as expected, the results agree.

29. $\begin{cases} 2x - y = -9 \\ x + 2y = 8 \end{cases}$ Then, $|D| = \begin{vmatrix} 2 & -1 \\ 1 & 2 \end{vmatrix} = 5, |D_x| = \begin{vmatrix} -9 & -1 \\ 8 & 2 \end{vmatrix} = -10,$ and

$|D_y| = \begin{vmatrix} 2 & -9 \\ 1 & 8 \end{vmatrix} = 25.$ Hence, $x = \dfrac{|D_x|}{|D|} = \dfrac{-10}{5} = -2, y = \dfrac{|D_y|}{|D|} = \dfrac{25}{5} = 5,$ and so the solution

is $(-2, 5)$.

31. $\begin{cases} x - 6y = 3 \\ 3x + 2y = 1 \end{cases}$ Then, $|D| = \begin{vmatrix} 1 & -6 \\ 3 & 2 \end{vmatrix} = 20, |D_x| = \begin{vmatrix} 3 & -6 \\ 1 & 2 \end{vmatrix} = 12,$ and

$|D_y| = \begin{vmatrix} 1 & 3 \\ 3 & 1 \end{vmatrix} = -8.$ Hence, $x = \dfrac{|D_x|}{|D|} = \dfrac{12}{20} = 0.6, y = \dfrac{|D_y|}{|D|} = \dfrac{-8}{20} = -0.4,$ and so the solution

is $(0.6, -0.4)$.

33. $\begin{cases} 0.4x + 1.2y = 0.4 \\ 1.2x + 1.6y = 3.2 \end{cases}$ Then, $|D| = \begin{vmatrix} 0.4 & 1.2 \\ 1.2 & 1.6 \end{vmatrix} = -0.8$, $|D_x| = \begin{vmatrix} 0.4 & 1.2 \\ 3.2 & 1.6 \end{vmatrix} = -3.2$, and

$|D_y| = \begin{vmatrix} 0.4 & 0.4 \\ 1.2 & 3.2 \end{vmatrix} = 0.8$. Hence, $x = \dfrac{|D_x|}{|D|} = \dfrac{-3.2}{-0.8} = 4$, $y = \dfrac{|D_y|}{|D|} = \dfrac{0.8}{-0.8} = -1$, and so the

solution is $(4, -1)$.

35. $\begin{cases} x - y + 2z = 0 \\ \quad 3x + z = 11 \\ -x + 2y = 0 \end{cases}$ Then, expanding by the second row,

$|D| = \begin{vmatrix} 1 & -1 & 2 \\ 3 & 0 & 1 \\ -1 & 2 & 0 \end{vmatrix} = -3\begin{vmatrix} -1 & 2 \\ 2 & 0 \end{vmatrix} - 1\begin{vmatrix} 1 & -1 \\ -1 & 2 \end{vmatrix} = 12 - 1 = 11,$

$|D_x| = \begin{vmatrix} 0 & -1 & 2 \\ 11 & 0 & 1 \\ 0 & 2 & 0 \end{vmatrix} = -11\begin{vmatrix} -1 & 2 \\ 2 & 0 \end{vmatrix} = 44$, $|D_y| = \begin{vmatrix} 1 & 0 & 2 \\ 3 & 11 & 1 \\ -1 & 0 & 0 \end{vmatrix} = 11\begin{vmatrix} 1 & 2 \\ -1 & 0 \end{vmatrix} = 22,$

and $|D_z| = \begin{vmatrix} 1 & -1 & 0 \\ 3 & 0 & 11 \\ -1 & 2 & 0 \end{vmatrix} = -11\begin{vmatrix} 1 & -1 \\ -1 & 2 \end{vmatrix} = -11$. Therefore, $x = \frac{44}{11} = 4$, $y = \frac{22}{11} = 2$,

$z = \frac{-11}{11} = -1$, and so the solution is $(4, 2, -1)$.

37. $\begin{cases} 2x_1 + 3x_2 - 5x_3 = 1 \\ x_1 + x_2 - x_3 = 2 \\ \quad 2x_2 + x_3 = 8 \end{cases}$ Then, expanding by the third row,

$|D| = \begin{vmatrix} 2 & 3 & -5 \\ 1 & 1 & -1 \\ 0 & 2 & 1 \end{vmatrix} = -2\begin{vmatrix} 2 & -5 \\ 1 & -1 \end{vmatrix} + \begin{vmatrix} 2 & 3 \\ 1 & 1 \end{vmatrix} = -6 - 1 = -7,$

$|D_{x_1}| = \begin{vmatrix} 1 & 3 & -5 \\ 2 & 1 & -1 \\ 8 & 2 & 1 \end{vmatrix} = \begin{vmatrix} 1 & -1 \\ 2 & 1 \end{vmatrix} - 3\begin{vmatrix} 2 & -1 \\ 8 & 1 \end{vmatrix} - 5\begin{vmatrix} 2 & 1 \\ 8 & 2 \end{vmatrix} = 3 - 30 + 20 = -7,$

$|D_{x_2}| = \begin{vmatrix} 2 & 1 & -5 \\ 1 & 2 & -1 \\ 0 & 8 & 1 \end{vmatrix} = -8\begin{vmatrix} 2 & -5 \\ 1 & -1 \end{vmatrix} + \begin{vmatrix} 2 & 1 \\ 1 & 2 \end{vmatrix} = -24 + 3 = -21$, and

$|D_{x_3}| = \begin{vmatrix} 2 & 3 & 1 \\ 1 & 1 & 2 \\ 0 & 2 & 8 \end{vmatrix} = -2\begin{vmatrix} 2 & 1 \\ 1 & 2 \end{vmatrix} + 8\begin{vmatrix} 2 & 3 \\ 1 & 1 \end{vmatrix} = -6 - 8 = -14$. Thus, $x_1 = \frac{-7}{-7} = 1$,

$x_2 = \frac{-21}{-7} = 3$, $x_3 = \frac{-14}{-7} = 2$, and so the solution is $(1, 3, 2)$.

39. $\begin{cases} \frac{1}{3}x - \frac{1}{5}y + \frac{1}{2}z = \frac{7}{10} \\ -\frac{2}{3}x + \frac{2}{5}y + \frac{3}{2}z = \frac{11}{10} \\ x - \frac{4}{5}y + z = \frac{9}{5} \end{cases} \Leftrightarrow \begin{cases} 10x - 6y + 15z = 21 \\ -20x + 12y + 45z = 33 \\ 5x - 4y + 5z = 9 \end{cases}$

Then, $|D| = \begin{vmatrix} 10 & -6 & 15 \\ -20 & 12 & 45 \\ 5 & -4 & 5 \end{vmatrix} = 10 \begin{vmatrix} 12 & 45 \\ -4 & 5 \end{vmatrix} + 6 \begin{vmatrix} -20 & 45 \\ 5 & 5 \end{vmatrix} + 15 \begin{vmatrix} -20 & 12 \\ 5 & -4 \end{vmatrix}$

$= 2400 - 1950 + 300 = 750,$

$|D_x| = \begin{vmatrix} 21 & -6 & 15 \\ 33 & 12 & 45 \\ 9 & -4 & 5 \end{vmatrix} = 21 \begin{vmatrix} 12 & 45 \\ -4 & 5 \end{vmatrix} + 6 \begin{vmatrix} 33 & 45 \\ 9 & 5 \end{vmatrix} + 15 \begin{vmatrix} 33 & 12 \\ 9 & -4 \end{vmatrix}$

$= 5040 - 1440 - 3600 = 0,$

$|D_y| = \begin{vmatrix} 10 & 21 & 15 \\ -20 & 33 & 45 \\ 5 & 9 & 5 \end{vmatrix} = 10 \begin{vmatrix} 33 & 45 \\ 9 & 5 \end{vmatrix} - 21 \begin{vmatrix} -20 & 45 \\ 5 & 5 \end{vmatrix} + 15 \begin{vmatrix} -20 & 33 \\ 5 & 9 \end{vmatrix}$

$= -2400 + 6825 - 5175 = -750,$ and

$|D_z| = \begin{vmatrix} 10 & -6 & 21 \\ -20 & 12 & 33 \\ 5 & -4 & 9 \end{vmatrix} = 10 \begin{vmatrix} 12 & 33 \\ -4 & 9 \end{vmatrix} + 6 \begin{vmatrix} -20 & 33 \\ 5 & 9 \end{vmatrix} + 21 \begin{vmatrix} -20 & 12 \\ 5 & -4 \end{vmatrix}$

$= 2400 - 2070 + 420 = 750.$

Therefore, $x = 0$, $y = -1$, $z = 1$, and so the solution is $(0, -1, 1)$.

41. $\begin{cases} 3y + 5z = 4 \\ 2x - z = 10 \\ 4x + 7y = 0 \end{cases}$ Then, $|D| = \begin{vmatrix} 0 & 3 & 5 \\ 2 & 0 & -1 \\ 4 & 7 & 0 \end{vmatrix} = -3 \begin{vmatrix} 2 & -1 \\ 4 & 0 \end{vmatrix} + 5 \begin{vmatrix} 2 & 0 \\ 4 & 7 \end{vmatrix} = -12 + 70 = 58,$

$|D_x| = \begin{vmatrix} 4 & 3 & 5 \\ 10 & 0 & -1 \\ 0 & 7 & 0 \end{vmatrix} = -7 \begin{vmatrix} 4 & 5 \\ 10 & -1 \end{vmatrix} = 378,$

$|D_y| = \begin{vmatrix} 0 & 4 & 5 \\ 2 & 10 & -1 \\ 4 & 0 & 0 \end{vmatrix} = 4 \begin{vmatrix} 4 & 5 \\ 10 & -1 \end{vmatrix} = -216,$ and

$|D_z| = \begin{vmatrix} 0 & 3 & 4 \\ 2 & 0 & 10 \\ 4 & 7 & 0 \end{vmatrix} = 4 \begin{vmatrix} 3 & 4 \\ 0 & 10 \end{vmatrix} - 7 \begin{vmatrix} 0 & 4 \\ 2 & 10 \end{vmatrix} = 120 + 56 = 176.$

Thus, $x = \frac{189}{29}$, $y = -\frac{108}{29}$, and $z = \frac{88}{29}$, and so the solution is $\left(\frac{189}{29}, -\frac{108}{29}, \frac{88}{29} \right)$.

43. $\begin{cases} x + y + z + w = 0 \\ 2z + w = 0 \\ y - z = 0 \\ x + 2z = 1 \end{cases}$ Then $|D| = \begin{vmatrix} 1 & 1 & 1 & 1 \\ 2 & 0 & 0 & 1 \\ 0 & 1 & -1 & 0 \\ 1 & 0 & 2 & 0 \end{vmatrix} = -1 \begin{vmatrix} 2 & 0 & 1 \\ 0 & -1 & 0 \\ 1 & 2 & 0 \end{vmatrix} - 1 \begin{vmatrix} 1 & 1 & 1 \\ 2 & 0 & 1 \\ 1 & 2 & 0 \end{vmatrix}$

$= -\left(2 \begin{vmatrix} -1 & 0 \\ 2 & 0 \end{vmatrix} + 1 \begin{vmatrix} 0 & 1 \\ -1 & 0 \end{vmatrix} \right) - \left(-1 \begin{vmatrix} 2 & 1 \\ 1 & 0 \end{vmatrix} - 2 \begin{vmatrix} 1 & 1 \\ 2 & 1 \end{vmatrix} \right)$

$= -2(0) - 1(1) + 1(-1) + 2(-1) = -4,$

$|D_x| = \begin{vmatrix} 0 & 1 & 1 & 1 \\ 0 & 0 & 0 & 1 \\ 0 & 1 & -1 & 0 \\ 1 & 0 & 2 & 0 \end{vmatrix} = -1 \begin{vmatrix} 1 & 1 & 1 \\ 0 & 0 & 1 \\ 1 & -1 & 0 \end{vmatrix} = -1(-1) \begin{vmatrix} 1 & 1 \\ 1 & -1 \end{vmatrix} = -2,$

$$|D_y| = \begin{vmatrix} 1 & 0 & 1 & 1 \\ 2 & 0 & 0 & 1 \\ 0 & 0 & -1 & 0 \\ 1 & 1 & 2 & 0 \end{vmatrix} = 1 \begin{vmatrix} 1 & 1 & 1 \\ 2 & 0 & 1 \\ 0 & -1 & 0 \end{vmatrix} = 1 \begin{vmatrix} 0 & 1 \\ -1 & 0 \end{vmatrix} - 2 \begin{vmatrix} 1 & 1 \\ -1 & 0 \end{vmatrix} = 1 - 2(1) = -1,$$

$$|D_z| = \begin{vmatrix} 1 & 1 & 0 & 1 \\ 2 & 0 & 0 & 1 \\ 0 & 1 & 0 & 0 \\ 1 & 0 & 1 & 0 \end{vmatrix} = -1 \begin{vmatrix} 1 & 1 & 1 \\ 2 & 0 & 1 \\ 0 & 1 & 0 \end{vmatrix} = -1 \begin{vmatrix} 0 & 1 \\ 1 & 0 \end{vmatrix} + 2 \begin{vmatrix} 1 & 1 \\ 1 & 0 \end{vmatrix} = -1(-1) + 2(-1) = -1, \text{ and}$$

$$|D_w| = \begin{vmatrix} 1 & 1 & 1 & 0 \\ 2 & 0 & 0 & 0 \\ 0 & 1 & -1 & 0 \\ 1 & 0 & 2 & 1 \end{vmatrix} = 1 \begin{vmatrix} 1 & 1 & 1 \\ 2 & 0 & 0 \\ 0 & 1 & -1 \end{vmatrix} = -2 \begin{vmatrix} 1 & 1 \\ 1 & -1 \end{vmatrix} = -2(-2) = 4. \text{ Hence, we have}$$

$x = \dfrac{|D_x|}{|D|} = \dfrac{-2}{-4} = \dfrac{1}{2}; \ y = \dfrac{|D_y|}{|D|} = \dfrac{-1}{-4} = \dfrac{1}{4}; \ z = \dfrac{|D_z|}{|D|} = \dfrac{-1}{-4} = \dfrac{1}{4}; \ w = \dfrac{|D_w|}{|D|} = \dfrac{4}{-4} = -1, \text{ and the}$

solution is $\left(\frac{1}{2}, \frac{1}{4}, \frac{1}{4}, -1\right)$.

45. $\begin{vmatrix} a & 0 & 0 & 0 & 0 \\ 0 & b & 0 & 0 & 0 \\ 0 & 0 & c & 0 & 0 \\ 0 & 0 & 0 & d & 0 \\ 0 & 0 & 0 & 0 & e \end{vmatrix} = a \begin{vmatrix} b & 0 & 0 & 0 \\ 0 & c & 0 & 0 \\ 0 & 0 & d & 0 \\ 0 & 0 & 0 & e \end{vmatrix} = ab \begin{vmatrix} c & 0 & 0 \\ 0 & d & 0 \\ 0 & 0 & e \end{vmatrix} = abc \begin{vmatrix} d & 0 \\ 0 & e \end{vmatrix} = abcde.$

47. $\begin{vmatrix} x & 12 & 13 \\ 0 & x-1 & 23 \\ 0 & 0 & x-2 \end{vmatrix} = 0 \quad \Leftrightarrow \quad (x-2)\begin{vmatrix} x & 12 \\ 0 & x-1 \end{vmatrix} = 0 \quad \Leftrightarrow \quad (x-2) \cdot x(x-1) = 0 \quad \Leftrightarrow$

$x = 0, 1$ or 2.

49. $\begin{vmatrix} 1 & 0 & x \\ x^2 & 1 & 0 \\ x & 0 & 1 \end{vmatrix} = 0 \quad \Leftrightarrow \quad 1\begin{vmatrix} 1 & 0 \\ 0 & 1 \end{vmatrix} + x\begin{vmatrix} x^2 & 1 \\ x & 0 \end{vmatrix} = 0 \quad \Leftrightarrow \quad 1 - x^2 = 0 \quad \Leftrightarrow \quad x^2 = 1 \quad \Leftrightarrow$

$x = \pm 1.$

51. Area $= \pm\dfrac{1}{2}\begin{vmatrix} 0 & 0 & 1 \\ 6 & 2 & 1 \\ 3 & 8 & 1 \end{vmatrix} = \pm\dfrac{1}{2}\begin{vmatrix} 6 & 2 \\ 3 & 8 \end{vmatrix}$

$= \pm\dfrac{1}{2}(48 - 6) = \dfrac{1}{2}(42) = 21.$

53. Area $= \pm\frac{1}{2}\begin{vmatrix} -1 & 3 & 1 \\ 2 & 9 & 1 \\ 5 & -6 & 1 \end{vmatrix}$

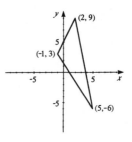

$= \pm\frac{1}{2}\left[-1\begin{vmatrix} 9 & 1 \\ -6 & 1 \end{vmatrix} - 3\begin{vmatrix} 2 & 1 \\ 5 & 1 \end{vmatrix} + 1\begin{vmatrix} 2 & 9 \\ 5 & -6 \end{vmatrix} \right]$

$= \pm\frac{1}{2}[-1(9+6) - 3(2-5) + 1(-12-45)]$

$= \pm\frac{1}{2}[-15 - 3(-3) + (-57)] = \pm\frac{1}{2}[-63]$

$= \frac{63}{2}$.

55. $\begin{vmatrix} 1 & x & x^2 \\ 1 & y & y^2 \\ 1 & z & z^2 \end{vmatrix} = 1\begin{vmatrix} y & y^2 \\ z & z^2 \end{vmatrix} - 1\begin{vmatrix} x & x^2 \\ z & z^2 \end{vmatrix} + 1\begin{vmatrix} x & x^2 \\ y & y^2 \end{vmatrix}$

$= yz^2 - y^2z - (xz^2 - x^2z) + (xy^2 - xy^2)$

$= yz^2 - y^2z - xz^2 - x^2z + xy^2 - xy^2 + xyz - xyz$

$= xyz - xz^2 - y^2z + yz^2 - x^2y + x^2z + zy^2 - xyz$

$= z(xy - xz - y^2 + yz) - x(xy - xz - y^2 + yz)$

$= (z - x)(xy - xz - y^2 + yz)$

$= (z - x)[x(y - z) - y(y - z)]$

$= (z - x)(x - y)(y - z)$

57. (a) If three points lie on a line then the area of the "triangle" they determine is 0, that is,

Area $= \pm\frac{1}{2}\begin{vmatrix} a_1 & b_1 & 1 \\ a_2 & b_2 & 1 \\ a_3 & b_3 & 1 \end{vmatrix} = 0 \quad \Leftrightarrow \quad \begin{vmatrix} a_1 & b_1 & 1 \\ a_2 & b_2 & 1 \\ a_3 & b_3 & 1 \end{vmatrix} = 0.$ If the points are not collinear, then

the point form a triangle, and the area of the triangle determined by these points $\neq 0$. If

$\begin{vmatrix} a_1 & b_1 & 1 \\ a_2 & b_2 & 1 \\ a_3 & b_3 & 1 \end{vmatrix} = 0$ then since Area $= \pm\frac{1}{2}\begin{vmatrix} a_1 & b_1 & 1 \\ a_2 & b_2 & 1 \\ a_3 & b_3 & 1 \end{vmatrix} = \pm\frac{1}{2}(0) = 0.$ So the "triangle" has no

area, and the points are collinear.

(b) (i) $\begin{vmatrix} -6 & 4 & 1 \\ 2 & 10 & 1 \\ 6 & 13 & 1 \end{vmatrix} = \begin{vmatrix} 2 & 10 \\ 6 & 13 \end{vmatrix} - \begin{vmatrix} -6 & 4 \\ 6 & 13 \end{vmatrix} + \begin{vmatrix} -6 & 4 \\ 2 & 10 \end{vmatrix}$

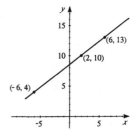

$= (26 - 60) - (-78 - 24) + (-60 - 8)$

$= -34 + 104 - 68 = 0.$

Thus these points are collinear.

(c)   (i) $\begin{vmatrix} -5 & 10 & 1 \\ 2 & 6 & 1 \\ 15 & -2 & 1 \end{vmatrix} = \begin{vmatrix} 2 & 6 \\ 15 & -2 \end{vmatrix} - \begin{vmatrix} -5 & 10 \\ 15 & -2 \end{vmatrix} + \begin{vmatrix} -5 & 10 \\ 2 & 6 \end{vmatrix}$

$$= (-4 - 90) - (10 - 150) + (-30 - 20)$$

$$= -94 + 140 - 50 = -4$$

These points are not collinear.

59.   (a)   If A is a matrix with a row or column consisting entirely of zeros, then if we expand the determinant by this row or column, we get $|A| = 0 \cdot |A_{1j}| - 0 \cdot |A_{2j}| + \cdots - 0 \cdot |A_{nj}| = 0$.

(b)   Use the principle that if matrix B is a square matrix obtained from A by adding a multiple of one row to another, or a multiple of one column to another, then $|A| = |B|$. If we let B be the matrix obtained by subtracting the two rows (or columns) that are the same, then matrix B will have a row or column that consists entirely of zeros. So $|B| = 0 \quad \Rightarrow \quad |A| = 0$.

(c)   Again use the principle that if matrix B is a square matrix obtained from A by adding a multiple of one row to another, or a multiple of one column to another, then $|A| = |B|$. If we let B be the matrix obtained by subtracting the proper multiple of the row (or column) from the other similar row (or column), then matrix B will have a row or column that consists entirely of zeros. So $|B| = 0 \quad \Rightarrow \quad |A| = 0$.

Exercises 8.8

1. $x \leq 2$

3. $y > x$

5. $y \geq 2x + 2$

7. $2x - y \leq 8$

9. $4x + 5y < 25$

11. $y > x^2 + 1$

13. $\begin{cases} x + y \leq 4 \\ \quad y \geq x \end{cases}$ The vertices occur where $\begin{cases} x + y = 4 \\ \quad y = x \end{cases}$.

Substituting, we have $2x = 4 \iff x = 2$. Since $y = x$, the vertex is $(2, 2)$, and the solution set is not bounded.

15. $\begin{cases} y < \frac{1}{4}x + 2 \\ y \geq 2x - 5 \end{cases}$ The vertex occurs where $\begin{cases} y = \frac{1}{4}x + 2 \\ y = 2x - 5 \end{cases}$

Substituting for y gives $\frac{1}{4}x + 2 = 2x - 5 \quad \Leftrightarrow \quad \frac{7}{4}x = 7 \quad \Leftrightarrow$
$x = 4$, so $y = 3$. Hence, the vertex is $(4, 3)$, and the solution is not bounded.

17. $\begin{cases} x \geq 0 \\ y \geq 0 \\ 3x + 5y \leq 15 \\ 3x + 2y \leq 9 \end{cases}$ From the graph, the points $(3, 0)$, $(0, 3)$ and

$(0, 0)$ are vertices, and the fourth vertex occurs where the lines
$3x + 5y = 15$ and $3x + 2y = 9$ intersect. Subtracting these two
equations gives $3y = 6 \quad \Leftrightarrow \quad y = 2$, and so $x = \frac{5}{3}$. Thus, the
fourth vertex is $\left(\frac{5}{3}, 2\right)$, and the solution set is bounded.

19. $\begin{cases} y < 9 - x^2 \\ y \geq x + 3 \end{cases}$ The vertices occur where $\begin{cases} y = 9 - x^2 \\ y = x + 3 \end{cases}$.

Substituting for y gives $9 - x^2 = x + 3 \quad \Leftrightarrow \quad x^2 + x - 6 = 0$
$\Leftrightarrow \quad (x - 2)(x + 3) = 0 \quad \Rightarrow \quad x = -3, x = 2$. Therefore,
he vertices are $(-3, 0)$ and $(2, 5)$, and the solution set is bounded.

21. $\begin{cases} x^2 + y^2 \leq 4 \\ x - y > 0 \end{cases}$ The vertices occur where $\begin{cases} x^2 + y^2 = 4 \\ x - y = 0 \end{cases}$.

Since $x - y = 0 \quad \Leftrightarrow \quad x = y$, substituting for x gives
$y^2 + y^2 = 4 \quad \Leftrightarrow \quad y^2 = 2 \quad \Rightarrow \quad y = \pm\sqrt{2}$, and $x = \pm\sqrt{2}$.
Therefore, the vertices are $(-\sqrt{2}, -\sqrt{2})$ and $(\sqrt{2}, \sqrt{2})$, and
the solution set is bounded.

23. $\begin{cases} x^2 - y \leq 0 \\ 2x^2 + y \leq 12 \end{cases}$ The vertices occur where $\begin{cases} x^2 - y = 0 \\ 2x^2 + y = 12 \end{cases}$

$\Leftrightarrow \quad \begin{cases} 2x^2 - 2y = 0 \\ 2x^2 + y = 12 \end{cases}$. Subtracting the equations gives $3y = 12$

$\Leftrightarrow \quad y = 4$, and $x = \pm 2$. Thus, the vertices are $(2, 4)$ and $(-2, 4)$,
and the solution set is bounded.

25. $\begin{cases} x + 2y \le 14 \\ 3x - y \ge 0 \\ x - y \ge 2 \end{cases}$ We now find the vertices of the region by solving pairs of the corresponding equations.

$\begin{cases} x + 2y = 14 \\ x - y = 2 \end{cases}$ Subtracting the second equation from the first gives $3y = 12 \iff y = 4$, and $x = 6$.

$\begin{cases} 3x - y = 0 \\ x - y = 2 \end{cases}$ Subtracting the second equation from the first gives $2x = -2 \iff x = -1$, and $y = -3$.

Therefore, the vertices are $(6, 4)$ and $(-1, -3)$, and the solution set is not bounded.

27. $\begin{cases} x \ge 0 \\ y \ge 0 \\ x \le 5 \\ x + y \le 7 \end{cases}$ The points of intersection are $(0, 7)$, $(0, 0)$, $(7, 0)$,

$(5, 2)$, and $(5, 0)$. However, the point $(7, 0)$ is not in the solution set. Therefore, the vertices are $(0, 7)$, $(0, 0)$, $(5, 0)$, and $(5, 2)$, and the solution set is bounded.

29. $\begin{cases} y > x + 1 \\ x + 2y \le 12 \\ x + 1 > 0 \end{cases}$ We now find the vertices of the region by solving pairs of the corresponding equations.

Using $x = -1$ and substituting for x in the line $y = x + 1$ gives the point $(-1, 0)$. Substituting for x in the line $x + 2y = 12$ gives the point $(-1, \frac{13}{2})$.

$\begin{cases} y = x + 1 \\ x + 2y = 12 \end{cases}$ From the first equation, $x = y - 1$, and

substituting for x into the second equation gives $y - 1 + 2y = 12 \iff 3y = 13 \iff y = \frac{13}{3}$, and $x = \frac{10}{3}$. So the vertices are $(-1, 0)$, $(-1, \frac{13}{2})$, and $(\frac{10}{3}, \frac{13}{3})$, and none of these vertices are in the solution set. The solution set is bounded.

31. $\begin{cases} x^2 + y^2 \le 8 \\ x \ge 2 \\ y \ge 0 \end{cases}$ The intersection points are $(2, \pm 2)$, $(2, 0)$, and

$(2\sqrt{2}, 0)$. However, since $(2, -2)$ is not part of the solution set, the vertices are $(2, 2)$, $(2, 0)$, and $(2\sqrt{2}, 0)$. The solution set is bounded.

33. $\begin{cases} x^2 + y^2 < 9 \\ x + y > 0 \\ x \le 0 \end{cases}$ Substituting $x = 0$ into the equations $x^2 + y^2 = 9$

and $x + y = 0$ gives the vertices $(0, \pm 3)$ and $(0, 0)$.

To find the points of intersection for the equations $\begin{cases} x^2 + y^2 = 9 \\ x + y = 0 \end{cases}$

we solve for $x = -y$ and substitute into the first equation. This

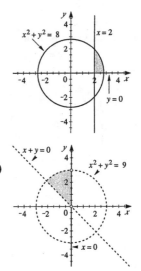

gives $(-y)^2 + y^2 = 9 \Rightarrow y = \pm\frac{3\sqrt{2}}{2}$. The points $(0, -3)$ and $\left(\frac{3\sqrt{2}}{2}, -\frac{3\sqrt{2}}{2}\right)$ lie away from the solution set, so the vertices are $(0,0)$, $(0,3)$, and $\left(-\frac{3\sqrt{2}}{2}, \frac{3\sqrt{2}}{2}\right)$. (Note that the vertices are not solutions in this case.) The solution set is bounded.

35. $\begin{cases} y \geq x - 3 \\ y \geq -2x + 6 \\ y \leq 8 \end{cases}$

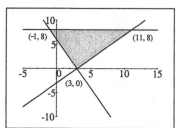

Using the graphing calculator we find the region as shown. The vertices are $(3, 0)$, $(-1, 8)$, and $(11, 8)$.

37. $\begin{cases} y \geq 6x - x^2 \\ x + y \geq 4 \end{cases}$

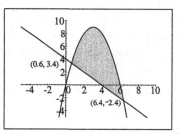

Using the graphing calculator we find the region as shown. The vertices are $(0.6, 3.4)$ and $(6.4, -2.4)$.

39. Let x be the number of fiction books published in a year, and y be the number of nonfiction books. Then, the following system of inequalities holds:

$\begin{cases} x \geq 0 \\ y \geq 0 \\ x + y \leq 100 \, . \\ y \geq 20 \\ x \geq y \end{cases}$ From the graph, we see that the vertices are $(50, 50)$, $(80, 20)$ and $(20, 20)$.

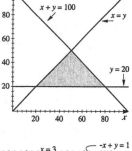

41. $\begin{cases} x + 2y > 4 \\ -x + y < 1 \\ x + 3y \leq 9 \, . \\ x < 3 \end{cases}$

We solve the system using the first method, that is, shading the solution to each inequality. However, since this text is published in black and white, we shade the region with lines perpendicular to the boundary. As you can see, as the number of inequalities in the system increases, it gets harder to locate the region where <u>all</u> the shaded parts overlap.

In the second method, if a region is shaded, then it does not satisfy at least one equality. As a result, the region that is left unshaded satisfies each inequality, and is the solution to the system of inequalities. This makes it easier to locate the solution set.

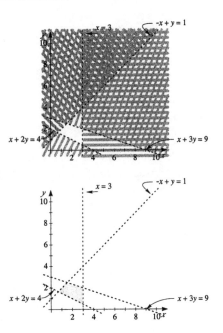

To finish, we find the vertices of the solution set. The line $x = 3$ intersects the line $x + 2y = 4$ at $\left(3, \frac{1}{2}\right)$ and the line $x + 3y = 9$ at $(3, 2)$. To find where the lines $-x + y = 1$ and $x + 2y = 4$ intersect, we add the two equations, which gives $3y = 5 \iff y = \frac{5}{3}$, and $x = \frac{2}{3}$. To find where the lines $-x + y = 1$ and $x + 3y = 9$ intersect, we add the two equations, which gives $4y = 10 \iff y = \frac{10}{4} = \frac{5}{2}$, and $x = \frac{3}{2}$. The vertices are $\left(3, \frac{1}{2}\right)$, $(3, 2)$, $\left(\frac{2}{3}, \frac{5}{3}\right)$, and $\left(\frac{3}{2}, \frac{5}{2}\right)$, and the solution set is bounded.

Exercises 8.9

1. $\dfrac{1}{(x-1)(x+2)} = \dfrac{A}{x-1} + \dfrac{B}{x+2}$

3. $\dfrac{x^2 - 3x + 5}{(x-2)^2(x+4)} = \dfrac{A}{x-2} + \dfrac{B}{(x-2)^2} + \dfrac{C}{x+4}$

5. $\dfrac{x^2}{(x-3)(x^2+4)} = \dfrac{A}{x-3} + \dfrac{Bx+C}{x^2+4}$

7. $\dfrac{x^3 - 4x^2 + 2}{(x^2+1)(x^2+2)} = \dfrac{Ax+B}{x^2+1} + \dfrac{Cx+D}{x^2+2}$

9. $\dfrac{x^3 + x + 1}{x(2x-5)^3(x^2+2x+5)^2} = \dfrac{A}{x} + \dfrac{B}{2x-5} + \dfrac{C}{(2x-5)^2} + \dfrac{D}{(2x-5)^3} +$

   $\dfrac{Ex+F}{x^2+2x+5} + \dfrac{Gx+H}{(x^2+2x+5)^2}$

11. $\dfrac{2}{(x-1)(x+1)} = \dfrac{A}{x-1} + \dfrac{B}{x+1}$. Multiplying by $(x-1)(x+1)$, we get

    $2 = A(x+1) + B(x-1) \quad \Leftrightarrow \quad 2 = Ax + A + Bx - B$. Thus

    $\begin{cases} A + B = 0 \\ A - B = 2 \end{cases}$. Adding we get $2A = 2 \quad \Leftrightarrow \quad A = 1$. Now $A + B = 0 \quad \Leftrightarrow \quad B = -A$, so

    $B = -1$. Thus, the required partial fraction decomposition is $\dfrac{2}{(x-1)(x+1)} = \dfrac{1}{x-1} - \dfrac{1}{x+1}$.

13. $\dfrac{5}{(x-1)(x+4)} = \dfrac{A}{x-1} + \dfrac{B}{x+4}$. Multiplying by $(x-1)(x+4)$, we get

    $5 = A(x+4) + B(x-1) \quad \Leftrightarrow \quad 5 = Ax + 4A + Bx - B$. Thus

    $\begin{cases} A + B = 0 \\ 4A - B = 5 \end{cases}$. Now $A + B = 0 \quad \Leftrightarrow \quad B = -A$, so substituting, we get $4A - (-A) = 5 \quad \Leftrightarrow$

    $5A = 5 \quad \Leftrightarrow \quad A = 1$ and $B = -1$. The required partial fraction decomposition is

    $\dfrac{5}{(x-1)(x+4)} = \dfrac{1}{x-1} - \dfrac{1}{x+4}$.

15. $\dfrac{12}{x^2-9} = \dfrac{12}{(x-3)(x+3)} = \dfrac{A}{x-3} + \dfrac{B}{x+3}$. Multiplying by $(x-3)(x+3)$, we get

    $12 = A(x+3) + B(x-3) \quad \Leftrightarrow \quad 12 = Ax + 3A + Bx - 3B$. Thus

    $\begin{cases} A + B = 0 \\ 3A - 3B = 12 \end{cases} \quad \Leftrightarrow \quad \begin{cases} A + B = 0 \\ A - B = 4 \end{cases}$. Adding we get $2A = 4 \quad \Leftrightarrow \quad A = 2$. So

    $2 + B = 2 \quad \Leftrightarrow \quad$ and $B = -2$. The required partial fraction decomposition is

    $\dfrac{12}{x^2-9} = \dfrac{2}{x-3} - \dfrac{2}{x+3}$.

17. $\dfrac{4}{x^2 - 4} = \dfrac{4}{(x-2)(x+2)} = \dfrac{A}{x-2} + \dfrac{B}{x+2}$. Multiplying by $x^2 - 4$, we get

$4 = A(x+2) + B(x-2) = (A+B)x + (2A - 2B)$, and so

$\begin{cases} A + B = 0 \\ 2A - 2B = 4 \end{cases} \Leftrightarrow \begin{cases} A + B = 0 \\ A - B = 2 \end{cases}$. Adding we get $2A = 2 \quad \Leftrightarrow \quad A = 1$, and $B = -1$.

Therefore, $\dfrac{4}{x^2 - 4} = \dfrac{1}{x-2} - \dfrac{1}{x+2}$.

19. $\dfrac{x + 14}{x^2 - 2x - 8} = \dfrac{x + 14}{(x-4)(x+2)} = \dfrac{A}{x-4} + \dfrac{B}{x+2}$. Hence,

$x + 14 = A(x+2) + B(x-4) = (A+B)x + (2A - 4B)$, and so

$\begin{cases} A + B = 1 \\ 2A - 4B = 14 \end{cases} \Leftrightarrow \begin{cases} 2A + 2B = 2 \\ A - 2B = 7 \end{cases}$. Adding, we get $3A = 9 \quad \Leftrightarrow \quad A = 3$. So

$(3) + B = 1 \quad \Leftrightarrow \quad B = -2$. Therefore, $\dfrac{x + 14}{x^2 - 2x - 8} = \dfrac{3}{x-4} - \dfrac{2}{x+2}$.

21. $\dfrac{x}{8x^2 - 10x + 3} = \dfrac{x}{(4x-3)(2x-1)} = \dfrac{A}{4x-3} + \dfrac{B}{2x-1}$. Hence,

$x = A(2x-1) + B(4x-3) = (2A + 4B)x + (-A - 3B)$, and so

$\begin{cases} 2A + 4B = 1 \\ -A - 3B = 0 \end{cases} \Leftrightarrow \begin{cases} 2A + 4B = 1 \\ -2A - 6B = 0 \end{cases}$. Adding, we get $-2B = 1 \quad \Leftrightarrow \quad B = -\frac{1}{2}$, and

$A = \frac{3}{2}$. Therefore, $\dfrac{x}{8x^2 - 10x + 3} = \dfrac{\frac{3}{2}}{4x-3} - \dfrac{\frac{1}{2}}{2x-1}$.

23. $\dfrac{9x^2 - 9x + 6}{2x^3 - x^2 - 8x + 4} = \dfrac{9x^2 - 9x + 6}{(x-2)(x+2)(2x-1)} = \dfrac{A}{x-2} + \dfrac{B}{x+2} + \dfrac{C}{2x-1}$. Thus,

$\begin{aligned} 9x^2 - 9x + 6 &= A(x+2)(2x-1) + B(x-2)(2x-1) + C(x-2)(x+2) \\ &= A(2x^2 + 3x - 2) + B(2x^2 - 5x + 2) + C(x^2 - 4) \\ &= (2A + 2B + C)x^2 + (3A - 5B)x + (-2A + 2B - 4C). \end{aligned}$

This leads to a system with the following matrix representation:

$\begin{bmatrix} 2 & 2 & 1 & 9 \\ 3 & -5 & 0 & -9 \\ -2 & 2 & -4 & 6 \end{bmatrix} \begin{smallmatrix} R_2 + R_3 \to R_2 \\ R_1 + R_3 \to R_1 \end{smallmatrix} \begin{bmatrix} 0 & 4 & -3 & 15 \\ 1 & -3 & -4 & -3 \\ -2 & 2 & -4 & 6 \end{bmatrix} \xrightarrow{R_1 \leftrightarrow R_2}$

$\begin{bmatrix} 1 & -3 & -4 & -3 \\ 0 & 4 & -3 & 15 \\ -2 & 2 & -4 & 6 \end{bmatrix} \xrightarrow{R_3 + 2R_1 \to R_3} \begin{bmatrix} 1 & -3 & -4 & -3 \\ 0 & 4 & -3 & 15 \\ 0 & -4 & -12 & 0 \end{bmatrix} \xrightarrow{R_3 + R_2 \to R_3}$

$\begin{bmatrix} 1 & -3 & -4 & -3 \\ 0 & 4 & -3 & 15 \\ 0 & 0 & -15 & 15 \end{bmatrix}$.

Hence, $-15C = 15 \Leftrightarrow C = -1$; $4B + 3 = 15 \Leftrightarrow B = 3$; and $A - 9 + 4 = -3 \Leftrightarrow A = 2$.

Therefore, $\dfrac{9x^2 - 9x + 6}{2x^3 - x^2 - 8x + 4} = \dfrac{2}{x-2} + \dfrac{3}{x+2} - \dfrac{1}{2x-1}$.

25. $\dfrac{x^2+1}{x^3+x^2} = \dfrac{x^2+1}{x^2(x+1)} = \dfrac{A}{x} + \dfrac{B}{x^2} + \dfrac{C}{x+1}$. Hence,

$x^2 + 1 = Ax(x+1) + B(x+1) + Cx^2 = (A+C)x^2 + (A+B)x + B$, and so $B = 1$;

$A + 1 = 0 \Leftrightarrow A = -1$; and $-1 + C = 1 \Leftrightarrow C = 2$. Therefore, $\dfrac{x^2+1}{x^3+x^2} = \dfrac{-1}{x} + \dfrac{1}{x^2} + \dfrac{2}{x+1}$.

27. $\dfrac{2x}{4x^2+12x+9} = \dfrac{2x}{(2x+3)^2} = \dfrac{A}{2x+3} + \dfrac{B}{(2x+3)^2}$. Hence,

$2x = A(2x+3) + B = 2Ax + (3A+B)$. So $2A = 2 \Leftrightarrow A = 1$; and $3(1) + B = 0 \Leftrightarrow B = -3$.

Therefore, $\dfrac{2x}{4x^2+12x+9} = \dfrac{1}{2x+3} - \dfrac{3}{(2x+3)^2}$.

29. $\dfrac{4x^2-x-2}{x^4+2x^3} = \dfrac{4x^2-x-2}{x^3(x+2)} = \dfrac{A}{x} + \dfrac{B}{x^2} + \dfrac{C}{x^3} + \dfrac{D}{x+2}$. Hence,

$4x^2 - x - 2 = Ax^2(x+2) + Bx(x+2) + C(x+2) + Dx^3$

$\qquad = (A+D)x^3 + (2A+B)x^2 + (2B+C)x + 2C.$

So $2C = -2 \Leftrightarrow C = -1$; $2B - 1 = -1 \Leftrightarrow B = 0$; $2A + 0 = 4 \Leftrightarrow A = 2$; and $2 + D = 0 \Leftrightarrow$

$D = -2$. Therefore, $\dfrac{4x^2-x-2}{x^4+2x^3} = \dfrac{2}{x} - \dfrac{1}{x^3} - \dfrac{2}{x+2}$.

31. $\dfrac{-10x^2+27x-14}{(x-1)^3(x+2)} = \dfrac{A}{x+2} + \dfrac{B}{x-1} + \dfrac{C}{(x-1)^2} + \dfrac{D}{(x-1)^3}$. Thus,

$-10x^2 + 27x - 14 = A(x-1)^3 + B(x+2)(x-1)^2 + C(x+2)(x-1) + D(x+2)$

$= A(x^3 - 3x^2 + 3x - 1) + B(x+2)(x^2 - 2x + 1) + C(x^2 + x - 2) + D(x+2)$

$= A(x^3 - 3x^2 + 3x - 1) + B(x^3 - 3x + 2) + C(x^2 + x - 2) + D(x+2)$

$= (A+B)x^3 + (-3A+C)x^2 + (3A - 3B + C + D)x + (-A + 2B - 2C + 2D)$, which leads

to the following system of equations:

$$\begin{bmatrix} 1 & 1 & 0 & 0 & 0 \\ -3 & 0 & 1 & 0 & -10 \\ 3 & -3 & 1 & 1 & 27 \\ -1 & 2 & -2 & 2 & -14 \end{bmatrix} \xrightarrow[\substack{R_2+3R_1 \to R_2,\ R_3-3R_1 \to R_3 \\ R_4+R_1 \to R_4}]{} \begin{bmatrix} 1 & 1 & 0 & 0 & 0 \\ 0 & 3 & 1 & 0 & -10 \\ 0 & -6 & 1 & 1 & 27 \\ 0 & 3 & -2 & 2 & -14 \end{bmatrix}$$

$$\xrightarrow[\substack{R_3+2R_2 \to R_3 \\ R_4-R_2 \to R_4}]{} \begin{bmatrix} 1 & 1 & 0 & 0 & 0 \\ 0 & 3 & 1 & 0 & -10 \\ 0 & 0 & 3 & 1 & 7 \\ 0 & 0 & -3 & 2 & -4 \end{bmatrix} \xrightarrow[\substack{R_4+R_3 \to R_4}]{} \begin{bmatrix} 1 & 1 & 0 & 0 & 0 \\ 0 & 3 & 1 & 0 & -10 \\ 0 & 0 & 3 & 1 & 7 \\ 0 & 0 & 0 & 3 & 3 \end{bmatrix}.$$

Hence, $3D = 3 \Leftrightarrow D = 1$; $3C + 1 = 7 \Leftrightarrow C = 2$; $3B + 2 = -10 \Leftrightarrow B = -4$; and $A - 4 = 0$

$\Leftrightarrow A = 4$. Therefore, $\dfrac{-10x^2+27x-14}{(x-1)^3(x+2)} = \dfrac{4}{x+2} - \dfrac{4}{x-1} + \dfrac{2}{(x-1)^2} + \dfrac{1}{(x-1)^3}$.

33. $\dfrac{3x^3+22x^2+53x+41}{(x+2)^2(x+3)^2} = \dfrac{A}{x+2} + \dfrac{B}{(x+2)^2} + \dfrac{C}{x+3} + \dfrac{D}{(x+3)^2}$. Thus,

$3x^3 + 22x^2 + 53x + 41 = A(x+2)(x+3)^2 + B(x+3)^2 + C(x+2)^2(x+3) + D(x+2)^2$

$= A(x^3 + 8x^2 + 21x + 18) + B(x^2 + 6x + 9) + C(x^3 + 7x^2 + 16x + 12) + D(x^2 + 4x + 4)$

$= (A+C)x^3 + (8A + B + 7C + D)x^2 + (21A + 6B + 16C + 4D)x +$

$(18A + 9B + 12C + 4D)$, so we must solve the system:

$$\begin{bmatrix} 1 & 0 & 1 & 0 & 3 \\ 8 & 1 & 7 & 1 & 22 \\ 21 & 6 & 16 & 4 & 53 \\ 18 & 9 & 12 & 4 & 41 \end{bmatrix} \xrightarrow[\text{R}_4-18\text{R}_1 \to \text{R}_4]{\text{R}_2-8\text{R}_1 \to \text{R}_2,\ \text{R}_3-21\text{R}_1 \to \text{R}_3} \begin{bmatrix} 1 & 0 & 1 & 0 & 3 \\ 0 & 1 & -1 & 1 & -2 \\ 0 & 6 & -5 & 4 & -10 \\ 0 & 9 & -6 & 4 & -13 \end{bmatrix}$$

$$\xrightarrow[\text{R}_4-9\text{R}_2 \to \text{R}_4]{\text{R}_3-6\text{R}_2 \to \text{R}_3} \begin{bmatrix} 1 & 0 & 1 & 0 & 3 \\ 0 & 1 & -1 & 1 & -2 \\ 0 & 0 & 1 & -2 & 2 \\ 0 & 0 & 3 & -5 & 5 \end{bmatrix} \xrightarrow{\text{R}_4-3\text{R}_3 \to \text{R}_4} \begin{bmatrix} 1 & 0 & 1 & 0 & 3 \\ 0 & 1 & -1 & 1 & -2 \\ 0 & 0 & 1 & -2 & 2 \\ 0 & 0 & 0 & 1 & -1 \end{bmatrix}.$$

Hence, $D = -1$; $C + 2 = 2 \Leftrightarrow C = 0$; $B - 0 - 1 = -2 \Leftrightarrow B = -1$; and $A + 0 = 3 \Leftrightarrow$

$A = 3$. Therefore, $\dfrac{3x^3 + 22x^2 + 53x + 41}{(x+2)^2(x+3)^2} = \dfrac{3}{x+2} - \dfrac{1}{(x+2)^2} - \dfrac{1}{(x+3)^2}.$

35. $\dfrac{x-3}{x^3+3x} = \dfrac{x-3}{x(x^2+3)} = \dfrac{A}{x} + \dfrac{Bx+C}{x^2+3}$. Hence, $x - 3 = A(x^2+3) + Bx^2 + Cx$

     $= (A+B)x^2 + Cx + 3A$. So $3A = -3 \Leftrightarrow A = -1$; $C = 1$; and $-1 + B = 0 \Leftrightarrow B = 1$.

     Therefore, $\dfrac{x-3}{x^3+3x} = -\dfrac{1}{x} + \dfrac{x+1}{x^2+3}.$

37. $\dfrac{2x^3+7x+5}{(x^2+x+2)(x^2+1)} = \dfrac{Ax+B}{x^2+x+2} + \dfrac{Cx+D}{x^2+1}$. Thus,

     $2x^3 + 7x + 5 = (Ax+B)(x^2+1) + (Cx+D)(x^2+x+2)$

     $= Ax^3 + Ax + Bx^2 + B + Cx^3 + Cx^2 + 2Cx + Dx^2 + Dx + 2D$

     $= (A+C)x^3 + (B+C+D)x^2 + (A+2C+D)x + (B+2D)$. We must solve the system:

$$\begin{bmatrix} 1 & 0 & 1 & 0 & 2 \\ 0 & 1 & 1 & 1 & 0 \\ 1 & 0 & 2 & 1 & 7 \\ 0 & 1 & 0 & 2 & 5 \end{bmatrix} \xrightarrow[\text{R}_4-\text{R}_2 \to \text{R}_4]{\text{R}_3-\text{R}_1 \to \text{R}_3} \begin{bmatrix} 1 & 0 & 1 & 0 & 2 \\ 0 & 1 & 1 & 1 & 0 \\ 0 & 0 & 1 & 1 & 5 \\ 0 & 0 & -1 & 1 & 5 \end{bmatrix} \xrightarrow{\text{R}_4+\text{R}_3 \to \text{R}_4} \begin{bmatrix} 1 & 0 & 1 & 0 & 2 \\ 0 & 1 & 1 & 1 & 0 \\ 0 & 0 & 1 & 1 & 5 \\ 0 & 0 & 0 & 2 & 10 \end{bmatrix}$$

Hence, $2D = 10 \Leftrightarrow D = 5$; $C + 5 = 5 \Leftrightarrow C = 0$; $B + 0 + 5 = 0 \Leftrightarrow B = -5$; and $A + 0 = 2$

$\Leftrightarrow A = 2$. Therefore, $\dfrac{2x^3+7x+5}{(x^2+x+2)(x^2+1)} = \dfrac{2x-5}{x^2+x+2} + \dfrac{5}{x^2+1}.$

39. $\dfrac{x^4+x^3+x^2-x+1}{x(x^2+1)^2} = \dfrac{A}{x} + \dfrac{Bx+C}{x^2+1} + \dfrac{Dx+E}{(x^2+1)^2}$. Hence,

     $x^4 + x^3 + x^2 - x + 1 = A(x^2+1)^2 + (Bx+C)x(x^2+1) + x(Dx+E)$

     $= A(x^4+2x^2+1) + (Bx^2+Cx)(x^2+1) + Dx^2 + Ex$

     $= A(x^4+2x^2+1) + Bx^4 + Bx^2 + Cx^3 + Cx + Dx^2 + Ex$

     $= (A+B)x^4 + Cx^3 + (2A+B+D)x^2 + (C+E)x + A.$

Hence, $A = 1$; $1 + B = 1 \Leftrightarrow B = 0$; $C = 1$; $2 + 0 + D = 1 \Leftrightarrow D = -1$; and $1 + E = -1$

$\Leftrightarrow E = -2$. Therefore, $\dfrac{x^4+x^3+x^2-x+1}{x(x^2+1)^2} = \dfrac{1}{x} + \dfrac{1}{x^2+1} - \dfrac{x+2}{(x^2+1)^2}.$

41. We must first get a proper rational function. Using long division, we have:

$$x^3 - 2x^2 + x - 2 \overline{\smash{\big)}\, x^5 - 2x^4 + x^3 + 0x^2 + x + 5} \quad \overset{\displaystyle x^2}{}$$
$$\underline{x^5 - 2x^4 + x^3 - 2x^2}$$
$$2x^2 + x + 5.$$

Therefore, $\dfrac{x^5 - 2x^4 + x^3 + x + 5}{x^3 - 2x^2 + x - 2} = x^2 + \dfrac{2x^2 + x + 5}{x^3 - 2x^2 + x - 2} = x^2 + \dfrac{2x^2 + x + 5}{(x - 2)(x^2 + 1)}$

$= x^2 + \dfrac{A}{x - 2} + \dfrac{Bx + C}{x^2 + 1}$. Hence, $2x^2 + x + 5 = A(x^2 + 1) + (Bx + C)(x - 2)$

$= Ax^2 + A + Bx^2 + Cx - 2Bx - 2C = (A + B)x^2 + (C - 2B)x + (A - 2C)$. Equating coefficients, we get the system:

$$\begin{bmatrix} 1 & 1 & 0 & 2 \\ 0 & -2 & 1 & 1 \\ 1 & 0 & -2 & 5 \end{bmatrix} \xrightarrow{R_3 - R_1 \to R_3} \begin{bmatrix} 1 & 1 & 0 & 2 \\ 0 & -2 & 1 & 1 \\ 0 & -1 & -2 & 3 \end{bmatrix} \xrightarrow[-R_3 \leftrightarrow R_2]{R_2 - 2R_3 \to R_2} \begin{bmatrix} 1 & 1 & 0 & 2 \\ 0 & 1 & 2 & -3 \\ 0 & 0 & 5 & -5 \end{bmatrix}.$$

Therefore, $5C = -5 \Leftrightarrow C = -1, B - 2 = -3 \Leftrightarrow B = -1$, and $A - 1 = 2 \Leftrightarrow$

$A = 3$. Therefore, $\dfrac{x^5 - 2x^4 + x^3 + x + 5}{x^3 - 2x^2 + x - 2} = x^2 + \dfrac{3}{x - 2} - \dfrac{x + 1}{x^2 + 1}$.

43. $\dfrac{ax + b}{x^2 - 1} = \dfrac{A}{x - 1} + \dfrac{B}{x + 1}$. Hence, $ax + b = A(x + 1) + B(x - 1) = (A + B)x + (A - B)$. So

$\begin{cases} A + B = a \\ A - B = b \end{cases}$. Adding, we get $2A = a + b \Leftrightarrow A = \dfrac{a + b}{2}$. Substituting, we get

$B = a - A = \dfrac{2a}{2} - \dfrac{a + b}{2} = \dfrac{a - b}{2}$. Therefore, $A = \dfrac{a + b}{2}$ and $B = \dfrac{a - b}{2}$.

45. (a) The expression $\dfrac{x}{x^2 + 1} + \dfrac{1}{x + 1}$ is already a partial fraction decomposition. The denominator in the first term is a quadratic which can't be factored and the degree of the numerator is less than 2. The denominator of the second term is linear and the numerator is a constant.

(b) The term $\dfrac{x}{(x + 1)^2}$ can be decomposed further, since the numerator and denominator both have

linear factors. $\dfrac{x}{(x + 1)^2} = \dfrac{A}{x + 1} + \dfrac{B}{(x + 1)^2}$. Hence, $x = A(x + 1) + B = Ax + (A + B)$.

So $A = 1, B = -1$, and $\dfrac{x}{(x + 1)^2} = \dfrac{1}{x + 1} + \dfrac{-1}{(x + 1)^2}$.

(c) The expression $\dfrac{1}{x + 1} + \dfrac{2}{(x + 1)^2}$ is already a partial fraction decomposition, since each numerator is constant.

(d) The expression $\dfrac{x + 2}{(x^2 + 1)^2}$ is already a partial fraction decomposition, since the denominator is the square of a quadratic which can't be factored and the degree of the numerator is less than 2.

Review Exercises for Chapter 8

1. $\begin{cases} 3x - y = 5 \\ 2x + y = 5 \end{cases}$ Adding, we get $5x = 10$ $\Leftrightarrow$ $x = 2$.
So $2(2) + y = 5$ $\Leftrightarrow$ $y = 1$. Thus the solution is $(2, 1)$.

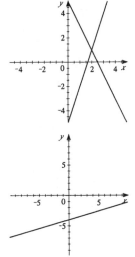

3. $\begin{cases} 2x - 7y = 28 \\ y = \frac{2}{7}x - 4 \end{cases}$ $\Leftrightarrow$ $\begin{cases} 2x - 7y = 28 \\ 2x - 7y = 28 \end{cases}$ Since these
equations represent the same line, any point on this line will satisfy
the system. Thus the solution are $\left(x, \frac{2}{7}x - 4\right)$, where x is any real
number.

5. $\begin{cases} 2x - y = 1 \\ x + 3y = 10 \\ 3x + 4y = 15 \end{cases}$ Solving the first equation for y, we get
$y = -2x + 1$. Substituting into the second equation gives
$x + 3(-2x + 1) = 10$ $\Leftrightarrow$ $-5x = 7$ $\Leftrightarrow$ $x = -\frac{7}{5}$. So
$y = -\left(-\frac{7}{5}\right) + 1 = \frac{12}{5}$. Checking the point $\left(-\frac{7}{5}, \frac{12}{5}\right)$ in the third
equation we have $3\left(-\frac{7}{5}\right) + 4\left(\frac{12}{5}\right) \overset{?}{=} 15$ but $-\frac{21}{5} + \frac{48}{5} \neq 15$.
Thus, there is no solution, and the lines do not intersect at one point.

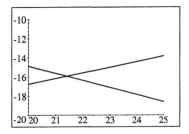

7. $\begin{cases} y = x^2 + 2x \\ y = 6 + x \end{cases}$ Substituting for y gives $6 + x = x^2 + 2x$ $\Leftrightarrow$ $x^2 + x - 6 = 0$. Factoring we
have $(x - 2)(x + 3) = 0$. Thus $x = 2$ or -3. If $x = 2$, then $y = 8$, and if $x = -3$, then $y = 3$.
Thus the solutions are $(-3, 3)$ and $(2, 8)$.

9. $\begin{cases} 3x + \dfrac{4}{y} = 6 \\ x - \dfrac{8}{y} = 4 \end{cases}$ Adding twice the first equation to the second equation gives $7x = 16$ $\Leftrightarrow$
$x = \frac{16}{7}$. So $\frac{16}{7} - \frac{8}{y} = 4$ $\Leftrightarrow$ $16y - 56 = 28y$ $\Leftrightarrow$ $-12y = 56$ $\Leftrightarrow$
$y = -\frac{14}{3}$. Thus the solution is $\left(\frac{16}{7}, -\frac{14}{3}\right)$.

11. $\begin{cases} 0.32x + 0.43y = 0 \\ 7x - 12y = 341 \end{cases}$ $\Leftrightarrow$ $\begin{cases} y = -\dfrac{32}{43}x \\ y = \dfrac{7x - 341}{12} \end{cases}$

The solution is $(21.41, -15.93)$.

13. $\begin{cases} x - y^2 = 10 \\ x = \frac{1}{22}y + 12 \end{cases}$ $\Leftrightarrow$ $\begin{cases} y = \pm\sqrt{x - 10} \\ y = 22(x - 12) \end{cases}$

The solutions are $(11.94, -1.39)$ and $(12.07, 1.44)$.

15. $\begin{bmatrix} 1 & 1 & 2 & 6 \\ 2 & 0 & 5 & 12 \\ 1 & 2 & 3 & 9 \end{bmatrix}$ $\xrightarrow[R_3 - R_1 \to R_3]{R_2 - 2R_1 \to R_2}$ $\begin{bmatrix} 1 & 1 & 2 & 6 \\ 0 & -2 & 1 & 0 \\ 0 & 1 & 1 & 3 \end{bmatrix}$ $\xrightarrow{R_3 \leftrightarrow R_2}$

$\begin{bmatrix} 1 & 1 & 2 & 6 \\ 0 & 1 & 1 & 3 \\ 0 & -2 & 1 & 0 \end{bmatrix}$ $\xrightarrow{R_3 + 2R_2 \to R_3}$ $\begin{bmatrix} 1 & 1 & 2 & 6 \\ 0 & 1 & 1 & 3 \\ 0 & 0 & 3 & 6 \end{bmatrix}$

Therefore, $3z = 6$ $\Leftrightarrow$ $z = 2$; $y + 2 = 3$ $\Leftrightarrow$ $y = 1$; and $x + 1 + 4 = 6$ $\Leftrightarrow$ $x = 1$. Hence, the solution is $(1, 1, 2)$.

17. $\begin{bmatrix} 1 & -2 & 3 & 1 \\ 2 & -1 & 1 & 3 \\ 2 & -7 & 11 & 2 \end{bmatrix}$ $\xrightarrow[R_3 - 2R_1 \to R_3]{R_2 - 2R_1 \to R_2}$ $\begin{bmatrix} 1 & -2 & 3 & 1 \\ 0 & 3 & -5 & 1 \\ 0 & -3 & 5 & 0 \end{bmatrix}$ $\xrightarrow{R_3 + R_2 \to R_3}$

$\begin{bmatrix} 1 & -2 & 3 & 1 \\ 0 & 3 & -5 & 1 \\ 0 & 0 & 0 & 1 \end{bmatrix}$

Therefore, the system is inconsistent and has no solution.

19. $\begin{bmatrix} 1 & -3 & 1 & 4 \\ 4 & -1 & 15 & 5 \end{bmatrix}$ $\xrightarrow{R_2 - 4R_1 \to R_2}$ $\begin{bmatrix} 1 & -3 & 1 & 4 \\ 0 & 11 & 11 & -11 \end{bmatrix}$ $\xrightarrow{\frac{1}{11}R_2}$ $\begin{bmatrix} 1 & -3 & 1 & 4 \\ 0 & 1 & 1 & -1 \end{bmatrix}$

Thus, the system has infinitely many solutions given by $z = t$, $y + t = -1$ $\Leftrightarrow$ $y = -1 - t$, and $x + 3(1 + t) + t = 4$ $\Leftrightarrow$ $x = 1 - 4t$. Therefore, the solutions are $(1 - 4t, -1 - t, t)$, where t is any real number.

21. $\begin{bmatrix} -1 & 4 & 1 & 8 \\ 2 & -6 & 1 & -9 \\ 1 & -6 & -4 & -15 \end{bmatrix}$ $\xrightarrow{R_1 \leftrightarrow R_3}$ $\begin{bmatrix} 1 & -6 & -4 & -15 \\ 2 & -6 & 1 & -9 \\ -1 & 4 & 1 & 8 \end{bmatrix}$ $\xrightarrow[R_3 + R_1 \to R_3]{R_2 - 2R_1 \to R_2}$

$\begin{bmatrix} 1 & -6 & -4 & -15 \\ 0 & 6 & 9 & 21 \\ 0 & -2 & -3 & -7 \end{bmatrix}$ $\xrightarrow[\frac{1}{6}R_2]{3R_3 + R_2 \to R_3}$ $\begin{bmatrix} 1 & -6 & -4 & -15 \\ 0 & 1 & \frac{3}{2} & \frac{7}{2} \\ 0 & 0 & 0 & 0 \end{bmatrix}$

Thus, the system has infinitely many solutions given by $z = t$, $y + \frac{3}{2}t = \frac{7}{2}$ $\Leftrightarrow$ $y = \frac{7}{2} - \frac{3}{2}t$, and $x - 6(\frac{7}{2} - \frac{3}{2}t) - 4t = -15$ $\Leftrightarrow$ $x = 6 - 5t$. Therefore, the solutions are $(6 - 5t, \frac{7}{2} - \frac{3}{2}t, t)$, where t is any real number.

23. Let x be the amount in the 6% account, and y be the amount in the 7% account. Thus, the system is:

$\begin{cases} y = 2x \\ 0.06x + 0.07y = 600 \end{cases}$.

Substituting gives $0.06x + 0.07(2x) = 600$ $\Leftrightarrow$ $0.2x = 600$ $\Leftrightarrow$ $x = 3000$. So $y = 2(3000) = 6000$. Hence, the man has \$3,000 invested at 6% and \$6,000 invested at 7%.

In Exercises 25 – 35:

$$A = \begin{bmatrix} 2 & 0 & -1 \end{bmatrix}$$

$$B = \begin{bmatrix} 1 & 2 & 4 \\ -2 & 1 & 0 \end{bmatrix}$$

$$C = \begin{bmatrix} \frac{1}{2} & 3 \\ 2 & \frac{3}{2} \\ -2 & 1 \end{bmatrix}$$

$$D = \begin{bmatrix} 1 & 4 \\ 0 & -1 \\ 2 & 0 \end{bmatrix}$$

$$E = \begin{bmatrix} 2 & -1 \\ -\frac{1}{2} & 1 \end{bmatrix}$$

$$F = \begin{bmatrix} 4 & 0 & 2 \\ -1 & 1 & 0 \\ 7 & 5 & 0 \end{bmatrix}$$

$$G = \begin{bmatrix} 5 \end{bmatrix}$$

25. $A + B$ cannot be performed because the matrix dimensions $(1 \times 3$ and $2 \times 3)$ are not compatible.

27. $2C + 3D = 2 \begin{bmatrix} \frac{1}{2} & 3 \\ 2 & \frac{3}{2} \\ -2 & 1 \end{bmatrix} + 3 \begin{bmatrix} 1 & 4 \\ 0 & -1 \\ 2 & 0 \end{bmatrix} = \begin{bmatrix} 1 & 6 \\ 4 & 3 \\ -4 & 2 \end{bmatrix} + \begin{bmatrix} 3 & 12 \\ 0 & -3 \\ 6 & 0 \end{bmatrix} = \begin{bmatrix} 4 & 18 \\ 4 & 0 \\ 2 & 2 \end{bmatrix}$

29. $G A = \begin{bmatrix} 5 \end{bmatrix} \begin{bmatrix} 2 & 0 & -1 \end{bmatrix} = \begin{bmatrix} 10 & 0 & -5 \end{bmatrix}$

31. $B C = \begin{bmatrix} 1 & 2 & 4 \\ -2 & 1 & 0 \end{bmatrix} \begin{bmatrix} \frac{1}{2} & 3 \\ 2 & \frac{3}{2} \\ -2 & 1 \end{bmatrix} = \begin{bmatrix} -\frac{7}{2} & 10 \\ 1 & -\frac{9}{2} \end{bmatrix}$

33. $B F = \begin{bmatrix} 1 & 2 & 4 \\ -2 & 1 & 0 \end{bmatrix} \begin{bmatrix} 4 & 0 & 2 \\ -1 & 1 & 0 \\ 7 & 5 & 0 \end{bmatrix} = \begin{bmatrix} 30 & 22 & 2 \\ -9 & 1 & -4 \end{bmatrix}$

35. $(C + D)E = \left(\begin{bmatrix} \frac{1}{2} & 3 \\ 2 & \frac{3}{2} \\ -2 & 1 \end{bmatrix} + \begin{bmatrix} 1 & 4 \\ 0 & -1 \\ 2 & 0 \end{bmatrix} \right) \begin{bmatrix} 2 & -1 \\ -\frac{1}{2} & 1 \end{bmatrix}$

$$= \begin{bmatrix} \frac{3}{2} & 7 \\ 2 & \frac{1}{2} \\ 0 & 1 \end{bmatrix} \begin{bmatrix} 2 & -1 \\ -\frac{1}{2} & 1 \end{bmatrix} = \begin{bmatrix} -\frac{1}{2} & \frac{11}{2} \\ \frac{15}{4} & -\frac{3}{2} \\ -\frac{1}{2} & 1 \end{bmatrix}$$

37. $D = \begin{bmatrix} 1 & 4 \\ 2 & 9 \end{bmatrix}$. Then, $|D| = 1(9) - 2(4) = 1$, and so $D^{-1} = \begin{bmatrix} 9 & -4 \\ -2 & 1 \end{bmatrix}$.

39. $D = \begin{bmatrix} 4 & -12 \\ -2 & 6 \end{bmatrix}$. Then, $|D| = 4(6) - 2(12) = 0$, and so D has no inverse.

41. $D = \begin{bmatrix} 3 & 0 & 1 \\ 2 & -3 & 0 \\ 4 & -2 & 1 \end{bmatrix}$. Then, $|D| = 1 \begin{vmatrix} 2 & -3 \\ 4 & -2 \end{vmatrix} + 1 \begin{vmatrix} 3 & 0 \\ 2 & -3 \end{vmatrix} = -4 + 12 - 9 = -1$. So D^{-1} exists .

$$\begin{bmatrix} 3 & 0 & 1 & 1 & 0 & 0 \\ 2 & -3 & 0 & 0 & 1 & 0 \\ 4 & -2 & 1 & 0 & 0 & 1 \end{bmatrix} \xrightarrow{R_1 - R_2 \rightarrow R_1} \begin{bmatrix} 1 & 3 & 1 & 1 & -1 & 0 \\ 2 & -3 & 0 & 0 & 1 & 0 \\ 4 & -2 & 1 & 0 & 0 & 1 \end{bmatrix} \begin{array}{l} R_2 - 2R_1 \rightarrow R_2 \\ R_3 - 4R_1 \rightarrow R_3 \end{array}$$

$$\begin{bmatrix} 1 & 3 & 1 & 1 & -1 & 0 \\ 0 & -9 & -2 & -2 & 3 & 0 \\ 0 & -14 & -3 & -4 & 4 & 1 \end{bmatrix} \xrightarrow[-2R_3]{-3R_2} \begin{bmatrix} 1 & 3 & 1 & 1 & -1 & 0 \\ 0 & 27 & 6 & 6 & -9 & 0 \\ 0 & 28 & 6 & 8 & -8 & -2 \end{bmatrix} \xrightarrow{R_3 - R_2 \rightarrow R_3}$$

$$\begin{bmatrix} 1 & 3 & 1 & 1 & -1 & 0 \\ 0 & 27 & 6 & 6 & -9 & 0 \\ 0 & 1 & 0 & 2 & 1 & -2 \end{bmatrix} \xrightarrow[\frac{1}{9}R_3]{R_3 \leftrightarrow R_2} \begin{bmatrix} 1 & 3 & 1 & 1 & -1 & 0 \\ 0 & 1 & 0 & 2 & 1 & -2 \\ 0 & 9 & 2 & 2 & -3 & 0 \end{bmatrix} \xrightarrow[R_1 - 3R_2 \rightarrow R_1]{R_3 - 9R_2 \rightarrow R_3}$$

$$\begin{bmatrix} 1 & 0 & 1 & -5 & -4 & 6 \\ 0 & 1 & 0 & 2 & 1 & -2 \\ 0 & 0 & 2 & -16 & -12 & 18 \end{bmatrix} \xrightarrow[R_1 - R_3 \rightarrow R_1]{\frac{1}{2}R_3} \begin{bmatrix} 1 & 0 & 0 & 3 & 2 & -3 \\ 0 & 1 & 0 & 2 & 1 & -2 \\ 0 & 0 & 1 & -8 & -6 & 9 \end{bmatrix}.$$

Thus, $D^{-1} = \begin{bmatrix} 3 & 2 & -3 \\ 2 & 1 & -2 \\ -8 & -6 & 9 \end{bmatrix}$.

43. $\begin{bmatrix} 12 & -5 \\ 5 & -2 \end{bmatrix} \begin{bmatrix} x \\ y \end{bmatrix} = \begin{bmatrix} 10 \\ 17 \end{bmatrix}$. If we let $A = \begin{bmatrix} 12 & -5 \\ 5 & -2 \end{bmatrix}$, then $A^{-1} = \frac{1}{-24+25} \begin{bmatrix} -2 & 5 \\ -5 & 12 \end{bmatrix}$

$= \begin{bmatrix} -2 & 5 \\ -5 & 12 \end{bmatrix}$, and so $\begin{bmatrix} x \\ y \end{bmatrix} = \begin{bmatrix} -2 & 5 \\ -5 & 12 \end{bmatrix} \begin{bmatrix} 10 \\ 17 \end{bmatrix} = \begin{bmatrix} 65 \\ 154 \end{bmatrix}$. Therefore, the solution is $(65, 154)$.

45. $|D| = \begin{vmatrix} 2 & 7 \\ 6 & 16 \end{vmatrix} = 32 - 42 = -10$; $|D_x| = \begin{vmatrix} 13 & 7 \\ 30 & 16 \end{vmatrix} = 208 - 210 = -2$; and

$|D_y| = \begin{vmatrix} 2 & 13 \\ 6 & 30 \end{vmatrix} = 60 - 78 = -18$. Therefore, $x = \frac{-2}{-10} = \frac{1}{5}$ and $y = \frac{-18}{-10} = \frac{9}{5}$, and so the solution is $(\frac{1}{5}, \frac{9}{5})$.

47. $|D| = \begin{vmatrix} 2 & -1 & 5 \\ -1 & 7 & 0 \\ 5 & 4 & 3 \end{vmatrix} = 5 \begin{vmatrix} -1 & 7 \\ 5 & 4 \end{vmatrix} + 3 \begin{vmatrix} 2 & -1 \\ -1 & 7 \end{vmatrix} = -195 + 39 = -156$;

$|D_x| = \begin{vmatrix} 0 & -1 & 5 \\ 9 & 7 & 0 \\ -9 & 4 & 3 \end{vmatrix} = 5 \begin{vmatrix} 9 & 7 \\ -9 & 4 \end{vmatrix} + 3 \begin{vmatrix} 0 & -1 \\ 9 & 7 \end{vmatrix} = 495 + 27 = 522$;

$|D_y| = \begin{vmatrix} 2 & 0 & 5 \\ -1 & 9 & 0 \\ 5 & -9 & 3 \end{vmatrix} = 5 \begin{vmatrix} -1 & 9 \\ 5 & -9 \end{vmatrix} + 3 \begin{vmatrix} 2 & 0 \\ -1 & 9 \end{vmatrix} = -180 + 54 = -126$; and

$|D_z| = \begin{vmatrix} 2 & -1 & 0 \\ -1 & 7 & 9 \\ 5 & 4 & -9 \end{vmatrix} = -9 \begin{vmatrix} 2 & -1 \\ 5 & 4 \end{vmatrix} - 9 \begin{vmatrix} 2 & -1 \\ -1 & 7 \end{vmatrix} = -117 - 117 = -234.$

Therefore, $x = \frac{522}{-156} = -\frac{87}{26}$, $y = \frac{-126}{-156} = \frac{21}{26}$, and $z = \frac{-234}{-156} = \frac{3}{2}$, and so the solution is $\left(-\frac{87}{26}, \frac{21}{26}, \frac{3}{2}\right)$.

49. $\begin{cases} x^2 + y^2 < 9 \\ \quad x + y < 0 \end{cases}$ The vertices occur where $y = -x$. By

substitution, $x^2 + x^2 = 9 \;\Leftrightarrow\; x = \pm\frac{3}{\sqrt{2}}$, and so $y = \mp\frac{3}{\sqrt{2}}$.

Therefore, the vertices are $\left(\frac{3}{\sqrt{2}}, -\frac{3}{\sqrt{2}}\right)$ and $\left(-\frac{3}{\sqrt{2}}, \frac{3}{\sqrt{2}}\right)$ and

the solution set is bounded.

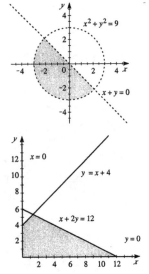

51. $\begin{cases} x \geq 0, \ y \geq 0 \\ x + 2y \leq 12 \\ \quad\ \ y \leq x + 4 \end{cases}$ The intersection points are $(-4, 0)$, $(0, 4)$,

$\left(\frac{4}{3}, \frac{16}{3}\right)$, $(0, 6)$, $(0, 0)$, and $(12, 0)$. Since the points $(-4, 0)$ and

$(0, 6)$ are not in the solution set, the vertices are $(0, 4)$, $\left(\frac{4}{3}, \frac{16}{3}\right)$,

$(12, 0)$, and $(0, 0)$. The solution set is bounded.

53. $\begin{bmatrix} -1 & 1 & 1 & a \\ 1 & -1 & 1 & b \\ 1 & 1 & -1 & c \end{bmatrix} \xrightarrow{-R_1} \begin{bmatrix} 1 & -1 & -1 & -a \\ 1 & -1 & 1 & b \\ 1 & 1 & -1 & c \end{bmatrix} \begin{array}{l} R_2 - R_1 \rightarrow R_2 \\ R_3 - R_1 \rightarrow R_3 \end{array}$

$\begin{bmatrix} 1 & -1 & -1 & -a \\ 0 & 0 & 2 & a+b \\ 0 & 2 & 0 & a+c \end{bmatrix} \xrightarrow{R_2 \leftrightarrow R_3} \begin{bmatrix} 1 & -1 & -1 & -a \\ 0 & 2 & 0 & a+c \\ 0 & 0 & 2 & a+b \end{bmatrix}$

Thus, $z = \dfrac{a+b}{2}$; $y = \dfrac{a+c}{2}$; and $x - \dfrac{a+c}{2} - \dfrac{a+b}{2} = -a \Leftrightarrow x = \dfrac{b+c}{2}$. The solution is

$\left(\dfrac{b+c}{2}, \dfrac{a+c}{2}, \dfrac{a+b}{2}\right)$.

55. $\begin{bmatrix} 1 & 1 & 12 \\ k & -1 & 0 \\ -1 & 1 & 2k \end{bmatrix} \xrightarrow{R_3 + R_1 \rightarrow R_3} \begin{bmatrix} 1 & 1 & 12 \\ k & -1 & 0 \\ 0 & 2 & 12 + 2k \end{bmatrix}$

Thus, $2y = 12 + 2k \;\Leftrightarrow\; y = 6 + k$ and $x = \frac{6+k}{k}$. So $\frac{6+k}{k} + 6 + k = 12 \Rightarrow$

$6 + k + 6k + k^2 = 12k \;\Leftrightarrow\; k^2 - 5k + 6 = 0 \;\Leftrightarrow\; (k-3)(k-2) = 0 \;\Rightarrow\; k = 2$ or $k = 3$.

57. $\dfrac{3x+1}{x^2 - 2x - 15} = \dfrac{3x+1}{(x-5)(x+3)} = \dfrac{A}{x-5} + \dfrac{B}{x+3}$. Thus, $3x + 1 = A(x+3) + B(x-5)$

$= x(A + B) + (3A - 5B)$, and so

$\begin{cases} A + B = 3 \\ 3A - 5B = 1 \end{cases} \Leftrightarrow \begin{cases} -3A - 3B = -9 \\ \ \ 3A - 5B = 1 \end{cases}$. Adding, we have $-8B = -8 \;\Leftrightarrow\; B = 1$, and

$A = 2$. Hence, $\dfrac{3x+1}{x^2 - 2x - 15} = \dfrac{2}{x-5} + \dfrac{1}{x+3}$.

59. $\dfrac{2x - 4}{x(x-1)^2} = \dfrac{A}{x} + \dfrac{B}{x-1} + \dfrac{C}{(x-1)^2}$. Then, $2x - 4 = A(x-1)^2 + Bx(x-1) + Cx$

$= Ax^2 - 2Ax + A + Bx^2 - Bx + Cx = x^2(A + B) + x(-2A - B + C) + A$. So $A = -4$;

$-4 + B = 0 \Leftrightarrow B = 4$; and $8 - 4 + C = 2 \Leftrightarrow C = -2$. Therefore,

$$\frac{2x - 4}{x(x-1)^2} = -\frac{4}{x} + \frac{4}{x-1} - \frac{2}{(x-1)^2}.$$

Chapter 8 Test

1. Let w be the speed of the wind and a be the speed of the airplane in still air, in km per hour. Then the speed of the of the plane flying against the wind is $a - w$, and the speed of the plane flying with the wind is $a + w$. Using $distance = time \times rate$, we get the system

$$\begin{cases} 600 = 2.5(a - w) \\ 300 = \frac{50}{60}(a + w) \end{cases} \Leftrightarrow \begin{cases} 240 = a - w \\ 360 = a + w \end{cases}.$$

Adding the two equations, we get $600 = 2a \quad \Leftrightarrow \quad a = 300$. So $360 = 300 + w \quad \Leftrightarrow \quad w = 60$. Thus the speed of the airplane in still air is 300 km/h and the speed of the wind is 60 km/h.

2. $\begin{cases} 3x - y = 10 \\ 2x + 5y = 1 \end{cases}$ Multiplying the first equation by 5 and then adding gives $17x = 51 \quad \Leftrightarrow$
$x = 3$. So $3(3) - y = 10 \quad \Leftrightarrow \quad y = -1$. Thus, the solution is $(3, -1)$, the system is linear, and it is neither inconsistent nor dependent.

3. $\begin{cases} x - y + 9z = -8 \\ x - 4z = 7 \\ 3x - y + z = 5 \end{cases}$ This system is linear and has the following matrix representation.

$$\begin{bmatrix} 1 & -1 & 9 & -8 \\ 1 & 0 & -4 & 7 \\ 3 & -1 & 1 & 5 \end{bmatrix} \begin{array}{c} R_2 \to R_2 - R_1 \\ \xrightarrow{\hspace{1cm}} \\ R_3 \to R_3 - 3R_1 \end{array} \begin{bmatrix} 1 & -1 & 9 & -8 \\ 0 & 1 & -13 & 15 \\ 0 & 2 & -26 & 29 \end{bmatrix} \xrightarrow{R_3 \to R_3 - 2R_2}$$

$$\begin{bmatrix} 1 & -1 & 9 & -8 \\ 0 & 1 & -13 & 15 \\ 0 & 0 & 0 & -1 \end{bmatrix}.$$ The third row states $0 = -1$, which is false. Hence, the system is inconsistent.

4. $\begin{cases} 2x - y + z = 0 \\ 3x + 2y - 3z = 1 \\ x - 4y + 5z = -1 \end{cases}$ This system is linear and has the following matrix representation.

$$\begin{bmatrix} 2 & -1 & 1 & 0 \\ 3 & 2 & -3 & 1 \\ 1 & -4 & 5 & -1 \end{bmatrix} \xrightarrow{R_1 \leftrightarrow R_3} \begin{bmatrix} 1 & -4 & 5 & -1 \\ 3 & 2 & -3 & 1 \\ 2 & -1 & 1 & 0 \end{bmatrix} \begin{array}{c} R_2 - 3R_1 \to R_2 \\ \xrightarrow{\hspace{1cm}} \\ R_3 - 2R_1 \to R_3 \end{array}$$

$$\begin{bmatrix} 1 & -4 & 5 & -1 \\ 0 & 14 & -18 & 4 \\ 0 & 7 & -9 & 2 \end{bmatrix} \xrightarrow{2R_3 - R_2 \to R_3} \begin{bmatrix} 1 & -4 & 5 & -1 \\ 0 & 14 & -18 & 4 \\ 0 & 0 & 0 & 0 \end{bmatrix}.$$

Then, $14y - 18z = 4 \quad \Leftrightarrow \quad y = \frac{2}{7} + \frac{9}{7}z$; $x - 4\left(\frac{2}{7} + \frac{9}{7}z\right) + 5z = -1 \quad \Leftrightarrow \quad x = \frac{1}{7} + \frac{1}{7}z$; and so the solutions are $\left(\frac{1}{7} + \frac{1}{7}z, \frac{2}{7} + \frac{9}{7}z, z\right)$ where z is any real number. The system is dependent.

5. $\begin{cases} 2x^2 + y^2 = 6 \\ 3x^2 - 4y = 11 \end{cases}$ Solving the second equation for x^2, we get $x^2 = \dfrac{11 + 4y}{3}$. Substituting into

the first equation gives $2\left(\dfrac{11 + 4y}{3}\right) + y^2 = 6 \quad \Leftrightarrow \quad 22 + 8y + 3y^2 = 18 \quad \Leftrightarrow$

$3y^2 + 8y + 4 = 0 \quad \Leftrightarrow \quad (3y + 2)(y + 2) = 0 \quad \Rightarrow \quad y = -\frac{2}{3}, y = -2$. Then $y = -\frac{2}{3} \quad \Rightarrow$

$x^2 = \frac{11 - \frac{8}{3}}{3} = \frac{25}{9} \quad \Rightarrow \quad x = \pm \frac{5}{3}$, and $y = -2 \quad \Rightarrow \quad x^2 = \frac{11 - 8}{3} = 1 \quad \Rightarrow \quad x = \pm 1$.

Therefore, the solutions are $\left(\frac{5}{3}, -\frac{2}{3}\right)$, $\left(-\frac{5}{3}, -\frac{2}{3}\right)$, $(1, -2)$ and $(-1, -2)$, and the system is nonlinear.

6. Let x, y, z represent the price per pound of the peaches, cherries, and pears respectively. Then, the system of equations is

$$\begin{cases} 4x + 3y + z = 9 \\ 2x + y + 3z = 6 \\ 2x + 2y + 2z = 7 \end{cases}$$ and the matrix representation is: $\begin{bmatrix} 4 & 3 & 1 & 9 \\ 2 & 1 & 3 & 6 \\ 2 & 2 & 2 & 7 \end{bmatrix}$ $\xrightarrow{R_1 \leftrightarrow R_3}$ $\begin{bmatrix} 2 & 2 & 2 & 7 \\ 2 & 1 & 3 & 6 \\ 4 & 3 & 1 & 9 \end{bmatrix}$

$\xrightarrow[R_3 - 2R_1 \to R_3]{R_2 - 2R_1 \to R_2}$ $\begin{bmatrix} 2 & 2 & 2 & 7 \\ 0 & -1 & 1 & -1 \\ 0 & -1 & -3 & -5 \end{bmatrix}$ $\xrightarrow{R_3 - R_2 \to R_3}$ $\begin{bmatrix} 2 & 2 & 2 & 7 \\ 0 & -1 & 1 & -1 \\ 0 & 0 & -4 & -4 \end{bmatrix}$

Thus, $-4z = 4 \iff z = 1$; $-y + 1 = -1 \iff y = 2$; and $2x + 2(2) + 2(1) = 7 \iff 2x = 1 \iff x = 0.50$. Hence, peaches are 50¢ per pound, cherries are \$2 per pound, and pears are \$1 per pound.

In problems 7 – 14, the matrices A, B, and C are defined as follows:

$$A = \begin{bmatrix} 2 & 3 \\ 2 & 4 \end{bmatrix} \qquad B = \begin{bmatrix} 2 & 4 \\ -1 & 1 \\ 3 & 0 \end{bmatrix} \qquad C = \begin{bmatrix} 1 & 0 & 4 \\ -1 & 1 & 2 \\ 0 & 1 & 3 \end{bmatrix}$$

7. $A + B$ is undefined because A is 2×2 and B is 3×2, so they have incompatible dimensions.

8. $A B$ is undefined because A is 2×2 and B is 3×2, so they have incompatible dimensions.

9. $BA - 3B = \begin{bmatrix} 2 & 4 \\ -1 & 1 \\ 3 & 0 \end{bmatrix} \begin{bmatrix} 2 & 3 \\ 2 & 4 \end{bmatrix} - 3 \begin{bmatrix} 2 & 4 \\ -1 & 1 \\ 3 & 0 \end{bmatrix} = \begin{bmatrix} 12 & 22 \\ 0 & 1 \\ 6 & 9 \end{bmatrix} - \begin{bmatrix} 6 & 12 \\ -3 & 3 \\ 9 & 0 \end{bmatrix} = \begin{bmatrix} 6 & 10 \\ 3 & -2 \\ -3 & 9 \end{bmatrix}$

10. $CBA = \begin{bmatrix} 1 & 0 & 4 \\ -1 & 1 & 2 \\ 0 & 1 & 3 \end{bmatrix} \begin{bmatrix} 2 & 4 \\ -1 & 1 \\ 3 & 0 \end{bmatrix} \begin{bmatrix} 2 & 3 \\ 2 & 4 \end{bmatrix} = \begin{bmatrix} 14 & 4 \\ 3 & -3 \\ 8 & 1 \end{bmatrix} \begin{bmatrix} 2 & 3 \\ 2 & 4 \end{bmatrix} = \begin{bmatrix} 36 & 58 \\ 0 & -3 \\ 18 & 28 \end{bmatrix}$

11. $A = \begin{bmatrix} 2 & 3 \\ 2 & 4 \end{bmatrix} \iff A^{-1} = \frac{1}{8-6} \begin{bmatrix} 4 & -3 \\ -2 & 2 \end{bmatrix} = \begin{bmatrix} 2 & -\frac{3}{2} \\ -1 & 1 \end{bmatrix}$

12. B^{-1} does not exist since B is not a square matrix.

13. $\det(B)$ is not defined since B is not a square matrix.

14. $\det(C) = \begin{vmatrix} 1 & 0 & 4 \\ -1 & 1 & 2 \\ 0 & 1 & 3 \end{vmatrix} = 1 \begin{vmatrix} 1 & 2 \\ 1 & 3 \end{vmatrix} + 4 \begin{vmatrix} -1 & 1 \\ 0 & 1 \end{vmatrix} = 1 - 4 = -3$

15. The system $\begin{cases} 4x - 3y = 10 \\ 3x - 2y = 30 \end{cases}$ is equivalent to the matrix equation $\begin{bmatrix} 4 & -3 \\ 3 & -2 \end{bmatrix} \begin{bmatrix} x \\ y \end{bmatrix} = \begin{bmatrix} 10 \\ 30 \end{bmatrix}$.

We have $|D| = \begin{vmatrix} 4 & -3 \\ 3 & -2 \end{vmatrix} = 4(-2) - 3(-3) = 1$. So $D^{-1} = \begin{bmatrix} -2 & 3 \\ -3 & 4 \end{bmatrix}$, and

$\begin{bmatrix} x \\ y \end{bmatrix} = \begin{bmatrix} -2 & 3 \\ -3 & 4 \end{bmatrix} \begin{bmatrix} 10 \\ 30 \end{bmatrix} = \begin{bmatrix} 70 \\ 90 \end{bmatrix}$. Therefore, $x = 70$ and $y = 90$.

16. $\begin{cases} 2x - z = 14 \\ 3x - y + 5z = 0 \\ 4x + 2y + 3z = -2 \end{cases}$

Then, $\det(D) = \begin{vmatrix} 2 & 0 & -1 \\ 3 & -1 & 5 \\ 4 & 2 & 3 \end{vmatrix} = 2\begin{vmatrix} -1 & 5 \\ 2 & 3 \end{vmatrix} - 1\begin{vmatrix} 3 & -1 \\ 4 & 2 \end{vmatrix} = -26 - 10 = -36;$

$\det(D_x) = \begin{vmatrix} 14 & 0 & -1 \\ 0 & -1 & 5 \\ -2 & 2 & 3 \end{vmatrix} = 14\begin{vmatrix} -1 & 5 \\ 2 & 3 \end{vmatrix} - 1\begin{vmatrix} 0 & -1 \\ 4 & 2 \end{vmatrix} = -182 + 2 = -180;$

$\det(D_y) = \begin{vmatrix} 2 & 14 & -1 \\ 3 & 0 & 5 \\ 4 & -2 & 3 \end{vmatrix} = -3\begin{vmatrix} 14 & -1 \\ -2 & 3 \end{vmatrix} - 5\begin{vmatrix} 2 & 14 \\ 4 & -2 \end{vmatrix} = -120 + 300 = 180;$ and

$\det(D_z) = \begin{vmatrix} 2 & 0 & 14 \\ 3 & -1 & 0 \\ 4 & 2 & -2 \end{vmatrix} = 2\begin{vmatrix} -1 & 0 \\ 2 & -2 \end{vmatrix} + 14\begin{vmatrix} 3 & -1 \\ 2 & 2 \end{vmatrix} = 4 + 140 = 144.$

Therefore, $x = \frac{-180}{-36} = 5$, $y = \frac{180}{-36} = -5$, $z = \frac{144}{-36} = -4$, and so the solution is $(5, -5, -4)$.

17. $|A| = \begin{vmatrix} 1 & 4 & 1 \\ 0 & 2 & 0 \\ 1 & 0 & 1 \end{vmatrix} = 2\begin{vmatrix} 1 & 1 \\ 1 & 1 \end{vmatrix} = 0;$ $|B| = \begin{vmatrix} 1 & 4 & 0 \\ 0 & 2 & 0 \\ -3 & 0 & 1 \end{vmatrix} = 2\begin{vmatrix} 1 & 0 \\ -3 & 1 \end{vmatrix} = 2.$

Since $|A| = 0$, A does not have an inverse, and since $|B| \neq 0$, B does have an inverse.

$\begin{bmatrix} 1 & 4 & 0 & 1 & 0 & 0 \\ 0 & 2 & 0 & 0 & 1 & 0 \\ -3 & 0 & 1 & 0 & 0 & 1 \end{bmatrix} \xrightarrow{R_3+3R_1 \to R_3} \begin{bmatrix} 1 & 4 & 0 & 1 & 0 & 0 \\ 0 & 2 & 0 & 0 & 1 & 0 \\ 0 & 12 & 1 & 3 & 0 & 1 \end{bmatrix} \xrightarrow[R_3-6R_2 \to R_3]{R_1-2R_2 \to R_1}$

$\begin{bmatrix} 1 & 0 & 0 & 1 & -2 & 0 \\ 0 & 2 & 0 & 0 & 1 & 0 \\ 0 & 0 & 1 & 3 & -6 & 1 \end{bmatrix} \xrightarrow{\frac{1}{2}R_2} \begin{bmatrix} 1 & 0 & 0 & 1 & -2 & 0 \\ 0 & 1 & 0 & 0 & \frac{1}{2} & 0 \\ 0 & 0 & 1 & 3 & -6 & 1 \end{bmatrix}.$

Therefore, $B^{-1} = \begin{bmatrix} 1 & -2 & 0 \\ 0 & \frac{1}{2} & 0 \\ 3 & -6 & 1 \end{bmatrix}.$

18. (a) $\begin{cases} 2x + y \leq 8 \\ x - y \geq -2 \\ x + 2y \geq 4 \end{cases}$

From the graph, the points $(4, 0)$ and $(0, 2)$ are vertices. The third vertex occurs where the lines $2x + y = 8$ and $x - y = -2$ intersect. Adding these two equations gives $3x = 6 \Leftrightarrow x = 2$, and so $y = 8 - 2(2) = 4$. Thus the third vertex is $(2, 4)$.

(b) $\begin{cases} x^2 - 5 + y \leq 0 \\ y \leq 5 + 2x \end{cases}$

Substituting $y = 5 + 2x$ into the first equation gives $x^2 - 5 + (5 + 2x) = 0 \Leftrightarrow x^2 + 2x = 0 \Leftrightarrow x(x + 2) = 0 \Leftrightarrow x = 0$ or $x = -2$. If $x = 0$, then $y = 5 + 2(0) = 5$, and if $x = -2$, then $y = 5 + 2(-2) = 1$. Thus the vertices are $(0, 5)$ and $(-2, 1)$.

19. $\dfrac{4x-1}{(x-1)^2(x+2)} = \dfrac{A}{x-1} + \dfrac{B}{(x-1)^2} + \dfrac{C}{x+2}$. Thus,

$4x - 1 = A(x-1)(x+2) + B(x+2) + C(x-1)^2$

$= A(x^2 + x - 2) + B(x+2) + C(x^2 - 2x + 1)$

$= (A+C)x^2 + (A + B - 2C)x + (-2A + 2B + C)$, which leads to the following system of

equations:

$$\begin{cases} A + C = 0 \\ A + B - 2C = 4 \\ -2A + 2B + C = -1 \end{cases}$$
So
$\begin{bmatrix} 1 & 0 & 1 & 0 \\ 1 & 1 & -2 & 4 \\ -2 & 2 & 1 & -1 \end{bmatrix}$
$\xrightarrow{R_1 \leftrightarrow R_2}$
$\begin{bmatrix} 1 & 1 & -2 & 4 \\ 1 & 0 & 1 & 0 \\ -2 & 2 & 1 & -1 \end{bmatrix}$

$\xrightarrow[R_3 + 2R_1 \to R_3]{R_2 - R_1 \to R_2}$
$\begin{bmatrix} 1 & 1 & -2 & 4 \\ 0 & -1 & 3 & -4 \\ 0 & 4 & -3 & 7 \end{bmatrix}$
$\xrightarrow{R_3 + 4R_2 \to R_3}$
$\begin{bmatrix} 1 & 1 & -2 & 4 \\ 0 & -1 & 3 & -4 \\ 0 & 0 & 9 & -9 \end{bmatrix}$.

Therefore, $9C = -9 \Leftrightarrow C = -1$; $-B - 3 = -4 \Leftrightarrow B = 1$; and $A + 1 + 2 = 4 \Leftrightarrow A = 1$.

Therefore, $\dfrac{4x-1}{(x-1)^2(x+2)} = \dfrac{1}{x-1} + \dfrac{1}{(x-1)^2} - \dfrac{1}{x+2}$.

20. $\begin{cases} 2x^2 + y^2 = 16 \\ y = x^4 - 4x^3 + 6x^2 - 4x \end{cases}$
We graph the system
$\begin{cases} y = \pm\sqrt{16 - 2x^2} \\ y = x^4 - 4x^3 + 6x^2 - 4x \end{cases}$.

The solutions are approximately $(-0.49, 3.93)$ and $(2.34, 2.24)$.

Focus on Modeling

1.

Vertex	$M = 200 - x - y$	
$(0,2)$	$200 - (0) - (2) = 198$	← maximum value
$(0,5)$	$200 - (0) - (5) = 195$	← minimum value
$(4,0)$	$200 - (4) - (0) = 196$	

Thus the maximum value is 198, and the minimum value is 195.

3. $$\begin{cases} x \geq 0, y \geq 0 \\ 2x + y \leq 10 \\ 2x + 4y \leq 28 \end{cases}$$

The objective function is $P = 140 - x + 3y$.

From the graph, the vertices are $(0,0)$, $(5,0)$, $(2,6)$, and $(0,7)$.

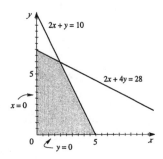

Vertex	$P = 140 - x + 3y$	
$(0,0)$	$140 - (0) + 3(0) = 140$	
$(5,0)$	$140 - (5) + 3(0) = 135$	← minimum value
$(2,6)$	$140 - (2) + 3(6) = 156$	
$(0,7)$	$140 - (0) + 3(7) = 161$	← maximum value

Thus the maximum value is 161, and the minimum value is 135.

5. Let t be the number of tables made daily and c be the number of chairs made daily. Then the data given can be summarized by the following table:

	Tables, t	Chairs, c	available time
carpentry	2 h	3 h	108 h
finishing	1 h	$\frac{1}{2}$ h	20 h
Profit	\$35	\$20	

Thus we wish to maximize the total profit, $P = 35t + 20c$, subject to the constraints:

$$\begin{cases} 2t + 3c \leq 108 \\ t + \frac{1}{2}c \leq 20 \\ t \geq 0, c \geq 0. \end{cases}$$

Thus we wish to maximize the total profit, $P = 35t + 20c$, subject to the constraints:

From the graph, the vertices occur at $(0,0)$, $(20,0)$, $(0,36)$, and $(3,34)$.

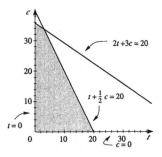

Vertex	$P = 35t + 20c$	
$(0,0)$	$35(0) + 20(0) = 0$	
$(20,0)$	$35(20) + 20(0) = 700$	
$(0,36)$	$35(0) + 20(36) = 720$	
$(3,34)$	$35(3) + 20(34) = 785$	← maximum value

Hence, 3 tables and 34 chairs should be produced daily for a maximum profit of \$785.

7. Let x be the number of crates of oranges and y be the number of crates of grapefruit. Then the data given can be summarized by the following table:

	oranges	grapefruit	available
volume	4 ft^3	6 ft^3	300 ft^3
weight	80 lb	100 lb	5600 lb
Profit	$2.50	$4.00	

In addition, $x \geq y$. Thus we wish to maximize the total profit, $P = 2.5x + 4y$, subject to the constraints:

$$\begin{cases} x \geq 0, y \geq 0 \\ x \geq y \\ 4x + 6y \leq 300 \\ 80x + 100y \leq 5600. \end{cases}$$

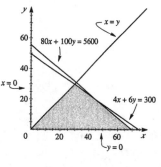

From the graph, the vertices occur at $(0,0)$, $(30,30)$, $(45,20)$, and $(70,0)$.

Vertex	$P = 2.5x + 4y$	
$(0,0)$	$2.5(0) + 4(0) = 0$	
$(30,30)$	$2.5(30) + 4(30) = 195$	← maximum value
$(45,20)$	$2.5(45) + 4(20) = 192.5$	
$(70,0)$	$2.5(70) + 4(0) = 175$	

Thus, she should carry 30 crates of oranges and 30 crates of grapefruit for a maximum profit of $195.

9. Let x be the number of stereo sets shipped from Long Beach to Santa Monica and y be the number of stereo sets shipped from Long Beach to El Toro. Thus, $15 - x$ sets must be shipped to Santa Monica from Pasadena and $19 - y$ sets to El Toro from Pasadena. Thus $x \geq 0$, $y \geq 0$, $15 - x \geq 0$, $19 - y \geq 0$, $x + y \leq 24$, and $(15 - x) + (19 - y) \leq 18$. Simplifying, we get the inequalities (constraints):

$$\begin{cases} x \geq 0, y \geq 0 \\ x \leq 15, y \leq 19 \\ x + y \leq 24 \\ x + y \geq 16 \end{cases}$$

The objective function is the cost,
$C = 5x + 6y + 4(15 - x) + 5.5(19 - y) = x + 0.5y + 164.5$,
which we wish to minimize. From the graph, the vertices occur at $(0,16)$, $(0,19)$, $(5,19)$, $(15,9)$, and $(15,1)$.

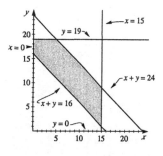

Vertex	$C = x + 0.5y + 164.5$	
$(0,16)$	$(0) + 0.5(16) + 164.5 = 172.5$	← minimum value
$(0,19)$	$(0) + 0.5(19) + 164.5 = 174$	
$(5,19)$	$(5) + 0.5(19) + 164.5 = 179$	
$(15,9)$	$(15) + 0.5(9) + 164.5 = 184$	
$(15,1)$	$(15) + 0.5(1) + 164.5 = 180$	

The minimum cost is $172.50 and occurs when $x = 0$, $y = 16$. Hence, 0 sets should be shipped from Long Beach to Santa Monica, 16 from Long Beach to El Toro, 15 from Pasadena to Santa Monica, and 3 from Pasadena to El Toro.

11. Let x be the number of bags of standard mixtures and y be the number of bags of deluxe mixtures.
     Then the data can be summarized by the following table:

	standard	deluxe	available
cashews	100 g	150 g	15 kg
peanuts	200 g	50 g	20 kg
selling price	$1.95	$2.20	

Thus the total revenue, which we want to maximize, is given by $R = 1.95x + 2.25y$. We have the
following constraints:

$$\begin{cases} x \geq 0, y \geq 0 \\ x \geq y \\ 0.1x + 0.15y \leq 15 \\ 0.2x + 0.05y \leq 20 \end{cases} \quad \Leftrightarrow \quad \begin{cases} x \geq 0, y \geq 0 \\ x \geq y \\ 10x + 15y \leq 1500 \\ 20x + 5y \leq 2000. \end{cases}$$

From the graph, the vertices occur at $(0,0)$, $(60,60)$, $(90,40)$, and
$(100,0)$.

Vertex	$R = 1.95x + 2.25y$	
$(0,0)$	$1.96(0) + 2.25(0) = 0$	
$(60,60)$	$1.95(60) + 2.25(60) = 252$	
$(90,40)$	$1.95(90) + 2.25(40) = 265.5$	← maximum revenue
$(100,0)$	$1.95(100) + 2.25(0) = 195$	

Hence, he should pack 90 bags of standard and 40 bags of deluxe mixture for a maximum revenue of
$265.50.

13. Let x be the amount in municipal bonds and y be the amount in bank certificates, both in dollars.
     Then, $12000 - x - y$ is the amount in high-risk bonds. So our constraints can be stated as:

$$\begin{cases} x \geq 0, y \geq 0 \\ 12,000 - x - y \geq 0 \\ x \geq 3y \\ 12000 - x - y \leq 2000 \end{cases} \quad \Leftrightarrow \quad \begin{cases} x \geq 0, y \geq 0 \\ x + y \leq 12,000 \\ x \geq 3y \\ x + y \geq 10,000. \end{cases}$$

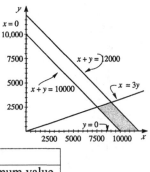

From the graph, the vertices occur at $(7500, 2500)$, $(10000, 0)$,
$(12000, 0)$, and $(9000, 3000)$. The objective function is
$P = 0.07x + 0.08y + 0.12(12000 - x - y)$
$= 1440 - 0.05x - 0.04y$, which we wish to maximize.

Vertex	$P = 1440 - 0.05x - 0.04y$	
$(7500, 2500)$	$1440 - 0.05(7500) - 0.04(2500) = 965$	← maximum value
$(10000, 0)$	$1440 - 0.05(10000) - 0.04(0) = 940$	
$(12000, 0)$	$1440 - 0.05(12000) - 0.04(0) = 840$	
$(9000, 3000)$	$1440 - 0.05(9000) - 0.04(3000) = 870$	

Hence, she should invest $7500 in municipal bonds, $2500 in bank certificates, and the remaining
$2000 in high-risk bonds for a maximum yield of $965.

15. Let g be the number of games published and e be the number of educational programs published.
     Then the number of utility programs published is $36 - g - e$. Hence we wish to maximize profit,
     $P = 5000g + 8000e + 6000(36 - g - e) = 216,000 - 1000g + 2000e$, subject to the constraints:

$$\begin{cases} g \geq 4, e \geq 0 \\ 36 - g - e \geq 0 \\ 36 - g - e \leq 2e \end{cases} \quad \Leftrightarrow \quad \begin{cases} g \geq 4, e \geq 0 \\ g + e \leq 36 \\ g + 3e \geq 36. \end{cases}$$

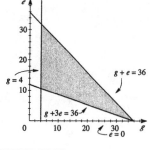

From the graph, the vertices are at $\left(4, \frac{32}{3}\right)$, $(4, 32)$, and $(36, 0)$.
The objective function is $P = 216{,}000 - 1000g + 2000e$.

Vertex	$P = 216{,}000 - 1000g + 2000e$	
$\left(4, \frac{32}{3}\right)$	$216{,}000 - 1000(4) + 2000\left(\frac{32}{3}\right) = 233{,}333.33$	
$(4, 32)$	$216{,}000 - 1000(4) + 2000(32) = 276{,}000$	← maximum value
$(36, 0)$	$216{,}000 - 1000(36) + 2000(0) = 180{,}000$	

So, they should publish 4 games, 32 educational programs, and 0 utility programs for a maximum profit of \$276,000 annually.

Chapter Nine
Exercises 9.1

1. III. Graph that opens to the right and is not as wide as the graph for Exercise 5.

3. II. Graph opens downward and is not wider than the graph represent in Exercise 6.

5. VI. Graph opens up to the right and is wider than the graph represent in Exercise 1.

7. $y^2 = 4x$. Then $4p = 4 \quad \Leftrightarrow \quad p = 1$.
    Focus: $(1, 0)$
    Directrix: $x = -1$
    Focal diameter: 4

9. $x^2 = 9y$. Then $4p = 9 \quad \Leftrightarrow \quad p = \frac{9}{4}$.
    Focus: $\left(0, \frac{9}{4}\right)$
    Directrix: $y = -\frac{9}{4}$
    Focal diameter: 9

11. $y = 5x^2 \quad \Leftrightarrow \quad x^2 = \frac{1}{5}y$. Then $4p = \frac{1}{5} \quad \Leftrightarrow \quad p = \frac{1}{20}$.
    Focus: $\left(0, \frac{1}{20}\right)$
    Directrix: $y = -\frac{1}{20}$
    Focal diameter: $\frac{1}{5}$

13. $x = -8y^2 \quad \Leftrightarrow \quad y^2 = -\frac{1}{8}x$. Then $4p = -\frac{1}{8} \quad \Leftrightarrow \quad p = -\frac{1}{32}$.
    Focus: $\left(-\frac{1}{32}, 0\right)$
    Directrix: $x = \frac{1}{32}$
    Focal diameter: $\frac{1}{8}$

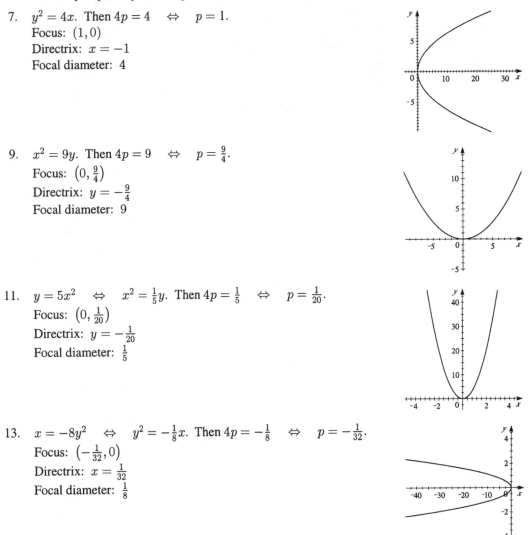

15. $x^2 + 6y = 0 \iff x^2 = -6y$. Then $4p = -6 \iff p = -\frac{3}{2}$.

Focus: $\left(0, -\frac{3}{2}\right)$

Directrix: $y = \frac{3}{2}$

Focal diameter: 6

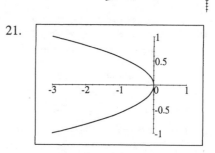

17. $5x + 3y^2 = 0 \iff y^2 = -\frac{5}{3}x$. Then $4p = -\frac{5}{3} \iff p = -\frac{5}{12}$.

Focus: $\left(-\frac{5}{12}, 0\right)$

Directrix: $x = \frac{5}{12}$

Focal diameter: $\frac{5}{3}$

19.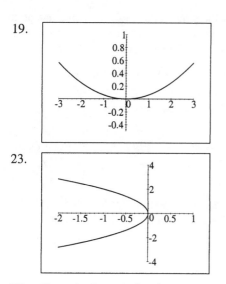

21.

23.

25. Since the focus is $(0, 2)$, $p = 2 \iff 4p = 8$. Hence, the equation of the parabola is $x^2 = 8y$.

27. Since the focus is $(-8, 0)$, $p = -8 \iff 4p = -32$. Hence, the equation of the parabola is $y^2 = -32x$.

29. Since the directrix is $x = 2$, $p = -2 \iff 4p = -8$. Hence, the equation of the parabola is $y^2 = -8x$.

31. Since the directrix is $y = -10$, $p = 10 \iff 4p = 40$. Hence, the equation of the parabola is $x^2 = 40y$.

33. The focus is on the positive x-axis, so the parabola opens horizontally with $2p = 2 \iff 4p = 4$. So the equation of the parabola is $y^2 = 4x$.

35. Since the parabola opens upward with focus 5 units from the vertex, the focus is $(5, 0)$. So $p = 5 \iff 4p = 20$. Thus the equation of the parabola is $x^2 = 20y$.

37. $p = 2$ $\Leftrightarrow$ $4p = 8$. Since the parabola opens upward, its equation is $x^2 = 8y$.

39. $p = 4$ $\Leftrightarrow$ $4p = 16$. Since the parabola opens to the left, its equation is $y^2 = -16x$.

41.   The focal diameter is $4p = \frac{3}{2} + \frac{3}{2} = 3$. Since the parabola opens to the left, its equation is
      $y^2 = -3x$.

43.   The equation of the parabola has the form $y^2 = 4px$. Since the parabola passes through the point
      $(4, -2)$, $(-2)^2 = 4p(4)$ $\Leftrightarrow$ $4p = 1$, and so the equation is $y^2 = x$.

45.   The area of the shaded region is $width \times height = 4p \times p = 8$, and so $p^2 = 2$ $\Leftrightarrow$ $p = -\sqrt{2}$
      (because the parabola opens downward). Therefore, the equation is $x^2 = 4py = -4\sqrt{2}\,y$ $\Leftrightarrow$
      $x^2 = -4\sqrt{2}\,y$.

47.   (a)   Since the focal diameter is 12 cm, $4p = 12$. Hence, the parabola has equation $y^2 = 12x$.

      (b)   At a point 20 cm horizontally from the vertex, the parabola passes through the point $(20, y)$,
            and hence from part (a), $y^2 = 12(20)$ $\Leftrightarrow$ $y^2 = 240$ $\Leftrightarrow$ $y = \pm 4\sqrt{15}$. Thus,
            $|CD| = 8\sqrt{15} \approx 31$ cm.

49.   With the vertex at the origin, the top of one tower will be at the point $(300, 150)$. Inserting this point
      into the equation $x^2 = 4py$ gives $(300)^2 = 4p(150)$ $\Leftrightarrow$ $90000 = 600p$ $\Leftrightarrow$ $p = 150$. So the
      equation of the parabolic part of the cables is $x^2 = 4(150)y$ $\Leftrightarrow$ $x^2 = 600y$.

51.   (a)   Since a parabola with directrix $y = -p$ has equation $x^2 = 4py$, we have the following.
            The directrix is $y = \frac{1}{2}$ $\Rightarrow$ $p = -\frac{1}{2}$, so the equation is $x^2 = 4\left(-\frac{1}{2}\right)y$ $\Leftrightarrow$ $x^2 = -2y$.
            The directrix is $y = 1$ $\Rightarrow$ $p = -1$, so the equation is $x^2 = 4(-1)y$ $\Leftrightarrow$ $x^2 = -4y$.
            The directrix is $y = 4$ $\Rightarrow$ $p = -4$, so the equation is $x^2 = 4(-4)y$ $\Leftrightarrow$ $x^2 = -16y$.
            The directrix is $y = 8$ $\Rightarrow$ $p = -8$, so the equation is $x^2 = 4(-8)y$ $\Leftrightarrow$ $x^2 = -32y$.

      (b)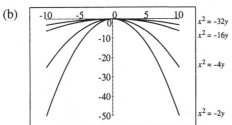

            As the directrix moves further from the vertex,
            the parabola get flatter.

53.   Yes. If a cone intersects a plane that is parallel to a line on the cone, the resulting curve is a
      parabola (as shown on page 735 of the text).

Exercises 9.2

1. II. Major axis is horizontal, vertices at $(\pm 4, 0)$.

3. I. Major axis is the vertical, vertices at $(0, \pm 2)$.

5. $\dfrac{x^2}{25} + \dfrac{y^2}{9} = 1$. This ellipse has $a = 5$, $b = 3$, and so
    $c^2 = a^2 - b^2 = 16 \quad \Leftrightarrow \quad c = 4$.
    Vertices: $(\pm 5, 0)$; foci: $(\pm 4, 0)$; eccentricity: $e = \frac{c}{a} = \frac{4}{5} = 0.8$;
    length of the major axis: $2a = 10$; length of the minor axis: $2b = 6$

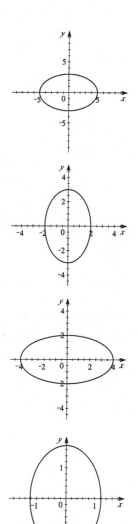

7. $9x^2 + 4y^2 = 36 \quad \Leftrightarrow \quad \dfrac{x^2}{4} + \dfrac{y^2}{9} = 1$. This ellipse has $a = 3$,
    $b = 2$, and so $c^2 = 9 - 4 = 5 \quad \Leftrightarrow \quad c = \sqrt{5}$.
    Vertices: $(0, \pm 3)$; foci: $(0, \pm\sqrt{5})$; eccentricity: $e = \frac{c}{a} = \frac{\sqrt{5}}{3}$;
    length of the major axis: $2a = 6$; length of the minor axis: $2b = 4$

9. $x^2 + 4y^2 = 16 \quad \Leftrightarrow \quad \dfrac{x^2}{16} + \dfrac{y^2}{4} = 1$. This ellipse has $a = 4$,
    $b = 2$, and so $c^2 = 16 - 4 = 12 \quad \Leftrightarrow \quad c = 2\sqrt{3}$.
    Vertices: $(\pm 4, 0)$; foci: $(\pm 2\sqrt{3}, 0)$; eccentricity:
    $e = \frac{c}{a} = \frac{2\sqrt{3}}{4} = \frac{\sqrt{3}}{2}$; length of the major axis: $2a = 8$; length of
    the minor axis: $2b = 4$.

11. $2x^2 + y^2 = 3 \quad \Leftrightarrow \quad \dfrac{x^2}{\frac{3}{2}} + \dfrac{y^2}{3} = 1$. This ellipse has $a = \sqrt{3}$,
    $b = \sqrt{\frac{3}{2}}$, and so $c^2 = 3 - \frac{3}{2} = \frac{3}{2} \quad \Leftrightarrow \quad c = \sqrt{\frac{3}{2}}$.
    Vertices: $\left(0, \pm\sqrt{3}\right)$; foci: $\left(0, \pm\sqrt{\frac{3}{2}}\right)$; eccentricity:
    $e = \frac{c}{a} = \dfrac{\sqrt{\frac{3}{2}}}{\sqrt{3}} = \dfrac{1}{\sqrt{2}} = \dfrac{\sqrt{2}}{2}$; length of the major axis: $2a = 2\sqrt{3}$
    length of the minor axis: $2b = 2\sqrt{\frac{3}{2}} = \sqrt{6}$.

13. $x^2 + 4y^2 = 1$ $\Leftrightarrow$ $\dfrac{x^2}{1} + \dfrac{y^2}{\frac{1}{4}} = 1$. This ellipse has $a = 1$, $b = \frac{1}{2}$,

and so $c^2 = 1 - \frac{1}{4} = \frac{3}{4}$ $\Leftrightarrow$ $c = \frac{\sqrt{3}}{2}$.

Vertices: $(\pm 1, 0)$; foci: $\left(\pm\frac{\sqrt{3}}{2}, 0\right)$; eccentricity:

$e = \frac{c}{a} = \frac{\sqrt{3}/2}{1} = \frac{\sqrt{3}}{2}$; length of the major axis: $2a = 2$; length

of the minor axis: $2b = 1$.

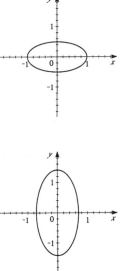

15. $\frac{1}{2}x^2 + \frac{1}{8}y^2 = \frac{1}{4}$ $\Leftrightarrow$ $2x^2 + \frac{1}{2}y^2 = 1$ $\Leftrightarrow$ $\dfrac{x^2}{\frac{1}{2}} + \dfrac{y^2}{2} = 1$.

This ellipse has $a = \sqrt{2}$, $b = \frac{1}{\sqrt{2}}$, and so $c^2 = 2 - \frac{1}{2} = \frac{3}{2}$

$\Leftrightarrow$ $c = \sqrt{\frac{3}{2}}$.

Vertices: $(0, \pm\sqrt{2})$; foci: $\left(0, \pm\sqrt{\frac{3}{2}}\right)$; eccentricity:

$= \frac{c}{a} = \dfrac{\sqrt{\frac{3}{2}}}{\sqrt{2}} = \frac{1}{2}\sqrt{3}$; length of the major axis: $2a = 2\sqrt{2}$;

length of the minor axis: $2b = \sqrt{2}$.

17. $y^2 = 1 - 2x^2$ $\Leftrightarrow$ $2x^2 + y^2 = 1$ $\Leftrightarrow$ $\dfrac{x^2}{\frac{1}{2}} + \dfrac{y^2}{1} = 1$. This

ellipse has $a = 1$, $b = \frac{1}{\sqrt{2}}$, and so $c^2 = 1 - \frac{1}{2} = \frac{1}{2}$ $\Leftrightarrow$ $c = \frac{1}{\sqrt{2}}$.

Vertices: $(0, \pm 1)$; foci: $\left(0, \pm\frac{1}{\sqrt{2}}\right)$; eccentricity:

$e = \frac{c}{a} = \dfrac{\frac{1}{\sqrt{2}}}{1} = \frac{1}{\sqrt{2}}$; length of the major axis: $2a = 2$; length of

the minor axis: $2b = \sqrt{2}$.

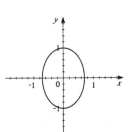

19. This ellipse has a horizontal major axis with $a = 5$ and $b = 4$, so the equation is $\dfrac{x^2}{(5)^2} + \dfrac{y^2}{(4)^2} = 1$

$\Leftrightarrow$ $\dfrac{x^2}{25} + \dfrac{y^2}{16} = 1$.

21. This ellipse has a vertical major axis with $c = 2$ and $b = 2$. So $a^2 = c^2 + b^2 = 2^2 + 2^2 = 8$ $\Leftrightarrow$

$a = 2\sqrt{2}$. So the equation is $\dfrac{x^2}{(2)^2} + \dfrac{y^2}{\left(2\sqrt{2}\right)^2} = 1$ $\Leftrightarrow$ $\dfrac{x^2}{4} + \dfrac{y^2}{8} = 1$.

23. This ellipse has a horizontal major axis with $a = 16$, so the equation of the ellipse is of the form

$\dfrac{x^2}{16^2} + \dfrac{y^2}{b^2} = 1$. Substituting the point $(8, 6)$ into the equation, we get $\dfrac{64}{256} + \dfrac{36}{b^2} = 1$ $\Leftrightarrow$

$\dfrac{36}{b^2} = 1 - \dfrac{1}{4}$ $\Leftrightarrow$ $\dfrac{36}{b^2} = \dfrac{3}{4}$ $\Leftrightarrow$ $b^2 = \dfrac{4(36)}{3} = 48$. Thus, the equation of the ellipse is

$\dfrac{x^2}{256} + \dfrac{y^2}{48} = 1$

25. $\dfrac{x^2}{25} + \dfrac{y^2}{20} = 1 \quad \Leftrightarrow \quad \dfrac{y^2}{20} = 1 - \dfrac{x^2}{25} \quad \Leftrightarrow$

$y^2 = 20 - \dfrac{4x^2}{5} \quad \Rightarrow \quad y = \pm\sqrt{20 - \dfrac{4x^2}{5}}.$

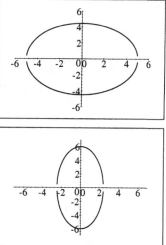

27. $6x^2 + y^2 = 36 \quad \Leftrightarrow \quad y^2 = 36 - 6x^2$

$\Rightarrow \quad y = \pm\sqrt{36 - 6x^2}.$

29. The foci are $(\pm4, 0)$, and the vertices are $(\pm5, 0)$. Thus, $c = 4$ and $a = 5$, and so $b^2 = 25 - 16 = 9$. Therefore, the equation of the ellipse is $\dfrac{x^2}{25} + \dfrac{y^2}{9} = 1$.

31. The length of the major axis is $2a = 4 \quad \Leftrightarrow \quad a = 2$, the length of the minor axis is $2b = 2 \quad \Leftrightarrow$ $b = 1$, and the foci are on the y-axis. Therefore, the equation of the ellipse is $x^2 + \dfrac{y^2}{4} = 1$.

33. The foci are $(0, \pm2)$, and the length of the minor axis is $2b = 6 \quad \Leftrightarrow \quad b = 3$. Thus, $a^2 = 4 + 9 = 13$. Since the foci are on the y-axis, the equation is $\dfrac{x^2}{9} + \dfrac{y^2}{13} = 1$.

35. The endpoints of the major axis are $(\pm10, 0) \quad \Leftrightarrow \quad a = 10$, and the distance between the foci is $2c = 6 \quad \Leftrightarrow \quad c = 3$. Therefore, $b^2 = 100 - 9 = 91$, and so the equation of the ellipse is $\dfrac{x^2}{100} + \dfrac{y^2}{91} = 1$.

37. The length of the major axis is 10, so $2a = 10 \quad \Leftrightarrow \quad a = 5$, and the foci are on the x-axis, so the form of the equation is $\dfrac{x^2}{25} + \dfrac{y^2}{b^2} = 1$. Since the ellipse passes through $\left(\sqrt{5}, 2\right)$, we know that

$\dfrac{\left(\sqrt{5}\right)^2}{25} + \dfrac{(2)^2}{b^2} = 1 \quad \Leftrightarrow \quad \dfrac{5}{25} + \dfrac{4}{b^2} = 1 \quad \Leftrightarrow \quad \dfrac{4}{b^2} = \dfrac{4}{5} \quad \Leftrightarrow \quad b^2 = 5$, and so the equation is $\dfrac{x^2}{25} + \dfrac{y^2}{5} = 1$.

39. Since the foci are $(\pm1.5, 0)$, we have $c = \dfrac{3}{2}$. Since the eccentricity is $0.8 = \dfrac{c}{a}$, we have $a = \dfrac{\frac{3}{2}}{\frac{4}{5}} = \dfrac{15}{8}$, and so $b^2 = \dfrac{225}{64} - \dfrac{9}{4} = \dfrac{225 - 16 \cdot 9}{64} = \dfrac{81}{64}$. Therefore, the equation of the ellipse is $\dfrac{x^2}{\left(15/8\right)^2} + \dfrac{y^2}{81/64} = 1$

$\Leftrightarrow \quad \dfrac{64x^2}{225} + \dfrac{64y^2}{81} = 1.$

41. $\begin{cases} 4x^2 + y^2 = 4 \\ 4x^2 + 9y^2 = 36 \end{cases}$ Subtracting the first equation from the second

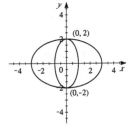

equation gives $8y^2 = 32$ $\Leftrightarrow$ $y^2 = 4$ $\Leftrightarrow$ $y = \pm 2$.

Substituting $y = \pm 2$ in the first equation gives $4x^2 + (\pm 2)^2 = 4$

$\Leftrightarrow$ $x = 0$, and so the points of intersection are $(0, \pm 2)$.

43. Using the perihelion, $a - c = 147{,}000{,}000$, while using the aphelion, $a + c = 153{,}000{,}000$.
     Adding, we have $2a = 300{,}000{,}000$ $\Leftrightarrow$ $a = 150{,}000{,}000$. So $b^2 = a^2 - c^2$
     $= (150 \times 10^6)^2 - (3 \times 10^6)^2 = 22{,}491 \times 10^{12} = 2.2491 \times 10^{16}$. Thus the equation of the orbit is

     $$\frac{x^2}{2.2500 \times 10^{16}} + \frac{y^2}{2.2491 \times 10^{16}} = 1.$$

45. Using the perilune, $a - c = 1075 + 68 = 1143$, and using the apolune,
     $a + c = 1075 + 195 = 1270$. Adding, we get $2a = 2413$ $\Leftrightarrow$ $a = 1206.5$. So
     $c = 1270 - 1206.5$ $\Leftrightarrow$ $c = 63.5$. Therefore, $b^2 = (1206.5)^2 - (63.5)^2 = 1{,}451{,}610$. Since
     $a^2 \approx 1{,}455{,}642$, the equation of Apollo 11's orbit is $\dfrac{x^2}{1{,}455{,}642} + \dfrac{y^2}{1{,}451{,}610} = 1$.

47. From the diagram, $a = 40$ and $b = 20$, and so the equation of the ellipse whose top half is the
     window is $\dfrac{x^2}{1600} + \dfrac{y^2}{400} = 1$. Since the ellipse passes through the point $(25, h)$, by substituting, we
     have $\dfrac{25^2}{1600} + \dfrac{h^2}{400} = 1$ $\Leftrightarrow$ $625 + 4y^2 = 1600$ $\Leftrightarrow$ $y = \dfrac{\sqrt{975}}{2} = \dfrac{5\sqrt{39}}{2} \approx 15.61$. Therefore,
     the window is approximately 15.6 inches high at the specified point.

49. The foci are $(\pm c, 0)$, where $c^2 = a^2 - b^2$. The endpoints of one latus rectum are the points $(c, \pm k)$,
     and the length is $2k$. Substituting this point into the equation, we get $\dfrac{c^2}{a^2} + \dfrac{k^2}{b^2} = 1$ $\Leftrightarrow$

     $\dfrac{k^2}{b^2} = 1 - \dfrac{c^2}{a^2} = \dfrac{a^2 - c^2}{a^2}$ $\Leftrightarrow$ $k^2 = \dfrac{b^2(a^2 - c^2)}{a^2}$. Since $b^2 = a^2 - c^2$, the last equation becomes

     $k^2 = \dfrac{b^4}{a^2}$ $\Rightarrow$ $k = \dfrac{b^2}{a}$. Thus, the length of the latus rectum is $2k = 2\left(\dfrac{b^2}{a}\right) = \dfrac{2b^2}{a}$.

51. (a) $x^2 + ky^2 = 100$ $\Leftrightarrow$ $ky^2 = 100 - x^2$

          $\Rightarrow$ $y = \pm \frac{1}{k}\sqrt{100 - x^2}$. For the top

          half, we graph $y = \frac{1}{k}\sqrt{100 - x^2}$ for

          $k = 4, 10, 25$, and 50.

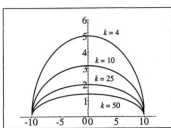

     (b) This family of ellipses have common major axes and vertices, and the eccentricity increases as
          k increases.

53. We start with the flashlight perpendicular to the wall; this shape is a circle. As the angle of elevation
     increases, the shape of the light changes to an ellipse. When the flashlight is angled so that the outer
     edge of the light cone is parallel to the wall, the shape of the light is a parabola. Finally, as the angle
     of elevation increases further, the shape of the light is hyperbolic.

Exercises 9.3

1. III. Opens horizontally, vertices at $(\pm 2, 0)$.

3. II. Opens vertically, vertices at $(0, \pm 3)$.

5. The hyperbola $\dfrac{x^2}{4} - \dfrac{y^2}{16} = 1$ has $a = 2$, $b = 4$, and $c^2 = 16 + 4$ $\Rightarrow$ $c = 2\sqrt{5}$.

   Vertices: $(\pm 2, 0)$; foci: $(\pm 2\sqrt{5}, 0)$; asymptotes: $y = \pm \frac{4}{2}x$ $\Leftrightarrow$ $y = \pm 2x$.

7. The hyperbola $\dfrac{y^2}{1} - \dfrac{x^2}{25} = 1$ has $a = 1$, $b = 5$, and $c^2 = 1 + 25 = 26$ $\Rightarrow$ $c = \sqrt{26}$.

   Vertices: $(0, \pm 1)$; foci: $(0, \pm\sqrt{26})$; asymptotes: $y = \pm \frac{1}{5}x$.

9. The hyperbola $x^2 - y^2 = 1$ has $a = 1$, $b = 1$, and $c^2 = 1 + 1 = 2$ $\Rightarrow$ $c = \sqrt{2}$.

   Vertices: $(\pm 1, 0)$; foci: $(\pm\sqrt{2}, 0)$; asymptotes: $y = \pm x$.

11. The hyperbola $25y^2 - 9x^2 = 225$ $\Leftrightarrow$ $\dfrac{y^2}{9} - \dfrac{x^2}{25} = 1$ has $a = 3$, $b = 5$, and $c^2 = 25 + 9 = 34$ $\Rightarrow$ $c = \sqrt{34}$.

   Vertices: $(0, \pm 3)$; foci: $(0, \pm\sqrt{34})$; asymptotes: $y = \pm \frac{3}{5}x$.

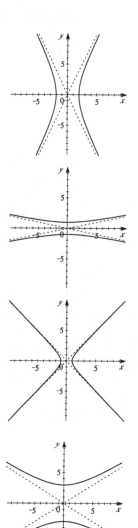

13. The hyperbola $x^2 - 4y^2 - 8 = 0 \Leftrightarrow \dfrac{x^2}{8} - \dfrac{y^2}{2} = 1$ has

$a = \sqrt{8}$, $b = \sqrt{2}$, and $c^2 = 8 + 2 = 10 \Rightarrow c = \sqrt{10}$.

Vertices: $(\pm 2\sqrt{2}, 0)$; foci: $(\pm\sqrt{10}, 0)$; asymptotrees: $y = \pm\dfrac{\sqrt{2}}{\sqrt{8}}x$

$\Leftrightarrow y = \pm\frac{1}{2}x$.

15. The hyperbola $4y^2 - x^2 = 1 \Leftrightarrow \dfrac{y^2}{\frac{1}{4}} - x^2 = 1$ has $a = \dfrac{1}{2}$,

$b = 1$, and $c^2 = \frac{1}{4} + 1 = \frac{5}{4} \Rightarrow c = \frac{1}{2}\sqrt{5}$.

Vertices: $(0, \pm\frac{1}{2})$; foci: $(0, \pm\frac{1}{2}\sqrt{5})$; asymptotes: $y = \pm\dfrac{\frac{1}{2}}{1}x$

$\Leftrightarrow y = \pm\frac{1}{2}x$.

17. From the graph, the foci are $(\pm 4, 0)$, and the vertices are $(\pm 2, 0)$, so $c = 4$ and $a = 2$. Thus, $b^2 = 16 - 4 = 12$, and since the vertices are on the x-axis, the equation of the hyperbola is $\dfrac{x^2}{4} - \dfrac{y^2}{12} = 1$.

19. From the graph, the vertices are $(0, \pm 4)$, the foci are on the y-axis, and the hyperbola passes through the point $(3, -5)$. So the equation is of the form $\dfrac{y^2}{16} - \dfrac{x^2}{b^2} = 1$. Substituting the point $(3, -5)$, we have $\dfrac{(-5)^2}{16} - \dfrac{(3)^2}{b^2} = 1 \Leftrightarrow \dfrac{25}{16} - 1 = \dfrac{9}{b^2} \Leftrightarrow \dfrac{9}{16} = \dfrac{9}{b^2} \Leftrightarrow b^2 = 16$. Thus, the equation of the hyperbola is $\dfrac{y^2}{16} - \dfrac{x^2}{16} = 1$.

21. The vertices are $(\pm 3, 0)$, so $a = 3$. Since the asymptotes are $y = \pm\frac{1}{2}x = \pm\frac{b}{a}x$, we have $\frac{b}{3} = \frac{1}{2}$ $\Leftrightarrow b = \frac{3}{2}$. Since the vertices are on the x-axis, the equation is $\dfrac{x^2}{3^2} - \dfrac{y^2}{(3/2)^2} = 1 \Leftrightarrow \dfrac{x^2}{9} - \dfrac{4y^2}{9} = 1$.

23. $x^2 - 2y^2 = 8 \Leftrightarrow 2y^2 = x^2 - 8 \Leftrightarrow$ $y^2 = \dfrac{x^2}{2} - 4 \Rightarrow y = \pm\sqrt{\dfrac{x^2}{2} - 4}$.

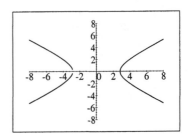

25. $\dfrac{y^2}{2} - \dfrac{x^2}{6} = 1 \quad\Leftrightarrow\quad \dfrac{y^2}{2} = \dfrac{x^2}{6} + 1 \quad\Leftrightarrow$

$y^2 = \dfrac{x^2}{3} + 2 \quad\Rightarrow\quad y = \pm\sqrt{\dfrac{x^2}{3} + 2}.$

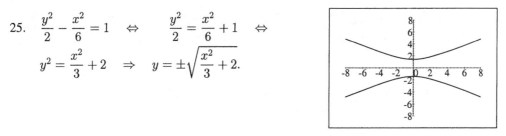

27. The foci are $(\pm 5, 0)$, and the vertices are $(\pm 3, 0)$, so $c = 5$ and $a = 3$. Then $b^2 = 25 - 9 = 16$, and since the vertices are on the x-axis, the equation of the hyperbola is $\dfrac{x^2}{9} - \dfrac{y^2}{16} = 1$.

29. The foci are $(0, \pm 2)$, and the vertices are $(0, \pm 1)$, so $c = 2$ and $a = 1$. Then $b^2 = 4 - 1 = 3$, and since the vertices are on the y-axis, the equation is $y^2 - \dfrac{x^2}{3} = 1$.

31. The vertices are $(\pm 1, 0)$, and the asymptotes are $y = \pm 5x$, so $a = 1$. The asymptotes are $y = \pm\dfrac{b}{a}x$, so $\dfrac{b}{1} = 5 \quad\Leftrightarrow\quad b = 5$. Therefore, the equation of the hyperbola is $x^2 - \dfrac{y^2}{25} = 1$.

33. The foci are $(0, \pm 8)$, and the asymptotes are $y = \pm\dfrac{1}{2}x$, so $c = 8$. The asymptotes are $y = \pm\dfrac{a}{b}x$, so $\dfrac{a}{b} = \dfrac{1}{2}$ and $b = 2a$. Since $a^2 + b^2 = c^2 = 64$, we have $a^2 + 4a^2 = 64 \quad\Leftrightarrow\quad a^2 = \dfrac{64}{5}$ and $b^2 = 4a^2 = \dfrac{256}{5}$. Thus, the equation of the hyperbola is $\dfrac{y^2}{64/5} - \dfrac{x^2}{256/5} = 1 \quad\Leftrightarrow$

$\dfrac{5y^2}{64} - \dfrac{5x^2}{256} = 1.$

35. The asymptotes of the hyperbola are $y = \pm x$ so $b = a$. Since the hyperbola passes through the point $(5, 3)$, its foci are on the x-axis, and the equation is of the form, $\dfrac{x^2}{a^2} - \dfrac{y^2}{a^2} = 1$, so it follows that $\dfrac{25}{a^2} - \dfrac{9}{a^2} = 1 \quad\Leftrightarrow\quad a^2 = 16 = b^2$. Therefore, the equation of the hyperbola is $\dfrac{x^2}{16} - \dfrac{y^2}{16} = 1$.

37. The foci are $(\pm 5, 0)$, and the length of the transverse axis is 6, so $c = 5$ and $2a = 6 \quad\Leftrightarrow\quad a = 3$. Thus, $b^2 = 25 - 9 = 16$, and the equation is $\dfrac{x^2}{9} - \dfrac{y^2}{16} = 1$.

39. (a) The hyperbola $x^2 - y^2 = 5 \quad\Leftrightarrow\quad \dfrac{x^2}{5} - \dfrac{y^2}{5} = 1$ has $a = \sqrt{5}$ and $b = \sqrt{5}$. Thus, the asymptotes are $y = \pm x$, and their slopes are $m_1 = 1$ and $m_2 = -1$. Since $m_1 \times m_2 = -1$, the asymptotes are perpendicular.

   (b) Since the asymptotes are perpendicular to each other, they must be of slope ± 1, so $a = b$. Therefore, $c^2 = 2a^2 \quad\Leftrightarrow\quad a^2 = \dfrac{c^2}{2}$, and since the vertices are on the x-axis, the equation is $\dfrac{x^2}{\frac{1}{2}c^2} - \dfrac{y^2}{\frac{1}{2}c^2} = 1 \quad\Leftrightarrow\quad x^2 - y^2 = \dfrac{c^2}{2}.$

41. $\sqrt{(x + c)^2 + y^2} - \sqrt{(x - c)^2 + y^2} = \pm 2a$. Let us consider the positive case only. Then $\sqrt{(x + c)^2 + y^2} = 2a + \sqrt{(x - c)^2 + y^2}$, and squaring both sides gives

$x^2 + 2cx + c^2 + y^2 = 4a^2 + 4a\sqrt{(x-c)^2 + y^2} + x^2 - 2cx + c^2 + y^2 \quad \Leftrightarrow$
$4a\sqrt{(x-c)^2 + y^2} = 4cx - 4a^2.$ Dividing by 4 and squaring both sides gives
$a^2(x^2 - 2cx + c^2 + y^2) = c^2x^2 - 2a^2cx + a^4 \quad \Leftrightarrow$
$a^2x^2 - 2a^2cx + a^2c^2 + a^2y^2 = c^2x^2 - 2a^2cx + a^4 \quad \Leftrightarrow \quad a^2x^2 + a^2c^2 + a^2y^2 = c^2x^2 + a^4.$
Rearranging the order, we have $c^2x^2 - a^2x^2 - a^2y^2 = a^2c^2 - a^4 \quad \Leftrightarrow$
$(c^2 - a^2)x^2 - a^2y^2 = a^2(c^2 - a^2).$ The negative case gives the same result.

43. $d(AB) = 500 = 2c \quad \Leftrightarrow \quad c = 250.$

(a) Since $\Delta t = 2640$ and $v = 980$, then $\Delta d = d(PA) - d(PB) = v\,\Delta t$
$= (980 \text{ ft/}\mu s) \cdot (2640 \ \mu s) = 2{,}587{,}200 \text{ ft} = 490 \text{ mi.}$

(b) $c = 250,\ 2a = 490 \quad \Leftrightarrow \quad a = 245$, and the foci are on the y-axis. Then,
$b^2 = 250^2 - 245^2 = 2475.$ Hence, the equation is $\dfrac{y^2}{60{,}025} - \dfrac{x^2}{2475} = 1.$

(c) Since P is due east of A, $c = 250$ is the y-coordinate of P. Therefore, P is at $(x, 250)$, and so
$\dfrac{250^2}{245^2} - \dfrac{x^2}{2475} = 1 \quad \Leftrightarrow \quad x^2 = 2475\left(\dfrac{250^2}{245^2} - 1\right) \approx 102.05.$ Then, $x \approx 10.1$, and so P is
approximately 10.1 miles from A.

45. (a) From the equation, we have $a^2 = k$ and $b^2 = 16 - k$. Thus, $c^2 = a^2 + b^2 = k + 16 - k = 16$
$\Rightarrow \quad c = \pm 4.$ Thus the foci of the family of hyperbolas are $(0, \pm 4).$

(b) $\dfrac{y^2}{k} - \dfrac{x^2}{16-k} = 1 \quad \Leftrightarrow \quad y^2 = k\left(1 + \dfrac{x^2}{16-k}\right) \quad \Rightarrow$

$y = \pm\sqrt{k + \dfrac{kx^2}{16-k}}.$ For the top branch, we graph

$y = \sqrt{k + \dfrac{kx^2}{16-k}},\ k = 1, 4, 8, 12.$

As k increases, the hyperbola gets steeper and narrower, and the vertices move further apart.

47. The wall is parallel to the axis of the cone of light coming from the top of the shade, so the
intersection of the wall and the cone of light is a hyperbola. In the case of the flashlight, hold it
parallel to the ground to form a hyperbola.

Exercises 9.4

1. The ellipse $\dfrac{(x-2)^2}{9} + \dfrac{(y-1)^2}{4} = 1$ is obtained from the ellipse

   $\dfrac{x^2}{9} + \dfrac{y^2}{4} = 1$ by shifting it 2 units to the right and 1 unit upward. So

   $a = 3$, $b = 2$, and $c = \sqrt{9-4} = \sqrt{5}$.

   Center: $(2, 1)$; foci: $(2 \pm \sqrt{5}, 1)$; vertices: $(2 \pm 3, 1)$, so the vertices
   are $(-1, 1)$ and $(5, 1)$; length of the major axis: $2a = 6$; length of
   the minor axis: $2b = 4$.

3. The ellipse $\dfrac{x^2}{9} + \dfrac{(y+5)^2}{25} = 1$ is obtained from the ellipse

   $\dfrac{x^2}{9} + \dfrac{y^2}{4} = 1$ by shifting it 5 units downward. So $a = 5$, $b = 3$, and

   $c = \sqrt{25-9} = 4$.
   Center: $(0, -5)$; foci: $(0, -5 \pm 4) = (0, -9)$ and $(0, -1)$; vertices:
   $(0, -5 \pm 5)$, so the vertices are $(0, -10)$ and $(0, 0)$; length of the
   major axis: $2a = 10$; length of the minor axis: $2b = 6$.

5. The parabola $(x-3)^2 = 8(y+1)$ is obtained from the parabola
   $x^2 = 8y$ by shifting it 3 units to the right and 1 unit down. So $4p = 8$
   $\Leftrightarrow \quad p = 2$.
   Vertex: $(3, -1)$; focus: $(3, -1 + 2) = (3, 1)$; directrix:
   $y = -1 - 2 = -3$.

7. The parabola $-4\left(x + \tfrac{1}{2}\right)^2 = y \quad \Leftrightarrow \quad \left(x + \tfrac{1}{2}\right)^2 = -\tfrac{1}{4}y$ is
   obtained from the parabola $x^2 = -\tfrac{1}{4}y$ by shifting it $\tfrac{1}{2}$ unit to the
   left. So $4p = -\tfrac{1}{4} \quad \Leftrightarrow \quad p = -\tfrac{1}{16}$.
   Vertex: $\left(-\tfrac{1}{2}, 0\right)$; focus: $\left(-\tfrac{1}{2}, 0 - \tfrac{1}{16}\right) = \left(-\tfrac{1}{2}, -\tfrac{1}{16}\right)$; directrix:
   $y = 0 + \tfrac{1}{16} = \tfrac{1}{16}$.

9. The hyperbola $\dfrac{(x+1)^2}{9} - \dfrac{(y-3)^2}{16} = 1$ is obtained from the

   yperbola $\dfrac{x^2}{9} - \dfrac{y^2}{16} = 1$ by shifting it 1 unit to the left and 3 units

   up. So $a = 3$, $b = 4$, and $c = \sqrt{9+16} = 5$.
   Center: $(-1, 3)$; foci: $(-1 \pm 5, 3)$, so the foci are $(-6, 3)$ and $(4, 3)$,
   vertices: $(-1 \pm 3, 3)$, so the vertices are $(-4, 3)$ and $(2, 3)$;
   asymptotes: $(y - 3) = \pm\tfrac{4}{3}(x+1) \quad \Leftrightarrow \quad y = \pm\tfrac{4}{3}(x+1) + 3$
   $\Leftrightarrow \quad 3y = 4x + 13$ and $3y = -4x + 5$.

11. The hyperbola $y^2 - \dfrac{(x+1)^2}{4} = 1$ is obtained from hyperbola

$y^2 - \frac{x^2}{4} = 1$ by shifting it 1 to the unit left. So $a = 1$, $b = 2$, and

$c = \sqrt{1+4} = \sqrt{5}$.

Center: $(-1, 0)$; foci: $(-1, \pm\sqrt{5})$, so the foci are $(-1, -\sqrt{5})$ and

$(-1, \sqrt{5})$; vertices: $(-1, \pm 1)$, so the vertices are $(-1, -1)$ and

$(-1, 1)$; asymptotes: $y = \pm\frac{1}{2}(x+1) \quad \Leftrightarrow \quad y = \frac{1}{2}(x+1)$ and $y = -\frac{1}{2}(x+1)$.

13. This is a parabola that opens down with its vertex at $(0, 4)$, so its equation is of the form
$x^2 = a(y - 4)$. Since $(1, 0)$ is a point on this parabola, we have $(1)^2 = a(0 - 4) \quad \Leftrightarrow \quad 1 = -4a$
$\Leftrightarrow \quad a = -\frac{1}{4}$. Thus, the equation is $x^2 = -\frac{1}{4}(y - 4)$.

15. This is an ellipse with the major axis parallel to the x-axis, with one vertex at $(0, 0)$, the other vertex
at $(10, 0)$, and one focus at $(8, 0)$. The center is at $\left(\frac{0+10}{2}, 0\right) = (5, 0)$, $a = 5$, and $c = 3$ (the distance
from one focus to the center). So $b^2 = a^2 - c^2 = 25 - 9 = 16$. Thus, the equation is
$\dfrac{(x - 5)^2}{25} + \dfrac{y^2}{16} = 1$.

17. This is a hyperbola with center $(0, 1)$ and vertices $(0, 0)$ and $(0, 2)$. Since a is the distance form the
center to a vertex, we have $a = 1$. The slope of the given asymptote is 1, so $\frac{a}{b} = 1 \quad \Leftrightarrow \quad b = 1$.
Thus, the equation of the hyperbola is $(y - 1)^2 - x^2 = 1$.

19. $9x^2 - 36x + 4y^2 = 0 \quad \Leftrightarrow \quad 9(x^2 - 4x + 4) - 36 + 4y^2 = 0 \quad \Leftrightarrow$

$9(x - 2)^2 + 4y^2 = 36 \quad \Leftrightarrow \quad \dfrac{(x - 2)^2}{4} + \dfrac{y^2}{9} = 1$. This is an

ellipse that has $a = 3$, $b = 2$, and $c = \sqrt{9 - 4} = \sqrt{5}$.

Center: $(2, 0)$; foci: $(2, \pm\sqrt{5})$; vertices: $(2, \pm 3)$; length of major
axis: $2a = 6$; length of minor axis: $2b = 4$.

21. $x^2 - 4y^2 - 2x + 16y = 20 \quad \Leftrightarrow$

$(x^2 - 2x + 1) - 4(y^2 - 4y + 4) = 20 + 1 - 16 \quad \Leftrightarrow$

$(x - 1)^2 - 4(y - 2)^2 = 5 \quad \Leftrightarrow \quad \dfrac{(x - 1)^2}{5} - \dfrac{(y - 2)^2}{\frac{5}{4}} = 1$. This

is a hyperbola that has $a = \sqrt{5}$, $b = \frac{1}{2}\sqrt{5}$, and $c = \sqrt{5 + \frac{5}{4}} = \frac{5}{2}$.

Center: $(1, 2)$; foci: $\left(1 \pm \frac{5}{2}, 2\right)$, so the foci are $\left(-\frac{3}{2}, 2\right)$ and $\left(\frac{7}{2}, 2\right)$; vertices: $(1 \pm \sqrt{5}, 2)$; asymptotes
$y - 2 = \pm\frac{1}{2}(x - 1) \quad \Leftrightarrow \quad y = \pm\frac{1}{2}(x - 1) + 2 \quad \Leftrightarrow \quad y = \frac{1}{2}x + \frac{3}{2}$ and $y = -\frac{1}{2}x + \frac{5}{2}$.

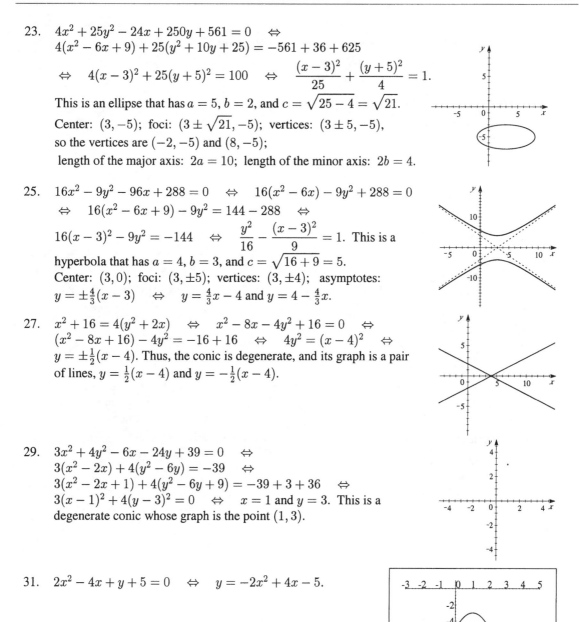

23. $4x^2 + 25y^2 - 24x + 250y + 561 = 0 \quad \Leftrightarrow$
$4(x^2 - 6x + 9) + 25(y^2 + 10y + 25) = -561 + 36 + 625$

$\Leftrightarrow \quad 4(x - 3)^2 + 25(y + 5)^2 = 100 \quad \Leftrightarrow \quad \dfrac{(x - 3)^2}{25} + \dfrac{(y + 5)^2}{4} = 1.$

This is an ellipse that has $a = 5$, $b = 2$, and $c = \sqrt{25 - 4} = \sqrt{21}.$
Center: $(3, -5)$; foci: $(3 \pm \sqrt{21}, -5)$; vertices: $(3 \pm 5, -5)$,
so the vertices are $(-2, -5)$ and $(8, -5)$;
length of the major axis: $2a = 10$; length of the minor axis: $2b = 4$.

25. $16x^2 - 9y^2 - 96x + 288 = 0 \quad \Leftrightarrow \quad 16(x^2 - 6x) - 9y^2 + 288 = 0$
$\Leftrightarrow \quad 16(x^2 - 6x + 9) - 9y^2 = 144 - 288 \quad \Leftrightarrow$

$16(x - 3)^2 - 9y^2 = -144 \quad \Leftrightarrow \quad \dfrac{y^2}{16} - \dfrac{(x - 3)^2}{9} = 1.$ This is a

hyperbola that has $a = 4$, $b = 3$, and $c = \sqrt{16 + 9} = 5$.
Center: $(3, 0)$; foci: $(3, \pm 5)$; vertices: $(3, \pm 4)$; asymptotes:
$y = \pm \frac{4}{3}(x - 3) \quad \Leftrightarrow \quad y = \frac{4}{3}x - 4$ and $y = 4 - \frac{4}{3}x.$

27. $x^2 + 16 = 4(y^2 + 2x) \quad \Leftrightarrow \quad x^2 - 8x - 4y^2 + 16 = 0 \quad \Leftrightarrow$
$(x^2 - 8x + 16) - 4y^2 = -16 + 16 \quad \Leftrightarrow \quad 4y^2 = (x - 4)^2 \quad \Leftrightarrow$
$y = \pm \frac{1}{2}(x - 4)$. Thus, the conic is degenerate, and its graph is a pair
of lines, $y = \frac{1}{2}(x - 4)$ and $y = -\frac{1}{2}(x - 4)$.

29. $3x^2 + 4y^2 - 6x - 24y + 39 = 0 \quad \Leftrightarrow$
$3(x^2 - 2x) + 4(y^2 - 6y) = -39 \quad \Leftrightarrow$
$3(x^2 - 2x + 1) + 4(y^2 - 6y + 9) = -39 + 3 + 36 \quad \Leftrightarrow$
$3(x - 1)^2 + 4(y - 3)^2 = 0 \quad \Leftrightarrow \quad x = 1$ and $y = 3$. This is a
degenerate conic whose graph is the point $(1, 3)$.

31. $2x^2 - 4x + y + 5 = 0 \quad \Leftrightarrow \quad y = -2x^2 + 4x - 5.$

33. $9x^2 + 36 = y^2 + 36x + 6y \quad \Leftrightarrow \quad x^2 - 36x + 36 = y^2 + 6y$
     $\Leftrightarrow \quad 9x^2 - 36x + 45 = y^2 + 6y + 9 \quad \Leftrightarrow$
     $9(x^2 - 4x + 5) = (y + 3)^2 \quad \Leftrightarrow$
     $y + 3 = \pm\sqrt{9(x^2 - 4x + 5)} \quad \Leftrightarrow$
     $y = -3 \pm 3\sqrt{x^2 - 4x + 5}.$

35. $4x^2 + y^2 + 4(x - 2y) + F = 0 \quad \Leftrightarrow \quad 4(x^2 + x) + (y^2 - 8y) = -F \quad \Leftrightarrow$
     $4(x^2 + x + \frac{1}{4}) + (y^2 - 8y + 16) = 16 + 1 - F \quad \Leftrightarrow \quad 4(x + \frac{1}{2})^2 + (y - 1)^2 = 17 - F.$

   (a) For an ellipse, $17 - F > 0 \quad \Leftrightarrow \quad F < 17.$

   (b) For a single point, $17 - F = 0 \quad \Leftrightarrow \quad F = 17.$

   (c) For the empty set, $17 - F < 0 \quad \Leftrightarrow \quad F > 17.$

37. (a) $x^2 = 4p(y + p)$, for $p = -2, -\frac{3}{2}, -1, -\frac{1}{2}, \frac{1}{2}, 1, \frac{3}{2}, 2.$

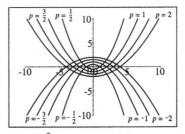

   (b) The graph of $x^2 = 4p(y + p)$ is obtained by shifting the graph of $x^2 = 4py$ vertically $-p$ units
        so that the vertex is at $(0, -p)$. The focus of $x^2 = 4py$ is at $(0, p)$, so this point is also shifted
        $-p$ units vertically to the point $(0, p - p) = (0, 0)$. Thus, the focus is located at the origin.

   (c) The parabolas become narrower as the vertex moves toward the origin.

Exercises 9.5

1. $(x, y) = (1, 1)$, $\phi = 45°$. Then, $X = x \cos \phi + y \sin \phi = 1 \cdot \frac{1}{\sqrt{2}} + 1 \cdot \frac{1}{\sqrt{2}} = \sqrt{2}$, and
   $Y = -x \sin \phi + y \cos \phi = -1 \cdot \frac{1}{\sqrt{2}} + 1 \cdot \frac{1}{\sqrt{2}} = 0$. Therefore, the XY-coordinates of the given point
   are $(X, Y) = (\sqrt{2}, 0)$.

3. $(x, y) = (3, -\sqrt{3})$, $\phi = 60°$. Then, $X = x \cos \phi + y \sin \phi = 3 \cdot \frac{1}{2} - \sqrt{3} \cdot \frac{\sqrt{3}}{2} = 0$, and
   $Y = -x \sin \phi + y \cos \phi = -3 \cdot \frac{\sqrt{3}}{2} - \sqrt{3} \cdot \frac{1}{2} = -2\sqrt{3}$. Therefore, the XY-coordinates of the
   given point are $(X, Y) = (0, -2\sqrt{3})$.

5. $(x, y) = (0, 2)$, $\phi = 55°$. Then, $X = x \cos \phi + y \sin \phi = 0 \cos 55° + 2 \sin 55° \approx 1.6383$ and
   $Y = -x \sin \phi + y \cos \phi = -0 \sin 55° + 2 \cos 55° \approx 1.1472$. Therefore, the XY-coordinates of the
   given point are approximately $(X, Y) = (1.6383, 1.1472)$.

7. $x^2 - 3y^2 = 4$, $\phi = 60°$. Then $x = X \cos 60° - Y \sin 60° = \frac{X}{2} - \frac{\sqrt{3}Y}{2}$ and
   $y = X \sin 60° + Y \cos 60° = \frac{\sqrt{3}X}{2} + \frac{Y}{2}$. Substituting these values into the equation, we get
   $\left(\frac{X}{2} - \frac{\sqrt{3}Y}{2}\right)^2 - 3\left(\frac{\sqrt{3}X}{2} + \frac{Y}{2}\right)^2 = 4$ $\Leftrightarrow$ $\frac{X^2}{4} - \frac{\sqrt{3}XY}{2} + \frac{3Y^2}{4} - 3\left(\frac{3X^2}{4} + \frac{\sqrt{3}XY}{2} + \frac{Y^2}{4}\right) = 4$ $\Leftrightarrow$
   $\frac{X^2}{4} - \frac{9}{4}X^2 + \frac{3Y^2}{4} - \frac{3Y^2}{4} - \frac{\sqrt{3}XY}{2} - \frac{3\sqrt{3}XY}{2} = 4$ $\Leftrightarrow$ $-2X^2 - 2\sqrt{3}XY = 4$ $\Leftrightarrow$
   $X^2 + \sqrt{3}XY = -2$.

9. $x^2 - y^2 = 2y$, $\phi = \cos^{-1}\left(\frac{3}{5}\right)$. So $\cos \phi = \frac{3}{5}$ and $\sin \phi = \frac{4}{5}$. Then,
   $(X \cos \phi - Y \sin \phi)^2 - (X \sin \phi + Y \cos \phi)^2 = 2(X \sin \phi + Y \cos \phi)$ $\Leftrightarrow$
   $\left(\frac{3X}{5} - \frac{4Y}{5}\right)^2 - \left(\frac{4X}{5} + \frac{3Y}{5}\right)^2 = 2\left(\frac{4X}{5} + \frac{3Y}{5}\right)$ $\Leftrightarrow$
   $\frac{9X^2}{25} - \frac{24XY}{25} + \frac{16Y^2}{25} - \frac{16X^2}{25} - \frac{24XY}{25} - \frac{9Y^2}{25} = \frac{8X}{5} + \frac{6Y}{5}$ $\Leftrightarrow$
   $\frac{-7X^2}{25} - \frac{48XY}{25} + \frac{7Y^2}{25} - \frac{8X}{5} - \frac{6Y}{5} = 0$ $\Leftrightarrow$ $7Y^2 - 48XY - 7X^2 - 40X - 30Y = 0$

11. $x^2 + 2\sqrt{3}xy - y^2 = 4$, $\phi = 30°$. Then $x = X \cos 30° - Y \sin 30° = \frac{\sqrt{3}}{2}X - \frac{1}{2}Y$
    $= \frac{1}{2}\left(\sqrt{3}X - Y\right)$, and $y = X \sin 30° + Y \cos 30° = \frac{1}{2}X + \frac{\sqrt{3}}{2}Y = \frac{1}{2}(X + \sqrt{3}Y)$. Substituting
    these values into the equation, we get
    $\left[\frac{1}{2}\left(\sqrt{3}X - Y\right)\right]^2 + 2\sqrt{3}\left[\frac{1}{2}\left(\sqrt{3}X - Y\right)\right]\left[\frac{1}{2}\left(X + \sqrt{3}Y\right)\right] - \left[\frac{1}{2}\left(X + \sqrt{3}Y\right)\right]^2 = 4$ $\Leftrightarrow$
    $\left(\sqrt{3}X - Y\right)^2 + 2\sqrt{3}\left(\sqrt{3}X - Y\right)\left(X + \sqrt{3}Y\right) - \left(X + \sqrt{3}Y\right)^2 = 16$ $\Leftrightarrow$
    $\left(3X^2 - 2\sqrt{3}XY + Y^2\right) + \left(6X^2 + 4\sqrt{3}XY - 6Y^2\right) - \left(X^2 + 2\sqrt{3}XY + 3Y^2\right) = 16$ $\Leftrightarrow$
    $8X^2 - 8Y^2 = 16$ $\Leftrightarrow$ $\frac{X^2}{2} - \frac{Y^2}{2} = 1$. This is a hyperbola.

13. (a) $xy = 8$ $\Leftrightarrow$ $0x^2 + xy + 0y^2 = 8$. So $A = 0$, $B = 1$, $C = 0$, and so the discriminant is
    $B^2 - 4AC = 1^2 - 4(0)(0) = 1$. Since the discriminant is positive the equation represents a
    hyperbola.

(b) $\cot 2\phi = \frac{A-C}{B} = 0$ $\Rightarrow$ $2\phi = 90°$ $\Leftrightarrow$ $\phi = 45°$. Therefore, $x = \frac{X}{\sqrt{2}} - \frac{Y}{\sqrt{2}}$ and

$y = \frac{X}{\sqrt{2}} + \frac{Y}{\sqrt{2}}$. After substitution, the original equation becomes $\left(\frac{X}{\sqrt{2}} - \frac{Y}{\sqrt{2}}\right)\left(\frac{X}{\sqrt{2}} + \frac{Y}{\sqrt{2}}\right) = 8$

$\Leftrightarrow$ $\frac{(X-Y)(X+Y)}{2} = 8$ $\Leftrightarrow$ $\frac{X^2}{16} - \frac{Y^2}{16} = 1$. This is a hyperbola with $a = 4$, $b = 4$,

and $c = 4\sqrt{2}$. Hence, the vertices are at $V(\pm 4, 0)$ and the foci are at $F(\pm 4\sqrt{2}, 0)$.

(c)

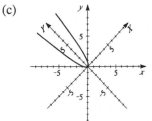

15. (a) $x^2 + 2xy + y^2 + x - y = 0$. So $A = 1$, $B = 2$, $C = 1$, and so the discriminant is
    $B^2 - 4AC = 2^2 - 4(1)(1) = 0$. Since the discriminant is zero the equation represents a
    parabola.

(b) $\cot 2\phi = \frac{A-C}{B} = 0$ $\Rightarrow$ $2\phi = 90°$ $\Leftrightarrow$ $\phi = 45°$. Therefore, $x = \frac{X}{\sqrt{2}} - \frac{Y}{\sqrt{2}}$ and

$y = \frac{X}{\sqrt{2}} + \frac{Y}{\sqrt{2}}$. After substitution, the original equation becomes:

$\left(\frac{X}{\sqrt{2}} - \frac{Y}{\sqrt{2}}\right)^2 + 2\left(\frac{X}{\sqrt{2}} - \frac{Y}{\sqrt{2}}\right)\left(\frac{X}{\sqrt{2}} + \frac{Y}{\sqrt{2}}\right) + \left(\frac{X}{\sqrt{2}} + \frac{Y}{\sqrt{2}}\right)^2 + \left(\frac{X}{\sqrt{2}} - \frac{Y}{\sqrt{2}}\right) - \left(\frac{X}{\sqrt{2}} + \frac{Y}{\sqrt{2}}\right) = 0$

$\Leftrightarrow$ $\frac{X^2}{2} - XY + \frac{Y^2}{2} + X^2 - Y^2 + \frac{X^2}{2} + XY + \frac{Y^2}{2} - \sqrt{2}Y = 0$ $\Leftrightarrow$ $2X^2 - \sqrt{2}Y = 0$

$\Leftrightarrow$ $X^2 = \frac{Y}{\sqrt{2}}$. This is a parabola that has $4p = \frac{1}{\sqrt{2}}$ and hence the focus is at $F\left(0, \frac{1}{4\sqrt{2}}\right)$.

(c)

17. (a) $x^2 + 2\sqrt{3}xy - y^2 + 2 = 0$. So $A = 1$, $B = 2\sqrt{3}$, $C = -1$, and so the discriminant is
    $B^2 - 4AC = (2\sqrt{3})^2 - 4(1)(-1) > 0$. Since the discriminant is positive the equation
    represents a hyperbola.

(b) $\cot 2\phi = \frac{A-C}{B} = \frac{1+1}{2\sqrt{3}} = \frac{1}{\sqrt{3}}$ $\Rightarrow$ $2\phi = 60°$ $\Leftrightarrow$ $\phi = 30°$. Therefore, $x = \frac{\sqrt{3}X}{2} - \frac{Y}{2}$

and $y = \frac{X}{2} + \frac{\sqrt{3}Y}{2}$. After substitution, the original equation becomes:

$\left(\frac{\sqrt{3}X}{2} - \frac{Y}{2}\right)^2 + 2\sqrt{3}\left(\frac{\sqrt{3}X}{2} - \frac{Y}{2}\right)\left(\frac{X}{2} + \frac{\sqrt{3}Y}{2}\right) - \left(\frac{X}{2} + \frac{\sqrt{3}Y}{2}\right)^2 + 2 = 0$ $\Leftrightarrow$

$\frac{3X^2}{4} - \frac{2\sqrt{3}XY}{4} + \frac{Y^2}{4} + \frac{\sqrt{3}}{2}\left(\sqrt{3}X^2 + 2XY - \sqrt{3}Y^2\right) - \frac{X^2}{4} - \frac{2\sqrt{3}XY}{4} - \frac{3Y^2}{4} + 2 = 0$ $\Leftrightarrow$

$X^2\left(\frac{3}{4} + \frac{3}{2} - \frac{1}{4}\right) + XY\left(-\frac{\sqrt{3}}{2} + \sqrt{3} - \frac{\sqrt{3}}{2}\right) + Y^2\left(\frac{1}{4} - \frac{3}{2} - \frac{3}{4}\right) = -2$ $\Leftrightarrow$

$2X^2 - 2Y^2 = -2$ $\Leftrightarrow$ $Y^2 - X^2 = 1$.

(c)

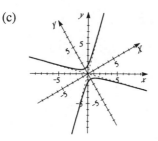

19. (a) $11x^2 - 24xy + 4y^2 + 20 = 0$. So $A = 11$, $B = -24$, $C = 4$, and so the discriminant is $B^2 - 4AC = (-24)^2 - 4(11)(4) > 0$. Since the discriminant is positive the equation represents a hyperbola.

(b) $\cot 2\phi = \frac{A-C}{B} = \frac{11-4}{-24} = \frac{-7}{24} \;\Rightarrow\; \cos 2\phi = \frac{-7}{25}$. Therefore, $\cos \phi = \sqrt{\frac{1+(-7/25)}{2}} = \frac{3}{5}$ and $\sin \phi = \sqrt{\frac{1-(-7/25)}{2}} = \frac{4}{5}$. Hence, $x = \frac{3X}{5} - \frac{4Y}{5}$ and $y = \frac{4X}{5} + \frac{3Y}{5}$. After substitution, the original equation becomes:

$11\left(\frac{3X}{5} - \frac{4Y}{5}\right)^2 - 24\left(\frac{3X}{5} - \frac{4Y}{5}\right)\left(\frac{4X}{5} + \frac{3Y}{5}\right) + 4\left(\frac{4X}{5} + \frac{3Y}{5}\right)^2 + 20 = 0 \;\Leftrightarrow$

$\frac{11}{25}(9X^2 - 24XY + 16Y^2) - \frac{24}{25}(12X^2 - 7XY - 12Y^2) + \frac{4}{25}(16X^2 + 24XY + 9Y^2) + 20 = 0 \;\Leftrightarrow\; X^2(99 - 288 + 64) + XY(-264 + 168 + 96) + Y^2(176 + 288 + 36) = -500$

$\Leftrightarrow\; -125X^2 + 500Y^2 = -500 \;\Leftrightarrow\; \frac{X^2}{4} - Y^2 = 1$.

(c)

Since $\cos 2\phi = -\frac{7}{25}$, we have $2\phi = \cos^{-1}\left(-\frac{7}{25}\right) \approx 106.26°$ and so $\phi \approx 53°$.

21. (a) $\sqrt{3}x^2 + 3xy = 3$. So $A = \sqrt{3}$, $B = 3$, $C = 0$, and so the discriminant is $B^2 - 4AC = (3)^2 - 4(\sqrt{3})(0) = 9$. Since the discriminant is positive the equation represents a hyperbola.

(b) $\cot 2\phi = \frac{A-C}{B} = \frac{1}{\sqrt{3}} \;\Rightarrow\; 2\phi = 60° \;\Leftrightarrow\; \phi = 30°$. Therefore, $x = \frac{\sqrt{3}X}{2} - \frac{Y}{2}$ and $y = \frac{X}{2} + \frac{\sqrt{3}Y}{2}$. After substitution, the equation becomes

$\sqrt{3}\left(\frac{\sqrt{3}X}{2} - \frac{Y}{2}\right)^2 + 3\left(\frac{\sqrt{3}X}{2} - \frac{Y}{2}\right)\left(\frac{X}{2} + \frac{\sqrt{3}Y}{2}\right) = 3 \;\Leftrightarrow$

$\frac{\sqrt{3}}{4}(3X^2 - 2\sqrt{3}XY + Y^2) + \frac{3}{4}(\sqrt{3}X^2 + 2XY - \sqrt{3}Y^2) = 3 \;\Leftrightarrow$

$X^2\left(\frac{3\sqrt{3}}{4} + \frac{3\sqrt{3}}{4}\right) + XY\left(\frac{-6}{4} + \frac{6}{4}\right) + Y^2\left(\frac{\sqrt{3}}{4} - \frac{3\sqrt{3}}{4}\right) = 3 \;\Leftrightarrow\; \frac{3\sqrt{3}X^2}{2} - \frac{\sqrt{3}Y^2}{2} = 3 \;\Leftrightarrow$

$\frac{\sqrt{3}X^2}{2} - \frac{Y^2}{2\sqrt{3}} = 1$. This is a hyperbola that has $a = \sqrt{\frac{2}{\sqrt{3}}}$ and $b = \sqrt{2\sqrt{3}}$.

(c)

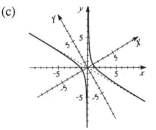

23. (a) $2\sqrt{3}x^2 - 6xy + \sqrt{3}x + 3y = 0$. So $A = 2\sqrt{3}$, $B = -6$, and $C = 0$, and so the discriminant is $B^2 - 4AC = (-6)^2 - 4(2\sqrt{3})(0) = 36$. Since the discriminant is positive the equation represents a hyperbola.

(b) $\cot 2\phi = \frac{A-C}{B} = \frac{2\sqrt{3}}{-6} = -\frac{1}{\sqrt{3}}$ $\Rightarrow$ $2\phi = 120°$ $\Leftrightarrow$ $\phi = 60°$. Therefore,

$x = \frac{X}{2} - \frac{\sqrt{3}Y}{2}$ and $y = \frac{\sqrt{3}X}{2} + \frac{Y}{2}$, and substituting gives

$2\sqrt{3}\left(\frac{X}{2} - \frac{\sqrt{3}Y}{2}\right)^2 - 6\left(\frac{X}{2} - \frac{\sqrt{3}Y}{2}\right)\left(\frac{\sqrt{3}X}{2} + \frac{Y}{2}\right) + \sqrt{3}\left(\frac{X}{2} - \frac{\sqrt{3}Y}{2}\right) + 3\left(\frac{\sqrt{3}X}{2} + \frac{Y}{2}\right) = 0$

$\Leftrightarrow$ $\frac{\sqrt{3}}{2}(X^2 - 2\sqrt{3}XY + 3Y^2) - \frac{3}{2}(\sqrt{3}X^2 - 2XY - \sqrt{3}Y^2) + \frac{\sqrt{3}}{2}(X - \sqrt{3}Y) +$

$\frac{3}{2}(\sqrt{3}X + Y) = 0$ $\Leftrightarrow$

$X^2\left(\frac{\sqrt{3}}{2} - \frac{3\sqrt{3}}{2}\right) + X\left(\frac{\sqrt{3}}{2} + \frac{3\sqrt{3}}{2}\right) + XY(-3 + 3) + Y^2\left(\frac{3\sqrt{3}}{2} + \frac{3\sqrt{3}}{2}\right) + Y\left(-\frac{3}{2} + \frac{3}{2}\right) = 0$

$\Leftrightarrow$ $-\sqrt{3}X^2 + 2\sqrt{3}X + 3\sqrt{3}Y^2 = 0$ $\Leftrightarrow$ $-X^2 + 2X + 3Y^2 = 0$ $\Leftrightarrow$
$3Y^2 - (X^2 - 2X + 1) = -1$ $\Leftrightarrow$ $(X - 1)^2 - 3Y^2 = 1$. This is a hyperbola that has

$a = 1$, $b = \frac{1}{\sqrt{3}}$, $c = \sqrt{1 + \frac{1}{3}} = \frac{2}{\sqrt{3}}$, and $C(1, 0)$.

(c)

25. (a) $52x^2 + 72xy + 73y^2 = 40x - 30y + 75$. So $A = 52$, $B = 72$, $C = 73$, and so the discriminant is $B^2 - 4AC = (72)^2 - 4(52)(73) = -10000$. Since the discriminant is negative the equation represents an ellipse.

(b) $\cot 2\phi = \frac{A-C}{B} = \frac{52-73}{72} = \frac{-7}{24}$. Therefore, as in Exercise 17(b), we get $\cos\phi = \frac{3}{5}$, $\sin\phi = \frac{4}{5}$, and $x = \frac{3X}{5} - \frac{4Y}{5}$, $y = \frac{4X}{5} + \frac{3Y}{5}$. By substitution,

$52\left(\frac{3X}{5} - \frac{4Y}{5}\right)^2 + 72\left(\frac{3X}{5} - \frac{4Y}{5}\right)\left(\frac{4X}{5} + \frac{3Y}{5}\right) + 73\left(\frac{4X}{5} + \frac{3Y}{5}\right)^2$
$= 40\left(\frac{3X}{5} - \frac{4Y}{5}\right) - 30\left(\frac{4X}{5} + \frac{3Y}{5}\right) + 75$ $\Leftrightarrow$
$\frac{52}{25}(9X^2 - 24XY + 16Y^2) + \frac{72}{25}(12X^2 - 7XY - 12Y^2) + \frac{73}{25}(16X^2 + 24XY + 9Y^2)$

$= 24X - 32Y - 24X - 18Y + 75$ $\Leftrightarrow$

$468X^2 + 832Y^2 + 864X^2 - 864Y^2 + 1168X^2 + 657Y^2 = -1250Y + 1875$ $\Leftrightarrow$
$2500X^2 + 625Y^2 + 1250Y = 1875$ $\Leftrightarrow$ $100X^2 + 25Y^2 + 50Y = 75$ $\Leftrightarrow$

$X^2 + \frac{(Y+1)^2}{4} = 1$. This is an ellipse with $a = 2$, $b = 1$, $c = \sqrt{4-1} = \sqrt{3}$, and center $C(0, -1)$.

(c)

27. (a) Discriminant $= B^2 - 4AC = (-4)^2 + 4(2)(2) = 0$. Since the discriminent is 0, the equation represents a parabola.

(b) $2x^2 - 4xy + 2y^2 - 5x - 5 = 0 \quad \Leftrightarrow$

$2y^2 - 4xy = -2x^2 + 5x + 5 \quad \Leftrightarrow$

$2(y^2 - 2xy) = -2x^2 + 5x + 5 \quad \Leftrightarrow$

$2(y^2 - 2xy + x^2) = -2x^2 + 5x + 5 + 2x^2 \quad \Leftrightarrow$

$2(y - x)^2 = 5x + 5 \quad \Leftrightarrow \quad (y - x)^2 = \frac{5}{2}x + \frac{5}{2} \quad \Rightarrow$

$y - x = \pm\sqrt{\frac{5}{2}x + \frac{5}{2}} \quad \Leftrightarrow \quad y = x \pm \sqrt{\frac{5}{2}x + \frac{5}{2}}.$

29. (a) Discriminant $= B^2 - 4AC = 10^2 + 4(6)(3) = 28 > 0$. Since the discriminent is positive, the equation represents a hyperbola.

(b) $6x^2 + 10xy + 3y^2 - 6y = 36 \quad \Leftrightarrow$

$3y^2 + 10xy - 6y = 36 - 6x^2 \quad \Leftrightarrow$

$3y^2 + 2(5x - 3)y = 36 - 6x^2 \quad \Leftrightarrow$

$y^2 + 2\left(\frac{5}{3}x - 1\right)y = 12 - 2x^2 \quad \Leftrightarrow$

$y^2 + 2\left(\frac{5}{3}x - 1\right)y + \left(\frac{5}{3}x - 1\right)^2 = \left(\frac{5}{3}x - 1\right)^2 + 12 - 2x^2$

$\Leftrightarrow \quad \left[y + \left(\frac{5}{3}x - 1\right)\right]^2 = \frac{25}{9}x^2 - \frac{10}{3}x + 1 + 12 - 2x^2$

$\Leftrightarrow \quad \left[y + \left(\frac{5}{3}x - 1\right)\right]^2 = \frac{7}{9}x^2 - \frac{10}{3}x + 13 \quad \Leftrightarrow \quad y + \left(\frac{5}{3}x - 1\right) = \pm\sqrt{\frac{7}{9}x^2 - \frac{10}{3}x + 13}$

$\Leftrightarrow \quad y = -\frac{5}{3}x + 1 \pm \sqrt{\frac{7}{9}x^2 - \frac{10}{3}x + 13}$

31. (a) $7x^2 + 48xy - 7y^2 - 200x - 150y + 600 = 0$. Then, $A = 7$, $B = 48$, and $C = -7$, and so the discriminant is $B^2 - 4AC = (48)^2 - 4(7)(7) > 0$. Since the discriminant is positive the equation represents a hyperbola.

We now find the equation in terms of XY-coordinates. We have $\cot 2\phi = \frac{A-C}{B} = \frac{7}{24} \quad \Rightarrow$ $\cos\phi = \frac{4}{5}$ and $\sin\phi = \frac{3}{5}$. Therefore, $x = \frac{4X}{5} - \frac{3Y}{5}$ and $y = \frac{3X}{5} + \frac{4Y}{5}$, and substitution gives

$7\left(\frac{4X}{5} - \frac{3Y}{5}\right)^2 + 48\left(\frac{4X}{5} - \frac{3Y}{5}\right)\left(\frac{3X}{5} + \frac{4Y}{5}\right) - 7\left(\frac{3X}{5} + \frac{4Y}{5}\right)^2 - 200\left(\frac{4X}{5} - \frac{3Y}{5}\right)$

$$- 150\left(\frac{3X}{5} + \frac{4Y}{5}\right) + 600 = 0 \quad \Leftrightarrow$$

$\frac{7}{25}(16X^2 - 24XY + 9Y^2) + \frac{48}{25}(12X^2 + 7XY - 12Y^2) - \frac{7}{25}(9X^2 + 24XY + 16Y^2)$

$$-160X + 120Y - 90X - 120Y + 600 = 0 \quad \Leftrightarrow$$

$$112X^2 - 168XY + 63Y^2 + 576X^2 + 336XY - 576Y^2 - 63X^2$$
$$- 168XY - 112Y^2 - 6250X + 15{,}000 = 0 \quad \Leftrightarrow$$
$$25X^2 - 25Y^2 - 250X + 600 = 0 \quad \Leftrightarrow \quad 25(X^2 - 10X + 25) - 25Y^2 = -600 + 625$$
$$\Leftrightarrow \quad (X-5)^2 - Y^2 = 1. \text{ This is a hyperbola that has } a = 1, b = 1, c = \sqrt{1+1} = \sqrt{2}, \text{ and}$$
its center at $C(5,0)$.

(b) In the XY-plane, the center is $C(5,0)$, the vertices are $V(5\pm1, 0) = V_1(4,0)$ and $V_2(6,0)$, and the foci are $F(5 \pm \sqrt{2}, 0)$. In the xy-plane, the center is
$$C\left(\tfrac{4}{5}\cdot 5 - \tfrac{3}{5}\cdot 0, \ \tfrac{3}{5}\cdot 5 + \tfrac{4}{5}\cdot 0\right) = C(4,3), \text{ the vertices are}$$
$$V_1\left(\tfrac{4}{5}\cdot 4 - \tfrac{3}{5}\cdot 0, \ \tfrac{3}{5}\cdot 4 + \tfrac{4}{5}\cdot 0\right) = V_1\left(\tfrac{16}{5}, \tfrac{12}{5}\right) \text{ and } V_2\left(\tfrac{4}{5}\cdot 6 - \tfrac{3}{5}\cdot 0, \ \tfrac{3}{5}\cdot 6 + \tfrac{4}{5}\cdot 0\right)$$
$$= V_2\left(\tfrac{24}{5}, \tfrac{18}{5}\right), \text{ and the foci are } F_1\left(4 + \tfrac{4}{5}\sqrt{2}, 3 + \tfrac{3}{5}\sqrt{2}\right) \text{ and } F_2\left(4 - \tfrac{4}{5}\sqrt{2}, 3 - \tfrac{3}{5}\sqrt{2}\right).$$

(c) In the XY-plane the equations of the asymptotes are $Y = X - 5$ and $Y = -X + 5$. In the xy-plane, these equations become $-x\cdot\tfrac{3}{5} + y\cdot\tfrac{4}{5} = x\cdot\tfrac{4}{5} + y\cdot\tfrac{3}{5} - 5 \quad \Leftrightarrow \quad y = 7x - 25$ and $-x\cdot\tfrac{3}{5} + y\cdot\tfrac{4}{5} = -\left(x\cdot\tfrac{4}{5} + y\cdot\tfrac{3}{5}\right) + 5 \quad \Leftrightarrow \quad y = -\tfrac{1}{7}x + \tfrac{25}{7}.$

33. We use the hint and eliminate the Y by adding:

$$\begin{aligned} x &= X\cos\phi - Y\sin\phi & \Leftrightarrow && x\cos\phi &= X\cos^2\phi - Y\sin\phi\cos\phi \\ y &= X\sin\phi + Y\cos\phi & \Leftrightarrow && \underline{y\sin\phi} &= X\sin^2\phi + Y\sin\phi\cos\phi \\ &&&& x\cos\phi + y\sin\phi &= X(\cos^2\phi + \sin^2\phi) \end{aligned}$$

$$\Leftrightarrow \quad x\cos\phi + y\sin\phi = X.$$

In a similar manner we eliminate the X by subtracting:

$$\begin{aligned} x &= X\cos\phi - Y\sin\phi & \Leftrightarrow && -x\sin\phi &= -X\cos\phi\sin\phi + Y\sin^2\phi \\ y &= X\sin\phi + Y\cos\phi & \Leftrightarrow && \underline{y\cos\phi} &= X\sin\phi\cos\phi + Y\cos^2\phi \\ &&&& -x\sin\phi + y\cos\phi &= Y(\cos^2\phi + \sin^2\phi) \end{aligned}$$

$$\Leftrightarrow \quad -x\sin\phi + y\cos\phi = Y. \text{ So } X = x\cos\phi + y\sin\phi \text{ and } Y = -x\sin\phi + y\cos\phi.$$

35. $Z = \begin{bmatrix} x \\ y \end{bmatrix}, Z' = \begin{bmatrix} X \\ Y \end{bmatrix}$, and $R = \begin{bmatrix} \cos\phi & -\sin\phi \\ \sin\phi & \cos\phi \end{bmatrix}$.

Thus $Z = RZ' \quad \Leftrightarrow \quad \begin{bmatrix} x \\ y \end{bmatrix} = \begin{bmatrix} \cos\phi & -\sin\phi \\ \sin\phi & \cos\phi \end{bmatrix}\begin{bmatrix} X \\ Y \end{bmatrix} = \begin{bmatrix} X\cos\phi - Y\sin\phi \\ X\sin\phi + Y\cos\phi \end{bmatrix}.$

Equating the entries in this matrix equation gives the first pair of rotation of axes formulas. Now
$$R^{-1} = \frac{1}{\cos^2\phi + \sin^2\phi}\begin{bmatrix} \cos\phi & \sin\phi \\ -\sin\phi & \cos\phi \end{bmatrix} = \begin{bmatrix} \cos\phi & \sin\phi \\ -\sin\phi & \cos\phi \end{bmatrix} \text{ and so } Z' = R^{-1}Z \quad \Leftrightarrow$$
$$\begin{bmatrix} X \\ Y \end{bmatrix} = \begin{bmatrix} \cos\phi & \sin\phi \\ -\sin\phi & \cos\phi \end{bmatrix}\begin{bmatrix} x \\ y \end{bmatrix} = \begin{bmatrix} x\cos\phi + y\sin\phi \\ -x\sin\phi + y\cos\phi \end{bmatrix}. \text{ Equating the entries in this matrix}$$
equation gives the second pair of rotation of axes formulas.

37. Let P be the point (x_1, y_1) and Q be the point (x_2, y_2) and let $P'(X_1, Y_1)$ and $Q'(X_2, Y_2)$ be the images of P and Q under the rotation of ϕ. So $X_1 = x_1\cos\phi + y_1\sin\phi$, $Y_1 = -x_1\sin\phi + y_1\cos\phi$, $X_2 = x_2\cos\phi + y_2\sin\phi$, and $Y_2 = -x_2\sin\phi + y_2\cos\phi$. Thus $d(P', Q') = \sqrt{(X_2 - X_1)^2 + (Y_2 - Y_1)^2}$ where

$(X_2 - X_1)^2 = [(x_2\cos\phi + y_2\sin\phi) - (x_1\cos\phi + y_1\sin\phi)]^2 = [(x_2 - x_1)\cos\phi + (y_2 - y_1)\sin\phi]^2$

$= (x_2 - x_1)^2\cos^2\phi + (x_2 - x_1)(y_2 - y_1)\sin\phi\cos\phi + (y_2 - y_1)^2\sin^2\phi$ and

$(Y_2 - Y_1)^2 = [(-x_2\sin\phi + y_2\cos\phi) - (-x_1\sin\phi + y_1\cos\phi)]^2$

$= [-(x_2 - x_1)\sin\phi + (y_2 - y_1)\cos\phi]^2$

$= (x_2 - x_1)^2\sin^2\phi - (x_2 - x_1)(y_2 - y_1)\sin\phi\cos\phi + (y_2 - y_1)^2\cos^2\phi$

So $(X_2 - X_1)^2 + (Y_2 - Y_1)^2 = (x_2 - x_1)^2\cos^2\phi + (x_2 - x_1)(y_2 - y_1)\sin\phi\cos\phi +$

$(y_2 - y_1)^2\sin^2\phi + (x_2 - x_1)^2\sin^2\phi - (x_2 - x_1)(y_2 - y_1)\sin\phi\cos\phi + (y_2 - y_1)^2\cos^2\phi$

$= (x_2 - x_1)^2\cos^2\phi + (y_2 - y_1)^2\sin^2\phi + (x_2 - x_1)^2\sin^2\phi + (y_2 - y_1)^2\cos^2\phi$

$= (x_2 - x_1)^2(\cos^2\phi + \sin^2\phi) + (y_2 - y_1)^2(\sin^2\phi + \cos^2\phi) = (x_2 - x_1)^2 + (y_2 - y_1)^2$. Putting

these equations together gives

$d(P', Q') = \sqrt{(X_2 - X_1)^2 + (Y_2 - Y_1)^2} = \sqrt{(x_2 - x_1)^2 + (y_2 - y_1)^2} = d(P, Q).$

Exercises 9.6

Solutions to Exercises 1 − 5 will vary. Some possible solutions are given.

1. $(3, \frac{\pi}{2})$ also has polar coordinates $(3, \frac{5\pi}{2})$ or $(-3, \frac{3\pi}{2})$.

3. $(-1, \frac{7\pi}{6})$ also has polar coordinates $(1, \frac{\pi}{6})$ or $(-1, -\frac{5\pi}{6})$.

5. $(-5, 0)$ also has polar coordinates $(5, \pi)$ or $(-5, 2\pi)$.

7. $(r, \theta) = (4, \frac{\pi}{6})$. So $x = r\cos\theta = 4\cos\frac{\pi}{6} = 4 \cdot \frac{\sqrt{3}}{2} = 2\sqrt{3}$ and $y = r\sin\theta = 4\sin\frac{\pi}{6} = 4 \cdot \frac{1}{2} = 2$.
   Thus, the rectangular coordinates are $(2\sqrt{3}, 2)$.

9. $(r, \theta) = (\sqrt{2}, -\frac{\pi}{4})$. So $x = r\cos\theta = \sqrt{2}\cos(-\frac{\pi}{4}) = \sqrt{2} \cdot \frac{1}{\sqrt{2}} = 1$, and $y = r\sin\theta = \sqrt{2}\sin(-\frac{\pi}{4})$
   $= \sqrt{2} \cdot \frac{-1}{\sqrt{2}} = -1$. Thus, the rectangular coordinates are $(1, -1)$.

11. $(r, \theta) = (5, 5\pi)$. So $x = r\cos\theta = 5\cos 5\pi = -5$, and $y = r\sin\theta = 5\sin 5\pi = 0$. Thus, the
    rectangular coordinates are $(-5, 0)$.

13. $(x, y) = (-1, 1)$. Since $r^2 = x^2 + y^2$, we have $r^2 = (-1)^2 + 1^2 = 2$, so $r = \sqrt{2}$. Now
    $\tan\theta = \frac{y}{x} = \frac{1}{-1} = -1$, so, since the point is in the second quadrant, $\theta = \frac{3\pi}{4}$. Thus, the polar
    coordinates are $(\sqrt{2}, \frac{3\pi}{4})$.

15. $(x, y) = (\sqrt{8}, \sqrt{8})$. Since $r^2 = x^2 + y^2$, we have $r^2 = (\sqrt{8})^2 + (\sqrt{8})^2 = 16$, so $r = 4$. Now
    $\tan\theta = \frac{y}{x} = \frac{\sqrt{8}}{\sqrt{8}} = 1$, so, since the point is in the first quadrant, $\theta = \frac{\pi}{4}$. Thus, the polar coordinates
    are $(4, \frac{\pi}{4})$.

17. $(x, y) = (3, 4)$. Since $r^2 = x^2 + y^2$, we have $r^2 = 3^2 + 4^2 = 25$, so $r = 5$. Now $\tan\theta = \dfrac{y}{x} = \dfrac{4}{3}$, so, since the point is in the first quadrant, $\theta = \tan^{-1}\frac{4}{3}$. Thus, the polar coordinates are $(5, \tan^{-1}\frac{4}{3})$.

19. $x = y \quad\Leftrightarrow\quad r\cos\theta = r\sin\theta \quad\Leftrightarrow\quad \tan\theta = 1$, and so $\theta = \frac{\pi}{4}$.

21. $y = x^2$. We substitute and then solve for r: $r\sin\theta = (r\cos\theta)^2 = r^2\cos^2\theta \quad\Leftrightarrow\quad \sin\theta = r\cos^2\theta$ $\Leftrightarrow\quad r = \dfrac{\sin\theta}{\cos^2\theta} = \tan\theta\sec\theta$.

23. $x = 4$. We substitute and then solve for r: $r\cos\theta = 4 \quad\Leftrightarrow\quad r = \dfrac{4}{\cos\theta} = 4\sec\theta$.

25. $r = 7$. But $r^2 = x^2 + y^2$, so $x^2 + y^2 = r^2 = 49$. Hence, the equivalent equation in rectangular coordinates is $x^2 + y^2 = 49$.

27. $r\cos\theta = 6$. But $x = r\cos\theta$, and so $x = 6$ is the equation.

29. $r^2 = \tan\theta$. Substituting $r^2 = x^2 + y^2$ and $\tan\theta = \dfrac{y}{x}$, we get $x^2 + y^2 = \dfrac{y}{x}$.

31. $r = \dfrac{1}{\sin\theta - \cos\theta} \quad\Rightarrow\quad r(\sin\theta - \cos\theta) = 1 \quad\Leftrightarrow\quad r\sin\theta - r\cos\theta = 1$, and since $r\cos\theta = x$ and $r\sin\theta = y$, we get $y - x = 1$.

33. $r = 1 + \cos\theta$. If we multiply both sides of this equation by r we get $r^2 = r + r\cos\theta$. Thus $r^2 - r\cos\theta = r$, and squaring both sides gives $(r^2 - r\cos\theta)^2 = r^2 \quad\Leftrightarrow\quad (x^2 + y^2 - x)^2 = x^2 + y^2$

35. $r = 2\sec\theta \quad\Leftrightarrow\quad r = 2\cdot\dfrac{1}{\cos\theta} \quad\Leftrightarrow\quad r\cos\theta = 2 \quad\Leftrightarrow\quad x = 2$.

37. $\sec\theta = 2 \quad\Leftrightarrow\quad \cos\theta = \frac{1}{2} \quad\Leftrightarrow\quad \theta = \pm\frac{\pi}{3} \quad\Leftrightarrow\quad \tan\theta = \pm\sqrt{3} \quad\Leftrightarrow\quad \dfrac{y}{x} = \pm\sqrt{3} \quad\Leftrightarrow$ $y = \pm\sqrt{3}x$.

39. VI   41. II   43. I

45. $r = 3$. Circle.   47. $\theta = -\frac{\pi}{2}$. Line.

49. $r = 6 \sin \theta$. Circle.

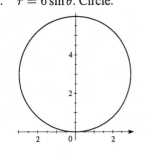

51. $r = -2 \cos \theta$. Circle.

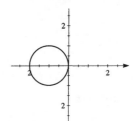

53. $r = 2 - 2 \cos \theta$. Cardioid.

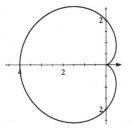

55. $r = -3 (1 + \sin \theta)$. Cardioid.

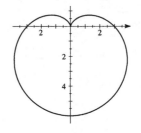

57. $r = \theta, \theta \geq 0$

59. $r = \sin 2\theta$

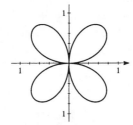

61. $r^2 = \cos 2\theta$

63. $r = 2 + \sin \theta$

65. $r = 2 + \sec \theta$

67. $r = \cos\left(\frac{\theta}{2}\right)$; Domain: $[0, 4\pi]$

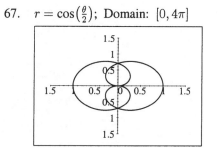

69. $r = 1 + 2\sin\left(\frac{\theta}{2}\right)$; Domain: $[0, 4\pi]$

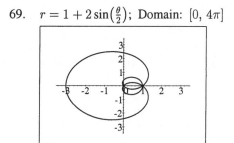

71. $r = 1 + \sin n\theta$. The number of loops is n.

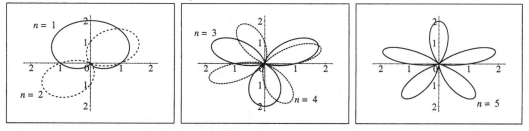

73. The graph of $r = \sin\left(\frac{\theta}{2}\right)$ is IV, since the graph must contain the points $(0, 0)$, $\left(\frac{1}{\sqrt{2}}, \frac{\pi}{2}\right)$, $(1, \pi)$, and so on.

75. The graph of $r = \theta \sin\theta$ is III, since for $\theta = \frac{\pi}{2}, \frac{5\pi}{2}, \frac{7\pi}{2}, \ldots$ the values of r are also $\frac{\pi}{2}, \frac{5\pi}{2}, \frac{7\pi}{2}, \ldots$. Thus the graph must cross the vertical axis at an infinite number of points.

77. (a) In rectangular coordinates, the points (r_1, θ_1) and (r_2, θ_2) are $(x_1, y_1) = (r_1 \cos\theta_1, r_1 \sin\theta_1)$ and $(x_2, y_2) = (r_2 \cos\theta_2, r_2 \sin\theta_2)$. Then, the distance between the points is

$$D = \sqrt{(x_1 - x_2)^2 + (y_1 - y_2)^2} = \sqrt{(r_1 \cos\theta_1 - r_2 \cos\theta_2)^2 + (r_1 \sin\theta_1 - r_2 \sin\theta_2)^2} =$$
$$\sqrt{r_1^2 \left(\cos^2\theta_1 + \sin^2\theta_1\right) + r_2^2 \left(\cos^2\theta_2 + \sin^2\theta_2\right) - 2r_1 r_2 \left(\cos\theta_1 \cos\theta_2 + \sin\theta_1 \sin\theta_2\right)} =$$
$$\sqrt{r_1^2 + r_2^2 - 2r_1 r_2 \cos(\theta_1 - \theta_2)}$$

(b) The distance between the points $(3, \frac{3\pi}{4})$ and $(-1, \frac{7\pi}{6})$ is

$$D = \sqrt{3^2 + (-1)^2 - 2(3)(-1)\cos(\tfrac{3\pi}{4} - \tfrac{7\pi}{6})} = \sqrt{9 + 1 + 6\cos(-\tfrac{5\pi}{12})} =$$
$$\sqrt{10 + 6\cos\tfrac{5\pi}{12}} \approx 3.40.$$

79. The graphs of $r = 1 + \sin(\theta - \frac{\pi}{6})$ and $r = 1 + \sin(\theta - \frac{\pi}{3})$ have the same shape as $r = 1 + \sin\theta$, rotated through angles of $\frac{\pi}{6}$ and $\frac{\pi}{3}$, respectively. Similarly, the graph of $r = f(\theta - \alpha)$ is the graph of $r = f(\theta)$ rotated by the angle α.

81. $y = 2 \quad \Leftrightarrow \quad r\sin\theta = 2 \quad \Leftrightarrow \quad r = 2\csc\theta$. The rectangular coordinate system gives the simpler equation here. It is easier to study lines in rectangular coordinates.

Exercises 9.7

1. Substituting $e = \frac{2}{3}$ and $d = 3$ into the general equation of a conic with vertical directrix, we get
$$r = \frac{\frac{2}{3} \cdot 3}{1 + \frac{2}{3}\cos\theta} \quad \Leftrightarrow \quad r = \frac{6}{3 + 2\cos\theta}.$$

3. Substituting $e = 1$ and $d = 2$ into the general equation of a conic with horizontal directrix, we get
$$r = \frac{1 \cdot 2}{1 + \sin\theta} \quad \Leftrightarrow \quad r = \frac{2}{1 + \sin\theta}.$$

5. $r = 5\sec\theta \quad \Leftrightarrow \quad r\cos\theta = 5 \quad \Leftrightarrow \quad x = 5.$ So $d = 5$ and $e = 4$ gives $r = \dfrac{4 \cdot 5}{1 + 4\cos\theta} \quad \Leftrightarrow$
$$r = \frac{20}{1 + 4\cos\theta}.$$

7. Since this is a parabola whose focus is at the origin and vertex at $(5, \pi/2)$, the directrix must be $y = 10$. So $d = 10$ and $e = 1$ gives $r = \dfrac{1 \cdot 10}{1 + \sin\theta} = \dfrac{10}{1 + \sin\theta}.$

9. (a) $r = \dfrac{4}{1 + 3\cos\theta} \quad \Rightarrow \quad e = 3$, thus the conic is a hyperbola.

   (b) The vertices occur where $\theta = 0$ and $\theta = \pi$.

   Now $\theta = 0 \quad \Rightarrow \quad r = \dfrac{4}{1 + 3\cos 0} = 1,$

   and $\theta = \pi \quad \Rightarrow \quad r = \dfrac{4}{1 + 3\cos\pi} = \dfrac{4}{-2} = -2.$

   Thus the vertices are $(1, 0)$ and $(-2, \pi)$.

11. (a) $r = \dfrac{2}{1 - \cos\theta} \quad \Rightarrow \quad e = 1$, thus the conic is a parabola.

    (b) Substituting $\theta = \pi$, we have
    $$r = \frac{2}{1 - \cos\pi} = \frac{2}{2} = 1. \text{ Thus the vertex is } (1, \pi).$$

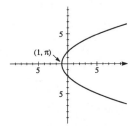

13. (a) $r = \dfrac{6}{2 + \sin\theta} \quad \Leftrightarrow \quad r = \dfrac{\frac{1}{2} \cdot 6}{1 + \frac{1}{2}\sin\theta} \quad \Rightarrow \quad e = \frac{1}{2}$, thus the conic is an ellipse.

(b) The vertices occur where $\theta = \frac{\pi}{2}$ and $\theta = \frac{3\pi}{2}$.

Now $\theta = \frac{\pi}{2}$ $\Rightarrow$ $r = \dfrac{6}{2 + \sin\frac{\pi}{2}} = \frac{6}{3} = 2,$

and $\theta = \frac{3\pi}{2}$ $\Rightarrow$ $r = \dfrac{6}{2 + \sin\frac{3\pi}{2}} = \frac{6}{1} = 6.$

Thus the vertices are $\left(2, \frac{\pi}{2}\right)$ and $\left(6, \frac{3\pi}{2}\right)$.

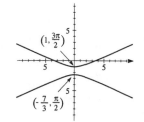

15. (a) $r = \dfrac{7}{2 - 5\sin\theta}$ $\Leftrightarrow$ $r = \dfrac{\frac{7}{2}}{1 - \frac{5}{2}\sin\theta}$ $\Rightarrow$ $e = \frac{5}{2}$, thus this conic is a hyperbola.

(b) The vertices occur where $\theta = \frac{\pi}{2}$ and $\theta = \frac{3\pi}{2}$.

$r = \dfrac{7}{2 - 5\sin\frac{\pi}{2}} = \frac{7}{-3} = -\frac{7}{3}$, and $\theta = \frac{3\pi}{2}$

$\Rightarrow$ $r = \dfrac{7}{2 - 5\sin\frac{3\pi}{2}} = \frac{7}{7} = 1.$

Thus the vertices are $\left(-\frac{7}{3}, \frac{\pi}{2}\right)$ and $\left(1, \frac{3\pi}{2}\right)$.

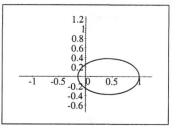

17. (a) $r = \dfrac{1}{4 - 3\cos\theta}$ $\Leftrightarrow$ $r = \dfrac{\frac{1}{4}}{1 - \frac{3}{4}\cos\theta}$

$\Rightarrow$ $e = \frac{3}{4}$. Since $ed = \frac{1}{4}$ we have

$d = \dfrac{\frac{1}{4}}{e} = \frac{4}{3} \cdot \frac{1}{4} = \frac{1}{3}$. Therefore the

eccentricity is $\frac{3}{4}$ and the directrix is

$x = -\frac{1}{3}$ $\Leftrightarrow$ $r = -\frac{1}{3}\sec\theta.$

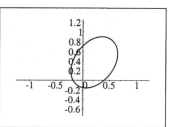

(b) We replace θ by $\theta - \frac{\pi}{3}$ to get

$r = \dfrac{1}{4 - 3\cos\left(\theta - \frac{\pi}{3}\right)}.$

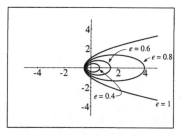

19. The ellipse is nearly circular when e is close to 0 and becomes more elongated as $e \to 1^-$. At $e = 1$, the curve becomes a parabola.

21. (a) Since the polar form of an ellipse with directrix $x = -d$ is $r = \dfrac{ed}{1 - e\cos\theta}$ we need to show that $ed = a(1 - e^2)$. From the proof of the Equivalent Description of Conics we have

$a^2 = \dfrac{e^2 d^2}{(1 - e^2)^2}$. Since the conic is an ellipse, $e < 1$ and so the variables a, d, and $(1 - e^2)$ are

all positive. Thus we can take the square roots of both sides. Thus $a^2 = \dfrac{e^2 d^2}{(1 - e^2)^2}$ $\Leftrightarrow$

$a = \dfrac{ed}{1 - e^2}$ $\Leftrightarrow$ $ed = a(1 - e^2)$. As a result $r = \dfrac{ed}{1 - e \cos\theta}$ $\Leftrightarrow$ $r = \dfrac{a(1 - e^2)}{1 - e \cos\theta}$.

(b) Since $2a = 2.99 \times 10^8$ we have $a = 1.495 \times 10^8$ so the polar equation for the earth's orbit

(using $e \approx 0.017$) is $r = \dfrac{1.495 \times 10^8 [1 - (0.017)^2]}{1 - 0.017 \cos\theta} \approx \dfrac{1.49 \times 10^8}{1 - 0.017 \cos\theta}$.

23. From Exercise 22, we have:
at perihelion, $r = 4.43 \times 10^9 = a(1 - e)$;
at aphelion, $r = 7.37 \times 10^9 = a(1 + e)$.

Dividing these equations gives $\dfrac{7.37 \times 10^9}{4.43 \times 10^9} = \dfrac{a(1 + e)}{a(1 - e)}$ $\Leftrightarrow$ $1.664 = \dfrac{1 + e}{1 - e}$ $\Leftrightarrow$

$1.664(1 - e) = 1 + e$ $\Leftrightarrow$ $1.664 - 1 = e + 1.664$ $\Leftrightarrow$ $0.664 = 2.664e$ $\Leftrightarrow$

$e = \frac{0.664}{2.664} \approx 0.25$.

25. The r-coordinate of the satellite will be it's distance from the focus (the center of the earth). From the r-coordinate we can easily calculate the height of the satellite

Exercises 9.8

1. (a) $x = 2t, y = t + 6$

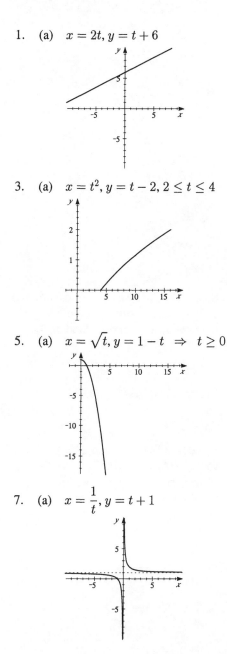

(b) Since $x = 2t$, $t = \dfrac{x}{2}$ and so $y = \dfrac{x}{2} + 6$

  $\Leftrightarrow$ $x - 2y + 12 = 0$.

3. (a) $x = t^2, y = t - 2, 2 \le t \le 4$

(b) Since $x = t^2$, $t = \sqrt{x}$ and since $2 \le t \le 4$ we have $4 \le x \le 16$. Thus $y = \sqrt{x} - 2$ with $4 \le x \le 16$.

5. (a) $x = \sqrt{t}, y = 1 - t \ \Rightarrow \ t \ge 0$

(b) Since $x = \sqrt{t}$, we have $x^2 = t$, and so $y = 1 - x^2$ with $x \ge 0$.

7. (a) $x = \dfrac{1}{t}, y = t + 1$

(b) Since $x = \dfrac{1}{t}$ we have $t = \dfrac{1}{x}$ and so $y = \dfrac{1}{x} + 1$.

9. (a) $x = 4t^2, y = 8t^3$

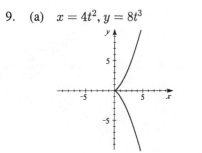

(b) Since $x = 4t^2$ we have
$x\sqrt{x} = 4t^2 \cdot 2t = 8t^3$, and so $y = x\sqrt{x}$.

11. (a) $x = 2\sin t, y = 2\cos t, 0 \le t \le \pi$

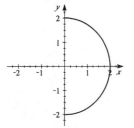

(b) $x^2 = (2\sin t)^2 = 4\sin^2 t$, and
$y^2 = (2\cos t)^2 = 4\cos^2 t$. Hence,
$x^2 + y^2 = 4\sin^2 t + 4\cos^2 t = 4 \quad \Leftrightarrow$
$x^2 + y^2 = 4$, where $x \ge 0$.

13. (a) $x = \sin^2 t, y = \sin^4 t$

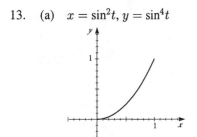

(b) Since $x = \sin^2 t$ we have $x^2 = \sin^4 t$ and
so $y = x^2$. But since $0 \le \sin^2 t \le 1$ we
only get the part of this parabola for
which $0 \le x \le 1$.

15. (a) $x = \cos t, y = \cos 2t$

(b) Since $x = \cos t$ we have $x^2 = \cos^2 t$ and
so $2x^2 - 1 = 2\cos^2 t - 1 = \cos 2t = y$.
Hence, the rectangular coordinate
equation is $y = 2x^2 - 1$, with
$-1 \le x \le 1$.

17. (a) $x = \sec t, y = \tan t, 0 \le t < \frac{\pi}{2} \quad \Rightarrow$
         $x \ge 1$ and $y \ge 0$.

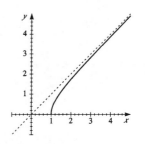

(b) $x^2 = \sec^2 t$, $y^2 = \tan^2 t$, and $y^2 + 1 = \tan^2 t + 1 = \sec^2 t = x^2$. Therefore, $y^2 + 1 = x^2$ ⇔ $x^2 - y^2 = 1$, $x \geq 1$, $y \geq 0$.

19. (a) $x = e^t$, $y = e^{-t}$ ⇒ $x > 0$, $y > 0$.   (b) $xy = e^t \cdot e^{-t} = e^0 = 1$. Hence, the equation is $xy = 1$, with $x > 0$, $y > 0$.

21. (a) $x = \cos^2 t$, $y = \sin^2 t$ (b) $x + y = \cos^2 t + \sin^2 t = 1$. Hence, the equation is $x + y = 1$ with $0 \leq x, y \leq 1$.

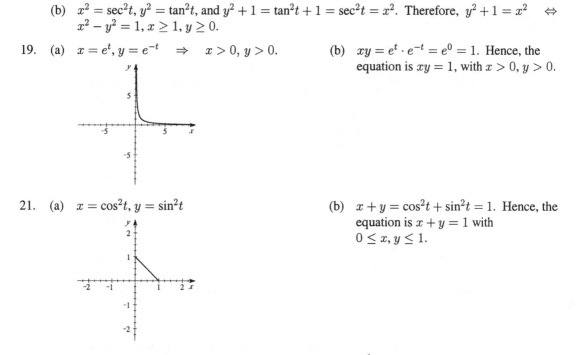

23. Since the line passes through the point $(4, -1)$ and has slope $\frac{1}{2}$, parametric equations for the line are $x = 4 + t$, $y = -1 + \frac{1}{2}t$.

25. Since the line passes through the points $(6, 7)$ and $(7, 8)$, its slope is $\frac{8-7}{7-6} = 1$. Thus, parametric equations for the line are $x = 6 + t$, $y = 7 + t$.

27. Since $\cos^2 t + \sin^2 t = 1$, we have $a^2 \cos^2 t + a^2 \sin^2 t = a^2$. If we let $x = a \cos t$ and $y = a \sin t$, then $x^2 + y^2 = a^2$. Hence, parametric equations for the circle are $x = a \cos t$, $y = a \sin t$.

29. $x = a \tan \theta$ ⇔ $\tan \theta = \dfrac{x}{a}$ ⇒ $\tan^2 \theta = \dfrac{x^2}{a^2}$. Also, $y = b \sec \theta$ ⇔ $\sec \theta = \dfrac{y}{b}$ ⇒ $\sec^2 \theta = \dfrac{y^2}{b^2}$. Since $\tan^2 \theta = \sec^2 \theta - 1$, we have $\dfrac{x^2}{a^2} = \dfrac{y^2}{b^2} - 1$ ⇔ $\dfrac{y^2}{b^2} - \dfrac{x^2}{a^2} = 1$, which is the equation of a hyperbola.

31. $x = t \cos t$, $y = t \sin t$, $t \geq 0$

t	x	y
0	0	0
$\frac{\pi}{4}$	$\frac{\pi\sqrt{2}}{8}$	$\frac{\pi\sqrt{2}}{8}$
$\frac{\pi}{2}$	0	$\frac{\pi}{2}$
$\frac{3\pi}{4}$	$-\frac{3\pi\sqrt{2}}{8}$	$\frac{3\pi\sqrt{2}}{8}$
π	$-\pi$	0

t	x	y
$\frac{5\pi}{4}$	$-\frac{5\pi\sqrt{2}}{8}$	$-\frac{5\pi\sqrt{2}}{8}$
$\frac{3\pi}{2}$	0	$-\frac{3\pi}{2}$
$\frac{7\pi}{4}$	$\frac{7\pi\sqrt{2}}{8}$	$-\frac{7\pi\sqrt{2}}{8}$
2π	2π	0

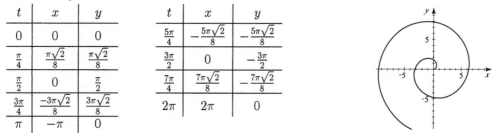

33. $x = \dfrac{3t}{1+t^3}, y = \dfrac{3t^2}{1+t^3}, t \neq -1$

t	x	y	t	x	y
-0.90	-9.96	8.97	-1.10	9.97	-10.97
-0.75	-3.89	2.92	-1.25	3.93	-4.92
-0.50	-1.71	0.86	-1.5	1.89	-2.84
0	0	0	-2	0.86	-1.71
0.5	1.33	0.67	-2.5	0.51	-1.28
1	1.5	1.5	-3	0.35	-1.04
1.5	1.03	1.54	-3.5	0.25	-0.88
2	0.67	1.33	-4	0.19	-0.76
2.5	0.45	1.13	-4.5	015	-0.67
3	0.32	0.96	-5	0.12	-0.60
4	0.18	0.74	-6	0.08	-0.50
5	0.12	0.60	-7	0.06	-0.43
6	0.08	0.50	-8	0.05	-0.38

As $t \to -1^-$ we have $x \to -\infty$ and $y \to \infty$.
As $t \to -1^+$ we have $x \to \infty$ and $y \to -\infty$.
As $t \to \infty$ we have $x \to 0^+$ and $y \to 0^+$.
As $t \to -\infty$ we have $x \to 0^+$ and $y \to 0^-$.

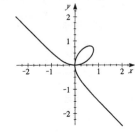

35. $x = (v_0 \cos \alpha)\, t, y = (v_0 \sin \alpha)\, t - 16t^2$. From the equation for x, $t = \dfrac{x}{v_0 \cos \alpha}$. Substituting into

the equation for y gives $y = (v_0 \sin \alpha) \dfrac{x}{v_0 \cos \alpha} - 16 \left(\dfrac{x}{v_0 \cos \alpha} \right)^2 = x \tan \alpha - \dfrac{16x^2}{v_0^2 \cos^2 \alpha}$. Thus the

equation is of the form $y = c_1 x - c_2 x^2$, where c_1 and c_2 are constants, so its graph is a parabola.

37. $x = \sin t, y = 2 \cos 3t$

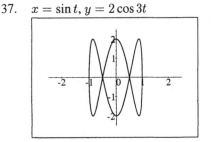

39. $x = 3 \sin 5t, y = 5 \cos 3t$

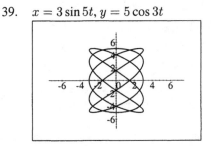

41. $x = \sin(\cos t), y = \cos t^{3/2}, 0 \leq t \leq 2\pi$

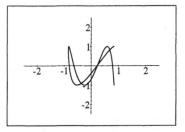

43.   (a) $r = e^{\theta/12}$, $0 \le \theta \le 4\pi$ $\Rightarrow$

(b)

      $x = e^{t/12} \cdot \cos t$ and $y = e^{t/12} \cdot \sin t$

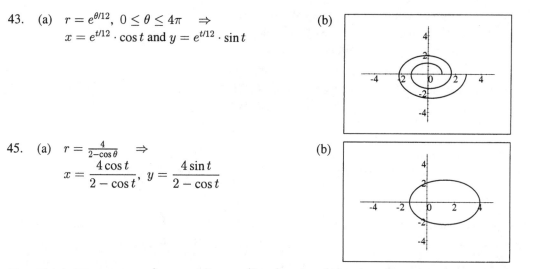

45.   (a) $r = \dfrac{4}{2 - \cos\theta}$ $\Rightarrow$

(b)

      $x = \dfrac{4\cos t}{2 - \cos t}$, $y = \dfrac{4\sin t}{2 - \cos t}$

47.   This is III, since $y = t^2 - t = (t^2 - t + \frac{1}{4}) - \frac{1}{4} = (t - \frac{1}{2})^2 - \frac{1}{4}$, and so $y \ge -\frac{1}{4}$ on this curve, while x is unbounded.

49.   This is II, since the values of x and y should oscillate about their values on the line $x = t$, $y = t$
      $\Leftrightarrow$ $y = x$.

51.   If we modify Figure 6 so that $|PC| = b$, then
      by the same reasoning as in Example 5, we see
      that $x = |OT| - |PQ| = a\theta - b\sin\theta$ and
      $y = |TC| - |CQ| = a - b\cos\theta$. We graph
      the case where $a = 3$ and $b = 2$.

53.   (a)   We first note that the center of circle C (the small
            circle) has coordinates $([a - b]\cos\theta, [a - b]\sin\theta)$.
            Now the arc PQ has the same length as the arc
            $P'Q$ (these two arcs are shown as thicker lines in
            the figure on the right). Thus $b\phi = a\theta$ $\Leftrightarrow$
            $\phi = \dfrac{a}{b}\theta$, and so $\phi - \theta = \dfrac{a}{b}\theta - \theta = \dfrac{a - b}{b}\theta$. Thus
            the x-coordinate of P is the x-coordinate of the
            center of circle C plus
            $b \cdot \cos(\phi - \theta) = b\cos\left(\dfrac{a - b}{b}\theta\right)$, and the y-
            coordinate of P is the y-coordinate of the center of
            circle C minus $b \cdot \sin(\phi - \theta) = b\sin\left(\dfrac{a - b}{b}\theta\right)$.
            So $x = (a - b)\cos\theta + b\cos\left(\dfrac{a - b}{b}\theta\right)$ and $y = (a - b)\sin\theta - b\sin\left(\dfrac{a - b}{b}\theta\right)$.

      (b)   If $a = 4b$, $b = \frac{a}{4}$, and $x = \frac{3}{4}a\cos\theta + \frac{1}{4}a\cos 3\theta$,

$y = \frac{3}{4}a \sin\theta - \frac{1}{4}a \sin 3\theta$. From Example 2 in Section 7.3, we see that $\cos 3\theta = 4\cos^3\theta - 3\cos\theta$. Similarly, one can prove that $\sin 3\theta = 3\sin\theta - 4\sin^3\theta$. Substituting, we get

$x = \frac{3}{4}a \cos\theta + \frac{1}{4}a \left(4\cos^3\theta - 3\cos\theta\right) = a\cos^3\theta$, and

$y = \frac{3}{4}a \sin\theta - \frac{1}{4}a \left(3\sin\theta - 4\sin^3\theta\right) = a\sin^3\theta$. Thus,

$x^{2/3} + y^{2/3} = a^{2/3}\cos^2\theta + a^{2/3}\sin^2\theta = a^{2/3}$, so $x^{2/3} + y^{2/3} = a^{2/3}$.

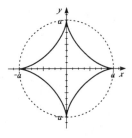

55. The polar coordinate equation for the circle is $r = 2a\sin\theta$. Thus the coordinates of Q are $x = r\cos\theta = 2a\sin\theta\cos\theta$ and $y = r\sin\theta = 2a\sin^2\theta$. The coordinates of R are $x = 2a\cot\theta$ and $y = 2a$. Since P is the midpoint of QR, we use the midpoint formula to get $x = a(\sin\theta\cos\theta + \cot\theta)$ and $y = a(1 + \sin^2\theta)$.

57. We use the equation for y from Example 5 and solve for θ. Thus for $0 \le \theta \le \pi$, $y = a(1 - \cos\theta)$

$\Leftrightarrow \dfrac{a - y}{a} = \cos\theta \quad \Leftrightarrow \quad \theta = \cos^{-1}\left(\dfrac{a - y}{a}\right)$. Substituting into the equation for x, we get:

$x = a\left[\cos^{-1}\left(\dfrac{a - y}{a}\right) - \sin\left(\cos^{-1}\left(\dfrac{a - y}{a}\right)\right)\right]$. However,

$\sin\left(\cos^{-1}\left(\dfrac{a - y}{a}\right)\right) = \sqrt{1 - \left(\dfrac{a - y}{a}\right)^2} = \dfrac{\sqrt{2ay - y^2}}{a}$. Thus

$x = a\left[\cos^{-1}\left(\dfrac{a - y}{a}\right) - \dfrac{\sqrt{2ay - y^2}}{a}\right]$, and we have $\dfrac{\sqrt{2ay - y^2} + x}{a} = \cos^{-1}\left(\dfrac{a - y}{a}\right) \quad \Rightarrow$

$1 - \dfrac{y}{a} = \cos\left(\dfrac{\sqrt{2ay - y^2} + x}{a}\right) \quad \Rightarrow \quad y = a\left[1 - \cos\left(\dfrac{\sqrt{2ay - y^2} + x}{a}\right)\right]$.

59. C: $x = t$, $y = t^2$. D: $x = \sqrt{t}$, $y = t$, $t \ge 0$. E: $x = \sin t$, $y = 1 - \cos^2 t$. F: $x = e^t$, $y = e^{2t}$.

(a) For C: $x = t$, $y = t^2 \quad \Rightarrow \quad y = x^2$.
    For D: $x = \sqrt{t}$, $y = t \quad \Rightarrow \quad y = x^2$.
    For E: $x = \sin t \quad \Rightarrow \quad x^2 = \sin^2 t = 1 - \cos^2 t = y$ and so $y = x^2$.
    For F: $x = e^t \quad \Rightarrow \quad x^2 = e^{2t} = y$ and so $y = x^2$. Therefore, the points on all four curves satisfy the same rectangular coordinate equation.

(b) The curve in C is the entire parabola
    $y = x^2$.

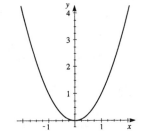

The curve in D is the right-half of the
parabola (because $t \geq 0$ and so $x \geq 0$).

The curve in E is the portion of the
parabola where $-1 \leq x \leq 1$.

The curve in F is the portion of the
parabola where $x > 0$.

Review Exercises for Chapter 9

1. $x^2 + 8y = 0 \iff x^2 = -8y.$ This is a parabola that has
    $4p = -8 \iff p = -2.$
    Vertex: $(0,0)$; focus: $(0,-2)$; directrix: $y = 2.$

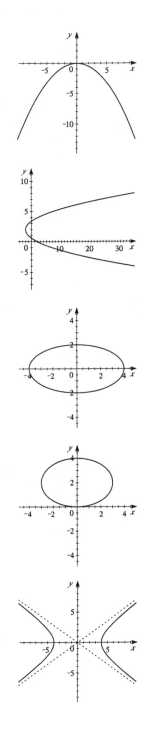

3. $x - y^2 + 4y - 2 = 0 \iff x - (y^2 - 4y + 4) - 2 = -4 \iff$
    $x - (y-2)^2 = -2 \iff (y-2)^2 = x + 2.$ This is a parabola
    that has $4p = 1 \iff p = \frac{1}{4}.$
    Vertex: $(-2,2)$; focus: $\left(-2+\frac{1}{4}, 2\right) = \left(-\frac{7}{4}, 2\right)$; directrix:
    $x = -2 - \frac{1}{4} = -\frac{9}{4}.$

5. $x^2 + 4y^2 = 16 \iff \dfrac{x^2}{16} + \dfrac{y^2}{4} = 1.$ This is an ellipse with
    $a = 4, b = 2,$ and $c = \sqrt{16 - 4} = 2\sqrt{3}.$
    Center: $(0,0)$; vertices: $(\pm 4, 0)$; foci: $(\pm 2\sqrt{3}, 0)$; length of the
    major axis: $2a = 8$; length of the minor axis: $2b = 4.$

7. $4x^2 + 9y^2 = 36y \iff 4x^2 + 9(y^2 - 4y + 4) = 36 \iff$
    $4x^2 + 9(y-2)^2 = 36 \iff \dfrac{x^2}{9} + \dfrac{(y-2)^2}{4} = 1.$ This is an
    ellipse with $a = 3, b = 2,$ and $c = \sqrt{9-4} = \sqrt{5}.$
    Center: $(0,2)$; vertices: $(\pm 3, 2)$; foci: $(\pm\sqrt{5}, 2)$; length of the
    major axis: $2a = 6$; length of the minor axis: $2b = 4.$

9. $x^2 - 2y^2 = 16 \iff \dfrac{x^2}{16} - \dfrac{y^2}{8} = 1.$ This is a hyperbola that has
    $a = 4, b = 2\sqrt{2},$ and $c = \sqrt{16+8} = \sqrt{24} = 2\sqrt{6}.$
    Center: $(0,0)$; vertices: $(\pm 4, 0)$; foci: $(\pm 2\sqrt{6}, 0)$; asymptotes:
    $y = \pm\frac{2\sqrt{2}}{4} x \iff y = \pm\frac{1}{\sqrt{2}} x.$

11. $9y^2 + 18y = x^2 + 6x + 18$ $\Leftrightarrow$

$9(y^2 + 2y + 1) = (x^2 + 6x + 9) + 9 - 9 + 18$ $\Leftrightarrow$.

$9(y + 1)^2 - (x + 3)^2 = 18$ $\Leftrightarrow$ $\dfrac{(y + 1)^2}{2} - \dfrac{(x + 3)^2}{18} = 1$. This is

a hyperbola that has $a = \sqrt{2}$, $b = 3\sqrt{2}$, and $c = \sqrt{2 + 18} = 2\sqrt{5}$.

Center: $(-3, -1)$; vertices: $(-3, -1 \pm \sqrt{2})$; foci:

$(-3, -1 \pm 2\sqrt{5})$; asymptotes: $y + 1 = \pm\frac{1}{3}(x + 3)$ $\Leftrightarrow$ $y = \frac{1}{3}x$

and $y = -\frac{1}{3}x - 2$.

13. This is a parabola that opens to the right with its vertex at $(0, 0)$ and the focus at $(2, 0)$. So $p = 2$, and the equation is $y^2 = 4(2)x$ $\Leftrightarrow$ $y^2 = 8x$.

15. From the graph, the center is $(0, 0)$, and the vertices are $(0, -4)$ and $(0, 4)$. Since a is the distance from the center to a vertex, we have $a = 4$. Because one focus is $(0, 5)$, we have $c = 5$, and since $c^2 = a^2 + b^2$, we have $25 = 16 + b^2$ $\Leftrightarrow$ $b^2 = 9$. Thus the equation of the hyperbola is
$\dfrac{y^2}{16} - \dfrac{x^2}{9} = 1$.

17. From the graph, the center of the ellipse is $(4, 2)$, and so $a = 4$ and $b = 2$. The equation is
$\dfrac{(x - 4)^2}{4^2} + \dfrac{(y - 2)^2}{2^2} = 1$ $\Leftrightarrow$ $\dfrac{(x - 4)^2}{16} + \dfrac{(y - 2)^2}{4} = 1$.

19. $\dfrac{x^2}{12} + y = 1$ $\Leftrightarrow$ $\dfrac{x^2}{12} = -(y - 1)$ $\Leftrightarrow$ $x^2 = -12(y - 1)$. This
is a parabola that has $4p = -12$ $\Leftrightarrow$ $p = -3$.

Vertex: $(0, 1)$; focus: $(0, 1 - 3) = (0, -2)$.

21. $x^2 - y^2 + 144 = 0$ $\Leftrightarrow$ $\dfrac{y^2}{144} - \dfrac{x^2}{144} = 1$. This is a hyperbola

that has $a = 12$, $b = 12$, and $c = \sqrt{144 + 144} = 12\sqrt{2}$.

Vertices: $(0, \pm 12)$; foci: $(0, \pm 12\sqrt{2})$.

23. $4x^2 + y^2 = 8(x + y)$ $\Leftrightarrow$ $4(x^2 - 2x) + (y^2 - 8y) = 0$ $\Leftrightarrow$
$4(x^2 - 2x + 1) + (y^2 - 8y + 16) = 4 + 16$ $\Leftrightarrow$

$4(x - 1)^2 + (y - 4)^2 = 20$ $\Leftrightarrow$ $\dfrac{(x - 1)^2}{5} + \dfrac{(y - 4)^2}{20} = 1$. This

is an ellipse that has $a = 2\sqrt{5}$, $b = \sqrt{5}$, and $c = \sqrt{20 - 5} = \sqrt{15}$.

Vertices: $(1, 4 \pm 2\sqrt{5})$; foci: $(1, 4 \pm \sqrt{15})$.

25. $x = y^2 - 16y \quad \Leftrightarrow \quad x + 64 = y^2 - 16y + 64 \quad \Leftrightarrow$

$(y-8)^2 = x + 64.$ This is a parabola that has $4p = 1 \quad \Leftrightarrow \quad p = \frac{1}{4}.$

Vertex: $(-64, 8)$; focus: $\left(-64 + \frac{1}{4}, 8\right) = \left(-\frac{255}{4}, 8\right).$

27. $2x^2 - 12x + y^2 + 6y + 26 = 0 \quad \Leftrightarrow$

$2(x^2 - 6x) + (y^2 + 6y) = -26 \quad \Leftrightarrow$

$2(x^2 - 6x + 9) + (y^2 + 6y + 9) = -26 + 18 + 9 \quad \Leftrightarrow$

$2(x-3)^2 + (y+3)^2 = 1 \quad \Leftrightarrow \quad \dfrac{(x-3)^2}{\frac{1}{2}} + (y+3)^2 = 1.$ This is

an ellipse that has $a = 1$, $b = \frac{1}{\sqrt{2}}$, and $c = \sqrt{1 - \frac{1}{2}} = \frac{1}{\sqrt{2}}.$

Vertices: $(3, -3 \pm 1)$, so the vertices are $(3, -4)$ and $(3, -2)$; foci:

$\left(3, -3 \pm \frac{1}{\sqrt{2}}\right).$

29. $9x^2 + 8y^2 - 15x + 8y + 27 = 0 \quad \Leftrightarrow \quad 9\left(x^2 - \frac{5}{3}x + \frac{25}{36}\right) + 8\left(y^2 + y + \frac{1}{4}\right) = -27 + \frac{25}{4} + 2 \quad \Leftrightarrow$

$9\left(x - \frac{5}{6}\right)^2 + 8\left(y + \frac{1}{2}\right)^2 = -\frac{75}{4}.$ However, since the left-hand side of the equation is greater than or

equal to 0, there is no point that satisfies this equation. The graph is empty.

31.   The parabola has focus $(0, 1)$ and directrix $y = -1$. Therefore, $p = 1$ and so $4p = 4$. Since the

focus is on the y-axis and the vertex is $(0, 0)$, the equation of the parabola is $x^2 = 4y.$

33.   The hyperbola has vertices $(0, \pm 2)$ and asymptotes $y = \pm \frac{1}{2}x$. Therefore, $a = 2$, and the foci are on

the y-axis. Since the slopes of the asymptotes are $\pm \frac{1}{2} = \pm \dfrac{a}{b} \quad \Leftrightarrow \quad b = 2a = 4$, the equation of

the hyperbola is $\dfrac{y^2}{4} - \dfrac{x^2}{16} = 1.$

35.   The ellipse has foci $F_1(1, 1)$ and $F_2(1, 3)$, and one vertex is on the x-axis. Thus, $2c = 3 - 1 = 2$

$\Leftrightarrow \quad c = 1$, and so the center of the ellipse is $C(1, 2)$. Also, since one vertex is on the x-axis,

$a = 2 - 0 = 2$, and thus $b^2 = 4 - 1 = 3$. So the equation of the ellipse is

$\dfrac{(x-1)^2}{3} + \dfrac{(y-2)^2}{4} = 1.$

37.   The ellipse has vertices $V_1(7, 12)$ and $V_2(7, -8)$ and passes through the point $P(1, 8)$. Thus,

$2a = 12 - (-8) = 20 \quad \Leftrightarrow \quad a = 10$, and the center is $\left(7, \frac{-8+12}{2}\right) = (7, 2)$. Thus the equation of

the ellipse has the form $\dfrac{(x-7)^2}{b^2} + \dfrac{(y-2)^2}{100} = 1.$ Since the point $P(1, 8)$ is on the ellipse,

$\dfrac{(1-7)^2}{b^2} + \dfrac{(8-2)^2}{100} = 1 \quad \Leftrightarrow \quad 3600 + 36b^2 = 100b^2 \quad \Leftrightarrow \quad 64b^2 = 3600 \quad \Leftrightarrow \quad b^2 = \dfrac{225}{4}.$

Therefore, the equation of the ellipse is $\dfrac{(x-7)^2}{225/4} + \dfrac{(y-2)^2}{100} = 1 \quad \Leftrightarrow$

$\dfrac{4(x-7)^2}{225} + \dfrac{(y-2)^2}{100} = 1.$

39. Since $(0,0)$ and $(1600,0)$ are both points on the parabola, the x-coordinate of the vertex is 800. And since the highest point it reaches is 3200, the y-coordinate of the vertex is 3200. Thus the vertex is $(800, 3200)$, and the equation is of the form $(x - 800)^2 = 4p(y - 3200)$. Substituting the point $(0,0)$, we get $(0 - 800)^2 = 4p(0 - 3200)$ $\Leftrightarrow$ $640000 = -12800p$ $\Leftrightarrow$ $p = -50$. So the equation is $(x - 800)^2 = 4(-50)(y - 3200)$ $\Leftrightarrow$ $(x - 800)^2 = -200(y - 3200)$.

41. The length of the major axis is $2a = 186{,}000{,}000$ $\Leftrightarrow$ $a = 93{,}000{,}000$. The eccentricity is $e = \frac{c}{a} = 0.017$, and so $c = 0.017(93{,}000{,}000) = 1{,}581{,}000$.

(a) The earth is closest to the sun when the distance is $a - c = 93{,}000{,}000 - 1{,}581{,}000$ $= 91{,}419{,}000$.

(b) The earth is furthest from the sun when the distance is $a + c = 93{,}000{,}000 + 1{,}581{,}000$ $= 94{,}581{,}000$.

43. (a) The graphs of $\dfrac{x^2}{16 + k^2} + \dfrac{y^2}{k^2} = 1$ for $k = 1, 2, 4$, and 8 are shown in the figure.

(b) $c^2 = (16 + k^2) - k^2 = 16$ $\Rightarrow$ $c = \pm 4$. Since the center is $(0, 0)$, the foci of each of the ellipses are $(\pm 4, 0)$.

45. (a) $x^2 + 4xy + y^2 = 1$. Then $A = 1$, $B = 4$, and $C = 1$, so the discriminant is $4^2 - 4(1)(1) = 12$. Since the discriminant is positive the equation represents a hyperbola.

(b) $\cot 2\phi = \frac{A-C}{B} = \frac{1-1}{4} = 0$ $\Rightarrow$ $2\phi = 90°$ $\Leftrightarrow$ $\phi = 45°$. Therefore, $x = \dfrac{X}{\sqrt{2}} - \dfrac{Y}{\sqrt{2}}$ and $y = \dfrac{X}{\sqrt{2}} + \dfrac{Y}{\sqrt{2}}$. Substituting into the original equation gives:

$\left(\dfrac{X}{\sqrt{2}} - \dfrac{Y}{\sqrt{2}}\right)^2 + 4\left(\dfrac{X}{\sqrt{2}} - \dfrac{Y}{\sqrt{2}}\right)\left(\dfrac{X}{\sqrt{2}} + \dfrac{Y}{\sqrt{2}}\right) + \left(\dfrac{X}{\sqrt{2}} + \dfrac{Y}{\sqrt{2}}\right)^2 = 1$ $\Leftrightarrow$

$\frac{1}{2}(X^2 - 2XY + Y^2) + 2(X^2 + XY - XY - Y^2) + \frac{1}{2}(X^2 + 2XY + Y^2) = 1$ $\Leftrightarrow$

$3X^2 - Y^2 = 1$ $\Leftrightarrow$ $\dfrac{X^2}{\frac{1}{3}} - Y^2 = 1$. This is a hyperbola that has $a = \dfrac{1}{\sqrt{3}}$, $b = 1$, and $c = \sqrt{\frac{1}{3} + 1} = \frac{2}{\sqrt{3}}$. Therefore, the hyperbola has vertices $V(\pm\frac{1}{\sqrt{3}}, 0)$ and foci $F(\pm\frac{2}{\sqrt{3}}, 0)$, in XY-coordinates.

(c)

47. (a) $7x^2 - 6\sqrt{3}xy + 13y^2 - 4\sqrt{3}x - 4y = 0$. Then $A = 7$, $B = -6\sqrt{3}$, and $C = 13$, so the discriminant is $(-6\sqrt{3})^2 - 4(7)(13) = -256$. Since the discriminant is negative the equation represents an ellipse.

(b) $\cot 2\phi = \dfrac{A-C}{B} = \dfrac{7-13}{-6\sqrt{3}} = \dfrac{1}{\sqrt{3}} \;\Rightarrow\; 2\phi = 60° \;\Leftrightarrow\; \phi = 30°.$ Therefore,

$x = \dfrac{\sqrt{3}X}{2} - \dfrac{Y}{2}$ and $y = \dfrac{X}{2} + \dfrac{\sqrt{3}Y}{2}.$ Substituting into the original equation gives:

$$7\left(\dfrac{\sqrt{3}X}{2} - \dfrac{Y}{2}\right)^2 - 6\sqrt{3}\left(\dfrac{\sqrt{3}X}{2} - \dfrac{Y}{2}\right)\left(\dfrac{X}{2} + \dfrac{\sqrt{3}Y}{2}\right) + 13\left(\dfrac{X}{2} + \dfrac{\sqrt{3}Y}{2}\right)^2$$

$$- 4\sqrt{3}\left(\dfrac{\sqrt{3}X}{2} - \dfrac{Y}{2}\right) - 4\left(\dfrac{X}{2} + \dfrac{\sqrt{3}Y}{2}\right) = 0 \;\Leftrightarrow$$

$\frac{7}{4}(3X^2 - 2\sqrt{3}XY + Y^2) - \frac{3\sqrt{3}}{2}(\sqrt{3}X^2 + 3XY - XY - \sqrt{3}Y^2)$

$\qquad + \frac{13}{4}(X^2 + 2\sqrt{3}XY + 3Y^2) - 6X + 2\sqrt{3}Y - 2X - 2\sqrt{3}Y = 0 \;\Leftrightarrow$

$X^2\left(\frac{21}{4} - \frac{9}{2} + \frac{13}{4}\right) - 8X + Y^2\left(\frac{7}{4} + \frac{9}{2} + \frac{39}{4}\right) = 0 \;\Leftrightarrow\; 4X^2 - 8X + 16Y^2 = 0 \;\Leftrightarrow$

$4(X^2 - 2X + 1) + 16Y^2 = 4 \;\Leftrightarrow\; (X-1)^2 + 4Y^2 = 1.$ This ellipse has $a = 1$, $b = \frac{1}{2}$,

and $c = \sqrt{1 - \frac{1}{4}} = \frac{1}{2}\sqrt{3}.$ Therefore, the vertices are at $V(1 \pm 1, 0) = V_1(0, 0)$ and $V_2(2, 0)$

and the foci are at $F\left(1 \pm \frac{1}{2}\sqrt{3}, 0\right).$

(c)

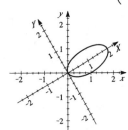

49. $5x^2 + 3y^2 = 60 \;\Leftrightarrow\; 3y^2 = 60 - 5x^2 \;\Leftrightarrow$

$y^2 = 20 - \frac{5}{3}x^2$

This conic is an ellipse.

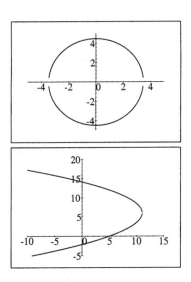

51. $6x + y^2 - 12y = 30 \;\Leftrightarrow\; y^2 - 12y = 30 - 6x \;\Leftrightarrow$

$y^2 - 12y + 36 = 66 - 6x \;\Leftrightarrow$

$(y - 6)^2 = 66 - 6x \;\Leftrightarrow\; y - 6 = \pm\sqrt{66 - 6x} \;\Leftrightarrow$

$y = 6 \pm \sqrt{66 - 6x}.$

This conic is a parabola.

53. (a)

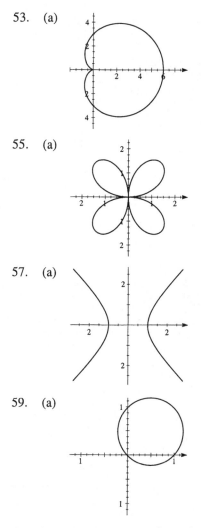

(b) $r = 3 + 3\cos\theta$ ⟺
$r^2 = 3r + 3r\cos\theta$ which gives
$x^2 + y^2 = 3\sqrt{x^2 + y^2} + 3x$ ⟺
$x^2 - 3x + y^2 = 3\sqrt{x^2 + y^2}$. Squaring
both sides gives
$(x^2 - 3x + y^2)^2 = 9(x^2 + y^2)$.

55. (a)

(b) $r = 2\sin 2\theta$ ⟺ $r = 2 \cdot 2\sin\theta\cos\theta$
⟺ $r^3 = 4r^2\sin\theta\cos\theta$ ⟺
$(r^2)^{3/2} = 4(r\sin\theta)(r\cos\theta)$ and so, since
$x = r\cos\theta$ and $y = r\sin\theta$ we get
$(x^2 + y^2)^{3/2} = 4xy$.

57. (a)

(b) $r^2 = \sec 2\theta = \dfrac{1}{\cos 2\theta} = \dfrac{1}{\cos^2\theta - \sin^2\theta}$
⟺ $r^2(\cos^2\theta - \sin^2\theta) = 1$ ⟺
$r^2\cos^2\theta - r^2\sin^2\theta = 1$ ⟺
$(r\cos\theta)^2 - (r\sin\theta)^2 = 1$ ⟺
$x^2 - y^2 = 1$.

59. (a)

(b) $r = \sin\theta + \cos\theta$ ⟺
$r^2 = r\sin\theta + r\cos\theta$ which gives
$x^2 + y^2 = y + x$ ⟺
$(x^2 - x + \tfrac{1}{4}) + (y^2 - y + \tfrac{1}{4}) = \tfrac{1}{2}$ ⟺
$\left(x - \tfrac{1}{2}\right)^2 + \left(y - \tfrac{1}{2}\right)^2 = \tfrac{1}{2}$.

61. Domain of θ shown is $[0, 6\pi]$.

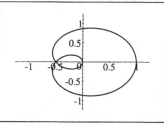

63. Domain of θ shown is $[0, 6\pi]$.

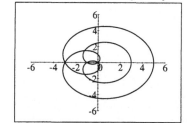

65. (a) $r = \dfrac{1}{1 - \cos\theta}$ $\Rightarrow$ $e = 1$. Therefore, this is a parabola.

    (b)

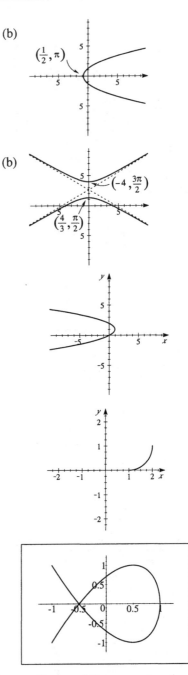

67. (a) $r = \dfrac{4}{1 + 2\sin\theta}$ $\Rightarrow$ $e = 2$. Therefore this is a hyperbola.

    (b)

69. $x = 1 - t^2, y = 1 + t$ $\Leftrightarrow$ $t = y - 1$.
Substituting for t gives $x = 1 - (y - 1)^2$
$\Leftrightarrow$ $(y - 1)^2 = 1 - x$ which is the
rectangular coordinate equation.

71. $x = 1 + \cos t$ $\Leftrightarrow$ $\cos t = x - 1$, and
$y = 1 - \sin t$ $\Leftrightarrow$ $\sin t = 1 - y$. Since
$\cos^2 t + \sin^2 t = 1$, it follows that
$(x - 1)^2 + (1 - y)^2 = 1$ $\Leftrightarrow$
$(x - 1)^2 + (y - 1)^2 = 1$. Since t is restricted
by $0 \le t \le \frac{\pi}{2}$, $1 + \cos 0 \le x \le 1 + \cos\frac{\pi}{2}$
$\Leftrightarrow$ $1 \le x \le 2$, and similarly, $0 \le y \le 1$.
(This is the lower right quarter of the circle.)

73. $x = \cos 2t, y = \sin 3t$

75. The coordinates of Q are $x = \cos\theta$ and $y = \sin\theta$. The coordinates of R are $x = 1$ and $y = \tan\theta$.
Hence, the midpoint P is $\left(\dfrac{1 + \cos\theta}{2}, \dfrac{\sin\theta + \tan\theta}{2}\right)$, so the parametric equations for the curve are
$x = \dfrac{1 + \cos\theta}{2}$ and $y = \dfrac{\sin\theta + \tan\theta}{2}$.

Chapter 9 Test

1. $x^2 = -12y$. This is a parabola that has $4p = -12$
   $\Leftrightarrow$ $p = -3$.

   Focus: $(0, -3)$; directrix: $y = 3$.

2. $\dfrac{x^2}{16} + \dfrac{y^2}{4} = 1$. This is an ellipse that has $a = 4$, $b = 2$, and
   $c = \sqrt{16 - 4} = 2\sqrt{3}$.

   Vertices: $(\pm 4, 0)$; foci: $(\pm 2\sqrt{3}, 0)$; length of the major axis: $2a = 8$;
   length of the minor axis: $2b = 4$.

3. $\dfrac{y^2}{9} - \dfrac{x^2}{16} = 1$. This is a hyperbola that has $a = 3$, $b = 4$, and
   $c = \sqrt{9 + 16} = 5$.

   Vertices: $(0, \pm 3)$; foci: $(0, \pm 5)$; asymptotes: $y = \pm \frac{3}{4} x$.

4. This is a parabola that opens to the left with its vertex at $(0, 0)$. So its equation is of the form
   $y^2 = 4px$ with $p < 0$. Substituting the point $(-4, 2)$, we have $2^2 = 4p(-4)$ $\Leftrightarrow$ $4 = -16p$
   $\Leftrightarrow$ $p = -\frac{1}{4}$. So the equation is $y^2 = 4\left(-\frac{1}{4}\right)x$ $\Leftrightarrow$ $y^2 = -x$.

5. This is an ellipse tangent to the x-axis at $(0, 0)$ and with one vertex at the point $(4, 3)$. The center is
   $(0, 3)$, and $a = 4$ and $b = 3$. Thus the equation is $\dfrac{x^2}{16} + \dfrac{(y - 3)^2}{9} = 1$.

6. This a hyperbola with a horizontal transverse axis, vertices at $(1, 0)$ and $(3, 0)$, and foci at $(0, 0)$ and
   $(4, 0)$. Thus the center is $(2, 0)$, and $a = 3 - 2 = 1$ and $c = 4 - 2 = 2$. Thus $b^2 = 2^2 - 1^2 = 3$. So
   the equation is $\dfrac{(x - 2)^2}{1^2} - \dfrac{y^2}{3} = 1$ $\Leftrightarrow$ $(x - 2)^2 - \dfrac{y^2}{3} = 1$.

7. $16x^2 + 36y^2 - 96x + 36y + 9 = 0$ $\Leftrightarrow$
   $16(x^2 - 6x) + 36(y^2 + y) = -9$ $\Leftrightarrow$
   $16(x^2 - 6x + 9) + 36\left(y^2 + y + \frac{1}{4}\right) = -9 + 144 + 9$ $\Leftrightarrow$
   $16(x - 3)^2 + 36\left(y + \frac{1}{2}\right)^2 = 144$ $\Leftrightarrow$ $\dfrac{(x - 3)^2}{9} + \dfrac{\left(y + \frac{1}{2}\right)^2}{4} = 1$.

   This is an ellipse that has $a = 3$, $b = 2$, and $c = \sqrt{9 - 4} = \sqrt{5}$.

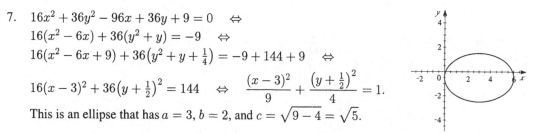

Center: $\left(3, -\frac{1}{2}\right)$; vertices: $\left(3 \pm 3, -\frac{1}{2}\right)$, so vertices are $\left(0, -\frac{1}{2}\right)$ and $\left(6, -\frac{1}{2}\right)$; foci: $(h \pm c, k)$ which are $\left(3 \pm \sqrt{5}, -\frac{1}{2}\right)$, or $\left(3 + \sqrt{5}, -\frac{1}{2}\right)$ and $\left(3 - \sqrt{5}, -\frac{1}{2}\right)$.

8. $9x^2 - 8y^2 + 36x + 64y = 164 \quad \Leftrightarrow \quad 9(x^2 + 4x) - 8(y^2 - 8y) = 164$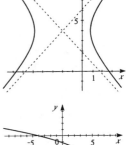
    $\Leftrightarrow \quad 9(x^2 + 4x + 4) - 8(y^2 - 8y + 16) = 164 + 36 - 128 \quad \Leftrightarrow$
    $9(x + 2)^2 - 8(y - 4)^2 = 72 \quad \Leftrightarrow \quad \dfrac{(x + 2)^2}{8} - \dfrac{(y - 4)^2}{9} = 1.$
    This conic is a hyperbola.

9. $2x + y^2 + 8y + 8 = 0 \quad \Leftrightarrow \quad y^2 + 8y + 16 = -2x - 8 + 16 \quad \Leftrightarrow$
    $(y + 4)^2 = -2(x - 4)$. This is a parabola that has $4p = -2 \quad \Leftrightarrow$
    $p = -\frac{1}{2}$.
    Vertex: $(4, -4)$; focus: $\left(4 - \frac{1}{2}, -4\right) = \left(\frac{7}{2}, -4\right)$. No asymptotes.

10. The hyperbola has foci $(0, \pm 5)$ and asymptotes $y = \pm\frac{3}{4}x$. Since the foci are $(0, \pm 5)$, $c = 5$, the foci are on the y-axis, and the center is $(0, 0)$. Also, since $y = \pm\frac{3}{4}x = \pm\dfrac{a}{b}x$, it follows that $\dfrac{a}{b} = \frac{3}{4} \quad \Leftrightarrow$
    $a = \frac{3}{4}b$. Then $c^2 = 5^2 = 25 = a^2 + b^2 = \left(\frac{3}{4}b\right)^2 + b^2 = \frac{25}{16}b^2 \quad \Leftrightarrow \quad b^2 = 16$, and by substitution,
    $a = \frac{3}{4}(4) = 3$. Therefore, the equation of the hyperbola is $\dfrac{y^2}{9} - \dfrac{x^2}{16} = 1$.

11. The parabola has focus $(2, 4)$ and directrix the x-axis $(y = 0)$. Therefore, $2p = 4 - 0 = 4 \quad \Leftrightarrow$
    $p = 2 \quad \Leftrightarrow \quad 4p = 8$, and the vertex is $(2, 4 - p) = (2, 2)$. Hence, the equation of the parabola is
    $(x - 2)^2 = 8(y - 2) \quad \Leftrightarrow \quad x^2 - 4x + 4 = 8y - 16 \quad \Leftrightarrow \quad x^2 - 4x - 8y + 20 = 0.$

12. We place the vertex of the parabola at the origin, so the parabola contains the points $(3, \pm 3)$, and the equation is of the form $y^2 = 4px$. Substituting the point $(3, 3)$, we get $3^2 = 4p(3) \quad \Leftrightarrow \quad 9 = 12p$
    $\Leftrightarrow \quad p = \frac{3}{4}$. So the focus is $\left(\frac{3}{4}, 0\right)$, and we should place the light bulb $\frac{3}{4}$ inches from the vertex.

13. (a) $5x^2 + 4xy + 2y^2 = 18$. Then $A = 5$, $B = 4$, and $C = 2$, so the discriminant is
        $(4)^2 - 4(5)(2) = -24$. Since the discriminant is negative the equation represents an ellipse.

    (b) $\cot 2\phi = \dfrac{A - C}{B} = \dfrac{5 - 2}{4} = \frac{3}{4}$. Thus, $\cos 2\phi = \frac{3}{5}$ and so $\cos\phi = \sqrt{\dfrac{1 + (3/5)}{2}} = \dfrac{2}{\sqrt{5}}$,
        $\sin\phi = \sqrt{\dfrac{1 - (3/5)}{2}} = \dfrac{1}{\sqrt{5}}$. It follows that $x = \dfrac{2X}{\sqrt{5}} - \dfrac{Y}{\sqrt{5}}$ and $y = \dfrac{X}{\sqrt{5}} + \dfrac{2Y}{\sqrt{5}}$. By substitution,
        $5\left(\dfrac{2X}{\sqrt{5}} - \dfrac{Y}{\sqrt{5}}\right)^2 + 4\left(\dfrac{2X}{\sqrt{5}} - \dfrac{Y}{\sqrt{5}}\right)\left(\dfrac{X}{\sqrt{5}} + \dfrac{2Y}{\sqrt{5}}\right) + 2\left(\dfrac{X}{\sqrt{5}} + \dfrac{2Y}{\sqrt{5}}\right)^2 = 18$
        $\Leftrightarrow \quad 4X^2 - 4XY + Y^2 + \frac{4}{5}(2X^2 + 4XY - XY - 2Y^2) + \frac{2}{5}(X^2 + 4XY + 4Y^2) = 18$
        $\Leftrightarrow \quad X^2\left(4 + \frac{8}{5} + \frac{2}{5}\right) + XY\left(-4 + \frac{12}{5} + \frac{8}{5}\right) + Y^2\left(1 - \frac{8}{5} + \frac{4}{5}\right) = 18 \quad \Leftrightarrow \quad 6X^2 + Y^2 = 18$
        $\Leftrightarrow \quad \dfrac{X^2}{3} + \dfrac{Y^2}{18} = 1$. This is an ellipse that has $a = 3\sqrt{2}$ and $b = \sqrt{3}$.

(c)

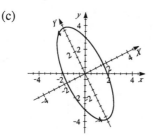

Since $\cos 2\phi = \frac{3}{5}$ we have $2\phi = \cos^{-1}\frac{3}{5} \approx 53.13°$ so $\phi \approx 27°$.

(d) In XY-coordinates, the vertices are $V(0, \pm 3\sqrt{2})$. Therefore, in xy-coordinates, the vertices are $x = \frac{-3\sqrt{2}}{\sqrt{5}}$ and $y = \frac{6\sqrt{2}}{\sqrt{5}}$ $\Rightarrow$ $V_1\left(\frac{-3\sqrt{2}}{\sqrt{5}}, \frac{6\sqrt{2}}{\sqrt{5}}\right)$, and $x = \frac{3\sqrt{2}}{\sqrt{5}}$ and $y = -\frac{6\sqrt{2}}{\sqrt{5}}$ $\Rightarrow$ $V_2\left(\frac{3\sqrt{2}}{\sqrt{5}}, \frac{-6\sqrt{2}}{\sqrt{5}}\right)$.

14. $r = 2 + \cos\theta$. This is a limacon.

15. $r = 2\cos\theta - 4\sin\theta$ $\Leftrightarrow$ $r^2 = 2r\cos\theta - 4r\sin\theta$ which gives $x^2 + y^2 = 2x - 4y$ $\Leftrightarrow$ $(x^2 - 2x + 1) + (y^2 + 4y + 4) = 5$ $\Leftrightarrow$ $(x-1)^2 + (y+2)^2 = 5$. The graph of this equation is a circle with center $(1, -2)$ and radius $\sqrt{5}$.

16. (a) Since focus of this conic is the origin and the directrix is $x = 2$, the conic has the form $r = \dfrac{ed}{1 + e\cos\theta}$. Subsituting $e = \frac{1}{2}$ and $d = 2$ we get $r = \dfrac{1}{1 + \frac{1}{2}\cos\theta}$ $\Leftrightarrow$ $r = \dfrac{2}{2 + \cos\theta}$.

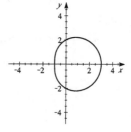

(b) $r = \dfrac{3}{2 - \sin\theta}$ $\Leftrightarrow$ $r = \dfrac{\frac{3}{2}}{1 - \frac{1}{2}\sin\theta}$. So $e = \frac{1}{2}$ and the conic is an ellipse.

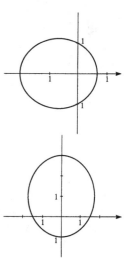

17.   (a) $x = 3\sin\theta + 3,\, y = 2\cos\theta,\, 0 \le \theta \le \pi$.

          From the work of part (b), we see that
          this is the half-ellipse shown on the right.

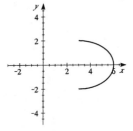

   (b) $x = 3\sin\theta + 3 \quad \Leftrightarrow \quad x - 3 = 3\sin\theta \quad \Leftrightarrow \quad \dfrac{x - 3}{3} = \sin\theta$. Squaring both sides gives

          $\dfrac{(x - 3)^2}{9} = \sin^2\theta$. Similarly, $y = 2\cos\theta \quad \Leftrightarrow \quad \dfrac{y}{2} = \cos\theta$, and squaring both sides gives

          $\dfrac{y^2}{4} = \cos^2\theta$. Since $\sin^2\theta + \cos^2\theta = 1$, it follows that $\dfrac{(x - 3)^2}{9} + \dfrac{y^2}{4} = 1$. Since $0 \le \theta \le \pi$,

          we get that $\sin\theta \ge 0$, so $3\sin\theta \ge 0 \quad \Rightarrow \quad 3\sin\theta + 3 \ge 3$, and so $x \ge 3$. Thus the curve
          consists only of the right half of the ellipse.

Focus on Modeling

1. From $x = (v_0\cos\theta)t$ we get $t = \dfrac{x}{v_0\cos\theta}$. Substituting this value for t into the equation for y, we get

$$y = (v_0\sin\theta)t - \tfrac{1}{2}gt^2 \quad\Leftrightarrow\quad y = (v_0\sin\theta)\left(\dfrac{x}{v_0\cos\theta}\right) - \tfrac{1}{2}g\left(\dfrac{x}{v_0\cos\theta}\right)^2 \quad\Leftrightarrow$$

$y = \tan\theta\, x - \dfrac{g}{2v_0^2\cos^2\theta}\,x^2$. This shows that y is a quadratic function of x, so its graph is a parabola as long as $\theta \neq 90°$. When $\theta = 90°$, the path of the projectile is a straight line up (then down).

3. (a) We use the equation $t = \dfrac{2v_0\sin\theta}{g}$ from page 682 of the text. Substituting $g \approx 32$ ft/s^2, $\theta = 5°$, and $v_0 = 1000$, we get $t = \dfrac{2 \cdot 1000 \cdot \sin 5°}{32} \approx 5.447$ seconds.

   (b) Substituting the given values into $y = (v_0\sin\theta)t - \tfrac{1}{2}gt^2$, we get $y = 87.2t - 16t^2$. The maximum value of y is attained at the vertex of the parabola; thus
   $y = 87.2t - 16t^2 = -16(t^2 - 5.45t) \quad\Leftrightarrow\quad y = -16[t^2 - 2(2.725)t + 7.425625] + 118.7$.
   Thus the greatest height is 118.7 ft.

   (c) The rocket hits the ground after 5.447 s, so substituting this into the expression for the horizontal distance gives $x = (1000\cos 5°)\,5.447 = 5426$ ft.

   (d)

   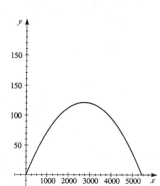

5. We use the equation of the parabola from Exercise 1 and find its vertex: $y = \tan\theta\, x - \dfrac{g}{2v_0^2\cos^2\theta}\,x^2$

$$\Leftrightarrow \quad y = -\dfrac{g}{2v_0^2\cos^2\theta}\left[x^2 - \dfrac{2v_0^2\sin\theta\cos\theta\, x}{g}\right] \quad\Leftrightarrow$$

$$y = -\dfrac{g}{2v_0^2\cos^2\theta}\left[x^2 - \dfrac{2v_0^2\sin\theta\cos\theta\, x}{g} + \left(\dfrac{v_0^2\sin\theta\cos\theta}{g}\right)^2\right] + \dfrac{g}{2v_0^2\cos^2\theta}\cdot\left(\dfrac{v_0^2\sin\theta\cos\theta}{g}\right)^2 \quad\Leftrightarrow$$

$$y = -\dfrac{g}{2v_0^2\cos^2\theta}\left[x - \dfrac{v_0^2\sin\theta\cos\theta}{g}\right]^2 + \dfrac{v_0^2\sin^2\theta}{2g}.$$ Thus the vertex is at $\left(\dfrac{v_0^2\sin\theta\cos\theta}{g}, \dfrac{v_0^2\sin^2\theta}{2g}\right)$ so

the maximum height is $\dfrac{v_0^2\sin^2\theta}{2g}$.

7. In Problem 6 we derived the equations
    $x = (v_0\cos\theta - w)t$,
    $y = (v_0\sin\theta)t - \frac{1}{2}gt^2$. We plot the graphs for
    the given values of v_0, w, and θ in the figure to
    the right. The projectile will be blown
    backwards if the horizontal component of its
    velocity is less than the speed of the wind, that
    is, $32\cos\theta < 24 \quad \Leftrightarrow \quad \cos\theta < \frac{3}{4} \quad \Rightarrow$
    $\theta > 41.4°$.
    The optimal firing angle appears to be
    between 15° and 30°. We graph the trajectory
    for $\theta = 20°$, $\theta = 23°$, and $\theta = 25°$. The
    solution appears to be close to 23°.

Chapter Ten
Exercises 10.1

1. $a_n = n + 1$. Then $a_1 = 1 + 1 = 2$; $a_2 = 2 + 1 = 3$; $a_3 = 3 + 1 = 4$; $a_4 = 4 + 1 = 5$; and $a_{100} = 100 + 1 = 101$.

3. $a_n = \dfrac{1}{n+1}$. Then $a_1 = \dfrac{1}{1+1} = \dfrac{1}{2}$; $a_2 = \dfrac{1}{2+1} = \dfrac{1}{3}$; $a_3 = \dfrac{1}{3+1} = \dfrac{1}{4}$; $a_4 = \dfrac{1}{4+1} = \dfrac{1}{5}$; and $a_{100} = \dfrac{1}{100+1} = \dfrac{1}{101}$.

5. $a_n = \dfrac{(-1)^n}{n^2}$. Then $a_1 = \dfrac{(-1)^1}{1^2} = -1$; $a_2 = \dfrac{(-1)^2}{2^2} = \dfrac{1}{4}$; $a_3 = \dfrac{(-1)^3}{3^2} = -\dfrac{1}{9}$; $a_4 = \dfrac{(-1)^4}{4^2} = \dfrac{1}{16}$; and $a_{100} = \dfrac{(-1)^{100}}{100^2} = \dfrac{1}{10{,}000}$.

7. $a_n = 1 + (-1)^n$. Then $a_1 = 1 + (-1)^1 = 0$; $a_2 = 1 + (-1)^2 = 2$; $a_3 = 1 + (-1)^3 = 0$; $a_4 = 1 + (-1)^4 = 2$; and $a_{100} = 1 + (-1)^{100} = 2$.

9. $a_n = n^n$. Then $a_1 = 1^1 = 1$; $a_2 = 2^2 = 4$; $a_3 = 3^3 = 27$; $a_4 = 4^4 = 256$; and $a_{100} = 100^{100} = 10^{200}$.

11. $a_n = 2(a_{n-1} - 2)$ and $a_1 = 3$. Then $a_2 = 2[(3) - 2] = 2$; $a_3 = 2[(2) - 2] = 0$; $a_4 = 2[(0) - 2] = -4$; and $a_5 = 2[(-4) - 2] = -12$.

13. $a_n = 2a_{n-1} + 1$ and $a_1 = 1$. Then $a_2 = 2(1) + 1 = 3$; $a_3 = 2(3) + 1 = 7$; $a_4 = 2(7) + 1 = 15$; and $a_5 = 2(15) + 1 = 31$.

15. $a_n = a_{n-1} + a_{n-2}$; $a_1 = 1$; and $a_2 = 2$. Then $a_3 = 2 + 1 = 3$; $a_4 = 3 + 2 = 5$; and $a_5 = 5 + 3 = 8$.

17. (a) $a_1 = 7$ $a_2 = 11$ (b)
    $a_3 = 15$ $a_4 = 19$
    $a_5 = 23$ $a_6 = 27$
    $a_7 = 31$ $a_8 = 35$
    $a_9 = 39$ $a_{10} = 43$

19. (a) $a_1 = 12$ $a_2 = 6$ (b)
    $a_3 = 4$ $a_4 = 3$
    $a_5 = 2.4$ $a_6 = 2$
    $a_7 = 1.714$ $a_8 = 1.5$
    $a_9 = 1.333$ $a_{10} = 1.2$

21. (a) $a_1 = 2$ $a_2 = 0.5$
       $a_3 = 2$ $a_4 = 0.5$
       $a_5 = 2$ $a_6 = 0.5$
       $a_7 = 2$ $a_8 = 0.5$
       $a_9 = 2$ $a_{10} = 0.5$

(b)

23. $2, 4, 8, 16, \ldots$. All are powers of 2, so $a_1 = 2$, $a_2 = 2^2$, $a_3 = 2^3$, $a_4 = 2^4$, ... Thus $a_n = 2^n$.

25. $1, 4, 7, 10, \ldots$. The difference between any two consecutive terms is 3, so $a_1 = 3(1) - 2$,
$a_2 = 3(2) - 2$, $a_3 = 3(3) - 2$, $a_4 = 3(4) - 2$, ... Thus $a_n = 3n - 2$.

27. $1, \frac{3}{4}, \frac{5}{9}, \frac{7}{16}, \frac{9}{25}, \ldots$. We consider the numerator separately from the denominator. The numerators
of the terms differ by 2, and the denominators are perfect squares. So $a_1 = \dfrac{2(1) - 1}{1^2}$,
$a_2 = \frac{2(2)-1}{2^2}$, $a_3 = \dfrac{2(3) - 1}{3^2}$, $a_4 = \dfrac{2(4) - 1}{4^2}$, $a_5 = \dfrac{2(5) - 1}{5^2}$, $\ldots$. Thus $a_n = \dfrac{2n - 1}{n^2}$.

29. $0, 2, 0, 2, 0, 2, \ldots$. These terms alternate between 0 and 2. So $a_1 = 1 - 1$, $a_2 = 1 + 1$, $a_3 = 1 - 1$,
$a_4 = 1 + 1$, $a_5 = 1 - 1$, $a_6 = 1 + 1$, ... Thus $a_n = 1 + (-1)^n$.

31. $a_1 = 1$, $a_2 = 3$, $a_3 = 5$, $a_4 = 7, \ldots$. Therefore, $a_n = 2n - 1$. So $S_1 = 1$; $S_2 = 1 + 3 = 4$;
$S_3 = 1 + 3 + 5 + = 9$; $S_4 = 1 + 3 + 5 + 7 = 16$; $S_5 = 1 + 3 + 5 + 7 + 9 = 25$; and
$S_6 = 1 + 3 + 5 + 7 + 9 + 11 = 36$.

33. $a_1 = \frac{1}{3}$, $a_2 = \frac{1}{3^2}$, $a_3 = \frac{1}{3^3}$, $a_4 = \frac{1}{3^4}, \ldots$. Therefore, $a_n = \frac{1}{3^n}$. So $S_1 = \frac{1}{3}$; $S_2 = \frac{1}{3} + \frac{1}{3^2} = \frac{4}{9}$;
$S_3 = \frac{1}{3} + \frac{1}{3^2} + \frac{1}{3^3} = \frac{13}{27}$; $S_4 = \frac{1}{3} + \frac{1}{3^2} + \frac{1}{3^3} + \frac{1}{3^4} = \frac{40}{81}$; and $S_5 = \frac{1}{3} + \frac{1}{3^2} + \frac{1}{3^3} + \frac{1}{3^4} + \frac{1}{3^5} = \frac{121}{243}$;
$S_6 = \frac{1}{3} + \frac{1}{3^2} + \frac{1}{3^3} + \frac{1}{3^4} + \frac{1}{3^5} + \frac{1}{3^6} = \frac{364}{729}$.

35. $a_n = \frac{2}{3^n}$. So $S_1 = \frac{2}{3}$; $S_2 = \frac{2}{3} + \frac{2}{3^2} = \frac{8}{9}$; $S_3 = \frac{2}{3} + \frac{2}{3^2} + \frac{2}{3^3} = \frac{26}{27}$; and $S_4 = \frac{2}{3} + \frac{2}{3^2} + \frac{2}{3^3} + \frac{2}{3^4} = \frac{80}{81}$.
Therefore, $S_n = \frac{3^n - 1}{3^n}$.

37. $a_n = \sqrt{n} - \sqrt{n+1}$. So $S_1 = \sqrt{1} - \sqrt{2} = \underline{1 - \sqrt{2}}$;
$S_2 = \left(\sqrt{1} - \sqrt{2}\right) + \left(\sqrt{2} - \sqrt{3}\right) = 1 + \left(-\sqrt{2} + \sqrt{2}\right) - \sqrt{3} = \underline{1 - \sqrt{3}}$;
$S_3 = \left(\sqrt{1} - \sqrt{2}\right) + \left(\sqrt{2} - \sqrt{3}\right) + \left(\sqrt{3} - \sqrt{4}\right)$
$\quad = 1 + \left(-\sqrt{2} + \sqrt{2}\right) + \left(-\sqrt{3} + \sqrt{3}\right) - \sqrt{4} = \underline{1 - \sqrt{4}}$;
$S_4 = \left(\sqrt{1} - \sqrt{2}\right) + \left(\sqrt{2} - \sqrt{3}\right) + \left(\sqrt{3} - \sqrt{4}\right) + \left(\sqrt{4} - \sqrt{5}\right)$
$\quad = 1 + \left(-\sqrt{2} + \sqrt{2}\right) + \left(-\sqrt{3} + \sqrt{3}\right) + \left(-\sqrt{4} + \sqrt{4}\right) - \sqrt{5} = \underline{1 - \sqrt{5}}$. Therefore,
$S_n = \left(\sqrt{1} - \sqrt{2}\right) + \left(\sqrt{2} - \sqrt{3}\right) + \cdots + \left(\sqrt{n} - \sqrt{n+1}\right)$
$\quad = 1 + \left(-\sqrt{2} + \sqrt{2}\right) + \left(-\sqrt{3} + \sqrt{3}\right) + \cdots + \left(-\sqrt{n} + \sqrt{n}\right) - \sqrt{n+1} = \underline{1 - \sqrt{n+1}}$.

39. $\displaystyle\sum_{k=1}^{4} k = 1 + 2 + 3 + 4 = 10$

41. $\displaystyle\sum_{k=1}^{3}\frac{1}{k}=1+\frac{1}{2}+\frac{1}{3}=\frac{6}{6}+\frac{3}{6}+\frac{2}{6}=\frac{11}{6}$

43. $\displaystyle\sum_{i=1}^{8}[1+(-1)^i]=0+2+0+2+0+2+0+2=8$

45. $\displaystyle\sum_{k=1}^{5}2^{k-1}=2^0+2^1+2^2+2^3+2^4=1+2+4+8+16=31$

47. 385   49. 46,438   51. 22

53. $\displaystyle\sum_{k=1}^{5}\sqrt{k}=\sqrt{1}+\sqrt{2}+\sqrt{3}+\sqrt{4}+\sqrt{5}$

55. $\displaystyle\sum_{k=0}^{6}\sqrt{k+4}=\sqrt{4}+\sqrt{5}+\sqrt{6}+\sqrt{7}+\sqrt{8}+\sqrt{9}+\sqrt{10}$

57. $\displaystyle\sum_{k=3}^{100}x^k=x^3+x^4+x^5+\cdots+x^{100}$

59. $\displaystyle 1+2+3+4+\cdots+100=\sum_{k=1}^{100}k$

61. $\displaystyle 1^2+2^2+3^2+\cdots+10^2=\sum_{k=1}^{10}k^2$

63. $\displaystyle\frac{1}{1\cdot 2}+\frac{1}{2\cdot 3}+\frac{1}{3\cdot 4}+\cdots+\frac{1}{999\cdot 1000}=\sum_{k=1}^{999}\frac{1}{k(k+1)}$

65. $\displaystyle 1+x+x^2+x^3+\cdots+x^{100}=\sum_{k=0}^{100}x^k$

67. $\sqrt{2},\ \sqrt{2\sqrt{2}},\ \sqrt{2\sqrt{2\sqrt{2}}},\ \sqrt{2\sqrt{2\sqrt{2\sqrt{2}}}},\ \ldots$. We simplify each term in an attempt to determine a formula for a_n. So $a_1=2^{1/2}$; $a_2=\sqrt{2\cdot 2^{1/2}}=\sqrt{2^{3/2}}=2^{3/4}$; $a_3=\sqrt{2\cdot 2^{3/4}}=\sqrt{2^{7/4}}=2^{7/8}$; $a_4=\sqrt{2\cdot 2^{7/8}}=\sqrt{2^{15/8}}=2^{15/16}$; $\ldots$. Thus $a_n=2^{(2^n-1)/2^n}$.

69. (a) $a_n=n^2$. Then $a_1=1^2=1$, $a_2=2^2=4$, $a_3=3^2=9$, $a_4=4^2=16$.

    (b) $a_n=n^2+(n-1)(n-2)(n-3)(n-4)$;
        $a_1=1^2+(1-1)(1-2)(1-3)(1-4)=1+0(-1)(-2)(-3)=1$;
        $a_2=2^2+(2-1)(2-2)(2-3)(2-4)=4+1\cdot 0(-1)(-2)=4$;
        $a_3=3^2+(3-1)(3-2)(3-3)(3-4)=9+2\cdot 1\cdot 0(-1)=9$;
        $a_4=4^2+(4-1)(4-2)(4-3)(4-4)=16+3\cdot 2\cdot 1\cdot 0=16$.
        Hence, the sequences agree in the first four terms. However, for the second sequence,
        $a_5=5^2+(5-1)(5-2)(5-3)(5-4)=25+4\cdot 3\cdot 2\cdot 1=49$, and for the first sequence,
        $a_5=5^2=25$, and thus the sequences disagree from the fifth term on.

    (c) $a_n=n^2+(n-1)(n-2)(n-3)(n-4)(n-5)(n-6)$ agrees with $a_n=n^2$ in the first six terms only.

    (d) $a_n=2^n$ and $b_n=2^n+(n-1)(n-2)(n-3)(n-4)$.

71. $a_n = a_{n-a_{n-1}} + a_{n-a_{n-2}}$; $a_1 = 1$; and $a_2 = 1$. So

$a_3 = a_{3-1} + a_{3-1} = a_2 + a_2 = 1 + 1 = 2$;

$a_4 = a_{4-2} + a_{4-1} = a_2 + a_3 = 1 + 2 = 3$;

$a_5 = a_{5-3} + a_{5-2} = a_2 + a_3 = 1 + 2 = 3$;

$a_6 = a_{6-3} + a_{6-3} = a_3 + a_3 = 2 + 2 = 4$;

$a_7 = a_{7-4} + a_{7-3} = a_3 + a_4 = 2 + 3 = 5$;

$a_8 = a_{8-5} + a_{8-4} = a_3 + a_4 = 2 + 3 = 5$;

$a_9 = a_{9-5} + a_{9-5} = a_4 + a_4 = 3 + 3 = 6$;

$a_{10} = a_{10-6} + a_{10-5} = a_4 + a_5 = 3 + 3 = 6$.

The definition of a_n depends on the <u>values</u> of certain preceding terms. So a_n is the sum of two preceding terms whose choice depends on the <u>values</u> of a_{n-1} and a_{n-2} (not on $n - 1$ and $n - 2$).

Exercises 10.2

1. (a) $a_1 = 5 + 2(1 - 1) = 5$
   $a_2 = 5 + 2(2 - 1) = 5 + 2 = 7$
   $a_3 = 5 + 2(3 - 1) = 5 + 4 = 9$
   $a_4 = 5 + 2(4 - 1) = 5 + 6 = 11$
   $a_5 = 5 + 2(5 - 1) = 5 + 8 = 13$

   (c)

   (b) The common difference is 2.

3. (a) $a_1 = \frac{5}{2} - (1 - 1) = \frac{5}{2}$
   $a_2 = \frac{5}{2} - (2 - 1) = \frac{3}{2}$
   $a_3 = \frac{5}{2} - (3 - 1) = \frac{1}{2}$
   $a_4 = \frac{5}{2} - (4 - 1) = -\frac{1}{2}$
   $a_5 = \frac{5}{2} - (5 - 1) = -\frac{3}{2}$

   (c)

   (b) The common difference is -1.

5. $a = 3$, $d = 5$, $a_n = a + d(n - 1)$. So $a_{10} = 3 + 5(10 - 1) = 48$.

7. $a = \frac{5}{2}$, $d = -\frac{1}{2}$, $a_n = a + d(n - 1)$. So $a_{10} = \frac{5}{2} - \frac{1}{2}(10 - 1) = \frac{-4}{2} = -2$.

9. $a_4 - a_3 = 14 - 11 = 3$; $a_3 - a_2 = 11 - 8 = 3$; $a_2 - a_1 = 8 - 5 = 3$. This sequence is arithmetic with the common difference 3.

11. Since $a_2 - a_1 = 4 - 2 = 2$ and $a_4 - a_3 = 16 - 8 = 8$, the terms of the sequence do not have a common difference. This sequence is not arithmetic.

13. $a_4 - a_3 = -\frac{3}{2} - 0 = -\frac{3}{2}$; $a_3 - a_2 = 0 - \frac{3}{2} = -\frac{3}{2}$; $a_2 - a_1 = \frac{3}{2} - 3 = -\frac{3}{2}$. This sequence is arithmetic with the common difference $-\frac{3}{2}$.

15. $a_4 - a_3 = 7.7 - 6.0 = 1.7$; $a_3 - a_2 = 6.0 - 4.3 = 1.7$; $4. - a_1 = 4.3 - 2.6 = 1.7$. This sequence is arithmetic with the common difference 1.7.

17. $a_1 = 4 + 7(1) = 11$; $a_2 = 4 + 7(2) = 18$; $a_3 = 4 + 7(3) = 25$; $a_4 = 4 + 7(4) = 32$;
    $a_5 = 4 + 7(5) = 39$. This sequence is arithmetic, the common difference is $d = 7$ and
    $a_n = 4 + 7n = 4 + 7n - 7 + 7 = 11 + 7(n - 1)$.

19. $a_1 = \frac{1}{1+2(1)} = \frac{1}{3}$; $a_2 = \frac{1}{1+2(2)} = \frac{1}{5}$; $a_3 = \frac{1}{1+2(3)} = \frac{1}{7}$; $a_4 = \frac{1}{1+2(4)} = \frac{1}{9}$; $a_5 = \frac{1}{1+2(5)} = \frac{1}{11}$. Since
    $a_4 - a_3 = \frac{1}{9} - \frac{1}{7} = -\frac{2}{63}$ and $a_3 - a_2 = \frac{1}{7} - \frac{1}{3} = -\frac{2}{21}$, the terms of the sequence do not have a common difference. This sequence is not arithmetic.

21. $a_1 = 6(1) - 10 = -4$; $a_2 = 6(2) - 10 = 2$; $a_3 = 6(3) - 10 = 8$; $a_4 = 6(4) - 10 = 14$;
    $a_5 = 6(5) - 10 = 20$. This sequence is arithmetic, the common difference is $d = 6$ and
    $a_n = 6n - 10 = 6n - 6 + 6 - 10 = -4 + 6(n - 1)$.

23. $2, 5, 8, 11, \ldots$. Then $d = a_2 - a_1 = 5 - 2 = 3$; $a_5 = a_4 + 3 = 11 + 3 = 14$; $a_n = 2 + 3(n - 1)$; and $a_{100} = 2 + 3(99) = 299$.

25. $4, 9, 14, 19, \ldots$. Then $d = a_2 - a_1 = 9 - 4 = 5$; $a_5 = a_4 + 5 = 19 + 5 = 24$; $a_n = 4 + 5(n - 1)$; and $a_{100} = 4 + 5(99) = 499$.

27. $-12, -8, -4, 0, \ldots$. Then $d = a_2 - a_1 = -8 - (-12) = 4$; $a_5 = a_4 + 4 = 0 + 4 = 4$; $a_n = -12 + 4(n - 1)$; and $a_{100} = -12 + 4(99) = 384$.

29. $25, 26.5, 28, 29.5, \ldots$. Then $d = a_2 - a_1 = 26.5 - 25 = 1.5$; $a_5 = a_4 + 1.5 = 29.5 + 1.5 = 31$; $a_n = 25 + 1.5(n - 1)$; $a_{100} = 25 + 1.5(99) = 173.5$.

31. $2, 2 + s, 2 + 2s, 2 + 3s, \ldots$. Then $d = a_2 - a_1 = 2 + s - 2 = s$; $a_5 = a_4 + s = 2 + 3s + s = 2 + 4s$; $a_n = 2 + (n - 1)s$; and $a_{100} = 2 + 99s$.

33. $a_{10} = \frac{55}{2}$, $a_2 = \frac{7}{2}$, and $a_n = a + d(n - 1)$. Then $a_2 = a + d = \frac{7}{2} \quad \Leftrightarrow \quad d = \frac{7}{2} - a$. Substituting into $a_{10} = a + 9d = \frac{55}{2}$ gives $a + 9\left(\frac{7}{2} - a\right) = \frac{55}{2} \quad \Leftrightarrow \quad a = \frac{1}{2}$. Thus, the first term is $a_1 = \frac{1}{2}$.

35. $a_{100} = 98$ and $d = 2$. Note that $a_{100} = a + 99d = a + 99(2) = a + 198$. Since $a_{100} = 98$, we have $a + 198 = a_{100} = 98 \quad \Leftrightarrow \quad a = -100$. Hence, $a_1 = -100$, $a_2 = -100 + 2 = -98$, and $a_3 = -100 + 4 = -96$.

37. The arithmetic sequence is $1, 4, 7, \ldots$. So $d = 4 - 1 = 3$ and $a_n = 1 + 3(n - 1)$. Then $a_n = 88$ $\Leftrightarrow \quad 1 + 3(n - 1) = 88 \quad \Leftrightarrow \quad 3(n - 1) = 87 \quad \Leftrightarrow \quad n - 1 = 29 \quad \Leftrightarrow \quad n = 30$. So, 88 is the 30th term.

39. $a = 1$, $d = 2$, $n = 10$. Then $S_{10} = \frac{10}{2}[2a + (10 - 1)d] = \frac{10}{2}[2 \cdot 1 + 9 \cdot 2] = 100$.

41. $a = 4$, $d = 2$, $n = 20$. Then $S_{20} = \frac{20}{2}[2a + (20 - 1)d] = \frac{20}{2}[2 \cdot 4 + 19 \cdot 2] = 460$.

43. $a_1 = 55$, $d = 12$, $n = 10$. Then $S_{10} = \frac{10}{2}[2a + (10 - 1)d] = \frac{10}{2}[2 \cdot 55 + 9 \cdot 12] = 1090$.

45. $1 + 5 + 9 + \cdots + 401$ is a partial sum of an arithmetic series, where $a = 1$ and $d = 5 - 1 = 4$. The last term is $401 = a_n = 1 + 4(n - 1)$, so $n - 1 = 100 \quad \Leftrightarrow \quad n = 101$. So, the partial sum is $S_{101} = \frac{101}{2}(1 + 401) = 101 \cdot 201 = 20{,}301$.

47. $0.7 + 2.7 + 4.7 + \cdots + 56.7$ is a partial sum of an arithmetic series, where $a = 0.7$ and $d = 2.7 - 0.7 = 2$. The last term is $56.7 = a_n = 0.7 + 2(n - 1) \quad \Leftrightarrow \quad 28 = n - 1 \quad \Leftrightarrow$ $n = 29$. So, the partial sum is $S_{29} = \frac{29}{2}(0.7 + 56.7) = 832.3$.

49. $\displaystyle\sum_{k=0}^{10}(3 + 0.25k)$ is a partial sum of an arithmetic series, where $a = 3 + 0.25 \cdot 0 = 3$ and $d = 0.25$. The last term is $a_{11} = 3 + 0.25 \cdot 10 = 5.5$. So the partial sum is $S_{11} = \frac{11}{2}(3 + 5.5) = 46.75$.

51. The diminishing values of the computer form an arithmetic sequence with $a_1 = 12500$ and common difference $d = -1875$. Thus the value of the computer after 6 years is $a_7 = 12500 + (7 - 1)(-1875) = \$1250$.

53. The increasing values of the man's salary form an arithmetic sequence with $a_1 = 30000$ and common difference $d = 2300$. Then his total earnings for a ten-year period are $S_{10} = \frac{10}{2}[2(30000) + 9(2300)] = 403500$. Thus his total earnings for the 10 year period are $403,500.

55. The number of seats in the nth row is given by the nth term of an arithmetic sequence with $a_1 = 15$ and common difference $d = 3$. We need to find n such that $S_n = 870$. So we solve $870 = S_n = \frac{n}{2}[2(15) + (n-1)3]$ for n. We have $870 = \frac{n}{2}(27 + 3n)$ $\Leftrightarrow$ $1740 = 3n^2 + 27n$ $\Leftrightarrow$ $3n^2 + 27n - 1740 = 0$ $\Leftrightarrow$ $n^2 + 9n - 580 = 0$ $\Leftrightarrow$ $(x - 20)(x + 29) = 0$ $\Rightarrow$ $n = 20$ or $n = -29$. Since the number of rows is positive, the theater must have 20 rows.

57. The sequence is $16, 48, 80, \ldots$. This is an arithmetic sequence with $a = 16$ and $d = 48 - 16 = 32$.
    (a) The total distance after 6 seconds is $S_6 = \frac{6}{2}(32 + 5 \cdot 32) = 3 \cdot 192 = 576$ ft.
    (b) The total distance after n seconds is $S_n = \frac{n}{2}[32 + 32(n - 1)] = 16n^2$ ft.

59. Let x denote the length of the side between the length of the other two sides. Then the lengths of the three sides of the triangle are $x - a$, x, and $x + a$, for some $a > 0$. Since $x + a$ is the longest side, it is the hypotenuse, and by the Pythagorean Theorem, we know that $(x - a)^2 + x^2 = (x + a)^2$ $\Leftrightarrow$ $x^2 - 2ax + a^2 + x^2 = x^2 + 2ax + a^2$ $\Leftrightarrow$ $x^2 - 4ax = 0$ $\Leftrightarrow$ $x(x - 4a) = 0$ $\Rightarrow$ $x = 4a$ ($x = 0$ is not a possible solution). Thus, the lengths of the three sides are $x - a = 4a - a = 3a$, $x = 4a$, and $x + a = 4a + a = 5a$. The lengths $3a$, $4a$, $5a$ are proportional to $3, 4, 5$, and so the triangle is similar to a 3 - 4 - 5 triangle.

61. The sequence $1, \frac{3}{5}, \frac{3}{7}, \frac{1}{3}, \ldots$ is harmonic if $1, \frac{5}{3}, \frac{7}{3}, 3, \ldots$ forms an arithmetic sequence. Since $\frac{5}{3} - 1 = \frac{7}{3} - \frac{5}{3} = 3 - \frac{7}{3} = \frac{2}{3}$, the sequence of reciprocals is arithmetic and thus the original sequence is harmonic.

63. (a) We want an arithmetic sequence with 4 terms, so let $a_1 = 10$ and $a_4 = 18$. Since the sequence is arithmetic, $a_4 - a_1 = 3d = 18 - 10 = 8$ $\Leftrightarrow$ $3d = 8$ $\Leftrightarrow$ $d = \frac{8}{3}$. Therefore, $a_2 = 10 + \frac{8}{3} = \frac{38}{3}$ and $a_3 = 10 + 2\left(\frac{8}{3}\right) = \frac{46}{3}$ are the two arithmetic means between 10 and 18.

    (b) We want an arithmetic sequence with 5 terms, so let $a_1 = 10$ and $a_5 = 18$. Since the sequence is arithmetic, $a_5 - a_1 = 4d = 18 - 10 = 8$ $\Leftrightarrow$ $4d = 8$ $\Leftrightarrow$ $d = 2$. Therefore, $a_2 = 10 + 2 = 12$, $a_3 = 10 + 2(2) = 14$, and $a_4 = 10 + 3(2) = 16$ are the three arithmetic means between 10 and 18.

    (c) We want an arithmetic sequence with 6 terms, with the starting dosage $a_1 = 100$ and the final dosage $a_6 = 300$. Since the sequence is arithmetic, $a_6 - a_1 = 5d = 300 - 100 = 200$ $\Leftrightarrow$ $5d = 200$ $\Leftrightarrow$ $d = 40$. Therefore, $a_2 = 140$, $a_3 = 180$, $a_4 = 220$, $a_5 = 260$, and $a_6 = 300$. The patient should take 140 mg, then 180 mg, then 220 mg, then 260 mg, and finally arrive at 300 mg.

Exercises 10.3

1. (a) $a_1 = 5(2)^0 = 5$
   $a_2 = 5(2)^1 = 10$
   $a_3 = 5(2)^2 = 20$
   $a_4 = 5(2)^3 = 40$
   $a_5 = 5(2)^4 = 80$

   (c)

   (b) The common ratio is 2.

3. (a) $a_1 = \frac{5}{2}(-\frac{1}{2})^0 = \frac{5}{2}$
   $a_2 = \frac{5}{2}(-\frac{1}{2})^1 = -\frac{5}{4}$
   $a_3 = \frac{5}{2}(-\frac{1}{2})^2 = \frac{5}{8}$
   $a_4 = \frac{5}{2}(-\frac{1}{2})^3 = -\frac{5}{16}$
   $a_5 = \frac{5}{2}(-\frac{1}{2})^4 = \frac{5}{32}$

   (c)

   (b) The common ratio is $-\frac{1}{2}$.

5. $a = 3, r = 5$. So $a_n = ar^{n-1} = 3(5)^{n-1}$ and $a_4 = 3 \cdot 5^3 = 375$.

7. $a = \frac{5}{2}, r = -\frac{1}{2}$. So $a_n = ar^{n-1} = \frac{5}{2}(-\frac{1}{2})^{n-1}$ and $a_4 = \frac{5}{2} \cdot (-\frac{1}{2})^3 = -\frac{5}{16}$.

9. $\frac{a_2}{a_1} = \frac{4}{2} = 2; \frac{a_3}{a_2} = \frac{8}{4} = 2; \frac{a_4}{a_3} = \frac{16}{8} = 2$. Since these ratios are the same, the sequence is geometric with the common ratio 2.

11. $\frac{a_2}{a_1} = \frac{3/2}{3} = \frac{1}{2}; \frac{a_3}{a_2} = \frac{3/4}{3/2} = \frac{1}{2}; \frac{a_4}{a_3} = \frac{3/8}{3/4} = \frac{1}{2}$. Since these ratios are the same, the sequence is geometric with the common ratio $\frac{1}{2}$.

13. $\frac{a_2}{a_1} = \frac{1/3}{1/2} = \frac{2}{3}; \frac{a_4}{a_3} = \frac{1/5}{1/4} = \frac{4}{5}$. Since these ratios are not the same, this is not a geometric sequence.

15. $\frac{a_2}{a_1} = \frac{1.1}{1.0} = 1.1; \frac{a_3}{a_2} = \frac{1.21}{1.1} = 1.1; \frac{a_4}{a_3} = \frac{1.331}{1.21} = 1.1$. Since these ratios are the same, the sequence is geometric with the common ratio 1.1.

17. $a_1 = 2(3)^1 = 6; a_2 = 2(3)^2 = 18; a_3 = 2(3)^3 = 54; a_4 = 2(3)^4 = 162; a_5 = 2(3)^5 = 486$. This sequence is geometric , the common ratio is $r = 3$ and $a_n = a_1 r^{n-1} = 6(3)^{n-1}$.

19. $a_1 = \frac{1}{4}; a_2 = \frac{1}{4^2} = \frac{1}{16}; a_3 = \frac{1}{4^3} = \frac{1}{64}; a_4 = \frac{1}{4^4} = \frac{1}{256}; a_5 = \frac{1}{4^5} = \frac{1}{1024}$. This sequence is geometric , the common ratio is $r = \frac{1}{4}$ and $a_n = a_1 r^{n-1} = \frac{1}{4}(\frac{1}{4})^{n-1}$.

21. Since $\ln a^b = b \ln a$ we have: $a_1 = \ln(5^0) = \ln 1 = 0; a_2 = \ln(5^1) = \ln 5; a_3 = \ln(5^2) = 2 \ln 5; a_4 = \ln(5^3) = 3 \ln 5; a_5 = \ln(5^4) = 4 \ln 5$. Since $a_1 = 0$ and $a_2 \neq 0$, this sequence is not geometric.

23. $2, 6, 18, 54, \ldots$. Then $r = \dfrac{a_2}{a_1} = \dfrac{6}{2} = 3$; $a_5 = a_4 \cdot 3 = 54(3) = 162$; and $a_n = 2 \cdot 3^{n-1}$.

25. $0.3, -0.09, 0.027, -0.0081, \ldots$. Then $r = \dfrac{a_2}{a_1} = \dfrac{-0.09}{0.3} = -0.3$; $a_5 = a_4 \cdot (-0.3) =$
$-0.0081(-0.3) = 0.00243$; and $a_n = 0.3(-0.3)^{n-1}$.

27. $144, -12, 1, -\frac{1}{12}, \ldots$. Then $r = \dfrac{a_2}{a_1} = \dfrac{-12}{144} = -\frac{1}{12}$; $a_5 = a_4 \cdot \left(-\frac{1}{12}\right) = -\frac{1}{12}\left(-\frac{1}{12}\right) = \frac{1}{144}$;
$a_n = 144\left(-\frac{1}{12}\right)^{n-1}$.

29. $3, 3^{5/3}, 3^{7/3}, 27, \ldots$. Then $r = \dfrac{a_2}{a_1} = \dfrac{3^{5/3}}{3} = 3^{2/3}$; $a_5 = a_4 \cdot \left(3^{2/3}\right) = 27 \cdot 3^{2/3} = 3^{11/3}$; and
$a_n = 3\left(3^{2/3}\right)^{n-1} = 3 \cdot 3^{(2n-2)/3} = 3^{(2n+1)/3}$.

31. $1, s^{2/7}, s^{4/7}, s^{6/7}, \ldots$. Then $r = \dfrac{a_2}{a_1} = \dfrac{s^{2/7}}{1} = s^{2/7}$; $a_5 = a_4 \cdot s^{2/7} = s^{6/7} \cdot s^{2/7} = s^{8/7}$; and
$a_n = \left(s^{2/7}\right)^{n-1} = s^{(2n-2)/7}$.

33. $a_1 = 8$, $a_2 = 4$. Thus $r = \dfrac{a_2}{a_1} = \dfrac{4}{8} = \dfrac{1}{2}$ and $a_5 = a_1 r^{5-1} = 8\left(\dfrac{1}{2}\right)^4 = \dfrac{8}{16} = \dfrac{1}{2}$.

35. $r = \frac{2}{5}$, $a_4 = \frac{5}{2}$. Since $r = \dfrac{a_4}{a_3}$, we have $a_3 = \dfrac{a_4}{r} = \dfrac{\frac{5}{2}}{\frac{2}{5}} = \dfrac{25}{4}$.

37. The geometric sequence is $2, 6, 18, \ldots$. Thus $r = \dfrac{a_2}{a_1} = \dfrac{6}{2} = 3$. We need to find n so that
$a_n = 2 \cdot 3^{n-1} = 118{,}098 \quad \Leftrightarrow \quad 3^{n-1} = 59{,}049 \quad \Leftrightarrow \quad n - 1 = \log_3 59{,}049 = 10 \quad \Leftrightarrow \quad n = 11$.
Therefore, $118{,}098$ is the 11th term of the geometric sequence.

39. $a = 5$, $r = 2$, $n = 6$. Then $S_6 = 5\dfrac{1 - 2^6}{1 - 2} = (-5)(-63) = 315$.

41. $a_3 = 28$, $a_6 = 224$, $n = 6$. So $\dfrac{a_6}{a_3} = \dfrac{ar^5}{ar^2} = r^3$. So we have $r^3 = \dfrac{a_6}{a_3} = \dfrac{224}{28} = 8$, and hence $r = 2$.
Since $a_3 = a \cdot r^2$, we get $a = \dfrac{a_3}{r^2} = \dfrac{28}{2^2} = 7$. So $S_6 = 7\dfrac{1 - 2^6}{1 - 2} = (-7)(-63) = 441$.

43. $1 + 3 + 9 + \cdots + 2187$ is a partial sum of a geometric sequence, where $a = 1$ and $r = \dfrac{a_2}{a_1} = \dfrac{3}{1} = 3$.
Then the last term is $2187 = a_n = 1 \cdot 3^{n-1} \quad \Leftrightarrow \quad n - 1 = \log_3 2187 = 7 \quad \Leftrightarrow \quad n = 8$. So the
partial sum is $S_8 = (1)\dfrac{1 - 3^8}{1 - 3} = 3280$.

45. $\displaystyle\sum_{k=0}^{10} 3\left(\frac{1}{2}\right)^k$ is partial sum of a geometric sequence, where $a = 3$, $r = \frac{1}{2}$, and $n = 11$. So the partial sum
is $S_{11} = (3)\dfrac{1 - \left(\frac{1}{2}\right)^{11}}{1 - \left(\frac{1}{2}\right)} = 6\left[1 - \left(\frac{1}{2}\right)^{11}\right] = 5.997070313$.

47. Since the ball is dropped from a height of 80 feet, $a = 80$. Also since the ball rebounds three-fourths of the distance fallen, $r = \frac{3}{4}$. So on the nth bounce, the ball attains a height of $a_n = 80\left(\frac{3}{4}\right)^n$. Hence, on the 5th bounce, the ball goes $a_5 = 80\left(\frac{3}{4}\right)^5 = \frac{80 \cdot 243}{1024} \approx 19$ ft high.

49. Let a_n be the amount of water remaining at the nth stage. We start with 5 gallons, so $a = 5$. When 1 gallon, that is $\frac{1}{5}$ of the mixture, is removed, $\frac{4}{5}$ of the mixture (and hence $\frac{4}{5}$ of the water in the mixture) remains. Thus, $a_1 = 5 \cdot \frac{4}{5}$, $a_2 = 5 \cdot \frac{4}{5} \cdot \frac{4}{5}, \ldots$, and in general, $a_n = 5\left(\frac{4}{5}\right)^n$. The amount of water remaining after 3 repetitions is $a_3 = 5\left(\frac{4}{5}\right)^3 = \frac{64}{25}$, and after 5 repetitions is $a_5 = 5\left(\frac{4}{5}\right)^5 = \frac{1024}{625}$.

51. Let a_n be the height the ball reaches on the nth bounce. From the given information, a_n is the geometric sequence $a_n = 9 \cdot \left(\frac{1}{3}\right)^n$. (Notice that the ball hits the ground for the fifth time after the 4th bounce.)

 (a) $a_0 = 9$, $a_1 = 9 \cdot \frac{1}{3} = 3$, $a_2 = 9 \cdot \left(\frac{1}{3}\right)^2 = 1$, $a_3 = 9 \cdot \left(\frac{1}{3}\right)^3 = \frac{1}{3}$, and $a_4 = 9 \cdot \left(\frac{1}{3}\right)^4 = \frac{1}{9}$. The total distance traveled is $a_0 + 2a_1 + 2a_2 + 2a_3 + 2a_4 = 9 + 2 \cdot 3 + 2 \cdot 1 + 2 \cdot \frac{1}{3} + 2 \cdot \frac{1}{9} = \frac{161}{9} = 17\frac{8}{9}$ ft.

 (b) The total distance traveled at the instant the ball hits the ground for the nth time is
$$D_n = 9 + 2 \cdot 9 \cdot \frac{1}{3} + 2 \cdot 9 \cdot \left(\frac{1}{3}\right)^2 + 2 \cdot 9 \cdot \left(\frac{1}{3}\right)^3 + 2 \cdot 9 \cdot \left(\frac{1}{3}\right)^4 + \cdots + 2 \cdot 9 \cdot \left(\frac{1}{3}\right)^{n-1}$$
$$= 2\left[9 + 9 \cdot \frac{1}{3} + 9 \cdot \left(\frac{1}{3}\right)^2 + 9 \cdot \left(\frac{1}{3}\right)^3 + 9 \cdot \left(\frac{1}{3}\right)^4 + \cdots + 9 \cdot \left(\frac{1}{3}\right)^{n-1}\right] - 9$$
$$= 2\left[9 \cdot \frac{1 - \left(\frac{1}{3}\right)^n}{1 - \frac{1}{3}}\right] - 9 = 27\left[1 - \left(\frac{1}{3}\right)^n\right] - 9 = 18 - \left(\frac{1}{3}\right)^{n-3}.$$

53. $1 + \frac{1}{3} + \frac{1}{9} + \frac{1}{27} + \cdots$ is an infinite geometric series with $a = 1$ and $r = \frac{1}{3}$. Therefore, the sum of the series is $S = \dfrac{a}{1 - r} = \dfrac{1}{1 - \left(\frac{1}{3}\right)} = \dfrac{3}{2}$.

55. $1 - \frac{1}{3} + \frac{1}{9} - \frac{1}{27} + \cdots$ is an infinite geometric series with $a = 1$ and $r = -\frac{1}{3}$. Therefore, the sum of the series is $S = \dfrac{a}{1 - r} = \dfrac{1}{1 - \left(-\frac{1}{3}\right)} = \dfrac{3}{4}$.

57. $\dfrac{1}{3^6} + \dfrac{1}{3^8} + \dfrac{1}{3^{10}} + \dfrac{1}{3^{12}} + \cdots$ is an infinite geometric series with $a = \dfrac{1}{3^6}$ and $r = \dfrac{1}{3^2} = \dfrac{1}{9}$. Therefore, the sum of the series is $S = \dfrac{a}{1 - r} = \dfrac{\frac{1}{3^6}}{1 - \left(\frac{1}{9}\right)} = \dfrac{1}{3^6} \cdot \dfrac{9}{8} = \dfrac{1}{648}$.

59. $-\dfrac{100}{9} + \dfrac{10}{3} - 1 + \dfrac{3}{10} - \cdots$ is an infinite geometric series with $a = -\dfrac{100}{9}$ and $r = \dfrac{\frac{10}{3}}{-\frac{100}{9}} = \dfrac{3}{10}$.

 Therefore, the sum of the series is $S = \dfrac{a}{1 - r} = \dfrac{-\frac{100}{9}}{1 - \left(-\frac{3}{10}\right)} = \dfrac{-\frac{100}{9}}{\frac{13}{10}} = -\dfrac{100}{9} \cdot \dfrac{10}{13} = -\dfrac{1000}{117}$.

61. $0.777\ldots = \dfrac{7}{10} + \dfrac{7}{100} + \dfrac{7}{1000} + \cdots$ is an infinite geometric series with $a = \dfrac{7}{10}$ and $r = \dfrac{1}{10}$. Thus

 $0.777\ldots = \dfrac{a}{1 - r} = \dfrac{\frac{7}{10}}{1 - \frac{1}{10}} = \dfrac{7}{9}$.

63. $0.030303\ldots = \dfrac{3}{100} + \dfrac{3}{10,000} + \dfrac{3}{1,000,000} + \cdots$ is an infinite geometric series with $a = \dfrac{3}{100}$ and

     $r = \dfrac{1}{100}$. Thus $0.030303\ldots = \dfrac{a}{1-r} = \dfrac{\frac{3}{100}}{1 - \frac{1}{100}} = \dfrac{3}{99} = \dfrac{1}{33}$.

65. $0.\overline{112} = 0.112112112\ldots = \dfrac{112}{1000} + \dfrac{112}{1,000,000} + \dfrac{112}{1,000,000,000} + \cdots$ is an infinite geometric

     series with $a = \dfrac{112}{1000}$ and $r = \dfrac{1}{1000}$. Thus $0.112112112\ldots = \dfrac{a}{1-r} = \dfrac{\frac{112}{1000}}{1 - \frac{1}{1000}} = \dfrac{112}{999}$.

67.   Let a_n be the height the ball reaches on the nth bounce. We have $a_0 = 1$ and $a_n = \frac{1}{2}a_{n-1}$. Since
     the total distance d traveled includes the bounce up as well and the distance down, we have

     $d = a_0 + 2 \cdot a_1 + 2 \cdot a_2 + \ldots = 1 + 2\left(\frac{1}{2}\right) + 2\left(\frac{1}{2}\right)^2 + 2\left(\frac{1}{2}\right)^3 + 2\left(\frac{1}{2}\right)^4 + \cdots$

     $= 1 + 1 + \frac{1}{2} + \left(\frac{1}{2}\right)^2 + \left(\frac{1}{2}\right)^3 + \cdots = 1 + \sum\limits_{i=0}^{\infty}\left(\frac{1}{2}\right)^i = 1 + \dfrac{1}{1 - \frac{1}{2}} = 3$. Thus the total distance

     traveled is about 3m.

69.   (a)   If a square has side x, then the side of the square formed by joining the midpoints is (by the

        Pythagorean Theorem) $\sqrt{\left(\dfrac{x}{2}\right)^2 + \left(\dfrac{x}{2}\right)^2} = \sqrt{\dfrac{x^2}{4} + \dfrac{x^2}{4}} = \dfrac{x}{\sqrt{2}}$. In our case, $x = 1$ and the

        side of the first inscribed square is $\dfrac{1}{\sqrt{2}}$, the side of the second inscribed square is

        $\dfrac{1}{\sqrt{2}} \cdot \dfrac{1}{\sqrt{2}} = \left(\dfrac{1}{\sqrt{2}}\right)^2$, the side of the third inscribed square is $\left(\dfrac{1}{\sqrt{2}}\right)^3$, $\ldots$. Since this pattern

        continues, the total area of all the squares is $A = 1^2 + \left(\dfrac{1}{\sqrt{2}}\right)^2 + \left(\dfrac{1}{\sqrt{2}}\right)^4 + \left(\dfrac{1}{\sqrt{2}}\right)^6 + \cdots$

        $= 1 + \frac{1}{2} + \left(\frac{1}{2}\right)^2 + \left(\frac{1}{2}\right)^3 + \cdots = \frac{1}{1 - \frac{1}{2}} = 2$.

     (b)   As in part (a), the sides of the squares are 1, $\dfrac{1}{\sqrt{2}}$, $\left(\dfrac{1}{\sqrt{2}}\right)^2$, $\left(\dfrac{1}{\sqrt{2}}\right)^3$, $\ldots$. Thus the sum of the

        perimeters is $S = 4 \cdot 1 + 4 \cdot \dfrac{1}{\sqrt{2}} + 4 \cdot \left(\dfrac{1}{\sqrt{2}}\right)^2 + 4 \cdot \left(\dfrac{1}{\sqrt{2}}\right)^3 + \cdots$, which is an infinite

        geometric series with $a = 4$ and $r = \dfrac{1}{\sqrt{2}}$. Thus the sum of the perimeters is

        $S = \dfrac{4}{1 - \frac{1}{\sqrt{2}}} = \dfrac{4\sqrt{2}}{\sqrt{2}-1} = \dfrac{4\sqrt{2}}{\sqrt{2}-1} \cdot \dfrac{\sqrt{2}+1}{\sqrt{2}+1} = \dfrac{4 \cdot 2 + 4\sqrt{2}}{2-1} = 8 + 4\sqrt{2}$.

71.   Let a_n denote the area colored blue at nth stage. Since only the middle squares are colored blue,
     $a_n = \frac{1}{9} \times$ (area remaining yellow at the $(n-1)^{\text{st}}$ stage). Also, the area remaining yellow at the nth
     stage is $\frac{8}{9}$ of the area remaining yellow at the preceding stage. So $a_1 = \frac{1}{9}$, $a_2 = \frac{1}{9}\left(\frac{8}{9}\right)$, $a_3 = \frac{1}{9}\left(\frac{8}{9}\right)^2$,
     $a_4 = \frac{1}{9}\left(\frac{8}{9}\right)^3$, $\ldots$. Thus the total area colored blue $A = \frac{1}{9} + \frac{1}{9}\left(\frac{8}{9}\right) + \frac{1}{9}\left(\frac{8}{9}\right)^2 + \frac{1}{9}\left(\frac{8}{9}\right)^3 + \ldots$ is an

     infinite geometric series with $a = \frac{1}{9}$ and $r = \frac{8}{9}$. So the total area is $A = \dfrac{\frac{1}{9}}{1 - \frac{8}{9}} = 1$.

73. The sum is given by $(a + b) + (a^2 + 2b) + (a^3 + 3b) + \cdots + (a^{10} + 10b) =$

$(a + a^2 + a^3 + \cdots + a^{10}) + (b + 2b + 3b + \cdots + 10b) = a\dfrac{1 - a^9}{1 - a} + \dfrac{10}{2}(b + 10b)$

$= a\dfrac{1 - a^9}{1 - a} + 55b.$

75. Let $a_1, a_2, a_3, \ldots$ be a geometric sequence with common ratio r. Thus $a_2 = a_1 r$, $a_3 = a_1 \cdot r^2, \ldots,$

$a_n = a_1 \cdot r^{n-1}$. Hence, $\dfrac{1}{a_2} = \dfrac{1}{a_1 \cdot r} = \dfrac{1}{a_1} \cdot \dfrac{1}{r}$, $\dfrac{1}{a_3} = \dfrac{1}{a_1 \cdot r^2} = \dfrac{1}{a_1} \cdot \dfrac{1}{r^2} = \dfrac{1}{a_1} \cdot \left(\dfrac{1}{r}\right)^2, \ldots$

$\dfrac{1}{a_n} = \dfrac{1}{a_1 \cdot r^{n-1}} = \dfrac{1}{a_1} \cdot \dfrac{1}{r^{n-1}} = \dfrac{1}{a_1}\left(\dfrac{1}{r}\right)^{n-1}$, and so $\dfrac{1}{a_1}, \dfrac{1}{a_2}, \dfrac{1}{a_3}, \ldots$ is a geometric sequence with common ratio $\frac{1}{r}$.

77. Since $a_1, a_2, a_3, \ldots$ is an arithmetic sequence with common difference d, the terms can be expressed as $a_2 = a_1 + d$, $a_3 = a_1 + 2d, \ldots, a_n = a_1 + (n - 1)d$. So $10^{a_2} = 10^{a_1 + d} = 10^{a_1} \cdot 10^d$, $10^{a_3} = 10^{a_1 + 2d} = 10^{a_1} \cdot (10^d)^2, \ldots, 10^{a_n} = 10^{a_1 + (n-1)d} = 10^{a_1} \cdot (10^d)^{n-1}$, and so $10^{a_1}, 10^{a_2}, 10^{a_3}$, $\ldots$ is a geometric sequence with common ratio $r = 10^d$.

Exercises 10.4

1. $n = 10, R = \$1000, i = 0.06.$ So, $A_f = R\dfrac{(1+i)^n - 1}{i} = 1000\dfrac{(1+0.06)^{10} - 1}{0.06} = \$13,180.79.$

3. $n = 20, R = \$5000, i = 0.12.$ So, $A_f = R\dfrac{(1+i)^n - 1}{i} = 5000\dfrac{(1+0.12)^{20} - 1}{0.12} = \$360,262.21.$

5. $n = 16, R = \$300, i = \dfrac{0.08}{4} = 0.02.$ So, $A_f = R\dfrac{(1+i)^n - 1}{i} = 300\dfrac{(1+0.02)^{16} - 1}{0.02}$

    $= \$5,591.79.$

7. $A_f = \$2000, i = \dfrac{0.06}{12} = 0.005, n = 8.$ Then $R = \dfrac{iA_f}{(1+i)^n - 1} = \dfrac{(0.005)(2000)}{(1+0.005)^8 - 1} = \$245.66.$

9. $R = \$200, n = 20, i = \dfrac{0.09}{2} = 0.045.$ So, $A_p = R\dfrac{1-(1+i)^{-n}}{i} = (200)\dfrac{1-(1+0.045)^{-20}}{0.045}$

    $= \$2601.59.$

11. $A_p = \$12,000, i = \dfrac{0.105}{12} = 0.00875, n = 48.$ Then $R = \dfrac{iA_p}{1-(1+i)^{-n}} = \dfrac{(0.00875)(12000)}{1-(1+0.00875)^{-48}}$

    $= \$307.24.$

13. $A_p = \$100,000, i = \dfrac{0.08}{12} \approx 0.006667, n = 360.$ Then $R = \dfrac{iA_p}{1-(1+i)^{-n}}$

    $= \dfrac{(0.006667)(100,000)}{1-(1+0.006667)^{-360}} = \$733.76.$ Therefore, the total amount paid on this loan over the 30

    year period is $(360)(733.76) = \$264,153.60.$

15. $A_p = 100,000, n = 360, i = \frac{0.0975}{12} = 0.008125.$

    (a) $R = \dfrac{i A_p}{1-(1+i)^{-n}} = \dfrac{(0.008125)(100,000)}{1-(1+0.008125)^{-360}} = \$859.15.$

    (b)   The total amount that will be paid over the 30 year period is $(360)(859.15) = \$309,294.00.$

    (c) $R = \$859.15, i = \dfrac{0.0975}{12} = 0.008125, n = 360.$ So, $A_f = 859.15\dfrac{(1+0.008125)^{360} - 1}{0.008125}$

       $= \$1,841,519.29.$

17. $R = \$30, i = \dfrac{0.10}{12} \approx 0.008333, n = 12.$ Then $A_p = R\dfrac{1-(1+i)^{-n}}{i}$

    $= 30\dfrac{1-\left(1+0.008333\right)^{-12}}{0.008333} = \$341.24.$

19. $A_p = \$640, R = \$32, n = 24.$ We want to solve the equation $R = \dfrac{iA_p}{1-(1+i)^n}$ for the interest

    rate $i.$ Let x be the interest rate, then $i = \frac{x}{12}.$ So we can express R as a function of x by

$R(x) = \dfrac{\frac{x}{12} \cdot 640}{1 - \left(1 + \frac{x}{12}\right)^{-24}}$. We graph $R(x)$ and $y = 32$ in the rectangle $[0.12, 0.22] \times [30, 34]$. The x-coordinate of the intersection is about 0.1816, which corresponds to an interest rate of 18.16%.

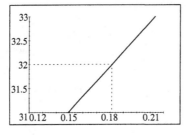

21. $A_p = \$189.99$, $R = \$10.50$, $n = 20$. We want to solve the equation $R = \dfrac{iA_p}{1 - (1+i)^n}$ for the interest rate i. Let x be the interest rate, then $i = \frac{x}{12}$. So we can express R as a function of x by $R(x) = \dfrac{\frac{x}{12} \cdot 189.99}{1 - \left(1 + \frac{x}{12}\right)^{-20}}$. We graph $R(x)$ and $y = 10.50$ in the rectangle $[0.10, 0.18] \times [10, 11]$. The x-coordinate of the intersection is about 0.1168, which corresponds to an interest rate of 11.68%.

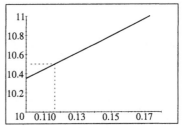

23.   (a)   The present value of the kth payment is $PV = \dfrac{R}{(1+i)^k}$. The amount of money to be invested now (A_p) to ensure an annuity in perpetuity is the (infinite) sum of the present values of each of the payments, as the following time line shows.

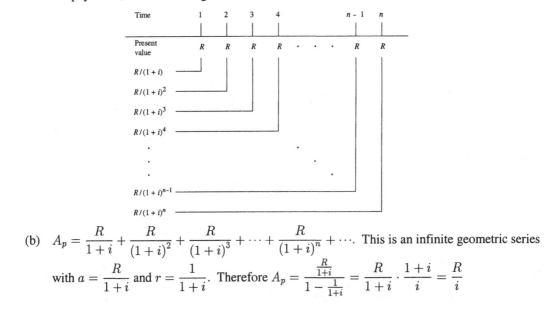

(b) $A_p = \dfrac{R}{1+i} + \dfrac{R}{(1+i)^2} + \dfrac{R}{(1+i)^3} + \cdots + \dfrac{R}{(1+i)^n} + \cdots$. This is an infinite geometric series

with $a = \dfrac{R}{1+i}$ and $r = \dfrac{1}{1+i}$. Therefore $A_p = \dfrac{\frac{R}{1+i}}{1 - \frac{1}{1+i}} = \dfrac{R}{1+i} \cdot \dfrac{1+i}{i} = \dfrac{R}{i}$

(c) Using the result from Part (b), we have $R = 5000$ and $i = 0.10$. Then $A_p = \dfrac{R}{i} = \dfrac{5000}{0.10}$
     $= \$50{,}000$.

(d) We are given two different time periods: the interest is compounded quarterly, while the annuity is paid yearly. In order to use the formula in Part (b), we need to find the effective annual interest rate produced by 8% interest compounded quarterly, which is $\left(1 + \frac{i}{n}\right)^n - 1$. Now $i = 8\%$ and it is compounded quarterly, $n = 4$, so the effective annual yield is $(1 + 0.02)^4 - 1 \approx 0.08243216$. Thus by the formula in Part (b), the amount that must be invested is $A_p = \dfrac{3000}{0.08243216} = \$36{,}393.56$.

Exercises 10.5

1. Let $P(n)$ denote the statement $2 + 4 + 6 + \cdots + 2n = n(n+1)$.

    Step 1 $P(1)$ is the statement that $2 = 1(1+1)$, which is true.

    Step 2 Assume that $P(k)$ is true; that is, $2 + 4 + 6 + \cdots + 2k = k(k+1)$. We want to use this to show that $P(k+1)$ is true. Now,

    $$2 + 4 + 6 + \cdots + 2k + 2(k+1) =$$
    $$k(k+1) + 2(k+1) = \qquad\qquad\qquad \text{induction hypothesis}$$
    $$(k+1)(k+2) = (k+1)[(k+1)+1].$$

    Thus, $P(k+1)$ follows from $P(k)$. So by the Principle of Mathematical Induction, $P(n)$ is true for all n.

3. Let $P(n)$ denote the statement $5 + 8 + 11 + \cdots + (3n+2) = \dfrac{n(3n+7)}{2}$.

    Step 1 We need to show that $P(1)$ is true. But $P(1)$ says that $5 = \frac{1 \cdot (3 \cdot 1 + 7)}{2}$, which is true.

    Step 2 Assume that $P(k)$ is true; that is, $5 + 8 + 11 + \cdots + (3k+2) = \dfrac{k(3k+7)}{2}$. We want to use this to show that $P(k+1)$ is true. Now,

    $$5 + 8 + 11 + \cdots + (3k+2) + [3(k+1)+2] =$$
    $$\frac{k(3k+7)}{2} + (3k+5) = \qquad\qquad\qquad \text{induction hypothesis}$$
    $$\frac{3k^2 + 7k}{2} + \frac{6k+10}{2} =$$
    $$\frac{3k^2 + 13k + 10}{2} = \frac{(3k+10)(k+1)}{2} = \frac{(k+1)[3(k+1)+7]}{2}.$$

    Thus, $P(k+1)$ follows from $P(k)$. So by the Principle of Mathematical Induction, $P(n)$ is true for all n

5. Let $P(n)$ denote the statement $1 \cdot 2 + 2 \cdot 3 + 3 \cdot 4 + \cdots + n(n+1) = \dfrac{n(n+1)(n+2)}{3}$.

    Step 1 $P(1)$ is the statement that $1 \cdot 2 = \frac{1 \cdot (1+1) \cdot (1+2)}{3}$, which is true.

    Step 2 Assume that $P(k)$ is true; that is, $1 \cdot 2 + 2 \cdot 3 + 3 \cdot 4 + \cdots + k(k+1) = \dfrac{k(k+1)(k+2)}{3}$. We want to use this to show that $P(k+1)$ is true. Now,

    $$1 \cdot 2 + 2 \cdot 3 + 3 \cdot 4 + \cdots + k(k+1) + (k+1)[(k+1)+1] =$$
    $$\frac{k(k+1)(k+2)}{3} + (k+1)(k+2) = \qquad\qquad\qquad \text{induction hypothesis}$$
    $$\frac{k(k+1)(k+2)}{3} + \frac{3(k+1)(k+2)}{3} = \frac{(k+1)(k+2)(k+3)}{3}.$$

    Thus, $P(k+1)$ follows from $P(k)$. So by the Principle of Mathematical Induction, $P(n)$ is true for all n.

7. Let $P(n)$ denote the statement $1^3 + 2^3 + 3^3 + \cdots + n^3 = \dfrac{n^2(n+1)^2}{4}$.

Step 1 $P(1)$ is the statement that $1^3 = \frac{1^2 \cdot (1+1)^2}{4}$, which is clearly true.

Step 2 Assume that $P(k)$ is true; that is, $1^3 + 2^3 + 3^3 + \cdots + k^3 = \dfrac{k^2(k+1)^2}{4}$. We want to use this to show that $P(k+1)$ is true. Now,

$1^3 + 2^3 + 3^3 + \cdots + k^3 + (k+1)^3 =$

$\dfrac{k^2(k+1)^2}{4} + (k+1)^3 =$ induction hypothesis

$\dfrac{(k+1)^2[k^2 + 4(k+1)]}{4} =$

$\dfrac{(k+1)^2[k^2 + 4k + 4]}{4} = \dfrac{(k+1)^2(k+2)^2}{4} = \dfrac{(k+1)^2[(k+1)+1]^2}{4}$.

Thus, $P(k+1)$ follows from $P(k)$. So by the Principle of Mathematical Induction, $P(n)$ is true for all n.

9. Let $P(n)$ denote the statement $2^3 + 4^3 + 6^3 + \cdots + (2n)^3 = 2n^2(n+1)^2$.

Step 1 $P(1)$ is true since $2^3 = 2(1)^2(1+1)^2 = 2 \cdot 4 = 8$.

Step 2 Assume that $P(k)$ is true; that is, $2^3 + 4^3 + 6^3 + \cdots + (2k)^3 = 2k^2(k+1)^2$. We want to use this to show that $P(k+1)$ is true. Now,

$2^3 + 4^3 + 6^3 + \cdots + (2k)^3 + [2(k+1)]^3 =$

$2k^2(k+1)^2 + [2(k+1)]^3 =$ induction hypothesis

$2k^2(k+1)^2 + 8(k+1)(k+1)^2 =$

$(k+1)^2(2k^2 + 8k + 8) = 2(k+1)^2(k+2)^2 = 2(k+1)^2[(k+1)+1]^2$.

Thus, $P(k+1)$ follows from $P(k)$. So by the Principle of Mathematical Induction, $P(n)$ is true for all n.

11. Let $P(n)$ denote the statement $1 \cdot 2 + 2 \cdot 2^2 + 3 \cdot 2^3 + 4 \cdot 2^4 + \cdots + n \cdot 2^n = 2[1 + (n-1)2^n]$.

Step 1 $P(1)$ is the statement that $1 \cdot 2 = 2[1 + 0]$, which is clearly true.

Step 2 Assume that $P(k)$ is true; that is,

$1 \cdot 2 + 2 \cdot 2^2 + 3 \cdot 2^3 + 4 \cdot 2^4 + \cdots + k \cdot 2^k = 2[1 + (k-1)2^k]$. We want to use this to show that $P(k+1)$ is true. Now,

$1 \cdot 2 + 2 \cdot 2^2 + 3 \cdot 2^3 + 4 \cdot 2^4 + \cdots + k \cdot 2^k + (k+1) \cdot 2^{(k+1)} =$

$2[1 + (k-1)2^k] + (k+1) \cdot 2^{(k+1)} =$ induction hypothesis

$2[1 + (k-1) \cdot 2^k + (k+1) \cdot 2^k] =$

$2[1 + 2k \cdot 2^k] = 2[1 + k \cdot 2^{k+1}] = 2\{1 + [(k+1) - 1]2^{k+1}\}$.

Thus $P(k+1)$ follows from $P(k)$. So by the Principle of Mathematical Induction, $P(n)$ is true for all n.

13. Let $P(n)$ denote the statement $n^2 + n$ is divisible by 2.

Step 1 $P(1)$ is the statement that $1^2 + 1 = 2$ is divisible by 2, which is clearly true.

Step 2 Assume that $P(k)$ is true; that is, $k^2 + k$ is divisible by 2. Now,

$(k+1)^2 + (k+1) = k^2 + 2k + 1 + k + 1 = (k^2 + k) + 2k + 2 = (k^2 + k) + 2(k+1)$.

By the induction hypothesis, $k^2 + k$ is divisible by 2, and clearly $2(k+1)$ is divisible by 2.

Thus, the sum is divisible by 2, so $P(k+1)$ true. Therefore, $P(k+1)$ follows from $P(k)$. So by the Principle of Mathematical Induction, $P(n)$ is true for all n.

15. Let $P(n)$ denote the statement that $n^2 - n + 41$ is odd.

Step 1 $P(1)$ is the statement that $1^2 - 1 + 41 = 41$ is odd, which is clearly true.

Step 2 Assume that $P(k)$ is true; that is, $k^2 - k + 41$ is odd. We want to use this to show that $P(k+1)$ is true. Now,
$(k+1)^2 - (k+1) + 41 = k^2 + 2k + 1 - k - 1 + 41 = (k^2 - k + 41) + 2k$, which is also odd because $k^2 - k + 41$ is odd by the induction hypothesis, $2k$ is always even, and an odd number plus an even number is always odd. Therefore, $P(k+1)$ follows from $P(k)$. So by the Principle of Mathematical Induction, $P(n)$ is true for all n.

17. Let $P(n)$ denote the statement that $8^n - 3^n$ is divisible by 5.

Step 1 $P(1)$ is the statement that $8^1 - 3^1 = 5$ is divisible by 5, which is clearly true.

Step 2 Assume that $P(k)$ is true; that is, $8^k - 3^k$ is divisible by 5. We want to use this to show that $P(k+1)$ is true. Now, $8^{k+1} - 3^{k+1} = 8 \cdot 8^k - 3 \cdot 3^k = 8 \cdot 8^k - (8-5) \cdot 3^k$
$= 8 \cdot (8^k - 3^k) + 5 \cdot 3^k$, which is divisible by 5 because $8^k - 3^k$ is divisible by 5 by our induction hypothesis, and $5 \cdot 3^k$ is divisible by 5. Thus $P(k+1)$ follows from $P(k)$. So by the Principle of Mathematical Induction, $P(n)$ is true for all n.

19. Let $P(n)$ denote the statement $n < 2^n$.

Step 1 $P(1)$ is the statement that $1 < 2^1 = 2$, which is clearly true.

Step 2 Assume that $P(k)$ is true; that is, $k < 2^k$. We want to use this to show that $P(k+1)$ is true. Adding 1 to both sides of $P(k)$ we have $k + 1 < 2^k + 1$. Since $1 < 2^k$ for $k \geq 1$, we have $2^k + 1 < 2^k + 2^k = 2 \cdot 2^k = 2^{k+1}$. Thus $k + 1 < 2^{k+1}$, which is exactly $P(k+1)$. Therefore, $P(k+1)$ follows from $P(k)$. So by the Principle of Mathematical Induction, $P(n)$ is true for all n.

21. Let $P(n)$ denote the statement $(1+x)^n \geq 1 + nx$, if $x > -1$.

Step 1 $P(1)$ is the statement that $(1+x)^1 \geq 1 + 1x$, which is clearly true.

Step 2 Assume that $P(k)$ is true; that is, $(1+x)^k \geq 1 + kx$. Now,
$(1+x)^{k+1} = (1+x)(1+x)^k \geq (1+x)(1+kx)$, by the induction hypothesis. Since $(1+x)(1+kx) = 1 + (k+1)x + kx^2 \geq 1 + (k+1)x$ (since $kx^2 \geq 0$), we have $(1+x)^{k+1} \geq 1 + (k+1)x$, which is $P(k+1)$. Thus $P(k+1)$ follows from $P(k)$. So the Principle of Mathematical Induction, $P(n)$ is true for all n.

23. Let $P(n)$ be the statement that $a_n = 5 \cdot 3^{n-1}$.

Step 1 $P(1)$ is the statement that $a_1 = 5 \cdot 3^0 = 5$, which is true.

Step 2 Assume that $P(k)$ is true; that is, $a_k = 5 \cdot 3^{k-1}$. We want to use this to show that $P(k+1)$ is true. Now, $a_{k+1} = 3a_k = 3 \cdot (5 \cdot 3^{k-1})$, by the induction hypothesis. Therefore, $a_{k+1} = 3 \cdot (5 \cdot 3^{k-1}) = 5 \cdot 3^k$, which is exactly $P(k+1)$. Thus, $P(k+1)$ follows from $P(k)$. So by the Principle of Mathematical Induction, $P(n)$ is true for all n.

25. Let $P(n)$ be the statement that $x - y$ is a factor of $x^n - y^n$ for all natural numbers n.

Step 1 $P(1)$ is the statement that $x - y$ is a factor of $x^1 - y^1$, which is clearly true.

Step 2 Assume that $P(k)$ is true; that is, $x - y$ is a factor of $x^k - y^k$. We want to use this to show that $P(k+1)$ is true. Now, $x^{k+1} - y^{k+1} = x^{k+1} - x^k y + x^k y - y^{k+1}$

$= x^k(x-y) + (x^k - y^k)y$, for which $x - y$ is a factor because $x - y$ is a factor of $x^k(x-y)$, and $x - y$ is a factor of $(x^k - y^k)y$, by the induction hypothesis. Thus $P(k+1)$ follows from $P(k)$. So by the Principle of Mathematical Induction, $P(n)$ is true for all n.

27. Let $P(n)$ denote the statement that F_{3n} is even for all natural numbers n.

Step 1 $P(1)$ is the statement that F_3 is even. Since $F_3 = F_2 + F_1 = 1 + 1 = 2$, this statement is true.

Step 2 Assume that $P(k)$ is true; that is, F_{3k} is even. We want to use this to show that $P(k+1)$ is true. Now, $F_{3(k+1)} = F_{3k+3} = F_{3k+2} + F_{3k+1} = F_{3k+1} + F_{3k} + F_{3k+1} = F_{3k} + 2 \cdot F_{3k+1}$, which is even because F_{3k} is even by the induction hypothesis, and $2 \cdot F_{3k+1}$ is even. Thus $P(k+1)$ follows from $P(k)$. So by the Principle of Mathematical Induction, $P(n)$ is true for all n.

29. Let $P(n)$ denote the statement that $F_1^2 + F_2^2 + F_3^2 + \cdots + F_n^2 = F_n \cdot F_{n+1}$.

Step 1 $P(1)$ is the statement that $F_1^2 = F_1 \cdot F_2$ or $1^2 = 1 \cdot 1$, which is true.

Step 2 Assume that $P(k)$ is true, that is, $F_1^2 + F_2^2 + F_3^2 + \cdots + F_k^2 = F_k \cdot F_{k+1}$. We want to use this to show that $P(k+1)$ is true. Now,

$$F_1^2 + F_2^2 + F_3^2 + \cdots + F_k^2 + F_{k+1}^2 =$$
$$F_k \cdot F_{k+1} + F_{k+1}^2 = \qquad\qquad \text{induction hypothesis}$$
$$F_{k+1}(F_k + F_{k+1}) = F_{k+1} \cdot F_{k+2}. \qquad \text{by definition of the Fibonacci sequence}$$

Thus $P(k+1)$ follows from $P(k)$. So by the Principle of Mathematical Induction, $P(n)$ is true for all n.

31. Let $P(n)$ denote the statement $\begin{bmatrix} 1 & 1 \\ 1 & 0 \end{bmatrix}^n = \begin{bmatrix} F_{n+1} & F_n \\ F_n & F_{n-1} \end{bmatrix}$.

Step 1 Since $\begin{bmatrix} 1 & 1 \\ 1 & 0 \end{bmatrix}^2 = \begin{bmatrix} 1 & 1 \\ 1 & 0 \end{bmatrix}\begin{bmatrix} 1 & 1 \\ 1 & 0 \end{bmatrix} = \begin{bmatrix} 2 & 1 \\ 1 & 1 \end{bmatrix} = \begin{bmatrix} F_3 & F_2 \\ F_2 & F_1 \end{bmatrix}$, it follows that $P(2)$ is true.

Step 2 Assume that $P(k)$ is true; that is, $\begin{bmatrix} 1 & 1 \\ 1 & 0 \end{bmatrix}^k = \begin{bmatrix} F_{k+1} & F_k \\ F_k & F_{k-1} \end{bmatrix}$. We show that $P(k+1)$ follows from this. Now,

$$\begin{bmatrix} 1 & 1 \\ 1 & 0 \end{bmatrix}^{k+1} = \begin{bmatrix} 1 & 1 \\ 1 & 0 \end{bmatrix}^k \begin{bmatrix} 1 & 1 \\ 1 & 0 \end{bmatrix} = \begin{bmatrix} F_{k+1} & F_k \\ F_k & F_{k-1} \end{bmatrix}\begin{bmatrix} 1 & 1 \\ 1 & 0 \end{bmatrix} \quad \text{(by the induction hypothesis)}$$
$$= \begin{bmatrix} F_{k+1} + F_k & F_{k+1} \\ F_k + F_{k-1} & F_k \end{bmatrix} = \begin{bmatrix} F_{k+2} & F_{k+1} \\ F_{k+1} & F_k \end{bmatrix}. \quad \text{(by definition of the Fibonacci sequence)}$$

Thus $P(k+1)$ follows from $P(k)$. So by the Principle of Mathematical Induction, $P(n)$ is true for all $n \geq 2$.

33. Since $F_1 = 1$, $F_2 = 1$, $F_3 = 2$, $F_4 = 3$, $F_5 = 5$, $F_6 = 8$, $F_7 = 13, \ldots$ our conjecture is that $F_n \geq n$, for all $n \geq 5$. Let $P(n)$ denote the statement that $F_n \geq n$.

Step 1 $P(5)$ is the statement that $F_5 = 5 \geq 5$, which is clearly true.

Step 2 Assume that $P(k)$ is true; that is, $F_k \geq k$, for some $k \geq 5$. We want to use this to show that $P(k+1)$ is true. Now, $F_{k+1} = F_k + F_{k-1} \geq k + F_{k-1}$ (by the induction hypothesis) $\geq k + 1$ (because $F_{k-1} \geq 1$). Thus $P(k+1)$ follows from $P(k)$. So by the Principle of Mathematical Induction, $P(n)$ is true for all $n \geq 5$.

35. (a) $P(n) = n^2 - n + 11$ is prime for all n. This is false as the case for $n = 11$ demonstrates: $P(11) = 11^2 - 11 + 11 = 121$, which is not prime since $11^2 = 121$.

(b) $n^2 > n$, for all $n \geq 2$. This is true. Let $P(n)$ denote the statement that $n^2 > n$.

Step 1 $P(2)$ is the statement that $2^2 = 4 > 2$, which is clearly true.

Step 2 Assume that $P(k)$ is true; that is, $k^2 > k$. We want to use this to show that $P(k+1)$ is true. Now $(k+1)^2 = k^2 + 2k + 1$. Using the induction hypothesis (to replace k^2), we have $k^2 + 2k + 1 > k + 2k + 1 = 3k + 1 > k + 1$, since $k \geq 2$. Therefore, $(k+1)^2 > k+1$, which is exactly $P(k+1)$. Thus $P(k+1)$ follows from $P(k)$. So by the Principle of Mathematical Induction, $P(n)$ is true for all n.

(c) $2^{2n+1} + 1$ is divisible by 3, for all $n \geq 1$. This is true. Let $P(n)$ denote the statement that $2^{2n+1} + 1$ is divisible by 3.

Step 1 $P(1)$ is the statement that $2^3 + 1 = 9$ is divisible by 3, which is clearly true.

Step 2 Assume that $P(k)$ is true; that is, $2^{2k+1} + 1$ is divisible by 3. We want to use this to show that $P(k+1)$ is true. Now, $2^{2(k+1)+1} + 1 = 2^{2k+3} + 1 = 4 \cdot 2^{2k+1} + 1$ $= (3+1)2^{2k+1} + 1 = 3 \cdot 2^{2k+1} + (2^{2k+1} + 1)$, which is divisible by 3 since $2^{2k+1} + 1$ is divisible by 3 by the induction hypothesis, and $3 \cdot 2^{2k+1}$ is clearly divisible by 3. Thus $P(k+1)$ follows from $P(k)$. So by the Principle of Mathematical Induction, $P(n)$ is true for all n.

(d) The statement $n^3 \geq (n+1)^2$ for all $n \geq 2$ is false. The statement fails when $n = 2$: $2^3 = 8 < (2+1)^2 = 9$.

(e) $n^3 - n$ is divisible by 3, for all $n \geq 2$. This is true. Let $P(n)$ denote the statement that $n^3 - n$ is divisible by 3.

Step 1 $P(2)$ is the statement that $2^3 - 2 = 6$ is divisible by 3, which is clearly true.

Step 2 Assume that $P(k)$ is true; that is, $k^3 - k$ is divisible by 3. We want to use this to show that $P(k+1)$ is true. Now, $(k+1)^3 - (k+1) = k^3 + 3k^2 + 3k + 1 - (k+1) = k^3 + 3k^2 + 2k = k^3 - k + 3k^2 + 2k + k = (k^3 - k) + 3(k^2 + k)$. The term $k^3 - k$ is divisible by 3 by our induction hypothesis, and the term $3(k^2 + k)$ is clearly divisible by 3. Thus $(k+1)^3 - (k+1)$ is divisible by 3, which is exactly $P(k+1)$. So by the Principle of Mathematical Induction, $P(n)$ is true for all n.

(f) $n^3 - 6n^2 + 11n$ is divisible by 6, for all $n \geq 1$. This is true. Let $P(n)$ denote the statement that $n^3 - 6n^2 + 11n$ is divisible by 6.

Step 1 $P(1)$ is the statement that $(1)^3 - 6(1)^2 + 11(1) = 6$ is divisible by 6, which is clearly true.

Step 2 Assume that $P(k)$ is true; that is, $k^3 - 6k^2 + 11k$ is divisible by 6. We show that $P(k+1)$ is then also true. Now, $(k+1)^3 - 6(k+1)^2 + 11(k+1)$ $= k^3 + 3k^2 + 3k + 1 - 6k^2 - 12k - 6 + 11k + 11 = k^3 - 3k^2 + 2k + 6$ $= k^3 - 6k^2 + 11k + (3k^2 - 9k + 6) = (k^3 - 6k^2 + 11k) + 3(k^2 - 3k + 2)$ $= (k^3 - 6k^2 + 11k) + 3(k-1)(k-2)$. In this last expression, the first term is divisible by 6 by our induction hypothesis. The second term is also divisible by 6. To see this, notice that $(k-1)$ and $(k-2)$ are consecutive natural numbers, and so one of them must be even (divisible by 2). Since 3 also appears in this second term, it follows that this term is divisible by 2 and 3 and so is divisible by 6. Thus $P(k+1)$ follows from $P(k)$. So by the Principle of Mathematical Induction, $P(n)$ is true for all n.

Exercises 10.6

1. $(x+y)^6 = x^6 + 6x^5 y + 15x^4 y^2 + 20x^3 y^3 + 15x^2 y^4 + 6xy^5 + y^6$

3. $\left(x + \dfrac{1}{x}\right)^4 = x^4 + 4x^3 \cdot \dfrac{1}{x} + 6x^2 \left(\dfrac{1}{x}\right)^2 + 4x \left(\dfrac{1}{x}\right)^3 + \left(\dfrac{1}{x}\right)^4 = x^4 + 4x^2 + 6 + \dfrac{4}{x^2} + \dfrac{1}{x^4}$

5. $(x-1)^5 = x^5 - 5x^4 + 10x^3 - 10x^2 + 5x - 1$

7. $(x^2 y - 1)^5 = (x^2 y)^5 - 5(x^2 y)^4 + 10(x^2 y)^3 - 10(x^2 y)^2 + 5x^2 y - 1$
     $= x^{10} y^5 - 5x^8 y^4 + 10x^6 y^3 - 10x^4 y^2 + 5x^2 y - 1$

9. $(2x - 3y)^3 = (2x)^3 - 3(2x)^2 3y + 3 \cdot 2x(3y)^2 - (3y)^3 = 8x^3 - 36x^2 y + 54xy^2 - 27y^3$

11. $\left(\dfrac{1}{x} - \sqrt{x}\right)^5 = \left(\dfrac{1}{x}\right)^5 - 5\left(\dfrac{1}{x}\right)^4 \sqrt{x} + 10\left(\dfrac{1}{x}\right)^3 x - 10\left(\dfrac{1}{x}\right)^2 x\sqrt{x} + 5\left(\dfrac{1}{x}\right)x^2 - x^2\sqrt{x}$
     $= \dfrac{1}{x^5} - \dfrac{5}{x^{7/2}} + \dfrac{10}{x^2} - \dfrac{10}{x^{1/2}} + 5x - x^{5/2}$

13. $\dbinom{6}{4} = \dfrac{6!}{4! \, 2!} = \dfrac{6 \cdot 5 \cdot 4!}{2 \cdot 1 \cdot 4!} = 15$

15. $\dbinom{100}{98} = \dfrac{100!}{98! \, 2!} = \dfrac{100 \cdot 99 \cdot 98!}{98! \cdot 2 \cdot 1} = 4950$

17. $\dbinom{3}{1}\dbinom{4}{2} = \dfrac{3!}{1! \, 2!} \dfrac{4!}{2! \, 2!} = \dfrac{3 \cdot 2! \cdot 4 \cdot 3 \cdot 2!}{1 \cdot 2! \cdot 2 \cdot 1 \cdot 2!} = 18$

19. $\dbinom{5}{0} + \dbinom{5}{1} + \dbinom{5}{2} + \dbinom{5}{3} + \dbinom{5}{4} + \dbinom{5}{5} = (1+1)^5 = 2^5 = 32$

21. $(x + 2y)^4 = \dbinom{4}{0}x^4 + \dbinom{4}{1}x^3 \cdot 2y + \dbinom{4}{2}x^2 \cdot 4y^2 + \dbinom{4}{3}x \cdot 8y^3 + \dbinom{4}{4}16y^4$
     $= x^4 + 8x^3 y + 24x^2 y^2 + 32xy^3 + 16y^4$

23   $\left(1 + \dfrac{1}{x}\right)^6 = \dbinom{6}{0}1^6 + \dbinom{6}{1}1^5\left(\dfrac{1}{x}\right) + \dbinom{6}{2}1^4\left(\dfrac{1}{x}\right)^2 + \dbinom{6}{3}1^3\left(\dfrac{1}{x}\right)^3 + \dbinom{6}{4}1^2\left(\dfrac{1}{x}\right)^4$
     $+ \dbinom{6}{5}1\left(\dfrac{1}{x}\right)^5 + \dbinom{6}{6}\left(\dfrac{1}{x}\right)^6 = 1 + \dfrac{6}{x} + \dfrac{15}{x^2} + \dfrac{20}{x^3} + \dfrac{15}{x^4} + \dfrac{6}{x^5} + \dfrac{1}{x^6}$

25.   The first three terms in the expansion of $(x + 2y)^{20}$ are $\dbinom{20}{0}x^{20} = x^{20}$, $\dbinom{20}{1}x^{19} \cdot 2y = 40x^{19}y$,
     and $\dbinom{20}{2}x^{18} \cdot (2y)^2 = 760x^{18}y^2$.

27.   The last two terms in the expansion of $(a^{2/3} + a^{1/3})^{25}$ are $\dbinom{25}{24}a^{2/3} \cdot \left(a^{1/3}\right)^{24} = 25a^{26/3}$, and
     $\dbinom{25}{25}a^{25/3} = a^{25/3}$.

29. The middle term in the expansion of $(x^2+1)^{18}$ occurs when both terms are raised to the 9th power. So this term is $\binom{18}{9}(x^2)^9 1^9 = 48{,}620 x^{18}$.

31. The 24th term in the expansion of $(a+b)^{25}$ is $\binom{25}{23} a^2 b^{23} = 300 a^2 b^{23}$.

33. The 100th term in the expansion of $(1+y)^{100}$ is $\binom{100}{99} 1^1 \cdot y^{99} = 100 y^{99}$.

35. The term that contains x^4 in the expansion of $(x+2y)^{10}$ has exponent $r = 4$. So this term is $\binom{10}{4} x^4 \cdot (2y)^{10-4} = 13{,}440 x^4 y^6$.

37. The rth term is $\binom{12}{r} a^r (b^2)^{12-r} = \binom{12}{r} a^r b^{24-2r}$. Thus the term that contains b^8 occurs where

$24 - 2r = 8 \iff r = 8$. So the term is $\binom{12}{8} a^8 b^8 = 495 a^8 b^8$.

39. $x^4 + 4x^3 y + 6x^2 y^2 + 4xy^3 + y^4 = (x+y)^4$.

41. $8a^3 + 12a^2 b + 6ab^2 + b^3 = \binom{3}{0}(2a)^3 + \binom{3}{1}(2a)^2 b + \binom{3}{2} 2ab^2 + \binom{3}{3} b^3 = (2a+b)^3$.

43. $\dfrac{(x+h)^3 - x^3}{h} = \dfrac{x^3 + 3x^2 h + 3xh^2 + h^3 - x^3}{h} = \dfrac{3x^2 h + 3xh^2 + h^3}{h} = \dfrac{h(3x^2 + 3xh + h^2)}{h}$

$= 3x^2 + 3xh + h^2$.

45. $(1.01)^{100} = (1+0.01)^{100}$. Now the 1st term in the expansion is $\binom{100}{0} 1^{100} = 1$, and the 2nd term is

$\binom{100}{1} 1^{99}(0.01) = 1$, and the 3rd term is $\binom{100}{2} 1^{98}(0.01)^2 = 0.495$. Now each term is non-

negative, so $(1.01)^{100} = (1+0.01)^{100} > 1 + 1 + .0.495 > 2$. Thus $(1.01)^{100} > 2$.

47. $\binom{n}{1} = \dfrac{n!}{1!\,(n-1)!} = \dfrac{n(n-1)!}{1(n-1)!} = \dfrac{n}{1} = n. \quad \binom{n}{n-1} = \dfrac{n!}{(n-1)!\,1!} = \dfrac{n(n-1)!}{(n-1)!\,1} = n.$

Therefore, $\binom{n}{1} = \binom{n}{n-1} = n$.

49. (a) $\binom{n}{r-1} + \binom{n}{r} = \dfrac{n!}{(r-1)!\,[n-(r-1)]!} + \dfrac{n!}{r!\,(n-r)!}$.

(b) $\dfrac{n!}{(r-1)!\,[n-(r-1)]!} + \dfrac{n!}{r!\,(n-r)!} = \dfrac{r \cdot n!}{r \cdot (r-1)!\,(n-r+1)!} + \dfrac{(n-r+1)\,n!}{r!\,(n-r+1)(n-r)!}$

$= \dfrac{r \cdot n!}{r!\,(n-r+1)!} + \dfrac{(n-r+1)\,n!}{r!\,(n-r+1)!}$. Thus a common denominator is $r!\,(n-r+1)!$.

(c) Therefore, using the results of parts (a) and (b),

$\binom{n}{r-1} + \binom{n}{r} = \dfrac{n!}{(r-1)!\,[n-(r-1)]!} + \dfrac{n!}{r!\,(n-r)!} = \dfrac{r \cdot n!}{r!\,(n-r+1)!} + \dfrac{(n-r+1)\,n!}{r!\,(n-r+1)!}$

$= \dfrac{r \cdot n! + (n-r+1)n!}{r!\,(n-r+1)!} = \dfrac{n! \cdot (r+n-r+1)}{r!\,(n-r+1)!} = \dfrac{n! \cdot (n+1)}{r!\,(n+1-r)!}$

$$= \frac{(n+1)!}{r!(n+1-r)!} = \binom{n+1}{r}.$$

51. Notice that $(100!)^{101} = (100!)^{100} \cdot 100!$ and $(101!)^{100} = (101 \cdot 100!)^{100} = 101^{100} \cdot (100!)^{100}$. Now, $100! = 1 \cdot 2 \cdot 3 \cdot 4 \cdots \cdot 99 \cdot 100$ and $101^{100} = 101 \cdot 101 \cdot 101 \cdots \cdot 101$. Thus each of these last two expressions consists of 100 factors multiplied together, and since each factor in the product for 101^{100} is larger than each factor in the product for $100!$, it follows that $100! < 101^{100}$. Thus $(100!)^{100} \cdot 100! < (100!)^{100} \cdot 101^{100}$. So, $(100!)^{101} < (101!)^{100}$.

53. $0 = 0^n = (-1+1)^n$

$$= \binom{n}{0}(-1)^0(1)^n + \binom{n}{1}(-1)^1(1)^{n-1} + \binom{n}{2}(-1)^2(1)^{n-2} + \cdots + \binom{n}{n}(-1)^n(1)^0$$

$$= \binom{n}{0} - \binom{n}{1} + \binom{n}{2} - \cdots + (-1)^k\binom{n}{k} + \cdots + (-1)^n\binom{n}{n}.$$

Review Exercises for Chapter 10

1. $a_n = \dfrac{n^2}{n+1}$. Then $a_1 = \dfrac{1^2}{1+1} = \dfrac{1}{2}$; $a_2 = \dfrac{2^2}{2+1} = \dfrac{4}{3}$; $a_3 = \dfrac{3^2}{3+1} = \dfrac{9}{4}$; $a_4 = \dfrac{4^2}{4+1} = \dfrac{16}{5}$; and

   $a_{10} = \dfrac{10^2}{10+1} = \dfrac{100}{11}$.

3. $a_n = \dfrac{(-1)^n + 1}{n^3}$. Then $a_1 = \dfrac{(-1)^1 + 1}{1^3} = 0$; $a_2 = \dfrac{(-1)^2 + 1}{2^3} = \dfrac{2}{8} = \dfrac{1}{4}$; $a_3 = \dfrac{(-1)^3 + 1}{3^3} = 0$;

   $a_4 = \dfrac{(-1)^4 + 1}{4^3} = \dfrac{2}{64} = \dfrac{1}{32}$; and $a_{10} = \dfrac{(-1)^{10} + 1}{10^3} = \dfrac{1}{500}$.

5. $a_n = \dfrac{(2n)!}{2^n n!}$. Then $a_1 = \dfrac{(2 \cdot 1)!}{2^1 \cdot 1!} = 1$; $a_2 = \dfrac{(2 \cdot 2)!}{2^2 \cdot 2!} = 3$; $a_3 = \dfrac{(2 \cdot 3)!}{2^3 \cdot 3!} = \dfrac{6 \cdot 5 \cdot 4}{8} = 15$;

   $a_4 = \dfrac{(2 \cdot 4)!}{2^4 \cdot 4!} = \dfrac{8 \cdot 7 \cdot 6 \cdot 5}{16} = 105$; and $a_{10} = \dfrac{(2 \cdot 10)!}{2^{10} \cdot 10!} = 654{,}729{,}075$.

7. $a_n = a_{n-1} + 2n - 1$ and $a_1 = 1$. Then $a_2 = a_1 + 4 - 1 = 4$; $a_3 = a_2 + 6 - 1 = 9$;
   $a_4 = a_3 + 8 - 1 = 16$; $a_5 = a_4 + 10 - 1 = 25$; $a_6 = a_5 + 12 - 1 = 36$; and
   $a_7 = a_6 + 14 - 1 = 49$.

9. $a_n = a_{n-1} + 2a_{n-2}$, $a_1 = 1$ and $a_2 = 3$. Then $a_3 = a_2 + 2a_1 = 5$; $a_4 = a_3 + 2a_2 = 11$;
   $a_5 = a_4 + 2a_3 = 21$; $a_6 = a_5 + 2a_4 = 43$; and $a_7 = a_6 + 2a_5 = 85$.

11. (a) $a_1 = 2(1) + 5 = 7$ (b)
    $a_2 = 2(2) + 5 = 9$
    $a_3 = 2(3) + 5 = 11$
    $a_4 = 2(4) + 5 = 13$
    $a_5 = 2(5) + 5 = 15$

    (c) This sequence is arithmetic, the common difference is 2.

13. (a) $a_1 = \dfrac{3^1}{2^2} = \dfrac{3}{4}$ (b)

    $a_2 = \dfrac{3^2}{2^3} = \dfrac{9}{8}$

    $a_3 = \dfrac{3^3}{2^4} = \dfrac{27}{16}$

    $a_4 = \dfrac{3^4}{2^5} = \dfrac{81}{32}$

    $a_5 = \dfrac{3^5}{2^6} = \dfrac{243}{64}$

    (c) This sequence is geometric, the common ratio is $\dfrac{3}{2}$.

15. $5, 5.5, 6, 6.5, \ldots$. Since $5.5 - 5 = 6 - 5.5 = 6.5 - 6 = 0.5$, this is an arithmetic sequence with
    $a_1 = 5$ and $d = 0.5$. Then $a_5 = a_4 + 0.5 = 7$.

17. $\sqrt{2}, 2\sqrt{2}, 3\sqrt{2}, 4\sqrt{2}, \ldots$. Since $2\sqrt{2} - \sqrt{2} = 3\sqrt{2} - 2\sqrt{2} = 4\sqrt{2} - 3\sqrt{2} = \sqrt{2}$, this is an arithmetic sequence with $a_1 = \sqrt{2}$ and $d = \sqrt{2}$. Then $a_5 = a_4 + \sqrt{2} = 4\sqrt{2} + \sqrt{2} = 5\sqrt{2}$.

19. $t - 3, t - 2, t - 1, t, \ldots$. Since $(t - 2) - (t - 3) = (t - 1) - (t - 2) = t - (t - 1) = 1$, this is an arithmetic sequence with $a_1 = t - 3$ and $d = 1$. Then $a_5 = a_4 + 1 = t + 1$.

21. $\frac{3}{4}, \frac{1}{2}, \frac{1}{3}, \frac{2}{9}, \ldots$. Since $\frac{\frac{1}{2}}{\frac{3}{4}} = \frac{\frac{1}{3}}{\frac{1}{2}} = \frac{\frac{2}{9}}{\frac{1}{3}} = \frac{2}{3}$, this is a geometric sequence with $a_1 = \frac{3}{4}$ and $r = \frac{2}{3}$.

Then $a_5 = a_4 \cdot r = \frac{2}{9} \cdot \frac{2}{3} = \frac{4}{27}$.

23. $3, 6i, -12, -24i, \ldots$. Since $\dfrac{6i}{3} = 2i$, $\dfrac{-12}{6i} = \dfrac{-2}{i} = \dfrac{-2i}{i^2} = 2i$, $\dfrac{-24i}{-12} = 2i$, this is a geometric sequence with common ratio $r = 2i$.

25. $a_6 = 17 = a + 5d$ and $a_4 = 11 = a + 3d$. Then, $a_6 - a_4 = 17 - 11$ $\Leftrightarrow$ $(a + 5d) - (a + 3d) = 6$ $\Leftrightarrow$ $6 = 2d$ $\Leftrightarrow$ $d = 3$. Substituting into $11 = a + 3d$ gives $11 = a + 3 \cdot 3$, and so $a = 2$. Thus $a_2 = a + (2 - 1)d = 2 + 3 = 5$.

27. $a_3 = 9$ and $r = \frac{3}{2}$. Then $a_5 = a_3 \cdot r^2 = 9 \cdot \left(\frac{3}{2}\right)^2 = \frac{81}{4}$.

29.   Let a_{mc} denote the term of the geometric series that is the frequency of middle C. Then $a_{mc} = 256$ and $a_{mc+1} = 512$. Since this is a geometric sequence, $r = \frac{512}{256} = 2$, and so $a_{mc-2} = \dfrac{a_{mc}}{r^2}$

$= \dfrac{256}{2^2} = 64$.

31.   Let a_n be the number of bacteria in the dish at the end of $5n$ seconds. So, $a_0 = 3$, $a_1 = 3 \cdot 2$, $a_2 = 3 \cdot 2^2$, $a_3 = 3 \cdot 2^3$, $\ldots$. Then, clearly, a_n is a geometric sequence with $r = 2$ and $a = 3$. Thus at the end of $60 = 5(12)$ seconds, the number of bacteria is $a_{12} = 3 \cdot 2^{12} = 12{,}288$.

33.   Suppose that the common ratio in the sequence $a_1, a_2, a_3, \ldots$ is r. Also, suppose that the common ratio in the sequence $b_1, b_2, b_3, \ldots$ is s. Then $a_n = a_1 r^{n-1}$ and $b_n = b_1 s^{n-1}$, $n = 1, 2, 3, \ldots$. Thus $a_n b_n = a_1 r^{n-1} \cdot b_1 s^{n-1} = (a_1 b_1)(rs)^{n-1}$. So the sequence $a_1 b_1, a_2 b_2, a_3 b_3, \ldots$ is geometric with first term $a_1 b_1$ and common ratio rs.

35.   (a) $6, x, 12, \ldots$ is arithmetic if $x - 6 = 12 - x$ $\Leftrightarrow$ $2x = 18$ $\Leftrightarrow$ $x = 9$.

      (b) $6, x, 12, \ldots$ is geometric if $\dfrac{x}{6} = \dfrac{12}{x}$ $\Leftrightarrow$ $x^2 = 72$ $\Leftrightarrow$ $x = \pm 6\sqrt{2}$.

37. $\displaystyle\sum_{k=3}^{6} (k + 1)^2 = (3 + 1)^2 + (4 + 1)^2 + (5 + 1)^2 + (6 + 1)^2 = 16 + 25 + 36 + 49 = 126$

39. $\displaystyle\sum_{k=1}^{6} (k + 1)2^{k-1} = 2 \cdot 2^0 + 3 \cdot 2^1 + 4 \cdot 2^2 + 5 \cdot 2^3 + 6 \cdot 2^4 + 7 \cdot 2^5 =$
$2 + 6 + 16 + 40 + 96 + 224 = 384$

41. $\displaystyle\sum_{k=1}^{10} (k - 1)^2 = 0^2 + 1^2 + 2^2 + 3^2 + 4^2 + 5^2 + 6^2 + 7^2 + 8^2 + 9^2$

43. $\displaystyle\sum_{k=1}^{50} \frac{3^k}{2^{k+1}} = \frac{3}{2^2} + \frac{3^2}{2^3} + \frac{3^3}{2^4} + \frac{3^4}{2^5} + \cdots + \frac{3^{49}}{2^{50}} + \frac{3^{50}}{2^{51}}$

45. $3 + 6 + 9 + 12 + \cdots + 99 = 3(1) + 3(2) + 3(3) + \cdots + 3(33) = \displaystyle\sum_{k=1}^{33} 3k$

47. $1 \cdot 2^3 + 2 \cdot 2^4 + 3 \cdot 2^5 + 4 \cdot 2^6 + \cdots + 100 \cdot 2^{102} = (1)2^{(1)+2} + (2)2^{(2)+2} + (3)2^{(3)+2} + (4)2^{(4)+2}$

$+ \cdots + (100)2^{(100)+2} = \displaystyle\sum_{k=1}^{100} k \cdot 2^{k+2}$

49. $1 + 0.9 + (0.9)^2 + \cdots + (0.9)^5$ is a geometric series with $a = 1$ and $r = \frac{0.9}{1} = 0.9$. Thus, the sum of

the series is $S_6 = \dfrac{1 - (0.9)^6}{1 - 0.9} = \dfrac{1 - 0.531441}{0.1} = 4.68559$.

51. $\sqrt{5} + 2\sqrt{5} + 3\sqrt{5} + \cdots + 100\sqrt{5}$ is an arithmetic series with $a = \sqrt{5}$ and $d = \sqrt{5}$. Then

$100\sqrt{5} = a_n = \sqrt{5} + \sqrt{5}(n-1) \quad\Leftrightarrow\quad n = 100$. So the sum is

$S_{100} = \frac{100}{2}\left(\sqrt{5} + 100\sqrt{5}\right) = 50(101\sqrt{5}) = 5050\sqrt{5}$.

53. $\displaystyle\sum_{n=0}^{6} 3 \cdot (-4)^n$ is a geometric series with $a = 3$, $r = -4$, and $n = 7$. Therefore, the sum of the series

is $S_7 = 3 \cdot \dfrac{1 - (-4)^7}{1 - (-4)} = \dfrac{3}{5}(1 + 4^7) = 9831$.

55. We have an arithmetic sequence with $a = 7$ and $d = 3$. Then $S_n = 325 = \dfrac{n}{2}[2a + (n-1)d]$

$= \dfrac{n}{2}[14 + 3(n-1)] = \dfrac{n}{2}(11 + 3n) \quad\Leftrightarrow\quad 650 = 3n^2 + 11n \quad\Leftrightarrow\quad (3n + 50)(n - 13) = 0$

$\Leftrightarrow\quad n = 13$ (because $n = -\frac{50}{3}$ is inadmissible). Thus, 13 terms must be added.

57. This is a geometric sequence with $a = 2$ and $r = 2$. Then

$S_{15} = 2 \cdot \dfrac{1 - 2^{15}}{1 - 2} = 2(2^{15} - 1) = 65{,}534$, and so the total number of ancestors is 65,534.

59. $A = 10{,}000$, $i = 0.03$, and $n = 4$. Thus, $10{,}000 = R\dfrac{(1.03)^4 - 1}{0.03} \quad\Leftrightarrow\quad R = \dfrac{10{,}000 \cdot 0.03}{(1.03)^4 - 1}$

$= \$2390.27$.

61. $1 - \frac{2}{5} + \frac{4}{25} - \frac{8}{125} + \cdots$ is a geometric series with $a = 1$ and $r = -\frac{2}{5}$. Therefore, the sum is

$S = \dfrac{a}{1 - r} = \dfrac{1}{1 - \left(-\frac{2}{5}\right)} = \dfrac{5}{7}$.

63. $1 + \dfrac{1}{3^{1/2}} + \dfrac{1}{3} + \dfrac{1}{3^{3/2}} + \cdots$ is an infinite geometric series with $a = 1$ and $r = \dfrac{1}{\sqrt{3}}$. Thus, the sum is

$S = \dfrac{1}{1 - \left(\frac{1}{\sqrt{3}}\right)} = \dfrac{\sqrt{3}}{\sqrt{3} - 1} = \dfrac{1}{2}(3 + \sqrt{3})$.

65. Let $P(n)$ denote the statement that $1 + 4 + 7 + \cdots + (3n - 2) = \dfrac{n(3n - 1)}{2}$.

Step 1 $P(1)$ is the statement that $1 = \dfrac{1[3(1)-1]}{2} = \dfrac{1 \cdot 2}{2}$, which is true.

Step 2 Assume that $P(k)$ is true; that is, $1 + 4 + 7 + \cdots + (3k-2) = \dfrac{k(3k-1)}{2}$. We want to use this to show that $P(k+1)$ is true. Now,

$$1 + 4 + 7 + 10 + \cdots + (3k-2) + [3(k+1)-2] =$$
$$\dfrac{k(3k-1)}{2} + 3k + 1 = \qquad\qquad \text{induction hypothesis}$$
$$\dfrac{k(3k-1)}{2} + \dfrac{6k+2}{2} = \dfrac{3k^2 - k + 6k + 2}{2} =$$
$$\dfrac{3k^2 + 5k + 2}{2} = \dfrac{(k+1)(3k+2)}{2} = \dfrac{(k+1)[3(k+1)-1]}{2}.$$

Thus, $P(k+1)$ follows from $P(k)$. So by the Principle of Mathematical Induction, $P(n)$ is true for all n.

67. Let $P(n)$ denote the statement that $\left(1 + \dfrac{1}{1}\right)\left(1 + \dfrac{1}{2}\right)\left(1 + \dfrac{1}{3}\right) \cdots \left(1 + \dfrac{1}{n}\right) = n + 1.$

Step 1 $P(1)$ is the statement that $\left(1 + \dfrac{1}{1}\right) = 1 + 1$, which is clearly true.

Step 2 Assume that $P(k)$ is true; that is, $\left(1 + \dfrac{1}{1}\right)\left(1 + \dfrac{1}{2}\right)\left(1 + \dfrac{1}{3}\right) \cdots \left(1 + \dfrac{1}{k}\right) = k + 1$. We want to use this to show that $P(k+1)$ is true. Now,

$$\left(1 + \tfrac{1}{1}\right)\left(1 + \tfrac{1}{2}\right)\left(1 + \tfrac{1}{3}\right) \cdots \left(1 + \tfrac{1}{k}\right)\left(1 + \tfrac{1}{k+1}\right) =$$
$$\left[\left(1 + \tfrac{1}{1}\right)\left(1 + \tfrac{1}{2}\right)\left(1 + \tfrac{1}{3}\right) \cdots \left(1 + \tfrac{1}{k}\right)\right]\left(1 + \tfrac{1}{k+1}\right) =$$
$$(k+1)\left(1 + \tfrac{1}{k+1}\right) = (k+1) + 1. \qquad \text{induction hypothesis}$$

Thus, $P(k+1)$ follows from $P(k)$. So by the Principle of Mathematical Induction, $P(n)$ is true for all n.

69. $a_{n+1} = 3a_n + 4$ and $a_1 = 4$. Let $P(n)$ denote the statement that $a_n = 2 \cdot 3^n - 2$.

Step 1 $P(1)$ is the statement that $a_1 = 2 \cdot 3^1 - 2 = 4$, which is clearly true.

Step 2 Assume that $P(k)$ is true; that is, $a_k = 2 \cdot 3^k - 2$. We want to use this to show that $P(k+1)$ is true. Now,

$$\begin{aligned}
a_{k+1} &= 3a_k + 4 &&\text{definition of } a_{k+1}\\
&= 3(2 \cdot 3^k - 2) + 4 &&\text{induction hypothesis}\\
&= 2 \cdot 3^{k+1} - 6 + 4\\
&= 2 \cdot 3^{k+1} - 2.
\end{aligned}$$

Thus $P(k+1)$ follows from $P(k)$. So by the Principle of Mathematical Induction, $P(n)$ is true for all n.

71. Let $P(n)$ denote the statement that $n! > 2^n$, for all natural numbers $n \geq 4$.

Step 1 $P(4)$ is the statement that $4! = 24 > 2^4 = 16$, which is true.

Step 2 Assume that $P(k)$ is true; that is, $k! > 2^k$. We want to use this to show that $P(k+1)$ is true. Now.

$$(k+1)! = (k+1)k!$$
$$> (k+1) \cdot 2^k \qquad \text{induction hypothesis}$$
$$> 2 \cdot 2^k \qquad \text{because } k+1 > 2 \text{ (for } k \geq 4)$$
$$= 2^{k+1}.$$

Thus $P(k+1)$ follows from $P(k)$. So by the Principle of Mathematical Induction, $P(n)$ is true for all $n \geq 4$.

73. $\dbinom{10}{2} + \dbinom{10}{6} = \dfrac{10!}{2!\,8!} + \dfrac{10!}{6!\,4!} = \dfrac{10 \cdot 9}{2} + \dfrac{10 \cdot 9 \cdot 8 \cdot 7}{4 \cdot 3 \cdot 2} = 45 + 210 = 255.$

75. $\displaystyle\sum_{k=0}^{8} \binom{8}{k}\binom{8}{8-k} = 2\binom{8}{0}\binom{8}{8} + 2\binom{8}{1}\binom{8}{7} + 2\binom{8}{2}\binom{8}{6} + 2\binom{8}{3}\binom{8}{5} + \binom{8}{4}\binom{8}{4}$

$= 2 + 2 \cdot 8^2 + 2 \cdot (28)^2 + 2 \cdot (56)^2 + (70)^2 = 12{,}870.$

77. $(2x+y)^4 = \dbinom{4}{0}(2x)^4 + \dbinom{4}{1}(2x)^3 y + \dbinom{4}{2}(2x)^2 y^2 + \dbinom{4}{3} \cdot 2xy^3 + \dbinom{4}{4}y^4$

$= 16x^4 + 32x^3 y + 24x^2 y^2 + 8xy^3 + y^4.$

79. The first three terms in the expansion of $(b^{-2/3} + b^{1/3})^{20}$ are $\dbinom{20}{0}(b^{-2/3})^{20} = b^{-40/3}$;

$\dbinom{20}{1}(b^{-2/3})^{19}\,(b^{1/3}) = 20b^{-37/3}$; and $\dbinom{20}{2}(b^{-2/3})^{18}(b^{1/3})^2 = 190b^{-34/3}.$

Chapter 10 Test

1. $a_1 = 1^2 - 1 = 0$; $a_2 = 2^2 - 1 = 3$; $a_3 = 3^2 - 1 = 8$; $a_4 = 4^2 - 1 = 15$; and $a_{10} = 10^2 - 1 = 99$.

2. $a_{n+2} = (a_n)^2 - a_{n+1}$, $a_1 = 1$ and $a_2 = 1$. Then $a_3 = a_1^2 - a_2 = 1^2 - 1 = 0$, $a_4 = a_2^2 - a_3 = 1^2 - 0 = 1$, and $a_5 = a_3^2 - a_4 = 0^2 - 1 = -1$.

3. $d = 76 - 80 = -4$. So $a_4 = a_3 + (-4) = 72 + (-4) = 68$ and $a_n = a_1 + (n-1)d = 80 + (n-1)(-4) = 84 - 4n$.

4. Since $a_n = a_1 \, r^{n-1}$, we substitute $a_1 = 25$, $a_4 = \frac{1}{5}$, and $n = 4$ and solve for r. This gives $\frac{1}{5} = 25 \, r^3$
    $\Leftrightarrow \quad r^3 = \frac{1}{125} = \frac{1}{5^3} \quad \Leftrightarrow \quad r = \frac{1}{5}$. So the common ratio is $\frac{1}{5}$ and $a_5 = a_1 r^4 = 25 \left(\frac{1}{5}\right)^4 = \frac{1}{25}$.

5. (a) If $a_1, a_2, a_3, \ldots$ is an arithmetic sequence, then the sequence $a_1^2, a_2^2, a_3^2, \ldots$ is also arithmetic. This statement is FALSE. For a counterexample, consider $a_1 = 1$, $a_2 = 2$, $a_3 = 3\ldots$. Then $a_1, a_2, a_3, \ldots$ is an arithmetic sequence with $a = 1$ and $d = 1$. However, the sequence $a_1^2, a_2^2, a_3^2, \ldots$ becomes $1, 4, 9, \ldots$, which is NOT arithmetic because there is no common difference.

    (b) If $a_1, a_2, a_3, \ldots$ is a geometric sequence, then the sequence $a_1^2, a_2^2, a_3^2, \ldots$ is also geometric. This statement is TRUE. Let the common ratio for the geometric series $a_1, a_2, a_3, \ldots$ be r so that $a_n = a_1 r^{n-1}$, $n = 1, 2, 3, \ldots$. Then $a_n^2 = (a_1 r^{n-1})^2 = (a_1^2)(r^2)^{n-1}$. Therefore, the sequence $a_1^2, a_2^2, a_3^2, \ldots$ is geometric with common ratio r^2.

6. (a) The nth partial sum an arithmetic sequence is $S_n = \dfrac{n}{2}(a + a_n)$ or $S_n = \dfrac{n}{2}[2a + (n-1)d]$.

    (b) $a_1 = 10$ and $a_{10} = 2$. Then $S_{10} = \frac{10}{2}(10 + 2) = 60$.

    (c) Since $S_{10} = \frac{10}{2}(2 \cdot 10 + 9d) = 60$, then $5(20 + 9d) = 60 \quad \Leftrightarrow \quad d = -\frac{8}{9}$, and so the common difference is $-\frac{8}{9}$. Then $a_{100} = a + 99d = 10 - \frac{8}{9} \cdot 99 = -78$.

7. (a) The nth partial sum a geometric sequence is $S_n = a \dfrac{1 - r^n}{1 - r}$, where $r \neq 1$.

    (b) The geometric series $\dfrac{1}{3} + \dfrac{2}{3^2} + \dfrac{2^2}{3^3} + \dfrac{2^3}{3^4} + \cdots + \dfrac{2^9}{3^{10}}$ has $a = \frac{1}{3}$, $r = \frac{2}{3}$, and $n = 10$. So

    $$S_{10} = \frac{1}{3} \cdot \frac{1 - \left(\frac{2}{3}\right)^{10}}{1 - \left(\frac{2}{3}\right)} = \frac{1}{3} \cdot 3 \left(1 - \frac{1024}{59{,}049}\right) = \frac{58{,}025}{59{,}049}.$$

8. The infinite geometric series $1 + \dfrac{1}{2^{1/2}} + \dfrac{1}{2} + \dfrac{1}{2^{3/2}} + \cdots$ has $a = 1$ and $r = 2^{-1/2} = \frac{1}{\sqrt{2}}$. Thus,
    $S = \dfrac{1}{1 - \left(\frac{1}{\sqrt{2}}\right)} = \dfrac{\sqrt{2}}{\sqrt{2} - 1} = \dfrac{\sqrt{2}}{\sqrt{2} - 1} \cdot \dfrac{\sqrt{2} + 1}{\sqrt{2} + 1} = 2 + \sqrt{2}$.

9. Let $P(n)$ denote the statement that $1^2 + 2^2 + 3^2 + \cdots + n^2 = \dfrac{n(n+1)(2n+1)}{6}$.

    <u>Step 1</u> Show that $P(1)$ is true. But $P(1)$ says that $1^2 = \frac{1 \cdot 2 \cdot 3}{6}$, which is true.

<u>Step 2</u> Assume that $P(k)$ is true; that is, $1^2 + 2^2 + 3^2 + \cdots + k^2 = \dfrac{k(k+1)(2k+1)}{6}$. We want to use this to show that $P(k+1)$ is true. Now,

$$1^2 + 2^2 + 3^2 + \cdots + k^2 + (k+1)^2 = \frac{k(k+1)(2k+1)}{6} + (k+1)^2 \qquad \text{induction hypothesis}$$

$$= \frac{k(k+1)(2k+1) + 6(k+1)^2}{6}$$

$$= \frac{(k+1)(2k^2 + k) + (6k+6)(k+1)}{6}$$

$$= \frac{(k+1)(2k^2 + k + 6k + 6)}{6}$$

$$= \frac{(k+1)(2k^2 + 7k + 6)}{6}$$

$$= \frac{(k+1)(k+2)(2k+3)}{6}$$

$$= \frac{(k+1)[(k+1)+1][2(k+1)+1]}{6}.$$

Thus $P(k+1)$ follows from $P(k)$. So by the Principle of Mathematical Induction, $P(n)$ is true for all n.

10. (a) $\displaystyle\sum_{n=1}^{5}(1 - n^2) = (1 - 1^2) + (1 - 2^2) + (1 - 3^2) + (1 - 4^2) + (1 - 5^2)$
$= 0 - 3 - 8 - 15 - 24 = -50$

(b) $\displaystyle\sum_{n=3}^{6}(-1)^n 2^{n-2} = (-1)^3 2^{3-2} + (-1)^4 2^{4-2} + (-1)^5 2^{5-2} + (-1)^6 2^{6-2}$
$= -2 + 4 - 8 + 16 = 10$

11. $(2x + y^2)^5 = \dbinom{5}{0}(2x)^5 + \dbinom{5}{1}(2x)^4 y^2 + \dbinom{5}{2}(2x)^3 (y^2)^2 + \dbinom{5}{3}(2x)^2 (y^2)^3 + \dbinom{5}{4}(2x)(y^2)^4$

$+ \dbinom{5}{5}(y^2)^5 = 32x^5 + 80x^4 y^2 + 80x^3 y^4 + 40x^2 y^6 + 10xy^8 + y^{10}.$

12. $\dbinom{10}{3}(3x)^3(-2)^7 = 120 \cdot 27x^3(-128) = -414{,}720x^3.$

Focus on Problem Solving

1. By dividing the successive gnomons into squares with side 1, we see that the sum of their areas is $1 + 3 + 5 + \cdots + (2n - 1) = n^2$, because the total area is the area of an $n \times n$ square.

3. Using the formula for the sum of cubes on page 635, we have
$$1^3 + 2^3 + \cdots + (n-1)^3 + n^3 = (1 + 2 + \cdots + n)^2$$
$$1^3 + 2^3 + \cdots + (n-1)^3 = (1 + 2 + \cdots + (n-1))^2.$$
Subtracting gives $n^3 = (1 + 2 + \cdots + n)^2 - (1 + 2 + \cdots + (n-1))^2$.

5. Since all rows have the same sum, S, and there are n rows, the total sum is nS. But this total sum must be $1 + 2 + 3 + \cdots + n^2 = \dfrac{n^2(n^2 + 1)}{2}$ (using the formula for the sum of an arithmetic series or the formula in Example 2 in Section 9.5). Therefore, $nS = \dfrac{n^2(n^2 + 1)}{2} \iff S = \dfrac{n(n^2 + 1)}{2}$.

7. (a) At each stage, each side is replaced by 4 shorter sides, each of length $\frac{1}{3}$ having the length of a side at the previous stage. Writing S_0 and L_0 for the number of sides and the length of the side of the initial figure, we have

$$
\begin{array}{ll}
S_0 = 3 & L_0 = 1 \\
S_1 = 3 \cdot 4 & L_1 = \frac{1}{3} \\
S_2 = 3 \cdot 4^2 & L_2 = \frac{1}{3^2} \\
S_3 = 3 \cdot 4^3 & L_3 = \frac{1}{3^3} \\
\vdots & \vdots
\end{array}
$$

In general, we have $S_n = 3 \cdot 4^n$ and $L_n = \dfrac{1}{3^n}$. The area of each of the small triangles that are added at a given stage is $\frac{1}{9}$th of the area of the triangle added at the preceding stage. Let a be the area of the original triangle. Then the area a_n of each of the small triangles added at stage n is $a_n = a \cdot \dfrac{1}{9^n} = \dfrac{a}{9^n}$. Since a small triangle is added to each side at every stage, it follows that the total area A_n added to the figure at the nth stage is
$$A_n = S_{n-1} \cdot a_n = 3 \cdot 4^{n-1} \cdot \dfrac{a}{9^n} = a \cdot \dfrac{4^{n-1}}{3^{2n-1}}.$$
Writing A_0 for the area of the original triangle, we see that the total area enclosed by the snowflake curve is
$$A = A_0 + A_1 + A_2 + A_3 + \cdots = a + a \cdot \tfrac{1}{3} + a \cdot \tfrac{4}{3^3} + a \cdot \tfrac{4^2}{3^5} + a \cdot \tfrac{4^3}{3^7} + \cdots$$
$$= a + \frac{a}{3}\left(1 + \frac{4}{3^2} + \frac{4^2}{3^4} + \frac{4^3}{3^6} + \cdots\right). \text{ The sum in the brackets is an infinite geometric series}$$
with the first term 1 and the common ratio $\frac{4}{3^2}$. Thus $1 + \frac{4}{3^2} + \frac{4^2}{3^4} + \frac{4^3}{3^6} + \cdots = \frac{1}{1 - (4/3^2)} = \frac{9}{5}$. So the area enclosed by the snowflake curve is $A = a + \frac{a}{3} \cdot \frac{9}{5} = \frac{8}{5}a$. It remains to find the area, a, of the original triangle. This area can be easily found using $Area = \frac{1}{2}(base)(height)$
$$= \tfrac{1}{2} \cdot 1 \cdot \cos 60° = \tfrac{1}{2} \cdot \frac{\sqrt{3}}{2} = \frac{\sqrt{3}}{4}. \text{ Thus } a = \frac{\sqrt{3}}{4}. \text{ Finally, } A = \tfrac{8}{5}a = \tfrac{8}{5} \cdot \frac{\sqrt{3}}{4} = \frac{2\sqrt{3}}{5}.$$

(b) At each stage, each side is replaced by 4 shorter sides, each having length $\frac{1}{3}$ of the length of a side at the previous stage. In general, we have $S_n = 3 \cdot 4^n$ and $L_n = \dfrac{1}{3^n}$. Thus the length of the

perimeter at the nth stage is $P_n = S_n \cdot L_n = 3 \cdot 4^n \cdot \dfrac{1}{3^n} = \dfrac{4^n}{3^{n-1}}$. But P_n is a geometric sequence with $r = \frac{4}{3} > 1$, so $P_n \to \infty$ as $n \to \infty$.

9. (a) The number of 1×1 squares is 6^2, the number of 2×2 squares is 5^2, the number of 3×3 squares is 4^2, the number of 4×4 squares is 3^2, the number of 5×5 squares is 2^2, and there is just one 6×6 square. So the total number of squares is $1^2 + 2^2 + 3^2 + 4^2 + 5^2 + 6^2 = 91$. For an $n \times n$ grid, the number is $1^2 + 2^2 + 3^2 + \cdots + n^2 = \dfrac{n(n+1)(2n+1)}{6}$. (See Exercise 4 in Section 9.5.)

(b) A rectangle is determined by 2 vertical lines and 2 horizontal lines. For an $n \times n$ grid, the 2 vertical lines can be chosen in $C(n+1,2)$ ways and the horizontal lines can also be chosen in $C(n+1,2)$ ways (see Section 10.2 for the definition of $C(n,r)$). So the number of rectangles is $C(n+1,2) \cdot C(n+1,2) = \left[\dfrac{n(n+1)}{2} \right]^2$. For a 6×6 grid, the number is $\left(\frac{6 \cdot 7}{2} \right)^2 = 441$.

Chapter Eleven
Exercises 11.1

1. By the Fundamental Counting Principle, the number of possible single-scoop ice cream cones is $\left(\begin{smallmatrix} \text{number of ways to} \\ \text{choose the flavor} \end{smallmatrix}\right) \cdot \left(\begin{smallmatrix} \text{number of ways to} \\ \text{choose the type of cone} \end{smallmatrix}\right) = 4 \cdot 3 = 12.$

3. By the Fundamental Counting Principle, the possible number of 3-letter words is $\left(\begin{smallmatrix} \text{number of ways to} \\ \text{choose the 1st letter} \end{smallmatrix}\right) \cdot \left(\begin{smallmatrix} \text{number of ways to} \\ \text{choose the 2nd letter} \end{smallmatrix}\right) \cdot \left(\begin{smallmatrix} \text{number of ways to} \\ \text{choose the 3rd letter} \end{smallmatrix}\right).$

   (a) Since repetitions are allowed, we have 4 choices for each letter. Thus there are $4 \cdot 4 \cdot 4 = 64$ words.

   (b) Since repetitions are *not* allowed, we have 4 choices for the 1st letter, 3 choices for the 2nd letter, and 2 choices for the 3rd letter. Thus there are $4 \cdot 3 \cdot 2 = 24$ words.

5. Since there are four choices for each of the five questions, by the Fundamental Counting Principle there are $4 \cdot 4 \cdot 4 \cdot 4 \cdot 4 = 1024$ different ways the test can be completed.

7. Since a runner can only finish once, there are no repetitions. And since we are assuming that there is no tie, the number of different finishes is $\left(\begin{smallmatrix} \text{number of ways to} \\ \text{choose the 1st runner} \end{smallmatrix}\right) \cdot \left(\begin{smallmatrix} \text{number of ways to} \\ \text{choose the 2nd runner} \end{smallmatrix}\right) \cdot \left(\begin{smallmatrix} \text{number of ways to} \\ \text{choose the 3rd runner} \end{smallmatrix}\right) \cdot \left(\begin{smallmatrix} \text{number of ways to} \\ \text{choose the 4th runner} \end{smallmatrix}\right) \cdot \left(\begin{smallmatrix} \text{number of ways to} \\ \text{choose the 5th runner} \end{smallmatrix}\right) = 5 \cdot 4 \cdot 3 \cdot 2 \cdot 1 = 120.$

9. Since there are 6 main courses, there are 6 ways to choose a main course. Likewise, there are 8 drinks and 3 desserts so there are 8 ways to choose a drink and 3 ways to choose a dessert. So the number of different meals consisting of a main course, a drink, and a dessert is $\left(\begin{smallmatrix} \text{number of ways to} \\ \text{choose the main course} \end{smallmatrix}\right) \cdot \left(\begin{smallmatrix} \text{number of ways to} \\ \text{choose a drink} \end{smallmatrix}\right) \cdot \left(\begin{smallmatrix} \text{number of ways to} \\ \text{choose a dessert} \end{smallmatrix}\right) = (6)(8)(3) = 144.$

11. By the Fundamental Counting Principle, the number of different routes from town A to town D via towns B and C is $\left(\begin{smallmatrix} \text{number of routes} \\ \text{from A to B} \end{smallmatrix}\right) \cdot \left(\begin{smallmatrix} \text{number of routes} \\ \text{from B to C} \end{smallmatrix}\right) \cdot \left(\begin{smallmatrix} \text{number of routes} \\ \text{from C to D} \end{smallmatrix}\right) = (4)(5)(6) = 120.$

13. The number of possible sequences of heads and tails when a coin is flipped 5 times is $\left(\begin{smallmatrix} \text{number of possible} \\ \text{outcomes on the 1st flip} \end{smallmatrix}\right) \cdot \left(\begin{smallmatrix} \text{number of possible} \\ \text{outcomes on the 2nd flip} \end{smallmatrix}\right) \cdot \left(\begin{smallmatrix} \text{number of possible} \\ \text{outcomes on the 3rd flip} \end{smallmatrix}\right) \cdot \left(\begin{smallmatrix} \text{number of possible} \\ \text{outcomes on the 4th flip} \end{smallmatrix}\right) \cdot \left(\begin{smallmatrix} \text{number of possible} \\ \text{outcomes on the 5th flip} \end{smallmatrix}\right) = (2)(2)(2)(2)(2) = 2^5 = 32.$ (Here there are only two choices, heads or tails, for each flip.)

15. Since there are six different faces on each die, the number of possible outcomes when a red die and a blue die and a white die are rolled is $\left(\begin{smallmatrix} \text{number of possible} \\ \text{outcomes on the red die} \end{smallmatrix}\right) \cdot \left(\begin{smallmatrix} \text{number of possible} \\ \text{outcomes on the blue die} \end{smallmatrix}\right) \cdot \left(\begin{smallmatrix} \text{number of possible} \\ \text{outcomes on the white die} \end{smallmatrix}\right) = (6)(6)(6) = 6^3 = 216.$

17. The number of possible skirt-blouse-shoe outfits is $\left(\begin{smallmatrix} \text{number of ways} \\ \text{to choose a skirt} \end{smallmatrix}\right) \cdot \left(\begin{smallmatrix} \text{number of ways} \\ \text{to choose a blouse} \end{smallmatrix}\right) \cdot \left(\begin{smallmatrix} \text{number of ways} \\ \text{to choose shoes} \end{smallmatrix}\right) = (5)(8)(12) = 480.$

19. The number of possible ID numbers of one letter followed by two digits is $\left(\begin{smallmatrix} \text{number of ways} \\ \text{to choose a letter} \end{smallmatrix}\right) \cdot \left(\begin{smallmatrix} \text{number of ways} \\ \text{to choose a digit} \end{smallmatrix}\right) \cdot \left(\begin{smallmatrix} \text{number of ways} \\ \text{to choose a digit} \end{smallmatrix}\right) = (26)(10)(10) = 2600.$ Since $2600 < 2844$, it is not possible to give each of the company's employees a different ID number using this scheme.

21. The number of different California license plates possible is $\left(\begin{smallmatrix} \text{number of ways to} \\ \text{choose a nonzero digit} \end{smallmatrix}\right) \cdot \left(\begin{smallmatrix} \text{number of ways} \\ \text{to choose 3 letters} \end{smallmatrix}\right) \cdot \left(\begin{smallmatrix} \text{number of ways} \\ \text{to choose 3 digits} \end{smallmatrix}\right) = (9)(26^3)(10^3) = 158,184,000.$

23. There are two possible ways to answer each question on a true-false test. Thus the possible number of different ways to complete a true-false test containing 10 questions is

$$\left(\begin{smallmatrix}\text{number of ways}\\\text{to answer question 1}\end{smallmatrix}\right) \cdot \left(\begin{smallmatrix}\text{number of ways}\\\text{to answer question 2}\end{smallmatrix}\right) \cdots \left(\begin{smallmatrix}\text{number of ways}\\\text{to answer question 10}\end{smallmatrix}\right) = 2^{10} = 1024.$$

25. The number of different classifications possible is

$$\left(\begin{smallmatrix}\text{number of ways}\\\text{to choose a major}\end{smallmatrix}\right) \cdot \left(\begin{smallmatrix}\text{number of ways to}\\\text{choose a minor}\end{smallmatrix}\right) \cdot \left(\begin{smallmatrix}\text{number of ways}\\\text{to choose a year}\end{smallmatrix}\right) \cdot \left(\begin{smallmatrix}\text{number of ways}\\\text{to choose a sex}\end{smallmatrix}\right) = (32)(32)(4)(2) = 8192.$$ To

see that there are 32 ways to choose a minor, we start with 32 fields, subtract the major (you can not major and minor in the same subject), and then add one for the possibility of *NO MINOR*.

27. The number of possible license plates of two letters followed by three digits is

$$\left(\begin{smallmatrix}\text{number of ways to}\\\text{choose 2 letters}\end{smallmatrix}\right) \cdot \left(\begin{smallmatrix}\text{number of ways}\\\text{to choose 3 digits}\end{smallmatrix}\right) = (26^2)(10^3) = 676,000.$$ Since $676,000 < 8,000,000$, there will

not be enough different license plates for the state's 8 million registered cars.

29. Since a student can hold only one office, the number of ways that a president, a vice-president and a secretary can be chosen from a class of 30 students is

$$\left(\begin{smallmatrix}\text{number of ways}\\\text{to choose a president}\end{smallmatrix}\right) \cdot \left(\begin{smallmatrix}\text{number of ways to}\\\text{choose a vice-president}\end{smallmatrix}\right) \cdot \left(\begin{smallmatrix}\text{number of ways}\\\text{to choose a secretary}\end{smallmatrix}\right) = (30)(29)(28) = 24,360.$$

31. The number of ways a chairman, vice-chairman, and a secretary can be chosen if the chairman must be a Democrat and the vice-chairman must be a Republican is

$$\left(\begin{smallmatrix}\text{number of ways to}\\\text{choose a Dem. chairman}\\\text{from the 10 Dem.}\end{smallmatrix}\right) \cdot \left(\begin{smallmatrix}\text{number of ways to choose}\\\text{a Rep. vice-chairman}\\\text{from the 7 Rep}\end{smallmatrix}\right) \cdot \left(\begin{smallmatrix}\text{number of ways to choose}\\\text{a secretary from the}\\\text{remaining 15 members}\end{smallmatrix}\right) = (10)(7)(15) = 1050.$$

33. The possible number of 5-letter words formed using the letters A, B, C, D, E, F, and G is calculated as follows:

    (a) If repetition of letters is allowed, then there are 7 ways to pick each letter in the word. Thus the number of 5-letter words is

    $$\left(\begin{smallmatrix}\text{number of ways to}\\\text{choose the 1st letter}\end{smallmatrix}\right) \cdot \left(\begin{smallmatrix}\text{number of ways to}\\\text{choose the 2nd letter}\end{smallmatrix}\right) \cdots \left(\begin{smallmatrix}\text{number of ways to}\\\text{choose the 5th letter}\end{smallmatrix}\right) = 7^5 = 16,807.$$

    (b) If no letter can be repeated in a word, then the number of 5-letter words is

    $$\left(\begin{smallmatrix}\text{number of ways to}\\\text{choose the 1st letter}\end{smallmatrix}\right) \cdot \left(\begin{smallmatrix}\text{number of ways to}\\\text{choose the 2nd letter}\end{smallmatrix}\right) \cdots \left(\begin{smallmatrix}\text{number of ways to}\\\text{choose the 5th letter}\end{smallmatrix}\right) = (7)(6)(5)(4)(3) = 2520.$$

    (c) If each word must begin with the letter A, then the number of 5-letter words (letters can be repeated) is

    $$\left(\begin{smallmatrix}\text{number of ways to}\\\text{choose the letter A}\end{smallmatrix}\right) \cdot \left(\begin{smallmatrix}\text{number of ways to}\\\text{choose the 2nd letter}\end{smallmatrix}\right) \cdots \left(\begin{smallmatrix}\text{number of ways to}\\\text{choose the 5th letter}\end{smallmatrix}\right) = (1)(7)(7)(7)(7) = 7^4 = 2401.$$

    (d) If the letter C must be in the middle, then the number of 5-letter words (letters can be repeated) is

    $$\left(\begin{smallmatrix}\text{number of ways to}\\\text{choose the 1st letter}\end{smallmatrix}\right) \cdot \left(\begin{smallmatrix}\text{number of ways to}\\\text{choose the 2nd letter}\end{smallmatrix}\right) \cdot \left(\begin{smallmatrix}\text{number of ways to}\\\text{choose the letter C}\end{smallmatrix}\right) \cdot \left(\begin{smallmatrix}\text{number of ways to}\\\text{choose the 4th letter}\end{smallmatrix}\right) \cdot \left(\begin{smallmatrix}\text{number of ways to}\\\text{choose the 5th letter}\end{smallmatrix}\right)$$
    $$= (7)(7)(1)(7)(7) = 7^4 = 2401.$$

    (e) If the middle letter must be a vowel, then the number of 5-letter words is $(7)(7)(2)(7)(7)$
    $$= 2 \cdot 7^4 = 4802.$$

35. The number of possible variable names is

$$\left(\begin{smallmatrix}\text{number of ways to}\\\text{choose a letter}\end{smallmatrix}\right) \cdot \left(\begin{smallmatrix}\text{number of ways to choose}\\\text{a letter or a digit}\end{smallmatrix}\right) = (26)(36) = 936.$$

37.   The number of ways 4 men and 4 women may be seated in a row of 8 seats is calculated as follows:

(a)   If the women are to be seated together and the men together, then the number of ways they can
      be seated is $\left(\begin{smallmatrix}\text{number of ways to seat the}\\ \text{women first and the men second}\end{smallmatrix}\right) + \left(\begin{smallmatrix}\text{number of ways to seat the}\\ \text{the men first and the women second}\end{smallmatrix}\right)$
      $$= (4)(3)(2)(1)(4)(3)(2)(1) + (4)(3)(2)(1)(4)(3)(2)(1) = (4!)(4!) + (4!)(4!) = 576 + 576$$
      $$= 1152.$$

(b)   If they are to be seated alternately by gender , then the number of ways they can be seated is
      $\left(\begin{smallmatrix}\text{number of ways to seat them}\\ \text{alternately if a woman is first}\end{smallmatrix}\right) + \left(\begin{smallmatrix}\text{number of ways to seat them}\\ \text{alternately if a man is first}\end{smallmatrix}\right)$
      $$= (4)(4)(3)(3)(2)(2)(1)(1) + (4)(4)(3)(3)(2)(2)(1)(1) = 1152.$$

39.   The number of ways that 8 mathematics books and 3 chemistry books may be placed on a shelf if the
      math books are to be next to each other and the chemistry books next to each other is
      $\left(\begin{smallmatrix}\text{number of ways to place them}\\ \text{if the math books are first}\end{smallmatrix}\right) + \left(\begin{smallmatrix}\text{number of ways to place them}\\ \text{if the chemistry books are first}\end{smallmatrix}\right) = (8!)(3!) + (3!)(8!) = 483,840.$

41.   In order for a number to be odd, the last digit must be odd. In this case, it must be a 1. Thus, the
      other two digits must be chosen from the three digits 2, 4, and 6. So, the number of 3-digit odd
      numbers that can be formed using the digits 1, 2, 4, and 6, if no digit may be used more than once is
      $\left(\begin{smallmatrix}\text{number of ways}\\ \text{to choose a digit}\\ \text{from the 3 digits}\end{smallmatrix}\right) \cdot \left(\begin{smallmatrix}\text{number of ways}\\ \text{to choose from the}\\ \text{2 remaining digits}\end{smallmatrix}\right) \cdot \left(\begin{smallmatrix}\text{number of ways}\\ \text{to choose}\\ \text{an odd digit}\end{smallmatrix}\right) = (3)(2)(1) = 6.$

43.   (a)   From Exercise 6 the number of seven-digit phone numbers is 8,000,000. Under the old rules,
            the possible number of telephone area codes consisting of 3 digits with the given conditions is
            $(8)(2)(10) = 160$. So the possible number of area code + telephone number combinations
            under the old rules is $160 \cdot 8,000,000 = 1,280,000,000$.

      (b)   Under the new rules, where the second digit can be any number, the number of area codes
            possible is $(8)(10)(10) = 800$. Thus the possible number of area code + telephone number
            combinations under the new rules is $800 \cdot 8,000,000 = 6,400,000,000$.

      (c)   Although over $1\frac{1}{4}$ billion telephone numbers may seem to be enough for a population of
            300,000,000, so many individuals and businesses now have multiple lines for fax, Internet
            access, and cellular phones that this number has proven insufficient.

      (d)   There are now more "new" area codes than "old" area codes. Numerous answers are possible.

Exercises 11.2

1. $P(8,3) = \dfrac{8!}{(8-3)!} = \dfrac{8!}{5!} = 8 \cdot 7 \cdot 6 = 336$

3. $P(11,4) = \dfrac{11!}{(11-4)!} = \dfrac{11!}{7!} = 11 \cdot 10 \cdot 9 \cdot 8 = 7920$

5. $P(100,1) = \dfrac{100!}{(100-1)!} = \dfrac{100!}{99!} = 100$

7.   We need the number of ways of selecting three students *in order* for the positions of president, vice president, and secretary from the 15 students in the class. Since a student cannot hold more than one position, this number is $P(15,3) = \dfrac{15!}{(15-3)!} = \dfrac{15!}{12!} = 15 \cdot 14 \cdot 13 = 2730.$

9.   Since a person cannot occupy more than one chair at a time, the number of ways of seating 6 people from 10 people in a row of 6 chairs is $P(10,6) = 10 \cdot 9 \cdot 8 \cdot 7 \cdot 6 \cdot 5 = 151{,}200.$

11. The number of ways of selecting 3 objects in order (a 3-letter word) from 6 distinct objects (the 6 letters) assuming that the letters cannot be repeated is $P(6,3) = 6 \cdot 5 \cdot 4 = 120.$

13. The number of ways of selecting 3 objects in order (a 3-digit number) from 4 distinct objects (the 4 digits) with no repetition of the digits is $P(4,3) = 4 \cdot 3 \cdot 2 = 24.$

15. The number of ways of ordering 9 distinct objects (the contestants) is $P(9,9) = 9! = 362{,}880.$ Here a runner cannot finish more than once, so no repetitions are allowed, and order is important.

17. The number of ways of ordering 1000 distinct objects (the contestants) taking 3 at a time is $P(1000,3) = 1000 \cdot 999 \cdot 998 = 997{,}002{,}000.$ We are assuming that a person cannot win more than once, that is, there are no repetitions.

19. We first place Jack in the first seat, and then seat the remaining 4 students. Thus the number of these arrangements is $\left(\begin{smallmatrix} \text{number of ways to} \\ \text{seat Jack in the 1}^{\text{st}}\text{ seat} \end{smallmatrix} \right) \cdot \left(\begin{smallmatrix} \text{number of ways to seat} \\ \text{the remaining 4 students} \end{smallmatrix} \right) = P(1,1) \cdot P(4,4) = 1!\,4! = 24.$

21. Here we have 6 letters, of which 3 are A's, 2 are B's, and 1 is a C. Thus the number of distinguishable permutations is $\dfrac{6!}{3!\,2!\,1!} = \dfrac{(6)(5)(4)(3!)}{(2)(3!)} = 60.$

23. Here we have 5 letters, of which 2 are A's, 1 is a B, 1 is a C, and 1 is a D. Thus the number of distinguishable permutations is $\dfrac{5!}{2!\,1!\,1!\,1!} = \dfrac{(5)(4)(3)(2!)}{2!} = 60.$

25. Here we have 6 objects, of which 2 are blue marbles and 4 are red marbles. Thus the number of distinguishable permutations is $\dfrac{6!}{2!\,4!} = \dfrac{(6)(5)(4!)}{2 \cdot 4!} = 15.$

27. The number of distinguishable permutations of 12 objects (the 12 coins), from like groups of size 4 (the pennies), of size 3 (the nickels), of size 2 (the dimes) and of size 3 (the quarters) is $\dfrac{12!}{4!\,3!\,2!\,3!} = 277{,}200.$

29. The number of distinguishable permutations of 12 objects (the 12 ice cream cones) from like groups of size 3 (the vanilla cones), of size 2 (the chocolate cones), of size 4 (the strawberry cones), and of size 5 (the butterscotch cones) is $\dfrac{14!}{3!\,2!\,4!\,5!} = 2{,}522{,}520$.

31. The number of distinguishable permutations of 8 objects (the 8 cleaning tasks) from like groups of size 5, 2, and 1 workers, respectively is $\dfrac{8!}{5!\,2!\,1!} = 168$.

33. $C(8,3) = \dfrac{8!}{3!\,(8-3)!} = \dfrac{8!}{3!\,5!} = \dfrac{8 \cdot 7 \cdot 6}{3 \cdot 2 \cdot 1} = 56$

35. $C(11,4) = \dfrac{11!}{4!\,7!} = \dfrac{11 \cdot 10 \cdot 9 \cdot 8}{4 \cdot 3 \cdot 2 \cdot 1} = 330$

37. $C(100,1) = \dfrac{100!}{1!\,99!} = \dfrac{100}{1} = 100$

39. We want the number of ways of choosing a group of three from a group of six. This number is $C(6,3) = \dfrac{6!}{3!\,3!} = 20$.

41. We want the number of ways of choosing a group of six people from a group of ten people. The number of combinations of 10 objects (10 people) taken 6 at a time is $C(10,6) = \dfrac{10!}{6!\,4!} = 210$.

43. We want the number of ways of choosing a group (the 5-card hand) where order of selection is not important. The number of combinations of 52 objects (the 52 cards) taken 5 at a time is $C(52,5) = \dfrac{52!}{5!\,47!} = 2{,}598{,}960$.

45. The order of selection is not important, hence we must calculate the number of combinations of 10 objects (the 10 questions) taken 7 at a time, this gives $C(10,7) = \dfrac{10!}{7!\,3!} = 120$.

47. We assume that the order in which he plays the pieces in the recital is *not* important, so the number of combinations of 12 objects (the 12 pieces) taken 8 at a time is $C(12,8) = \dfrac{12!}{8!\,4!} = 495$.

49. We are just interested in the group of seven students taken from the class of 30 students, not the order in which they are picked. Thus the number is $C(30,7) = \dfrac{30!}{7!\,23!} = 2{,}035{,}800$.

51. We first take Jack out of the class of 30 students and select the 7 students from the remaining 29 students. Thus there are $C(29,7) = \dfrac{29!}{7!\,22!} = 1{,}560{,}780$ ways to pick the 7 students for the field trip.

53. We must count the number of different ways to choose the group of 6 numbers from the 53 numbers. There are $C(53,6) = \dfrac{53!}{6!\,47!} = 22{,}957{,}480$ possible tickets, so it would cost \$22,957,480.

55. (a) The number of ways to select 5 of the 8 objects is $C(8,5) = \dfrac{8!}{5!\,3!} = 56$.

    (b) A set with 8 elements has $2^8 = 256$ subsets.

57. Each subset of toppings constitutes a different way a hamburger can be ordered. Since a set with 10 elements has $2^{10} = 1024$ subsets, there are 1024 different ways to order a hamburger.

59. We pick the two men from the group of ten men, and we pick the two women from the group of ten women. So the number of ways 2 men and 2 women can be chosen is
$$\left(\begin{smallmatrix} \text{number of ways to pick} \\ \text{2 of the 10 men} \end{smallmatrix} \right) \cdot \left(\begin{smallmatrix} \text{number of ways to pick} \\ \text{2 of the 10 women} \end{smallmatrix} \right) = C(10, 2) \cdot C(10, 2) = (45)(45) = 2025.$$

61. The leading and supporting roles are different (order counts), while the extra roles are not (order doesn't count). Also, the male roles must be filled by the male actors and the female roles filled by the female actresses. Thus, number of ways the actors and actresses can be chosen is
$$\left(\begin{smallmatrix} \text{number of ways the} \\ \text{leading and the supporting} \\ \text{actors can be chosen} \end{smallmatrix} \right) \cdot \left(\begin{smallmatrix} \text{number of ways the} \\ \text{leading and supporting} \\ \text{actresses can be chosen} \end{smallmatrix} \right) \cdot \left(\begin{smallmatrix} \text{number of ways to choose} \\ \text{5 of 8 male extras} \end{smallmatrix} \right) \cdot \left(\begin{smallmatrix} \text{number of ways to choose} \\ \text{3 of 10 female extras} \end{smallmatrix} \right)$$
$$= P(10, 2) \cdot P(12, 2) \cdot C(8, 5) \cdot C(10, 3) = (90)(132)(56)(120) = 79,833,600.$$

63. To order a pizza, we must make several choices. First the size (4 choices), the type of crust (2 choices), and then the toppings. Since there are 14 toppings, the number of possible choices is the number of subsets of the 14 toppings, that is 2^{14} choices. So by the Fundamental Counting Principle, the number of possible pizzas is $(4)(2) \cdot 2^{14} = 131,072.$

65. We treat John and Jane as one object and Mike and Molly as one object, so we need the number of ways of permuting 8 objects. We then multiply this by the number of ways of arranging John and Jane within their group and arranging Mike and Molly within their group. Thus the number of possible arrangements is $P(8, 8) \cdot P(2, 2) \cdot P(2, 2) = 8! \cdot 2! \cdot 2! = 161,280$.

67. (a) To find the number of ways the men and women can be seated we first select and place a man in the first seat and then arrange the other 7 people. Thus we get
$$\left(\begin{smallmatrix} \text{select 1 of} \\ \text{the 4 men} \end{smallmatrix} \right) \cdot \left(\begin{smallmatrix} \text{arrange the} \\ \text{remaining 7 people} \end{smallmatrix} \right) = C(4, 1) \cdot P(7, 7) = 4 \cdot 7! = 20,160.$$

    (b) To find the number of ways the men and women can be seated we first select and place a woman in the first and last seats and then arrange the other 6 people. Thus we get
$$\left(\begin{smallmatrix} \text{arrange 2 of} \\ \text{the 4 women} \end{smallmatrix} \right) \cdot \left(\begin{smallmatrix} \text{arrange the} \\ \text{remaining 6 people} \end{smallmatrix} \right) = P(4, 2) \cdot P(6, 6) = 6 \cdot 6! = 8,640.$$

69. The number of ways the top finalist can be chosen is
$$\left(\begin{smallmatrix} \text{number of ways to choose} \\ \text{the 6 semifinalists from the 30} \end{smallmatrix} \right) \cdot \left(\begin{smallmatrix} \text{number of ways to choose} \\ \text{the 2 finalist from the 6} \end{smallmatrix} \right) \cdot \left(\begin{smallmatrix} \text{number of ways to pick} \\ \text{the top finalist from the 2} \end{smallmatrix} \right)$$
$$= C(30, 6) \cdot C(6, 2) \cdot C(2, 1) = (593775)(15)(2) = 17,813,250.$$

71. We find the number of committees that can be formed and subtract those committees that contain the two picky people. There are $C(10, 4)$ ways to select the committees without restrictions. The number of committees that contain the two picky people is $C(8, 2)$ because once we place these two people on the committee, then we need only choose two more members from the remaining eight candidates to complete the committee. Thus the number of committees that do not contain these two people is $C(10, 4) - C(8, 2) = 210 - 28 = 182.$

73. We show two methods to solve this exercise.
    Method 1: We consider the number of 5 member committees that can be formed from the 26 interested people and subtract off those that contain no teacher and those that contain no students. Thus the number of committees is
$$C(26, 5) - C(12, 5) - C(14, 5) = 65,780 - 792 - 2002 = 62,986.$$

Method 2: In the method we construct all the committees that are possible. Thus the number of

committees is $\begin{pmatrix} \text{committees} \\ \text{with 1 student} \\ \text{and 4 teachers} \end{pmatrix} + \begin{pmatrix} \text{committees} \\ \text{with 2 students} \\ \text{and 3 teachers} \end{pmatrix} + \begin{pmatrix} \text{committees} \\ \text{with 3 students} \\ \text{and 2 teachers} \end{pmatrix} + \begin{pmatrix} \text{committees} \\ \text{with 4 students} \\ \text{and 1 teacher} \end{pmatrix}$

$= C(14,1) \cdot C(12,4) + C(14,2) \cdot C(12,3) + C(14,3) \cdot C(12,2) + C(14,4) \cdot C(12,1)$

$= (14)(495) + (91)(220) + (364)(66) + (1001)(12) = 6,930 + 20,020 + 24,024 + 12,012$

$= 62,986.$

75. We are only interested in selecting a set of three marbles to give to Luke and a set of two marbles to
     give to Mark, not the order in which we hand out the marbles. Since both $C(10,3) \cdot C(7,2)$ and
     $C(10,2) \cdot C(8,3)$ count the number of ways this can be done, these numbers must be equal.
     (Calculating these values shows that they are indeed equal.) In general, if we wish to find two
     distinct sets of k and r objects selected from n objects ($k + r \leq n$), then we can either first select the
     k objects from the n objects and then select the r objects from the $n - k$ remaining objects, or we
     can first select the r objects from the n objects and then the k objects from the $n - r$ remaining

     objects. Thus $\binom{n}{r} \cdot \binom{n-r}{k} = \binom{n}{k} \cdot \binom{n-k}{r}$.

Exercises 11.3

1. Let H stand for head and T for tails.

   (a) The sample space is $S = \{HH, HT, TH, TT\}$.

   (b) Let E be the event of getting exactly two heads, so $E = \{HH\}$. Then $P(E) = \dfrac{n(E)}{n(S)} = \frac{1}{4}$.

   (c) Let F be the event of getting at least one head. Then $F = \{HH, HT, TH\}$, and
   $$P(F) = \frac{n(F)}{n(S)} = \tfrac{3}{4}.$$

   (d) Let G be the event of getting exactly one head, that is, $G = \{HT, TH\}$. Then
   $$P(G) = \frac{n(G)}{n(S)} = \tfrac{2}{4} = \tfrac{1}{2}.$$

3. (a) Let E be the event of rolling a six. Then $P(E) = \dfrac{n(E)}{n(S)} = \frac{1}{6}$.

   (b) Let F be the event of rolling an even number. Then $F = \{2, 4, 6\}$. So
   $$P(F) = \frac{n(F)}{n(S)} = \tfrac{3}{6} = \tfrac{1}{2}.$$

   (c) Let G be the event of rolling a number greater than 5. Since 6 is the only face greater than 5,
   $$P(G) = \frac{n(G)}{n(S)} = \tfrac{1}{6}.$$

5. (a) Let E be the event of choosing a king. Since a deck has 4 kings, $P(E) = \dfrac{n(E)}{n(S)} = \frac{4}{52} = \frac{1}{13}$.

   (b) Let F be the event of choosing a face card. Since there are 3 face cards per suit and 4 suits,
   $$P(F) = \frac{n(F)}{n(S)} = \tfrac{12}{52} = \tfrac{3}{13}.$$

   (c) Let F be the event of choosing a face card. Then $P(F') = 1 - P(F) = 1 - \tfrac{3}{13} = \tfrac{10}{13}$.

7. (a) Let E be the event of selecting a red ball. Since the jar contains 5 red balls,
   $$P(E) = \frac{n(E)}{n(S)} = \tfrac{5}{8}.$$

   (b) Let F be the event of selecting a yellow ball. Since there is only one yellow ball,
   $$P(F') = 1 - P(F) = 1 - \frac{n(F)}{n(S)} = 1 - \tfrac{1}{8} = \tfrac{7}{8}.$$

   (c) Let G be the event of selecting a black ball. Since there are no black balls in the jar,
   $$P(G) = \frac{n(G)}{n(S)} = \tfrac{0}{8} = 0.$$

9. (a) Let E be the event of drawing a red sock. Since 3 pairs are red, the drawer contains 6 red socks, and so $P(E) = \dfrac{n(E)}{n(S)} = \frac{6}{18} = \frac{1}{3}$.

   (b) Let F be the event of drawing another red sock. Since there are 17 socks left of which 5 are red, $P(F) = \dfrac{n(F)}{n(S)} = \frac{5}{17}$.

11. (a) Let E be the event of choosing a "T". Since 3 of the 16 letters are T's, $P(E) = \frac{3}{16}$.

(b) Let F be the event of choosing a vowel. Since there are 6 vowels, $P(F) = \frac{6}{16} = \frac{3}{8}$.

(c) Let F be the event of choosing a vowel. Then $P(F') = 1 - \frac{3}{8} = \frac{5}{8}$.

13. Let E be the event of choosing 5 cards of the same suit. Since there are 4 suits and 13 cards in each suit, $n(E) = 4 \cdot C(13,5)$. Also by Exercise 43, Section 10.2, $n(S) = C(52,5)$. Therefore,
$$P(E) = \frac{4 \cdot C(13,5)}{C(52,5)} = \frac{5,148}{2,598,960} \approx 0.00198.$$

15. Let E be the event of dealing a royal flush (ace, king, queen, jack, and 10 of the same suit). Since there is only one such sequence for each suit, there are only 4 royal flushes, so
$$P(E) = \frac{4}{C(52,5)} = \frac{4}{2,598,960} \approx 1.53908 \times 10^{-6}.$$

17. (a) Let B stand for "boy" and G stand for "girl". Then $S = \{$BBBB, GBBB, BGBB, BBGB, BBBG, GGBB, GBGB, GBBG, BGGB, BGBG, BBGG, BGGG, GBGG, GGBG, GGGB, GGGG$\}$.

(b) Let E be the event that the couple has only boys. Then $E = \{$BBBB$\}$ and $P(E) = \frac{1}{16}$.

(c) Let F be the event that the couple has 2 boys and 2 girls. Then $F = \{$GGBB, GBGB, GBBG, BGGB, BGBG, BBGG$\}$, so $P(F) = \frac{6}{16} = \frac{3}{8}$.

(d) Let G be the event that the couple has 4 children of the same sex. Then $G = \{$BBBB, GGGG$\}$, and $P(G) = \frac{2}{16} = \frac{1}{8}$.

(e) Let H be the event that the couple has at least 2 girls. Then H' is the event that the couple has fewer than two girls. Thus, $H' = \{$BBBB, GBBB, BGBB, BBGB, BBBG$\}$, so $n(H') = 5$, and $P(H) = 1 - P(H') = 1 - \frac{5}{16} = \frac{11}{16}$.

19. Let E be the event that the ball lands in an odd numbered slot. Since there are 18 odd numbers between 1 and 36, $P(E) = \frac{18}{38} = \frac{9}{19}$.

21. Let E be the event of picking the 6 winning numbers. Since there is only one way to pick these,
$$P(E) = \frac{1}{C(49,6)} = \frac{1}{13,983,816} \approx 7.15 \times 10^{-8}.$$

23. The sample space consist of all possible True-False combinations, so $n(S) = 2^{10}$.

(a) Let E be the event that the student answers all 10 questions correctly. Since there is only one way to answer all 10 questions correctly, $P(E) = \frac{1}{2^{10}} = \frac{1}{1024}$.

(b) Let F be the event that the student answers exactly 7 questions correctly. The number of ways to answer exactly 7 of the 10 questions correctly is the number of ways to choose 7 of the 10 questions, so $n(F) = C(10,7)$. Therefore, $P(E) = \frac{C(10,7)}{2^{10}} = \frac{120}{1024} = \frac{15}{128}$.

25. (a) Let E be the event that the monkey types "Hamlet" as his first word. Since "Hamlet" contains 6 letters and there are 48 typewriter keys, $P(E) = \frac{1}{48^6} \approx 8.18 \times 10^{-11}$.

(b) Let F be the event that the monkey types "to be or not to be" as his first words. Since this phrase has 18 characters (including the blanks), $P(F) = \frac{1}{48^{18}} \approx 5.47 \times 10^{-31}$.

27. Let E be the event that the monkey will arrange the 11 blocks to spell "PROBABILITY" as his first word. The number of ways of arranging these blocks is the number of distinguishable permutations

of 11 blocks. Since there are two blocks labeled `B' and two blocks labeled `I', the number of distinguishable permutations is $\frac{11!}{2!\,2!}$. Only one of these arrangements spells the word "PROBABILITY'. Thus $P(E) = \dfrac{1}{\frac{11!}{2!\,2!}} = \frac{2!\,2!}{11!} \approx 1.00 \times 10^{-7}$.

29. (a) Let E be the event that the pea is tall. Since tall is dominant, $E = \{\text{TT, Tt, tT}\}$. So $P(E) = \frac{3}{4}$.

    (b) E' is the event that the pea is short. So $P(E') = 1 - P(E) = 1 - \frac{3}{4} = \frac{1}{4}$.

31. (a) YES, the events are mutually exclusive since a person cannot be both male and female.

    (b) NO, the events are not mutually exclusive since a person can be both tall and blond.

33. (a) YES, the events are mutually exclusive since the number cannot be both even and odd. So $P(E \cup F) = P(E) + P(F) = \frac{3}{6} + \frac{3}{6} = 1$.

    (b) NO, the events are not mutually exclusive since 6 is both even and greater than 4. So $P(E \cup F) = P(E) + P(F) - P(E \cap F) = \frac{3}{6} + \frac{2}{6} - \frac{1}{6} = \frac{2}{3}$.

35. (a) NO, the events E and F are not mutually exclusive since the Jack, Queen, and King of spades are both face cards and spades. So $P(E \cup F) = P(E) + P(F) - P(E \cap F) = \frac{13}{52} + \frac{12}{52} - \frac{3}{52} = \frac{11}{26}$.

    (b) YES, the events E and F are mutually exclusive since the card cannot be both a heart and a spade. So $P(E \cup F) = P(E) + P(F) = \frac{13}{52} + \frac{13}{52} = \frac{1}{2}$.

37. (a) Let E be the event that the spinner stops on red. Since 12 of the regions are red, $P(E) = \frac{12}{16} = \frac{3}{4}$.

    (b) Let F be the event that the spinner stops on an even number. Since 8 of the regions are even-numbered, $P(F) = \frac{8}{16} = \frac{1}{2}$.

    (c) Since 4 of the even-numbered regions are red, $P(E \cup F) = P(E) + P(F) - P(E \cap F)$ $= \frac{3}{4} + \frac{1}{2} - \frac{4}{16} = 1$.

39. Let E be the event that the ball lands in an odd numbered slot and F be the event that it lands in a slot with a number higher than 31. Since there are two odd-numbered slots with numbers greater than 31, $P(E \cup F) = P(E) + P(F) - P(E \cap F) = \frac{18}{38} + \frac{5}{38} - \frac{2}{38} = \frac{21}{38}$.

41. Let E be the event that the committee is all male and F the event it is all female. The sample space is the set of all ways that 5 people can be chosen from the group of 14. These events are mutually exclusive, so $P(E \cup F) = P(E) + P(F) = \dfrac{C(6,5)}{C(14,5)} + \dfrac{C(8,5)}{C(14,5)} = \frac{6+56}{2002} = \frac{31}{1001}$.

43. Let E be the event that the marble is red and F be the event that the number is odd-numbered. Then E' is the event that the marble is blue, and F' is the event that the marble is even-numbered.

    (a) $P(E) = \frac{6}{16} = \frac{3}{8}$

    (b) $P(F) = \frac{8}{16} = \frac{1}{2}$

    (c) $P(E \cup F) = P(E) + P(F) - P(E \cap F) = \frac{6}{16} + \frac{8}{16} - \frac{3}{16} = \frac{11}{16}$

    (d) $P(E' \cup F') = P(E') + P(F') - P(E' \cap F') = \frac{10}{16} + \frac{8}{16} - \frac{5}{16} = \frac{13}{16}$.

45. (a) YES, the first roll does not influence the outcome of the second roll.

(b) The probability of getting a six on both rolls is $P(E \cap F) = P(E) \cdot P(F) = \left(\frac{1}{6}\right)\left(\frac{1}{6}\right) = \frac{1}{36}$.

47. (a) Let E_A and E_B be the event that the respective spinners stop on a purple region. Since these events are independent, $P(E_A \cap E_B) = P(E_A) \cdot P(E_B) = \frac{1}{4} \cdot \frac{2}{8} = \frac{1}{16}$.

(b) Let F_A and F_B be the event that the respective spinners stop on a blue region. Since these events are independent, $P(F_A \cap F_B) = P(F_A) \cdot P(F_B) = \frac{1}{4} \cdot \frac{1}{8} = \frac{1}{32}$.

49. Let E be the event of getting a 1 on the first roll, and let F be the event of getting an even number on the second roll. Since these events are independent, $P(E \cap F) = P(E) \cdot P(F) = \frac{1}{6} \cdot \frac{3}{6} = \frac{1}{12}$.

51. Let E be the event that the player wins on spin 1, and let F be the event that the player wins on spin 2. What happens on the first spin does not influence what happens on the second spin, so the events are independent. Thus, $P(E \cap F) = P(E) \cdot P(F) = \frac{1}{38} \cdot \frac{1}{38} = \frac{1}{1444}$.

53. Let E, F and G denote the events of rolling two ones on the first, second, and third rolls, respectively, of a pair of dice. The events are independent, so
$P(E \cap F \cap G) = P(E) \cdot P(F) \cdot P(G) = \frac{1}{36} \cdot \frac{1}{36} \cdot \frac{1}{36} = \frac{1}{36^3} \approx 2.14 \times 10^{-5}$.

55. The probability of getting 2 red balls by picking from jar B is $\left(\frac{5}{7}\right)\left(\frac{4}{6}\right) = \frac{10}{21}$. The probability of getting 2 red balls by picking one ball from each jar is $\left(\frac{3}{7}\right)\left(\frac{5}{7}\right) = \frac{15}{49}$. The probability of getting 2 red balls after putting all balls in one jar is $\left(\frac{8}{14}\right)\left(\frac{7}{13}\right) = \frac{4}{13}$. Hence, picking both balls from jar B gives the greatest probability.

57. Let E be the event that two of the students have the same birthday. It is easier to consider the complementary event E': no two students have the same birthday. Then
$P(E') = \dfrac{\text{number of ways to assign 8 different birthdays}}{\text{number of ways to assign 8 birthdays}} = \dfrac{P(365, 8)}{365^8}$
$= \frac{365 \cdot 364 \cdot 363 \cdot 362 \cdot 361 \cdot 360 \cdot 359 \cdot 358}{365 \cdot 365 \cdot 365 \cdot 365 \cdot 365 \cdot 365 \cdot 365 \cdot 365} \approx 0.92566$. So $P(E) = 1 - P(E') \approx 0.07434$.

59. Let E be the event that she opens the lock within an hour. The number of combinations she can try in one hour is $10 \cdot 60 = 600$. The number of possible combinations is $P(40,3)$ assuming that no number can be repeated. Thus $P(E) = \dfrac{600}{P(40,3)} = \dfrac{600}{59,280} = \dfrac{5}{494} \approx 0.010$.

61. Let E be the event that Paul stands next to Phyllis. To find $n(E)$ we treat Paul and Phyllis as one object and find the number of ways to arrange the 19 objects and then multiply the result by the number of ways to arrange Paul and Phyllis. So $n(E) = 19! \cdot 2!$. The sample space is all the ways that 20 people can be arranged. Thus $P(E) = \dfrac{19! \cdot 2!}{20!} = \dfrac{2}{20} = 0.10$.

63. The sample space for the genders of Mrs. Smith's children is $S_S = \{(b,g), (b,b)\}$, where we list the first born first. The sample space for the genders of Mrs. Jones' children is
$S_J = \{(b,g), (g,b), (b,b)\}$. Thus, the probability that Mrs. Smith's other child is a boy is $\frac{1}{2}$, while the probability that Mrs. Jones' other child is a boy is $\frac{1}{3}$. The reason there is a difference is that we *know* that Mrs. Smith's first born is a boy.

Exercises 11.4

1. Mike gets \$2 with probability $\frac{1}{2}$ and \$1 with probability $\frac{1}{2}$. Thus, $E = (2)\left(\frac{1}{2}\right) + (1)\left(\frac{1}{2}\right) = 1.5$, and so his expected winnings are \$1.50 per game.

3. Since the probability of drawing the ace of spades is $\frac{1}{52}$, the expected value of this game is
   $E = (100)\left(\frac{1}{52}\right) + (-1)\left(\frac{51}{52}\right) = \frac{49}{52} \approx 0.94$. So your expected winnings are \$0.94 per game.

5. Since the probability that Carol rolls a six is $\frac{1}{6}$, the expected value of this game is
   $E = (3)\left(\frac{1}{6}\right) + (0.50)\left(\frac{5}{6}\right) = \frac{5.5}{6} \approx 0.9167$. So Carol expects to win \$0.92 per game.

7. Since the probability that the die shows an even number equals the probability that that die shows an odd number, the expected value of this game is $E = (2)\left(\frac{1}{2}\right) + (-2)\left(\frac{1}{2}\right) = 0$. So Tom should expect to break even after playing this game many times.

9. Since it cost 50¢ to play, if you get a silver dollar, you only win $1 - 0.50 = \$.50$. Thus the expected value of this game is $E = (0.50)\left(\frac{2}{10}\right) + (-0.50)\left(\frac{8}{10}\right) = -0.30$. So your expected winnings are $-\$0.30$ per game. In other words, you should expect to lose \$0.30 per game.

11. You can either win \$35 or lose \$1, so the expected value of this game is
    $E = (35)\left(\frac{1}{38}\right) + (-1)\left(\frac{37}{38}\right) = -\frac{2}{38} = -0.0526$. Thus the expected value is $-\$0.0526$ per game.

13. By the rules of the game, a player can win \$10, \$5, \$0 or lose \$100. Thus the expected value of this game is $E = (10)\left(\frac{10}{100}\right) + (5)\left(\frac{10}{100}\right) + (-100)\left(\frac{2}{100}\right) + (0)\left(\frac{78}{100}\right) = -0.50$. So the expected winnings per game are $-\$0.50$.

15. If the stock goes up to \$20, she expects to make $\$20 - \$5 = \$15$. And if the stock falls to \$1, then she has lost $\$5 - \$1 = \$4$. So the expected value of her profit is $E = (15)(0.1) - (4)(0.9) = -2.1$. Thus, her expected profit per share is $-\$2.10$, that is, she should expect to lose \$2.10 per share. She did not make a wise investment.

17. There are $C(49, 6)$ ways to select a group of six numbers from the group of 49 numbers, of which only one is a winning set. Thus the expected value of this game is
    $$E = (10^6 - 1)\left(\frac{1}{C(49,6)}\right) + (-1)\left(1 - \frac{1}{C(49,6)}\right) \approx -\$0.93.$$

19. Let x be the fair price to pay to play this game. Then the game is fair whenever $E = 0 \Leftrightarrow$
    $(13 - x)\left(\frac{4}{52}\right) + (-x)\left(\frac{48}{52}\right) = 0 \Leftrightarrow 52 - 52x = 0 \Leftrightarrow x = 1$. Thus, a fair price to pay to play this game is \$1.

Review Exercises for Chapter 11

1. The number of possible outcomes is $\left(\begin{smallmatrix}\text{number of outcomes}\\\text{when a coin is tossed}\end{smallmatrix}\right) \cdot \left(\begin{smallmatrix}\text{number of outcomes}\\\text{a die is rolled}\end{smallmatrix}\right) \cdot \left(\begin{smallmatrix}\text{number of ways}\\\text{to draw a card}\end{smallmatrix}\right)$
    $= (2)(6)(52) = 624.$

3. (a) Order is not important, and there are no repetitions, so the number of different two-element
        subsets is $C(5,2) = \dfrac{5!}{2!\,3!} = \dfrac{5\cdot 4}{2} = 10.$

    (b) Order is important, and there are no repetitions, so the number of different two-letter words is
        $P(5,2) = \frac{5!}{3!} = 20.$

5. You earn a score of 70% by answering exactly 7 of the 10 questions correctly. The number of
    different ways to answer the questions correctly is $C(10,7) = \dfrac{10!}{7!\,3!} = 120.$

7. You must choose two of the ten questions to omit, and the number of ways of choosing these two
    questions is $C(10,2) = \dfrac{10!}{2!\,8!} = 45.$

9. The maximum number of employees using this security system is
    $\left(\begin{smallmatrix}\text{number of choices}\\\text{for the first letter}\end{smallmatrix}\right) \cdot \left(\begin{smallmatrix}\text{number of choices}\\\text{for the second letter}\end{smallmatrix}\right) \cdot \left(\begin{smallmatrix}\text{number of choices}\\\text{for the third letter}\end{smallmatrix}\right) = (26)(26)(26) = 17{,}576.$

11. We could count the number of ways of choosing 7 of the flips to be HEADS; equivalently we could
    count the number of ways of choosing 3 of the flips to be TAILS. Thus, the number of different
    ways this can occur is $C(10,7) = C(10,3) = \dfrac{10!}{3!\,7!} = 120.$

13. Let x be the number of people in the group. Then $C(x,2) = 10 \quad\Leftrightarrow\quad \dfrac{x!}{2!(x-2)!} = 10 \quad\Leftrightarrow$
    $\dfrac{x!}{(x-2)!} = 20 \quad\Leftrightarrow\quad x(x-1) = 20 \quad\Leftrightarrow\quad x^2 - x - 20 = 0 \quad\Leftrightarrow\quad (x-5)(x+4) = 0 \quad\Leftrightarrow$
    $x = 5$ or $x = -4.$ So there are 5 people in this group.

15. A letter can be represented by a sequence of length 1, a sequence of length 2, or a sequence of length
    3. Since each symbol is either a dot or a dash, the possible number of letters is
    $\left(\begin{smallmatrix}\text{number of letters}\\\text{using 3 symbols}\end{smallmatrix}\right) + \left(\begin{smallmatrix}\text{number of letters}\\\text{using 2 symbols}\end{smallmatrix}\right) + \left(\begin{smallmatrix}\text{number of letters}\\\text{using 1 symbol}\end{smallmatrix}\right) = 2^3 + 2^2 + 2 = 14.$

17. (a) Since we cannot choose a major and a minor in the same subject, the number of ways a student
        can select a major and a minor is $P(16,2) = 16 \cdot 15 = 240.$

    (b) Again, since we cannot have repetitions and the order of selection is important, the number of
        ways to select a major, a first minor, and a second minor is $P(16,3) = 16 \cdot 15 \cdot 14 = 3360.$

    (c) When we select a major and 2 minors, the order in which we choose the minors is not
        important. Thus the number of ways to select a major and 2 minors is
        $\left(\begin{smallmatrix}\text{number of ways}\\\text{to select a major}\end{smallmatrix}\right) \cdot \left(\begin{smallmatrix}\text{number of ways to}\\\text{select two minors}\end{smallmatrix}\right) = 16 \cdot C(15,2) = 16 \cdot 105 = 1680.$

19. Since the letters are distinct, the number of anagrams of the word TRIANGLE is $8! = 40{,}320.$

21. (a) The possible number of committees is $C(18,7) = 31{,}824.$

(b) Since we must select the 4 men from the group 10 men and the 3 women from the group of 8 women, the possible number of committees is $\left(\begin{smallmatrix}\text{number of ways to}\\\text{choose 4 of 10 men}\end{smallmatrix}\right) \cdot \left(\begin{smallmatrix}\text{number of ways to}\\\text{choose 3 of 8 women}\end{smallmatrix}\right)$

$= C(10,4) \cdot C(8,3) = 210 \cdot 56 = 11,760$

(c) We remove Susie from the group of 18, so the possible number of committees is
$C(17,7) = 19,448.$

(d) The possible number of committees is
$\left(\begin{smallmatrix}\text{possible number of}\\\text{committees with 5 women}\end{smallmatrix}\right) + \left(\begin{smallmatrix}\text{possible number of}\\\text{committees with 6 women}\end{smallmatrix}\right) + \left(\begin{smallmatrix}\text{possible number of}\\\text{committees with 7 women}\end{smallmatrix}\right)$
$= C(8,5) \cdot C(10,2) + C(8,6) \cdot C(10,1) + C(8,7) \cdot C(10,0) = 56 \cdot 45 + 28 \cdot 10 + 8 \cdot 1$
$= 2808.$

(e) Since the committee is to have 7 members, "at most two men" is the same as "at least five women" which we found in part (d). So the number is also 2808.

(f) We select the specific offices first, then complete the committee from the remaining members of the group. So the number of possible committees is
$\left(\begin{smallmatrix}\text{number of ways to choose}\\\text{a chairman, a vice-chairman, a secretary}\end{smallmatrix}\right) \cdot \left(\begin{smallmatrix}\text{number of ways to}\\\text{choose 4 other members}\end{smallmatrix}\right) = P(18,3) \cdot C(15,4)$
$= 4896 \cdot 1365 = 6,683,040.$

23. Let R_n denote the event that the nth ball is red and let W_n denote the event that the nth ball is white.

(a) $P(\text{both balls are red}) = P(R_1 \cap R_2) = P(R_1) \cdot P(R_2 \mid R_1) = \frac{10}{15} \cdot \frac{9}{14} = \frac{3}{7}.$

(b) <u>Solution 1</u>: The probability that one is white and that the other is red is
$\dfrac{\text{number of ways to select one white \& one red}}{\text{number of ways to select two balls}} = \dfrac{C(10,1) \cdot C(5,1)}{C(15,2)} = \dfrac{10}{21}.$

<u>Solution 2</u>: $P(\text{one white and one red}) = P(W_1 \cap R_2) + P(R_1 \cap W_2)$
$= P(W_1) \cdot P(R_2 \mid W_1) + P(R_1) \cdot P(W_2 \mid R_1) = \frac{5}{15} \cdot \frac{10}{14} + \frac{10}{15} \cdot \frac{5}{14} = \frac{10}{21}.$

(c) <u>Solution 1</u>: Let E be the event "at least one is red". Then E' is the event "both are white".
$P(E') = P(W_1 \cap W_2) = P(W_1) \cdot P(W_2 \mid W_1) = \frac{5}{15} \cdot \frac{4}{14} = \frac{2}{21}.$ Thus $P(E) = 1 - \frac{2}{21} = \frac{19}{21}.$

<u>Solution 2</u>: $P(\text{at least one is red}) = P(\text{one red and one white}) + P(\text{both red})$
$= \frac{10}{21} + \frac{9}{21} = \frac{19}{21}$ (from (a) and (b)).

(d) Since 5 of the 15 balls are both red and even-numbered, the probability that both balls are red and even-numbered is $\frac{5}{15} \cdot \frac{4}{14} = \frac{2}{21}.$

(e) Since 2 of the 15 balls are both white and odd-numbered, the probability that both are white is $\frac{2}{15} \cdot \frac{1}{14} = \frac{1}{105}.$

25. The probability that you select a mathematics book is $\dfrac{\begin{smallmatrix}\text{number of ways to select}\\\text{a mathematics book}\end{smallmatrix}}{\text{number of ways to select a book}} = \frac{4}{10}$
$= \frac{2}{5} = 0.4.$

27. (a) $P(\text{ace}) = \frac{4}{52} = \frac{1}{13}.$

(b) Let E be the event the card chosen is an ace, and let F be the event the card chosen is a jack. Then $P(E \cup F) = P(E) + P(F) = \frac{4}{52} + \frac{4}{52} = \frac{2}{13}.$

(c) Let E be the event the card chosen is an ace, and let F be the event the card chosen is a spade. Then $P(E \cup F) = P(E) + P(F) - P(E \cap F) = \frac{4}{52} + \frac{13}{52} - \frac{1}{52} = \frac{4}{13}.$

(d) Let E be the event the card chosen is an ace, and let F be the event the card chosen is a red card. Then $P(E \cap F) = \dfrac{n(E \cap F)}{n(S)} = \frac{2}{52} = \frac{1}{26}$.

29. (a) The probability the first die shows some number is 1, and the probability the second die shows the same number is $\frac{1}{6}$. So the probability each die shows the same number is $1 \cdot \frac{1}{6} = \frac{1}{6}$.

(b) By part (a), the event of showing the same number has probability of $\frac{1}{6}$, and the complement of this event is that the dice show different numbers. Thus the probability that the dice show different numbers is $1 - \frac{1}{6} = \frac{5}{6}$.

31. In the numbers game lottery, there are 1000 possible "winning" numbers.

(a) The probability that John wins \$500 is $\frac{1}{1000}$.

(b) There are $P(3, 3) = 6$ ways to arrange the digits "1", "5", "9". However, if John wins only \$50, it means that his number 159 was not the winning number. Thus the probability is $\frac{5}{1000} = \frac{1}{200}$.

33. There are 36 possible outcomes in rolling two dice and 6 ways in which both dice show the same numbers, namely, $(1, 1)$, $(2, 2)$, $(3, 3)$, $(4, 4)$, $(5, 5)$, and $(6, 6)$. So the expected value of this game is $E = (5)\left(\frac{6}{36}\right) + (-1)\left(\frac{30}{36}\right) = 0$.

35. Since Mary makes a guess as to the order of ratification of the 13 original states, the number of such guesses is $P(13, 13) = 13!$, while the probability that she guesses the correct order is $\frac{1}{13!}$. Thus the expected value is $E = (1,000,000)\left(\frac{1}{13!}\right) + (0)\left(\frac{13!-1}{13!}\right) = 0.00016$. So Mary's expected winnings are \$0.00016.

37. (a) Since there are only two colors of socks, any 3 socks must contain a matching pair.

(b) Method 1: If the two socks drawn form a matching pair then they are either both red or both blue. So $P(\text{choosing a matching pair}) = P(\text{both red or both blue})$
$$= P(\text{both red}) + P(\text{both blue}) = \frac{C(20, 2)}{C(50, 2)} + \frac{C(30, 2)}{C(50, 2)} \approx 0.51.$$

Method 2: The complement of choosing a matching pair is choosing one sock of each color. So $P(\text{choosing a matching pair}) = 1 - P(\text{different colors}) = 1 - \dfrac{C(20, 1) \cdot C(30, 1)}{C(50, 2)}$
$\approx 1 - .49 = 0.51$.

39. (a) $\begin{pmatrix} \text{number of different} \\ \text{zip codes} \end{pmatrix} = \begin{pmatrix} \text{number of ways to} \\ \text{choose the 1st digit} \end{pmatrix} \cdot \begin{pmatrix} \text{number of ways to} \\ \text{choose the 2nd digit} \end{pmatrix} \cdot \ \cdots\ \cdot \begin{pmatrix} \text{number of ways to} \\ \text{choose the 5th digit} \end{pmatrix}$
$= 10 \cdot 10 \cdot 10 \cdot 10 \cdot 10 = 10^5 = 100{,}000$.

(b) Since there are five numbers (0, 1, 6, 8 and 9) that can be read upside down, we have
$\begin{pmatrix} \text{number of different} \\ \text{zip codes} \end{pmatrix} = \begin{pmatrix} \text{number of ways to} \\ \text{choose the 1st digit} \end{pmatrix} \cdot \begin{pmatrix} \text{number of ways to} \\ \text{choose the 2nd digit} \end{pmatrix} \cdot \ \cdots\ \cdot \begin{pmatrix} \text{number of ways to} \\ \text{choose the 5th digit} \end{pmatrix} = 5^5 = 3125.$

(c) Let E be the event that a zip code can be read upside down. Then by parts (a) and (b),
$P(E) = \dfrac{n(E)}{n(S)} = \frac{5^5}{10^5} = \frac{1}{32}$.

(d) Suppose a zip code is turned upside down. Then the middle digit remains the middle digit, so it must be a digit that reads the same when turned upside down, that is, a 0, 1 or 8. Also, the last digit becomes the first digit, and the next to last digit becomes the second digit. Thus, once the first two digits are chosen, the last two are determined. Therefore, the number of zip codes that read the same upside down as right side up is

$$\left(\begin{smallmatrix}\text{number of ways to}\\\text{choose the 1}^{\text{st}}\text{ digit}\end{smallmatrix}\right) \cdot \left(\begin{smallmatrix}\text{number of ways to}\\\text{choose the 2}^{\text{nd}}\text{ digit}\end{smallmatrix}\right) \cdot \left(\begin{smallmatrix}\text{number of ways to}\\\text{choose the 3}^{\text{rd}}\text{ digit}\end{smallmatrix}\right) \cdot \left(\begin{smallmatrix}\text{number of ways to}\\\text{choose the 4}^{\text{th}}\text{ digit}\end{smallmatrix}\right) \cdot \left(\begin{smallmatrix}\text{number of ways to}\\\text{choose the 5}^{\text{th}}\text{ digit}\end{smallmatrix}\right)$$

$$= 5 \cdot 5 \cdot 3 \cdot 1 \cdot 1 = 75.$$

41. (a) Using the rule for the number of distinguishable combinations, the number of divisors of N is $(7+1)(2+1)(5+1) = 144$.

(b) An even divisor of N must contain 2 as a factor. Thus we place a 2 as one of the factors and count the number of distinguishable combinations of $M = 2^6 3^2 5^5$. So using the rule for the number of distinguishable combinations, the number of even divisors of N is $(6+1)(2+1)(5+1) = 126$.

(c) A divisor is a multiple of 6 if 2 is a factor and 3 is a factor. Thus we place a 2 as one of the factors and a 3 as one of the factors. Then we count the number of distinguishable combinations of $K = 2^6 3^1 5^5$. So using the rule for the number of distinguishable combinations, the number of even divisors of N is $(6+1)(1+1)(5+1) = 84$.

(d) Let E be the event that the divisor is even. Then using parts (a) and (b), $P(E) = \dfrac{n(E)}{n(S)}$

$$= \frac{126}{144} = \frac{7}{8}.$$

Chapter 11 Test

1. (a) If repetition is allowed, then each letter of the word can be chosen in 10 ways since there are 10 letters. Thus the number of possible 5 letter words is $10 \cdot 10 \cdot 10 \cdot 10 \cdot 10 = 10^5 = 100{,}000$.

   (b) If repetition is not allowed, then since order is important, we need the number of permutations of 10 objects (the 10 letters) taken 5 at a time. Therefore, the number of possible 5 letter words is $P(10, 5) = 10 \cdot 9 \cdot 8 \cdot 7 \cdot 6 = 30{,}240$.

2. There are three choices to be made: one choice each of a main course, a dessert, and a drink. Since a main course can be chosen in one of five ways, a dessert in one of three ways, and a drink in one of four ways, there are $5 \cdot 3 \cdot 4 = 60$ possible ways that a customer could order a meal.

3. (a) Order is important in the arrangement, therefore the number of ways to arrange $P(30, 4) = 657{,}720$.

   (b) Here we are interested in the group of books to be taken on vacation so order is not important, therefore the number of ways to choose these books is $C(30, 4) = 27{,}405$.

4. There are two choices to be made: choose a road to travel from Ajax to Barrie, and then choose a different road from Barrie to Ajax. Since there are 4 roads joining the two cities, we need the number of permutations of 4 objects (the roads) taken 2 at a time (the road there and the road back). This number is $P(4, 2) = 4 \cdot 3 = 12$.

5. A customer must choose a size of pizza and must make a choice of toppings. There are 4 sizes of pizza, and each choice of toppings from the 14 available corresponds to a subset of the 14 objects. Since a set with 14 objects has 2^{14} subsets, the number of different pizzas this parlor offers is $4 \cdot 2^{14} = 65{,}536$.

6. (a) We want the number of ways of arranging 4 distinct objects (the letters L, O, V, E). This is the number of permutations of 4 objects taken 4 at a time. Therefore, the number of anagrams of the word LOVE is $P(4, 4) = 4! = 24$.

   (b) We want the number of distinguishable permutations of 6 objects (the letters K, I, S, S, E, S) consisting of three like groups of size 1 and a like group of size 3 (the S's). Therefore, the number of different anagrams of the word KISSES is $\dfrac{6!}{1!\, 1!\, 1!\, 3!} = \dfrac{6!}{3!} = 120$.

7. We choose the officers first. Here order is important, because the officers are different. Thus there are $P(30, 3)$ ways to do this. Next we choose the other 5 members from the remaining 27 members. Here order is not important, so there are $C(27, 5)$ ways to do this. Therefore the number of ways that the board of directors can be chosen is
$P(30, 3) \cdot C(27, 5) = 30 \cdot 29 \cdot 28 \cdot \frac{27!}{5!\,22!} = 1{,}966{,}582{,}800$.

8. One card is drawn from a deck.

   (a) Since there are 26 red cards, the probability that the card is red is $\frac{26}{52} = \frac{1}{2}$.

   (b) Since there are 4 kings, the probability that the card is a king is $\frac{4}{52} = \frac{1}{13}$.

   (c) Since there are 2 red kings, the probability that the card is a red king is $\frac{2}{52} = \frac{1}{26}$.

9. Let R be the event that the ball chosen is red. Let E be the event that the ball chosen is even-numbered.

(a) Since 5 of the 13 balls are red, $P(R) = \frac{5}{13} \approx 0.3846$.

(b) Since 6 of the 13 balls are even-numbered, $P(E) = \frac{6}{13} \approx .4615$.

(c) $P(R \text{ or } E) = P(R) + P(E) - P(R \cap E) = \frac{5}{13} + \frac{6}{13} - \frac{2}{13} = \frac{9}{13} \approx 0.6923$.

10. Let E be the event of choosing 3 men. Then
$$P(E) = \frac{n(E)}{n(S)} = \frac{\text{number of ways to choose 3 men}}{\text{number of ways to choose 3 people}} = \frac{C(5,3)}{C(15,3)} \approx 0.022.$$

11. Two dice are rolled. Let E be the event of getting doubles. Since a double may occur in 6 ways,
$$P(E) = \frac{n(E)}{n(S)} = \frac{6}{36} = \frac{1}{6}.$$

12. There are 4 students and 12 astrological signs. Let E be the event that at least 2 have the same astrological sign. Then E' is the event that no 2 have the same astrological sign. It is easier to find E'. So $P(E') = \dfrac{\text{number of ways to assign 4 different astrological signs}}{\text{number of ways to assign 4 astrological signs}} = \dfrac{P(12,4)}{12^4}$
$= \frac{12 \cdot 11 \cdot 10 \cdot 9}{12 \cdot 12 \cdot 12 \cdot 12} = \frac{55}{96}$. Therefore, $P(E) = 1 - P(E') = 1 - \frac{55}{96} = \frac{41}{96} \approx 0.427$.

13. A deck of cards contains 4 aces, 12 face cards, and 36 other cards. So the probability of an ace is $\frac{4}{52} = \frac{1}{13}$, the probability of a face card is $\frac{12}{52} = \frac{3}{13}$, and the probability of a non-ace, non-face card is $\frac{36}{52} = \frac{9}{13}$. Thus the expected value of this game is $E = (10)\left(\frac{1}{13}\right) + (1)\left(\frac{3}{13}\right) + (-.5)\left(\frac{9}{13}\right) = \frac{8.5}{13}$
≈ 0.654, that is, about \$0.65.

Focus on Modeling

1. (a) You should find that with the switching strategy, you win about 90% of the time. The more games you play, the closer to 90% your winning ratio will be.

   (b) The probability that the contestant has selected the winning door to begin with is $\frac{1}{10}$, since there are ten doors and only one is a winner. So the probability that he has selected a losing door is $\frac{9}{10}$. If the contestant switches, he exchanges a losing door for a winning door (and vice versa), so the probability that he loses is now $\frac{1}{10}$, and the probability that he wins is now $\frac{9}{10}$.

3. (a) You should find that A wins about $\frac{7}{8}$ of the time. That is, if you play this game 80 times, A should win approximately 70 times.

   (b) The game will end when either A gets one more "head" or B gets three more "tails". Each toss is independent, and both "heads" and "tails" have probability $\frac{1}{2}$, so we obtain the following probabilities.

Outcome	Probability
H	$\frac{1}{2}$
TH	$\frac{1}{2} \cdot \frac{1}{2} = \frac{1}{4}$
TTH	$\frac{1}{2} \cdot \frac{1}{2} \cdot \frac{1}{2} = \frac{1}{8}$
TTT	$\frac{1}{2} \cdot \frac{1}{2} \cdot \frac{1}{2} = \frac{1}{8}$

   Since A wins for any outcome that ends in "heads", the probability that he wins is $\frac{1}{2} + \frac{1}{4} + \frac{1}{8} = \frac{7}{8}$.

5. With 1000 trials, you should obtain an estimate for π that is reasonably close to 3.1 or 3.2.

7. (a) We can use the following TI-83 program to model this experiment. It is a minor modification of the one given in Problem 5.

```
PROGRAM: PROB6
:0 → P
:For(N,1,1000)
:rand → X:rand → Y
:P+((X+Y)<1) → P
:End
:Disp "PROBABILITY IS APPROX"
:Disp P/1000
```

   You should find that the probability is very close to $\frac{1}{2}$.

   (b) Following the hint, the points in the square for which $x + y < 1$ are the ones that lie below the line $x + y = 1$. This triangle has area $\frac{1}{2}$ (it takes up half the square), so the probability that $x + y < 1$ is $\frac{1}{2}$.

Chapter Twelve
Exercises 12.1

1.

x	3.9	3.99	3.999	4.001	4.01	4.1
$f(x)$	0.25158	0.25016	0.25002	0.24998	0.24984	0.24845

$$\lim_{x \to 4} \frac{\sqrt{x} - 2}{x - 4} = 0.25$$

3.

x	0.9	0.99	0.999	1.001	1.01	1.1
$f(x)$	0.36900	0.33669	0.33367	0.3330	0.33002	0.30211

$$\lim_{x \to 1} \frac{x - 1}{x^3 - 1} = 0.33333$$

5.

x	± 1	± 0.5	± 0.1	± 0.05	± 0.01
$f(x)$	0.84147	0.95885	0.99833	0.99958	0.99998

$$\lim_{x \to 0} \frac{\sin x}{x} = 1$$

7.

x	-3.9	-3.99	-3.999	-4.001	-4.01	-4.1
$f(x)$	-1.11111	-1.01010	-1.00100	-0.99900	-0.99010	-0.90909

$$\lim_{x \to -4} \frac{x + 4}{x^2 + 7x + 12} = -1$$

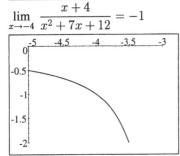

9.

x	-0.1	-0.01	-0.001	0.001	0.01	0.1
$f(x)$	0.44619	0.50396	0.51013	0.51152	0.51779	0.58496

$$\lim_{x \to 0} \frac{5^x - 3^x}{x} = 0.5108$$

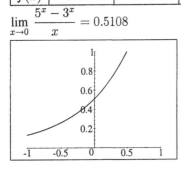

11.

x	0.9	0.99	0.999	1.001	1.01	1.1
$f(x)$	0.50878	0.50084	0.50008	0.49992	0.49917	0.49206

$$\lim_{x \to 1} \left(\frac{1}{\ln x} - \frac{1}{x-1} \right) = 0.5000$$

13. (a) $\displaystyle\lim_{x \to 1^-} f(x) = 2$ (b) $\displaystyle\lim_{x \to 1^+} f(x) = 3$

(c) $\displaystyle\lim_{x \to 1} f(x)$ does not exist since $\displaystyle\lim_{x \to 1^-} f(x) \neq \lim_{x \to 1^+} f(x)$

(d) $\displaystyle\lim_{x \to 5} f(x) = 4$ (e) $f(5)$ is not defined.

15. (a) $\displaystyle\lim_{t \to 0^-} g(t) = -1$ (b) $\displaystyle\lim_{t \to 0^+} g(t) = -2$

(c) $\displaystyle\lim_{t \to 0} g(t)$ does not exist since $\displaystyle\lim_{t \to 0^-} g(t) \neq \lim_{t \to 0^+} g(t))$

(d) $\displaystyle\lim_{t \to 2^-} g(t) = 2$ (e) $\displaystyle\lim_{t \to 2^+} g(t) = 0$

(f) $\displaystyle\lim_{t \to 2} g(t)$ does not exist since $\displaystyle\lim_{t \to 2^-} g(t) \neq \lim_{t \to 2^+} g(t)$

(g) $g(2) = 1$ (h) $\displaystyle\lim_{t \to 4} g(t) = 3$

17. $\displaystyle\lim_{x \to 1} \frac{x^3 + x^2 + 3x - 5}{2x^2 - 5x + 3} = -8.00$

19. $\displaystyle\lim_{x \to 0} \ln(\sin^2 x)$ does not exist

21. $\displaystyle\lim_{x\to 0} \cos \frac{1}{x}$ does not exist.

23. $f(x) = \begin{cases} x^2 & \text{if } x \le 2 \\ 6-x & \text{if } x > 2 \end{cases}$.

   (a) $\displaystyle\lim_{x\to 2^-} f(x) = 4$

   (b) $\displaystyle\lim_{x\to 2^+} f(x) = 4$

   (c) $\displaystyle\lim_{x\to 2} f(x) = 4$

25. $f(x) = \begin{cases} -x+3 & \text{if } x < -1 \\ 3 & \text{if } x \ge -1 \end{cases}$.

   (a) $\displaystyle\lim_{x\to -1^-} f(x) = 4$

   (b) $\displaystyle\lim_{x\to -1^+} f(x) = 3$

   (c) $\displaystyle\lim_{x\to -1} f(x)$ does not exist.

27. There are an infinite number of functions with the given conditions. An example of such a function is shown on the right.

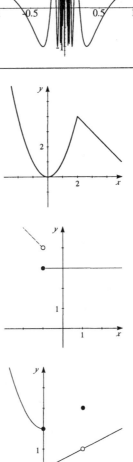

Exercises 12.2

1. (a) $\displaystyle\lim_{x\to a}[f(x)+h(x)] = \lim_{x\to a} f(x) + \lim_{x\to a} h(x) = -3+8 = 5$

   (b) $\displaystyle\lim_{x\to a}[f(x)]^2 = \left[\lim_{x\to a} f(x)\right]^2 = (-3)^2 = 9$

   (c) $\displaystyle\lim_{x\to a} \sqrt[3]{h(x)} = \sqrt[3]{\lim_{x\to a} h(x)} = \sqrt[3]{8} = 2$

   (d) $\displaystyle\lim_{x\to a} \frac{1}{f(x)} = \frac{1}{\displaystyle\lim_{x\to a} f(x)} = \frac{1}{-3}$

   (e) $\displaystyle\lim_{x\to a} \frac{f(x)}{h(x)} = \frac{\displaystyle\lim_{x\to a} f(x)}{\displaystyle\lim_{x\to a} h(x)} = \frac{-3}{8}$

   (f) $\displaystyle\lim_{x\to a} \frac{g(x)}{f(x)} = \frac{\displaystyle\lim_{x\to a} g(x)}{\displaystyle\lim_{x\to a} f(x)} = \frac{0}{-3} = 0$

   (g) $\displaystyle\lim_{x\to a} \frac{f(x)}{g(x)}$ does not exist since $\displaystyle\lim_{x\to a} g(x) = 0$.

   (h) $\displaystyle\lim_{x\to a} \frac{2f(x)}{h(x)-f(x)} = \frac{\displaystyle\lim_{x\to a}[2f(x)]}{\displaystyle\lim_{x\to a}[h(x)-f(x)]} = \frac{2\cdot\left[\displaystyle\lim_{x\to a} f(x)\right]}{\left[\displaystyle\lim_{x\to a} h(x)\right] - \left[\displaystyle\lim_{x\to a} f(x)\right]} = \frac{2(-3)}{8-(-3)} = \frac{-6}{11}$

3. $\displaystyle\lim_{x\to 4}(5x^2 - 2x + 3) = 5\lim_{x\to 4} x^2 - 2\lim_{x\to 4} x + \lim_{x\to 4} 3$ Laws 1, 2, and 3

   $\qquad\qquad\qquad\quad\; = 5(4)^2 - 2(4) + 3$ Special Limits 1, 2, and 3

   $\qquad\qquad\qquad\quad\; = 80 - 8 + 3 = 75$

5. $\displaystyle\lim_{x\to -1} \frac{x-2}{x^2 + 4x - 3} = \frac{\displaystyle\lim_{x\to -1} x - 2}{\displaystyle\lim_{x\to -1} x^2 + 4x - 3}$ Law 5

   $\qquad\qquad\qquad\quad = \frac{\displaystyle\lim_{x\to -1} x - \lim_{x\to -1} 2}{\displaystyle\lim_{x\to -1} x^2 + 4\lim_{x\to -1} x - \lim_{x\to -1} 3}$ Laws 1, 2, and 3

   $\qquad\qquad\qquad\quad = \frac{(-1) - 2}{(-1)^2 + 4(-1) - 3}$ Special Limits 1, 2, and 3

   $\qquad\qquad\qquad\quad = \frac{-3}{-6} = \frac{1}{2}$

7. $\displaystyle\lim_{t\to-2}(t+1)^9(t^2-1)=\left[\lim_{t\to-2}(t+1)^9\right]\left[\lim_{t\to-2}t^2-1\right]$ Law 4

$\displaystyle =\left[\lim_{t\to-2}t+1\right]^9\left[\lim_{t\to-2}t^2-1\right]$ Law 6

$\displaystyle =\left[\lim_{t\to-2}t+\lim_{t\to-2}1\right]^9\left[\lim_{t\to-2}t^2-\lim_{t\to-2}1\right]$ Laws 1, 2, and 3

$\displaystyle =[(-2)+1]^9[(-2)^2-1]$ Special Limits 1, 2, and 3

$\displaystyle =(-1)^9(4-1)=(-1)(3)=-3$

9. $\displaystyle\lim_{x\to2}\frac{x^2+x-6}{x-2}=\lim_{x\to2}\frac{(x-2)(x+3)}{x-2}=\lim_{x\to2}x+3=5$

11. $\displaystyle\lim_{x\to2}\frac{x^2-x+6}{x+2}=\frac{(2)^2-(2)+6}{(2)+2}=\frac{8}{4}=2$

13. $\displaystyle\lim_{t\to-3}\frac{t^2-9}{2t^2+7t+3}=\lim_{t\to-3}\frac{(t-3)(t+3)}{(t+3)(2t+1)}=\lim_{t\to-3}\frac{t-3}{2t+1}=\frac{(-3)-3}{2(-3)+1}=\frac{-6}{-5}=\frac{6}{5}$

15. $\displaystyle\lim_{h\to0}\frac{(2+h)^3-8}{h}=\lim_{h\to0}\frac{8+12h+6h^2+h^3-8}{h}=\lim_{h\to0}\frac{12h+6h^2+h^3}{h}$

$\displaystyle =\lim_{h\to0}\frac{h(12+6h+h^2)}{h}=\lim_{h\to0}12+6h+h^2=12$

17. $\displaystyle\lim_{x\to7}\frac{\sqrt{x+2}-3}{x-7}=\lim_{x\to7}\frac{\left(\sqrt{x+2}-3\right)\left(\sqrt{x+2}+3\right)}{(x-7)\left(\sqrt{x+2}+3\right)}=\lim_{x\to7}\frac{x+2-9}{(x-7)\left(\sqrt{x+2}+3\right)}$

$\displaystyle =\lim_{x\to7}\frac{x-7}{(x-7)\sqrt{x+2}+3}=\lim_{x\to7}\frac{1}{\sqrt{x+2}+3}=\frac{1}{\sqrt{7+2}+3}=\frac{1}{6}$

19. $\displaystyle\lim_{x\to-4}\frac{\frac14+\frac1x}{4+x}=\lim_{x\to-4}\frac{\left(\frac14+\frac1x\right)4x}{(4+x)4x}=\lim_{x\to-4}\frac{x+4}{(4+x)4x}=\lim_{x\to-4}\frac{1}{4x}=\frac{1}{4(-4)}=-\frac{1}{16}$

21. $\displaystyle\lim_{x\to1}\frac{x^2-1}{\sqrt{x}-1}=\lim_{x\to1}\frac{(x-1)(x+1)\left(\sqrt{x}+1\right)}{\left(\sqrt{x}-1\right)\left(\sqrt{x}+1\right)}=\lim_{x\to1}\frac{(x-1)(x+1)\left(\sqrt{x}+1\right)}{x-1}$

$\displaystyle =\lim_{x\to1}(x+1)\left(\sqrt{x}+1\right)=[(1)+1]\left[\sqrt{1}+1\right]=2\cdot2=4$

23. $\displaystyle\lim_{x\to-1}\frac{x^2-x-2}{x^3-x}=\lim_{x\to-1}\frac{(x-2)(x+1)}{x(x-1)(x+1)}=\lim_{x\to-1}\frac{x-2}{x(x-1)}=\frac{(-1)-2}{(-1)[(-1)-1]}=\frac{-3}{2}$

25. (a)

From the graph $\displaystyle\lim_{x\to0}\frac{x}{\sqrt{1+3x}-1}=0.67$

(b)

x	-0.1	-0.01	-0.001	0.001	0.01	0.1
$f(x)$	0.61222	0.66163	0.66617	0.66717	0.67183	0.71339

(c) $\displaystyle\lim_{x\to0}\frac{x}{\sqrt{1+3x}-1}=\lim_{x\to0}\frac{x\left(\sqrt{1+3x}+1\right)}{\left(\sqrt{1+3x}-1\right)\left(\sqrt{1+3x}+1\right)}=\lim_{x\to0}\frac{x\left(\sqrt{1+3x}+1\right)}{(1+3x)-1}$

$\displaystyle=\lim_{x\to0}\frac{x\left(\sqrt{1+3x}+1\right)}{3x}=\lim_{x\to0}\frac{\sqrt{1+3x}+1}{3}=\frac{\sqrt{1+3(0)}+1}{3}=\frac{2}{3}$

27. $\displaystyle\lim_{x\to-4^-}|x+4|=\lim_{x\to-4^-}-(x+4)=0$ and $\displaystyle\lim_{x\to-4^+}|x+4|=\lim_{x\to-4^+}x+4=0$. Therefore $\displaystyle\lim_{x\to-4^+}|x+4|=0$.

29. $\displaystyle\lim_{x\to2^-}\frac{|x-2|}{x-2}=\lim_{x\to2^-}\frac{-(x-2)}{x-2}=-1$ and $\displaystyle\lim_{x\to2^+}\frac{|x-2|}{x-2}=\lim_{x\to2^+}\frac{x-2}{x-2}=1$. So $\displaystyle\lim_{x\to2}\frac{|x-2|}{x-2}$ does not exist.

31. $\displaystyle\lim_{x\to0^-}\left(\frac{1}{x}-\frac{1}{|x|}\right)=\lim_{x\to0^-}\left(\frac{1}{x}-\frac{1}{-x}\right)=\lim_{x\to0^-}\frac{2}{x}$ which does not exist.

33. (a) $\displaystyle\lim_{x\to2^-}f(x)=\lim_{x\to2^-}(x-1)=1$ and $\displaystyle\lim_{x\to2^+}f(x)=\lim_{x\to2^+}(x^2-4x+6)=2$.

(b) Since $\displaystyle\lim_{x\to2^-}f(x)\neq\lim_{x\to2^+}f(x)$, $\displaystyle\lim_{x\to2}f(x)$ does not exist.

(c)

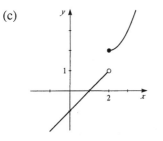

35. (a) The equation is true only for $x \neq 2$. That is, $x = 2$ is in the domain of $f(x) = x + 3$ but not in the domain of $g(x) = \dfrac{x^2 + x - 6}{x - 2}$.

    (b) When we take the limit we have $x \neq 2$.

37. (a) Many answers are possible, for example let $f(x) = \dfrac{x + 4}{x - 2}$ and $g(x) = \dfrac{x - 8}{x - 2}$. Then $\lim\limits_{x \to 2} f(x)$ and $\lim\limits_{x \to 2} g(x)$ both do not exist, but

$$\lim_{x \to 2} f(x) + g(x) = \lim_{x \to 2} \left(\frac{x + 4}{x - 2} + \frac{x - 8}{x - 2} \right) = \lim_{x \to 2} \frac{2x - 4}{x - 2} = \lim_{x \to 2} \frac{2(x - 2)}{x - 2} = \lim_{x \to 2} 2 = 2.$$

    (b) Many answers are possible, for example let $f(x) = \dfrac{|x - 2|}{x - 2}$ and $g(x) = \dfrac{x - 2}{|x - 2|}$. Then $\lim\limits_{x \to 2} f(x)$ and $\lim\limits_{x \to 2} g(x)$ both do not exist, but

$$\lim_{x \to 2} [f(x)g(x)] = \lim_{x \to 2} \left[\frac{|x - 2|}{x - 2} \cdot \frac{x - 2}{|x - 2|} \right] = \lim_{x \to 2} 1 = 1.$$

Exercises 12.3

1. $m = \lim\limits_{h \to 0} \dfrac{f(1+h) - f(1)}{h} = \lim\limits_{h \to 0} \dfrac{[3(1+h) + 4] - [3(1) + 4]}{h} = \lim\limits_{h \to 0} \dfrac{7 + 3h - 7}{h}$

$= \lim\limits_{h \to 0} \dfrac{3h}{h} = \lim\limits_{h \to 0} 3 = 3$

3. $m = \lim\limits_{h \to 0} \dfrac{f(-1+h) - f(-1)}{h} = \lim\limits_{h \to 0} \dfrac{[4(-1+h)^2 - 3(-1+h)] - [4(-1)^2 - 3(-1)]}{h}$

$= \lim\limits_{h \to 0} \dfrac{4 - 8h + 4h^2 + 3 - 3h - 7}{h} = \lim\limits_{h \to 0} \dfrac{-11h + 4h^2}{h}$

$= \lim\limits_{h \to 0} \dfrac{h(-11 + 4h)}{h} = \lim\limits_{h \to 0} (-11 + 4h) = -11$

5. $m = \lim\limits_{h \to 0} \dfrac{f(2+h) - f(2)}{h} = \lim\limits_{h \to 0} \dfrac{[2(2+h)^3] - [2(2)^3]}{h} = \lim\limits_{h \to 0} \dfrac{16 + 24h + 12h^2 + 2h^3 - 16}{h}$

$= \lim\limits_{h \to 0} \dfrac{24h + 12h^2 + 2h^3}{h} = \lim\limits_{h \to 0} \dfrac{h(24 + 12h + 2h^2)}{h} = \lim\limits_{h \to 0} \left(24 + 12h + 2h^2\right) = 24$

7. $m = \lim\limits_{h \to 0} \dfrac{[(-1+h) + (-1+h)^2] - [(-1) + (-1)^2]}{h} = \lim\limits_{h \to 0} \dfrac{-1 + h + 1 - 2h + h^2}{h}$

$= \lim\limits_{h \to 0} \dfrac{-h + h^2}{h} = \lim\limits_{h \to 0} \dfrac{h(-1 + h)}{h} = \lim\limits_{h \to 0} (-1 + h) = -1$

Thus an equation of the tangent line at $(-1, 0)$ is

$y - 0 = -1(x + 1) \quad \Leftrightarrow \quad y = -x - 1.$

9. $m = \lim\limits_{h \to 0} \dfrac{\dfrac{2+h}{2+h-1} - \dfrac{2}{2-1}}{h} = \lim\limits_{h \to 0} \dfrac{\left(\dfrac{2+h}{1+h} - 2\right)}{h} \cdot \dfrac{(1+h)}{(1+h)}$

$= \lim\limits_{h \to 0} \dfrac{2 + h - 2 - 2h}{h(1+h)} = \lim\limits_{h \to 0} \dfrac{-h}{h(1+h)} = \lim\limits_{h \to 0} \dfrac{-1}{1+h} = -1$

Thus an equation of the tangent line at $(2, 2)$ is

$y - 2 = -1(x - 2) \quad \Leftrightarrow \quad y = -x + 4.$

11. $m = \lim\limits_{h \to 0} \dfrac{\sqrt{(1+h)+3} - \sqrt{1+3}}{h} = \lim\limits_{h \to 0} \dfrac{\sqrt{h+4} - 2}{h} = \lim\limits_{h \to 0} \dfrac{\left(\sqrt{h+4} - 2\right)\left(\sqrt{h+4} + 2\right)}{h\left(\sqrt{h+4} + 2\right)}$

$= \lim\limits_{h \to 0} \dfrac{h+4-4}{h\left(\sqrt{h+4}+2\right)} = \lim\limits_{h \to 0} \dfrac{h}{h\left(\sqrt{h+4}+2\right)} = \lim\limits_{h \to 0} \dfrac{1}{\sqrt{h+4}+2} = \dfrac{1}{4}$

Thus an equation of the tangent line at $(1, 2)$ is

$y - 2 = \tfrac{1}{4}(x - 1) \quad \Leftrightarrow \quad y = \tfrac{1}{4}x + \tfrac{7}{4}.$

13. $f'(2) = \lim\limits_{h \to 0} \dfrac{f(2+h) - f(2)}{h} = \lim\limits_{h \to 0} \dfrac{[1 - 3(2+h)^2] - [1 - 3(2)^2]}{h}$

$= \lim\limits_{h \to 0} \dfrac{1 - 12 - 12h - 3h^2 + 11}{h} = \lim\limits_{h \to 0} \dfrac{-12h - 3h^2}{h} = \lim\limits_{h \to 0} \dfrac{h(-12 - 3h)}{h}$

$= \lim\limits_{h \to 0} (-12 - 3h) = -12$

15. $g'(1) = \lim\limits_{h \to 0} \dfrac{g(1+h) - g(1)}{h} = \lim\limits_{h \to 0} \dfrac{(1+h)^4 - (1)^4}{h}$

$= \lim\limits_{h \to 0} \dfrac{4h + 6h^2 + 4h^3 + h^4}{h} = \lim\limits_{h \to 0} \dfrac{h(4 + 6h + 4h^2 + h^3)}{h}$

$= \lim\limits_{h \to 0} (4 + 6h + 4h^2 + h^3) = 4$

17. $F'(4) = \lim\limits_{h \to 0} \dfrac{F(4+h) - F(4)}{h} = \lim\limits_{h \to 0} \dfrac{\left[\dfrac{1}{\sqrt{4+h}}\right] - \left[\dfrac{1}{\sqrt{4}}\right]}{h} = \lim\limits_{h \to 0} \dfrac{\dfrac{1}{\sqrt{4+h}} - \dfrac{1}{2}}{h}$

$= \lim\limits_{h \to 0} \dfrac{\left(\dfrac{1}{\sqrt{4+h}} - \dfrac{1}{2}\right)2\sqrt{4+h}}{h \cdot 2\sqrt{4+h}} = \lim\limits_{h \to 0} \dfrac{2 - \sqrt{4+h}}{2h\sqrt{4+h}}$

$= \lim\limits_{h \to 0} \dfrac{\left(2 - \sqrt{4+h}\right)\left(2 + \sqrt{4+h}\right)}{2h\sqrt{4+h}\left(2 + \sqrt{4+h}\right)} = \lim\limits_{h \to 0} \dfrac{4 - (4+h)}{2h\sqrt{4+h}\left(2 + \sqrt{4+h}\right)}$

$= \lim\limits_{h \to 0} \dfrac{-h}{2h\sqrt{4+h}\left(2 + \sqrt{4+h}\right)} = \lim\limits_{h \to 0} \dfrac{-1}{2\sqrt{4+h}\left(2 + \sqrt{4+h}\right)} = -\dfrac{1}{16}$

19. $f'(a) = \lim\limits_{x \to a} \dfrac{f(x) - f(a)}{x - a} = \lim\limits_{x \to a} \dfrac{[x^2 + 2x] - [a^2 + 2a]}{x - a}$

$= \lim\limits_{x \to a} \dfrac{x^2 + 2x - a^2 - 2a}{x - a} = \lim\limits_{x \to a} \dfrac{x^2 - a^2 + 2x - 2a}{x - a} = \lim\limits_{x \to a} \dfrac{(x - a)(x + a) + 2(x - a)}{x - a}$

$= \lim\limits_{x \to a} \dfrac{(x - a)[(x + a) + 2]}{x - a} = \lim\limits_{x \to a} (x + a + 2) = 2a + 2$

21. $f'(a) = \lim\limits_{x \to a} \dfrac{f(x) - f(a)}{x - a} = \lim\limits_{x \to a} \dfrac{\left[\dfrac{x}{x+1}\right] - \left[\dfrac{a}{a+1}\right]}{x - a}$

$= \lim\limits_{x \to a} \dfrac{\left(\left[\dfrac{x}{x+1}\right] - \left[\dfrac{a}{a+1}\right]\right)(a+1)(x+1)}{(x - a)(a+1)(x+1)}$

$= \lim\limits_{x \to a} \dfrac{x(a+1) - a(x+1)}{(x - a)(a+1)(x+1)} = \lim\limits_{x \to a} \dfrac{ax + x - ax - a}{(x - a)(a+1)(x+1)} = \lim\limits_{x \to a} \dfrac{x - a}{(x - a)(a+1)(x+1)}$

$= \lim\limits_{x \to a} \dfrac{1}{(a+1)(x+1)} = \dfrac{1}{(a+1)^2}$

23.   (a) $f'(a) = \lim\limits_{x \to a} \dfrac{f(x) - f(a)}{x - a} = \lim\limits_{x \to a} \dfrac{[x^3 - 2x + 4] - [a^3 - 2a + 4]}{x - a}$

$= \lim\limits_{x \to a} \dfrac{x^3 - 2x + 4 - a^3 + 2a - 4}{x - a} = \lim\limits_{x \to a} \dfrac{x^3 - a^3 - 2x + 2a}{x - a}$

$= \lim\limits_{x \to a} \dfrac{(x - a)(x^2 + ax + a^2) - 2(x - a)}{x - a} = \lim\limits_{x \to a} \dfrac{(x - a)(x^2 + ax + a^2 - 2)}{x - a}$

$= \lim\limits_{x \to a}(x^2 + ax + a^2 - 2) = 3a^2 - 2$

(b) $f(0) = 0^3 - 2(0) + 4 = 4$ and $f'(0) = 3(0)^2 - 2 = -2$. So the equation of line tangent to $f(x)$ at $x = 0$ is $y - 4 = -2(x - 0) \quad \Leftrightarrow \quad y = -2x + 4$.

$f(1) = 1^3 - 2(1) + 4 = 3$ and $f'(1) = 3(1)^2 - 2 = 1$. So the equation of line tangent to $f(x)$ at $x = 1$ is $y - 3 = 1(x - 1) \quad \Leftrightarrow \quad y = x + 2$

$f(2) = 2^3 - 2(2) + 4 = 8$ and $f'(2) = 3(2)^2 - 2 = 10$. So the equation of line tangent to $f(x)$ at $x = 2$ is $y - 8 = 10(x - 2) \quad \Leftrightarrow \quad y = 10x - 12$

(c)

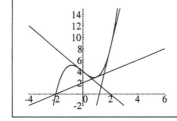

25.   Let $s(t) = 40t - 16t^2$

$v(2) = \lim\limits_{t \to 2} \dfrac{(40t - 16t^2) - 16}{t - 2} = \lim\limits_{t \to 2} \dfrac{-16t^2 + 40t - 16}{t - 2} = \lim\limits_{t \to 2} \dfrac{-8(2t^2 - 5t + 2)}{t - 2}$

$= \lim\limits_{t \to 2} \dfrac{-8(t - 2)(2t - 1)}{t - 2} = -8 \lim\limits_{t \to 2}(2t - 1) = -8(3) = -24$

Thus, the instantaneous velocity when $t = 2$ is -24 ft/s.

27. $v(a) = \lim\limits_{h \to 0} \dfrac{s(a+h) - s(a)}{h} = \lim\limits_{h \to 0} \dfrac{[4(a+h)^3 + 6(a+h) + 2] - [4a^3 + 6a + 2]}{h}$

$= \lim\limits_{h \to 0} \dfrac{4a^3 + 12a^2h + 12ah^2 + 4h^3 + 6a + 6h + 2 - 4a^3 - 6a - 2}{h}$

$= \lim\limits_{h \to 0} \dfrac{12a^2h + 12ah^2 + 4h^3 + 6h}{h} = \lim\limits_{h \to 0} \dfrac{h(12a^2 + 12ah + 4h^2 + 6)}{h}$

$= \lim\limits_{h \to 0} \left(12a^2 + 12ah + 4h^2 + 6\right) = 12a^2 + 6$ m/s

So $v(1) = 12(1)^2 + 6 = 18$ m/s, $v(2) = 12(2)^2 + 6 = 54$ m/s, and $v(3) = 12(3)^2 + 6 = 114$ m/s.

29. The slope of the tangent (that is, the rate of change in temperature with respect to time) at $t = 1$ h seems to be about $\frac{147-106}{90-30} \approx 0.7°$F/min.

31. (a) For the time interval $[10, 15]$ the average rate is $\dfrac{250 - 444}{15 - 10} = -38.8$ gal/min.

For the time interval $[15, 20]$ the average rate is $\dfrac{111 - 250}{20 - 15} = -27.8$ gal/min.

(b) $V'(15) \approx \frac{-38.8-27.8}{2} = -33.3$ gal/min.

33. $g'(0)$ is the only negative value. The slope at $x = 4$ is smaller than the slope at $x = 2$ and both are smaller than the slope at $x = -2$. Thus, $g'(0) < 0 < g'(4) < g'(2) < g'(-2)$.

Exercises 12.4

1. (a) $\lim\limits_{x\to\infty} f(x) = -1$ and $\lim\limits_{x\to-\infty} f(x) = 2$.

   (b) Horizontal asymptotes: $y = -1$ and $y = 2$.

3. $\lim\limits_{x\to\infty} \dfrac{6}{x} = 0$

5. $\lim\limits_{x\to\infty} \dfrac{2x+1}{5x-1} = \lim\limits_{x\to\infty} \dfrac{2+\dfrac{1}{x}}{5-\dfrac{1}{x}} = \dfrac{\lim\limits_{x\to\infty}2 + \lim\limits_{x\to\infty}\dfrac{1}{x}}{\lim\limits_{x\to\infty}5 - \lim\limits_{x\to\infty}\dfrac{1}{x}} = \dfrac{2+0}{5-0} = \dfrac{2}{5}$

7. $\lim\limits_{x\to\infty} \dfrac{4x^2+1}{2+3x^2} = \lim\limits_{x\to\infty} \dfrac{4+\dfrac{1}{x^2}}{\dfrac{2}{x^2}+3} = \dfrac{\lim\limits_{x\to\infty}4 + \lim\limits_{x\to\infty}\dfrac{1}{x^2}}{\lim\limits_{x\to\infty}\dfrac{2}{x^2} + \lim\limits_{x\to\infty}3} = \dfrac{4+0}{0+3} = \dfrac{4}{3}$

9. $\lim\limits_{t\to\infty} \dfrac{8t^3+t}{(2t-1)(2t^2+1)} = \lim\limits_{t\to\infty} \dfrac{8+\dfrac{1}{t^2}}{\left(\dfrac{2t-1}{t}\right)\left(\dfrac{2t^2+1}{t^2}\right)} = \lim\limits_{t\to\infty} \dfrac{8+\dfrac{1}{t^2}}{\left(2-\dfrac{1}{t}\right)\left(2+\dfrac{1}{t^2}\right)}$

$$= \dfrac{\lim\limits_{t\to\infty}8 + \lim\limits_{t\to\infty}\dfrac{1}{t^2}}{\left[\lim\limits_{t\to\infty}\left(2-\dfrac{1}{t}\right)\right]\left[\lim\limits_{t\to\infty}\left(2+\tfrac{1}{t^2}\right)\right]}$$

$$= \dfrac{\lim\limits_{t\to\infty}8 + \lim\limits_{t\to\infty}\dfrac{1}{t^2}}{\left[\lim\limits_{t\to\infty}2 - \lim\limits_{t\to\infty}\dfrac{1}{t}\right]\left[\lim\limits_{t\to\infty}2 + \lim\limits_{t\to\infty}\dfrac{1}{t^2}\right]} = \dfrac{8+0}{(2-0)(2+0)} = 2$$

11. $\lim\limits_{x\to\infty} \dfrac{x^4}{1-x^2+x^3} = \lim\limits_{x\to\infty} \dfrac{1}{\dfrac{1}{x^4}-\dfrac{1}{x^2}+\dfrac{1}{x}} = \dfrac{\lim\limits_{x\to\infty}1}{\lim\limits_{x\to\infty}\dfrac{1}{x^4} - \lim\limits_{x\to\infty}\dfrac{1}{x^2} + \lim\limits_{x\to\infty}\dfrac{1}{x}} = \dfrac{1}{0}$ so the limit does not

   exists.

13. $\lim\limits_{x\to-\infty} \left(\dfrac{x-1}{x+1}+6\right) = \lim\limits_{x\to-\infty} \left(\dfrac{1-\dfrac{1}{x}}{1+\dfrac{1}{x}}+6\right) = \lim\limits_{x\to-\infty} \dfrac{1-\dfrac{1}{x}}{1+\dfrac{1}{x}} + \lim\limits_{x\to-\infty}6$

$$= \dfrac{\lim\limits_{x\to-\infty}1 - \lim\limits_{x\to-\infty}\dfrac{1}{x}}{\lim\limits_{x\to-\infty}1 + \lim\limits_{x\to-\infty}\dfrac{1}{x}} + \lim\limits_{x\to-\infty}6 = \dfrac{1-0}{1+0}+6 = 7$$

15.

x	-10	-100	-1000
$\dfrac{\sqrt{x^2+4x}}{4x+1}$	-0.1986	-0.2456	-0.2496

From the table it appears that

$$\lim_{x\to-\infty}\frac{\sqrt{x^2+4x}}{4x+1}=-0.25$$

17.

x	10	100	1000
$\dfrac{x^5}{e^x}$	4.5399	3.720×10^{-34}	0

From the table it appears that

$$\lim_{x\to\infty}\frac{x^5}{e^x}=0$$

19. $\displaystyle\lim_{n\to\infty}a_n=\lim_{n\to\infty}\frac{1+n}{n+n^2}=\lim_{n\to\infty}\frac{\dfrac{1}{n^2}+\dfrac{1}{n}}{\dfrac{1}{n}+1}=\frac{\displaystyle\lim_{n\to\infty}\frac{1}{n^2}+\lim_{n\to\infty}\frac{1}{n}}{\displaystyle\lim_{n\to\infty}\frac{1}{n}+\lim_{n\to\infty}1}=\frac{0+0}{0+1}=0$

21. $a_n=\dfrac{n^2}{n+1}$ is divergent since $\displaystyle\lim_{n\to\infty}a_n=\lim_{n\to\infty}\frac{n^2}{n+1}=\lim_{n\to\infty}\frac{1}{\dfrac{1}{n}+\dfrac{1}{n^2}}=\frac{\displaystyle\lim_{n\to\infty}1}{\displaystyle\lim_{n\to\infty}\frac{1}{n}+\lim_{n\to\infty}\frac{1}{n^2}}=\frac{1}{0+0}$

    which is not defined.

23. $\displaystyle\lim_{n\to\infty}a_n=\lim_{n\to\infty}\frac{1}{3^n}=0$

25. $a_n=\sin(n\pi/2)$, because of the periodic nature of the sine function, the terms of this sequence repeat the sequence $1,0,-1,0$ infinitely often and so they don't approach any definite number. Therefore, $\displaystyle\lim_{n\to\infty}a_n$ does not exist, and the sequence is divergent.

27. $\displaystyle\lim_{n\to\infty}a_n=\lim_{n\to\infty}\frac{3}{n^2}\left[\frac{n(n+1)}{2}\right]=\lim_{n\to\infty}\frac{3}{2}\left(\frac{n}{n}\right)\left(\frac{n+1}{n}\right)=\lim_{n\to\infty}\frac{3}{2}(1)\left(1+\frac{1}{n}\right)$

$\qquad\qquad=\lim_{n\to\infty}\frac{3}{2}\cdot\lim_{n\to\infty}1\cdot\lim_{n\to\infty}\left(1+\frac{1}{n}\right)=\frac{3}{2}\cdot1\cdot1=\frac{3}{2}$

29. $\displaystyle\lim_{n\to\infty}a_n=\lim_{n\to\infty}\frac{24}{n^3}\left[\frac{n(n+1)(2n+1)}{6}\right]=\lim_{n\to\infty}4\left(\frac{n}{n}\right)\left(\frac{n+1}{n}\right)\left(\frac{2n+1}{n}\right)$

$\qquad\qquad=\lim_{n\to\infty}4(1)\left(1+\frac{1}{n}\right)\left(2+\frac{1}{n}\right)=4\lim_{n\to\infty}\left(1+\frac{1}{n}\right)\cdot\lim_{n\to\infty}\left(2+\frac{1}{n}\right)=4\cdot1\cdot2=8$

31. (a) $C(t)=\dfrac{\text{amount of salt}}{\text{liters of water}}=\dfrac{30\cdot25t}{5000+25t}=\dfrac{30t}{200+t}.$

(b) $\displaystyle\lim_{t\to\infty}\frac{30t}{200+t}=\lim_{t\to\infty}\frac{30}{\dfrac{200}{t}+1}=\frac{\displaystyle\lim_{t\to\infty}30}{\displaystyle\lim_{t\to\infty}\frac{200}{t}+\lim_{t\to\infty}1}=\frac{30}{0+1}=30\text{ g/L.}$

33. (a) $a_1=0$

$a_2=\sqrt{2+a_1}=\sqrt{2+0}=1.41421356$

$a_3=\sqrt{2+a_2}=\sqrt{3.41421356}=1.84775907$

$a_4=\sqrt{2+a_3}=\sqrt{3.84775907}=1.96157056$

$a_5=\sqrt{2+a_4}=\sqrt{3.96157056}=1.99036945$

$a_6=\sqrt{2+a_5}=\sqrt{3.99036945}=1.99759091$

$a_7=\sqrt{2+a_6}=\sqrt{3.99759091}=1.99939764$

$a_8=\sqrt{2+a_7}=\sqrt{3.99939764}=1.99984940$

$a_9=\sqrt{2+a_8}=\sqrt{3.99984940}=1.99996235$

$a_{10}=\sqrt{2+a_9}=\sqrt{3.99996235}=1.99999059$

From the table, it appears that $\displaystyle\lim_{n\to\infty}a_n=2.$

(b) Let $\displaystyle\lim_{n\to\infty}a_n=L.$ Then we can also have $\displaystyle\lim_{n\to\infty}a_{n=1}=L.$ Thus, we have $L=\displaystyle\lim_{n\to\infty}a_{n+1}=$
$\displaystyle\lim_{n\to\infty}\sqrt{2+a_n}=\sqrt{\lim_{n\to\infty}(2+a_n)}=\sqrt{\lim_{n\to\infty}2+\lim_{n\to\infty}a_n}=\sqrt{2+L}.$ So $L=\sqrt{2+L}\quad\Rightarrow$
$L^2=2+L\quad\Leftrightarrow\quad L^2-L-2=0\quad\Leftrightarrow\quad(L-2)(L+1)=0\quad\Leftrightarrow\quad L=2\text{ or }L=-1.$
But $L\geq 0,$ so $L\neq -1.$ Therefore, $\displaystyle\lim_{n\to\infty}a_n=2.$

Exercises 12.5

1. (a) Since f is increasing, we can obtain a lower estimate by using left endpoints. We are instructed to use five rectangles, so $n = 5$.

$$L_5 = \sum_{i=1}^{5} f(x_{i-1})\,\Delta x \quad (\Delta x = \tfrac{b-a}{n} = \tfrac{10-0}{5} = 2)$$
$$= f(x_0) \cdot 2 + f(x_1) \cdot 2 + f(x_2) \cdot 2 + f(x_3) \cdot 2 + f(x_4) \cdot 2$$
$$= 2[f(0) + f(2) + f(4) + f(6) + f(8)]$$
$$\approx 2(1 + 3 + 4.3 + 5.4 + 6.3) = 2(20) = 40$$

Since f is increasing, we can obtain an upper estimate by using right endpoints.

$$R_5 = \sum_{i=1}^{5} f(x_i)\,\Delta x$$
$$= f(x_1) \cdot 2 + f(x_2) \cdot 2 + f(x_3) \cdot 2 + f(x_4) \cdot 2 + f(x_5) \cdot 2$$
$$= 2[f(2) + f(4) + f(6) + f(8) + f(10)]$$
$$\approx 2(3 + 4.3 + 5.4 + 6.3\,7) = 2(26) = 52$$

Comparing R_5 to L_5, we see that we have added the rightmost rectangle, $f(10) \cdot 2$, to the sum and subtracting the area of the leftmost rectangle, $f(0) \cdot 2$, from the sum.

(b)
$$L_{10} = \sum_{i=1}^{10} f(x_{i-1})\,\Delta x \quad (\Delta x = \tfrac{10-0}{10} = 1)$$
$$= 1[f(x_0) + f(x_1) + \cdots + f(x_9)]$$
$$= f(0) + f(1) + \cdots + f(9)$$
$$\approx 1 + 2.1 + 3 + 3.7 + 4.3 + 4.9 + 5.4 + 5.8 + 6.3 + 6.7$$
$$= 43.2$$

$$R_{10} = \sum_{i=1}^{10} f(x_i)\,\Delta x$$
$$= L_{10} + 1 \cdot f(10) - 1 \cdot f(0) \quad \begin{bmatrix} \text{Add rightmost rectangle,} \\ \text{subtract leftmost} \end{bmatrix}$$
$$= 43.2 + 7 - 1 = 49.2$$

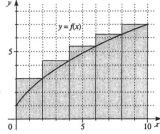

3. $R_4 = \sum_{i=1}^{4} f(x_i)\,\Delta x \quad (\Delta x = \frac{2-0}{4} = \frac{1}{2})$

$= f(\frac{1}{2}) \cdot \frac{1}{2} + f(1) \cdot \frac{1}{2} + f(\frac{3}{2}) \cdot \frac{1}{2} + f(2) \cdot \frac{1}{2}$

$= \frac{1}{2}[\frac{9}{4} + \frac{10}{4} + \frac{11}{4} + \frac{12}{4}] = \frac{42}{8} = \frac{21}{4}$

5. $R_6 = \sum_{i=1}^{6} f(x_i)\,\Delta x \quad (\Delta x = \frac{7-1}{6} = 1)$

$= f(2) \cdot 1 + f(3) \cdot 1 + f(4) \cdot 1 + f(5) \cdot 1 + f(6) \cdot 1 + f(7) \cdot 1$

$= 2 + \frac{4}{3} + 1 + \frac{4}{5} + \frac{4}{6} + \frac{4}{7} = \frac{223}{35} \approx 6.37$

7. (a) $R_4 = \sum_{i=1}^{4} f(x_i)\,\Delta x \quad (\Delta x = \frac{5-1}{4} = 1)$

$= f(x_1) \cdot 1 + f(x_2) \cdot 1 + f(x_3) \cdot 1 + f(x_4) \cdot 1$

$= f(2) + f(3) + f(4) + f(5)$

$= \frac{1}{2} + \frac{1}{3} + \frac{1}{4} + \frac{1}{5} = \frac{77}{60} = 1.28\overline{3}$

Since f is decreasing on $[1, 5]$, an underestimate is obtained
by the right endpoint approximation, R_4.

(b) $L_4 = \sum_{i=1}^{4} f(x_{i-1})\,\Delta x$

$= f(1) + f(2) + f(3) + f(4)$

$= 1 + \frac{1}{2} + \frac{1}{3} + \frac{1}{4} = \frac{25}{12} = 2.08\overline{3}$

L_4 is an overestimate. Alternatively, we could just add the

area of the leftmost rectangle and subtract the area of the
rightmost; that is,

$L_4 = R_4 + f91) \cdot 1 - f(5) \cdot 1.$

9. (a) $f(x) = 1 + x^2$ and $\Delta x = \frac{2-(-1)}{3} = 1$ so

$R_3 = f(0) \cdot 1 + f(1) \cdot 1 + f(2) \cdot 1 = 1[1 + 2 + 5] = 8$

If $\Delta x = \frac{2-(-1)}{6} = 0.5$ then

$R_6 = 0.5[f(-0.5) + f(0) + f(0.5) + f(1) + f(1.5) + f(2)]$

$= 0.5(1.25 + 1 + 1.25 + 2 + 3.25 + 5)$

$= 0.5(13.75) = 6.875$

(b) $L_3 = f(-1) \cdot 1 + f(0) \cdot 1 + f(1) \cdot 1 = 1[2 + 1 + 2] = 5$

$$L_6 = 0.5[f(-1) + f(-0.5) + f(0) + f(0.5) + f(1) + f(1.5)]$$
$$= 0.5(2 + 1.25 + 1 + 1.25 + 2 + 3.25)$$
$$= 0.5(10.75) = 5.375$$

11. $f(x) = 3x$ and $\Delta x = \dfrac{5-0}{n} = \dfrac{5}{n}$ and $x_k = \dfrac{5k}{n}$

$$A = \lim_{n\to\infty}\sum_{k=1}^{n} f(x_k)\,\Delta x = \lim_{n\to\infty}\sum_{k=1}^{n} 3\left(\frac{5k}{n}\right) \cdot \frac{5}{n}$$

$$= \lim_{n\to\infty}\sum_{k=1}^{n}\frac{75k}{n^2} = \lim_{n\to\infty}\frac{75}{n^2}\sum_{k=1}^{n}k = \lim_{n\to\infty}\frac{75}{n^2}\cdot\frac{n(n+1)}{2}$$

$$= \lim_{n\to\infty}\frac{75(n+1)}{2n} = \lim_{n\to\infty}\frac{75}{2}\left(1+\frac{1}{n}\right) = \frac{75}{2}(1+0) = \frac{75}{2}$$

Using geometry the area of the triangle $= \frac{1}{2}(5)(15) = \frac{75}{2}$.

13. $f(x) = 3x^2$, $a = 0$, $b = 2$, $\Delta x = \frac{2-0}{n} = \frac{2}{n}$, and $x_k = \frac{2k}{n}$

$$A = \lim_{n\to\infty}\sum_{k=1}^{n} f(x_k)\,\Delta x = \lim_{n\to\infty}\sum_{k=1}^{n} 3\left(\frac{2k}{n}\right)^2 \cdot \frac{2}{n} = \lim_{n\to\infty}\sum_{k=1}^{n}\frac{24k^2}{n^3} = \lim_{n\to\infty}\frac{24}{n^3}\cdot\sum_{k=1}^{n}k^2$$

$$= \lim_{n\to\infty}\frac{24}{n^3}\cdot\frac{n(n+1)(2n+1)}{6} = \lim_{n\to\infty}\frac{4(2n^2+3n+1)}{n^2} = \lim_{n\to\infty}4\left(2+\frac{3}{n}+\frac{1}{n^2}\right)$$

$$= 4(2+0+0) = 8$$

15. $f(x) = x^3 + 2$, $a = 0$, $b = 5$, $\Delta x = \frac{5-0}{n} = \frac{5}{n}$, and $x_k = \frac{5k}{n}$

$$A = \lim_{n\to\infty}\sum_{k=1}^{n} f(x_k)\,\Delta x = \lim_{n\to\infty}\sum_{k=1}^{n}\left[\left(\frac{5k}{n}\right)^3 + 2\right]\cdot\frac{5}{n} = \lim_{n\to\infty}\sum_{k=1}^{n}\left[\frac{625k^3}{n^4} + \frac{10}{n}\right]$$

$$= \lim_{n\to\infty}\left[\frac{625}{n^4}\cdot\sum_{k=1}^{n}k^3 + \frac{10}{n}\cdot\sum_{k=1}^{n}1\right] = \lim_{n\to\infty}\left(\frac{625}{n^4}\cdot\frac{n^2(n+1)^2}{4} + \frac{10}{n}\cdot n\right)$$

$$= \lim_{n\to\infty}\left[\frac{625(n^2+2n+1)}{4n^2} + 10\right] = \lim_{n\to\infty}\left[\frac{625}{4}\left(1+\frac{2}{n}+\frac{1}{n^2}\right) + 10\right]$$

$$= \tfrac{625}{4}(1+0+0) + 10 = \tfrac{665}{4} = 166.25$$

17. $f(x) = x + 6x^2$, $a = 1$, $b = 4$, $\Delta x = \frac{4-1}{n} = \frac{3}{n}$, and $x_k = 1 + \frac{3k}{n}$

$$A = \lim_{n \to \infty} \sum_{k=1}^{n} f(x_k)\,\Delta x = \lim_{n \to \infty} \sum_{k=1}^{n} \left[\left(1 + \frac{3k}{n}\right) + 6\left(1 + \frac{3k}{n}\right)^2 \right] \cdot \frac{3}{n}$$

$$= \lim_{n \to \infty} \sum_{k=1}^{n} \left[\frac{3}{n} + \frac{9k}{n^2} + \frac{18}{n} + \frac{108k}{n^2} + \frac{162k^2}{n^3} \right]$$

$$= \lim_{n \to \infty} \left[\frac{21}{n} \sum_{k=1}^{n} 1 + \frac{117}{n^2} \sum_{k=1}^{n} k + \frac{162}{n^3} \sum_{k=1}^{n} k^2 \right]$$

$$= \lim_{n \to \infty} \left(\frac{21}{n} \cdot n + \frac{117}{n^2} \cdot \frac{n(n+1)}{2} + \frac{162}{n^3} \cdot \frac{n(n+1)(2n+1)}{6} \right)$$

$$= \lim_{n \to \infty} \left(21 + \frac{117}{2} \cdot \frac{(n+1)}{n} + 27 \cdot \frac{2n^2 + 3n + 1}{n^2} \right)$$

$$= \lim_{n \to \infty} \left[21 + \frac{117}{2}\left(1 + \frac{1}{n}\right) + 27\left(2 + \frac{3}{n} + \frac{1}{n^2}\right) \right] = 21 + \frac{117}{2} + 54 = 133.5$$

19. For regions with straight boundaries we draw a vertical line through each vertex. This creates triangles and trapezoids whose area is easily found. For regions with curved boundaries, we must use the limit process to determine the area.

Review Exercises for Chapter 12

1.

x	1.9	1.99	1.999	2.001	2.01	2.1
$f(x)$	1.11111	1.01010	1.00100	0.99990	0.99100	0.90909

$$\lim_{x \to 2} \frac{x-2}{x^2 - 3x + 2} = 1$$

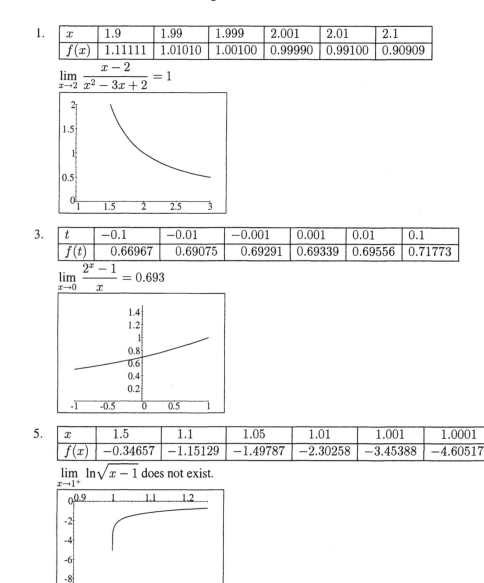

3.

t	-0.1	-0.01	-0.001	0.001	0.01	0.1
$f(t)$	0.66967	0.69075	0.69291	0.69339	0.69556	0.71773

$$\lim_{x \to 0} \frac{2^x - 1}{x} = 0.693$$

5.

x	1.5	1.1	1.05	1.01	1.001	1.0001
$f(x)$	-0.34657	-1.15129	-1.49787	-2.30258	-3.45388	-4.60517

$\lim_{x \to 1^+} \ln \sqrt{x-1}$ does not exist.

7. (a) $\lim_{x \to 2^+} f(x)$ does not exist, since f does not converge to a finite value.

    (b) $\lim_{x \to -3^+} f(x) = 2.4$

    (c) $\lim_{x \to -3^-} f(x) = 2.4$

    (d) $\lim_{x \to -3} f(x) = 2.4$

(e) $\displaystyle\lim_{x\to 4} f(x) = 0.5$

(f) $\displaystyle\lim_{x\to\infty} f(x) = 1$

(g) $\displaystyle\lim_{x\to -\infty} f(x) = 2$

(h) $\displaystyle\lim_{x\to 0} f(x)f(x) = \left(\lim_{x\to 0} f(x)\right)\left(\lim_{x\to 0} f(x)\right) = 0\cdot 0 = 0$

9. $\displaystyle\lim_{x\to 2}\frac{x+1}{x-3} = \frac{2+1}{2-3} = -3$

11. $\displaystyle\lim_{x\to 3}\frac{x^2+x-12}{x-3} = \lim_{x\to 3}\frac{(x-3)(x+4)}{x-3} = \lim_{x\to 3}(x+4) = 3+4 = 7$

13. $\displaystyle\lim_{u\to 0}\frac{(u+1)^2-1}{u} = \lim_{u\to 0}\frac{u^2+2u+1-1}{u} = \lim_{u\to 0}\frac{u^2+2u}{u} = \lim_{u\to 0}(u+2) = 0+2 = 2$

15. $\displaystyle\lim_{x\to 3^-}\frac{x-3}{|x-3|} = \lim_{x\to 3^-}\frac{x-3}{-(x-3)} = \lim_{x\to 3^-} -1 = -1$

17. $\displaystyle\lim_{x\to\infty}\frac{2x}{x-4} = \lim_{x\to\infty}\frac{2}{1-\dfrac{4}{x}} = \frac{2}{1-0} = 2$

19. $\displaystyle\lim_{x\to\infty}\cos^2 x$ does not exist since cosine squared alternates between 0 and 1.

21. $\displaystyle f'(4) = \lim_{h\to 0}\frac{f(4+h)-f(4)}{h} = \lim_{h\to 0}\frac{[3(4+h)-5]-[3(4)-5]}{h}$

$\displaystyle = \lim_{h\to 0}\frac{12+3h-5-12+5}{h} = \lim_{h\to 0}\frac{3h}{h} = \lim_{h\to 0} 3 = 3$

23. $\displaystyle f'(16) = \lim_{h\to 0}\frac{f(16+h)-f(16)}{h} = \lim_{h\to 0}\frac{\sqrt{16+h}-\sqrt{16}}{h}$

$\displaystyle = \lim_{h\to 0}\frac{\left(\sqrt{16+h}-4\right)}{h}\cdot\frac{\left(\sqrt{16+h}+4\right)}{\left(\sqrt{16+h}+4\right)} = \lim_{h\to 0}\frac{16+h-16}{h\left(\sqrt{16+h}+4\right)}$

$\displaystyle = \lim_{h\to 0}\frac{h}{h\left(\sqrt{16+h}+4\right)} = \lim_{h\to 0}\frac{1}{\sqrt{16+h}+4} = \frac{1}{8}$

25. (a) $\displaystyle f'(a) = \lim_{x\to a}\frac{f(x)-f(a)}{x-a} = \lim_{x\to a}\frac{[6-2x]-[6-2a]}{x-a} = \lim_{x\to a}\frac{6-2x-6+2a}{x-a} = \lim_{x\to a}\frac{-2x+2a}{x-a}$

$\displaystyle = \lim_{x\to a}\frac{-2(x-a)}{x-a} = \lim_{x\to a} -2 = -2$

(b) So $f'(2) = -2$ and $f'(-2) = -2$.

27. (a) $f'(a) = \lim\limits_{x \to a} \dfrac{f(x) - f(a)}{x - a} = \lim\limits_{x \to a} \dfrac{\sqrt{x+6} - \sqrt{a+6}}{x - a}$

$= \lim\limits_{x \to a} \dfrac{(\sqrt{x+6} - \sqrt{a+6})(\sqrt{x+6} + \sqrt{a+6})}{(x-a)(\sqrt{x+6} + \sqrt{a+6})} \lim\limits_{x \to a} \dfrac{x+6-a-6}{(x-a)(\sqrt{x+6} + \sqrt{a+6})}$

$= \lim\limits_{x \to a} \dfrac{x-a}{(x-a)(\sqrt{x+6} + \sqrt{a+6})} = \lim\limits_{x \to a} \dfrac{1}{\sqrt{x+6} + \sqrt{a+6}} = \dfrac{1}{2\sqrt{a+6}}$

(b) So $f'(2) = \dfrac{1}{2\sqrt{2+6}} = \dfrac{1}{4\sqrt{2}} = \dfrac{\sqrt{2}}{8}$ and $f'(-2) = \dfrac{1}{2\sqrt{-2+6}} = \dfrac{1}{4}$.

29. $m = \lim\limits_{h \to 0} \dfrac{f(1+h) - f(1)}{h} = \lim\limits_{h \to 0} \dfrac{[4(1+h) - (1+h)^2] - [4(1) - (1)^2]}{h}$

$= \lim\limits_{h \to 0} \dfrac{4 + 4h - 1 - 2h - h^2 - 3}{h} = \lim\limits_{h \to 0} \dfrac{2h - h^2}{h}$

$= \lim\limits_{h \to 0} \dfrac{h(2-h)}{h} = \lim\limits_{h \to 0} (2-h) = 2$

So the equation of the line tangent to $y = 4x - x^2$ at $(1,3)$ is $y - 3 = 2(x - 1)$ $\Leftrightarrow$ $y = 2x + 1$.

31. $m = \lim\limits_{h \to 0} \dfrac{f(3+h) - f(3)}{h} = \lim\limits_{h \to 0} \dfrac{[2(3+h)] - [2(3)]}{h}$

$= \lim\limits_{h \to 0} \dfrac{6 + 2h - 6}{h} = \lim\limits_{h \to 0} \dfrac{2h}{h} = \lim\limits_{h \to 0} 2 = 2$

So the equation of the line tangent to $y = 2x$ at $(3,6)$ is $y - 6 = 2(x - 3)$ $\Leftrightarrow$ $y = 2x$.

33. $m = \lim\limits_{h \to 0} \dfrac{f(2+h) - f(2)}{h} = \lim\limits_{h \to 0} \dfrac{\frac{1}{2+h} - \frac{1}{2}}{h} = \lim\limits_{h \to 0} \dfrac{\left(\frac{1}{2+h} - \frac{1}{2}\right)}{h} \cdot \dfrac{2(2+h)}{2(2+h)}$

$= \lim\limits_{h \to 0} \dfrac{2 - (2+h)}{2h(2+h)} = \lim\limits_{h \to 0} \dfrac{-h}{2h(2+h)} = \lim\limits_{h \to 0} \dfrac{-1}{2(2+h)} = -\dfrac{1}{4}$

So the equation of the line tangent to $y = \dfrac{1}{x}$ at $(2, \frac{1}{2})$ is $y - \frac{1}{2} = -\frac{1}{4}(x - 2)$ $\Leftrightarrow$ $y = -\frac{1}{4}x + 1$.

35. (a) $v(2) = \lim\limits_{t \to 2} \dfrac{h(t) - h(2)}{t - 2} = \lim\limits_{t \to 2} \dfrac{[640 - 16t^2] - [640 - 16(2)^2]}{t - 2}$

$= \lim\limits_{t \to 2} \dfrac{640 - 16t^2 - 640 + 64}{t - 2} = \lim\limits_{t \to 2} \dfrac{-16t^2 + 64}{t - 2} = \lim\limits_{t \to 2} \dfrac{-16(t+2)(t-2)}{t - 2}$

$= \lim\limits_{t \to 2} -16(t+2) = 64$ ft/s

(b) $v(a) = \lim\limits_{t \to a} \dfrac{h(t) - h(a)}{t - a} = \lim\limits_{t \to a} \dfrac{[640 - 16t^2] - [640 - 16a^2]}{t - a}$

$= \lim\limits_{t \to a} \dfrac{640 - 16t^2 - 640 + 16a^2}{t - a} = \lim\limits_{t \to a} \dfrac{-16t^2 + 16a^2}{t - a} = \lim\limits_{t \to a} \dfrac{-16(t+a)(t-a)}{t - a}$

$= \lim\limits_{t \to a} \dfrac{58h - 1.66ah - 0.83h^2}{h} = \lim\limits_{t \to a} \dfrac{h(58 - 1.66a - 0.83h)}{h}$

$= \lim\limits_{t \to a} -16(t+a) = -32a$ ft/s

(c) $h(t) = 0$ when $640 - 16t^2 = 0$ $\Leftrightarrow$ $-16(t^2 - 40) = 0$ $\Leftrightarrow$ $t^2 = 40$ $\Rightarrow$
$t = \sqrt{40} \approx 6.32$ s (since $t \geq 0$).

(d) $v(6.32) = -32(6.32) = -202.4$ ft/s.

37. $\displaystyle\lim_{n\to\infty} a_n = \lim_{n\to\infty} \frac{n}{5n+1} = \lim_{n\to\infty} \frac{1}{5 + \dfrac{1}{n}} = \frac{1}{5+0} = \frac{1}{5}$

39. $\displaystyle\lim_{n\to\infty} a_n = \lim_{n\to\infty} \left(\frac{n(n+1)}{2n^2} \right) = \lim_{n\to\infty} \frac{1}{2} \left(\frac{n}{n} \right) \left(\frac{n+1}{n} \right) = \lim_{n\to\infty} \frac{1}{2} (1) \left(1 + \frac{1}{n} \right)$

$\displaystyle = \lim_{n\to\infty} \frac{1}{2} \cdot \lim_{n\to\infty} 1 \cdot \lim_{n\to\infty} \left(1 + \frac{1}{n} \right) = \frac{1}{2} \cdot 1 \cdot 1 = \frac{1}{2}$

41. The sequence $a_n = \cos\left(\dfrac{n\pi}{2} \right)$ is the sequence $0, -1, 0, 1, 0, -1, 0, 1, 0, -1, 0, 1, \ldots$ which does not go to any one value. Thus this sequence does not converge.

43. $f(x) = \sqrt{x}$ and $\Delta x = 0.5$.

$\displaystyle R_6 = \sum_{i=1}^{6} f(x_i)\, \Delta x$

$= f(x_1) \cdot 0.5 + f(x_2) \cdot 0.5 + f(x_3) \cdot 0.5 + f(x_4) \cdot 0.5 + f(x_5) \cdot 0.5 + f(x_6) \cdot 0.5$

$= 0.5[f(0.5) + f(1) + f(1.5) + f(2) + f(2.5) + f(3)]$

$\approx 0.5(0.7071 + 1 + 1.2247 + 1.4142 + 1.5811 + 1.7320) = 0.5(7.6591) = 3.8296$

45. $f(x) = 2x + 3$, $a = 0$, $b = 2$, $\Delta x = \frac{2-0}{n} = \frac{2}{n}$, and $x_k = \frac{2k}{n}$

$\displaystyle A = \lim_{n\to\infty} \sum_{k=1}^{n} f(x_k)\, \Delta x = \lim_{n\to\infty} \sum_{k=1}^{n} \left[2\left(\frac{2k}{n} \right) + 3 \right] \cdot \frac{2}{n} = \lim_{n\to\infty} \sum_{k=1}^{n} \left[\frac{8k}{n^2} + \frac{6}{n} \right]$

$\displaystyle = \lim_{n\to\infty} \left[\frac{8}{n^2} \cdot \sum_{k=1}^{n} k + \frac{6}{n} \cdot \sum_{k=1}^{n} 1 \right] = \lim_{n\to\infty} \left(\frac{8}{n^2} \cdot \frac{n(n+1)}{2} + \frac{6}{n} \cdot n \right)$

$\displaystyle = \lim_{n\to\infty} \left[\frac{4(n+1)}{n} + 6 \right] = \lim_{n\to\infty} \left[4\left(1 + \frac{1}{n} \right) + 6 \right]$

$= 4(1+0) + 6 = 10$

47. $f(x) = x^2 - x$, $a = 1$, $b = 2$, $\Delta x = \frac{2-1}{n} = \frac{1}{n}$, and $x_k = 1 + \frac{k}{n}$

$$A = \lim_{n \to \infty} \sum_{k=1}^{n} f(x_k)\,\Delta x = \lim_{n \to \infty} \sum_{k=1}^{n} \left[\left(1 + \frac{k}{n}\right)^2 - \left(1 + \frac{k}{n}\right) \right] \cdot \frac{1}{n}$$

$$= \lim_{n \to \infty} \sum_{k=1}^{n} \left[1 + \frac{2k}{n} + \frac{k^2}{n^2} - 1 - \frac{k}{n} \right] \cdot \frac{1}{n} = \lim_{n \to \infty} \sum_{k=1}^{n} \left[\frac{k}{n^2} + \frac{k^2}{n^3} \right] = \lim_{n \to \infty} \left[\sum_{k=1}^{n} \frac{k}{n^2} + \sum_{k=1}^{n} \frac{k^2}{n^3} \right]$$

$$= \lim_{n \to \infty} \left[\frac{1}{n^2} \sum_{k=1}^{n} k + \frac{1}{n^3} \sum_{k=1}^{n} k^2 \right] = \lim_{n \to \infty} \left[\frac{1}{n^2} \cdot \frac{n(n+1)}{2} + \frac{1}{n^3} \cdot \frac{n(n+1)(2n+1)}{6} \right]$$

$$= \lim_{n \to \infty} \left(\frac{1}{2} \cdot \frac{(n+1)}{n} + \frac{1}{6} \cdot \frac{2n^2 + 3n + 1}{n^2} \right) = \lim_{n \to \infty} \left[\frac{1}{2}\left(1 + \frac{1}{n}\right) + \frac{1}{6}\left(2 + \frac{3}{n} + \frac{1}{n^2}\right) \right]$$

$$= \frac{1}{2}(1 + 0) + \frac{1}{6}(2 + 0 + 0) = \frac{5}{6} = 0.8\overline{3}$$

Chapter 12 Test

1. (a)

x	-0.1	-0.01	-0.001	0.001	0.01	0.1
$f(x)$	0.50335	0.50003	0.50000	0.50000	0.50003	0.50335

$$\lim_{x \to 0} \frac{x}{\sin 2x} = 0.5$$

   (b)

2. (a) $\displaystyle\lim_{x \to -1^-} f(x) = \lim_{x \to -1^-} 1 = 1$

   (b) $\displaystyle\lim_{x \to -1^+} f(x) = \lim_{x \to -1^+} x^2 = (-1)^2 = 1$

   (c) $\displaystyle\lim_{x \to -1} f(x) = 1$

   (d) $\displaystyle\lim_{x \to 0^-} f(x) = \lim_{x \to 0^-} x^2 = (0)^2 = 0$

   (e) $\displaystyle\lim_{x \to 0^+} f(x) = \lim_{x \to 0^+} x^2 = (0)^2 = 0$

   (f) $\displaystyle\lim_{x \to 0} f(x) = 0$

   (g) $\displaystyle\lim_{x \to 2^-} f(x) = \lim_{x \to 2^-} x^2 = (2)^2 = 4$

   (h) $\displaystyle\lim_{x \to 2^+} f(x) = \lim_{x \to 2^+} (4 - x) = 4 - (2) = 2$

   (i) $\displaystyle\lim_{x \to 2} f(x)$ does not exist since $\displaystyle\lim_{x \to 2^-} f(x) \neq \lim_{x \to 2^+} f(x)$.

3. (a) $\displaystyle\lim_{x \to 2} \frac{x^2 + 2x - 8}{x - 2} = \lim_{x \to 2} \frac{(x - 2)(x + 4)}{x - 2} = \lim_{x \to 2} (x + 4) = 2 + 4 = 6$

   (b) $\displaystyle\lim_{x \to 2} \frac{x^2 - 2x - 8}{x + 2} = \frac{2^2 - 2(2) - 8}{2 + 2} = -2$

   (c) $\displaystyle\lim_{x \to 2} \frac{1}{x - 2}$ does not exist because $\left| \dfrac{1}{x-2} \right|$ grows without bounds as $x \to 2$.

   (d) $\displaystyle\lim_{x \to 2^-} \frac{x - 2}{|x - 2|} = \lim_{x \to 2^-} \frac{x - 2}{-(x - 2)} = \lim_{x \to 2^-} -1 = -1$ and

   $\displaystyle\lim_{x \to 2^+} \frac{x - 2}{|x - 2|} = \lim_{x \to 2^+} \frac{x - 2}{x - 2} = \lim_{x \to 2^+} 1 = 1$. Since $\displaystyle\lim_{x \to 2^-} \frac{x - 2}{|x - 2|} \neq \lim_{x \to 2^+} \frac{x - 2}{|x - 2|}$,

   $\displaystyle\lim_{x \to 2} \frac{x - 2}{|x - 2|}$ does not exist.

(e). $\displaystyle\lim_{z\to 4}\frac{\sqrt{z}-2}{z-4}=\lim_{z\to 4}\frac{\sqrt{x}-2}{\left(\sqrt{x}+2\right)\left(\sqrt{x}-2\right)}=\lim_{z\to 4}\frac{1}{\sqrt{x}+2}=\frac{1}{\sqrt{4}+2}=\frac{1}{4}$

(f) $\displaystyle\lim_{x\to\infty}\frac{2x^2-4}{x^2+x}=\lim_{x\to\infty}\frac{2-\dfrac{4}{x^2}}{1-\dfrac{1}{x}}=\ =\ \frac{2-0}{1-0}=2$

4. (a) $f(x)=x^2-2x$ so

$$f'(x)=\lim_{h\to 0}\frac{f(x+h)-f(x)}{h}=\lim_{h\to 0}\frac{[(x+h)^2-2(x+h)]-[x^2-2x]}{h}$$

$$=\lim_{h\to 0}\frac{x^2+2hx+h^2-2x-2h-x^2+2x}{h}=\lim_{h\to 0}\frac{2hx+h^2-2h}{h}$$

$$=\lim_{h\to 0}\frac{h(2x+h-2)}{h}=\lim_{h\to 0}(2x+h-2)=2x-2$$

(b) $f'(-1)=2(-1)-2=-4$
$f'(1)=2(1)-2=0$
$f'(2)=2(2)-2=2$

5. $\displaystyle m=\lim_{h\to 0}\frac{f(9+h)-f(9)}{h}=\lim_{h\to 0}\frac{\sqrt{9+h}-\sqrt{9}}{h}=\lim_{h\to 0}\frac{\sqrt{9+h}-3}{h}$

$$=\lim_{h\to 0}\frac{\left(\sqrt{9+h}-3\right)}{h}\cdot\frac{\left(\sqrt{9+h}+3\right)}{\left(\sqrt{9+h}+3\right)}=\lim_{h\to 0}\frac{(9+h)-9}{h\left(\sqrt{9+h}+3\right)}=\lim_{h\to 0}\frac{h}{h\left(\sqrt{9+h}+3\right)}$$

$$=\lim_{h\to 0}\frac{1}{\sqrt{9+h}+3}=\frac{1}{3+3}=\frac{1}{6}$$

So the equation of the line tangent to $f(x)=\sqrt{x}$ at $(9,3)$ is $y-3=\frac{1}{6}(x-9)\quad\Leftrightarrow\quad y=\frac{1}{6}x+\frac{3}{2}$.

6. (a) $\displaystyle\lim_{n\to\infty}a_n=\lim_{n\to\infty}\frac{n}{n^2+4}=\lim_{n\to\infty}\frac{\dfrac{1}{n}}{1+\dfrac{4}{n^2}}=\lim_{n\to\infty}\frac{0}{1+0}=0$

(b) The sequence $a_n=\sec n\pi$ is the sequence $-1,1,-1,1,-1,1,\ldots$ which does not go to any one value. Thus this sequence does not converge.

7. (a) $f(x)=4-x^2$ and $\Delta x=\frac{1-0}{5}=0.2$.

$$R_5=\sum_{k=1}^{5}f(x_k)\,\Delta x=f(0.2)\cdot 0.2+f(0.4)\cdot 0.2+f(0.6)\cdot 0.2+f(0.8)\cdot 0.2+f(1)\cdot 0.2$$

$$=0.2(3.96+3.84+3.64+3.36+3)=0.2(17.8)=3.56$$

(b) $f(x) = 4 - x^2$, $a = 0$, $b = 1$, $\Delta x = \frac{1-0}{n} = \frac{1}{n}$, and $x_k = \frac{k}{n}$

$$A = \lim_{n\to\infty} \sum_{k=1}^{n} f(x_k)\,\Delta x = \lim_{n\to\infty} \sum_{k=1}^{n} \left[4 - \left(\frac{k}{n}\right)^2 \right] \cdot \frac{1}{n} = \lim_{n\to\infty} \sum_{k=1}^{n} \left[\frac{1}{n} - \frac{k^2}{n^3} \right]$$

$$= \lim_{n\to\infty} \left[\frac{4}{n} \cdot \sum_{k=1}^{n} 1 - \frac{1}{n^3} \cdot \sum_{k=1}^{n} k^2 \right] = \lim_{n\to\infty} \left(\frac{4}{n} \cdot n - \frac{1}{n^3} \cdot \frac{n(n+1)(2n+1)}{6} \right)$$

$$= \lim_{n\to\infty} \left[4 - \frac{1}{6}\left(\frac{n+1}{n}\right)\left(\frac{2n+1}{n}\right) \right] = \lim_{n\to\infty} \left[4 - \frac{1}{6}\left(1+\frac{1}{n}\right)\left(2+\frac{1}{n}\right) \right]$$

$$= 4 - \tfrac{1}{6}(1+0)(2+0) = \tfrac{11}{3}$$

Focus on Modeling

1. *Work = force × distance* so the work moving the tree the kth internal is $w_k = f(x_k)\Delta x$. With
   $f(x) = 1500 + 10x - \frac{1}{2}x^2$, $a = 0$, $b = 40$, $\Delta x = \frac{40-0}{n} = \frac{40}{n}$, and $x_k = \frac{40k}{n}$

$$W = \lim_{n\to\infty}\sum_{k=1}^{n}f(x_k)\,\Delta x = \lim_{n\to\infty}\sum_{k=1}^{n}\left[1500 + 10\left(\frac{40k}{n}\right) - \frac{1}{2}\left(\frac{40k}{n}\right)^2\right]\cdot\frac{40}{n}$$

$$= \lim_{n\to\infty}\sum_{k=1}^{n}\left[\frac{60{,}000}{n} + \frac{16{,}000k}{n^2} - \frac{32{,}000k^2}{n^3}\right]$$

$$= \lim_{n\to\infty}\left[\frac{60{,}000}{n}\sum_{k=1}^{n}1 + \frac{16{,}000}{n^2}\sum_{k=1}^{n}k - \frac{32{,}000}{n^3}\sum_{k=1}^{n}k^2\right]$$

$$= \lim_{n\to\infty}\left(\frac{60{,}000}{n}\cdot n + \frac{16{,}000}{n^2}\cdot\frac{n(n+1)}{2} - \frac{32{,}000}{n^3}\cdot\frac{n(n+1)(2n+1)}{6}\right)$$

$$= \lim_{n\to\infty}\left(60{,}000 + 8{,}000\cdot\frac{n+1}{n} - \frac{16{,}000}{3}\cdot\frac{(n+1)(2n+1)}{n^2}\right)$$

$$= \lim_{n\to\infty}\left[60{,}000 + 8{,}000\cdot\left(1+\frac{1}{n}\right) - \frac{16{,}000}{3}\cdot\left(1+\frac{1}{n}\right)\left(2+\frac{1}{n}\right)\right]$$

$$= 60{,}000 + 8{,}000 - \frac{32{,}000}{3} = 57{,}333.33 \text{ ft-lbs}$$

3. (a) The force on the kth strip is $375x_k\Delta x$, to find the force exerted on the window panel we must
   sum up the strips giving us $\displaystyle\lim_{n\to\infty}\sum_{k=1}^{n}375x_k\,\Delta x$

   (b) The area under the graph of $p(x) = 375x$ between $x = 0$ and $x = 4$.

   (c) Using $\Delta x = \frac{4}{n}$, and $x_k = \frac{4k}{n}$

$$P = \lim_{n\to\infty}\sum_{k=1}^{n}375x_k\,\Delta x = \lim_{n\to\infty}\sum_{k=1}^{n}375\left(\frac{4k}{n}\right)\cdot\frac{4}{n} = \lim_{n\to\infty}\sum_{k=1}^{n}\left[\frac{6000k}{n^2}\right]$$

$$= \lim_{n\to\infty}\left[\frac{6000}{n^2}\sum_{k=1}^{n}k\right] = \lim_{n\to\infty}\left(\frac{6000}{n^2}\cdot\frac{n(n+1)}{2}\right) = \lim_{n\to\infty}\left[3000\left(\frac{n+1}{n}\right)\right]$$

$$= \lim_{n\to\infty}\left[3000\left(1+\frac{1}{n}\right)\right] = 3000 \text{ lb.}$$

   (d) The area of kth strip is $3\Delta x$, so the pressure on the kth strip is $187.5x_k\Delta x$.
   Now using $\Delta x = \frac{4}{n}$, and $x_k = \frac{4k}{n}$, we have

$$P = \lim_{n\to\infty}\sum_{k=1}^{n}187.5x_k\,\Delta x = \lim_{n\to\infty}\sum_{k=1}^{n}187.5\left(\frac{4k}{n}\right)\cdot\frac{4}{n} = \lim_{n\to\infty}\sum_{k=1}^{n}\left[\frac{3000k}{n^2}\right]$$

$$= \lim_{n\to\infty}\left[\frac{3000}{n^2}\sum_{k=1}^{n}k\right] = \lim_{n\to\infty}\left(\frac{3000}{n^2}\cdot\frac{n(n+1)}{2}\right) = \lim_{n\to\infty}\left[1500\left(\frac{n+1}{n}\right)\right]$$

$$= \lim_{n\to\infty}\left[1500\left(1+\frac{1}{n}\right)\right] = 1500 \text{ lb.}$$

5. (a) $D(t) = 61 + \frac{6}{5}t - \frac{1}{25}t^2$, $a = 0$, $b = 24$, $\Delta x = \frac{24-0}{n} = \frac{24}{n}$, and $x_k = \frac{24k}{n}$

$$\textbf{heating} = \lim_{n\to\infty} \sum_{k=1}^{n} D(t_k)\,\Delta t = \lim_{n\to\infty} \sum_{k=1}^{n} \left[61 + \frac{6}{5}\left(\frac{24k}{n}\right) - \frac{1}{25}\left(\frac{24k}{n}\right)^2 \right] \cdot \frac{24}{n}$$

$$= \lim_{n\to\infty} \sum_{k=1}^{n} \left[\frac{1464}{n} + \frac{3456k}{5n^2} - \frac{13824k^2}{25n^3} \right]$$

$$= \lim_{n\to\infty} \left[\frac{1464}{n}\sum_{k=1}^{n} 1 + \frac{3456}{5n^2}\sum_{k=1}^{n} k - \frac{13824}{25n^3}\sum_{k=1}^{n} k^2 \right]$$

$$= \lim_{n\to\infty} \left(\frac{1464}{n}\cdot n + \frac{3456}{5n^2}\cdot\frac{n(n+1)}{2} - \frac{13824}{25n^3}\cdot\frac{n(n+1)(2n+1)}{6} \right)$$

$$= \lim_{n\to\infty} \left(1464 + \frac{1728}{5}\cdot\frac{n+1}{n} - \frac{2304}{25}\cdot\frac{(n+1)(2n+1)}{n^2} \right)$$

$$= \lim_{n\to\infty} \left[1464 + \frac{1728}{5}\cdot\left(1+\frac{1}{n}\right) - \frac{2304}{25}\cdot\left(1+\frac{1}{n}\right)\left(2+\frac{1}{n}\right) \right]$$

$$= 1464 + \frac{1728}{5} - \frac{4608}{25} = 1625.28 \text{ heating degree-hours.}$$

(b) $D(t) = 61 + \frac{6}{5}t - \frac{1}{25}t^2 = -\frac{1}{25}(t^2 - 30t) + 61 = -\frac{1}{25}(t^2 - 30t + 225) + 61 + 9$
$= -\frac{1}{25}(t-15)^2 + 70$. Thus the maximum temperature during the day was $70°$.

(c) $D(t) = 50 + 5t - \frac{1}{4}t^2$, $a = 0$, $b = 24$, $\Delta x = \frac{24-0}{n} = \frac{24}{n}$, and $x_k = \frac{24k}{n}$

$$\textbf{heating} = \lim_{n\to\infty} \sum_{k=1}^{n} D(t_k)\,\Delta t = \lim_{n\to\infty} \sum_{k=1}^{n} \left[50 + 5\left(\frac{24k}{n}\right) - \frac{1}{4}\left(\frac{24k}{n}\right)^2 \right] \cdot \frac{24}{n}$$

$$= \lim_{n\to\infty} \sum_{k=1}^{n} \left[\frac{1200}{n} + \frac{2880k}{n^2} - \frac{3456k^2}{n^3} \right]$$

$$= \lim_{n\to\infty} \left[\frac{1200}{n}\sum_{k=1}^{n} 1 + \frac{2880}{n^2}\sum_{k=1}^{n} k - \frac{3456}{n^3}\sum_{k=1}^{n} k^2 \right]$$

$$= \lim_{n\to\infty} \left(\frac{1200}{n}\cdot n + \frac{2880}{n^2}\cdot\frac{n(n+1)}{2} - \frac{3456}{n^3}\cdot\frac{n(n+1)(2n+1)}{6} \right)$$

$$= \lim_{n\to\infty} \left(1200 + 1440\cdot\frac{n+1}{n} - 576\cdot\frac{(n+1)(2n+1)}{n^2} \right)$$

$$= \lim_{n\to\infty} \left[1200 + 1440\cdot\left(1+\frac{1}{n}\right) - 576\cdot\left(1+\frac{1}{n}\right)\left(2+\frac{1}{n}\right) \right]$$

$$= 1200 + 1440 - 1152 = 1488 \text{ heating degree-hours.}$$

(d) $D(t) = 50 + 5t - \frac{1}{4}t^2 = -\frac{1}{4}(t^2 - 20t) + 50 = -\frac{1}{4}(t^2 - 20t + 100) + 50 + 25$
$= -\frac{1}{4}(t-10)^2 + 75$. Thus the maximum temperature during the day was $75°$.

(e) The day described in (c) was "hotter" since the heating degree-hours were more, meaning the average temperature of that day was higher.